ESSENTIALS
OF STATISTICS
FOR THE BEHAVIORAL
SCIENCES
FOURTH EDITION

ABOUT THE AUTHORS

Frederick J Gravetter is Professor of Psychology at the State University of New York College at Brockport. Specializing in statistics, experimental design, and cognitive psychology, he has taught at Brockport since the early 1970s. Dr. Gravetter has chaired many commitees and served as Chair of the Department of Psychology for six years. He has published many research articles on such topics as stimulus response learning and perception. Dr. Gravetter has also published textbooks on statistics applied to psychology and the behavioral sciences.

Nicki and Fred

Larry B. Wallnau is Professor of Psychology at the State University of New York College at Brockport. The recipient of grants and awards in both research and teaching, Dr. Wallnau has published numerous research articles, primarily on the effect of psychotropic drugs. With Dr. Gravetter, he co-authored *Essentials of Statistics for the Behavioral Sciences*. He also has provided editorial consulting for publishers such as Allyn and Bacon and Harper & Row and for journals such as *Pharmacology Biochemistry and Behavior, Psychology & Behavior, Journal of Comparative Psychology,* and *Psychobiology*.

Nico and Larry

ESSENTIALS
OF STATISTICS
FOR THE BEHAVIORAL
SCIENCES
FOURTH EDITION

FREDERICK J GRAVETTER

State University of New York
College at Brockport

LARRY B. WALLNAU

State University of New York
College at Brockport

WADSWORTH
TM
THOMSON LEARNING

Australia • Canada • Mexico • Singapore • Spain • United Kingdom • United States

WADSWORTH

THOMSON LEARNING

Sponsoring Editor: *Vicki Knight*
Editorial Assistant: *Julie Dillemuth, Dan Moneypenny*
Marketing Manager: *Joanne Terhaar*
Marketing Assistant: *Justine Ferguson*
Production Editor: *Kirk Bomont*
Production Service: *Helen Walden*
Manuscript Editor: *Helen Walden*

Permissions Editor: *Sue Ewing*
Cover Art: *Vassily Kandinsky, "Subdued Glow" © 2001 Artists Rights Society (ARS), New York/ADAGP, Paris*
Print Buyer: *Vena Dyer*
Typesetting: *Clarinda Company*
Printing and Binding: *Transcontinental Printing*

For more information about this or any other Wadsworth product, contact:
WADSWORTH
511 Forest Lodge Road
Pacific Grove, CA 93950 USA
www.wadsworth.com
1-800-423-0563 (Thomson Learning Academic Resource Center)

For permission to use material from this work, contact us by:
Web: www.thomsonrights.com
Fax: 1-800-730-2215
Phone: 1-800-730-2214

Printed in Canada

10   9   8   7   6   5   4   3

Library of Congress Cataloging-in-Publication Data

Gravetter, Frederick J.
    Essentials of statistics for the behavioral sciences / Frederick J. Gravetter, Larry B. Wallnau.—4th ed.
        p.   cm.
    Includes bibliographical references and index.
    ISBN 0-534-58617-1
        1. Social sciences—Statistical methods. I. Wallnau, Larry B. II. Title.
HA29.G726 2002
519.5'024'3—dc21   2001026423

THIS BOOK IS PRINTED ON ACID-FREE RECYCLED PAPER

CONTENTS IN BRIEF

CONTENTS

CHAPTER 4   **VARIABILITY**   76

CHAPTER 5   ***z*-SCORES: LOCATION OF SCORES AND STANDARDIZED DISTRIBUTIONS**   103

CHAPTER 6   **PROBABILITY**   121

CHAPTER 7   **PROBABILITY AND SAMPLES: THE DISTRIBUTION OF SAMPLE MEANS**   144

PREFACE

There are three kinds of lies: Lies, damned lies, and statistics

We have used this quote in previous editions because it is timeless as well as humorous. It is attributed by Mark Twain to Benjamin Disraeli and reflects a commonly held belief that statistics (or perhaps even statisticians) should not be trusted. Unfortunately, this mistrust does have at least some basis in reality. In this book, we shall see that statistical techniques are tools that we use to organize information and to make inferences from our data. Like any other tool, however, statistics can be misused, which can result in misleading, distorted, or incorrect conclusions. It is no small wonder, then, that we are sometimes skeptical when a statistician presents findings. However, if we understand the correct uses of statistical techniques, then we will recognize those situations in which statistical procedures have been incorrectly applied. We can decide which statistical reports are more believable. By understanding statistical techniques, we can examine someone else's results, understand how they were analyzed, and arrive at our own thoughtful conclusion about the study. Therefore, the goal of this book is to teach not only the methods of statistics, but also how to apply these methods appropriately. Finally, a certain amount of mistrust is healthy; that is, we should critically examine information and data before we accept its implications. As you will see, statistical techniques help us look at data with a critical eye and a questioning mind.

For those of you who are familiar with previous editions of *Essentials of Statistics for the Behavioral Sciences,* you will notice that some changes have been made. These changes are summarized in the section entitled "To the Instructor." In revising this text, our students have been foremost in our minds. Over the years, they have provided honest and useful feedback. Their hard work and perseverance has made our writing and teaching most rewarding. We sincerely thank them. Students who are using this edition should please read the section of the preface entitled "To the Student."

ANCILLARIES Ancillaries for this edition include the following:
- *Study Guide:* Contains chapter overviews, learning objectives, new terms and concepts, new formulas, step-by-step procedures for problem solving, study hints and cautions, self-tests, and review. The Study Guide contains answers to the self-test questions.

- *Instructor's Manual:* Contains test items, as well as solutions to all end-of-chapter problems included in the text.
- *Transparency CD-ROM:* Includes about 90 tables and figures taken directly from the text. Electronic; in Powerpoint.

ACKNOWLEDGMENTS

It takes a lot of good, hard-working people to produce a book. Our friends at Wadsworth have made an enormous contribution to this textbook. We thank our editor, Vicki Knight, who has been most supportive and encouraging; editorial assistants Dan Moneypenny and Julie Dillemuth; production editor Kirk Bomont; cover designer Vernon Boes; Jennifer Wilkinson, who edited the supplements; and marketing manager, Joanne Terhaar.

Special thanks also go to Helen Walden who shepherded us through production and to Roxy Peck who checked our computations and made many helpful suggestions during the preparation of the manuscript.

Reviewers play a very important role in the development of a manuscript. Accordingly, we offer our appreciation to the following colleagues for their thoughtful reviews: Holly Arrow, University of Oregon; Deborah M. Clawson, Catholic University of America; Andrea M. Karkowski, Capital University; Maureen McCarthy, Austin Peay State University; David K. Meagher, City University of New York-Brooklyn College; Craig A. Mertler, Bowling Green State University; Kerri Pickel, Ball State University; Robert Pred, Temple University; and Peter H. Wood, Bowling Green State University.

A Special Note of Thanks Our family members have endured weekends and evenings when we were not available because we were immersed in writing and proof-reading. This endeavor would be impossible were it not for their support, encouragement, and patience. Heartfelt thanks go to Debbie, Justin, Melissa, Megan, JoAnn, and Nico.

TO THE INSTRUCTOR

Those of you familiar with the third edition of *Essentials of Statistics for the Behavioral Sciences* will notice several changes in the fourth edition. A general summary of the revisions follows:
- Sections on measuring and describing *effect size* using Cohen's d and r-squared have been added to most of the hypothesis-testing chapters (Chapters 10, 11, 13, and 16).
- Chapter 14 now includes an introduction to repeated-measures analysis of variance in addition to the two-factor analysis.
- New *On the Computer* sections demonstrating and explaining SPSS and Minitab printouts have been added to several chapters (Chapters 10, 11, 13, 14, 15, and 16).
- Throughout the text, we attempted to eliminate excessively technical and "nonessential" elements.

The following are examples of the specific and noteworthy revisions:

Chapter 1
- Removed nonstatistical material on theories, hypothesis, and hypothetical constructs.
- Added new examples showing the kinds of data obtained from correlation, experimental, and quasi-experimental studies.

Chapter 3
- Clarified the section on the weighed mean.
- Added a more conceptual explanation of how adding or removing a score affects the mean.
- Removed the section using interpolation to find the median.
- Expanded the section on when to use the mode.

Chapter 4
- Added a section discussing the concept of biased and unbiased statistics.
- Simplified the section discussing how variance is related to inferential statistics.

Chapter 5
- Simplified the sections introducing the *z*-score formula and explaining the process of standardizing distributions.

Chapter 6
- Eliminated the section on percentiles and percentile ranks.

Chapter 7
- Revised the final section describing how standard error is used in inferential statistics so that it creates a link to the hypothesis tests in Chapter 8.

Chapter 9
- Created a new Box 9.1 that discusses how standard deviation and standard error are both derived from variance.
- Created a new Box 9.2 that presents an analogy for the standard error based on the accuracy (error) of predicting coin tosses.

Chapter 10
- Created a new Box 10.1 stressing that pooled variance is the average of the two sample variances.
- Added a new *On the Computer* section showing how the independent-measures *t* test appears in SPSS and Minitab printouts.
- Added a new section on *effect size* introducing Cohen's *d* and *r*-squared (percentage of variance accounted for.)

Chapter 11
- Added a new *On the Computer* section showing how the repeated-measures *t* test appears in SPSS and Minitab printouts.
- Added a new section on *effect size* demonstrating Cohen's *d* and *r*-squared (percentage of variance accounted for) for the repeated-measures *t*.
- Revised the section showing the advantages of a repeated-measures design, stressing the reduction of error by removing individual differences.

Chapter 12
- Eliminated the section demonstrating estimation with *z*-scores. The chapter now focuses on the three *t* tests (single sample, independent-measures, and repeated-measures).
- Added new figures (12.5 and 12.8) showing how an interval estimate can be viewed as a range of values on the scale of measurement.

- Added a new section discussing the relationships between estimation, hypothesis tests, and effect size.

Chapter 13
- Added a new *On the Computer* section showing how analysis of variance appears in SPSS and Minitab printouts.
- Added a new section demonstrating the use of *r*-squared to measure effect size in an analysis of variance.
- Added a new figure (13.9) to demonstrate the concepts of between-treatments and within-treatments variance.
- Expanded the section on post hoc tests to include a discussion of planned versus unplanned tests and to introduce Tukey's HSD test along with Scheffé test.
- Eliminated the section on the relationship between ANOVA and *t* tests.

Chapter 14
- Added a section presenting repeated-measures ANOVA as well as two-factor ANOVA.
- Added an *On the Computer* section showing SPSS and Minitab printouts for both ANOVAs.

Chapter 15
- Added a box (15.2) discussing reliability of measurement.
- Revised the section on the strength of a relationship to connect correlations to the measure of effect size (*r*-squared) presented in earlier chapters.
- Added an *On the Computer* section showing how correlations appear in SPSS and Minitab printouts.

Chapter 16
- Added an *On the Computer* section showing the test for independence in SPSS and Minitab printouts.

TO THE STUDENT   There is a common (and usually unfair) belief that visits to the dentist will be associated with fear and pain, even though dentists perform a service of great benefit to us. Although you initially may have similar fears and anxieties about this course, we could argue that a statistics course also performs a beneficial service. This is evident when one considers that our world has become information-laden and information-dependent. The media informs us of the latest findings on nutrition and health, global warming, economic trends, aging and memory, effects of television violence on children, success or failure of new welfare programs, and so on. All these data-gathering efforts provide an enormous and unmanageable amount of information. Enter the statisticians, who use statistical procedures to analyze, organize, and interpret vast amounts of data. Having a basic understanding of a variety of statistical procedures will help you to understand these findings, to examine the data critically, and to question the statisticians about what they have done.

What about the fear of taking statistics? One way to deal with the fear is to get plenty of practice. You will notice that this book provides you with a number of opportunities to repeat the techniques you will be learning, in the form of learning checks, examples, demonstrations, and end-of-chapter problems. We encourage you to take advantage of these opportunities. Also, we encourage you to read the text rather than just memorize the formulas. We have taken great pains to present each statistical procedure in a conceptual context that explains why the procedure was developed and when it should be used. If you read this material and gain an understanding of the basic concepts underlying a statistical formula, you will find that learning the formula and how to use it will be much easier. In the following section, "Study Hints," we provide advice that we give our own students. Ask your instructor for advice as well; we are sure other instructors will have ideas of their own.

Study Hints   You may find some of these tips helpful, as our own students have reported.

- You will learn (and remember) much more if you study for short periods several times per week rather than try to condense all of your studying into one long session. For example, it is far more effective to study half an hour every night than to have a single $3\frac{1}{2}$-hour study session once a week. We cannot even work on *writing* this book without frequent rest breaks.
- Do some work before class. Keep a little ahead of the instructor by reading the appropriate sections before they are presented in class. Although you may not fully understand what you read, you will have a general idea of the topic, which will make the lecture easier to follow. Also, you can identify material that is particularly confusing and then be sure the topic is clarified in class.
- Pay attention and think during class. Although this advice seems obvious, often it is not practiced. Many students spend so much time trying to write down every example presented or every word spoken by the instructor that they do not actually understand and process what is being said. Check with your instructor. There may not be a need to copy every example presented in class, especially if there are many examples like it in the text. Sometimes, we tell our students to put their pens and pencils down for a moment and just listen.
- Test yourself regularly. Do not wait until the end of the chapter or the end of the week to check your knowledge. After each lecture, work some of the end-of-chapter problems, and do the Learning Checks. Review the Demonstration Problems, and be sure you can define the Key Terms. If you are having trouble, get your questions answered *immediately* (reread the section, go to your instructor, or ask questions in class). By doing so, you will be able to move ahead to new material.
- Do not kid yourself! Avoid denial. Many students observe their instructor solve problems in class and think to themselves, "This looks easy, I understand it." Do you really understand it? Can you really do the problem on your own without having to leaf through the pages of a chapter? Although there is nothing wrong with using examples in the text as models for solving problems, you should try working a problem with your book closed to test your level of mastery.
- We realize that many students are embarassed to ask for help. It is our biggest challenge as instructors. You must find a way to overcome this aversion. Perhaps contacting the instructor directly would be a good starting point, if asking questions in class is too anxiety-provoking. You could be pleasantly surprised to find that your instructor does not yell, scold, or bite! Also, your instructor might know of another student who can offer assistance. Peer tutoring can be very helpful.

Over the years, students in our classes have given us many helpful suggestions. We learn from them. If you have any suggestions or comments about this book, you can send a note to us at the Department of Psychology, SUNY College at Brockport, 350 New Campus Drive, Brockport, NY 14420. Also, we can be reached by e-mail at fgravett@po.brockport.edu and lwallnau@po.brockport.edu.

Frederick J Gravetter
Larry B. Wallnau

CHAPTER 1

INTRODUCTION TO STATISTICS

CONTENTS

1.1   STATISTICS, SCIENCE, AND OBSERVATIONS

The procedure is actually quite simple. First you arrange things into different groups depending on their makeup. Of course, one pile may be sufficient, depending on how much there is to do. If you have to go somewhere else due to lack of facilities, that is the next step; otherwise you are pretty well set. It is important not to overdo any particular endeavor. That is, it is better to do too few things at once than too many. In the short run this may not seem important, but complications from doing too many can easily arise. A mistake can be expensive as well. The manipulation of the appropriate mechanisms should be self-explanatory, and we need not dwell on it here. At first the whole procedure will seem complicated. Soon, however, it will become just another facet of life. It is difficult to foresee any end to the necessity for this task in the immediate future, but then one never can tell.*

The preceding paragraph was adapted from a psychology experiment reported by Bransford and Johnson (1972). If you have not read the paragraph yet, go back and read it now.

You probably find the paragraph a little confusing, and most of you probably think it is describing some obscure statistical procedure. Actually, this paragraph describes the everyday task of doing laundry. Now that you know the topic of the paragraph, try reading it again—it should make sense now.

Why did we begin a statistics textbook with a paragraph about washing clothes? Our goal is to demonstrate the importance of context—when not in the proper context, even the simplest material can appear difficult and confusing. In the Bransford and Johnson experiment, people who knew the topic before reading the paragraph were able to recall 73% more than people who did not know that it was about doing laundry. When you have the appropriate background, it is much easier to fit new material into your memory and to recall it later. As you work through the topics in this book, remember that all statistical methods were developed to serve a purpose. The purpose for each statistical procedure provides a background or context for the details of the formulas and calculations. If you understand why a new procedure is needed, you will find it much easier to learn the procedure.

The objectives for this first chapter are to provide an introduction to the topic of statistics and to give you some background for the rest of the book. We will discuss the role of statistics within the general field of scientific inquiry, and we will introduce some of the vocabulary and notation that are necessary for the statistical methods that follow.

Incidentally, we cannot promise that statistics will be as easy as washing clothes. But if you begin each new topic within the proper context, you should eliminate some unnecessary confusion.

DEFINITIONS OF STATISTICS

By one common definition, *statistics* are facts and figures. A quick glance at a newspaper, for example, yields statistics that deal with crime rates, birth rates, average income, average snowfall, and so on. These statistics generally are informative and time saving because they condense large quantities of information into a few simple figures or statements. For example, the average snowfall in Chicago during the month of January is based on many observations made over many years. Few people would be interested in

---

*Bransford, J. D., and Johnson, M. K. (1972). Contextual prerequisites for understanding: Some investigations of comprehension and recall. *Journal of Verbal Learning and Verbal Behavior, 11,* 717–726. Copyright by Academic Press. Reprinted by permission.

seeing a complete list of day-by-day snowfall amounts for the past 50 years. Even fewer people would be able to make much sense of all those numbers at a quick glance. But nearly everyone can understand and appreciate the meaning of an average.

In this book, however, we will use another definition of the term *statistics.* When researchers use the word *statistics,* they are referring to a set of mathematical procedures that are used to organize, summarize, and interpret information.

DEFINITION

The term *statistics* refers to a set of methods and rules for organizing, summarizing, and interpreting information.

Caution: The term *statistics* (plural) is used as a general reference for the entire set of statistical procedures. Later, we will use the term *statistic* (singular) to refer to a specific type of statistical method.

Statistical procedures help ensure that the information or observations are presented and interpreted in an accurate and informative way. In somewhat grandiose terms, statistics help researchers to bring order out of chaos. In addition, statistics provide researchers with a set of standardized techniques that are recognized and understood throughout the scientific community. Thus, the statistical methods used by one researcher will be familiar to other researchers, who can accurately interpret the statistical analyses with a full understanding of how the analysis was done and what the results signify.

1.2   POPULATIONS AND SAMPLES

WHAT ARE THEY?

Scientific research typically begins with a general question about a specific group (or groups) of individuals. For example, a researcher may be interested in the effect of divorce on the self-esteem of preteen children. Or a researcher may want to examine the attitudes of men toward abortion versus those of women. In the first example, the researcher is interested in the group of *preteen children.* In the second example, the researcher wants to compare the group of *men* to the group of *women.* In statistical terminology, the entire group that a researcher wishes to study is called a *population.*

DEFINITION

A *population* is the set of all individuals of interest for a particular study.

Usually, populations are quite large—for example, the number of women on the planet Earth. A researcher might be more specific, limiting the population to women who are registered voters in the United States. Perhaps the investigator would like to study the population consisting of women who are heads of state. Populations can obviously vary in size from extremely large to very small, depending on how the investigator defines the population. The population being studied should always be identified by the researcher. In addition, the population need not consist of people—it could be a population of rats, corporations, parts produced in a factory, or anything else an investigator wants to study.

Although research questions concern an entire population, it is usually impossible for a researcher to examine every single individual in the population of interest. Therefore, researchers typically select a smaller, more manageable group from the population and limit their studies to the individuals in the selected group. In statistical terms, a set of individuals selected from a population is called a *sample.* A sample is intended to be representative of its population, and a sample should always be identified in terms of the population from which it was selected.

DEFINITION

A *sample* is a set of individuals selected from a population, usually intended to represent the population in a research study.

Just as we saw with populations, samples can vary in size. For example, one study might examine a sample of only 10 children in a preschool program, and another study might use a sample of over 1000 people representing the population of a major city.

Before we move on, there is one additional point that we should make about samples and populations. Thus far we have defined populations and samples in terms of *individuals*. For example, we have discussed a population of preteen children and a sample of preschool children. You should be forewarned, however, that we will also refer to populations or samples of *scores*. The change from individuals to scores is usually very straightforward because research typically involves measuring each individual and recording a score (measurement) for that individual. Thus, each sample (or population) of individuals produces a corresponding sample (or population) of scores. Occasionally, a set of scores is called a *statistical population* or a *statistical sample* to differentiate it from a population or a sample of individuals. A noteworthy report of this distinction is presented by Hyman (1993).

PARAMETERS AND STATISTICS

When describing data it is necessary to distinguish whether the data come from a population or a sample. A characteristic that describes a population—for example, the population average— is called a *parameter*. On the other hand, a characteristic that describes a sample is called a *statistic*. Thus, the average score for a sample is an example of a statistic. Typically, the research process begins with a question about a population parameter. However, the actual data come from a sample and are used to compute sample statistics.

DEFINITIONS

A *parameter* is a value, usually a numerical value, that describes a population. A parameter may be obtained from a single measurement, or it may be derived from a set of measurements from the population.

A *statistic* is a value, usually a numerical value, that describes a sample. A statistic may be obtained from a single measurement, or it may be derived from a set of measurements from the sample.

As we will see later, statisticians frequently use different symbols for a parameter and a statistic. By using different symbols, we can readily tell whether a characteristic, such as an average, is describing a population or a sample.

DESCRIPTIVE AND INFERENTIAL STATISTICAL METHODS

The task of answering a research question begins by gathering information. In science, information is gathered by making observations and recording measurements for the individuals being studied. The measurement or observation obtained for each individual is called a *datum,* or, more commonly, a *score* or *raw score*. The complete set of scores or measurements is called the *data set* or simply the *data*. After data are obtained, statistical methods are used to organize and interpret the data.

DEFINITIONS

Data (plural) are measurements or observations. A *data set* is a collection of measurements or observations. A *datum* (singular) is a single measurement or observation and is commonly called a *score* or *raw score.*

Although researchers have developed a variety of different statistical procedures to organize and interpret data, these different procedures can be classified into two general categories. The first category, *descriptive statistics,* consists of statistical procedures that are used to simplify and summarize data.

DEFINITION   *Descriptive statistics* are statistical procedures that are used to summarize, organize, and simplify data.

Descriptive statistics are techniques that take raw scores and organize or summarize them in a form that is more manageable. Often the scores are organized in a table or a graph so that it is possible to see the entire set of scores. Another common technique is to summarize a set of scores by computing an average. Note that even if the data set has hundreds of scores, the average provides a single descriptive value for the entire set.

The second general category of statistical techniques is called *inferential statistics.* Inferential statistics are methods that use sample data to make general statements about a population.

DEFINITION   *Inferential statistics* consist of techniques that allow us to study samples and then make generalizations about the populations from which they were selected.

Because populations are typically too large to observe every individual, a sample is selected. By analyzing the results from the sample, we hope to make general statements about the population. Typically, researchers use sample statistics as the basis for drawing conclusions about population parameters.

One problem with using samples, however, is that a sample provides only limited information about the population. It gives us just a "glimpse" of the population. Of great importance, however, is the notion that a sample should be *representative* of its population. That is, the general characteristics of the sample should be consistent with the characteristics of the population. The method of selecting a sample (as we shall see in Chapter 6) helps ensure that a sample is representative. Even so, a sample is not expected to give a perfectly accurate picture of the whole population. There usually is some discrepancy between a sample statistic and the corresponding population parameter. This discrepancy is called *sampling error,* and it creates another problem to be addressed by inferential statistics.

DEFINITION   *Sampling error* is the discrepancy, or amount of error, that exists between a sample statistic and the corresponding population parameter.

The concept of sampling error will be discussed in more detail in Chapter 7, but, for now, you should realize that a statistic obtained from a sample generally will not be identical to the corresponding population parameter. Suppose, for example, that a class of 30 students has an average exam score of 76.3. If you selected a sample of 4 students from this class and computed the average exam score for the sample, would you expect to obtain a value exactly equal to 76.3? It should be obvious that the sample of 4 students probably will not have the same average as the entire class. To make the situation even more complex, suppose that you select another sample of 4 students and compute the average score for them. Would you expect the second sample to have exactly the same average score as the first sample? Again, it should be clear that the two samples will probably not be identical. This is the general concept of sampling error. There typically will be some error or discrepancy between a sample statistic and the corresponding population parameter. Furthermore, if you compare one sample with another, there typically will be differences between the sample statistics even though the samples come from the same population.

One common example of sampling error is the error associated with a sample proportion. For example, in newspaper articles reporting results from political polls, you frequently find statements such as this:

> Candidate Brown leads the poll with 51% of the vote. Candidate Jones has 42% approval, and the remaining 7% are undecided. This poll was taken from a sample of registered voters and has a margin of error of plus-or-minus 4 percentage points.

The "margin of error" is the sampling error. A sample of voters was selected, and 51% of the individuals in the sample expressed a preference for candidate Brown. Thus, the 51% is a sample statistic. Because the sample is only a small part of the total population of voters, you should not expect the sample value to be exactly equal to the population parameter. A statistic always has some "margin of error," which is defined as sampling error.

The following example shows the general stages of a research study and demonstrates how descriptive statistics and inferential statistics are used to organize and interpret the data. At the end of the example, note how sampling error can affect the interpretation of experimental results, and consider why inferential statistical methods are needed to deal with this problem.

EXAMPLE 1.1

Figure 1.1 shows an overview of a research situation and the role that descriptive and inferential statistics play. In the example, a researcher is examining the effects of a cold medication on reaction time. The researcher begins with the population of college students. It is known from past research that this population has an average reaction time of 200 milliseconds. The researcher selects a sample from the population, administers the cold medication to each individual, and then measures each person's reaction time. The scores from this sample make up the data for the study.

Next, descriptive statistics are used to simplify the data. The researcher could use a graph to display the entire set of scores, or the researcher could simply calculate the average score for the sample. In this example, the students who received the cold medication had an average reaction time of 215 milliseconds.

After the researcher has described the sample data, the next step is to interpret the outcome; that is, the researcher must use the sample data to reach a general conclusion about the population. This is the job of inferential statistics. In this example, the data seem to indicate that the cold medication increases reaction time. Specifically, the sample with medication had an average reaction time that is 15 milliseconds longer than the average for the general population (an average of 215 milliseconds versus an average of 200 milliseconds). However, you must remember that the average for the sample is a *sample statistic* and, therefore, has a margin of error (sampling error).

To illustrate the concept of sampling error, suppose that the researcher had selected a *different* sample of students. A new sample would produce different scores and would almost certainly have a different average. A new sample might even produce an average reaction time that is faster than 200 milliseconds. The point of this argument is that there are differences from one sample to another and no single sample will give a perfectly accurate picture of the population. This is the general idea behind the concept of sampling error. For this research study, inferential statistics would be used to help the researcher decide between the following two interpretations of the data:

FIGURE 1.1

The role of statistics in research.

Step 1 Data Collection: A sample of college students is selected from the population. The cold medication (the treatment) is given to each individual in the sample. Each individual's reaction time is measured. The data consist of reaction time scores for a sample of students who have taken the cold medication.

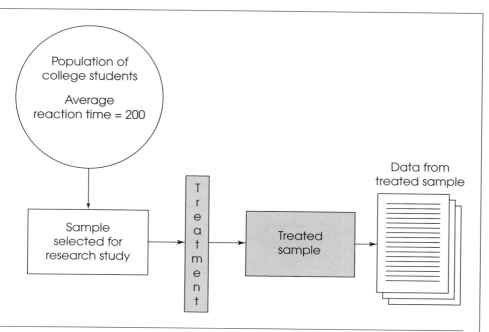

Step 2 Descriptive Statistics: Organize and simplify. The data can be organized in a graph or they can be summarized by calculating the average score.

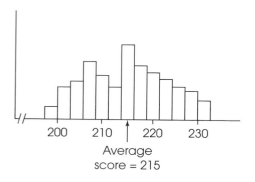

Step 3 Inferential Statistics: Interpret the results.

The sample data show an average reaction time that is 15 points higher than the average for the general population. Is the 15-point difference simply due to chance (sampling error) or does it indicate that the medication has an effect on reaction time? Inferential statistics will help us decide between these two interpretations.

1. The 15-point difference between the sample and the original population is simply due to chance (sampling error) and does not indicate that the medication has any real effect on reaction time. After all, sample is not expected to be exactly identical to its population and the 15-point difference is within the normal margin of error. If additional samples were tested, there would not be any consistent pattern of results: sometimes the sample average would be higher than 200 and sometimes it would be lower.

2. The 15-point difference is more than chance (greater than sampling error) and indicates that the medication does have a real effect on reaction time. If the researcher continued to select and test new samples, the data would show a consistent pattern of longer reaction times for people who received the cold medication.

Note that the magnitude of the sampling error is an important factor in the interpretation of the research results. For the situation described in Example 1.1, the sampling error would determine how much difference is reasonable to expect just by chance between the sample average and the population average. If a reasonable margin of error was found to be 15 points (or more), then we would conclude that the data do not provide convincing evidence that the medication affects reaction time. However, if the margin of error was small—for example, around 5 points—then we could conclude that the 15-point difference is more than chance and, therefore, indicates that the medication does influence reaction time. Determining the magnitude of the sampling error will be an important part of inferential statistics.

LEARNING CHECK ◆

1. What is a *population,* and what is a *sample*?

2. A characteristic that describes a population, such as the population average, is called a(n) _____.

3. The relationship between a population and a parameter is the same as the relationship between a sample and a(n) _____.

4. Statistical techniques are classified into two general categories. What are the two categories called, and what is the general purpose for the techniques in each category?

5. Briefly define the concept of sampling error.

ANSWERS

1. The population is the entire set of individuals of interest for a particular research study. The sample is the specific set of individuals selected to participate in the study. The sample is selected from the population and is expected to be representative of the population.

2. parameter

3. statistic

4. The two categories are descriptive statistics and inferential statistics. Descriptive techniques are intended to organize, simplify, and summarize data. Inferential techniques use sample data to reach general conclusions about populations.

5. Sampling error is the error or discrepancy between the value obtained for a sample statistic and the value for the corresponding population parameter. ◆

1.3 THE SCIENTIFIC METHOD AND THE DESIGN OF RESEARCH STUDIES

RELATIONSHIPS BETWEEN VARIABLES

Science attempts to discover orderliness in the universe. Even people of ancient civilizations noted regularity in the world around them—the change of seasons, changes in the moon's phases, changes in the tides—and they were able to make many observations to document these orderly changes. Something that can change or have different values is called a *variable.*

DEFINITION

A *variable* is a characteristic or condition that changes or has different values for different individuals.

Variables may be characteristics that differ from one individual to another, such as height, weight, gender, or personality. Variables also can be environmental conditions that change, such as temperature, time of day, or the size of the room where the research is being conducted.

When variables are measured, the resulting values are often identified by letters, usually X and Y. For example, the variable height could be identified by the letter X, and shoe size could be identified by Y. It is reasonable to expect a consistent relationship between these two variables. As X changes, Y also changes in a predictable way.

A value that does not change or vary is called a *constant*. For example, an instructor may adjust the exam scores for a class by adding 4 points to each student's score. Because every individual gets the same 4 points, this value is a constant.

DEFINITION

A *constant* is a characteristic or condition that does not vary but is the same for every individual.

In a research study, it is common to control variables by holding them constant. For example, a research study may examine only 10-year-old children who are all tested in the same room at 2 P.M. In this study, the subjects' age, the room, and the time of day are all constant.

Science involves a search for relationships between variables. For example, there is a relationship between the amount of rainfall and crop growth. Rainfall is one of the variables. It varies from year to year and season to season. Crop growth is the other variable. Some years, the cornstalks seem short and stunted; other years, they are tall and full. When there is very little rainfall, the crops are short and shriveled. When rain is ample, the crops show vigorous growth. Note that in order to document the relationship, one must make observations—that is, measurements of the amount of rainfall and size of the crops.

THE CORRELATIONAL METHOD

The simplest way to look for relationships between variables is to make observations of the two variables as they exist naturally for a set of individuals. This is called the *correlational method.*

DEFINITION

With the *correlational method,* two variables are observed to see whether there is a relationship.

Suppose, for example, that a researcher wants to examine the relationship between violence on television and the behavior of children who watch the TV violence. A large sample of children is obtained and the researcher interviews each child to determine how much violent TV the child watches. Then the researcher observes each child during a school recess to record incidences of aggressive or violent behavior. Note that the correlational method simply involves measuring two different variables for each individual. After the measurements are obtained, the researcher examines the data to see whether there are any consistent trends or patterns. For example, the data may show that the kids who watch the most TV violence also tend to be the kids who show the most aggressive and violent behavior. In this case, the data would show a relationship between the two variables.

When a correlational study shows a relationship between two variables, it is often tempting to conclude that one variable is causing changes in the other variable. For example, it would be tempting to conclude that viewing TV violence causes children to behave violently. However, this conclusion is not justified. A limitation of the correlational method is that it simply describes the relationship—it does not explain the cause-and-effect mechanism of the relationship. For example, it may be that children who are violent and aggressive simply prefer to watch TV programs that are also violent.

To establish a cause-and-effect relationship, it is necessary to exert a much greater level of control over the variables being studied. This is accomplished by the experimental method. We shall see that the experimental method is a highly structured, systematic approach to the study of relationships between variables.

THE EXPERIMENTAL METHOD

The goal of the *experimental method* is to establish a cause-and-effect relationship between two variables. That is, the method is intended to show that changes in one variable are *caused* by changes in the other variable. To accomplish this goal, the experimental method has two distinguishing characteristics:

In more complex experiments, a researcher may systematically manipulate more than one variable and may observe more than one variable. Here we are considering the simplest case, where only one variable is manipulated and only one variable is observed.

1. The researcher *manipulates* one of the variables and observes the second variable to determine whether or not the manipulation causes changes to occur.
2. The researcher must exercise some *control* over the research situation to ensure that other, extraneous variables do not influence the relationship being examined.

To demonstrate these two characteristics, consider an experiment in which a researcher is examining the effects of room temperature on memory performance. The purpose of the experiment is to determine whether changes in room temperature *cause* changes in memory performance.

The researcher manipulates temperature by creating two or more different treatment conditions. For example, our researcher could set the temperature at 70° for one condition and then change the temperature to 90° for a second condition. The experiment would consist of observing the memory performance for a group of individuals (often called *subjects* or *participants*) in the 70° room and comparing their scores with those of another group that is tested in the 90° room. The structure of this experiment is shown in Figure 1.2.

To be able to say that differences in memory performance are caused by temperature, the researcher must rule out any other possible explanations for the difference. That is, any other variables that might affect memory performance must be controlled.

FIGURE 1.2

The structure of an experiment. Volunteers are randomly assigned to one of two treatment conditions: a 70° room or a 90° room. A list of words is presented and the subjects are tested by writing down as many words as they can remember from the list. A difference between groups is attributed to the treatment (the temperature of the room).

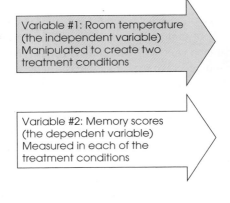

Variable #1: Room temperature (the independent variable) Manipulated to create two treatment conditions

70° Room	90° Room
17	12
19	10
16	14
12	15
17	13
18	12
15	11
16	13

Variable #2: Memory scores (the dependent variable) Measured in each of the treatment conditions

Any difference?

Researchers typically use two basic techniques to control variables. First, the researcher could use *random assignment* so that each subject has an equal chance of being assigned to each of the treatment conditions. Random assignment helps assure that the subjects in one treatment condition are not substantially different from the subjects in another treatment condition. For example, a researcher should not assign all the young subjects to one condition and all the old subjects to another. If this were done, the researcher could not be sure that the difference in memory performance was caused by temperature; instead, it could be caused by age differences. Second, the experimental method requires that the treatment conditions be identical except for the one variable that is being manipulated. This is accomplished by *controlling* or *holding constant* any other variables that might influence performance. For example, the researcher should test both groups of subjects at the same time of day, in the same room, with the same instructions, and so on. Again, the goal is to eliminate the contribution of all other variables, except temperature, that might account for the difference in memory performance.

DEFINITION

In the *experimental method,* one variable is manipulated while another variable is observed and measured. To establish a cause-and-effect relationship between the two variables, an experiment attempts to eliminate or minimize the effect of all other variables by using *random assignment* and by *controlling* or *holding constant* other variables that might influence the results.

THE INDEPENDENT AND DEPENDENT VARIABLES

Specific names are used for the two variables that are studied by the experimental method. The variable that is manipulated by the experimenter is called the *independent variable.* It can be identified as the treatment conditions to which subjects are assigned. For the example in Figure 1.2, the temperature of the room is the independent variable. The variable that is observed to assess a possible effect of the manipulation is the *dependent variable.*

DEFINITIONS

The *independent variable* is the variable that is manipulated by the researcher. In behavioral research, the independent variable usually consists of the two (or more) treatment conditions to which subjects are exposed.

The *dependent variable* is the one that is observed for changes in order to assess the effect of the treatment.

In psychological research, the dependent variable is typically a measurement or score obtained for each subject. For the temperature experiment (Figure 1.2), the dependent variable is the number of words recalled on the learning test. Differences between groups in performance on the dependent variable suggest that the manipulation had an effect. That is, changes in the dependent variable *depend* on the independent variable.

An experimental study evaluates the relationship between two variables by manipulating one variable (the independent variable) and measuring one variable (the dependent variable). Note that in an experiment only one variable is actually measured. You should realize that this is very different from a correlational study, where both variables are measured and the data consist of two separate scores for each individual.

Often an experiment will include a condition in which the subjects do not receive any treatment. The scores from these subjects are then compared with scores from subjects who do receive the treatment. The goal of this type of study is to demonstrate that the treatment has an effect by showing that the scores in the treatment condition are substantially different from the scores in the no-treatment condition. In this kind of research, the no-treatment condition is called the *control condition* and the treatment condition is called the *experimental condition.*

DEFINITIONS

Individuals in a *control condition* do not receive the experimental treatment. Instead, they either receive no treatment or they receive a neutral, placebo treatment. The purpose of a control condition is to provide a baseline for comparison with the experimental condition.

Individuals in the *experimental condition* do receive the experimental treatment.

Note that the independent variable always consists of at least two values. (Something must have at least two different values before you can say that it is "variable.") For the temperature experiment (Figure 1.2), the independent variable is the temperature of the room, 70° versus 90°. For an experiment with an experimental group and a control group, the independent variable would be treatment versus no treatment.

THE QUASI-EXPERIMENTAL METHOD

As the name implies, the *quasi-experimental* method concerns research studies that are almost, but not quite, real experiments. You should recall that in a true experiment, the researcher manipulates one variable to create treatment conditions that can be compared. The manipulated variable is called the independent variable. In quasi-experimental research, there is no manipulation of an independent variable. Instead, one of the variables is used to define groups or conditions that can be compared. The variable that defines the groups is a naturally occurring, nonmanipulated variable that is usually a *subject variable* or a *time variable.*

A *subject variable* is a characteristic such as age or gender that varies from one subject to another. For example, a researcher might want to measure verbal ability scores for a group of 5-year-old girls and compare them with verbal scores for a group of 5-year-old boys. The structure of this study is shown in Figure 1.3(a). Note that the study uses one variable to create two groups to be compared (like an experiment), but the groups were not created by manipulating a variable. Specifically, a researcher cannot randomly assign subjects to two groups and then make one group into males and make the second group into females.

A *time variable* simply involves comparing individuals at different points in time. For example, a researcher may measure depression before therapy and then again after therapy. This study is comparing two groups of scores (before versus after) but the two groups were not created by manipulating a variable. See Figure 1.3(b). Specifically, the researcher cannot control or manipulate the passage of time.

Research studies using the quasi-experimental method are similar to those using the experimental method because they both use one variable to create groups or conditions, and then they both measure a second variable to obtain scores within each group or condition (see Figures 1.2 and 1.3). In an experimental study, the groups are created by manipulating an independent variable. For example, a researcher manipulates temperature to create a 70° room for one group and a 90° room for another group. In a quasi-experimental study, the researcher simply uses a nonmanipulated variable to define the groups. The variable defining the groups is called a *quasi-independent variable.* For example, a researcher compares vocabulary scores for a group of 4-year-old girls versus

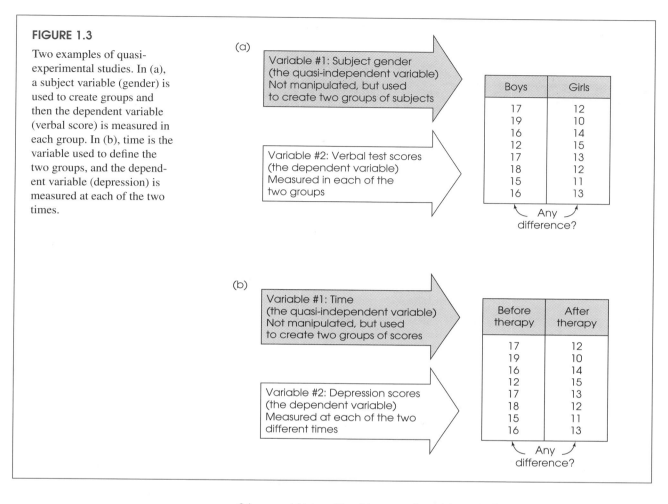

FIGURE 1.3

Two examples of quasi-experimental studies. In (a), a subject variable (gender) is used to create groups and then the dependent variable (verbal score) is measured in each group. In (b), time is the variable used to define the two groups, and the dependent variable (depression) is measured at each of the two times.

a group of 4-year-old boys. For this example, subject gender (male/female) is the quasi-independent variable.

DEFINITIONS

Instead of using an independent variable to create treatment conditions, a *quasi-experimental* research study uses a nonmanipulated variable to define the conditions that are being compared. The nonmanipulated variable is usually a subject variable (such as male versus female) or a time variable (such as before treatment versus after treatment).

The nonmanipulated variable that defines the conditions is called a *quasi-independent variable*.

As a final note, you should realize that because a quasi-experimental study does not include the manipulation of an independent variable, the researcher does not have full control over the variables. Therefore, you cannot make a cause-and-effect conclusion based on the results from a quasi-experimental study. For example, even if depression scores are lower after therapy than they were before therapy, you cannot conclude that the therapy is responsible for the change. Other factors may have caused the change. In particular, it is always possible that the people got better simply with the passage of time. Remember that a cause-and-effect relationship can be established only with a true experiment.

1. A researcher interviews parents to determine the amount of sugar consumed by their children. In addition, each child is observed on the playground to obtain a measure of activity level. The researcher finds that children with higher levels of sugar consumption also tend to have higher levels of activity. Is this an example of the experimental method or the correlational method?

2. What two elements are necessary for a research study to be an experiment?

3. The results from an experiment indicate that increasing the amount of indoor lighting during the winter months results in significantly lower levels of depression. Identify the independent variable and the dependent variable for this study.

ANSWERS

1. This is a correlational study. The researcher is simply observing the variables.

2. First, the researcher must manipulate one of the two variables being studied. Second, all other variables that might influence the results must be controlled.

3. The independent variable is the amount of indoor lighting, and the dependent variable is a measure of depression for each individual.

1.4 SCALES OF MEASUREMENT

WHAT IS A MEASUREMENT?

It should be obvious by now that data collection requires that we make measurements of our observations. Measurement involves either categorizing events (qualitative measurement) or using numbers to characterize the size of the event (quantitative measurement). Several types of scales are associated with measurements. The distinctions among the scales are important because they underscore the limitations of certain types of measurements and because certain statistical procedures are appropriate for data collected on some scales but not on others. If you were interested in people's heights, for example, you could measure a group of individuals by simply classifying them into three categories: tall, medium, and short. However, this simple classification would not tell you much about the actual heights of the individuals, and these measurements would not give you enough information to calculate an average height for the group. Although the simple classification would be adequate for some purposes, you would need more sophisticated measurements before you could answer more detailed questions. In this section, we examine four different scales of measurement, beginning with the simplest and moving to the most sophisticated.

NOMINAL SCALE

A *nominal scale* of measurement labels observations so that they fall into different categories.

DEFINITION

A *nominal scale* consists of a set of categories that have different names. Measurements on a nominal scale label and categorize observations but do not make any quantitative distinctions between observations.

The word *nominal* means "having to do with names." Measurements that are made on this scale involve naming things. For example, if we wish to know the sex of a person responding to a questionnaire, we would measure it on a nominal scale consisting of two categories. A researcher observing the behavior of a group of infant monkeys might categorize responses as playing, grooming, feeding, acting aggressively, or showing submissiveness. Again, this instance typifies a nominal scale of measurement. The nominal scale consists of qualitative distinctions.

If two individuals are measured on a nominal scale, it is possible to determine whether the two measurements are the same or different. However, if the measurements are different, you cannot determine how big the difference is, and you cannot say that one measurement is "more" or "less" than the other. A nominal scale consists of *qualitative* differences. It does not provide any information about *quantitative* differences between individuals.

Although the categories on a nominal scale are not quantitative values, they are occasionally represented by numbers. For example, the rooms or offices in a building may be identified by numbers. You should realize that the room numbers are simply names and do not reflect any quantitative information. Room 109 is not necessarily bigger than room 100 and certainly not 9 points bigger. It also is fairly common to use numerical values as a code for nominal categories when data are entered into computer programs. For example, the data from a survey may code males with a 0 and females with a 1. Again, the numerical values are simply names and do not represent any quantitative difference.

ORDINAL SCALE

In an *ordinal scale* of measurement, the categories that make up the scale not only have separate names (as in a nominal scale), but also are ranked in terms of magnitude. Thus, as the word *ordinal* implies, observations measured on an ordinal scale are categorized and arranged in rank order.

DEFINITION

An *ordinal scale* consists of a set of categories that are organized in an ordered sequence. Measurements on an ordinal scale rank observations in terms of size or magnitude.

For example, a job supervisor is asked to rank employees in terms of how well they perform their work. The resulting data will tell us who the supervisor considers the best worker, the second best, and so on. However, the data provide no information about the amount that the workers differ in job performance. The data may reveal that Jan, who is ranked second, is viewed as doing better work than Joe, who is ranked third. However, the data do not reveal *how much* better. This is a limitation of measurements on an ordinal scale. Thus, an ordinal scale provides information about the direction of difference between two measurements, but it does not reveal the magnitude of the difference.

INTERVAL AND RATIO SCALES

An *interval scale* of measurement consists of an ordered set of categories (like an ordinal scale), with the additional requirement that the categories form a series of intervals that are all exactly the same size. The additional feature of equal-sized intervals makes it possible to compute distances between values on an interval scale. On a ruler, for example, a 1-inch interval is the same size at every location on the ruler, and a 4-inch distance is exactly the same size no matter where it is measured on the ruler. Thus, the advantage of an interval scale (compared to nominal or ordinal) is that it allows you to measure *how much difference* there is between two individual scores.

A *ratio scale* of measurement has all the features of an interval scale but adds an absolute zero point. That is, on a ratio scale, a value of zero indicates *none* (a complete absence) of the variable being measured. The advantage of an absolute zero is that ratios of numbers on the scale reflect ratios of magnitude for the variable being measured. Thus, a ratio scale not only allows you to measure the difference between two individuals, but also allows you to describe the difference in terms of ratios. For example, you can state that one measurement is three times larger than another, or you can say that one score is only half as large as another. The distinction between an interval and a ratio scale is demonstrated in Example 1.2.

DEFINITIONS

An *interval scale* consists of ordered categories where all of the categories are intervals of exactly the same size. In an interval scale, equal differences between numbers on the scale reflect equal differences in magnitude. However, ratios of magnitudes are not meaningful.

A *ratio scale* is an interval scale with the additional feature of an absolute zero point. In a ratio scale, ratios of numbers reflect ratios of magnitude.

EXAMPLE 1.2

A researcher obtains measurements of height for a group of 8-year-old boys. Initially, the researcher simply records each child's height in inches, obtaining values such as 44, 51, 49, and so on. These initial measurements constitute a ratio scale. A value of zero represents no height (absolute zero). Also, it is possible to use these measurements to form ratios. For example, a child who is 80 inches tall is twice as tall as a 40-inch-tall child.

Now suppose the researcher converts the initial measurements into a new scale by calculating the difference between each child's actual height and the average height for this age group. A child who is 1 inch taller than average now gets a score of +1; a child 4 inches taller than average gets a score of +4. Similarly, a child who is 2 inches shorter than average gets a score of −2. The new scores constitute an interval scale of measurement. A score of zero no longer indicates an absence of height; now it simply means average height.

Note that both sets of scores involve measurement in inches, and you can compute differences, or intervals, on either scale. For example, there is a 6-inch difference in height between two boys who measure 57 and 51 inches tall on the first scale. Likewise, there is a 6-inch difference between two boys who measure +9 and +3 on the second scale. However, you should also note that ratio comparisons are not possible on the second scale. For example, a boy who measures +9 is *not* three times as tall as a boy who measures +3.

For most statistical applications, the distinction between an interval scale and a ratio scale is not particularly important. As we have seen, the process of measuring inches on a ruler can produce either interval scores or ratio scores depending on how the ruler is used. If you begin measuring at ground level (starting at zero) the ruler will produce ratio scores. On the other hand, measuring distances from an arbitrary (nonzero) point produces interval scores. However, the values from either scale allow basic arithmetic operations that permit us to calculate differences between scores, to sum scores, and to calculate average scores. For this reason, most dependent variables we will encounter are measured on either an interval or a ratio scale. Finally, you should realize that the distinction between different scales of measurement is often unclear when considering specific measurements. For example, the scores resulting from an IQ test are usually treated as measurements on an interval scale, but many researchers believe that IQ scores are more accurately described as ordinal data. An IQ score of 105 is clearly greater than a score of 100, but there is some question concerning *how much* difference in intelligence is reflected in the 5-point difference between these two scores.

1.5   DISCRETE AND CONTINUOUS VARIABLES

WHAT ARE THEY, AND HOW DO THEY DIFFER?

The variables in a study can be characterized by the type of values that can be assigned to them. A *discrete variable* consists of separate, indivisible categories. For this type of variable, there are no intermediate values between two adjacent categories. Consider the values displayed when dice are rolled. Between neighboring values—for example, seven dots and eight dots—no other values can ever be observed.

DEFINITION

A *discrete variable* consists of separate, indivisible categories. No values can exist between two neighboring categories.

Discrete variables are commonly restricted to whole countable numbers—for example, the number of children in a family or the number of students attending class. If you observe class attendance from day to day, you may find 18 students one day and 19 students the next day. However, it is impossible ever to observe a value between 18 and 19. A discrete variable may also consist of observations that differ qualitatively. For example, a psychologist observing patients may classify some as having panic disorders, others as having dissociative disorders, and some as having psychotic disorders. The type of disorder is a discrete variable because there are distinct and finite categories that can be observed.

On the other hand, many variables are not discrete. Variables such as time, height, and weight are not limited to a fixed set of separate, indivisible categories. You can measure time, for example, in hours, minutes, seconds, or fractions of seconds. These variables are called *continuous* because they can be divided into an infinite number of fractional parts.

DEFINITION

A *continuous variable* is divisible into an infinite number of fractional parts. For a continuous variable, there are an infinite number of possible values that fall between any two observed values.

Suppose, for example, that a researcher is measuring the amount of time required to solve a mental arithmetic problem. Because time is a continuous variable, it can be pictured as a continuous line (see Figure 1.4). Note that there are an infinite number of possible points on the line without any gaps or separations between neighboring points. For any two different points on the line, it is always possible to find a third value that is between the two points.

Two other factors apply to continuous variables:

1. When measuring a continuous variable, it should be very rare to obtain identical measurements for two different individuals. Because a continuous variable has

FIGURE 1.4

Representation of time has a continuous number line. Note that there are an infinite number of possible values with no gaps in the line.

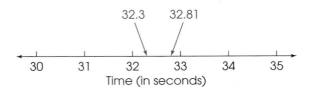

an infinite number of possible values, it should be almost impossible for two people to have exactly the same score. If the data show a substantial number of tied scores, then you should suspect that the measurement procedure is very crude or that the variable is not really continuous.

2. When measuring a continuous variable, each measurement category is actually an *interval* that must be defined by boundaries. For example, two people who both claim to weigh 150 pounds are probably not *exactly* the same weight. However, they are both around 150 pounds. One person may actually weigh 149.6 and the other actually weighs 150.3. Thus, a score of 150 is not a specific point on the scale but instead it is an interval (see Figure 1.5). To differentiate a score of 150 from a score of 149 or 151, we must set up boundaries on the scale of measurement. These boundaries are called *real limits* and are positioned exactly halfway between adjacent scores. Thus, a score of $X = 150$ pounds is actually an interval bounded by a lower real limit of 149.5 at the bottom and an upper real limit of 150.5 at the top. Any individual whose weight falls between these real limits will be assigned a score of $X = 150$.

DEFINITION

Real limits are the boundaries of intervals for scores that are represented on a continuous number line. The real limit separating two adjacent scores is located exactly halfway between the scores. Each score has two real limits. The *upper real limit* is at the top of the interval, and the *lower real limit* is at the bottom.

FIGURE 1.5

When measuring weight to the nearest whole pound, 149.6 and 150.3 are assigned the value of 150 (top). Any value in the interval between 149.5 and 150.5 is given the value of 150.

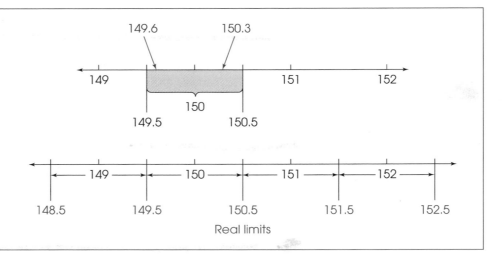

Real limits will be used later for constructing graphs and for various calculations with continuous scales. For now, however, you should realize that real limits are necessary whenever measuring a continuous variable.

1. The local fast-food restaurant offers small, medium, and large soft drinks. What kind of scale is used to measure the size of the drinks?

2. The Scholastic Aptitude Test (SAT) most likely measures aptitude on a(n) _____ scale.

3. In a study on perception of facial expressions, subjects must classify the emotions displayed in photographs of people as anger, sadness, joy, disgust, fear, or surprise. Emotional expression is measured on a(n) _____ scale.

4. A researcher studies the factors that determine how many children couples decide to have. The variable, number of children, is a _____ (discrete/continuous) variable.

5. An investigator studies how concept-formation ability changes with age. Age is a _____ (discrete/continuous) variable.

6. a. When measuring weight to the nearest pound, what are the real limits for a score of $X = 150$ pounds?

   b. When measuring weight to the nearest $\frac{1}{2}$ pound, what are the real limits for a score of $X = 144.5$ pounds?

ANSWERS   1. ordinal   2. interval   3. nominal   4. discrete   5. continuous

6. a. 149.5 and 150.5   b. 144.25 and 144.75

1.6   STATISTICAL NOTATION

Measurements of behavior usually will provide data composed of numerical values. These numbers form the basis of the computations that are done for statistical analyses. There is a standardized notation system for statistical procedures, and it is used to identify terms in equations and mathematical operations. Some general mathematical operations, notation, and basic algebra are outlined in the review section of Appendix A. There is also a skills assessment exam (page A-2) to help you determine whether you need the basic mathematics review. Here, we introduce some statistical notation that is used throughout this book. In subsequent chapters, additional notation will be introduced as it is needed.

SCORES   Making observations of a dependent variable in a study will typically yield values or scores for each subject. Raw scores are the original, unchanged scores obtained in the study. Scores for a particular variable are represented by the letter X. For example, if performance in your statistics course is measured by tests and you obtain a 35 on the

X
37
35
35
30
25
17
16

first test, then we could state that $X = 35$. A set of scores can be presented in a column that is headed by X. For example, quiz scores from your class might be listed as shown in the margin.

When observations are made for two variables, there will be two scores for each subject. The data can be presented as two lists labeled X and Y for the two variables. For example, observations of people's height in inches (variable X) and weight in pounds (variable Y) can be presented in the following manner. Each X, Y pair represents the observations made of a single subject.

X	Y
72	165
68	151
67	160
68	146
70	160
66	133

It is also useful to specify how many scores are in a set. We will use an uppercase letter N to represent the number of scores in a population and a lowercase letter n to represent the number of scores in a sample. Throughout the remainder of the book you will notice that we often will use notational differences to distinguish between samples and populations. For the height and weight data in the preceding table, $n = 6$ for both variables. You should realize that by using a lowercase letter n, we are implying that these data are a sample.

SUMMATION NOTATION

Many of the computations required in statistics will involve adding a set of scores. Because this procedure is used so frequently, a special notation is used to refer to the sum of a set of scores. The Greek letter *sigma,* or Σ, is used to stand for summation. The expression ΣX means to add all the scores for variable X. The summation sign Σ can be read as "the sum of." Thus, ΣX is read "the sum of the scores." For the following set of quiz scores,

$$10, \quad 6, \quad 7, \quad 4$$

$\Sigma X = 27$ and $N = 4$.

To use summation notation correctly, you should keep in mind the following two points:

1. The summation sign Σ is always followed by a symbol or mathematical expression. The symbol or expression identifies exactly which values are to be summed. To compute ΣX, for example, the symbol following the summation sign is X, and the task is to find the sum of the X values. On the other hand, to compute $\Sigma(X - 1)^2$, the summation sign is followed by a relatively complex mathematical expression, so your first task is to calculate all of the $(X - 1)^2$ values and then sum the results.

2. The summation process is often included with several other mathematical operations, such as multiplication or squaring. To obtain the correct answer, it is

essential that the different operations be done in the correct sequence. Following is a list showing the correct *order of operations* for performing mathematical operations. Most of this list should be familiar, but you should note that we have inserted the summation process as the fourth operation in the list.

More information on the order of operations for mathematics is available in the Math Review appendix, page A-3.

Order of Mathematical Operations

1. Any calculation contained within parentheses is done first.
2. Squaring (or raising to other exponents) is done second.
3. Multiplying and/or dividing is done third. A series of multiplication and/or division operations should be done in order from left to right.
4. Summation using the Σ notation is done next.
5. Finally, any other addition and/or subtraction is done.

The following examples demonstrate how summation notation will be used in most of the calculations and formulas we will present in this book.

EXAMPLE 1.3

A set of four scores consists of values 3, 1, 7, and 4. We will compute ΣX, ΣX^2, and $(\Sigma X)^2$ for these scores. To help demonstrate the calculations, we have constructed a *computational table* showing the original scores (the X values) in the first column. Additional columns can then be used to show additional steps that may be required in the calculation. The following table shows the squared scores (the X^2 values) that are needed to compute ΣX^2.

X	X^2
3	9
1	1
7	49
4	16

The first calculation, ΣX, does not include any parentheses, squaring, or multiplication, so we go directly to the summation operation. The X values are listed in the first column of the table, and we simply sum the values in this column:

$$\Sigma X = 3 + 1 + 7 + 4 = 15$$

To compute ΣX^2, the correct order of operations is to square each score and then find the sum of the squared values. The computational table shows the original scores and the results obtained from squaring (the first step in the calculation). The second step is to find the sum of the squared values, so we simply add the numbers in the X^2 column (see Box 1.1).

$$\Sigma X^2 = 9 + 1 + 49 + 16 = 75$$

The final calculation, $(\Sigma X)^2$, includes parentheses, so the first step is to perform the calculation inside the parentheses. Thus, we first find ΣX and then square this sum. Earlier, we computed $\Sigma X = 15$, so

$$(\Sigma X)^2 = (15)^2 = 225$$

1.1   COMPUTING ΣX^2 WITH A CALCULATOR

THE SUM of squared scores, ΣX^2, is a common expression in many statistical calculations. The following steps outline the most efficient procedure for using a typical, inexpensive hand calculator to find this sum. We assume that your calculator has one memory where you can store and retrieve information. *Caution:* The following instructions work for most calculators but not for every model. If you encounter trouble, don't panic—check your manual or talk with your instructor.

1. Clear the calculator memory. You may press the memory-clear key (usually MC) or simply turn the calculator off and then back on.

2. Enter the first score.

3. Press the multiply key ($\times$); then press the equals key ($=$). The squared score should appear in the display.

(Note that you do not need to enter a number twice to square it. Just follow the sequence: number-times-equals.)

4. Put the squared value into the calculator memory. For most calculators, you press the key labeled M+.

5. Enter the next score, square it, and add it to memory (steps 2, 3, and 4). (Note that you do not need to clear the display between scores.)

6. Continue this process for the full set of scores. Then retrieve the total, ΣX^2, from memory by pressing the memory-recall key (usually labeled MR).

Check this procedure with a simple set of scores, such as 1, 2, 3. You should find $\Sigma X^2 = 14$.

EXAMPLE 1.4   We will use the same set of four scores from Example 1.3 and compute $\Sigma(X - 1)$ and $\Sigma(X - 1)^2$. The following computational table will help demonstrate the calculations.

X	$(X - 1)$	$(X - 1)^2$	
3	2	4	The first column lists the
1	0	0	original scores, the second
7	6	36	column lists the $(X - 1)$
4	3	9	values, and the third column
			shows the $(X - 1)^2$ values.

To compute $\Sigma(X - 1)$, the first step is to perform the operation inside the parentheses. Thus, we begin by subtracting 1 point from each of the X values. The resulting values are listed in the middle column of the table. The next step is to sum the $(X - 1)$ values.

$$\Sigma(X - 1) = 2 + 0 + 6 + 3 = 11$$

The calculation of $\Sigma(X - 1)^2$ requires three steps. The first step (inside parentheses) is to subtract 1 point from each X value. The results from this step are shown in the middle column of the computational table. The second step is to square each of the $(X - 1)$ values. The results from this step are shown in the third column of the table. The final step is to sum the $(X - 1)^2$ values to obtain

$$\Sigma(X - 1)^2 = 4 + 0 + 36 + 9 = 49$$

Note that this calculation requires squaring before summing. A common mistake is to sum the $(X - 1)$ values and then square the total. Be careful!

EXAMPLE 1.5   In both of the preceding examples and in many other situations, the summation operation is the last step in the calculation. According to the order of operations, parentheses, exponents, and multiplication all come before summation. However, there are situations in which extra addition and subtraction are completed after the summation. For this example, we will use the same scores that appeared in the previous two examples, and we will compute $\Sigma X - 1$.

With no parentheses, exponents, or multiplication, the first step is the summation. Thus, we begin by computing ΣX. Earlier, we found $\Sigma X = 15$. The next step is to subtract 1 point from the total. For these data,

$$\Sigma X - 1 = 15 - 1 = 14$$

EXAMPLE 1.6   For this example, each individual has two scores. The first score is identified as X, and the second score is Y. With the help of the following computational table, we will compute ΣX, ΣY, and ΣXY.

X	Y	XY
3	5	15
1	3	3
7	4	28
4	2	8

To find ΣX, simply sum the values in the X column.

$$\Sigma X = 3 + 1 + 7 + 4 = 15$$

Similarly, ΣY is the sum of the Y values.

$$\Sigma Y = 5 + 3 + 4 + 2 = 14$$

To compute ΣXY, the first step is to multiply X times Y for each individual. The resulting products (XY values) are listed in the third column of the table. Finally, we sum the products to obtain

$$\Sigma XY = 15 + 3 + 28 + 8 = 54$$

LEARNING CHECK ◆   For the data in the margin, find each value requested.

X
4
3
5
2

1. ΣX 2. ΣX^2 3. $(\Sigma X)^2$ 4. $\Sigma X - 2$ 5. $\Sigma(X - 2)$

6. $\Sigma(X - 2)^2$ 7. N

ANSWERS   1. 14   2. 54   3. 196   4. 12   5. 6   6. 14   7. 4   ◆

ON THE WEB

THERE IS a Web site that provides additional help, practice, and general information about the topics presented in this book. The Web site can be reached directly at **www.wadsworth.com**. The opening page of the site provides access to all of the products made available by Wadsworth Publishing Company, and you are welcome to explore the entire site. To gain access to the information about statistics, you need to click on the *disciplines* box and then highlight *psychology* in the list of options. When you get to the psychology page, we suggest that you focus on the series of chapter-by-chapter practice quizzes that have been prepared specifically for this book and the series of statistics workshops that follow the main subject areas in this book.

Practice Quizzes   Practice quizzes, consisting of 10 multiple-choice items for each chapter, can be reached from the psychology home page by selecting the *choose quiz* option, and then clicking on *Gravetter/Wallnau Essentials 4e*. You can also find the quizzes by using the *choose area* option. To follow this path, first select *research methods and statistics*, then choose *statistics*, then click on *Gravetter/Wallnau Essentials 4e*, and finally, select *practice quizzes*. We suggest that you try each quiz as soon as you finish the chapter and use the results to help identify which sections you need to review. The quizzes are also a good study tool to use as a final check immediately before a class exam.

Workshops   The Web site also provides access to a series of statistics workshops developed by Glenn Meyer of Trinity University. These "workshops" are entertaining, easy-to-understand, real-world examples and analogies for the major statistics concepts presented in this book. The workshops present specific statistical procedures in the context of everyday living and often give a concrete and practical view of topics that may seem totally abstract and theoretical. The first workshop covers topics that will be presented in Chapters 3 and 4. When we reach that point in the book, we will remind you again about the workshops. To find the workshops from the psychology home page, begin with the *choose area* option and select *research methods and statistics*, then choose *statistics*, then click on *Gravetter/Wallnau Essentials 4e*, and finally, select *workshops*.

At the end of each chapter we will remind you about the Practice Quizzes and, where appropriate, we will direct you to the related Workshop. You can begin right now with Quiz 1.

SUMMARY

1. The term *statistics* is used to refer to methods for organizing, summarizing, and interpreting data.

2. Scientific questions usually concern a population that is the entire set of individuals one wishes to study. Usually, populations are so large that it is impossible to examine every individual, so most research is conducted with samples. A sample is a group selected from a population, usually for purposes of a research study.

3. Statistical methods can be classified into two broad categories: descriptive statistics, which organize and summarize data, and inferential statistics, which use sample data to draw inferences about populations.

4. The correlational method looks for interrelationships between variables but cannot determine the cause-and-effect nature of the relationship. The experimental method is able to establish causes and effects in a relationship.

5. In the experimental method, one variable (the independent variable) is manipulated, and another variable (the dependent variable) is observed for changes that may occur as a result of the manipulation. All other variables are controlled or held constant.

6. A measurement scale consists of a set of categories that are used to classify individuals. A nominal scale consists of categories that differ only in name and are not differentiated in terms of magnitude or direction. In an ordinal scale, the categories are differentiated in terms of direction, forming an ordered series. An interval scale consists of an ordered series of categories where the categories are all equal-sized intervals. With an interval scale, it is possi-

ble to differentiate direction and magnitude (or distance) between categories. Finally, a ratio scale is an interval scale where the zero point indicates none of the variable being measured. With a ratio scale, ratios of measurements reflect ratios of magnitude.

7. A discrete variable is one that can have only a finite number of values between any two values. It typically consists of whole numbers that vary in countable steps. A continuous variable can have an infinite number of values between any two values.

8. For a continuous variable, each score corresponds to an interval on the scale. The boundaries that separate intervals are called real limits. The real limits are located exactly halfway between adjacent scores.

9. The letter X is used to represent scores for a variable. If a second variable is used, Y represents its scores. The letter N is used as the symbol for the number of scores in a set. The Greek letter *sigma* (Σ) is used to stand for summation. Therefore, the expression ΣX is read "the sum of the scores."

KEY TERMS

statistics	descriptive statistics	independent variable	ordinal scale
population	inferential statistics	dependent variable	interval scale
sample	sampling error	control group	ratio scale
population parameter	variable	experimental group	discrete variable
sample statistic	constant	quasi-experimental method	continuous variable
data	correlational method	quasi-independent variable	real limits
raw score	experimental method	nominal scale	computational table

---

FOCUS ON PROBLEM SOLVING

1. It may help to simplify summation notation if you observe that the summation sign is always followed by a symbol (or symbolic expression)—for example, ΣX or $\Sigma(X + 3)$. This symbol specifies which values you are to add. If you use the symbol as a column heading and list all the appropriate values in the column, your task is simply to add up the numbers in the column. To find $\Sigma(X + 3)$, for example, you will need a column headed by $(X + 3)$. List all of the $(X + 3)$ values in the column and then find the total for the column.

2. Often, summation notation is part of a relatively complex mathematical expression that requires several steps of calculation. In this case, the best procedure is to use a computational table. Begin with the X values listed in the first column, then create a new column of values for each step in the calculation. For example, computing $\Sigma(X - 1)^2$ requires three steps and will use a computational table with three columns (see Example 1.4). The first column simply lists the original scores, X values.

STEP 1   The first step in the calculation is to subtract 1 from each X. A new column is added to the computational table to list each of the $(X - 1)$ values.

STEP 2   The second step is to square each $(X - 1)$ value. Again, a new column is added to list each of the $(X - 1)^2$ values.

STEP 3   The third step is to sum the $(X - 1)^2$ values, so you simply add the numbers in the $(X - 1)^2$ column.

DEMONSTRATION 1.1

SUMMATION NOTATION

A set of data consists of the following scores:

$$7, \quad 3, \quad 9, \quad 5, \quad 4$$

For these data, find the following values:

a. ΣX **b.** $(\Sigma X)^2$ **c.** ΣX^2 **d.** $\Sigma X + 5$ **e.** $\Sigma(X - 2)$

a. *Compute* ΣX. To compute ΣX, we simply add all of the scores in the group. For these data, we obtain

$$\Sigma X = 7 + 3 + 9 + 5 + 4 = 28$$

b. *Compute* $(\Sigma X)^2$. The key to determining the value of $(\Sigma X)^2$ is the presence of parentheses. The rule is to perform the operations that are inside the parentheses first.
   Step 1: Find the sum of the scores, ΣX.
   Step 2: Square the total.
We have already determined that ΣX is 28. Squaring this total, we obtain

$$(\Sigma X)^2 = (28)^2 = 784$$

c. *Compute* ΣX^2. Calculating the sum of the squared scores, ΣX^2, involves two steps.
   Step 1: Square each score.
   Step 2: Sum the squared values.
   These steps are most easily accomplished by constructing a computational table. The first column has the heading X and lists the scores. The second column is labeled X^2 and contains the squared value for each score. For this example, the table is shown in the margin.
   To find the value for ΣX^2, we sum the X^2 column.

X	X^2
7	49
3	9
9	81
5	25
4	16

$$\Sigma X^2 = 49 + 9 + 81 + 25 + 16 = 180$$

d. *Compute* $\Sigma X + 5$. In this expression, there are no parentheses. Thus, the summation sign is applied only to the X values.
   Step 1: Find the sum of X.
   Step 2: Add the constant 5 to the total from step 1.
Earlier we found that the sum of the scores is 28. For $\Sigma X + 5$, we obtain the following.

$$\Sigma X + 5 = 28 + 5 = 33$$

e. *Compute* $\Sigma(X - 2)$. The summation sign is followed by an expression with parentheses. In this case, $X - 2$ is treated as a single expression, and the summation sign applies to the $(X - 2)$ values.
   Step 1: Subtract 2 from every score.
   Step 2: Sum these new values.
   This problem can be done by using a computational table with two columns, headed X and $X - 2$, respectively. To determine the value for $\Sigma(X - 2)$, we sum the $X - 2$ column.

X	$X - 2$
7	5
3	1
9	7
5	3
4	2

$$\Sigma(X - 2) = 5 + 1 + 7 + 3 + 2 = 18$$

PROBLEMS

*1. Statistical methods are classified into two major categories: descriptive and inferential. Describe the general purpose for the statistical methods in each category.

2. Define the terms population, sample, parameter, and statistic, and explain how these terms are related to each other.

3. Describe the difference between an experimental research study and a quasi-experimental research study.

4. Identify the two elements of an experiment that make this type of research study different from other research methods.

5. Define the concept of *sampling error.* Be sure that your definition includes the concepts of *statistic* and *parameter.*

6. In general, research attempts to establish and explain relationships between variables. What terms are used to identify the two variables in an experiment? Define each term.

7. A researcher reports that individuals who survived one heart attack and were given daily doses of aspirin were significantly less likely to suffer a second heart attack than survivors who did not take aspirin. For this study, identify the independent variable and the dependent variable.

8. A developmental psychologist conducts a research study comparing vocabulary skills for 5-year-old boys and 5-year-old girls. Is this study an *experiment?* Explain why or why not.

9. A researcher studying sensory processes manipulates the loudness of a buzzer and measures how quickly subjects respond to the sound at different levels of intensity. Identify the independent and dependent variables for this study.

10. A researcher would like to evaluate the claim that large doses of vitamin C can help prevent the common cold. One group of subjects is given a large dose of the vitamin (500 mg per day), and a second group is given a placebo (sugar pill). The researcher records the number of colds each individual experiences during the 3-month winter season.
  a. Identify the dependent variable for this study.
  b. Is the dependent variable discrete or continuous?
  c. What scale of measurement (nominal, ordinal, interval, or ratio) is used to measure the dependent variable?

d. What research method is being used (experimental or correlational)?

11. A researcher prepares three lists of 40 words. One list contains all one-syllable words. The second list is all two-syllable words, and the third list consists of three-syllable words. Research subjects are given 5 minutes to study each list, and then must list as many words as they can recall. The researcher is interested in the relationship between recall and the number of syllables per word.
  a. Identify the independent variable for this experiment. What scale of measurement is used for the independent variable?
  b. Identify the dependent variable for this experiment. What scale of measurement is used for the dependent variable?

12. A researcher would like to examine the relationship between exposure to light and mood. In one section of an office building, the intensity of the lighting is increased by 50% for a 2-week period and in another section of the same building, the lighting is reduced by 25%. At the end of the 2-week period, the workers in both sections are given a mood inventory test. Identify the independent and the dependent variables for this study.

13. A researcher is comparing two brands of medication intended to reduce stomach acid. Before eating a very spicy meal, one group of people is given brand *X*, and another group is given brand *Y*. Two hours after eating, each person is asked to rate his or her level of indigestion using the following scale: no stomach upset, mild indigestion, moderate indigestion, severe indigestion.
  a. What is the independent variable for this study, and what scale of measurement is used for this variable?
  b. What is the dependent variable for this study, and what scale of measurement is used for this variable?

14. A researcher studying the effects of environment on mood asks subjects to sit alone in a waiting room for 15 minutes at the beginning of an experiment. Half of the subjects are assigned to a room with dark blue walls, and the other half are assigned to a room with bright yellow walls. After 15 minutes in the waiting room, each subject is brought into the lab and given a mood-assessment questionnaire.
  a. Identify the independent and dependent variables for this study.
  b. What scale of measurement is used for the independent variable?

15. Define and differentiate between a discrete variable and a continuous variable.

---

*Solutions for odd-numbered problems are provided in Appendix C.

16. A questionnaire asks individuals to report age, sex, eye color, and height. For each of the four variables:
  a. Classify the variable as either discrete or continuous.
  b. Identify the scale of measurement that probably would be used.

17. A researcher measures two individuals and then uses the resulting scores to make a statement comparing the two individuals. For each of the following statements, identify the scale of measurement (nominal, ordinal, interval, ratio) that the researcher used.
  a. I can only say that the two individuals are different.
  b. I can say that one individual scored 6 points higher than the other.
  c. I can say that one individual scored higher than the other, but I cannot specify how much higher.
  d. I can say that the score for one individual is twice as large as the score for the other individual.

18. For the following scores, find the value of each expression:
  a. ΣX
  b. ΣX^2
  c. $(\Sigma X)^2$
  d. $\Sigma(X - 1)$

X
4
2
6
1

19. Two scores, X and Y, are recorded for each of $n = 4$ subjects. For these scores, find the value of each expression:
  a. ΣX
  b. ΣY
  c. ΣXY

Subject	X	Y
A	3	2
B	4	1
C	2	3
D	6	4

20. Use summation notation to express each of the following calculations:
  a. Sum the scores, and then add 3 points to the total.
  b. Subtract 2 points from each score, and square the result. Then sum the squared values.
  c. Square each score, and sum the squared values. Then subtract 10 points from the sum.

21. Each of the following summation expressions requires a specific sequence of mathematical operations. For each expression, state in words the sequence of operations necessary to perform the specified calculations. For example, the expression $\Sigma(X + 1)$ instructs you to add 1 point to each score and then sum the resulting values.
  a. $\Sigma X - 4$
  b. ΣX^2
  c. $\Sigma(X + 4)^2$

22. For the following set of scores, find the value of each expression:
  a. ΣX
  b. ΣX^2
  c. $\Sigma(X + 1)$
  d. $\Sigma(X + 1)^2$

X
2
3
0
6

23. For the following set of scores, find the value of each expression:
  a. ΣX
  b. ΣX^2
  c. $\Sigma(X + 3)$

X
4
-2
0
-1
-4

24. For the following set of scores, find the value of each expression:
  a. ΣX
  b. ΣY
  c. ΣXY

X	Y
-2	4
1	5
4	2
-4	3

25. Statistical calculations often use summation with the following general structure: $\Sigma(X - 4)^2$.
  a. What is the first step for this computation? What is the second step? The third?
  b. Compute $\Sigma(X - 4)^2$ for the following set of scores: 3, 1, 8, 2, 6.
  c. Compute $\Sigma(X - 4)$ for the same set of scores.

CHAPTER 2

FREQUENCY DISTRIBUTIONS

The following items are considered essential background material for this chapter. If you doubt your knowledge of any of these items, you should review the appropriate chapter or section before proceeding.

- Proportions (math review, Appendix A)
  - Fractions
  - Decimals
  - Percentages
- Scales of measurement (Chapter 1): nominal, ordinal, interval, and ratio
- Continuous and discrete variables (Chapter 1)

CONTENTS

2.1   INTRODUCTION

When a researcher finishes the data collection phase of an experiment, the results usually consist of pages of numbers. The immediate problem for the researcher is to organize the scores into some comprehensible form so that any patterns in the data can be seen easily and communicated to others. This is the job of descriptive statistics: to simplify the organization and presentation of data. One of the most common procedures for organizing a set of data is to place the scores in a frequency distribution.

DEFINITION   A *frequency distribution* is an organized tabulation of the number of individual scores located in each category on the scale of measurement.

A frequency distribution takes a disorganized set of scores and places them in order from highest to lowest, grouping together all individual scores that are the same. If the highest score is $X = 10$, for example, the frequency distribution groups together all the 10s, then all the 9s, then the 8s, and so on. Thus, a frequency distribution allows the researcher to see "at a glance" the entire set of scores. It shows whether the scores are generally high or low and whether they are concentrated in one area or spread out across the entire scale and generally provides an organized picture of the data. In addition to providing a picture of the entire set of scores, a frequency distribution allows the researcher to see the location of any individual score relative to all of the other scores in the set.

A frequency distribution can be structured either as a table or as a graph, but in either case, the distribution presents the same two elements:

1. The set of categories that make up the original measurement scale

2. A record of the frequency, or number of individuals in each category

Thus, a frequency distribution presents a picture of how the individual scores are distributed on the measurement scale—hence the name *frequency distribution*.

2.2   FREQUENCY DISTRIBUTION TABLES

It is customary to list scores from highest to lowest, but this is an arbitrary arrangement. Many computer programs will list scores from lowest to highest.

The simplest frequency distribution table presents the measurement scale by listing the measurement categories (X values) in a column from highest to lowest. Beside each X value, we indicate the frequency, or the number of times the score occurred in the data. It is customary to use an X as the column heading for the scores and an f as the column heading for the frequencies. An example of a frequency distribution table follows.

EXAMPLE 2.1   The following set of $N = 20$ scores was obtained from a 10-point statistics quiz. We will organize these scores by constructing a frequency distribution table. Scores:

8, 9, 8, 7, 10, 9, 6, 4, 9, 8,

7, 8, 10, 9, 8, 6, 9, 7, 8, 8

X	f
10	2
9	5
8	7
7	3
6	2
5	0
4	1

1. The highest score is $X = 10$, and the lowest score is $X = 4$. Therefore, the first column of the table will list the scale of measurement (X values) from 10 down to 4. Note that all of the possible values are listed in the table. For example, no one had a score of $X = 5$, but this value is included.

2. The frequency associated with each score is recorded in the second column. For example, two people had scores of $X = 6$, so there is a 2 in the f column beside $X = 6$.

Because the table organizes the scores, it is possible to see very quickly the general quiz results. For example, there were only two perfect scores, but most of the class had high grades (8s and 9s). With one exception (the score of $X = 4$), it appears that the class has learned the material fairly well.

Note that the X values in a frequency distribution table represent the scale of measurement, *not* the actual set of scores. For example, the X column shows only one value for $X = 10$, but the frequency column indicates that there are actually two values of $X = 10$. Also, the X column shows a value of $X = 5$, but the frequency column indicates that there are actually no scores of $X = 5$.

You also should note that the frequencies can be used to find the total number of scores in the distribution. By adding up the frequencies, you will obtain the total number of individuals:

$$\Sigma f = N$$

OBTAINING ΣX FROM A FREQUENCY DISTRIBUTION TABLE

There may be times when you need to compute the sum of the scores, ΣX, or perform other computations for a set of scores that has been organized into a frequency distribution table. Such calculations can present a problem because many students tend to disregard the frequencies and use only the values listed in the X column of the table. However, this practice is incorrect because it ignores the information provided by the frequency (f) column.

When it is necessary to perform calculations for scores that have been organized into a frequency distribution table, the safest procedure is to take the individual scores out of the table before you begin any computations. Consider the frequency distribution table for Example 2.1. The table shows that the distribution has two 10s, five 9s, seven 8s, and so on. If you simply list all of the individual scores, then you can safely proceed with calculations such as finding ΣX or ΣX^2. Note that the complete set contains $N = \Sigma f = 20$ scores and your list should contain 20 values. For example, to compute ΣX you simply add all 20 of the scores:

$$\Sigma X = 10 + 10 + 9 + 9 + 9 + 9 + 9 + 8 + 8$$
$$+ 8 + 8 + 8 + 8 + 8 + \cdots$$

For the data in Example 2.1, you should obtain $\Sigma X = 158$. Try it yourself. Similarly, to obtain ΣX^2 you simply square each of the 20 scores and then add the squared values.

$$\Sigma X^2 = 10^2 + 10^2 + 9^2 + 9^2 + 9^2 + 9^2 + 9^2 + 8^2 + 8^2$$
$$+ 8^2 + 8^2 + 8^2 + 8^2 + 8^2 + \cdots$$

This time you should obtain $\Sigma X^2 = 1288$.

An alternative way to get ΣX from a frequency distribution table is to multiply each X value by its frequency and then add these products. This sum may be expressed in symbols as ΣfX. The computation is summarized as follows for the data in Example 2.1:

Caution: Doing calculations within the table works well for ΣX but can lead to errors for more complex formulas.

X	f	fX	
10	2	20	(The two 10s total 20)
9	5	45	(The five 9s total 45)
8	7	56	(The seven 8s total 56)
7	3	21	(The three 7s total 21)
6	2	12	(The two 6s total 12)
5	0	0	(There are no 5s)
4	1	4	(The one 4 totals 4)

$$\Sigma fX = 158$$

No matter which method you use to find ΣX, the important point is that you must use the information given in the frequency column.

PROPORTIONS AND PERCENTAGES

In addition to the two basic columns of a frequency distribution, there are other measures that describe the distribution of scores and can be incorporated into the table. The two most common are proportion and percentage.

Proportion measures the fraction of the total group that is associated with each score. In Example 2.1, there were two individuals with $X = 6$. Thus, 2 out of 20 people had $X = 6$, so the proportion is $2/20 = 0.10$. In general, the proportion associated with each score is

$$\text{proportion} = p = \frac{f}{N}$$

Because proportions describe the frequency (f) in relation to the total number (N), they often are called *relative frequencies*. Although proportions can be expressed as fractions (for example, 2/20), they more commonly appear as decimals. A column of proportions, headed with a p, can be added to the basic frequency distribution table (see Example 2.2).

In addition to using frequencies (f) and proportions (p), researchers often describe a distribution of scores with percentages. For example, an instructor might describe the results of an exam by saying that 15% of the class earned As, 23% Bs, and so on. To compute the percentage associated with each score, you first find the proportion (p) and then multiply by 100:

$$\text{percentage} = p(100) = \frac{f}{N}(100)$$

Percentages can be included in a frequency distribution table by adding a column headed with % (see Example 2.2).

EXAMPLE 2.2 The frequency distribution table from Example 2.1 is repeated here. This time we have added columns showing the proportion (p) and the percentage (%) associated with each score.

X	f	$p = f/N$	$\% = p(100)$
10	2	2/20 = 0.10	10%
9	5	5/20 = 0.25	25%
8	7	7/20 = 0.35	35%
7	3	3/20 = 0.15	15%
6	2	2/20 = 0.10	10%
5	0	0/20 = 0	0%
4	1	1/20 = 0.05	5%

GROUPED FREQUENCY DISTRIBUTION TABLES

When the scores are whole numbers, the total number of rows for a regular table can be obtained by finding the difference between the highest and the lowest scores and adding 1:

rows = highest − lowest + 1

When a set of data covers a wide range of values, it is unreasonable to list all the individual scores in a frequency distribution table. For example, a set of exam scores ranges from a low of $X = 41$ to a high of $X = 96$. These scores cover a range of over 50 points. If we were to list all the individual scores, it would take 56 rows to complete the frequency distribution table. Although this would organize and simplify the data, the table would be long and cumbersome. Remember, the purpose for constructing a table is to obtain a relatively simple, organized picture of the data. This can be accomplished by grouping the scores into intervals and then listing the intervals in the table instead of listing each individual score. For example, we could construct a table showing the number of students who had scores in the 90s, the number with scores in the 80s, and so on. The result is called a *grouped frequency distribution table* because we are presenting groups of scores rather than individual values. The groups, or intervals, are called *class intervals.*

There are several rules that help guide you in the construction of a grouped frequency distribution table. These rules should be considered guidelines rather than absolute requirements, but they do help produce a simple, well-organized, and easily understood table.

RULE 1 The grouped frequency distribution table should have about 10 class intervals. If a table has many more than 10 intervals, it becomes cumbersome and defeats the purpose of a frequency distribution table. On the other hand, if you have too few intervals, you begin to lose information about the distribution of the scores. At the extreme, with only 1 interval, the table would not tell you anything about how the scores are distributed. Remember, the purpose of a frequency distribution is to help you see the data. With too few or too many intervals, the table will not provide a clear picture. You should note that 10 intervals is a general guide. If you are constructing a table on a blackboard, for example, you probably will want only 5 or 6 intervals. If the table is to be printed in a scientific report, you may want 12 or 15 intervals. In each case, your goal is to present a table that is easy to see and understand.

RULE 2 The width of each interval should be a relatively simple number. For example, 2, 5, 10, or 20 would be a good choice for the interval width. Note that it is easy to count by 5s or 10s. These numbers are easy to understand and make it possible for someone to see quickly how you have divided the range.

RULE 3   Each class interval should start with a score that is a multiple of the width. If you decide to use an interval width of 10 points, for example, you should use a multiple of 10 as the lowest score in each interval. Thus, the bottom interval might start with 30, and successive intervals would start with 40, 50, and so on as you move up the scale. The goal is to make it easier for someone to understand how the table was constructed.

RULE 4   All intervals should be the same width. They should cover the range of scores completely, with no gaps and no overlaps, so that any particular score belongs in exactly one interval.

The application of these rules is demonstrated in Example 2.3.

EXAMPLE 2.3   An instructor has obtained the set of $N = 25$ exam scores shown here. To help organize these scores, we will place them in a frequency distribution table. Scores:

82, 75, 88, 93, 53, 84, 87, 58, 72, 94, 69, 84, 61,

91, 64, 87, 84, 70, 76, 89, 75, 80, 73, 78, 60

Remember, the number of rows is determined by

highest − lowest + 1

The first step is to determine the range of scores. For these data, the smallest score is $X = 53$ and the largest score is $X = 94$, so a total of 42 rows would be needed for a table that lists each individual score. Because 42 rows would not provide a simple table, we will have to group the scores into class intervals.

The best method for finding a good interval width is a systematic trial-and-error approach that uses rules 1 and 2 simultaneously. According to rule 1, we want about 10 intervals; according to rule 2, we want the interval width to be a simple number. For this example, the scores cover a range of 42 points, so we will try several different interval widths to see how many intervals are needed to cover this range. For example, if we try a width of 2, how many intervals would it take to cover the range of scores? With each interval only 2 points wide, we would need 21 intervals to cover the range. This is too many. What about an interval width of 5? What about a width of 10? The following table shows how many intervals would be needed for these possible widths:

To find the number of intervals, divide the range by the width and round up any fractions.

Width	Number of intervals needed to cover a range of 42 values	
2	21	(too many)
5	9	(OK)
10	5	(too few)

Note that an interval width of 5 will result in about 10 intervals, which is exactly what we want.

The next step is to actually identify the intervals. In this example, we have decided to use an interval width of 5 points. According to rule 3, each of the class intervals should start with a multiple of 5. Because the lowest score for these data is $X = 53$, the

TABLE 2.1

A grouped frequency distribution table showing the data from Example 2.3. The original scores range from a high of $X = 94$ to a low of $X = 53$. This range has been divided into 9 intervals, with each interval exactly 5 points wide. The frequency column (f) lists the number of individuals with scores in each of the class intervals.

X	f
90–94	3
85–89	4
80–84	5
75–79	4
70–74	3
65–69	1
60–64	3
55–59	1
50–54	1

gaps of 5

bottom interval would start at 50 and go to 54. Note that the lowest score, $X = 50$, is a multiple of 5. Also note that the interval contains five values (50, 51, 52, 53, 54), so it does have a width of 5 points. The next interval would start at 55 (also a multiple of 5) and go to 59. The complete frequency distribution table showing all of the class intervals is presented in Table 2.1.

Once the class intervals are listed, you complete the table by adding a column of frequencies. The values in the frequency column indicate the number of individuals whose scores are located in that class interval. For this example, there were three students with scores in the 60–64 interval, so the frequency for this class interval is $f = 3$ (see Table 2.1).

Finally, you should note that after the scores have been placed in a grouped table, you lose information about the specific value for any individual score. For example, Table 2.1 shows that one person had a score between 65 and 69, but the table does not identify the exact value for the score. In general, the wider the class intervals are, the more information is lost. In Table 2.1 the interval width is 5 points and the table shows that there are three people with scores in the lower 60s and one person with a score in the upper 60s. This information would be lost if the interval width was increased to 10 points. With an interval width of 10, all of the 60s would be grouped together into one interval labeled 60–69. The table would show a frequency of four people in the 60–69 interval, but it would not tell whether the scores were in the upper 60s or the lower 60s.

LEARNING CHECK

1. Place the following scores in a frequency distribution table:

    2, 3, 1, 2, 5, 4, 5, 5, 1, 4, 2, 2

2. A set of scores ranges from a high of $X = 142$ to a low of $X = 65$.
    a. Explain why it would not be reasonable to display these scores in a *regular* frequency distribution table.
    b. Determine what interval width is most appropriate for a grouped frequency distribution for this set of scores.
    c. What range of values would form the bottom interval for the grouped table?

3. Find the values for N and ΣX for the population of scores in the following frequency distribution table:

X	f
5	1
4	3
3	5
2	2
1	2

4. Using only the frequency distribution table presented in Table 2.1, how many individuals had a score of $X = 73$?

ANSWERS   1.

X	f
5	3
4	2
3	1
2	4
1	2

2. **a.** It would require a table with 78 rows to list all the individual score values. This is too many rows.

   b. An interval width of 10 points is probably best. With a width of 10, it would require 8 intervals to cover the range of scores. In some circumstances, an interval width of 5 points (requiring 16 intervals) might be appropriate.

   c. With a width of 10, the bottom interval would be 60–69.

3. There are $N = 13$ scores summarized in the table ($\Sigma f = 13$). The 13 scores sum to $\Sigma X = 38$.

4. After a set of scores has been summarized in a grouped table, you cannot determine the frequency for any specific score. There is no way to determine how many individuals had $X = 73$ from the table alone. (You can say that *at most* three people had $X = 73$.)   ◆

2.3 FREQUENCY DISTRIBUTION GRAPHS

A frequency distribution graph is basically a picture of the information available in a frequency distribution table. We will consider several different types of graphs, but all start with two perpendicular lines called axes. The horizontal line is called the X-axis, or the abscissa. The vertical line is called the Y-axis, or the ordinate. The scale of measurement (X values) is listed along the X-axis in increasing value from left to right. The frequencies are listed on the Y-axis in increasing value from bottom to top. As a general rule, the point where the two axes intersect should have a value of zero for both the scores and the frequencies. A final general rule is that the graph should be constructed so that its height (Y-axis) is approximately two-thirds to three-quarters of its length (X-axis). Violating these guidelines can result in graphs that give a misleading picture of the data (see Box 2.1).

HISTOGRAMS AND BAR GRAPHS

The first type of graph we will consider is called either a histogram or a bar graph. For this type of graph, you simply draw a bar above each X value so that the height of the bar corresponds to the frequency of the score. As you will see, the choice of using a histogram or a bar graph is determined by the scale of measurement.

Remember that interval and ratio scales consist of a series of numerical categories like the inches on a ruler or the seconds on a stopwatch.

Histograms   When a frequency distribution graph is showing data from an interval or a ratio scale, the bars are drawn so that adjacent bars touch each other. The touching bars produce a continuous figure, which emphasizes the continuity of the variable. This type of frequency distribution graph is called a histogram. An example of a histogram is presented in Figure 2.1.

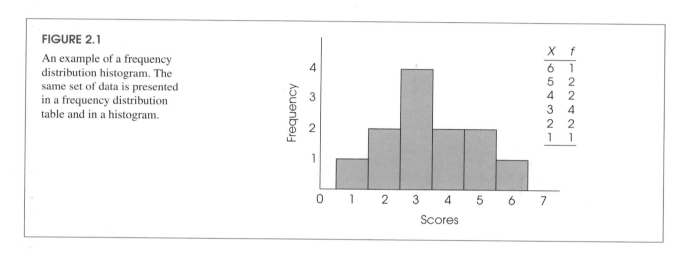

FIGURE 2.1

An example of a frequency distribution histogram. The same set of data is presented in a frequency distribution table and in a histogram.

X	f
6	1
5	2
4	2
3	4
2	2
1	1

DEFINITION

For a *histogram,* a vertical bar is drawn above each score so that

1. The height of the bar corresponds to the frequency.
2. The width of the bar extends to the real limits of the score.

A histogram is used when the data are measured on an interval or a ratio scale.

When data have been grouped into class intervals, you can construct a frequency distribution histogram by drawing a bar above each interval so that the width of the bar extends to the real limits of the interval (the lower real limit of the lowest score and the upper real limit of the highest score in the interval). This process is demonstrated in Figure 2.2.

Bar graphs   When you are presenting the frequency distribution for data from a nominal or an ordinal scale, the graph is constructed so that there is some space between the bars. In this case, the separate bars emphasize that the scale consists of separate, distinct categories. The resulting graph is called a bar graph. An example of a frequency distribution bar graph is given in Figure 2.3.

FIGURE 2.2

An example of a frequency distribution histogram for grouped data. The same set of data is presented in a grouped frequency distribution table and in a histogram.

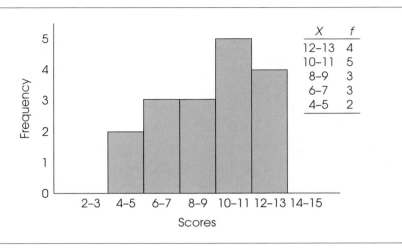

X	f
12–13	4
10–11	5
8–9	3
6–7	3
4–5	2

DEFINITION   For a *bar graph,* a vertical bar is drawn above each score (or category) so that

1. The height of the bar corresponds to the frequency.
2. There is a space separating each bar from the next.

A bar graph is used when the data are measured on a nominal or an ordinal scale.

FREQUENCY DISTRIBUTION POLYGONS

Instead of a histogram, many researchers prefer to display a frequency distribution using a polygon.

DEFINITION   In a *frequency distribution polygon,* a single dot is drawn above each score so that

1. The dot is centered above the score.
2. The vertical location (height) of the dot corresponds to the frequency.

A continuous line is then drawn connecting these dots. The graph is completed by drawing a line down to the *X*-axis (zero frequency) at a point just beyond each end of the range of scores.

FIGURE 2.3

A bar graph showing the distribution of personality types in a sample of college students. Because personality type is a discrete variable measured on a nominal scale, the graph is drawn with space between the bars.

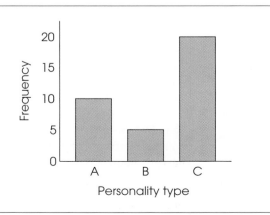

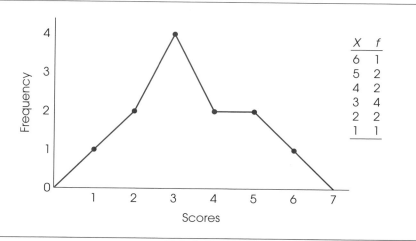

FIGURE 2.4

An example of a frequency distribution polygon. The same set of data is presented in a frequency distribution table and in a polygon. Note that these data are shown in a histogram in Figure 2.1.

X	f
6	1
5	2
4	2
3	4
2	2
1	1

As with a histogram, the frequency distribution polygon is intended for use with interval or ratio scales. An example of a polygon is shown in Figure 2.4. A polygon also can be used with data that have been grouped into class intervals. In this case, you position the dots directly above the midpoint of each class interval. An example of a frequency distribution polygon with grouped data is shown in Figure 2.5.

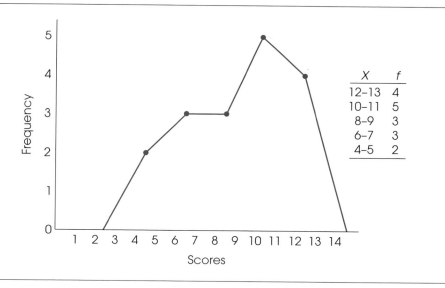

FIGURE 2.5

An example of a frequency distribution polygon for grouped data. The same set of data is presented in a grouped frequency distribution table and in a polygon. Note that these data are shown in a histogram in Figure 2.2.

X	f
12–13	4
10–11	5
8–9	3
6–7	3
4–5	2

RELATIVE FREQUENCIES AND SMOOTH CURVES

Often, it is impossible to construct a frequency distribution for a population because there are simply too many individuals for a researcher to obtain measurements and frequencies for the entire group. In this case, it is customary to draw a frequency distribution graph, showing *relative frequencies* (proportions) on the vertical axis. For example, a researcher may know that a particular species of animal has three times as many females as males in the population. This fact could be displayed in a bar graph by simply making the bar above "female" three times as tall as the bar above "male." Note that the actual frequencies are unknown but that the relative frequencies of males and females can still be presented in a graph.

For populations where the scores are measured on interval or ratio scales, it is customary to show the relative frequencies with a smooth curve instead of the series of bars or lines that make up histograms or polygons. The smooth curve indicates that the graph is not showing a specific series of real frequencies but rather is showing a distribution that is not limited to one specific set of data. One commonly occurring population distribution is the normal curve. The word *normal* refers to a specific shape that can be precisely defined by an equation. Less precisely, we can describe a normal distribution as being symmetrical, with the greatest frequency in the middle and relatively smaller frequencies as you move toward either extreme. A good example of a normal distribution is the population distribution for IQ scores shown in Figure 2.6. Because normal-shaped distributions occur commonly and because this shape is mathematically guaranteed in certain situations, it will receive extensive attention throughout this book.

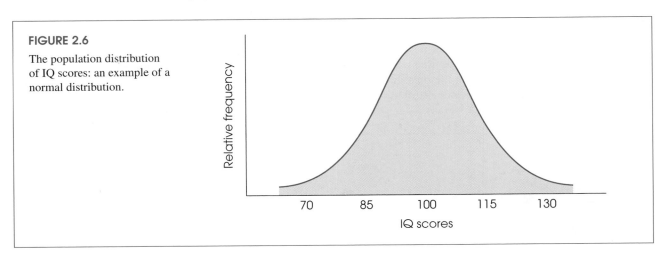

FIGURE 2.6

The population distribution of IQ scores: an example of a normal distribution.

In the future, we will be referring to *distributions of scores*. Whenever the term *distribution* appears, you should conjure up an image of a frequency distribution graph. The graph provides a picture showing exactly where the individual scores are located. To make this concept more concrete, you might find it useful to think of the graph as showing a pile of individuals. In Figure 2.6, for example, the pile is highest at an IQ score of around 100 because most people have "average" IQs. There are only a few individuals piled up with IQ scores above 130; it must be lonely at the top.

2.4   THE SHAPE OF A FREQUENCY DISTRIBUTION

Rather than drawing a complete frequency distribution graph, researchers often simply describe a distribution by listing its characteristics. There are three characteristics that completely describe any distribution: shape, central tendency, and variability. In simple terms, central tendency measures where the center of the distribution is located. Vari-

2.1 THE USE AND MISUSE OF GRAPHS

ALTHOUGH GRAPHS are intended to provide an accurate picture of a set of data, they can be used to exaggerate or misrepresent a set of scores. These misrepresentations generally result from failing to follow the basic rules for graph construction. The following example demonstrates how the same set of data can be presented in two entirely different ways by manipulating the structure of a graph.

For the past several years, the city has kept records of the number of major felonies. The data are summarized as follows:

Year	Number of major felonies
1998	218
1999	225
2000	229

These same data are shown in two different graphs in Figure 2.7. In the first graph, we have exaggerated the height, and we started numbering the Y-axis at 210 rather than at zero. As a result, the graph seems to indicate a rapid rise in the crime rate over the 3-year period. In the second graph, we have expanded the range of values on the Y-axis and used zero as the starting point. The result is a graph that shows little change in the crime rate over the 3-year period.

Which graph is correct? The answer is that neither one is very good. Remember that the purpose of a graph is to provide an accurate display of the data. Figure 2.7(a) exaggerates the differences between years, while the graph in Figure 2.7(b) conceals the differences. Some compromise is needed. You also should note that in some cases a graph may not be the best way to display information. For these data, for example, showing the numbers in a table would be better than either graph.

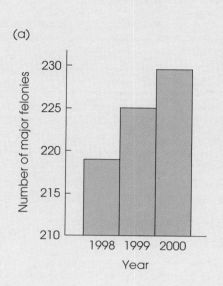

(a)

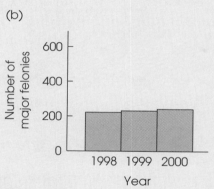

(b)

FIGURE 2.7

Two graphs showing the number of major felonies in a city over a 3-year period. Both graphs are showing exactly the same data. However, the first graph gives the appearance that the crime rate is high and rising rapidly. The second graph gives the impression that the crime rate is low and has not changed over the 3-year period.

ability tells whether the scores are spread over a wide range or are clustered together. Central tendency and variability will be covered in detail in Chapters 3 and 4. Technically, the shape of a distribution is defined by an equation that prescribes the exact relationship between each X and Y value on the graph. However, we will rely on a few less-precise terms that will serve to describe the shape of most distributions.

Nearly all distributions can be classified as being either symmetrical or skewed.

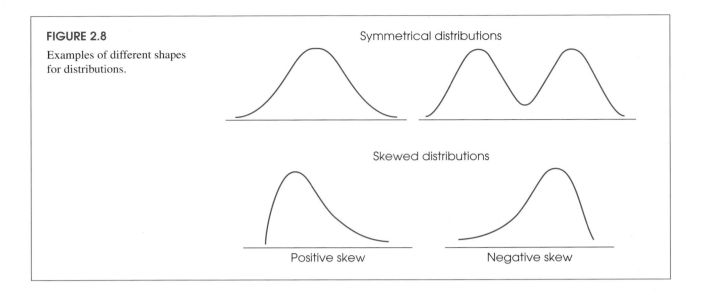

FIGURE 2.8

Examples of different shapes for distributions.

DEFINITIONS

In a *symmetrical distribution,* it is possible to draw a vertical line through the middle so that one side of the distribution is a mirror image of the other (see Figure 2.8).

In a *skewed distribution,* the scores tend to pile up toward one end of the scale and taper off gradually at the other end (see Figure 2.8).

The section where the scores taper off toward one end of a distribution is called the *tail* of the distribution.

A skewed distribution with the tail on the right-hand side is said to be *positively skewed* because the tail points toward the positive (above-zero) end of the *X*-axis. If the tail points to the left, the distribution is said to be *negatively skewed* (see Figure 2.8).

For a very difficult exam, most scores will tend to be low, with only a few individuals earning high scores. This will produce a positively skewed distribution. Similarly, a very easy exam will tend to produce a negatively skewed distribution, with most of the students earning high scores and only a few with low values.

LEARNING CHECK ◆

1. Sketch a frequency distribution histogram and a frequency distribution polygon for the data in the following table:

X	f
5	4
4	6
3	3
2	1
1	1

2. Describe the shape of the distribution in Exercise 1.

3. What type of graph would be appropriate to show the number of gold medals, silver medals, and bronze medals won by the United States during the 2000 Olympics?

4. What shape would you expect for the distribution of salaries for all employees of a major industry?

ANSWERS   1. The graphs are shown in Figure 2.9.

2. The distribution is negatively skewed.

3. A bar graph is appropriate for ordinal data.

4. The distribution probably would be positively skewed, with most employees earning an average salary and a relatively small number of top executives with very large salaries.   ◆

FIGURE 2.9

Answers to Learning Check Exercise 1.

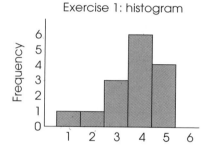

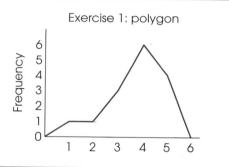

ON THE WEB

REMEMBER, A practice quiz for Chapter 2 is available on the Wadsworth Web site at **www.wadsworth.com**. You can use the quiz to test your knowledge on the material in this chapter and determine which parts of the chapter may need more study. For more information about finding the quizzes and workshops, see page 24.

SUMMARY

1. The goal of descriptive statistics is to simplify the organization and presentation of data. One descriptive technique is to place the data in a frequency distribution table or graph that shows exactly how many individuals (or scores) are located in each category on the scale of measurement.

2. A frequency distribution table lists the categories that make up the scale of measurement (the X values) in one column. Beside each X value, in a second column, is the frequency or number of individuals in that category. The table may include a proportion column showing the relative frequency for each category:

$$\text{proportion} = p = \frac{f}{n}$$

The table may also include a percentage column showing the percentage associated with each X value:

$$\text{percentage} = p(100) = \frac{f}{n}(100)$$

3. It is recommended that a frequency distribution table have a maximum of 10 to 15 rows to keep it simple. If the scores cover a range that is wider than this suggested maximum, it is customary to divide the range into sections called class intervals. These intervals are then listed in the frequency distribution table along with the frequency or number of individuals with scores in each interval. The result is called a grouped frequency distribution. The guidelines for constructing a grouped frequency distribution table are as follows:
   a. There should be about 10 intervals.
   b. The width of each interval should be a simple number (e.g., 2, 5, or 10).
   c. The bottom score in each interval should be a multiple of the width.
   d. All intervals should be the same width, and they should cover the range of scores with no gaps.

4. A frequency distribution graph lists scores on the horizontal axis and frequencies on the vertical axis. The type of graph used to display a distribution depends on the scale of measurement used. For interval or ratio scales, you should use a histogram or a polygon. For a histogram, a bar is drawn above each score so that the height of the bar corresponds to the frequency. Each bar extends to the real limits of the score so that adjacent bars touch. For a polygon, a dot is placed above the midpoint of each score or class interval so that the height of the dot corresponds to the frequency; then lines are drawn to connect the dots. Bar graphs are used with nominal or ordinal scales. Bar graphs are similar to histograms except that gaps are left between adjacent bars.

5. Shape is one of the basic characteristics used to describe a distribution of scores. Most distributions can be classified as either symmetrical or skewed. A skewed distribution that tails off to the right is said to be positively skewed. If it tails off to the left, it is negatively skewed.

KEY TERMS

frequency distribution	class interval	polygon	positively skewed distribution
grouped frequency distribution	histogram	relative frequency	negatively skewed distribution
	bar graph	symmetrical distribution	

FOCUS ON PROBLEM SOLVING

1. The reason for constructing frequency distributions is to put a disorganized set of raw data into a comprehensible, organized format. Because several different types of frequency distribution tables and graphs are available, one problem is deciding which type should be used. Tables have the advantage of being easier to construct, but graphs generally give a better picture of the data and are easier to understand.
   To help you decide exactly which type of frequency distribution is best, consider the following points:
   a. What is the range of scores? With a wide range, you will need to group the scores into class intervals.
   b. What is the scale of measurement? With an interval or a ratio scale, you can use a polygon or a histogram. With a nominal or an ordinal scale, you must use a bar graph.

2. When using a grouped frequency distribution table, a common mistake is to calculate the interval width by using the highest and lowest values that define each interval. For example, some students are tricked into thinking that an interval identified as 20–24 is only 4 points wide. To determine the correct interval width, you can

a. Count the individual scores in the interval. For this example, the scores are 20, 21, 22, 23, and 24 for a total of 5 values. Thus, the interval width is 5 points.

b. Use the real limits to determine the real width of the interval. For example, an interval identified as 20–24 has a lower real limit of 19.5 and an upper real limit of 24.5 (halfway to the next score). Using the real limits, the interval width is

$$24.5 - 19.5 = 5 \text{ points}$$

DEMONSTRATION 2.1

A GROUPED FREQUENCY DISTRIBUTION TABLE

For the following set of $N = 20$ scores, construct a grouped frequency distribution table. Use an interval width of 5 points, and include columns for f and p. Scores:

4,   8,   27,   16,   10,   22,   9,   13,   16,   12,

10,   9,   15,   17,   6,   14,   11,   18,   14,   11

X
25–29
20–24
15–19
10–14
5–9

STEP 1   Set up the class intervals.

The largest score in this distribution is $X = 27$, and the lowest is $X = 6$. Therefore, a frequency distribution table for these data would have 22 rows and would be too large. A grouped frequency distribution table would be better. We have asked specifically for an interval width of 5 points, and the resulting table (in the margin) will have five rows. Remember, the interval width is determined by the real limits of the interval. For example, the class interval 25–29 has an upper real limit of 29.5 and a lower real limit of 24.5. The difference between these two values is the width of the interval—namely, 5.

STEP 2   Determine the frequencies for each interval.

Examine the scores, and count how many fall into the class interval of 25–29. Cross out each score that you have already counted. Record the frequency for this class interval. Now repeat this process for the remaining intervals. The result is the following table:

X	f	
25–29	1	(The score $X = 27$)
20–24	1	($X = 22$)
15–19	5	(The scores $X = 16, 16, 15, 17,$ and 18)
10–14	9	($X = 14, 10, 13, 12, 10, 14, 11, 14,$ and 11)
5–9	4	($X = 8, 9, 9,$ and 6)

STEP 3   Compute the proportions.

The proportion (p) of scores contained in an interval is determined by dividing the frequency (f) of that interval by the number of scores (N) in the distribution. Thus, for each interval, we must compute the following:

$$p = \frac{f}{N}$$

This is demonstrated in the following table:

X	f	p
25–29	1	$f/N = 1/20 = 0.05$
20–24	1	$f/N = 1/20 = 0.05$
15–19	5	$f/N = 5/20 = 0.25$
10–14	9	$f/N = 9/20 = 0.45$
5–9	4	$f/N = 4/20 = 0.20$

PROBLEMS

1. Place the following scores in a frequency distribution table. Include columns for proportion (p) and percentage (%) in your table. Scores:

3, 1, 1, 2, 5, 4, 4, 5, 3, 5,

3, 2, 3, 4, 3, 3, 4, 3, 2, 3

2. What information is available about the data in a regular frequency distribution table that is not available in a grouped table?

3. Describe the difference in appearance between a bar graph and a histogram, and describe the circumstances under which each type of graph should be used.

4. Under what circumstances should you use a grouped frequency distribution instead of a regular frequency distribution?

5. Sketch a histogram and a polygon showing the distribution of scores presented in the following table:

X	f
5	4
4	6
3	5
2	3
1	2

6. During the first meeting with a statistics class, the professor asks three questions: How many of you have anxiety about taking this class? How many of you feel relaxed? How many of you are not sure how you feel? Twenty-two students indicated they had some level of anxiety, 8 were relaxed, and 10 not sure. Construct a bar graph for these data.

7. The following are reading comprehension scores for a third-grade class of 18 students:

5, 3, 5, 4, 5, 5, 4, 5, 2,

4, 5, 3, 5, 4, 5, 5, 3, 5

a. Place the scores in a frequency distribution table.
b. Sketch a histogram showing the distribution.
c. Using your graph, provide the following information:
  (1) Describe the shape of the distribution.
  (2) If a score of $X = 3$ is considered normal for third-graders, how would you describe the general reading level for this class?

8. An instructor obtained the following set of scores from a 10-point quiz for a class of 26 students:

9, 2, 3, 8, 10, 9, 9, 2, 1, 2, 9,

8, 2, 5, 2, 9, 9, 3, 2, 5, 7, 2,

10, 1, 2, 9

a. Place the scores in a frequency distribution table.
b. Sketch a histogram showing the distribution.
c. Using your graph, provide the following information:
  (1) Describe the shape of the distribution.
  (2) As a whole, how did the class do on the quiz? Were most scores high or low? Was the quiz easy or hard?

9. A set of scores has been organized into the following frequency distribution table. Find each of the following values for the original set of scores:
  a. N
  b. ΣX

X	f
5	4
4	3
3	3
2	0
1	2

10. For the set of scores shown in the following frequency distribution table,
  a. How many scores are in the distribution? ($N = $?)
  b. Find ΣX for this set of scores.

X	f
4	2
3	4
2	5
1	3

11. Find N, ΣX, and ΣX^2 for the set of scores in the following frequency distribution table:

X	f
5.	1
4.	3
3.	5
2	2
1	2

12. Find each value requested for the set of scores summarized in the following table:
  a. N
  b. ΣX
  c. ΣX^2

X	f
5	2
4	3
3	4
2	1
1	1

13. For the following set of scores:

2, 6, 3, 7, 11, 3, 4, 2, 5,

7, 4, 2, 5, 6, 2, 3, 4,

9, 4, 5, 3, 4, 6, 4, 3

  a. Construct a frequency distribution table.
  b. Sketch a histogram for these data.
  c. Sketch a polygon for these data.
  d. What is the shape of the distribution?

14. Three sets of data are described as follows:
  Set I: $N = 40$, highest score is $X = 93$, lowest score is $X = 52$
  Set II: $N = 62$, highest score is $X = 35$, lowest score is $X = 26$
  Set III: $N = 25$, highest score is $X = 890$, lowest score is $X = 230$
  For each set of data, identify whether a regular table or a grouped table should be used, and if a grouped table is necessary, identify the interval width that would be most appropriate.

15. Place the following set of scores in a grouped frequency distribution table using
  a. An interval width of 2.
  b. An interval width of 5.

23, 12, 16, 16, 17,

20, 14, 21, 18, 24,

18, 21, 22, 27, 21,

22, 23, 21, 30, 27

16. For the following scores, construct a frequency distribution table using
  a. An interval width of 5.
  b. An interval width of 10.

64, 75, 50, 67, 86, 66, 62, 64, 71,

47, 57, 74, 63, 67, 56, 65, 70, 87,

48, 50, 41, 66, 73, 60, 63, 45, 78,

68, 53, 75

17. For each of the following sets of scores:

		Set I						Set II		
3	5	4	2	1		3	9	14	10	
3	3	2	3	4		6	4	9	1	4

a. Construct a frequency distribution table for each set of data.
b. Sketch a histogram showing each frequency distribution.
c. Describe each distribution using the following characteristics:
   (1) What is the shape of the distribution?
   (2) What score best identifies the center (average) for the distribution?
   (3) Are the scores clustered together around a central point, or are the scores spread out across the scale?

18. For the following set of scores:

5, 6, 2, 3, 6, 5, 6, 4, 1, 5, 6,

3, 4

a. Construct a frequency distribution table.
b. Sketch a polygon showing the distribution.
c. Describe the distribution using the following characteristics:
   (1) What is the shape of the distribution?
   (2) What score best identifies the center (average) for the distribution?
   (3) Are the scores clustered together, or are they spread out across the scale?

19. For the following set of scores:

4, 6, 9, 5, 3, 8, 9, 4, 2, 5, 10,

7, 4, 9, 8, 3

a. Construct a frequency distribution table.
b. Sketch a polygon showing the distribution.
c. Describe the distribution using the following characteristics:
   (1) What is the shape of the distribution?
   (2) What score best identifies the center (average) for the distribution?
   (3) Are the scores clustered together, or are they spread out across the scale?

20. For the following set of quiz scores:

3, 5, 4, 6, 2, 3, 4, 1, 4, 3,

7, 7, 3, 4, 5, 8, 2, 4, 7, 10

a. Construct a frequency distribution table to organize the scores.
b. Draw a frequency distribution histogram for these data.

21. Construct a grouped frequency distribution table to organize the following set of scores:

206, 350, 590, 473, 450, 483,

112, 380, 584, 620, 743, 816,

685, 592, 712, 727, 686, 592,

542, 490, 684, 491, 520, 380

22. A psychologist would like to examine the effects of diet on intelligence. Two groups of rats are selected, with 12 rats in each group. One group is fed the regular diet of Rat Chow, whereas the second group has special vitamins and minerals added to their food. After 6 months, each rat is tested on a discrimination problem. The psychologist records the number of errors each animal makes before it solves the problem. The data from this experiment are as follows:

regular diet scores: 13, 11, 12, 13, 11,

9, 12, 10, 12, 14,

10, 12

special diet scores: 9, 8, 7, 8, 9, 10,

7, 8, 9, 6, 8, 10

a. Identify the independent variable and the dependent variable for this experiment.
b. Sketch a frequency distribution polygon for the group of rats with the regular diet. On the same graph (in a different color), sketch the distribution for the rats with the special diet.
c. From looking at your graph, would you say that the special diet had any effect on intelligence? Explain your answer.

23. Mental imagery has been shown to be very effective for improving memory. In one demonstration study, two groups of subjects were presented with a list of 20 words. One group was given instructions to use mental images to help them remember the words, and the second group was given no special instructions. After the list was presented, each subject was asked to recall as many words as possible. The scores for the two groups are as follows:

Imagery group				
18	19	18	17	19
13	20	17	18	18
20	18	14	19	16

No instruction group				
11	12	16	12	10
13	14	12	10	8
13	10	11	14	12

a. Sketch a histogram showing the distribution of scores for each group (two separate graphs).

b. Describe each graph by identifying the shape of the distribution and the approximate center of the distribution.

c. Based on the appearance of the two distributions, what is the effect of using mental images on the level of performance for this memory task?

24. Sketch a frequency distribution histogram for the following data:

X	f
15	2
14	5
13	6
12	3
11	2
10	1

25. The following data are quiz scores from two different sections of an introductory statistics course:

	Section I	
9	6	8
10	8	3
7	8	8
7	5	10
9	6	7

	Section II	
4	7	8
6	3	7
4	6	5
10	3	6
7	4	6

a. Organize the scores from each section in a frequency distribution histogram.

b. Describe the general differences between the two distributions.

CHAPTER 3

CENTRAL TENDENCY

TOOLS YOU WILL NEED

The following items are considered essential background material for this chapter. If you doubt your knowledge of any of these items, you should review the appropriate chapter or section before proceeding.

- Summation notation (Chapter 1)
- Frequency distributions (Chapter 2)

CONTENTS

3.1   INTRODUCTION

The goal in measuring central tendency is to describe a distribution of scores by determining a single value that identifies the center of the distribution. Ideally, this central value will be the score that is the best representative value for all of the individuals in the distribution.

DEFINITION   *Central tendency* is a statistical measure to determine a single score that defines the center of a distribution. The goal of central tendency is to find the single score that is most typical or most representative of the entire group.

In everyday language, the goal of central tendency is to find the "average" or "typical" individual. This average value can then be used to provide a simple description of the entire population or sample. For example, archeological discoveries indicate that the average height for men in the ancient Roman city of Pompeii was 5 feet 7 inches. Obviously, not all the men were exactly 5 feet 7 inches, but this average value provides a general description of the population. Measures of central tendency also are useful for making comparisons between groups of individuals or between sets of figures. For example, weather data indicate that for Seattle, Washington, the average yearly temperature is 53° and the average annual precipitation is 34 inches. By comparison, the average temperature in Miami, Florida is 76° and the average precipitation is 58.5 inches. The point of these examples is to demonstrate the great advantage of being able to describe a large set of data with a single, representative number. Central tendency characterizes what is typical for a large population and in doing so makes large amounts of data more digestible. Statisticians sometimes use the expression "number crunching" to illustrate this aspect of data description. That is, we take a distribution consisting of many scores and "crunch" them down to a single value that describes them all.

Unfortunately, there is no single standard procedure for determining central tendency. The problem is that no single measure will always produce a central, representative value in every situation. The three distributions shown in Figure 3.1 should help demonstrate this fact. Before we discuss the three distributions, take a moment to look at the figure, and try to identify the "center" or the "most representative score" for each distribution.

1. The first distribution [Figure 3.1(a)] is symmetrical, with the scores forming a distinct pile centered around $X = 5$. For this type of distribution, it is easy to identify the "center," and most people would agree that the value $X = 5$ is an appropriate measure of central tendency.

2. In the second distribution [Figure 3.1(b)], however, problems begin to appear. Now the scores form a negatively skewed distribution, piling up at the high end of the scale, around $X = 8$, but tapering off to the left all the way down to $X = 1$. Where is the "center" in this case? Some people might select $X = 8$ as the center because more individuals had this score than any other single value. However, $X = 8$ is clearly not in the middle of the distribution. In fact, the majority of the scores (10 out of 16) have values less than 8, so it seems reasonable that the "center" should be defined by a value that is less than 8.

3. Now consider the third distribution [Figure 3.1(c)]. Again, the distribution is symmetrical, but now there are two distinct piles of scores. Because the distribution is symmetrical, with $X = 5$ as the midpoint, you may choose $X = 5$ as the

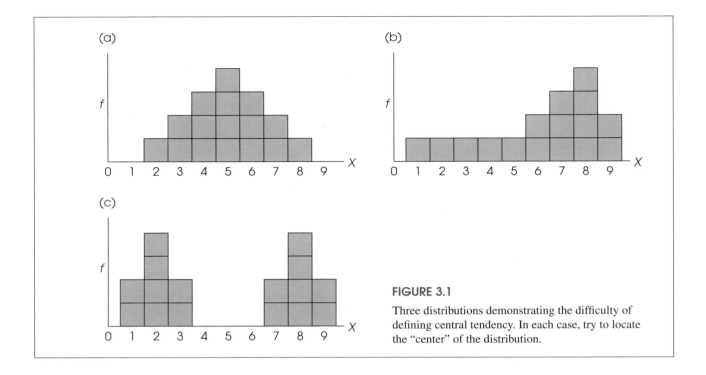

FIGURE 3.1

Three distributions demonstrating the difficulty of defining central tendency. In each case, try to locate the "center" of the distribution.

"center." However, none of the scores is located at $X = 5$ (or even close), so this value is not particularly good as a representative score. On the other hand, because there are two separate piles of scores, with one group centered at $X = 2$ and the other centered at $X = 8$, it is tempting to say that this distribution has two centers. But can there be two centers?

Clearly, there are problems defining the "center" of a distribution. Occasionally, you will find a nice, neat distribution like the one shown in Figure 3.1(a), where everyone will agree on the center. However, you should realize that other distributions are possible and that there may be different opinions concerning the definition of the center. To deal with these problems, statisticians have developed three different methods for measuring central tendency: the mean, the median, and the mode. They are computed differently and have different characteristics. To decide which of the three measures is best for any particular distribution, you should keep in mind that the general purpose of central tendency is to find the single most representative score. Each of the three measures we will present has been developed to work best in a specific situation. We will examine this issue in more detail after we define the three measures.

3.2   THE MEAN

The mean, commonly known as the arithmetic average, is computed by adding all the scores in the distribution and dividing by the number of scores. The mean for a population will be identified by the Greek letter mu, μ (pronounced "myoo"), and the mean for a sample will be identified by $\overline{X}$ (read "x-bar").

DEFINITION   The *mean* for a distribution is the sum of the scores divided by the number of scores.

The formula for the population mean is

$$\mu = \frac{\Sigma X}{N} \tag{3.1}$$

First, sum all the scores in the population, and then divide by N. For a sample, the computation is done the same way, but the formula uses symbols that signify sample values:

$$\text{sample mean} = \overline{X} = \frac{\Sigma X}{n} \tag{3.2}$$

In general, we will use Greek letters to identify characteristics of a population and letters of our own alphabet to stand for sample values. If a mean is identified with the symbol $\overline{X}$, you should realize that we are dealing with a sample. Also note that n is used as the symbol for the number of scores in the sample.

EXAMPLE 3.1   For a population of $N = 4$ scores,

$$3, \quad 7, \quad 4, \quad 6$$

the mean is

$$\mu = \frac{\Sigma X}{N} = \frac{20}{4} = 5$$

ALTERNATIVE DEFINITIONS
FOR THE MEAN

Although the procedure of adding the scores and dividing by the number provides a useful definition of the mean, there are two alternative definitions that may give you a better understanding of this important measure of central tendency.

The first alternative is to think of the mean as the amount each individual would get if the total (ΣX) were divided equally among all the individuals (N) in the distribution. This somewhat socialistic viewpoint is particularly useful in problems where you know the mean and must find the total. Consider the following example.

EXAMPLE 3.2   A group of $n = 6$ boys buys a box of baseball cards at a garage sale and discovers that the box contains a total of 180 cards. If the boys divide the cards equally among themselves, how many cards will each boy get? You should recognize that this problem represents the standard procedure for computing the mean. Specifically, the total (ΣX) is divided by the number (n) to produce the mean, $\frac{180}{6} = 30$ cards for each boy.

You should also recognize that this example demonstrates that it is possible to define the mean as the amount that each individual gets when the total is distributed equally. This new definition can be useful for some problems involving the mean. Consider the following example.

This time we have a group of $n = 4$ boys and we measure the amount of money that each boy has. The data produce a mean of $\overline{X} = \$5$. Given this information, what is the total amount of money for the whole group? Although you do not know exactly how much money each boy has, the new definition of the mean tells you that if they pool their money together and then distribute the total equally, each boy will get $5. For each of $n = 4$ boys to get $5, the total must be $4(\$5) = \$20$. To check this answer, use the formula for the mean:

$$\overline{X} = \frac{\Sigma X}{n} = \frac{\$20}{4} = \$5$$

The second alternative is to define the mean as the *balance point* for the distribution. Consider a population consisting of $N = 4$ scores: 2, 2, 6, and 10. Figure 3.2 shows this population drawn as a histogram with each score represented by a box that is sitting on a seesaw. If the seesaw is positioned so that it pivots at a point equal to the mean, then it will be balanced and will rest level.

FIGURE 3.2

The frequency distribution shown as a seesaw balanced at the mean.

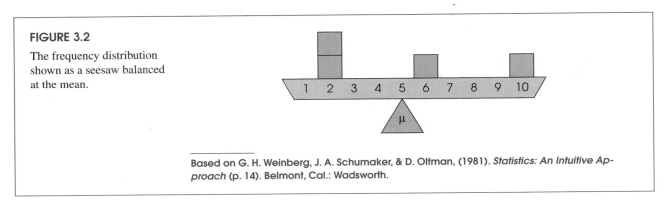

Based on G. H. Weinberg, J. A. Schumaker, & D. Oltman, (1981). *Statistics: An Intuitive Approach* (p. 14). Belmont, Cal.: Wadsworth.

The reason the seesaw is balanced over the mean becomes clear when we measure the distance of each box (score) from the mean:

Score	Distance from the mean
$X = 2$	3 points below the mean
$X = 2$	3 points below the mean
$X = 6$	1 point above the mean
$X = 10$	5 points above the mean

Notice that the mean balances the distances. That is, the total distance below the mean is the same as the total distance above the mean:

3 points below + 3 points below = 6 points below

1 point above + 5 points above = 6 points above

Because the mean serves as a balance point, the value of the mean will always be located somewhere between the highest score and the lowest score; that is, the mean can never be outside the range of scores. If the lowest score in a distribution is $X = 8$ and the highest is $X = 15$, then the mean *must* be between 8 and 15. If you calculate a value that is outside this range, then you have made an error.

THE WEIGHTED MEAN

Often it is necessary to combine two sets of scores and then find the overall mean for the combined group. Suppose that we begin with two separate samples. The first sample has $n = 12$ scores and $\overline{X} = 6$. The second sample has $n = 8$ and $\overline{X} = 7$. If the two samples are combined, what is the mean for the total group?

To calculate the overall mean, we will need two values: the overall sum of the scores for the combined group (ΣX) and the total number of scores in the combined group (n). To determine the overall sum, we will simply find the sum of the scores for the first sample (ΣX_1) and the sum for the second sample (ΣX_2) and then add the two sums together. Similarly, the total number of scores in the combined group can be found by adding the number in the first sample (n_1) and the number in the second sample (n_2). With these two values, we can compute the mean using the basic formula

$$\text{overall mean} = \overline{X} = \frac{\Sigma X (\text{overall sum for the combined group})}{n (\text{total number in the combined group})}$$

$$= \frac{\Sigma X_1 + \Sigma X_2}{n_1 + n_2}$$

The first sample has $n = 12$ and $\overline{X} = 6$. Therefore, the total for this sample must be $\Sigma X = 72$. (Remember that when the total is distributed equally, each person gets the mean. For each of 12 people to get $\overline{X} = 6$, the total must be 72.) In the same way, the second sample has $n = 8$ and $\overline{X} = 7$, so the total must be $\Sigma X = 56$. Using these values, we obtain an overall mean of

$$\text{overall mean} = \overline{X} = \frac{\Sigma X_1 + \Sigma X_2}{n_1 + n_2} = \frac{72 + 56}{12 + 8} = \frac{128}{20} = 6.4$$

The following table summarizes the calculations.

First sample	Second sample	Combined sample
$n = 12$	$n = 8$	$n = 20$ (12 + 8)
$\Sigma X = 72$	$\Sigma X = 56$	$\Sigma X = 128$ (72 + 56)
$\overline{X} = 6$	$\overline{X} = 7$	$\overline{X} = 6.4$

Note that the overall mean is not halfway between the original two sample means. Because the samples are not the same size, one will make a larger contribution to the total group and therefore will carry more weight in determining the overall mean. For this reason, the overall mean we have calculated is called the *weighted mean*. In this example, the overall mean of $\overline{X} = 6.4$ is closer to the value of $\overline{X} = 6$ (the larger sample) than it is to $\overline{X} = 7$ (the smaller sample).

In summary, when two samples are combined, the weighted mean is obtained as follows:

STEP 1 Determine the grand total of all the scores in both samples. This sum is obtained by adding the sum of the scores for the first sample (ΣX_1) and the sum of the scores for the second sample (ΣX_2).

STEP 2   Determine the total number of scores in both samples. This value is obtained by adding the number in the first sample (n_1) and the number in the second sample (n_2).

STEP 3   Divide the sum of all the scores (step 1) by the total number of scores (step 2). Expressed as an equation,

$$\text{weighted mean} = \frac{\text{combined sum}}{\text{combined } n} = \frac{\Sigma X_1 + \Sigma X_2}{n_1 + n_2}$$

COMPUTING THE MEAN FROM A FREQUENCY DISTRIBUTION TABLE

When a set of scores has been organized in a frequency distribution table, the calculation of the mean is usually easier if you first remove the individual scores from the table. Table 3.1 shows a distribution of quiz scores organized in a frequency distribution table. To compute the mean for this distribution, you must be careful to use both the X values in the first column and the frequencies in the second column. The values in the table show that the distribution consists of one 10, two 9s, four 8s, and one 6, for a total of $n = 8$ scores. Remember that you can determine the number of scores by adding the frequencies, $n = \Sigma f$. To find the sum of the scores, you must be careful to add all eight scores:

$$\Sigma X = 10 + 9 + 9 + 8 + 8 + 8 + 8 + 6 = 66$$

You can also find the sum by computing ΣfX (see p. 32).

Once you have found ΣX and n, you compute the mean as usual. For these data,

$$\overline{X} = \frac{\Sigma X}{n} = \frac{66}{8} = 8.25$$

TABLE 3.1

Statistics quiz scores for a section of $n = 8$ students

Quiz score (X)	f	fX
10	1	10
9	2	18
8	4	32
7	0	0
6	1	6

LEARNING CHECK ◆

1. A sample of $n = 8$ scores has a mean of $\overline{X} = 6$. What is ΣX for this sample?

2. Sample A has $n = 8$ and $\overline{X} = 14$. For sample B, $n = 20$ and $\overline{X} = 6$. If the two samples are combined, then
    a. The mean for the combined sample will be between 14 and 6. (True or false?)
    b. The mean for the combined sample will be closer to 14 than it is to 6. (True or false?)
    c. Calculate the mean for the combined sample.

3. Find n, ΣX, and $\overline{X}$ for the sample of scores shown in the following frequency distribution table:

X	f
4	2
3	4
2	3
1	1

ANSWERS   **1.** $\Sigma X = 48$

    2. a. True

      b. False

      c. $\overline{X} = \frac{232}{28} = 8.29$

    3. $n = 10$, $\Sigma X = 27$, and $\overline{X} = \frac{27}{10} = 2.7$ ◆

CHARACTERISTICS OF THE MEAN

The mean has many characteristics that will be important in future discussions. In general, these characteristics result from the fact that every score in the distribution contributes to the value of the mean. Specifically, every score must be added into the total in order to compute the mean. We will now discuss four of the more important characteristics.

Changing a score   Changing the value of any score will change the mean. For example, a sample of quiz scores for a psychology lab section consist of 9, 8, 7, 5, and 1. Note that the sample consists of $n = 5$ scores with $\Sigma X = 30$. The mean for this sample is

$$\overline{X} = \frac{\Sigma X}{n} = \frac{30}{5} = 6.00$$

Suppose the student who received the score of $X = 1$ returned a few days later and explained that she was ill on the day of the quiz. In fact, she went straight to the infirmary after class and was admitted for two days with the flu. Out of the goodness of the instructor's heart, the student was given a makeup quiz, and she received a score of $X = 8$. Changing the score from 1 to 8 creates a new distribution consisting of 9, 8, 7, 5, and 8. There are still $n = 5$ scores, but now $\Sigma X = 37$. The new mean is

$$\overline{X} = \frac{\Sigma X}{n} = \frac{37}{5} = 7.40$$

Notice that changing a single score in the sample has produced a new mean. You should recognize that changing any score will also change the value of ΣX (the sum of the scores), and thus will always change the value of the mean.

Introducing a new score or removing a score   In general, the mean is determined by two values: ΣX and N (or n). Whenever either of these values is changed, the mean also will be changed. In the preceding example, the value of one score was changed. This produced a change in the total (ΣX) and therefore changed the mean. If you add a new score (or take away a score), you will change both ΣX and n, and you must compute the new mean using the changed values.

    Usually, but not always, adding a new score or removing an existing score will change the mean. The exception is when the new score (or the removed score) is exactly equal to the mean. It is easy to visualize the effect of adding or removing a score if you remember that the mean is defined as the balance point for the distribution. Figure 3.3 shows a distribution of scores represented as boxes on a seesaw that is balanced at the mean, $\overline{X} = 7$. Imagine what would happen if we added a new score (a new box) at $X = 10$. Clearly, the seesaw would tip to the right and

FIGURE 3.3

A distribution of $N = 5$ scores that is balanced with a mean of $\mu = 7$.

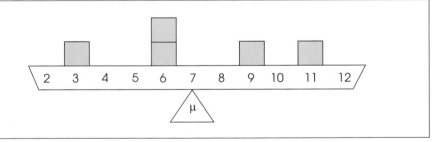

we would need to slide the pivot point (the mean) higher to restore balance. Thus, adding a new score that is larger than the current mean will cause an increase in the value of the mean.

Again using Figure 3.3, imagine what would happen if we removed the score (the box) that is located at $X = 9$. This time the seesaw would tip to the left and we would have to move the mean lower to restore balance. Thus, removing a score that is greater than the current mean will cause a decrease in the value of the mean.

Finally, consider what would happen to the seesaw if we added a new score (or removed an existing score) located exactly at the mean. It should be clear that the seesaw would not tilt in either direction so the mean would stay in exactly the same place.

The following example demonstrates exactly how the new mean is computed when a new score is added to an existing sample.

EXAMPLE 3.3

Remember that the mean is the amount each person gets when the total is divided equally. If each of four people has 7, then the total must be 28.

We begin with a sample of $n = 4$ scores with a mean of $\overline{X} = 7$. Notice that this sample must have $\Sigma X = 28$. The problem is to determine what happens to the sample mean if a new score of $X = 12$ is added to the sample.

To find the new sample mean, we must first determine the values for n and ΣX. In each case, we begin with the original sample and then consider the impact of adding a new score. The original sample had $n = 4$ scores, so adding one new score brings us to $n = 5$. Similarly, the original sample had $\Sigma X = 28$. We added $X = 12$, so the new total is $\Sigma X = 28 + 12 = 40$. Finally, the new mean is computed using the new values for n and ΣX.

$$\overline{X} = \frac{\Sigma X}{n} = \frac{40}{5} = 8$$

The entire process can be summarized as follows:

Original sample	New sample adding $X = 12$
$n = 4$	$n = 5$
$\Sigma X = 28$	$\Sigma X = 40$
$\overline{X} = 28/4 = 7$	$\overline{X} = 40/5 = 8$

TABLE 3.2

Amount of food (in grams) consumed before and after diet drug injections.

Rat's identification	Before drug consumption	After drug consumption
A	6	4
B	3	1
C	5	3
D	3	1
E	4	2
F	5	3
	$\Sigma X = 26$	$\Sigma X = 14$
	$\overline{X} = 4.33$	$\overline{X} = 2.33$

Adding or subtracting a constant from each score   If a constant value is added to every score in a distribution, the same constant will be added to the mean. Similarly, if you subtract a constant from every score, the same constant will be subtracted from the mean.

Consider the feeding scores for a sample of $n = 6$ rats shown in Table 3.2. The scores show the amount of food each rat ate during a 24-hour test period. The first column shows food consumption before the rats were injected with a diet drug. Note that the total amount is $\Sigma X = 26$ grams for $n = 6$ rats, so the mean is $\overline{X} = 4.33$. The following day, the rats are injected with an experimental drug that reduces appetite. Suppose that the effect of the drug is to subtract a constant (2 points) from each rat's feeding score. The resulting scores are shown in the final column in the table. Note that these scores (after the drug) total $\Sigma X = 14$ grams for $n = 6$ rats, so the new mean is $\overline{X} = 2.33$. Subtracting 2 points from each score has also subtracted 2 points from the mean, from $\overline{X} = 4.33$ to $\overline{X} = 2.33$. (It is important to note that experimental effects are practically never as simple as the adding or subtracting of a constant. Nonetheless, the principle of this characteristic of the mean is important and will be addressed in later chapters when we are using statistics to evaluate the effects of experimental manipulations.)

Multiplying or dividing each score by a constant   If every score in a distribution is multiplied by (or divided by) a constant value, the mean will change in the same way.

Multiplying (or dividing) each score by a constant value is a common method for changing the unit of measurement. To change a set of measurements from minutes to seconds, for example, you multiply by 60; to change from inches to feet, you divide by 12. Table 3.3 shows how a sample of $n = 5$ scores originally measured in yards would

TABLE 3.3

Measurement of five pieces of wood

Original measurement in yards	Conversion to feet (multiply by 3)
10	30
9	27
12	36
8	24
11	33
$\Sigma X = 50$	$\Sigma X = 150$
$\overline{X} = 10$ yards	$\overline{X} = 30$ feet

be transformed into a set of scores measured in feet. The first column shows the original scores with total $\Sigma X = 50$ and $\overline{X} = 10$ yards. In the second column, each of the original values has been multiplied by 3 (to change from yards to feet), and the resulting values total $\Sigma X = 150$, with $\overline{X} = 30$ feet. Multiplying each score by 3 has also caused the mean to be multiplied by 3. You should realize, however, that although the numerical values for the individual scores and the sample mean have been multiplied, the actual measurements are not changed.

LEARNING CHECK ◆

1. **a.** Compute the mean for the following sample of scores:

      6,   1,   8,   0,   5

   b. Add 4 points to each score, and then compute the mean.

   c. Multiply each of the original scores by 5, and then compute the mean.

2. A population has a mean of $\mu = 80$.

   a. If 6 points are added to every score, what would be the value for the new mean?

   b. If every score is multiplied by 2, what would be the value for the new mean?

3. A sample of $n = 5$ scores has a mean of $\overline{X} = 8$. If you add a new score of $X = 2$ to the sample, what value would you obtain for the new sample mean?

A N S W E R S

1. **a.** $\overline{X} = \frac{20}{5} = 4$ **b.** $\overline{X} = \frac{40}{5} = 8$ **c.** $\overline{X} = \frac{100}{5} = 20$

2. **a.** The new mean would be 86.

   b. The new mean would be 160.

3. The original sample has $n = 5$ and $\Sigma X = 40$. With the new score, the sample has $n = 6$ and $\Sigma X = 42$. The new mean is $\frac{42}{6} = 7$.   ◆

3.3 THE MEDIAN

The second measure of central tendency we will consider is called the *median.* The median is the score that divides a distribution exactly in half. Exactly one-half of the scores are less than or equal to the median, and exactly one-half are greater than or equal to the median.

DEFINITION

The *median* is the score that divides a distribution exactly in half. Exactly 50% of the individuals in a distribution have scores at or below the median.

By midpoint of the distribution we mean that the area in the graph is divided into two equal parts. We are *not* locating the midpoint between the highest and lowest X values.

Earlier, when we introduced the mean, we used specific symbols and notation to identify the mean and to differentiate a sample mean and a population mean. For the median, however, there are no symbols or notation. Instead, the median is simply identified by the word *median*. In addition, the definition and the computations for the median are identical for a sample and for a population.

The goal of the median is to determine the precise midpoint of a distribution. The commonsense goal is demonstrated in the following examples.

METHOD 1: WHEN *N* IS AN ODD NUMBER

With an odd number of scores, you list the scores in order (lowest to highest), and the median is the middle score in the list. Consider the following set of $N = 5$ scores, which have been listed in order:

$$3, \quad 5, \quad 8, \quad 10, \quad 11$$

The middle score is $X = 8$, so the median is equal to 8.0. In a graph, the median divides the space or area of the graph in half (Figure 3.4). The amount of area above the median consists of $2\frac{1}{2}$ "boxes," the same as the area below the median (shaded portion).

FIGURE 3.4

The median divides the area in the graph exactly in half.

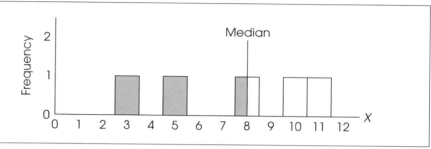

METHOD 2: WHEN *N* IS AN EVEN NUMBER

With an even number of scores in the distribution, you list the scores in order (lowest to highest) and then locate the median by finding the average of the middle two scores. Consider the following population:

$$3, \quad 3, \quad 4, \quad 5, \quad 7, \quad 8$$

Now we select the middle pair of scores (4 and 5), add them together, and divide by 2:

$$\text{median} = \frac{4 + 5}{2} = \frac{9}{2} = 4.5$$

In terms of a graph, we see again that the median divides the area of the distribution exactly in half (Figure 3.5). There are three scores (or boxes) above the median and three below the median.

FIGURE 3.5

The median divides the area in the graph exactly in half.

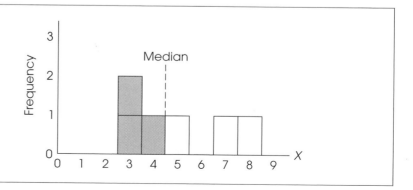

In each of the preceding examples, the median was computed by listing all the scores in order, from highest to lowest, and then finding the middle of the list. In each case, we also showed a figure demonstrating how the median divides a frequency distribution exactly in half. Whether the scores are represented in a list or in a graph, the key concept is that the median splits the scores into two groups that are exactly the same size (50% in each group). For this reason, the median is often used when a researcher wants to divide a sample into two groups; those with high scores and those with low scores. Using the median as a dividing line, a researcher can obtain one group of individuals with scores above the median and another group with scores below the median. This process is called a *median split* and provides a researcher with two equal-sized groups, one of high-scoring subjects and one of low-scoring subjects.

LEARNING CHECK ◆

1. Find the median for each distribution of scores:
   a. 3, 10, 8, 4, 10, 7, 6
   b. 13, 8, 10, 11, 12, 10

2. A distribution can have more than one median. (True or false?)

3. If you have a score of 52 on an 80-point exam, then you definitely scored above the median. (True or false?)

ANSWERS

1. a. The median is $X = 7$.
   b. The median is $X = 10.5$.

2. False

3. False. The value of the median would depend on where the scores are located.   ◆

3.4 THE MODE

The final measure of central tendency that we will consider is called the mode. In its common usage, the word *mode* means "the customary fashion" or "a popular style." The statistical definition is similar in that the mode is the most common observation among a group of scores.

DEFINITION

In a frequency distribution, the *mode* is the score or category that has the greatest frequency.

In a frequency distribution graph, the greatest frequency will appear as the tallest part of the figure. To find the mode, you simply identify the score located directly beneath the highest point in the distribution.

As with the median, there are no symbols or special notation used to identify the mode or to differentiate between a sample mode and a population mode. In addition, the definition of the mode is the same for either a population or a sample distribution.

The mode is a useful measure of central tendency because it can be used to determine the typical or average value for any scale of measurement, including a nominal

TABLE 3.4

Favorite restaurants named by a sample of $n = 100$ students

Caution: The mode is always a score or category, not a frequency. For this example, the mode is Luigi's, not $f = 42$.

Restaurant	f
College Grill	5
George & Harry's	16
Luigi's	42
Oasis Diner	18
Roxbury Inn	7
Sutter's Mill	12

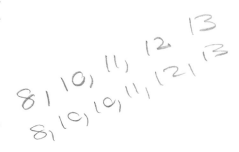

scale (see Chapter 1). Consider, for example, the data shown in Table 3.4. These data were obtained by asking a sample of 100 students to name their favorite restaurants in town. For these data, the mode is Luigi's, the restaurant (score) that was named most frequently as a favorite place. Although we can identify a modal response for these data, note that it would be impossible to compute a mean or a median. For example, you cannot add the scores to determine a mean (How much is 5 College Grills plus 42 Luigi's?). Also, the restaurants do not form any natural order. Although they are listed alphabetically in this example, they could be listed in any order. Thus, it is impossible to list them in order and determine a 50% point (median). In general, the mode is the only measure of central tendency that can be used with data from a nominal scale of measurement.

Although a distribution will have only one mean and only one median, it is possible to have more than one mode. Specifically, it is possible to have two or more scores that have the same highest frequency. In a frequency distribution graph, the different modes will correspond to distinct, equally high peaks. A distribution with two modes is said to be *bimodal,* and a distribution with more than two modes is called *multimodal.* Occasionally, a distribution with several equally high points is said to have no mode.

Technically, the mode is the score with the absolute highest frequency. However, the term *mode* is often used more casually to refer to scores with relatively high frequencies—that is, scores that correspond to peaks in a distribution even though the peaks are not the absolute highest points. For example, Figure 3.6 shows the number of fish caught at various times during the day. There are two distinct peaks in this distribution, one at 6 A.M. and one at 6 P.M. Each of these values is a mode in the distribution. Close inspection of the graph reveals that the two modes do not have identical

FIGURE 3.6

The relationship between time of day and number of fish caught.

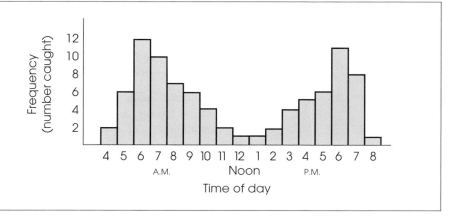

frequencies. Twelve fish were caught at 6 A.M. and 11 were caught at 6 P.M. Nonetheless, both of these points are called modes. Occasionally, the taller peak is called the *major mode,* and the shorter one is the *minor mode.*

LEARNING CHECK ◆

1. An instructor recorded the number of absences for each student in a class of 20 and obtained the frequency distribution shown in the following table.

Number of absences (X)	f
7	1
6	0
5	3
4	2
3	3
2	5
1	4
0	2

    a. Using the mean to define central tendency, what is the average number of absences for this class?

    b. Using the mode to define central tendency, what is the average number of absences for this class?

2. In a recent survey comparing picture quality for three brands of color televisions, 63 people preferred brand A, 29 people preferred brand B, and 58 people preferred brand C. What is the mode for this distribution?

3. It is possible for a distribution to have more than one mode. (True or false?)

ANSWERS   **1. a.** The mean is 2.65.

        b. The mode is $X = 2$ absences.

    2. The mode is brand A.

    3. True   ◆

3.5   SELECTING A MEASURE OF CENTRAL TENDENCY

How do you decide which measure of central tendency to use? The answer to this question depends on several factors. Before we discuss these factors, however, it should be noted that with many sets of data it is possible to compute two or even three different measures of central tendency. Often the three measures will produce similar results, but there are situations in which the results will be very different (see Section 3.6). Also, note that the mean is most often the preferred measure of central tendency. Because the mean uses every score in the distribution, it usually is a good representative value. Remember that the goal of central tendency is to find the single value that best represents the entire distribution. Besides being a good representative, the mean has the added advantage of being closely related to variance and standard deviation, the most common measures of variability (Chapter 4). This relationship makes the mean a valuable measure for purposes of inferential statistics. For these reasons, and others, the mean generally is considered to be the best of the three measures of central tendency. There are specific situations, however, where it is impossible to compute a mean or where the mean is not particularly representative. It is in these situations that the mode and the median are used.

WHEN TO USE THE MEDIAN

We will consider three situations in which the median serves as a valuable alternative to the mean. In each case, the data consist of numerical values (interval or ratio scales) for which you would normally compute the mean. However, each case also involves a special problem so that it is either impossible to compute the mean or calculation of the mean produces a value that is not central or not representative of the distribution.

Extreme scores or skewed distributions   The median is often used to measure and describe central tendency for skewed distributions and for other situations in which there are a few scores that are extremely high (or low) relative to the rest of the distribution. The problem comes from the fact that a few extreme scores can have a relatively large impact and cause the mean to be displaced away from the center of the distribution. For example, suppose a sample of $n = 10$ rats is tested in a maze and the researcher records the number of errors that each animal makes before it solves the maze. Hypothetical data are presented in Figure 3.7. Notice that most of the scores are clustered between 10 and 13, but there is one extreme score of $X = 100$ (a slow learner). The mean for this sample is

$$\overline{X} = \frac{\Sigma X}{n} = \frac{203}{10} = 20.3$$

Here the mean is not very representative of the scores in the distribution. In this example, the extreme score inflated the value of ΣX and distorted the mean.

   The median, on the other hand, is relatively unaffected by extreme scores. For this example, there are $n = 10$ scores, so there should be 5 scores on each side of the median.

FIGURE 3.7

Frequency distribution of errors committed before reaching learning criterion.

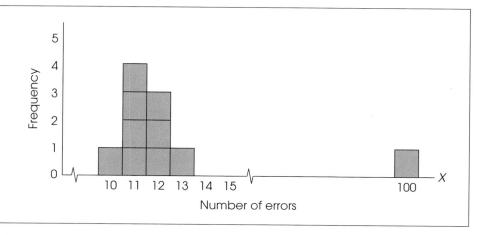

Looking at Figure 3.7, you should find that the median is 11.5. Notice that this is a representative value (most of the rats had scores around 11.5). Also notice that the median would not be changed even if the slow learner made 1000 errors instead of only 100.

Notice that the graph in Figure 3.7 shows two *breaks* in the X-axis. Rather than listing all the scores from 0 to 100, the graph jumps directly to the first score, which is $X = 10$, and then jumps directly from $X = 15$ to $X = 100$. The breaks shown in the X-axis are the conventional way of notifying the reader that some values have been omitted.

Because the median is not displaced by extreme scores, it is commonly used to report central tendency for skewed distributions. With very skewed distributions, the extreme values in the tail tend to displace the mean so that it is not representative. The median, on the other hand, is not influenced by extreme values and tends to stay anchored in the middle of the distribution. For example, the distribution of personal incomes is very skewed, with a small segment of the population earning incomes that are astronomical. These extreme values distort the mean so that it is not representative of the vast majority of actual incomes. Therefore, when statistics concerning income are reported, you usually will see the median income instead of the mean. As mentioned before, the median is preferred when extreme scores exist.

Undetermined values   Occasionally, you will encounter a situation in which an individual has an unknown or undetermined score. In psychology, this often occurs in learning experiments where you are measuring the number of errors an individual makes when solving a particular problem or the amount of time required for an individual to solve a particular problem. For example, suppose an experimenter asks a sample of $n = 6$ people to assemble a wooden puzzle as quickly as possible. The experimenter records how long (in minutes) it takes each individual to arrange all the pieces to complete the puzzle. Table 3.5 presents the outcome of this experiment.

TABLE 3.5

Amount of time to complete puzzle

Person	Time (min.)
1	8
2	11
3	12
4	13
5	17
6	Never finished

Notice that person 6 never completed the puzzle. After an hour, this person still showed no sign of solving the puzzle, so the experimenter stopped him or her. This person has an undetermined score. (There are two important points to be noted. First, the experimenter should not throw out this individual's score. The whole purpose for using a sample is to gain a picture of the population, and this individual tells us that part of the population cannot solve the puzzle. Second, this person should not be given a score of $X = 60$ minutes. Even though the experimenter stopped the individual after 1 hour, the person did not finish the puzzle. The score that is recorded is the amount of time needed to finish. For this individual, we do not know how long this would be.)

Number of children (X)	f
5 or more	3
4	2
3	2
2	3
1	6
0	4

Because of the undetermined score, it is impossible to compute ΣX for these data, so it is impossible to compute the mean. However, it is possible to compute the median. For these data, the median is 12.5. Three scores are below the median, and three scores (including the undetermined value) are above the median.

Open-ended distributions   A distribution is said to be *open-ended* when there is no upper limit (or lower limit) for one of the categories. The table in the margin provides an example of an open-ended distribution, showing the number of children in each family for a sample of $n = 20$ households. The top category in this distribution shows that three of the families have "5 or more" children. This is an open-ended category. Notice that it is impossible to compute a mean for these data because you cannot find ΣX (the total number of children for all 20 families). However, you can find the median. For these data, the median is 1.5 (exactly 50% of the families have fewer than 1.5 children).

WHEN TO USE THE MODE

We will consider three situations in which the mode is commonly used as an alternative to the mean, or is used in conjunction with the mean to describe central tendency.

Nominal scales   The primary advantage of the mode is that it can be used to measure and describe central tendency for data that are measured on a nominal scale. Recall that the categories that make up a nominal scale are differentiated only by name. Because nominal scales do not measure quantity, it is impossible to compute a mean or a median for data from a nominal scale. Therefore, the mode is the only option for describing central tendency for nominal data.

Discrete variables   Recall that discrete variables are those that exist only in whole, indivisible categories. Often, discrete variables are numerical values, such as the number of children in a family or the number of rooms in a house. When these variables produce numerical scores, it is possible to calculate means. In this situation, the calculated means will usually be fractional values that cannot actually exist. For example, computing means will generate results such as "the average family has 2.4 children and a house with 5.33 rooms." On the other hand, the mode always identifies the most typical case and, therefore, it produces more sensible measures of central tendency. Using the mode, our conclusion would be "the typical, or modal, family has 2 children and a house with 5 rooms." In many situations, especially with discrete variables, people are more comfortable using the realistic, whole-number values produced by the mode.

Describing shape   Because the mode requires little or no calculation, it is often included as a supplementary measure along with the mean or median as a no-cost extra. The value of the mode (or modes) in this situation is that it gives an indication of the shape of the distribution as well as a measure of central tendency. Remember that the mode identifies the location of the peak (or peaks) in the frequency distribution graph. For example, if you are told that a set of exam scores has a mean of 72 and a mode of 80, you should have a better picture of the distribution than would be available from the mean alone (see Section 3.6).

IN THE LITERATURE:
REPORTING MEASURES OF CENTRAL TENDENCY

Measures of central tendency are commonly used in the behavioral sciences to summarize and describe the results of a research study. For example, a researcher may report the sample means from two different treatments or the median score for a large sample. These values may be reported in verbal descriptions of the results, in tables, or in graphs.

In reporting the results, many behavioral science journals use guidelines adopted by the American Psychological Association (APA), as outlined in the *Publication Manual of the American Psychological Association* (1994). We will refer to the APA manual from time to time in describing how data and research results are reported in the scientific literature. The APA style typically uses the letter M as the symbol for the sample mean. Thus, a study might state

> The treatment group showed fewer errors ($M = 2.56$) on the task than the control group ($M = 11.76$).

When there are many means to report, tables with headings provide an organized and more easily understood presentation. Table 3.6 illustrates this point.

TABLE 3.6

The mean number of errors made on the task for treatment and control groups according to gender

	Treatment	Control
Females	1.45	8.36
Males	3.83	14.77

The median can be reported using the abbreviation *Mdn*, as in "Mdn = 8.5 errors," or it can simply be reported in narrative text, as follows:

> The median number of errors for the treatment group was 8.5, compared to a median of 13 for the control group.

There is no special symbol or convention for reporting the mode. If mentioned at all, the mode is usually just reported in narrative text.

> The modal hair color was blonde, with 23 out of 50 subjects in this category.

Graphs also can be used to report and compare measures of central tendency. Usually graphs are used to display values obtained for sample means, but occasionally you will see sample medians reported in graphs (modes are rarely, if ever, shown in a graph). The value of a graph is that it allows several means (or medians) to be shown simultaneously so it is possible to make quick comparisons between groups or treatment conditions. When preparing a graph, it is customary to list the values for the different groups or treatment conditions on the horizontal axis. Typically, these are the different values that make up the independent variable or the quasi-independent variable. Values for the dependent variable (the scores) are listed on the vertical axis. The means (or medians) are then displayed using a *line graph,* a *histogram,* or a *bar graph,* depending on the scale of measurement used for the independent variable.

Figure 3.8 is an example of a graph displaying the relationship between drug dose (the independent variable) and food consumption (the dependent variable). In this study, there were five different drug doses (treatment conditions) and they are listed along the horizontal axis. The five means appear as points in the graph. To construct this graph, a point was placed above each treatment condition so that the vertical position of the point corresponds to the mean score for the treatment condition. The points are then connected with straight lines and the resulting graph is called a *line graph.* A line graph is used when the values on the horizontal axis are measured on an interval or a ratio scale. An alternative to the line graph is a *histogram.* For this example, the histogram would show a bar above each drug dose so that the height of each bar corresponds to the mean food consumption for that group, and with no space between adjacent bars.

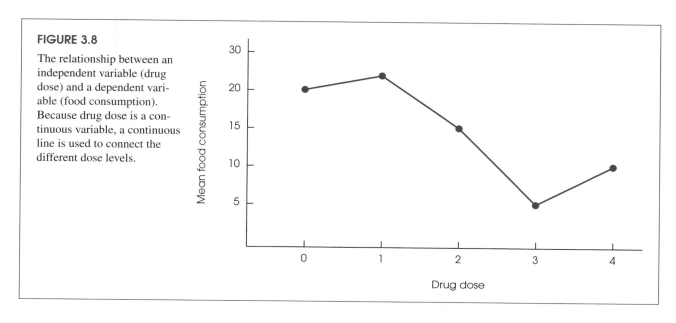

FIGURE 3.8

The relationship between an independent variable (drug dose) and a dependent variable (food consumption). Because drug dose is a continuous variable, a continuous line is used to connect the different dose levels.

Figure 3.9 shows a bar graph displaying the median selling price for single-family homes in different regions of the United States. Bar graphs are used to present means (or medians) when the groups or treatments shown on the *X*-axis are measured on a nominal or an ordinal scale. To construct a bar graph, you simply draw a bar directly above each group or treatment so that the height of the bar corresponds to the mean (or median) for that group or treatment. For a bar graph, a space is left between adjacent bars to indicate that the scale of measurement is nominal or ordinal.

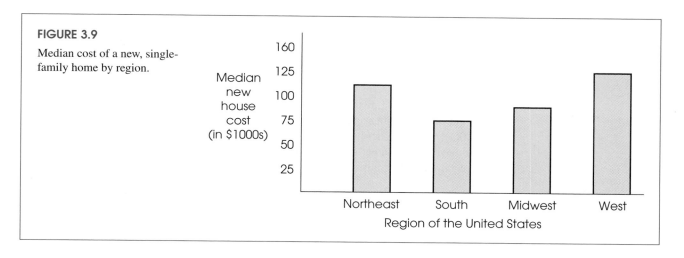

FIGURE 3.9

Median cost of a new, single-family home by region.

When constructing graphs of any type, you should recall the basic rules we introduced in Chapter 2:

1. The height of a graph should be approximately two-thirds to three-quarters of its length.

2. Normally, you start numbering both the *X*-axis and the *Y*-axis with zero at the point where the two axes intersect. However, when a value of zero is part of the

data, it is common to move the zero point away from the intersection so that the graph does not overlap the axes (see Figure 3.8).

More important, you should remember that the purpose of a graph is to give an accurate representation of the information in a set of data. Box 2.1 in Chapter 2 demonstrates what can happen when these basic principles are ignored.   ❑

3.6 CENTRAL TENDENCY AND THE SHAPE OF THE DISTRIBUTION

We have identified three different measures of central tendency, and often a researcher will calculate all three for a single set of data. Because the mean, the median, and the mode are all trying to measure the same thing (central tendency), it is reasonable to expect that these three values should be related. In fact, there are some consistent and predictable relationships among the three measures of central tendency. Specifically, there are situations in which all three measures will have exactly the same value. On the other hand, there are situations in which the three measures are guaranteed to be different. In part, the relationships among the mean, median, and mode are determined by the shape of the distribution. We will consider two general types of distributions.

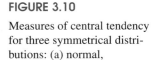

SYMMETRICAL DISTRIBUTIONS

For a *symmetrical distribution,* the right-hand side of the graph will be a mirror image of the left-hand side. By definition, the median will be exactly at the center of a symmetrical distribution because exactly half of the area in the graph will be on either side of the center. The mean also will be exactly at the center of a symmetrical distribution because each individual score in the distribution has a corresponding score on the other side (the mirror image), so that the average of these two values is exactly in the middle. Because all the scores can be paired in this way, the overall average will be exactly at the middle. For any symmetrical distribution, the mean and the median will be the same [Figure 3.10(a)].

If a symmetrical distribution has only one mode, then it must be exactly at the center, so that all three measures of central tendency will have the same value [see Figure 3.10(a)]. On the other hand, a bimodal distribution that is symmetrical [Figure 3.10(b)] will have the mean and the median together in the center with the modes on each side. A rectangular distribution [Figure 3.10 (c)] has no mode because all X values occur with

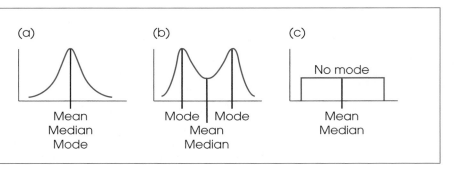

FIGURE 3.10

Measures of central tendency for three symmetrical distributions: (a) normal, (b) bimodal, and (c) rectangular.

(a)

Mean
Median
Mode

(b)

Mode | Mode
Mean
Median

(c)

No mode

Mean
Median

the same frequency. Still, the mean and the median will be in the center of the distribution and equivalent in value.

SKEWED DISTRIBUTIONS   Distributions are not always symmetrical. In fact, quite often they are lopsided, or *skewed*. For example, Figure 3.11(a) shows a *positively skewed distribution*. In this distribution, the peak (highest frequency) is on the left-hand side. This is the position of the mode. If you examine Figure 3.11(a) carefully, it should be clear that the vertical line drawn at the mode does not divide the distribution into two equal parts. In order to have exactly 50% of the distribution on each side, the median must be located to the right of the mode. Finally, the mean will be located to the right of median because it is influenced most by extreme scores and will be displaced farthest to the right by the scores in the tail. Therefore, in a positively skewed distribution, the mean will have the largest value, followed by the median and then the mode [see Figure 3.11(a)].

FIGURE 3.11

Measures of central tendency for skewed distributions.

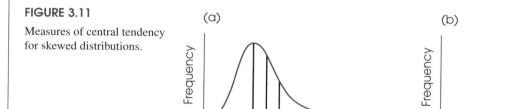

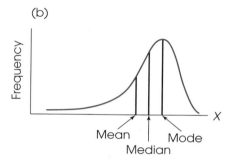

Negatively skewed distributions are lopsided in the opposite direction, with the scores piling up on the right-hand side and the tail tapering off to the left. The grades on an easy exam, for example, will tend to form a negatively skewed distribution [see Figure 3.11(b)]. For a distribution with negative skew, the mode is on the right-hand side (with the peak), while the mean is displaced on the left by the extreme scores in the tail. As before, the median is located between the mean and the mode. In order from highest value to lowest value, the three measures of central tendency will be the mode, the median, and the mean.

LEARNING CHECK ◆   1. Which measure of central tendency is most likely to be affected by one or two extreme scores in a distribution? ((mean), median, mode)

2. The mode is the correct way to measure central tendency for data from a nominal scale. ((True) or false?)

3. If a graph is used to show the means obtained from an experiment, the different treatment conditions (the independent variable) should be listed on the vertical axis. (True or (false?))

4. A distribution has a mean of 75 and a median of 70. This distribution is probably positively skewed. (True or false?)

ANSWERS   **1.** mean   **2.** True   **3.** False   **4.** True   ◆

ON THE WEB

NOW THAT you have finished Chapter 3, you can test your knowledge with the practice quiz that is available on the Wadsworth Web site at **www.wadsworth.com**. In addition, you can visit the workshop on Central Ten- dency and Variability to get a practical perspective on the concept of central tendency. For more information about finding the quizzes and workshops, see page 24.

SUMMARY

1. The purpose of central tendency is to determine the single value that identifies the center of the distribution and best represents the entire set of scores. The three standard measures of central tendency are the mode, the median, and the mean.

2. The mean is the arithmetic average. It is computed by summing all the scores and then dividing by the number of scores. Conceptually, the mean is obtained by dividing the total (ΣX) equally among the number of individuals (N or n). The mean can also be defined as the balance point for the distribution. The distances above the mean are exactly balanced by the distances below the mean. Although the calculation is the same for a population or a sample mean, a population mean is identified by the symbol μ, and a sample mean is identified by $\overline{X}$.

3. Changing any score in the distribution will cause the mean to be changed. When a constant value is added to (or subtracted from) every score in a distribution, the same constant value is added to (or subtracted from) the mean. If every score is multiplied by a constant, the mean will be multiplied by the same constant. In nearly all circumstances, the mean provides a good representative value and is the preferred measure of central tendency.

4. The median is the value that divides a distribution exactly in half. The median is the preferred measure of central tendency when a distribution has a few extreme scores that displace the value of the mean. The median also is used when there are undetermined (infinite) scores that make it impossible to compute a mean.

5. The mode is the most frequently occurring score in a distribution. It is easily located by finding the peak in a frequency distribution graph. For data measured on a nominal scale, the mode is the appropriate measure of central tendency. It is possible for a distribution to have more than one mode.

6. For symmetrical distributions, the mean will equal the median. If there is only one mode, then it also will have the same value.

7. For skewed distributions, the mode will be located toward the side where the scores pile up, and the mean will be pulled toward the extreme scores in the tail. The median will be located between these two values.

KEY TERMS

central tendency	median	bimodal distribution	positive skew
population mean (μ)	mode	multimodal distribution	negative skew
sample mean ($\overline{X}$)	major mode	symmetrical distribution	
weighted mean	minor mode	skewed distribution	

——— FOCUS ON PROBLEM SOLVING ———————————————

1. Because there are three different measures of central tendency, your first problem is to decide which one is best for your specific set of data. Usually the mean is the preferred measure, but the median may provide a more representative value if you are working with a skewed distribution. With data measured on a nominal scale, you must use the mode.

2. Although the three measures of central tendency appear to be very simple to calculate, there is always a chance for errors. The most common sources of error are listed next.

   a. Many students find it very difficult to compute the mean for data presented in a frequency distribution table. They tend to ignore the frequencies in the table and simply average the score values listed in the X column. You must use the frequencies and the scores! Remember, the number of scores is found by $N = \Sigma f$, and the sum of all N scores is found by ΣfX.

   b. The median is the midpoint of the distribution of scores, not the midpoint of the scale of measurement. For a 100-point test, for example, many students incorrectly assume that the median must be $X = 50$. To find the median, you must have the *complete set* of individual scores. The median separates the individuals into two equal-sized groups.

   c. The most common error with the mode is for students to report the highest frequency in a distribution rather than the score with the highest frequency. Remember, the purpose of central tendency is to find the most representative score. Therefore, for the following data, the mode is $X = 3$, not $f = 8$.

X	f
4	3
3	8
2	5
1	2

——— DEMONSTRATION 3.1 ———————————————

COMPUTING MEASURES OF CENTRAL TENDENCY

For the following sample data, find the mean, median, and mode. Scores:

$$5, \quad 6, \quad 9, \quad 11, \quad 5, \quad 11, \quad 8, \quad 14, \quad 2, \quad 11$$

Compute the mean. Calculating the mean involves two steps:

1. Obtain the sum of the scores, ΣX.
2. Divide the sum by the number of scores, n.

For these data, the sum of the scores is as follows:

$$\Sigma X = 5 + 6 + 9 + 11 + 5 + 11 + 8 + 14 + 2 + 11 = 82$$

We can also observe that $n = 10$. Therefore, the mean of this sample is obtained by

$$\overline{X} = \frac{\Sigma X}{n} = \frac{82}{10} = 8.2$$

Find the median. The median divides the distribution in half, in that half of the scores are above or equal to the median and half are below or equal to it. In this demonstration, $n = 10$. Thus, the median should be a value that has five scores above it and five scores below it.

1. Arrange the scores in order.

    2,   5,   5,   6,   8,   9,   11,   11,   11,   14

2. With an even number of scores, locate the midpoint between the middle two scores. The middle scores are $X = 8$ and $X = 9$. The median is the midpoint between 8 and 9.

$$\text{Median} = \frac{8 + 9}{2} = \frac{17}{2} = 8.5$$

Find the mode. The mode is the X value that has the highest frequency. Looking at the data, we can readily determine that $X = 11$ is the score that occurs most frequently.

PROBLEMS

1. Explain the general purpose for measuring central tendency.

2. Explain why there is more than one method for measuring central tendency. Why not use a single, standardized method for determining the "average" score?

3. Explain what is meant by each of the following statements:
    a. The mean is the *balance point* of the distribution.
    b. The median is the *midpoint* of the distribution.

4. Identify the circumstances in which the median rather than the mean is the preferred measure of central tendency.

5. Under what circumstances will the mean, the median, and the mode all have the same value?

6. Under what circumstances is the mode the preferred measure of central tendency?

7. Explain why the mean is often not a good measure of central tendency for a skewed distribution.

8. Find the mean, median, and mode for the following sample of scores:

    1,   4,   3,   5,   4,   2,   4,   2,   5,   3

9. Find the mean, median, and mode for the following sample of scores:

    6,   5,   3,   5,   4,   7,   5,   6,   5,   4

10. Find the mean, median, and mode for the set of scores in the following frequency distribution table:

X	f
5	2
4	5
3	3
2	2
1	2

11. Find the mean, median, and mode for the set of scores in the following frequency distribution table:

X	f
8	2
7	3
6	5
5	9
4	1

$= 16$
21

$\frac{116}{20}$
median

12. A population of $N = 8$ scores has a mean of $\mu = 12$. What is the value of ΣX for this population?

13. A sample of $n = 15$ scores has a mean of $\overline{X} = 7$. What is the value of ΣX for this sample?

14. A sample of $n = 6$ scores has a mean of $\overline{X} = 9$. If one of the scores is changed from $X = 2$ to $X = 14$, what will be the new value for the sample mean?

15. A set of eight scores has a mean of 20. If one of the scores is changed from $X = 42$ to $X = 2$, what will be the new value for the mean?

16. A sample of $n = 10$ scores has a mean of 7. If a new score of $X = 18$ is added to the sample, what will be the new value for the sample mean?

17. A population of $N = 5$ scores has a mean of $\mu = 6$. If a score of $X = 2$ is removed from the population, what will be the new value for the population mean?

18. A sample of $n = 8$ scores has a mean of $\overline{X} = 10$. One score is removed from the sample and the mean for the remaining scores is $\overline{X} = 6$. What is the value of the score that was removed? (*Hint:* Find ΣX for the original sample and for the new sample.)

19. A sample of $n = 5$ scores has a mean of $\overline{X} = 11$. After one new score is added to the sample, the new mean is $\overline{X} = 12$. What is the value of the new score?

20. A sample of $n = 4$ scores has a mean of $\overline{X} = 8$. A second sample of $n = 6$ scores has $\overline{X} = 12$. If the two samples are combined, what value will be obtained for the mean of the combined sample?

21. A sample of $n = 15$ scores has a mean of $\overline{X} = 30$. A second sample of $n = 5$ scores has a mean of 24. If the two samples are combined, what value will be obtained for the mean of the combined sample?

22. For each of the following situations, identify the measure of central tendency (mean, median, or mode) that would provide the best description of the "average" score.
  a. A researcher asks each individual in a sample of 50 adults to name his/her favorite season (summer, fall, winter, spring).
  b. An insurance company would like to determine how long people remain hospitalized after a routine appendectomy. The data from a large sample indicate that most people are released after two or three days but a few develop infections and stay in the hospital for weeks.
  c. A teacher measures scores on a standardized reading test for a sample of children from a middle-class, suburban elementary school.

23. A professor computed the mean, median, and mode for the exam scores from a class of $N = 20$ students. Identify which of the following statements *cannot* be true and explain your answer:
  a. None of the students had an exam score exactly equal to the mean.
  b. None of the students had an exam score exactly equal to the median.
  c. None of the students had an exam score exactly equal to the mode.

24. A professor computed the mean, median, and mode for the exam scores from a class of $N = 20$ students. Iden-

tify which of the following statements *cannot* be true and explain your answer.
  a. More than half the class had scores above the mode.
  b. More than half the class had scores above the median.
  c. More than half the class had scores above the mean.

25. Consider the following two sets of data:

  Set 1: 7, 6, 9, 5, 6, 11, 7, 5, 6, 8
  Set 2: 8, 6, 12, 7, 9, 6, 15, 6, 8, 7

  a. Sketch a histogram for the data in set 1 and compute the mean, median, and mode for these data.
  b. Sketch a histogram for the data in set 2 and compute the mean, median, and mode for these data.
  c. Which distribution is more skewed? How does the degree of skew relate to the measures of central tendency, especially the mean?

26. Research has demonstrated that the amount of sleep needed by the average person changes as a function of age. The following values show the mean hours of sleep needed at each age. Draw a line graph to show the relationship between age and amount of sleep.

  1 year, 13 hours

  5 years, 11 hours

  10 years, 10 hours

  15 years, $8\frac{1}{2}$ hours

  20 years, 8 hours

27. A researcher evaluated the taste of four leading brands of instant coffee by having a sample of individuals taste each coffee and then rate its flavor on a scale from 1 to 5 (1 = very bad and 5 = excellent). The results from this study are summarized as follows:

Coffee	Average rating
Brand A	2.5
Brand B	4.1
Brand C	3.2
Brand D	3.6

  a. Identify the independent variable and the dependent variable for this study.
  b. What scale of measurement was used for the independent variable (nominal, ordinal, interval, or ratio)?
  c. If the researcher used a graph to show the obtained relationship between the independent variable and the dependent variable, what kind of graph would be appropriate (line graph, histogram, bar graph)?
  d. Sketch a graph showing the results of this experiment.

CHAPTER 4

VARIABILITY

TOOLS YOU WILL NEED

The following items are considered essential background material for this chapter. If you doubt your knowledge of any of these items, you should review the appropriate chapter or section before proceeding.

- Summation notation (Chapter 1)
- Central tendency (Chapter 3)
  - Mean
  - Median

CONTENTS

4.1   INTRODUCTION

The term *variability* has much the same meaning in statistics as it has in everyday language; to say that things are variable means that they are not all the same. In statistics, our goal is to measure the amount of variability for a particular set of scores, a distribution. In simple terms, if the scores in a distribution are all the same, then there is no variability. If there are small differences between scores, the variability is small, and if there are big differences between scores, the variability is large.

DEFINITION

Variability provides a quantitative measure of the degree to which scores in a distribution are spread out or clustered together.

Figure 4.1 shows two distributions of familiar values: Figure 4.1(a) shows the distribution of adult heights (in inches), and Figure 4.1(b) shows the distribution of adult weights (in pounds). Note that the two distributions differ in terms of central tendency. The mean adult height is 68 inches (5 feet and 8 inches), and the mean adult weight is 150 pounds. In addition, note that the distributions differ in terms of variability. For example, most adult heights are clustered close together, within 5 or 6 inches of the mean. On the other hand, adult weights are spread over a much wider range. In the weight distribution, it is not unusual to find individuals who are located more than 30 pounds away from the mean, and it would not be surprising to find two individuals whose weights differ by more than 30 or 40 pounds. The goal for measuring variability is to describe how spread out the scores are in a distribution. In general, a good measure of variability will serve two purposes:

1. Variability describes the distribution. Specifically, it tells whether the scores are clustered close together or are spread out over a large distance. Usually, variability is defined in terms of *distance*. It tells how much distance to expect between one score and another or how much distance to expect between an individual

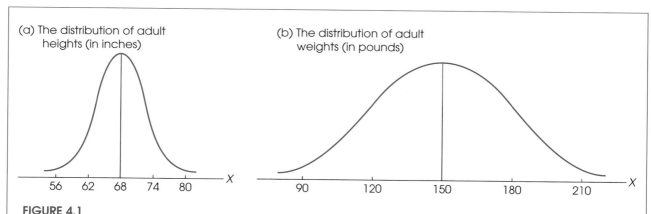

FIGURE 4.1

Population distributions of adult heights and adult weights.

Note: For simplicity, we have omitted the vertical axis for these graphs. As always, the height of any point on the curve indicates the relative frequency for that particular score.

score and the mean. For example, we know that most adults' heights are clustered close together within 5 or 6 inches of the average. Although heights that are more extreme exist, they are relatively rare.

2. Variability measures how well an individual score (or group of scores) represents the entire distribution. This aspect of variability is very important for inferential statistics where relatively small samples are used to answer questions about populations. For example, suppose that you selected a sample of one person to represent the entire population. Because most adult heights are within a few inches of the population average (the distances are small), there is a very good chance that you would select someone whose height is within 6 inches of the population mean. On the other hand, the scores are much more spread out (the distances are greater) in the distribution of adult weights. In this case, you probably would *not* obtain someone whose weight was within 6 pounds of the population mean. Thus, variability provides information about how much error to expect when you are using a sample to represent a population.

In this chapter, we will consider three different measures of variability: the range, the interquartile range, and the standard deviation. Of these three, the standard deviation (and the related measure of variance) is by far the most important.

4.2 THE RANGE

The range is the distance between the largest score (X_{max}) and the smallest score in the distribution (X_{min}). In determining this distance, you must also take into account the real limits of the maximum and minimum X values. The range therefore is computed as the difference between the upper real limit (URL) for X_{max} and the lower real limit (LRL) for X_{min}:

$$range = URL\ X_{max} - LRL\ X_{min}$$

DEFINITION

The *range* is the difference between the upper real limit of the largest (maximum) X value and the lower real limit of the smallest (minimum) X value.

For example, consider the following data:

3,   7,   12,   8,   5,   10

For these data, $X_{max} = 12$, with an upper real limit of 12.5, and $X_{min} = 3$, with a lower real limit of 2.5. Thus, the range equals

When the distribution consists of whole numbers, the range also can be obtained as follows:

range = highest X − lowest X + 1

$$range = URL\ X_{max} - LRL\ X_{min}$$

$$= 12.5 - 2.5 = 10$$

The range is perhaps the most obvious way of describing how spread out the scores are—simply find the distance between the maximum and the minimum scores. The problem with using the range as a measure of variability is that it is completely determined by the two extreme values and ignores the other scores in the distribution.

Because the range does not consider all the scores in the distribution, it often does not give an accurate description of the variability for the entire distribution. For this reason, the range is considered to be a crude and unreliable measure of variability.

4.3   THE INTERQUARTILE RANGE AND SEMI-INTERQUARTILE RANGE

In Chapter 3, we defined the median as the score that divides a distribution exactly in half. In a similar way, a distribution can be divided into four equal parts using quartiles. By definition, the first quartile ($Q1$) is the score that separates the lower 25% of the distribution from the rest. The second quartile ($Q2$) is the score that has exactly two quarters, or 50%, of the distribution below it. Note that the second quartile and the median are the same. Finally, the third quartile ($Q3$) is the score that separates the bottom three-quarters of the distribution from the top quarter.

The simplest method for finding the values of $Q1$, $Q2$, and $Q3$ is to construct a frequency distribution histogram where each score is represented by a box (see Figure 4.2). Then determine exactly how many boxes are needed to make up exactly one-quarter of the whole set. With a total of $n = 16$ scores (boxes), for example, one-quarter is exactly 4 boxes. In this case, the first quartile separates the lowest 4 boxes (25%) from the rest, the second quartile has exactly 8 boxes (50%) on each side, and the third quartile separates the lowest 12 boxes (75%) from the highest 4 boxes. Usually you can simply count boxes or fractions of boxes to locate $Q1$, $Q2$, and $Q3$.

After the quartiles have been determined, the *interquartile range* is defined as the distance between the first quartile and the third quartile. The interquartile range effectively ignores the top 25% and the bottom 25% of the distribution and measures the range covered by the middle 50% of the distribution.

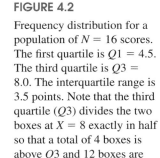

FIGURE 4.2

Frequency distribution for a population of $N = 16$ scores. The first quartile is $Q1 = 4.5$. The third quartile is $Q3 = 8.0$. The interquartile range is 3.5 points. Note that the third quartile ($Q3$) divides the two boxes at $X = 8$ exactly in half so that a total of 4 boxes is above $Q3$ and 12 boxes are below it.

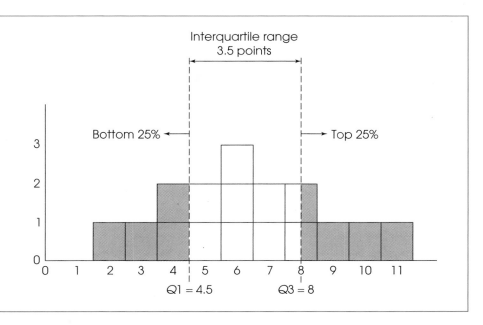

DEFINITION   The *interquartile range* is the distance between the first quartile and the third quartile:

$$\text{interquartile range} = Q3 - Q1$$

When the interquartile range is used to describe variability, it commonly is transformed into the *semi-interquartile range.* As the name implies, the semi-interquartile range is simply one-half of the interquartile range. Conceptually, the semi-interquartile range measures the distance from the middle of the distribution to the boundaries that define the middle 50%.

DEFINITION   The *semi-interquartile range* is one-half of the interquartile range:

$$\text{semi-interquartile range} = \frac{Q3 - Q1}{2}$$

EXAMPLE 4.1   Figure 4.2 shows a frequency distribution histogram for a set of 16 scores. For this distribution, the first quartile is $Q1 = 4.5$. Exactly 25% of the scores (4 out of 16) are located below $X = 4.5$. Similarly, the third quartile is $Q3 = 8.0$. Note that this value separates the bottom 75% of the distribution (12 out of 16 scores) from the top 25%. For this set of scores, the interquartile range is

$$Q3 - Q1 = 8.0 - 4.5 = 3.5$$

The semi-interquartile range is simply one-half of this distance:

$$\text{semi-interquartile range} = \frac{3.5}{2} = 1.75$$

Because the semi-interquartile range is derived from the middle 50% of a distribution, it is less likely to be influenced by extreme scores and therefore gives a better and more stable measure of variability than the range. Nevertheless, the semi-interquartile range does not take into account the actual distances between individual scores, so it does not give a complete picture of how scattered or clustered the scores are. Like the range, the semi-interquartile range is considered to be a somewhat crude measure of variability.

LEARNING CHECK ◆   1. For the following data, find the range and the semi-interquartile range:

3, 4, 5, 7, 9, 10, 11, 13

2. Consider the distribution of Exercise 1, except replace the score of 13 with a score of 100. What are the new values for the range and the semi-interquartile range? In comparing the answer to the one in Exercise 1, what can you conclude about these measures of variability?

ANSWERS   1. Range = URL X_{max} − LRL X_{min} = 13.5 − 2.5 = 11; semi-interquartile range = $(Q3 - Q1)/2 = (10.5 - 4.5)/2 = 3$.

2. Range = 98; semi-interquartile range = 3. The range is greatly affected by extreme scores in the distribution.   ◆

4.4 STANDARD DEVIATION AND VARIANCE FOR A POPULATION

The standard deviation is the most commonly used and the most important measure of variability. Standard deviation uses the mean of the distribution as a reference point and measures variability by considering the distance between each score and the mean. It determines whether the scores are generally near or far from the mean. That is, are the scores clustered together or scattered? In simple terms, the standard deviation approximates the average distance from the mean.

Although the concept of standard deviation is straightforward, the actual equations will appear complex. Therefore, we will begin by looking at the logic that leads to these equations. If you remember that our goal is to measure the standard, or typical, distance from the mean, then this logic and the equations that follow should be easier to remember.

STEP 1   The first step in finding the standard distance from the mean is to determine the deviation, or distance from the mean, for each individual score. By definition, the deviation for each score is the difference between the score and the mean.

DEFINITION   *Deviation* is distance and direction from the mean:

$$\text{deviation score} = X - \mu$$

A deviation score occasionally is identified by a lowercase letter x.

For a distribution of scores with $\mu = 50$, if your score is $X = 53$, then your deviation score is

$$X - \mu = 53 - 50 = 3$$

If your score is $X = 45$, then your deviation score is

$$X - \mu = 45 - 50 = -5$$

Note that there are two parts to a deviation score: the sign ($+$ or $-$) and the number. The sign tells the direction from the mean—that is, whether the score is located above ($+$) or below ($-$) the mean. The number gives the actual distance from the mean. For example, a deviation score of -6 corresponds to a score that is below the mean by 6 points.

STEP 2   Because our goal is to compute a measure of the standard distance from the mean, the obvious next step is to calculate the mean of the deviation scores. To compute this mean, first add up the deviation scores and then divide by N. We demonstrate this process in the following example.

EXAMPLE 4.2   We start with the following set of $N = 4$ scores. These scores add up to $\Sigma X = 12$, so the mean is $\mu = \frac{12}{4} = 3$. For each score, we have computed the deviation.

X	$X - \mu$
8	$+5$
1	-2
3	0
0	$\underline{-3}$
	$0 = \Sigma(X - \mu)$

Note that the deviation scores add up to zero. This should not be surprising if you re-member that the mean serves as a balance point for the distribution. The distances above the mean are equal to the distances below the mean (see page 54). Logically, the devia-tion scores must *always* add up to zero.

Because the mean deviation is always zero, it is of no value as a measure of variabil-ity. It is zero whether the scores are grouped together or are all scattered out. The mean deviation score provides no information about variability. (You should note, however, that the constant value of zero can be useful in other ways. Whenever you are working with deviation scores, you can check your calculations by making sure that the devia-tion scores add up to zero.)

STEP 3   The average of the deviation scores will not work as a measure of variability because it is always zero. Clearly, this problem results from the positive and negative values cancel-ing each other out. The solution is to get rid of the signs ($+$ and $-$). The standard proce-dure for accomplishing this is to square each deviation score. Using these squared values, you then compute the mean squared deviation, which is called *variance*.

DEFINITION   *Variance* = mean squared deviation. Variance is the mean of the squared devia-tion scores.

Note that the process of squaring deviation scores does more than simply get rid of plus and minus signs. It results in a measure of variability based on *squared* distances. Although variance is valuable for some of the *inferential* statistical methods covered later, the mean squared distance is not the best *descriptive* measure for variability.

STEP 4   Remember that our goal is to compute a measure of the standard distance from the mean. Variance, the mean squared deviation, is not exactly what we want. The final step simply makes a correction for having squared all the distances. The new measure, the standard deviation, is the square root of the variance.

DEFINITION   *Standard deviation* = $\sqrt{\text{variance}}$.

Technically, standard deviation is the square root of the mean squared deviation. Conceptually, however, standard deviation is easier to understand if you think of it as describing the typical distance of scores from the mean (that is, the typical $X - \mu$). As the name implies, standard deviation measures the standard, or typical, deviation score.

The concept of standard deviation (or variance) is the same for a sample as for a pop-ulation. However, the details of the calculations differ slightly, depending on whether you have data for a sample or a complete population. Therefore, we will first consider the formulas for measures of population variability.

SUM OF SQUARED DEVIATIONS (*SS*)   Variance, you should recall, is defined as the mean squared deviation. This mean is computed exactly the same way you compute any mean: First, find the sum, and then divide by the number of scores:

$$\text{variance} = \text{mean squared deviation} = \frac{\text{sum of squared deviations}}{\text{number of scores}}$$

The value in the numerator of this equation, the sum of the squared deviations, is a basic component of variability, and we will focus on it. To simplify things, it is identified by the notation SS (for sum of squared deviations), and it generally is referred to as the *sum of squares*.

DEFINITION   *SS*, or *sum of squares*, is the sum of the squared deviation scores.

You will need to know two formulas to compute SS. These formulas are algebraically equivalent (they always produce the same answer), but they look different and are used in different situations.

The first of these formulas is called the definitional formula because the terms in the formula literally define the process of adding up the squared deviations:

$$\text{definitional formula:} \quad SS = \Sigma(X - \mu)^2 \tag{4.1}$$

Note that the formula instructs you to perform a sequence of calculations:

1. Find each deviation score $(X - \mu)$.
2. Square each deviation score, $(X - \mu)^2$.
3. Sum the squared deviations.

The result is SS, the sum of the squared deviations. The following example demonstrates using this formula.

EXAMPLE 4.3   We will compute SS for the following set of $N = 4$ scores. These scores have a sum of $\Sigma X = 8$, so the mean is $\mu = \frac{8}{4} = 2$. The following table shows the deviation and the squared deviation for each score. The sum of the squared deviation is $SS = 22$.

X	$X - \mu$	$(X - \mu)^2$	
1	-1	1	$\Sigma X = 8$
0	-2	4	$\mu = 2$
6	$+4$	16	
1	-1	$\underline{1}$	
		$22 = \Sigma(X - \mu)^2$	

The second formula for SS is called the computational formula (or the machine formula) because it works directly with the scores (X values) and therefore is generally easier to use for calculations, especially with an electronic calculator:

$$\text{computational formula:} \quad SS = \Sigma X^2 - \frac{(\Sigma X)^2}{N} \tag{4.2}$$

The first part of this formula directs you to square each score and then add the squared values, ΣX^2. In the second part of the formula, you find the sum of the scores, ΣX, then square this total and, finally, divide the result by N (see Box 4.1). The use of this formula is shown in Example 4.4 with the same scores that we used to demonstrate the definitional formula.

4.1 COMPUTING *SS* WITH A CALCULATOR

THE COMPUTATIONAL formula for *SS* is intended to simplify calculations, especially when you are using an electronic calculator. The following steps outline the most efficient procedure for using a typical, inexpensive hand calculator to find *SS*. (We assume that your calculator has one memory, where you can store and retrieve information.) The computational formula for *SS* is presented here for easy reference.

$$SS = \Sigma X^2 - \frac{(\Sigma X)^2}{N}$$

STEP 1: The first term in the computational formula is ΣX^2. The procedure for finding this sum is described in Box 1.1 on page 22. Once you have calculated ΣX^2, write this sum on a piece of paper so you do not lose it. Leave ΣX^2 in the calculator memory, and go to the next step.

STEP 2: Now you must find the sum of the scores, ΣX. We assume that you can add a set of numbers with your calculator—just be sure to press the equals key (=) after the last score. Write this total on your paper. (*Note:* You may want to clear the calculator display before you begin this process. It is not necessary, but you may feel more comfortable starting with zero.)

STEP 3: Now you are ready to plug the sums into the formula. Your calculator should still have the sum of the scores, ΣX, in the display. If not, enter this value.

1. With ΣX in the display, you can compute $(\Sigma X)^2$ simply by pressing the multiply key ($\times$) and then the equals key (=).
2. Now you must divide the squared sum by N, the number of scores. Assuming that you have counted the number of scores, press the divide key ($\div$), enter N, and then press the equals key.

Your calculator display now shows $(\Sigma X)^2/N$. Write this number on your paper.

3. Finally, subtract the value of your calculator display from ΣX^2, which is in the calculator memory. You can do this by pressing the memory subtract key (usually M−). The value for *SS* is now in memory, and you can retrieve it by pressing the memory recall key (MR).

Try the whole procedure with a simple set of scores such as 1, 2, 3. You should obtain $SS = 2$ for these scores.

We asked you to write values at several steps during the calculation in case you make a mistake at some point. If you have written the values for ΣX^2, ΣX, and so on, you should be able to compute *SS* easily even if the contents of memory are lost.

E X A M P L E   4 . 4   The computational formula is used to calculate *SS* for the same set of $N = 4$ scores we used in Example 4.3. First, compute ΣX. Then square each score, and compute ΣX^2. These calculations are shown in the following table. The two sums are used in the formula to compute *SS*.

X	X^2
1	1
0	0
6	36
1	1
$\Sigma X = 8$	$\Sigma X^2 = 38$

$$SS = \Sigma X^2 - \frac{(\Sigma X)^2}{N}$$

$$= 38 - \frac{(8)^2}{4}$$

$$= 38 - \frac{64}{4}$$

$$= 38 - 16$$

$$= 22$$

Note that the two formulas produce exactly the same value for *SS*. Although the formulas look different, they are in fact equivalent.

The definitional formula for *SS* is the most direct way of calculating the sum of squares, but it can be awkward to use for most sets of data. In particular, if the mean is not a whole number, then the deviation scores will all be fractions or decimals, and the calculations become difficult. In addition, calculations with decimals or fractions introduce the opportunity for rounding error, which makes the results less accurate. For these reasons, the computational formula is used most of the time. If you have a small group of scores and the mean is a whole number, then the definitional formula is fine; otherwise, use the computational formula.

FORMULAS FOR POPULATION STANDARD DEVIATION AND VARIANCE

With the definition and calculation of *SS* behind you, the equations for variance and standard deviation become relatively simple. Remember, variance is defined as the mean squared deviation. The mean is the sum divided by *N*, so the equation for variance is

$$\text{variance} = \frac{SS}{N}$$

In the same way that sum of squares, or *SS*, is used to refer to the sum of squared deviations, the term *mean square,* or *MS*, is often used to refer to variance, which is the mean squared deviation.

Standard deviation is the square root of variance, so the equation for standard deviation is

$$\text{standard deviation} = \sqrt{\frac{SS}{N}}$$

There is one final bit of notation before we work completely through an example computing *SS*, variance, and standard deviation. Like the mean (μ), variance and standard deviation are parameters of a population and will be identified by Greek letters. To identify the standard deviation, we use the Greek letter sigma (the Greek letter *s*, standing for standard deviation). The capital letter sigma (Σ) has been used already, so we now use the lowercase sigma, σ:

$$\text{population standard deviation} = \sigma = \sqrt{\frac{SS}{N}} \tag{4.3}$$

The symbol for population variance should help you remember the relationship between standard deviation and variance. If you square the standard deviation, you will get the variance. The symbol for variance is sigma squared, σ^2:

$$\text{population variance} = \sigma^2 = \frac{SS}{N} \tag{4.4}$$

SUMMARY OF COMPUTATION FOR VARIANCE AND STANDARD DEVIATION

The following example demonstrates the complete process of calculating the variance and the standard deviation for a population of scores. Before we begin the example, however, we will briefly review the basic steps in the calculation.

STEP 1   Find the distance from the mean for each individual.

STEP 2   Square each distance.

STEP 3   Find the sum of the squared distances. This value is called *SS* or *sum of squares*. (*Note:* SS can also be obtained using the computational formula instead of steps 1–3.)

STEP 4   Find the mean of the squared distances. This value is called *variance* and measures the average squared distance from the mean.

STEP 5   Take the square root of the variance. This value is called *standard deviation* and provides a measure of the standard distance from the mean.

EXAMPLE 4.5   The following population of scores will be used to demonstrate the calculation of *SS*, variance, and standard deviation:

$$1, \quad 9, \quad 5, \quad 8, \quad 7$$

These five scores add up to $\Sigma X = 30$, so the mean is $\frac{30}{5} = 6$. Before doing any other calculations, remember that the purpose of standard deviation is to measure the standard distance from the mean. The scores we have been working with are shown in a histogram in Figure 4.3 so that you can see the variability more easily. Note that the scores closest to the mean are only 1 point away. Also, the score farthest from the mean is 5 points away. For this distribution, the largest distance from the mean is 5 points and the smallest distance is 1 point. Thus, the standard distance should be somewhere between 1 and 5. By looking at a distribution in this way, you should be able to make a rough estimate of the standard deviation. In this case, the standard deviation should be between 1 and 5, probably around 3 points.

FIGURE 4.3

A frequency distribution histogram for a population of $N = 5$ scores. The mean for this population is $\mu = 6$. The smallest distance from the mean is 1 point, and the largest distance is 5 points. The standard distance (or standard deviation) should be between 1 and 5 points.

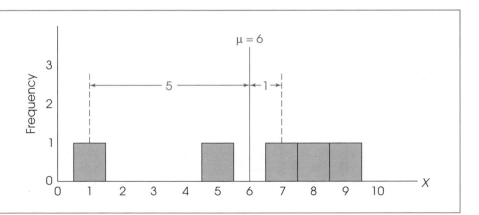

Making a preliminary judgment of standard deviation can help you avoid errors in calculation. If, for example, you worked through the formulas and ended up with a value of $\sigma = 12$, you should realize immediately that you have made an error. (If the largest deviation is only 5 points, then it is impossible for the standard deviation to be 12.)

Now we will start the calculations. The first step is to find *SS* for this set of scores. Because the mean is a whole number ($\mu = 6$), we can use the definitional formula for *SS*. Therefore, we first find each deviation, then square each deviation, then sum the squared deviations. This process is shown in the following table.

X	$X - \mu$	$(X - \mu)^2$	
1	-5	25	$\Sigma X = 30$
9	$+3$	9	$\mu = 6$
5	-1	1	
8	$+2$	4	
7	$+1$	$\underline{1}$	
		$40 = \Sigma(X - \mu)^2 = SS$	

For this set of scores, the sum of the squared deviations is $SS = 40$, so the variance is $\sigma^2 = 40/5 = 8$, and the standard deviation is $\sigma = \sqrt{8} = 2.83$. Note that the value for the standard deviation is in excellent agreement with our preliminary estimate of the standard distance from the mean.

LEARNING CHECK ◆

1. Write brief definitions of variance and standard deviation.

2. Find SS, variance, and standard deviation for the following population of $N = 5$ scores: 10, 10, 10, 10, 10. (*Note:* You should be able to answer this question without doing any calculations.)

3. **a.** Sketch a frequency distribution histogram for the following population of scores: 1, 3, 3, 9. Using this histogram, make an estimate of the standard deviation (i.e., the standard distance from the mean).

   b. Calculate SS, variance, and standard deviation for these scores. How well does your estimate from part (a) compare with the real standard deviation?

ANSWERS

1. Variance is the mean squared distance from the mean. Standard deviation is the square root of variance and provides a measure of the standard distance from the mean.

2. Because there is no variability in the population, SS, variance, and standard deviation are all equal to zero.

3. **a.** Your sketch should show a mean of $\mu = 4$. The score closest to the mean is $X = 3$, and the farthest score is $X = 9$. The standard deviation should be somewhere between 1 point and 5 points.

   b. For this population, $SS = 36$; the variance is $\frac{36}{4} = 9$; the standard deviation is $\sqrt{9} = 3$. ◆

GRAPHIC REPRESENTATION OF THE MEAN AND STANDARD DEVIATION

In frequency distribution graphs, we will identify the position of the mean by drawing a vertical line and labeling it with μ or $\overline{X}$ (see Figure 4.4). Because the standard deviation measures distance from the mean, it will be represented by a line drawn from the mean outward for a distance equal to the standard deviation (see Figure 4.4). For rough sketches, you can identify the mean with a vertical line in the middle of the distribution. The standard deviation line should extend approximately halfway from the mean to the most extreme score. (*Note:* In Figure 4.4 we show the standard deviation as a line pointing to the right. You should realize that we could have drawn the line pointing to the left, or we could have drawn two lines, with one pointing to the right and one pointing to the left. In each case, the goal is to show the standard distance from the mean.)

FIGURE 4.4

The graphic representation of a population with a mean of $\mu = 40$ and a standard deviation of $\mu = 4$.

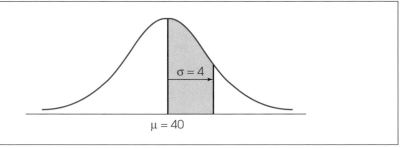

$\sigma = 4$

$\mu = 40$

4.5   STANDARD DEVIATION AND VARIANCE FOR SAMPLES

The goal of inferential statistics is to use the limited information from samples to draw general conclusions about populations. The basic assumption of this process is that samples should be representative of the populations from which they come. This assumption poses a special problem for variability because samples consistently tend to be less variable than their populations. An example of this general tendency is shown in Figure 4.5. The fact that a sample tends to be less variable than its population means that sample variability gives a *biased* estimate of population variability. This bias is in the direction of underestimating the population value rather than being right on the mark. To correct for this bias, it is necessary to make a simple adjustment in the calculation of variability when you are working with sample data. The intent of the adjustment is to make the resulting value for sample variability a more accurate estimate of the population variability.

A sample statistic is said to be *biased* if, on the average, it does not provide an accurate estimate of the corresponding population parameter.

FIGURE 4.5

The population of adult heights forms a normal distribution. If you select a sample from this population, you are most likely to obtain individuals who are near average in height. As a result, the scores in the sample will be less variable (spread out) than the scores in the population.

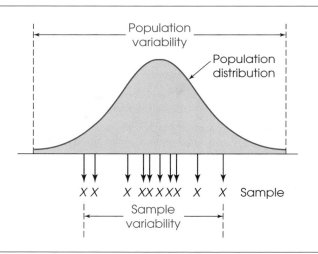

Population variability

Population distribution

X X   X XX X XX   X   X   Sample

Sample variability

The calculation of variance and standard deviation for a sample follows the same general process that was used to find population variance and standard deviation. Except for minor changes in notation, the first three steps in this process are exactly the same for a sample as they are for a population. That is, the calculation of *SS* is the same for a sample as it is for a population. The changes in notation involve using $\overline{X}$ for the sample mean instead of μ and using n instead of N for the number of scores. Thus, we find SS for a sample as follows:

STEP 1 Find the deviation for each score:

$$\text{sample deviation score} = X - \overline{X} \tag{4.5}$$

STEP 2 Square each deviation:

$$\text{squared deviation} = (X - \overline{X})^2$$

STEP 3 Sum the squared deviations:

$$SS = \Sigma(X - \overline{X})^2$$

We can summarize these three steps in a definitional formula for SS:

$$\text{definitional formula:} \quad SS = \Sigma(X - \overline{X})^2 \tag{4.6}$$

We can also obtain the value of SS using the computational formula. Using sample notation, this formula is

$$\text{computational formula:} \quad SS = \Sigma X^2 - \frac{(\Sigma X)^2}{n} \tag{4.7}$$

After you compute SS, however, it becomes critical to differentiate between samples and populations. To correct for the bias in sample variability, it is necessary to make an adjustment in the formulas for sample variance and standard deviation. With this in mind, sample variance (identified by the symbol s^2) is defined as

$$\text{sample variance} = s^2 = \frac{SS}{n - 1} \tag{4.8}$$

Sample standard deviation (identified by the symbol s) is simply the square root of the variance.

$$\text{sample standard deviation} = s = \sqrt{\frac{SS}{n - 1}} \tag{4.9}$$

Remember that sample variability tends to underestimate population variability unless some correction is made.

Note that these sample formulas use $n - 1$ instead of n. This adjustment is necessary to correct for the bias in sample variability. The effect of the adjustment is to increase the value you will obtain. Dividing by a smaller number ($n - 1$ instead of n) produces a larger result and makes sample variance an accurate, or unbiased, estimator of population variance.

The following example demonstrates the calculation of variance and standard deviation for a sample.

EXAMPLE 4.6 We have selected a sample of $n = 7$ scores. The scores are 1, 6, 4, 3, 8, 7, 6. The frequency distribution histogram for this sample is shown in Figure 4.6. Before we begin

FIGURE 4.6

The frequency distribution histogram for a sample of $n = 7$ scores. The sample mean is $\overline{X} = 5$. The smallest distance from the mean is 1 point, and the largest distance from the mean is 4 points. The standard distance (standard deviation) should be between 1 and 4 points.

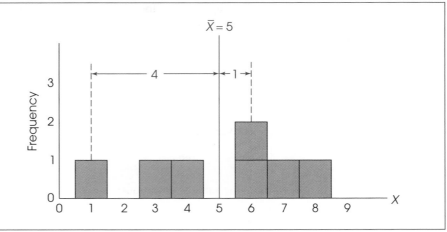

any calculations, you should be able to look at the sample distribution and make a preliminary estimate of the outcome. Remember that standard deviation measures the standard distance from the mean. For this sample, the mean is $\overline{X} = 5$ ($\frac{35}{7} = 5$). The scores closest to the mean are $X = 4$ and $X = 6$, both of which are exactly 1 point away. The score farthest from the mean is $X = 1$, which is 4 points away. With the smallest distance from the mean equal to 1 and the largest distance equal to 4, we should obtain a standard distance somewhere around 2.5 (between 1 and 4).

Now let's begin the calculations. First, we will find SS for this sample. Because there are only a few scores and the mean is a whole number, the definitional formula will be easy to use. You should try this formula for practice. Meanwhile, we will work with the computational formula.

Caution: The calculation of SS is the same for a sample and a population. Do not use $n - 1$ in the formula for SS.

X	X^2	
1	1	$\Sigma X = 35$
6	36	$\Sigma X^2 = 211$
4	16	
3	9	
8	64	
7	49	
6	36	

$$SS = \Sigma X^2 - \frac{(\Sigma X)^2}{n}$$

$$= 211 - \frac{(35)^2}{7}$$

$$= 211 - \frac{1225}{7}$$

$$= 211 - 175$$

$$= 36$$

SS for this sample is 36. You should obtain exactly the same answer using the definitional formula. Continuing the calculations,

$$\text{sample variance} = s^2 = \frac{SS}{n - 1} = \frac{36}{7 - 1} = 6$$

Finally, the standard deviation is

$$s = \sqrt{s^2} = \sqrt{6} = 2.45$$

Note that the value we obtained is in excellent agreement with our preliminary prediction.

---

1. **a.** Sketch a frequency distribution histogram for the following sample of scores: 1, 1, 9, 1. Using your histogram, make an estimate of the standard deviation for this sample.

   b. Calculate SS, variance, and standard deviation for this sample. How well does your estimate from part (a) compare with the real standard deviation?

2. If the scores in the previous exercise were for a population, what value would you obtain for SS?

3. Explain why the formulas for sample variance and standard deviation use $n - 1$ instead of n.

1. **a.** Your graph should show a sample mean of $\overline{X} = 3$. The score farthest from the mean is $X = 9$, and the closest score is $X = 1$. You should estimate the standard deviation to be between 2 points and 6 points.

   b. For this sample, $SS = 48$; the sample variance is $\frac{48}{3} = 16$; the sample standard deviation is $\sqrt{16} = 4$.

2. $SS = 48$ whether the data are from a sample or a population.

3. Sample variability is biased because the scores in a sample tend to be less variable than the scores in a population. To correct for this bias, the formulas divide by $n - 1$ instead of n. ◆

SAMPLE VARIABILITY AND DEGREES OF FREEDOM

If you have an entire population of scores, including the mean, then it is possible to find the deviation, $X - \mu$, for each individual score. However, when you have only a sample to work with, you must use the sample mean, $\overline{X}$, as the reference point for measuring deviations. This requires that you know the value of $\overline{X}$ before you can begin to compute deviations. However, if you know the value of $\overline{X}$, then you must also know the value of ΣX. For example, if you have a sample of $n = 3$ scores with a mean of $\overline{X} = 10$, then the three scores must have a total of $\Sigma X = 30$.

The fact that you must know $\overline{X}$ and ΣX before you can compute variability implies that not all of the scores in the sample are free to vary. Suppose, for example, you are taking a sample of $n = 3$ scores and you know that $\Sigma X = 30$ ($\overline{X} = 10$). Once you have identified the first two scores in the sample, the value of the third score is restricted. If the first scores were $X = 0$ and $X = 5$, then the last score would have to be $X = 25$ for the total to be $\Sigma X = 30$. Note that the first two scores in this sample could have any values but that the last score is restricted. As a result, the sample is said to have $n - 1$ degrees of freedom; that is, only $n - 1$ of the scores are free to vary.

DEFINITION

Degrees of freedom, or *df*, for sample variance are defined as

$$df = n - 1$$

where n is the number of scores in the sample.

The $n - 1$ degrees of freedom for a sample is the same $n - 1$ that is used in the formulas for sample variance and standard deviation. Remember that variance is defined as the mean squared deviation. As always, this mean is computed by finding the sum and dividing by the number of scores:

$$\text{mean} = \frac{\text{sum}}{\text{number}}$$

To calculate sample variance (mean squared deviation), we find the sum of the squared deviations (*SS*) and divide by the number of scores that are free to vary. This number is $n - 1 = df$.

$$s^2 = \frac{\text{sum of squared deviations}}{\text{number of scores free to vary}} = \frac{SS}{df} = \frac{SS}{n - 1}$$

Later in this book, we will use the concept of degrees of freedom in other situations. For now, remember that knowing the sample mean places a restriction on sample variability. Only $n - 1$ of the scores are free to vary; $df = n - 1$.

4.6   MORE ABOUT VARIANCE AND STANDARD DEVIATION

Variance and standard deviation are two of the most important elements in all of statistics. These two statistical measures are used extensively in both descriptive methods and inferential methods. Although variance and standard deviation can both be defined by mathematical formulas, it is much better to understand the concept behind these two measures and to understand how they are used. In the following sections, we will examine some of the uses and characteristics of the variance and the standard deviation.

BIASED AND UNBIASED STATISTICS

The formula for sample variance has been developed so that the value obtained for a sample variance will provide an *unbiased* estimate of the corresponding population variance. This does not mean that each individual sample variance will be exactly equal to its population variance. In fact, some sample variances will overestimate the population value and some will underestimate it. However, the *average* of all the sample variances will produce an accurate estimate of the population variance. This is the idea behind the concept of an unbiased statistic.

DEFINITIONS

A sample statistic is *unbiased* if the average value of the sample statistic, obtained over many different samples, is equal to the population parameter. On the other hand, if the average value for a sample statistic consistently underestimates or consistently overestimates the corresponding population parameter, then the statistic is *biased*.

The following example is intended to demonstrate the concept of an unbiased statistic. In addition, the example demonstrates another interesting point: Specifically, because the sample variance is unbiased, the sample standard deviation is biased. The problem is that the variance and standard deviation are related by a nonlinear square root relationship, so they cannot both be unbiased.

EXAMPLE 4.7

Technical note: We have structured this example to mimic "sampling with replacement," which will be covered in Chapter 6.

We begin with a population that consists of exactly $N = 6$ scores: 0, 0, 3, 3, 6, 6. With a few simple calculations you should be able to verify that this population has a mean of $\mu = 3$, a variance of $\sigma^2 = 6$, and a standard deviation of $\sigma = \sqrt{6} = 2.45$.

Next, we will select samples from this population so that each sample has exactly $n = 2$ scores. In fact, we will obtain every single possible sample with $n = 2$. The complete set of samples is listed in Table 4.1. Note that the samples are listed systematically to ensure that every possible sample is included. We begin by listing all the samples that have $X = 0$ as the first score, then all the samples with $X = 3$ as the first score, and so on. Note that the table shows a total of 9 samples.

Finally, we have computed the sample mean, $\overline{X}$, the sample variance, s^2, and the sample standard deviation, s, for each sample. You should verify our calculations by computing one or two of the values for yourself. The complete set of sample means, sample variances, and sample standard deviations are listed in the table.

Now, direct your attention to the column of sample variances. Although the population has a variance of $\sigma^2 = 6$, note that none of the samples has a variance exactly equal to 6. However, if you consider the complete set of samples, you will find that the 9 sample variances add up to a total of 54, so the average of the sample variances is $\frac{54}{9} = 6.00$. This is exactly what is meant by the concept of an unbiased estimate: On average, the sample values provide an accurate representation of the population. In this example, the average of the 9 sample variances is exactly equal to the population variance.

Now turn your attention to the column of sample standard deviations (s values). The population standard deviation is $\sigma = 2.45$ and none of the samples has exactly this same value. In addition, if you compute the average of the 9 sample standard deviations, you obtain $\frac{16.96}{9} = 1.88$. This time, the average of the sample values is not equal to the population value. In other words, the sample standard deviation does not provide an unbiased estimate of the population standard deviation.

Finally, consider the column of sample means. For this example, the population mean is $\mu = 3$ and a few of the samples have means that are identical to the popula-

---

TABLE 4.1

The set of all the possible samples for $n = 2$ selected from the population described in Example 4.7. The mean, the variance, and the standard deviation have been computed for each of the 9 samples.

Sample	First score	Second score	Mean $\overline{X}$	Variance s^2	Stand. dev. s
1	0	0	0.00	0.00	0.00
2	0	3	1.50	4.50	2.12
3	0	6	3.00	18.00	4.24
4	3	0	1.50	4.50	2.12
5	3	3	3.00	0.00	0.00
6	3	6	4.50	4.50	2.12
7	6	0	3.00	18.00	4.24
8	6	3	4.50	4.50	2.12
9	6	6	6.00	0.00	0.00

Sample statistics (spanning Mean, Variance, Stand. dev. columns)

tion value. In addition, when you add the 9 sample means you obtain a total of 27, so the average of the sample means is $\frac{27}{9} = 3.00$. Note that the average of the sample means is exactly the same as the population mean. Thus, the sample mean is also an unbiased statistic.

In summary, both the sample mean and the sample variance are examples of unbiased statistics. This fact makes the sample mean and sample variance extremely valuable for use in inferential statistics. Although no individual sample is likely to have a mean and variance exactly equal to the population values, on average, both the sample mean and the sample variance do provide accurate estimates of the corresponding population values.

The fact that the sample variance is unbiased and the sample standard deviation is not will have some consequences in future chapters. In particular, we will tend to use the sample standard deviation exclusively as a descriptive statistic; that is, the value of s will be used to describe the set of scores in a sample. However, when our focus shifts to inferential statistics, we will tend to use the sample variance. Thus, when we want to generalize from a sample to a population, we will use the sample variance because it provides an accurate and unbiased estimate of the population value.

STANDARD DEVIATION AND DESCRIPTIVE STATISTICS

Because the sample standard deviation is a biased statistic, it does not provide a perfectly accurate representation of the population standard deviation. Thus, we will avoid using the sample standard deviation when we are doing inferential statistics—that is, using sample values to answer questions about populations. On the other hand, the sample standard deviation does provide a perfectly accurate description of the sample data and, therefore, it will be used extensively as a descriptive statistic.

The general goal of descriptive statistics is to summarize and describe a set of data. The mean and the standard deviation are probably the most commonly used descriptive statistics. A research report, for example, typically will not list all of the individual scores but rather will summarize the data by reporting the mean and the standard deviation. When you are given these two descriptive statistics, you should be able to visualize the entire set of data. For example, consider a sample with a mean of $\overline{X} = 36$ and a standard deviation of $s = 4$. Although there are several different ways to picture the data, one simple technique is to imagine (or sketch) a histogram where each score is represented by a box in the graph.

We have constructed an example distribution in Figure 4.7. For this sample, the data can be pictured as a pile of boxes (scores), with the center of the pile located at the mean, $\overline{X} = 36$. The individual scores or boxes are scattered on both sides of the mean, with some boxes relatively close to the mean and some relatively far away. In this example, the standard deviation is $s = 4$, so most of the boxes are within 4 points of the mean and only a few boxes are located more than 4 points away from $\overline{X} = 36$ (see Figure 4.7).

Note that Figure 4.7 not only shows the mean and the standard deviation, it also uses these two values to reconstruct the underlying scale of measurement (the X values along the horizontal line). The scale of measurement helps complete the picture of the entire distribution and helps relate each individual score to the rest of the group. In this example, you should realize that a score of $X = 34$ is located near the center of the distribution, only slightly below the mean. On the other hand, a score of $X = 44$ is an extremely high score, located far out in the right-hand tail of the distribution.

The general point of this discussion is that the mean and the standard deviation are not simply abstract concepts or mathematical equations. Instead, these two values

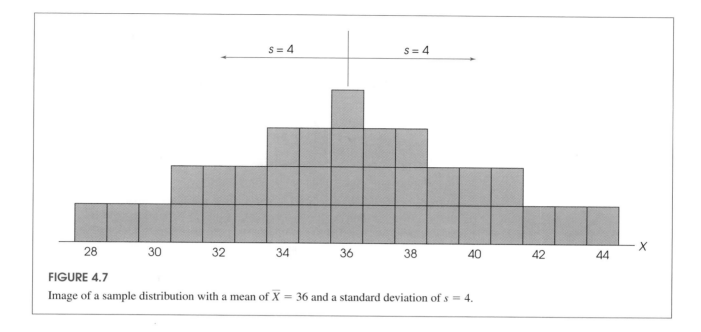

FIGURE 4.7

Image of a sample distribution with a mean of $\overline{X} = 36$ and a standard deviation of $s = 4$.

should be concrete and meaningful, especially in the context of a set of scores. Specifically, you should be able to see the mean and the standard deviation as if they were superimposed onto a graph showing the distribution of scores. The mean and the standard deviation are central concepts for most of the statistics that will be presented in the following chapters. A good understanding of these two statistics will help you with the more complex procedures that follow (see Box 4.2).

VARIANCE AND INFERENTIAL STATISTICS

In general terms, the goal of inferential statistics is to use the information from samples to answer questions about populations. Because the sample variance was specifically

 4.2   AN ANALOGY FOR THE MEAN AND THE STANDARD DEVIATION

ALTHOUGH THE basic concepts of the mean and the standard deviation are not overly complex, the following analogy often helps students gain a more complete understanding of these two statistical measures.

In our local community, the site for the new high school was selected because it provides a central location. An alternative site on the western edge of the community was considered, but this site was rejected because it would require extensive busing of students living on the east side of town. The location of the high school is analogous to the concept of the mean; that is, the mean is located in the center of the distribution of scores.

For each student in the community, it is possible to measure the distance between home and the new high school. Some students live only a few blocks from the new school, and others live as much as 3 miles away. The average distance that a student must travel to school was calculated to be 0.80 mile. The average distance from the school is analogous to the concept of the standard deviation; that is, the standard deviation measures the standard distance from an individual score to the mean.

constructed to provide an accurate and unbiased representation of the population variance, we will use the sample variance extensively in inferential techniques. In particular, the sample variance will serve two important roles.

1. Sample variance provides an indication of how accurately an individual score or a sample represents its population. When variance is small, all the individuals are clustered close together and any individual will serve as a reasonably accurate representative for the entire group. However, when variance is large, the scores are more scattered and it is much more likely to select an extreme individual who is not a good representative for the group. Thus, sample variance will be a critical component when we are determining how much error to expect when we are using a sample to represent an entire population.

2. Sample variance will have a direct impact on how easily we can detect meaningful patterns in sample data. Suppose, for example, that 15 people are given a new blood pressure medication and each person's blood pressure drops by about 20 points. Because everyone shows the same response (all the scores are around 20), the sample variance will be small. In this case, small variance is an indication of consistency, and a consistent pattern is very easy to see. Large variance, on the other hand, is an indication that there is no consistent effect. Using the blood pressure example again, suppose that some of the patients showed a decrease in blood pressure, some showed an increase, and some showed no change at all. In this case the scores are widely scattered, which means the variance is large and it is difficult to see any meaningful pattern in the data. In general, as sample variance increases it becomes more difficult to see any systematic patterns that might exist in the data. An analogy is to think of variance as the static that exists on a radio or the "snow" on a television screen. High variance makes it difficult to get a clear signal from the data.

TRANSFORMATIONS OF SCALE

Occasionally, it is convenient to transform a set of scores by adding a constant to each score or by multiplying each score by a constant value. This is done, for example, when you want to adjust a set of exam scores by adding a fixed amount to each individual's grade or when you want to change the scale of measurement (to convert from minutes to seconds, multiply each X by 60). What happens to the standard deviation when the scores are transformed in this manner?

The easiest way to determine the effect of a transformation is to remember that the standard deviation is a measure of distance. If you select any two scores and see what happens to the distance between them, you also will find out what happens to the standard deviation.

1. **Adding a constant to each score does not change the standard deviation.** If you begin with a distribution that has $\mu = 40$ and $\sigma = 10$, what happens to σ if you add 5 points to every score? Consider any two scores in this distribution: Suppose, for example, that these are exam scores and that you had $X = 41$ and your friend had $X = 43$. The distance between these two scores is $43 - 41 = 2$ points. After adding the constant, 5 points, to each score, your score would be $X = 46$, and your friend would have $X = 48$. The distance between scores is still 2 points. Adding a constant to every score will not affect any of the distances and therefore will not change the standard deviation. This fact can be seen clearly if you imagine a frequency distribution graph. For example, if you add 10 points to each score, then every score in the graph would move 10 points to the right. The result is that the entire distribution shifts to a new position 10 points up the scale. Note that the mean moves along with the scores and is increased by 10 points.

However, the variability does not change because each of the deviation scores $(X - \mu)$ does not change.

2. **Multiplying each score by a constant causes the standard deviation to be multiplied by the same constant.** Consider the same distribution of exam scores we looked at earlier. If $\mu = 40$ and $\sigma = 10$, what would happen to σ if each score were multiplied by 2? Again, we will look at two scores, $X = 41$ and $X = 43$, with a distance between them equal to 2 points. After all the scores have been multiplied by 2, these scores become $X = 82$ and $X = 86$. Now the distance between scores is 4 points, twice the original distance. Multiplying each score causes each distance to be multiplied, so the standard deviation also is multiplied by the same amount.

IN THE LITERATURE:
REPORTING THE STANDARD DEVIATION

In reporting the results of a study, the researcher often provides descriptive information for both central tendency and variability. The dependent variables in psychology research frequently involve measures taken on interval or ratio scales. Thus, the mean (central tendency) and the standard deviation (variability) are commonly reported together. In many journals, especially those following APA style, the symbol SD is used for the sample standard deviation. For example, the results might state:

> Children who viewed the violent cartoon displayed more aggressive responses ($M = 12.45$, $SD = 3.7$) than those who viewed the control cartoon ($M = 4.22$, $SD = 1.04$).

When reporting the descriptive measures for several groups, the findings may be summarized in a table. Table 4.2 illustrates the results of hypothetical data.

TABLE 4.2
The number of aggressive responses in male and female children after viewing cartoons.

| | Type of cartoon | |
	Violent	Control
Males	$M = 15.72$	$M = 6.94$
	$SD = 4.43$	$SD = 2.26$
Females	$M = 3.47$	$M = 2.61$
	$SD = 1.12$	$SD = 0.98$

Sometimes the table will also indicate the sample size, n, for each group. Remember that the purpose of the table is to present the data in an organized, concise, and accurate manner.   ❏

ON THE WEB

NOW THAT you have finished Chapter 4, you can test your knowledge with the practice quiz on the Wadsworth Web site at **www.wadsworth.com**. In addition, you can look at the workshop on central tendency and variability to get a practical perspective on these concepts. For more information about the quizzes and workshops, see page 24.

SUMMARY

1. The purpose of variability is to determine how spread out the scores are in a distribution. There are four basic measures of variability: the range, the semi-interquartile range, the variance, and the standard deviation.

   The range is the distance between the upper real limit of the largest X and the lower real limit of the smallest X in the distribution. The semi-interquartile range is one-half the distance between the first quartile and the third quartile. Variance is defined as the mean squared deviation. Standard deviation is the square root of the variance.

2. Standard deviation and variance are the most commonly used measures of variability. Both of these measures are based on the observation that each individual score can be described in terms of its deviation or distance from the mean. The standard deviation is a measure of the standard distance from the mean. The variance is the mean of the squared deviations—that is, the mean squared distance from the mean.

3. To calculate variance or standard deviation, you first need to find the sum of the squared deviations, SS. There are two methods for calculating SS:
   I. By definition, you can find SS using the following steps:
      a. Find the deviation $(X - \mu)$ for each score.
      b. Square each deviation.
      c. Sum the squared deviations.
      This process can be summarized in a formula as follows:

      definitional formula: $SS = \Sigma(X - \mu)^2$

   II. The sum of the squared deviations can also be found using a computational formula, which is especially useful when the mean is not a whole number:

      computational formula: $SS = \Sigma X^2 - \dfrac{(\Sigma X)^2}{N}$

4. Variance is the mean squared deviation and is obtained by finding the sum of the squared deviations and then dividing by the number. For a population, variance is

$$\sigma^2 = \frac{SS}{N}$$

For a sample, only $n - 1$ of the scores are free to vary (degrees of freedom or $df = n - 1$), so sample variance is

$$s^2 = \frac{SS}{n - 1} = \frac{SS}{df}$$

Using $n - 1$ in the sample formula makes the sample variance an accurate and unbiased estimate of the population variance.

5. Standard deviation is the square root of the variance. For a population, this is

$$\sigma = \sqrt{\frac{SS}{N}}$$

Sample standard deviation is

$$s = \sqrt{\frac{SS}{n - 1}} = \sqrt{\frac{SS}{df}}$$

6. Adding a constant value to every score in a distribution will not change the standard deviation. Multiplying every score by a constant, however, will cause the standard deviation to be multiplied by the same constant.

KEY TERMS

variability

range

interquartile range

semi-interquartile range

deviation score

population variance (σ^2)

population standard deviation (σ)

sample variance (s^2)

sample standard deviation (s)

sum of squares (SS)

degrees of freedom (df)

biased statistic

unbiased statistic

FOCUS ON PROBLEM SOLVING

---

1. The purpose of variability is to provide a measure of how spread out the scores are in a distribution. Usually this is described by the standard deviation. Because the calculations are relatively complicated, it is wise to make a preliminary estimate of the standard deviation before you begin. Remember, standard deviation provides a measure of the typical, or standard, distance from the mean. Therefore, the standard deviation must have a value somewhere between the largest and the smallest deviation scores. As a rule of thumb, the standard deviation should be about one-fourth of the range.

2. Rather than trying to memorize all the formulas for *SS*, variance, and standard deviation, you should focus on the definitions of these values and the logic that relates them to each other:

   SS is the sum of squared deviations.

   Variance is the mean squared deviation.

   Standard deviation is the square root of variance.

   The only formula you should need to memorize is the computational formula for *SS*.

3. If you heed the warnings in the following list, you may avoid some of the more common mistakes in solving variability problems.

   a. Because the calculation of standard deviation requires several steps of calculation, students often get lost in the arithmetic and forget what they are trying to compute. It helps to examine the data before you begin and make a rough estimate of the mean and the standard deviation.

   b. The standard deviation formulas for populations and samples are slightly different. Be sure that you know whether the data come from a sample or a population before you begin calculations.

   c. A common error is to use $n - 1$ in the computational formula for *SS* when you have scores from a sample. Remember, the *SS* formula always uses n (or N). After you compute *SS* for a sample, you must correct for the sample bias by using $n - 1$ in the formulas for variance and standard deviation.

DEMONSTRATION 4.1

COMPUTING MEASURES OF VARIABILITY

For the following sample data, compute the variance and the standard deviation. Scores:

$$10, \quad 7, \quad 6, \quad 10, \quad 6, \quad 15$$

The sample consists of $n = 6$ scores with $\Sigma X = 54$, so $\overline{X} = 54/6 = 9$.

STEP 1   Calculate the sum of squares, *SS*. For this demonstration we will use the definitional formula.

$$SS = \Sigma(X - \overline{X})^2$$

First, we find the distance from the mean for each score, $(X - \overline{X})$. Then we square each distance, $\Sigma(X - \overline{X})^2$. Finally, we sum the squared distances. The calculations are shown in the following computational table. For these data, the sum of the squared deviations is $SS = 60$.

X	$X - \overline{X}$	$(X - \overline{X})^2$
10	$+1$	1
7	-2	4
6	-3	9
10	$+1$	1
6	-3	9
15	$+6$	36

$$SS = 60$$

STEP 2 Compute the sample variance. Remember that when you are using sample data, you must use $df = n - 1$ in the formula for variance to ensure that the sample variance provides an unbiased representation of the population variance.

$$\text{Sample variance} = s^2 = \frac{SS}{n - 1} = \frac{SS}{df} = \frac{60}{5} = 12$$

STEP 3 Compute the sample standard deviation. Standard deviation is always determined by the square root of the variance.

$$\text{Sample standard deviation} = s = \sqrt{12} = 3.46$$

PROBLEMS

1. In words, explain what is measured by each of the following:
  a. *SS*
  b. Variance
  c. Standard deviation

2. A population has $\mu = 100$ and $\sigma = 20$. If you select a single score from this population, on the average, how close would it be to the population mean? Explain your answer.

3. Can *SS* ever have a value less than zero? Explain your answer.

4. In general, what does it mean for a sample to have a standard deviation of zero? Describe the scores in such a sample.

5. Explain what it means to say that the sample variance provides an *unbiased* estimate of the population variance.

6. A population of $N = 15$ scores has a standard deviation of 4.0. What is the variance for this population?

7. A sample of $n = 35$ scores has a variance of 100. What is the standard deviation for this sample?

8. A professor administers a 5-point quiz to a class of 40 students. The professor calculates a mean of 4.2 for the quiz with a standard deviation of 11.4. Although the mean is a

reasonable value, you should realize that the standard deviation is not. Explain why it appears that the professor made a mistake computing the standard deviation.

9. a. A sample of $n = 6$ scores has $SS = 60$. What is the variance for this sample?
  b. A population of $N = 6$ scores has $SS = 60$. What is the variance for this population?

10. For the following scores:

8,   4,   7,   1

  a. Calculate the mean. (Note that the value of the mean does not depend on whether the set of scores is considered to be a sample or a population.)
  b. Find the deviation for each score, and check that the deviations sum to zero.
  c. Square each deviation, and compute *SS*. (Again, note that the value of *SS* is independent of whether the set of scores is a sample or a population.)

11. There are two different formulas or methods that can be used to calculate *SS*.
  a. Under what circumstances is the definitional formula easy to use?
  b. Under what circumstances is the computational formula preferred?

12. Calculate *SS*, variance, and standard deviation for the following sample of $n = 4$ scores: 0, 3, 0, 3. (*Note:* The computational formula for *SS* works best with these scores.)

13. Calculate *SS*, variance, and standard deviation for the following sample of $n = 9$ scores: 2, 0, 0, 0, 0, 2, 0, 2, 0. (*Note:* The computational formula for *SS* works best with these scores.)

14. Calculate *SS*, variance, and standard deviation for the following population of $N = 6$ scores: 5, 0, 9, 3, 8, 5. (*Note:* The definitional formula for *SS* works well with these scores.)

15. Calculate *SS*, variance, and standard deviation for the following population of $N = 4$ scores: 6, 8, 0, 6. (*Note:* The definitional formula for *SS* works well with these scores.)

16. A distribution of scores has a mean of $\overline{X} = 42$.
  a. If the standard deviation is $s = 12$, would a score of $X = 48$ be considered an extreme value? Explain your answer.
  b. If the standard deviation is $s = 2$, would a score of $X = 48$ be considered an extreme value? Explain your answer.

17. On an exam with $\mu = 75$, you obtain a score of $X = 80$.
  a. Would you prefer that the exam distribution had $\sigma = 2$ or $\sigma = 10$? (Sketch each distribution, and locate the position of $X = 80$ in each one.)
  b. If your score is $X = 70$, would you prefer $\sigma = 2$ or $\sigma = 10$? (Again, sketch each distribution to determine how the value of σ affects your position relative to the rest of the class.)

18. Sketch a normal distribution (see Figure 4.4, p. 88) with $\mu = 50$ and $\sigma = 20$.
  a. Locate each of the following scores in your sketch, and indicate whether you consider each score to be an extreme value (high or low) or a central value:

  65,   55,   40,   47

  b. Make another sketch showing a distribution with $\mu = 50$, but this time with $\sigma = 2$. Now locate each of the four scores in the new distribution and indicate whether they are extreme or central. (*Note:* The value of the standard deviation can have a dramatic effect on the location of a score within a distribution.)

19. For the following population of scores:

  3, 4, 4, 1, 7, 3, 2, 6, 4, 2,
  1, 6, 3, 4, 5, 2, 5, 4, 3, 4

  a. Sketch a frequency distribution histogram.
  b. Find the range for the population. (*Hint:* You can use the formula for the range, or you can simply count the boxes or categories across the base of the histogram.)
  c. Find the interquartile range and the semi-interquartile range for the population.

20. For the following population of $N = 4$ scores:

  2,   0,   8,   2

  a. Use the definitional formula to compute *SS*, then find the population variance and the standard deviation.
  b. Add 3 points to each score; then compute *SS*, variance, and standard deviation for the new population.
  c. Multiply each of the original scores by 2; then compute *SS*, variance, and standard deviation for the new population.
  d. When a constant is added to each score, what happens to the deviation scores? What happens to the standard deviation?
  e. When each score is multiplied by a constant, what happens to the deviation scores? What happens to the standard deviation?

21. A sample of $n = 25$ scores has a variance of 100.
  a. Find the standard deviation for this sample.
  b. Find the value of *SS* for this sample. (Be careful to use the *sample* formula.)

22. For the following sample:

  5, 8, 3, 2, 7, 8, 6, 4, 9, 10,
  7, 3, 6, 6, 7, 5, 8, 4, 5, 7

  a. Calculate the range, the semi-interquartile range, and the standard deviation.
  b. Add 2 points to every score, and then compute the range, the semi-interquartile range, and the standard deviation. How is variability affected when a constant is added to every score?

23. For the following sample of $n = 8$ scores: 1, 2, 3, 4, 5, 6, 7, 8,
  a. Compute the range, the interquartile range, and the standard deviation. (*Note:* It may help to sketch a histogram showing the distribution.)
  b. Now we will modify the distribution by moving the two extreme scores closer to the center of the distribution. At one extreme, $X = 1$ will be changed to $X = 2$, and at the other extreme $X = 8$ will be changed to $X = 7$. (The new set of scores becomes: 2, 2, 3, 4, 5, 6, 7, 7.) Note that we are moving the scores closer together so the variability should be reduced. Again, compute the range, the interquartile

range, and the standard deviation and compare your answers with the results from part (a). You should find that changing the extreme scores will influence the range and the standard deviation but will have no effect on the interquartile range.

c. Now we will modify the original distribution (part a) by moving the two central scores out to the extremes. At one end, $X = 4$ will be changed to $X = 1$ and at the other end, $X = 5$ will be changed to $X = 8$. (The new set of scores becomes: 1, 1, 2, 3, 6, 7, 8, 8.) Because we are moving scores away from the center, the variability should increase. Again, compute the range, the interquartile range, and the standard deviation. You should find that changing central scores has an effect on the interquartile range and the standard deviation but has no effect on the range.

CHAPTER 5

z-SCORES: LOCATION OF SCORES AND STANDARDIZED DISTRIBUTIONS

TOOLS YOU WILL NEED

The following items are considered essential background material for this chapter. If you doubt your knowledge of any of these items, you should review the appropriate chapter and section before proceeding.

- The mean (Chapter 3)

- The standard deviation (Chapter 4)

- Basic algebra (math review, Appendix A)

CONTENTS

5.1   OVERVIEW

At this point, we have finished the basic elements of *descriptive statistics*. You should recall that descriptive statistics are techniques that attempt to describe and summarize a set of data. The primary descriptive techniques are the following:

1. Construct a frequency distribution that displays the entire set of data.
2. Compute one or two specific values, such as the mean and the standard deviation, that summarize the distribution.

A good understanding of these descriptive statistics will be a great help as we begin to introduce inferential statistics. In particular, whenever we talk about a set of scores, either a sample or a population, you should think of a frequency distribution graph with the scores centered around the mean and the standard deviation describing the typical distance from the mean.

In this chapter and in the next two chapters, we will develop the concepts and skills that form the foundation for inferential statistics. In general, these three chapters will establish formal, quantitative relationships between samples and populations. We will begin with the situation where the sample consists of a single score and then expand to samples of any size. After we have developed the relationships between samples and populations, we can use these relationships to begin inferential statistics. That is, we can begin to use sample data as the basis for drawing conclusions about populations. A brief summary of the next three chapters is as follows:

Chapter 5: We will present a method for describing the exact location of an individual score relative to the other scores in a distribution. This will enable us, for example, to determine precisely whether an individual IQ score is close to average, slightly above average, far below average, and so on.

Chapter 6: In this chapter, we will determine probability values associated with different locations in a distribution of scores. Thus, we will be able to identify a specific score as a central value and say that it is a high probability value. For example, we could determine that a specific IQ score is close to average and is the kind of value that would be expected over 80% of the time.

Chapter 7: In this chapter, we will take the basic skills from Chapters 5 and 6 and apply them to sample means instead of individual scores. Thus, we will be able to describe how any specific sample mean is related to other sample means, and we will be able to determine a probability for each sample mean. For example, we will be able to determine that an average IQ score above 120 is extremely high for a sample of $n = 25$ people and that a sample mean this extreme has a probability that is less than 1 in 1000.

5.2   INTRODUCTION TO z-SCORES

In the previous two chapters, we introduced the concepts of the mean and the standard deviation as methods for describing an entire distribution of scores. Now we will shift our attention to the individual scores within a distribution. In this chapter, we introduce a statistical technique that uses the mean and the standard deviation to transform each score (*X* value) into a *z-score* or a *standard score*. The purpose of z-scores, or standard scores, is to identify and describe the exact location of every score in a distribution.

The following example demonstrates why z-scores are useful and introduces the general concept of transforming *X* values into z-scores.

EXAMPLE 5.1   Suppose you received a score of $X = 76$ on a statistics exam. How did you do? It should be clear that you need more information to predict your grade. Your score of $X = 76$ could be one of the best scores in the class, or it might be the lowest score in the distribution. To find the location of your score, you must have information about the other scores in the distribution. It would be useful, for example, to know the mean for the class. If the mean were $\mu = 70$, you would be in a much better position than if the mean were $\mu = 85$. Obviously, your position relative to the rest of the class depends on the mean. However, the mean by itself is not sufficient to tell you the exact location of your score. Suppose you know that the mean for the statistics exam is $\mu = 70$ and your score is $X = 76$. At this point, you know that your score is above the mean, but you still do not know exactly where it is located. You may have the highest score in the class, or you may be only slightly above average. Figure 5.1 shows two possible distributions of exam scores. Both distributions have $\mu = 70$, but for one distribution, the standard deviation is $\sigma = 3$, and for the other, $\sigma = 12$. Note that the relative location of $X = 76$ is very different for these two distributions. When the standard deviation is $\sigma = 3$, your score of $X = 76$ is in the extreme right-hand tail, one of the highest scores in the distribution. However, in the other distribution, where $\sigma = 12$, your score is only slightly above average. Thus, your relative location within the distribution depends on the mean and the standard deviation as well as your actual score.

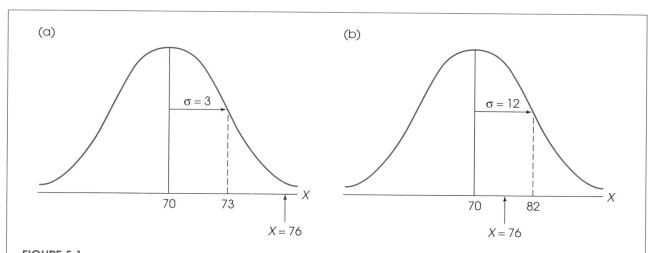

FIGURE 5.1

Two distributions of exam scores. For both distributions, $\mu = 70$, but for one distribution, $\sigma = 3$, and for the other, $\sigma = 12$. The position of $X = 76$ is very different for these two distributions.

The purpose of the preceding example is to demonstrate that a score *by itself* does not necessarily provide much information about its position within a distribution. These original, unchanged scores are often called *raw scores*. To make raw scores more meaningful, they are often transformed into new values that contain more information. This transformation is one purpose for z-scores. In particular, we will transform X values into z-scores so that the resulting z-scores tell exactly where the original scores are located.

A second purpose for z-scores is to *standardize* an entire distribution. A common example of a standardized distribution is the distribution of IQ scores. Although there are several different tests for measuring IQ, all of the tests are standardized so that they have a mean of 100 and a standard deviation of 15. Because all the different tests are standardized, it is possible to understand and compare IQ scores even though they come from different tests. For example, we all understand that an IQ score of 95 is a little below average, *no matter which IQ test was used.* Similarly, an IQ of 145 is extremely high, *no matter which IQ test was used.* In general terms, the process of standardizing takes different distributions and makes them equivalent. The advantage of this process is that it is possible to compare distributions even though they may have been quite different before standardization.

In summary, the process of transforming X values into z-scores serves two useful purposes:

1. Each z-score will tell the exact location of the original X value within the distribution.
2. The z-scores will form a standardized distribution that can be directly compared to other distributions that also have been transformed into z-scores.

Each of these purposes will be discussed in the following sections.

5.3 z-SCORES AND LOCATION IN A DISTRIBUTION

One of the primary purposes of a z-score is to describe the exact location of a score within a distribution. The z-score accomplishes this goal by transforming each X value into a signed number ($+$ or $-$) so that

1. The *sign* tells whether the score is located above ($+$) or below ($-$) the mean, and
2. The *number* tells the distance between the score and the mean in terms of the number of standard deviations.

Thus, in a distribution of standardized IQ scores with $\mu = 100$ and $\sigma = 15$, a score of $X = 130$ would be transformed into $z = +2.00$. The z value indicates that the score is located above the mean ($+$) by a distance of 2 standard deviations (30 points).

DEFINITION

A *z-score* specifies the precise location of each X value within a distribution. The sign of the z-score ($+$ or $-$) signifies whether the score is above the mean (positive) or below the mean (negative). The numerical value of the z-score specifies the distance from the mean by counting the number of standard deviations between X and μ.

Note that a z-score always consists of two parts: a sign ($+$ or $-$) and a magnitude. Both parts are necessary to describe completely where a raw score is located within a distribution.

FIGURE 5.2

The relationship between z-score values and locations in a population distribution.

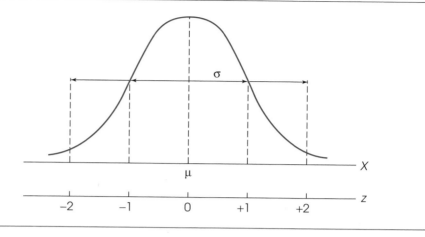

Whenever you are working with z-scores, you should imagine or draw a picture similar to Figure 5.2. Although not all distributions are normal, we will use the normal shape as an example when showing z-scores.

Figure 5.2 shows a population distribution with various positions identified by their z-score values. Note that all z-scores above the mean are positive and all z-scores below the mean are negative. The sign of a z-score tells you immediately whether the score is located above or below the mean. Also, note that a z-score of $z = +1.00$ corresponds to a position exactly 1 standard deviation above the mean. A z-score of $z = +2.00$ is always located exactly 2 standard deviations above the mean. The numerical value of the z-score tells you the number of standard deviations from the mean. Finally, note that Figure 5.2 does not give any specific values for the population mean or the standard deviation. The locations identified by z-scores are the same for *all distributions*, no matter what mean or standard deviation the distributions may have.

Now we can return to the two distributions shown in Figure 5.1 and use a z-score to describe the position of $X = 76$ within each distribution as follows:

In Figure 5.1(a), the score $X = 76$ corresponds to a z-score of $z = +2.00$. That is, the score is located *above* the mean by exactly 2 standard deviations.

In Figure 5.1(b), the score $X = 76$ corresponds to a z-score of $z = +0.50$. In this distribution, the score is located exactly $\frac{1}{2}$ standard deviation *above* the mean.

LEARNING CHECK

1. A negative z-score always indicates a location below the mean. (True or false?)

2. What z-score value identifies each of the following locations in a distribution?
   a. Above the mean by 2 standard deviations
   b. Below the mean by $\frac{1}{2}$ standard deviation
   c. Above the mean by $\frac{1}{4}$ standard deviation
   c. Below the mean by 3 standard deviations

3. For a population with $\mu = 50$ and $\sigma = 10$, find the z-score for each of the following scores:
   a. $X = 55$
   b. $X = 40$
   c. $X = 30$

4. For a population with $\mu = 50$ and $\sigma = 10$, find the X value corresponding to each of the following z-scores:

   a. $z = +1.00$

   b. $z = -0.50$

   c. $z = +2.00$

ANSWERS   1. True

2. **a.** $z = +2$

   b. $z = -\frac{1}{2}$ or -0.50

   c. $z = +\frac{1}{4}$ or $+0.25$

   d. $z = -3$

3. **a.** $z = +0.50$

   b. $z = -1.00$

   c. $z = -2.00$

4. **a.** $X = 60$

   b. $X = 45$

   c. $X = 70$ ◆

THE z-SCORE FORMULA

The z-score definition is adequate for transforming back and forth from X values to z-scores as long as the arithmetic is easy to do in your head. For more complicated values, it is best to have an equation to help structure the calculations. Fortunately, the relationship between X values and z-scores can be easily expressed in a formula. The formula for transforming scores into z-scores is

$$z = \frac{X - \mu}{\sigma} \qquad\qquad (5.1)$$

The numerator of the equation, $X - \mu$, is a *deviation score* (Chapter 4, page 81); it measures the distance in points between X and μ and indicates whether X is located above or below the mean. We divide this difference by σ because we want the z-score to measure distance in terms of standard deviation units. The formula performs exactly the same arithmetic that is used with the z-score definition, and it provides a structured equation to organize the calculations when the numbers are more difficult. The following examples demonstrate the use of the z-score formula.

EXAMPLE 5.2   A distribution of scores has a mean of $\mu = 100$ and a standard deviation of $\sigma = 10$. What z-score corresponds to a score of $X = 120$ in this distribution?

According to the definition, the z-score will have a value of $+2$ because the score is located above the mean by exactly 2 standard deviations. Using the z-score formula, we obtain

$$z = \frac{X - \mu}{\sigma} = \frac{120 - 100}{10} = \frac{20}{10} = 2.00$$

The formula produces exactly the same result that is obtained using the z-score definition.

EXAMPLE 5.3   A distribution of scores has a mean of $\mu = 86$ and a standard deviation of $\sigma = 7$. What z-score corresponds to a score of $X = 95$ in this distribution?

Note that this problem is not particularly easy, especially if you try to use the z-score definition and perform the calculations in your head. However, the z-score formula organizes the numbers and allows you to finish the final arithmetic with your calculator. Using the formula, we obtain

$$z = \frac{X - \mu}{\sigma} = \frac{95 - 86}{7} = \frac{9}{7} = 1.29$$

According to the formula, a score of $X = 95$ corresponds to $z = 1.29$. The z-score indicates a location that is above the mean (positive) by slightly more than $1\frac{1}{4}$ standard deviations.

DETERMINING A RAW SCORE (X) FROM A z-SCORE   Although the z-score equation (Formula 5.1) works well for transforming X values into z-scores, it can be awkward when you are trying to work in the opposite direction and change z-scores back into X values. Therefore, we will create a different formula to use when you need to transform z-scores into X values. To develop the new formula, we will begin with a sample problem.

For a distribution with a mean of $\mu = 60$ and a standard deviation of $\sigma = 5$, what X value corresponds to a z-score of $z = -2.00$?

To solve this problem, we will use the z-score definition and carefully monitor the step-by-step process. The value of the z-score indicates that X is located 2 standard deviations below the mean. Thus, the first step in the calculation is to determine the distance corresponding to 2 standard deviations. This distance is obtained by multiplying the z-score value (-2) by the standard deviation value (5). In symbols,

$$z\sigma = (-2)(5) = -10 \text{ points}$$

(Our score is located below the mean by 10 points.)

The next step is to start at the mean and go down by 10 points to find the value of X. In symbols,

$$X = \mu - 10 = 60 - 10 = 50$$

The two steps can be combined to form a single formula:

$$X = \mu + z\sigma \tag{5.2}$$

Note that the value of $z\sigma$ is the *deviation* of X. In the example, this value was -10, or 10 points below the mean. Formula 5.2 simply combines the mean and the deviation from the mean to determine the exact value of X.

Finally, you should realize that Formula 5.1 and Formula 5.2 are actually two different versions of the same equation. If you begin with either formula and use algebra to shuffle the terms around, you will soon end up with the other formula. We will leave this as an exercise for those who want to try it.

1. A distribution of scores has a mean of $\mu = 80$ and a standard deviation of $\sigma = 12$. Find the z-score value corresponding to each of the following scores. *Note:* You may use the z-score definition or Formula 5.1 to determine these values.

   a. $X = 98$ **b.** $X = 86$

   c. $X = 77$ **d.** $X = 75$

2. A distribution of scores has a mean of $\mu = 80$ and a standard deviation of $\sigma = 12$. Find the X value corresponding to each of the following z-scores. *Note:* You may use the z-score definition or Formula 5.2 to determine these values.

   a. $z = -1.25$ **b.** $z = 2.50$

   c. $z = -0.75$ **d.** $z = 1.00$

ANSWERS   **1. a.** $z = 1.50$ **b.** $z = 0.50$ **c.** $z = -0.25$ **d.** $z = -0.42$

   2. a. $X = 65$ **b.** $X = 110$ **c.** $X = 71$ **d.** $X = 92$

5.4   USING z-SCORES TO STANDARDIZE A DISTRIBUTION

It is possible to transform every X value in a distribution into a corresponding z-score. The result of this process is that the entire distribution of X scores is transformed into a distribution of z-scores (see Figure 5.3). The new distribution of z-scores has characteristics that make the z-*score transformation* a very useful tool. Specifically, if every X value is transformed into a z-score, then the distribution of z-scores will have the following properties:

   1. Shape. The shape of the z-score distribution will be the same as the original distribution of raw scores. If the original distribution is negatively skewed, for example, then the z-score distribution will also be negatively skewed. If the original distribution is normal, the distribution of z-scores will also be normal. Transforming raw scores into z-scores does not change anyone's position in the distribution. For example, any raw score that is above the mean by 1 standard deviation will be transformed to a z-score of $+1.00$, which is still above the mean by 1 standard deviation. Because each individual score stays in its same position within the distribution, the overall shape of the distribution does not change.

   2. The Mean. The z-score distribution will *always* have a mean of zero. In Figure 5.3, the original distribution of X values has a mean of $\mu = 100$. When this value, $X = 100$, is transformed into a z-score, the result is

$$z = \frac{X - \mu}{\sigma} = \frac{100 - 100}{10} = 0$$

Thus, the original population mean is transformed into a value of zero in the z-score distribution. The fact that the z-score distribution has a mean of zero makes it easy to iden-

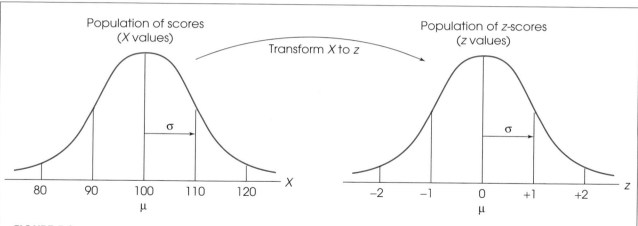

FIGURE 5.3

An entire population of scores is transformed into z-scores. The transformation does not change the shape of the population but the mean is transformed into a value of 0 and the standard deviation is transformed to a value of 1.

tify locations. Recall from the definition of z-scores that all positive values are above the mean and all negative values are below the mean. A value of zero makes the mean a convenient reference point.

3. The Standard Deviation. The distribution of z-scores will always have a standard deviation of 1. In Figure 5.3, the original distribution of X values has $\mu = 100$ and $\sigma = 10$. In this distribution, a value of $X = 110$ is above the mean by exactly 10 points or 1 standard deviation. When $X = 110$ is transformed, it becomes $z = +1.00$, which is above the mean by exactly 1 point in the z-score distribution. Thus, the standard deviation corresponds to a 10-point distance in the X distribution and is transformed into a 1-point distance in the z-score distribution. The advantage of having a standard deviation of 1 is that the numerical value of a z-score is exactly the same as the number of standard deviations from the mean. For example, a z-score value of 2 is exactly 2 standard deviations from the mean.

In Figure 5.3, we showed the z-score transformation as a process that changed a distribution of X values into a new distribution of z-scores. In fact, there is no need to create a whole new distribution. Instead, you can think of the z-score transformation as simply *re-labeling* the values along the X-axis. That is, after a z-score transformation, you still have the same distribution, but now each individual is labeled with a z-score instead of an X value. Figure 5.4 demonstrates this concept with a single distribution that has two sets of labels: the X values along one line and the corresponding z-scores along another line. Note that the mean for the distribution of z-scores is zero and the standard deviation is 1.

When *any* distribution (with any mean or standard deviation) is transformed into z-scores, the resulting distribution will always have a mean of $\mu = 0$ and a standard deviation of $\sigma = 1$. Because all z-score distributions have the same mean and the same standard deviation, the z-score distribution is called a *standardized distribution*.

DEFINITION   A *standardized distribution* is composed of scores that have been transformed to create predetermined values for μ and σ. Standardized distributions are used to make dissimilar distributions comparable.

FIGURE 5.4

Following a z-score transformation, the X-axis is relabeled in z-score units. The distance that is equivalent to 1 standard deviation on the X-axis (σ = 10 points in this example) corresponds to 1 point on the z-score scale.

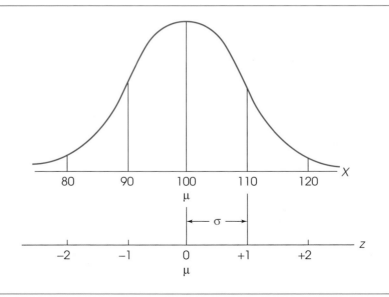

The advantage of standardizing is that it makes it possible to compare different scores or different individuals even though they may come from completely different distributions. We discuss the procedure for making comparisons in the following section.

USING z-SCORES FOR MAKING COMPARISONS

When two scores come from different distributions, it is impossible to make any direct comparison between them. Suppose, for example, Bob received a score of $X = 60$ on a psychology exam and a score of $X = 56$ on a biology test. For which course should Bob expect the better grade?

Because the scores come from two different distributions, you cannot make any direct comparison. Without additional information, it is even impossible to determine whether Bob is above or below the mean in either distribution. Before you can begin to make comparisons, you must know the values for the mean and standard deviation for each distribution. Suppose the biology scores had $\mu = 48$ and $\sigma = 4$, and the psychology scores had $\mu = 50$ and $\sigma = 10$. With this new information, you could sketch the two distributions, locate Bob's score in each distribution, and compare the two locations.

An alternative procedure is to standardize the two distributions by transforming both sets of scores into z-scores. If both distributions are transformed to z-scores, then both distributions will have $\mu = 0$ and $\sigma = 1$. Because the two distributions are now the same (at least they have the same mean and standard deviation) we can compare Bob's z-score for biology with his z-score for psychology.

In practice, it is not necessary to transform every score in a distribution to make comparisons between two scores. We need to transform only the two scores in question. In Bob's case, we must find the z-scores for his psychology and biology scores. For psychology, Bob's z-score is

Be sure to use the μ and σ values for the distribution to which X belongs.

$$z = \frac{X - \mu}{\sigma} = \frac{60 - 50}{10} = \frac{10}{10} = +1.0$$

For biology, Bob's *z*-score is

$$z = \frac{56 - 48}{4} = \frac{8}{4} = +2.0$$

Note that Bob's *z*-score for biology is $+2.0$, which means that his test score is 2 standard deviations above the class mean. On the other hand, his *z*-score is $+1.0$ for psychology, or 1 standard deviation above the mean. In terms of relative class standing, Bob is doing much better in the biology class. Note that it is meaningful to make a direct comparison of the two *z*-scores. A *z*-score of $+2.00$ *always* indicates a higher position than a *z*-score of $+1.00$ because all *z*-score values are based on a standardized distribution with a $\mu = 0$ and $\sigma = 1$.

LEARNING CHECK ◆

1. A normal-shaped distribution with $\mu = 50$ and $\sigma = 8$ is transformed into *z*-scores. Describe the shape, mean, and standard deviation for the *z*-score distribution.

2. Why is it possible to compare scores from different distributions after the distributions have been transformed into *z*-scores?

3. A set of mathematics exam scores has $\mu = 70$ and $\sigma = 8$. A set of English exam scores has $\mu = 74$ and $\sigma = 16$. For which exam would a score of $X = 78$ have a higher standing?

4. What is the advantage of having $\mu = 0$ for a distribution of *z*-scores?

ANSWERS

1. The *z*-score distribution would be normal (same shape) with $\mu = 0$ and $\sigma = 1$.

2. Comparison is possible because the two distributions will have the same mean ($\mu = 0$) and the same standard deviation ($\sigma = 1$) after transformation.

3. $z = 1.00$ for the mathematics exam, which is a higher standing than $z = 0.25$ for the English exam.

4. With $\mu = 0$, you know immediately that any positive value is above the mean and any negative value is below the mean.   ◆

5.5 OTHER STANDARDIZED DISTRIBUTIONS BASED ON *z*-SCORES

TRANSFORMING *z*-SCORES TO A DISTRIBUTION WITH A PREDETERMINED μ AND σ

Although *z*-score distributions have distinct advantages, many people find them cumbersome because they contain negative values and decimals. For these reasons, it is common to standardize a distribution by transforming *z*-scores to a distribution with a predetermined mean and standard deviation that are whole round numbers. The goal is to create a new (standardized) distribution that has "simple" values for the mean and standard deviation but does not change any individual's location within the distribution. Standardized scores of this type are frequently used in psychological or educational testing. For example, raw scores of the Scholastic Aptitude Test (SAT) are transformed to a standardized distribution that has $\mu = 500$ and $\sigma = 100$. For intelligence tests, raw scores are frequently converted to standard scores that have a mean of 100 and a standard deviation of 15. Because IQ tests are standardized so that they all have the same mean and standard deviation, it is possible to compare IQ scores even though they may come from different tests.

The procedure for standardizing a distribution to create new values for μ and σ involves a two-step process:

1. The original raw scores are transformed into z-scores.
2. The z-scores are then transformed into new X values so that the specific μ and σ are attained.

This procedure ensures that each individual has exactly the same z-score location in the new distribution as in the original distribution. The following example demonstrates the standardization procedure.

EXAMPLE 5.4 An instructor gives an exam to a psychology class. For this exam, the distribution of raw scores has a mean of $\mu = 57$ with $\sigma = 14$. The instructor would like to simplify the distribution by transforming all scores into a new, standardized distribution with $\mu = 50$ and $\sigma = 10$. To demonstrate this process, we will consider what happens to two specific students: Maria, who has a raw score of $X = 64$ in the original distribution; and Joe, whose original raw score is $X = 43$.

STEP 1 Transform each of the original raw scores into z-scores. For Maria, $X = 64$, so her z-score is

$$z = \frac{X - \mu}{\sigma} = \frac{64 - 57}{14} = +0.5$$

Remember, the values of μ and σ are for the distribution from which X was taken.

For Joe, $X = 43$, and his z-score is

$$z = \frac{X - \mu}{\sigma} = \frac{43 - 57}{14} = -1.0$$

STEP 2 Change the z-scores into standardized scores so that the new distribution has a mean of $\mu = 50$ and a standard deviation of $\sigma = 10$.

Maria's z-score, $z = +0.50$, indicates that she is located above the mean by $\frac{1}{2}$ standard deviation. In the new, standardized distribution, this location corresponds to $X = 55$ (above the mean by 5 points).

Joe's z-score, $z = -1.00$, indicates that he is located below the mean by exactly 1 standard deviation. In the new distribution, this location corresponds to $X = 40$ (below the mean by 10 points).

The results of this two-step transformation process are summarized in Table 5.1. Note that Joe, for example, has exactly the same z-score ($z = -1.00$) in both the origi-

TABLE 5.1

A demonstration of how two individual scores are changed when a distribution is standardized. See Example 5.4.

	Original scores $\mu = 57$ and $\sigma = 14$	z-score location	Standardized scores $\mu = 50$ and $\sigma = 10$
Maria	$X = 64$ $\longrightarrow$	$z = +0.50$ $\longrightarrow$	$X = 55$
Joe	$X = 43$ $\longrightarrow$	$z = -1.00$ $\longrightarrow$	$X = 40$

nal distribution and the new standardized distribution. This means that Joe's position relative to the other students in the class has not changed.

Figure 5.5 provides another demonstration of the general concept that standardizing a distribution does not change relative positions within the distribution. The figure shows the original distribution and the standardized distribution from Example 5.4. Note that the underlying z-score scale is the same for both distributions even though the scores (X values) are different. In both distributions, for example, a z-score of zero is located at the mean, $z = +1$ is one standard deviation above the mean, and so on. Also note that Joe's position in the standardized distribution is exactly the same as his position in the original distribution. By ensuring that each individual has the same z-score in both distributions, we can guarantee that each individual stays in the same position in both distributions. Because *all* of the individuals stay in the same positions relative to the rest of the scores, standardizing a distribution will not change the shape of the overall distribution—the process simply changes the values for the mean and the standard deviation.

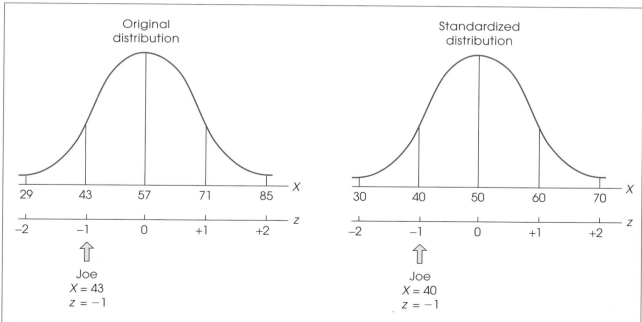

FIGURE 5.5

The original distribution and the standardized distribution from Example 5.4. Note that both distributions have the same underlying z-scores and that Joe's position in the new standardized distribution is exactly the same as his position in the original distribution.

LEARNING CHECK

1. A population has $\mu = 37$ and $\sigma = 2$. If this distribution is transformed into a new distribution with $\mu = 100$ and $\sigma = 20$, what new values will be obtained for each of the following scores: 35, 36, 37, 38, 39?

2. For the following population, $\mu = 7$ and $\sigma = 4$. Scores: 2, 4, 6, 10, 13.

   a. Transform this distribution so $\mu = 50$ and $\sigma = 20$.

   b. Compute μ and σ for the new population. (You should obtain $\mu = 50$ and $\sigma = 20$.)

ANSWERS   **1.** The five scores, 35, 36, 37, 38, and 39, are transformed into 80, 90, 100, 110, and 120, respectively.

  2. a. The original scores, 2, 4, 6, 10, and 13, are transformed into 25, 35, 45, 65, and 80, respectively.

     b. The new scores add up to $\Sigma X = 250$, so the mean is $\frac{250}{5} = 50$. The SS for the transformed scores is 2000, the variance is 400, and the new standard deviation is 20.   ◆

ON THE WEB

REMEMBER THAT a practice quiz for Chapter 5 is available on the Wadsworth Web site at **www.wadsworth.com.** You can use the quiz to test your knowledge on the material in this chapter and determine which parts of the chapter may need more study. In ad-dition, there is a workshop on z-scores that may give you a better understanding of this important statistical technique. For more information about the quizzes and workshops, see page 24.

SUMMARY

1. Each X value can be transformed into a z-score that specifies the exact location of X within the distribution. The sign of the z-score indicates whether the location is above (positive) or below (negative) the mean. The numerical value of the z-score specifies the number of standard deviations between X and μ.

2. The z-score formula is used to transform X values into z-scores:

$$z = \frac{X - \mu}{\sigma}$$

3. To transform z-scores back into X values, solve the z-score equation for X:

$$X = \mu + z\sigma$$

4. When an entire distribution of X values is transformed into z-scores, the result is a distribution of z-scores. The z-score distribution will have the same shape as the distribution of raw scores, and it always will have a mean of 0 and a standard deviation of 1.

5. When comparing raw scores from different distributions, it is necessary to standardize the distributions with a z-score transformation. The distributions will then be comparable because they will have the same parameters ($\mu = 0$, $\sigma = 1$). In practice, it is necessary to transform only those raw scores that are being compared.

3. In certain situations, such as in psychological testing, the z-scores are converted into standardized distributions that have a particular mean and standard deviation.

KEY TERMS

raw score

z-score

deviation score

z-score transformation

standardized distribution

standardized score

───── **FOCUS ON PROBLEM SOLVING** ─────

1. When you are converting an X value to a z-score (or vice versa), do not rely entirely on the formula. You can avoid careless mistakes if you use the definition of a z-score (sign and numerical value) to make a preliminary estimate of the answer before you begin computations. For example, a z-score of $z = -0.85$ identifies a score located *below* the mean by almost 1 standard deviation. When computing the X value for this z-score, be sure that your answer is smaller than the mean, and check that the distance between X and μ is slightly less than the standard deviation.

   A common mistake when computing z-scores is to forget to include the sign of the z-score. The sign is determined by the deviation score $(X - \mu)$ and should be carried through all steps of the computation. If, for example, the correct z-score is $z = -2.0$, then an answer of $z = 2.0$ is wrong. In the first case, the raw score is 2 standard deviations *below* the mean, but the second (and incorrect) answer indicates that the X value is 2 standard deviations *above* the mean. These are clearly different answers, and only one can be correct. What is the best advice to avoid careless errors? Sketch the distribution, showing the mean and the raw score (or z-score) in question. This way you will have a concrete frame of reference for each problem.

2. When comparing scores from distributions that have different standard deviations, it is important to be sure that you use the correct value for σ in the z-score formula. Use the σ value for the distribution from which the raw score in question was taken.

3. Remember, a z-score specifies a relative position within the context of a specific distribution. A z-score is a relative value, not an absolute value. For example, a z-score of $z = -2.0$ does not necessarily suggest a very low raw score—it simply means that the raw score is among the lowest within that specific group.

───── **DEMONSTRATION 5.1** ─────

TRANSFORMING X VALUES INTO z-SCORES

A distribution of scores has a mean of $\mu = 60$ with $\sigma = 12$. Find the z-score for $X = 75$.

STEP 1   Determine the sign of the z-score.
   First, determine whether X is above or below the mean. This will determine the sign of the z-score. For this demonstration, X is larger than (above) μ, so the z-score will be positive.

STEP 2   Find the distance between X and μ.
   The distance is obtained by computing a deviation score.

$$\text{deviation score} = X - \mu = 75 - 60 = 15$$

   Thus, the score, $X = 75$, is 15 points above μ.

STEP 3   Convert the distance to standard deviation units.
   Converting the distance from step 2 to σ units is accomplished by dividing the distance by σ. For this demonstration,

$$\frac{15}{12} = 1.25$$

   Thus, $X = 75$ is 1.25 standard deviations from the mean.

STEP 4   Combine the sign from step 1 with the number from step 2.
     The raw score is above the mean, so the z-score must be positive (step 1). For these
     data,

$$z = +1.25$$

     In using the z-score formula, the sign of the z-score will be determined by the sign of
     the deviation score, $X - \mu$. If X is larger than μ, the deviation score will be positive.
     However, if X is smaller than μ, the deviation score will be negative. For this demonstra-
     tion, Formula 5.1 is used as follows:

$$z = \frac{X - \mu}{\sigma} = \frac{75 - 60}{12} = \frac{+15}{12} = +1.25$$

DEMONSTRATION 5.2

CONVERTING z-SCORES TO X VALUES

For a population with $\mu = 60$ and $\sigma = 12$, what X value corresponds to $z = -0.50$?
In this situation we know the z-score and must find X.

STEP 1   Locate X in relation to the mean.
     The sign of the z-score is negative. This tells us that the X value we are looking for is
     below μ.

STEP 2   Determine the distance from the mean (deviation score).
     The magnitude of the z-score tells us how many standard deviations there are between X
     and μ. In this case, X is $\frac{1}{2}$ standard deviation from the mean. In this distribution, 1 standard
     deviation is 12 points ($\sigma = 12$). Therefore, X is one-half of 12 points from the mean, or

$$(0.5)(12) = 6 \text{ points}$$

STEP 3   Find the X value.
     Starting with the value of the mean, use the direction (step 1) and the distance (step 2)
     to determine the X value. For this demonstration, we want to find the score that is 6 points
     below $\mu = 60$. Therefore,

$$X = 60 - 6 = 54$$

     Formula 5.2 is used to convert a z-score to an X value. For this demonstration, we obtain
     the following, using the formula:

$$
\begin{aligned}
X &= \mu + z\sigma \\
&= 60 + (-0.50)(12) \\
&= 60 + (-6) = 60 - 6 \\
&= 54
\end{aligned}
$$

     Note that the sign of the z-score determines whether the deviation score is added to or sub-
     tracted from the mean.

PROBLEMS

1. Describe exactly what information is provided by a z-score.

2. A positively skewed distribution has $\mu = 80$ and $\sigma = 12$. If this entire distribution is transformed into z-scores, describe the shape, mean, and standard deviation for the resulting distribution of z-scores.

3. A distribution of scores has a mean of $\mu = 70$. In this distribution, a score of $X = 80$ is located 10 points above the mean.
   a. Assume that the standard deviation is $\sigma = 5$. Sketch the distribution and locate the position of $X = 80$. What z-score corresponds to $X = 80$?
   b. Now assume that the standard deviation is $\sigma = 20$. Again, sketch the distribution and locate the position of $X = 80$. Now what z-score corresponds to $X = 80$?

4. For a distribution of raw scores, $\mu = 45$. The z-score for $X = 55$ is computed, and a value of $z = -2.00$ is obtained. Regardless of the value for the standard deviation, why must this z-score be incorrect?

5. For a population with $\mu = 100$ and $\sigma = 20$,
   a. Find the z-score corresponding to each of the following X values:

   $X = 110$ $X = 140$ $X = 80$
   $X = 60$ $X = 105$ $X = 130$

   b. Find the X value corresponding to each of the following z-scores:

   $z = 2.50$ $z = -0.50$ $z = -1.50$
   $z = 0.25$ $z = -1.00$ $z = 0.75$

6. For a population with $\mu = 30$ and $\sigma = 4$,
   a. Find the z-score corresponding to each of the following X values:

   $X = 34$ $X = 36$ $X = 38$
   $X = 28$ $X = 22$ $X = 24$

   b. Find the X value corresponding to each of the following z-scores:

   $z = 0.75$ $z = 1.50$ $z = 2.50$
   $z = -0.25$ $z = -1.00$ $z = -1.25$

7. A population of scores has $\mu = 60$ and $\sigma = 12$. Find the z-score corresponding to each of the following X values from this population.

   $X = 66$ $X = 48$ $X = 84$
   $X = 55$ $X = 70$ $X = 75$

8. A population of scores has $\mu = 85$ and $\sigma = 20$. Find the raw score (X value) corresponding to each of the following z-scores in this population:

   $z = 1.25$ $z = -2.30$ $z = -1.50$
   $z = 0.60$ $z = -0.40$ $z = 2.10$

9. For a population with $\mu = 80$ and $\sigma = 20$,
   a. Find the z-score for each of the following X values. (*Note:* You should be able to find these values using the definition of a z-score. You should not need to use a formula or do any serious calculations.)

   $X = 75$ $X = 90$ $X = 110$
   $X = 95$ $X = 60$ $X = 40$

   b. Find the score (X value) that corresponds to each of the following z-scores. (*Note:* You should be able to find these values using the definition of a z-score. You should not need to use a formula or do any serious calculations.)

   $z = 2.50$ $z = -0.50$ $z = -1.50$
   $z = 0.25$ $z = -0.75$ $z = 1.00$

10. For a population with $\mu = 45$ and $\sigma = 7$, find the z-score for each of the following X values. (*Note:* You probably will need to use the formula and a calculator to find these values.)

   $X = 47$ $X = 35$ $X = 40$
   $X = 60$ $X = 55$ $X = 42$

11. A distribution of scores has a standard deviation of $\sigma = 10$. Find the z-score corresponding to each of the following values.
   a. A score that is 20 points above the mean.
   b. A score 10 points below the mean.
   c. A score 15 points above the mean.
   d. A score 30 points below the mean.

12. A score that is 12 points above the mean corresponds to a z-score of $Z = +2.00$. What is the standard deviation for this population?

13. For a population with $\mu = 90$, a raw score of $X = 93$ corresponds to $z = +0.50$. What is the standard deviation for this distribution?

14. For a population with $\mu = 60$, a score of $X = 52$ corresponds to $z = -2.00$. What is the standard deviation for this distribution?

15. For a population with $\sigma = 12$, a score of $X = 87$ corresponds to $z = -0.25$. What is the mean for this distribution?

16. For a population with $\sigma = 5$, a score of $X = 55$ corresponds to $z = 2.00$. What is the mean for this distribution?

17. For a population of exam scores, a score of $X = 58$ corresponds to $z = +0.50$ and a score of $X = 46$ corresponds to $z = -1.00$. Find the mean and the standard deviation for the population. (*Hint:* Sketch the distribution and locate the two scores in your sketch.)

18. In a distribution of scores, a raw score of $X = 43$ corresponds to $z = 1.00$ and a score of $X = 49$ corresponds to $z = 2.00$. Find the mean and the standard deviation for the distribution of scores.

19. A population has $\mu = 80$.
   a. If the standard deviation is $\sigma = 2$, would a score of $X = 86$ be described as a central score or an extremely high score?
   b. If the standard deviation is $\sigma = 12$, would a score of $X = 86$ be described as a central score or an extremely high score?

20. Suppose that you have a score of $X = 55$ on an exam with $\mu = 50$. Which standard deviation would give you the better grade: $\sigma = 5$ or $\sigma = 10$?

21. Answer the question in Problem 20, but this time assume that the mean for the exam is $\mu = 60$.

22. On Tuesday afternoon, Bill earned a score of $X = 73$ on an English test with $\mu = 65$ and $\sigma = 8$. The same day, John earned a score of $X = 63$ on a math test with $\mu = 57$ and $\sigma = 3$. Who should expect the better grade, Bill or John? Explain your answer.

23. Mary had two exams last week. She got a score of $X = 48$ on a statistics exam where the class averaged $\mu = 50$ with $\sigma = 8$, and she got a score of $X = 68$ on a biology exam where the class average was $\mu = 74$ with $\sigma = 3$. For which exam should Mary expect the better grade? Explain your answer.

24. A distribution with $\mu = 65$ and $\sigma = 6$ is being standardized to produce a new mean of $\mu = 50$ and a new standard deviation of $\sigma = 10$. Find the new standardized value for each of the following scores from the original distribution: 68, 59, 77, and 56.

25. A distribution with $\mu = 38$ and $\sigma = 4$ is being standardized to produce a new mean of $\mu = 100$ and a new standard deviation of $\sigma = 20$. Find the new standardized value for each of the following scores from the original distribution: 34, 36, 37, 41, and 46.

26. A population consists of the following scores:
   $$12, \quad 1, \quad 10, \quad 3, \quad 7, \quad 3$$
   a. Compute μ and σ for the population.
   b. Find the z-score for each raw score in the population.
   c. Transform each score into a new standardized value so that the standardized distribution has a mean of $\mu = 100$ and a standard deviation of $\sigma = 20$.

27. A population consists of the following $N = 6$ scores: 0, 4, 6, 1, 3, and 4.
   a. Compute μ and σ for the population.
   b. Find the z-score for each score in the population.
   c. Transform the original population into a new population of $N = 6$ scores with a mean of $\mu = 50$ and a standard deviation of $\sigma = 10$.

28. A population consists of the following $N = 5$ scores: 0, 6, 4, 3, and 12.
   a. Compute μ and σ for the population.
   b. Find the z-score for each score in the population.
   c. Transform the original population into a new population of $N = 5$ scores with a mean of $\mu = 60$ and a standard deviation of $\sigma = 8$.

CHAPTER 6 # PROBABILITY

TOOLS YOU WILL NEED

The following items are considered essential background material for this chapter. If you doubt your knowledge of any of these items, you should review the appropriate chapter or section before proceeding.

- Proportions (math review, Appendix A)
  - Fractions
  - Decimals
  - Percentages
- Basic algebra (math review, Appendix A)
- z-Scores (Chapter 5)

CONTENTS

6.1   INTRODUCTION TO PROBABILITY

In Chapter 1, we introduced the idea that research studies usually begin with a general question about an entire population, but the actual research is conducted using a sample. In this situation, the role of inferential statistics is to use the sample data as the basis for answering questions about the population. To accomplish this goal, inferential procedures are typically built around the concept of probability. Specifically, the relationships between samples and populations are usually defined in terms of probability. Suppose, for example, you are selecting a single marble from a jar that contains 50 black and 50 white marbles. (In this example, the jar of marbles is the *population* and the single marble to be selected is the *sample.*) Although you cannot guarantee the exact outcome of your sample, it is possible to talk about the potential outcomes in terms of probabilities. In this case, you have a fifty-fifty chance of getting either color. Now consider another jar (population) that has 90 black and only 10 white marbles. Again, you cannot specify the exact outcome of a sample, but now you know that the sample probably will be a black marble. By knowing the makeup of a population, we can determine the probability of obtaining specific samples. In this way, probability gives us a connection between populations and samples, and this connection will be the foundation for the inferential statistics to be presented in the chapters that follow.

You may have noticed that the preceding examples begin with a population and then use probability to describe the samples that could be obtained. This is exactly backward from what we want to do with inferential statistics. Remember, the goal of inferential statistics is to begin with a sample and then answer general questions about the population. We will reach this goal in a two-stage process. In the first stage, we develop probability as a bridge from population to samples. This stage involves identifying the types of samples that probably would be obtained from a specific population. Once this bridge is established, we simply reverse the probability rules to allow us to move from samples to populations (see Figure 6.1). The process of reversing the probability relationship can be demonstrated by considering again the two jars of marbles we looked at earlier. (Jar 1 has 50 black and 50 white marbles; jar 2 has 90 black and only 10 white marbles.) This time, suppose that you are blindfolded when the sample is selected and that your task is to use the sample to help you to decide which jar was used. If you select a sample of $n = 4$ marbles and all are black, where did the sample come from? It should be clear

FIGURE 6.1

The role of probability in inferential statistics. Probability is used to predict what kind of samples are likely to be obtained from a population. Thus, probability establishes a connection between samples and populations. Inferential statistics rely on this connection when they use sample data as the basis for making conclusions about populations.

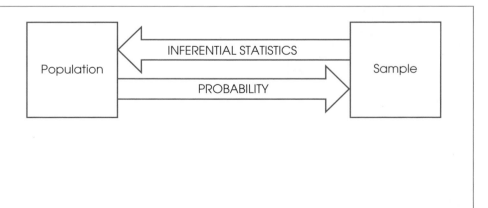

that it would be relatively unlikely (low probability) to obtain this sample from jar 1; in four draws, you almost certainly would get at least 1 white marble. On the other hand, this sample would have a high probability of coming from jar 2, where nearly all the marbles are black. Your decision therefore is that the sample probably came from jar 2. Note that you now are using the sample to make an inference about the population.

PROBABILITY DEFINITION

Probability is a huge topic that extends far beyond the limits of introductory statistics, and we will not attempt to examine it all here. Instead, we will concentrate on the few concepts and definitions that are needed for an introduction to inferential statistics. We begin with a relatively simple definition of probability.

DEFINITION

In a situation where several different outcomes are possible, we define the *probability* for any particular outcome as a fraction or proportion. If the possible outcomes are identified as *A*, *B*, *C*, *D*, and so on, then

$$\text{probability of } A = \frac{\text{number of outcomes classified as } A}{\text{total number of possible outcomes}}$$

For example, if you are selecting a card from a complete deck, there are 52 possible outcomes. The probability of selecting the king of hearts is $p = \frac{1}{52}$. The probability of selecting an ace is $p = \frac{4}{52}$ because there are 4 aces in the deck.

To simplify the discussion of probability, we will use a notation system that eliminates a lot of the words. The probability of a specific outcome will be expressed with a *p* (for probability) followed by the specific outcome in parentheses. For example, the probability of selecting a king from a deck of cards will be written as *p*(king). The probability of obtaining heads for a coin toss will be written as *p*(heads).

You should note that probability is defined as a proportion. This definition makes it possible to restate any probability problem as a proportion problem. For example, the probability problem "What is the probability of obtaining a king from a deck of cards?" can be restated as "Out of the whole deck, what proportion are kings?" In each case, the answer is $\frac{4}{52}$, or "4 out of 52." This translation from probability to proportion may seem trivial now, but it will be a great aid when the probability problems become more complex. In most situations, we are concerned with the probability of obtaining a particular sample from a population. The terminology of *sample* and *population* will not change the basic definition of probability. For example, the whole deck of cards can be considered as a population, and the single card we select is the sample.

The definition we are using identifies probability as a fraction or a proportion. If you work directly from this definition, the probability values you obtain will be expressed as fractions. For example, if you are selecting a card,

$$p(\text{spade}) = \tfrac{13}{52} = \tfrac{1}{4}$$

or if you are tossing a coin,

$$p(\text{heads}) = \tfrac{1}{2}$$

If you are unsure how to convert from fractions to decimals or percentages, you should review the section on proportions in the math review, Appendix A.

You should be aware that these fractions can be expressed equally well as either decimals or percentages:

$$p = \tfrac{1}{4} = 0.25 = 25\%$$
$$p = \tfrac{1}{2} = .050 = 50\%$$

By convention, probability values most often are expressed as decimal values, but you should realize that any of these three forms is acceptable.

You also should note that all the possible probability values are contained in a limited range. At one extreme, when an event never occurs, the probability is zero or 0%. At the other extreme, when an event always occurs, the probability is 1, or 100%. For example, suppose you have a jar containing 10 white marbles. The probability of randomly selecting a black marble is

$$p(\text{black}) = \tfrac{0}{10} = 0$$

The probability of selecting a white marble is

$$p(\text{white}) = \tfrac{10}{10} = 1$$

RANDOM SAMPLING

For the preceding definition of probability to be accurate, it is necessary that the outcomes be obtained by a process called random sampling.

DEFINITION

See the *Note* at the end of this section

A *random sample* must satisfy two requirements:

1. Each individual in the population must have an *equal chance* of being selected.
2. If more than one individual is to be selected for the sample, there must be *constant probability* for each and every selection.

Each of the two requirements for random sampling has some interesting consequences. The first assures that there is no bias in the selection process. For a population with N individuals, each individual must have the same probability, $p = 1/N$, of being selected. Note that the "equal chance" requirement applies to the *individuals* in the population. Earlier we considered an example using a jar of 90 black marbles and 10 white marbles. For a random sample from this jar, each of the 100 marbles must have an equal chance of being selected. In this case, each marble has a probability of $p = 1/100$. The individual probabilities are then combined to find the probability for specific *groups* or *categories* in the population; for example, the probability of obtaining a black marble is $p = 90/100$.

Finally, you should realize that the "equal chance" requirement prohibits you from using the definition of probability in situations where the *individual* outcomes are not equally likely. Consider, for example, the question of whether or not there is life on Mars. There are only two possible alternatives:

1. There is life on Mars.
2. There is no life on Mars.

With only two individual outcomes in the population of alternatives, you might conclude that the probability of life on Mars is $p = 1/2$. However, you should realize that these two individual outcomes are not equally likely, and, therefore, our definition of probability does not apply.

The second requirement also is more interesting than may be apparent at first glance. Consider, for example, the selection of $n = 2$ cards from a complete deck. For the first draw, the probability of obtaining the jack of diamonds is

$$p(\text{jack of diamonds}) = \tfrac{1}{52}$$

Now, for the second draw, what is the probability of obtaining the jack of diamonds? Assuming you still are holding the first card, there are two possibilities:

$$p(\text{jack of diamonds}) = \tfrac{1}{51} \text{ if the first card was not the jack of diamonds}$$

or

$$p(\text{jack of diamonds}) = 0 \text{ if the first card was the jack of diamonds}$$

In either case, the probability is different from its value for the first draw. This contradicts the requirement for random sampling that states the probability must stay constant. To keep the probabilities from changing from one selection to the next, it is necessary to replace each sample before you make the next selection. This solution is called *sampling with replacement*. The second requirement for random samples (constant probability) demands that you sample with replacement.

(*Note:* The definition that we are using identifies one type of random sampling, often called a *simple random sample* or an *independent random sample*. This kind of sampling is important for the mathematical foundation of many of the statistics we will encounter later. However, you should realize that other definitions exist for the concept of random sampling. In particular, it is very common to define random sampling without the requirement of constant probabilities—that is, without replacement. In addition, there are many different sampling techniques that are used when researchers are selecting individuals to participate in research studies.)

PROBABILITY AND FREQUENCY DISTRIBUTIONS

The situations in which we are concerned with probability usually will involve a population of scores that can be displayed in a frequency distribution graph. If you think of the graph as representing the entire population, then different portions of the graph will represent different portions of the population. Because probability and proportion are equivalent, a particular proportion of the graph corresponds to a particular probability in the population. Thus, whenever a population is presented in a frequency distribution graph, it will be possible to represent probabilities as proportions of the graph. The following example demonstrates the relationship between graphs and probabilities.

EXAMPLE 6.1

We will use a very simple population that contains only $N = 10$ scores with values 1, 1, 2, 3, 3, 4, 4, 4, 5, 6. This population is shown in the frequency distribution graph in Figure 6.2. If you are taking a random sample of $n = 1$ score from this population, what is the probability of obtaining a score greater than 4? In probability notation,

$$p(X > 4) = ?$$

Using the definition of probability, there are 2 scores that meet this criterion out of the total group of $N = 10$ scores, so the answer is $p = \tfrac{2}{10}$. This answer can be obtained directly from the frequency distribution graph if you recall that probability and proportion measure the same thing. Looking at the graph (Figure 6.2), what proportion of the population consists of scores greater than 4? The answer is the shaded part of the distribution—that is, 2 boxes out of the total of 10 boxes in the distribution. Note that we now are defining probability as the proportion of *area* in the frequency distribution graph. This provides a very concrete and graphic way of representing probability.

FIGURE 6.2

A frequency distribution histogram for a population that consists of $N = 10$ scores. The shaded part of the figure indicates the portion of the whole population that corresponds to scores greater than $X = 4$. The shaded portion is two-tenths ($p = \frac{2}{10}$) of the whole distribution.

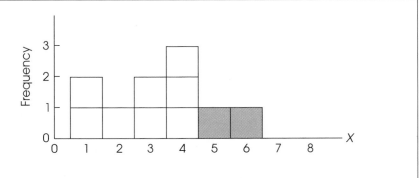

Using the same population once again, what is the probability of selecting a score less than 5? In symbols,

$$p(X < 5) = ?$$

Going directly to the distribution in Figure 6.2, we now want to know what part of the graph is not shaded. The unshaded portion consists of 8 out of the 10 boxes ($\frac{8}{10}$ of the area of the graph), so the answer is $p = \frac{8}{10}$.

LEARNING CHECK

1. The animal colony in the psychology department contains 20 male rats and 30 female rats. Of the 20 males, 15 are white and 5 spotted. Of the 30 females, 15 are white and 15 spotted. Suppose you randomly select 1 rat from this colony.
   a. What is the probability of obtaining a female?
   b. What is the probability of obtaining a white male?
   c. Which selection is more likely, a spotted male or a spotted female?

2. What is the purpose of sampling with replacement?

3. Suppose you are going to select a random sample of $n = 1$ score from the distribution in Figure 6.2. Find the following probabilities:
   a. $p(X > 2)$
   b. $p(X > 5)$
   c. $p(X < 3)$

ANSWERS

1. a. $p = 30/50 = 0.60$ b. $p = 15/50 = 0.30$
   c. A spotted female ($p = 0.30$) is more likely than a spotted male ($p = 0.10$).

2. Sampling with replacement is necessary to maintain constant probabilities for each and every selection.

3. a. $p = 7/10 = 0.70$ b. $p = 1/10 = 0.10$ c. $p = 3/10 = 0.30$

6.2   PROBABILITY AND THE NORMAL DISTRIBUTION

We first introduced the normal distribution in Chapter 2 as an example of a commonly occurring shape for population distributions. An example of a normal distribution is shown in Figure 6.3.

FIGURE 6.3

The normal distribution. The exact shape of the normal distribution is specified by an equation relating each X value (score) to each Y value (frequency). The equation is

$$Y = \frac{1}{\sqrt{2\pi\sigma^2}} \, e^{-(X-\mu)^2/2\sigma^2}$$

(π and e are mathematical constants.) In simpler terms, the normal distribution is symmetrical, with a single mode in the middle. The frequency tapers off as you move farther from the middle in either direction.

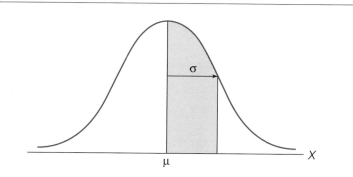

Note that the normal distribution is symmetrical, with the highest frequency in the middle and frequencies tapering off as you move toward either extreme. Although the exact shape for the normal distribution is defined by an equation (see Figure 6.3), the normal shape can also be described by the proportions of area contained in each section of the distribution. Statisticians often identify sections of a normal distribution by using z-scores. Figure 6.4 shows a normal distribution with several sections marked in z-score units. Recall that z-scores measure positions in a distribution in terms of standard deviations from the mean. (Thus, $z = +1$ is 1 standard deviation above the mean, $z = +2$ is 2 standard deviations above the mean, and so on.) The graph shows the percentage of scores that fall in each of these sections. For example, the section between the mean ($z = 0$) and the point that is 1 standard deviation above the mean ($z = 1$) makes up 34.13% of the scores. Similarly, 13.59% of the scores fall between 1 and 2 standard deviations from the mean. In this way it is possible to define a normal distribution in terms of its proportions; that is, a distribution is normal if and only if it has all the right proportions.

There are two additional points to be made about the distribution shown in Figure 6.4. First, you should realize that the sections on the left side of the distribution have exactly the same proportions as the corresponding sections on the right side because the normal distribution is symmetrical. Second, because the locations in the distribution are identified by z-scores, the proportions shown in the figure apply to *any normal distribution* regardless of the values for the mean and the standard deviation. Remember, when

FIGURE 6.4

The normal distribution
following a *z*-score
transformation.

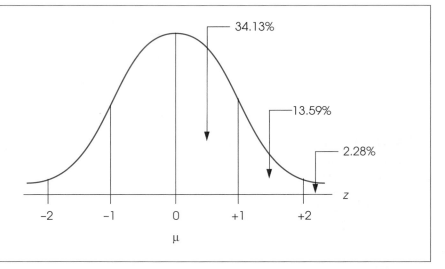

any distribution is transformed into *z*-scores, the mean becomes zero and the standard deviation becomes one.

Because the normal distribution is a good model for many naturally occurring distributions and because this shape is guaranteed in some circumstances (as you will see in Chapter 7), we will devote considerable attention to this particular distribution.

We introduce the process of answering probability questions about a normal distribution in the following example.

EXAMPLE 6.2   Adult heights form a normal distribution with a mean of 68 inches and a standard deviation of 6 inches. Given this information about the population and the known proportions for a normal distribution (Figure 6.4), we can determine the probability associated with specific samples. For example, what is the probability of randomly selecting an individual from this population who is taller than 6 feet 8 inches (*X* = 80 inches)?

Restating this question in probability notation, we get

$$p(X > 80) = ?$$

We will follow a step-by-step process to find the answer to this question.

1. First, the probability question is translated into a proportion question: Out of all possible adult heights, what proportion is greater than 80?

2. We know that "all possible adult heights" is simply the population distribution. This population is shown in Figure 6.5(a). The mean is $\mu = 68$, so the score $X = 80$ is to the right of the mean. Because we are interested in all heights greater than 80, we shade in the area to the right of 80. This area represents the proportion we are trying to determine.

3. Identify the exact position of $X = 80$ by computing a *z*-score. For this example,

$$z = \frac{X - \mu}{\sigma} = \frac{80 - 68}{6} = \frac{12}{6} = 2.00$$

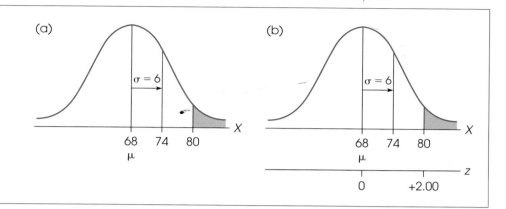

FIGURE 6.5

The distribution for
Example 6.2.

That is, a height of $X = 80$ inches is exactly 2 standard deviations above the mean and
corresponds to a z-score of $z = +2.00$ [see Figure 6.5(b)].

4. The proportion we are trying to determine may now be expressed in terms of
its z-score:

$$p(z > 2.00) = ?$$

According to the proportions shown in Figure 6.4, all normal distributions, regardless
of the values for μ and σ, will have 2.28% of the scores in the tail beyond $z = +2.00$.
Thus, for the population of adult heights,

$$p(X > 80) = p(z > +2.00) = 2.28\%$$

THE UNIT NORMAL TABLE   Before we attempt any more probability questions, we must introduce a more useful
tool than the graph of the normal distribution shown in Figure 6.4. The graph shows
proportions for only a few selected z-score values. A more complete listing of z-scores
and proportions is provided in the *unit normal table.* This table lists proportions of the
normal distribution for a full range of possible z-score values.

The complete unit normal table is provided in Appendix B, Table B.1, and a portion
of the table is reproduced in Figure 6.6. Note that the table is structured in a three-
column format. The first column (A) lists z-score values corresponding to different locations in a normal distribution. If you imagine a vertical line drawn through a normal
distribution, then the exact location of the line can be described by one of the z-score
values listed in column A. You should also realize that a vertical line will separate the
distribution into two sections: a larger section that we will call the *body* and a smaller
section called the *tail.* Columns B and C in the table identify the proportion of the distribution in each of the two sections. Column B presents the proportion in the body (the
larger portion), and column C presents the proportion in the tail. For example, you
should be able to use Figure 6.6 to verify that a vertical line drawn through a normal distribution at $z = +0.25$ will separate the distribution into two sections with the larger
section containing 0.5987 (59.87%) of the distribution and the smaller section contain-

FIGURE 6.6

A portion of the unit normal table. This table lists proportions of the normal distribution corresponding to each z-score value. Column A of the table lists z-scores. Column B lists the proportion in the body of the normal distribution up to the z-score value. Column C lists the proportion of the normal distribution that is located in the tail of the distribution beyond the z-score value.

(A) z	(B) Proportion in body	(C) Proportion in tail
0.00	0.5000	0.5000
0.01	0.5040	0.4960
0.02	0.5080	0.4920
0.03	0.5120	0.4880
0.21	0.5832	0.4168
0.22	0.5871	0.4129
0.23	0.5910	0.4090
0.24	0.5948	0.4052
0.25	0.5987	0.4013
0.26	0.6026	0.3974
0.27	0.6064	0.3936
0.28	0.6103	0.3897
0.29	0.6141	0.3859
0.30	0.6179	0.3821
0.31	0.6217	0.3783
0.32	0.6255	0.3745
0.33	0.6293	0.3707
0.34	0.6331	0.3669

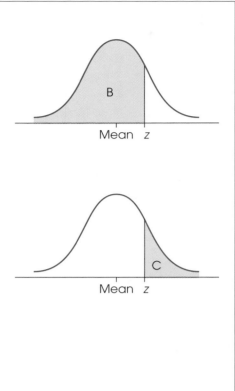

ing 0.4013 (40.13%) of the distribution. To make full use of the unit normal table, there are a few other facts to keep in mind:

1. The *body* always corresponds to the larger part of the distribution whether it is on the right-hand side or the left-hand side. Similarly, the *tail* is always the smaller section whether it is on the right or the left.

2. Because the normal distribution is symmetrical, the proportions on the right-hand side are exactly the same as the corresponding proportions on the left-hand side. For example, the proportion in the right-hand tail beyond $z = +1.00$ is exactly the same as the proportion in the left-hand tail beyond $z = -1.00$.

3. Although the z-score values will change signs ($+$ and $-$) from one side to the other, the proportions will always be positive. Thus, column C in the table always lists the proportion in the tail whether it is the right-hand tail or the left-hand tail.

4. For any specific z-score value, the two proportions (columns B and C) will always add to 1.00. The two parts of the distribution (body and tail) will always add to equal the whole distribution.

**PROBABILITIES,
PROPORTIONS,
AND z-SCORES**

The unit normal table lists relationships between z-score locations and proportions in a normal distribution. For any z-score location, you can use the table to look up the corresponding proportions. Similarly, if you know the proportions, you can use the table to look up the specific z-score location. Because we have defined probability as equivalent to proportion, you can also use the unit normal table to look up probabilities for normal distributions. The following examples demonstrate a variety of different ways that the unit normal table can be used.

Finding proportions/probabilities for specific z-score values   For each of the following examples, we begin with a specific z-score value and then use the unit normal table to find probabilities or proportions associated with the z-score.

EXAMPLE 6.3A   What proportion of the normal distribution corresponds to z-score values greater than $z = 1.00$? First, you should sketch the distribution and shade in the area you are trying to determine. This is shown in Figure 6.7(a). In this case, the shaded portion is the tail of the distribution beyond $z = 1.00$. To find this shaded area, you simply look up $z = 1.00$ in column A of the unit normal table. Then you read column C (tail) for the proportion. Using the table in Appendix B, you should find that the answer is 0.1587.

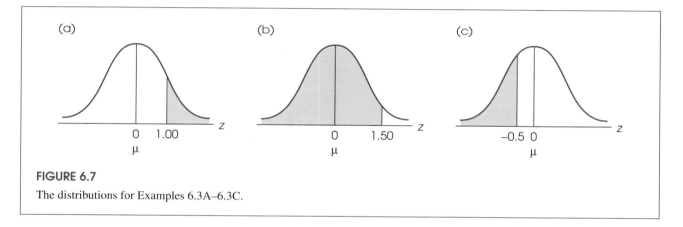

FIGURE 6.7

The distributions for Examples 6.3A–6.3C.

You also should notice that this same problem could have been phrased as a probability question. Specifically, we could have asked, "For a normal distribution, what is the probability of selecting a z-score value greater than $z = +1.00$?" Because probability is the same as proportion, the answer is $p(z > 1.00) = 0.1587$ (or 15.87%).

EXAMPLE 6.3B   For a normal distribution, what is the probability of selecting a z-score less than $z = 1.50$? In symbols, $p(z < 1.50) = ?$ Because probability is equivalent to proportion, our goal is to determine what proportion of the z-scores have values less than 1.50. A normal distribution is shown in Figure 6.7(b) and $z = 1.50$ is located in the distribution. Note that we have shaded all the values to the left of (less than) $z = 1.50$. This is the portion we trying to find. Clearly the shaded portion is more than 50% so it corresponds to the body of the distribution. Therefore, we find $z = 1.50$ in the unit normal table and read the proportion from column B. The answer is $p(z < 1.50) = 0.9332$ (or 93.32).

EXAMPLE 6.3C

Many problems will require that you find proportions for negative z-scores. For example, what proportion of the normal distribution corresponds to the tail beyond $z = -0.50$? That is, $p(z < -0.50)$. This portion has been shaded in Figure 6.7(c). To answer questions with negative z-scores, simply remember that the normal distribution is symmetrical with a z-score of zero at the mean, positive values to the right, and negative values to the left. The proportion in the left tail beyond $z = -0.50$ is identical to the proportion in the right tail beyond $z = +0.50$. To find this proportion, look up $z = 0.50$ in column A, and find the proportion in column C (tail). You should get an answer of 0.3085 (30.85%).

Moving to the left on the X-axis results in smaller X values and smaller z-scores. Thus, a z-score of −3.00 reflects a smaller value than a z-score of −1.

Finding the z-score location that corresponds to specific proportions   The preceding examples all involved using a z-score value in column A to look up a proportion in column B or C. You should realize, however, that the table also allows you to begin with a known proportion and then look up the corresponding z-score. In general, the unit normal table can be used for two purposes:

1. If you know a specific location (z-score) in a normal distribution, you can use the table to look up the corresponding proportions.
2. If you know a specific proportion (or proportions), you can use the table to look up the exact z-score location in the distribution.

   The following examples demonstrate how the table can be used to find specific z-scores if you begin with known proportions.

EXAMPLE 6.4A

For a normal distribution, what z-score separates the top 10% from the remainder of the distribution? To answer this question, we have sketched a normal distribution [Figure 6.8(a)] and drawn a vertical line that separates the highest 10% (approximately) from the rest. The problem is to locate the exact position of this line. For this distribution, we know that the tail contains 0.1000 (10%) and the body contains 0.9000 (90%). To find the z-score value, you simply locate 0.1000 in column C or 0.9000 in column B of the unit normal table. Note that you probably will not find the exact proportion, but you can use the closest value listed in the table. For example, you will not find 0.1000 listed in column C but you can use 0.1003, which is listed. Once you have found the correct proportion in the table, simply read the corresponding z-score. For

FIGURE 6.8

The distributions for Examples 6.4A and 6.4B.

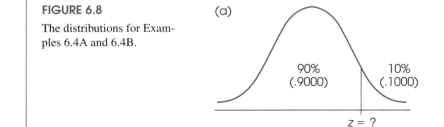

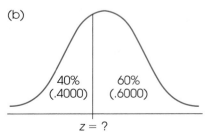

this example, the z-score that separates the extreme 10% in the tail is $z = 1.28$. At this point you must be careful because the table does not differentiate between the right-hand tail and the left-hand tail of the distribution. Specifically, the final answer could be either $z = +1.28$, which separates 10% in the right-hand tail, or the answer could be $z = -1.28$, which separates 10% in the left-hand tail. For this problem we want the right-hand tail (the highest 10%), so the z-score value is $z = +1.28$.

EXAMPLE 6.4B   For a normal distribution, what z-score value forms the boundary between the top 60% and the bottom 40% of the scores? Again, we have sketched a normal distribution [Figure 6.8(b)] and drawn a vertical line in the approximate location. For this example, slightly more than half of the distribution is on the right-hand side of the line. The problem is to find the z-score value that defines the exact location of the line. To find the z-score, you begin with the known proportions: 0.6000 in the body (column B) and 0.4000 in the tail (column C). These precise proportions are not found in the table, but the closest values that are listed are 0.5987 and 0.4013. Reading from column A, the corresponding z-score is $z = 0.25$. Once again, you must decide whether the final z-score answer is $+0.25$ or -0.25. Looking at the sketch [Figure 6.8(b)], you can see that the line is located below the mean, so the z-score value is $z = -0.25$.

You may have noticed that we have sketched distributions for each of the preceding problems. As a general rule, you should always sketch a distribution, locate the mean with a vertical line, and shade in the portion you are trying to determine. Look at your sketch. It will indicate which columns to use in the unit normal table. If you make a habit of drawing sketches, you will avoid careless errors in using the table.

LEARNING CHECK

1. Find the proportion of the normal distribution that is associated with the following sections of a graph:
    a. $z < +1.00$
    b. $z > +0.80$
    c. $z < -2.00$
    d. $z > -0.33$
    e. $z > -0.50$

2. For a normal distribution, find the z-score location that separates the distribution as follows:
    a. Separate the highest 30% from the rest of the distribution.
    b. Separate the lowest 40% from the rest of the distribution.
    c. Separate the highest 75% from the rest of the distribution.

ANSWERS   1. **a.** 0.8413   **b.** 0.2119   **c.** 0.0228   **d.** 0.6293   **e.** 0.6915
2. **a.** $z = 0.52$ **b.** $z = -0.25$ **c.** $z = -0.67$

PROBABILITIES, PROPORTIONS, AND SCORES (X VALUES)

In the preceding examples, we used the unit normal table to find probabilities and proportions corresponding to specific *z*-score values. In most situations, however, it will be necessary to find probabilities for specific *X* values. Consider the following example:

> It is known that IQ scores form a normal distribution with $\mu = 100$ and $\sigma = 15$. Given this information, what is the probability of randomly selecting an individual with an IQ score greater than 130?

This problem is asking for a specific probability or proportion of a normal distribution. However, before we can look up the answer in the unit normal table, we must first transform the IQ scores (*X* values) into *z*-scores. Thus, to solve this new kind of probability problem, we must add one new step to the process. Specifically, in order to answer probability questions about scores (*X* values) from a normal distribution, you must use the following two-step procedure:

1. Transform the *X* values into *z*-scores.
2. Use the unit normal table to look up the proportions corresponding to the *z*-score values.

This process is demonstrated in the following examples. Once again, we suggest that you sketch the distribution and shade the portion you are trying to find in order to avoid careless mistakes.

EXAMPLE 6.5

We will now answer the probability question about IQ scores that was presented earlier. Specifically, what is the probability of randomly selecting an individual with an IQ score greater than 130?

$$p(X > 130) = ?$$

Restated in terms of proportions, we want to find the proportion of the IQ distribution that corresponds to scores greater than 130. The distribution is drawn in Figure 6.9, and the portion we want has been shaded.

FIGURE 6.9

The distribution of IQ scores. The problem is to find the probability or proportion of the distribution corresponding to scores greater than 130.

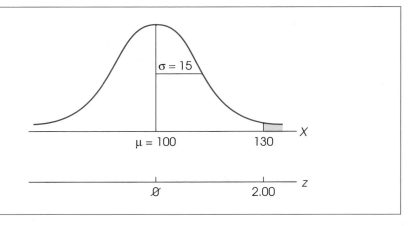

The first step is to change the X values into z-scores. In particular, the score of $X = 130$ is changed to

$$z = \frac{X - \mu}{\sigma} = \frac{130 - 100}{15} = \frac{30}{15} = 2.00$$

Next, look up the z-score value in the unit normal table. Because we want the proportion of the distribution in the tail beyond 130 (Figure 6.9), the answer will be found in column C. Consulting the table, we see that a z-score of 2.00 corresponds to a proportion of 0.0228. The probability of randomly selecting an individual with an IQ greater than 130 is 0.0228:

$$p(X > 130) = 0.0228 \text{ (or } 2.28\%)$$ 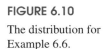 *want to see what's in the tail*

Finding proportions/probabilities located between two scores The next example demonstrates the process of finding the probability of selecting a score that is located *between* two specific values. This kind of problem is different from any of the previous examples because we are now looking for a proportion defined by a slice from the middle of the normal distribution. In particular, the final answer does not correspond to either the body or the tail of the distribution, which means that you cannot read the answer directly from the table. Instead, you must use the information in the table to calculate the final answer.

EXAMPLE 6.6   The distribution of SAT scores is normal with $\mu = 500$ and $\sigma = 100$. For this distribution, what is the probability of randomly selecting an individual with a score between $X = 600$ and $X = 700$? In probability notation, the problem is to find

$$p(600 < X < 700) = ?$$

The distribution of SAT scores is shown in Figure 6.10, with the appropriate area shaded. Remember, finding the probability is the same thing as finding the proportion

FIGURE 6.10

The distribution for Example 6.6.

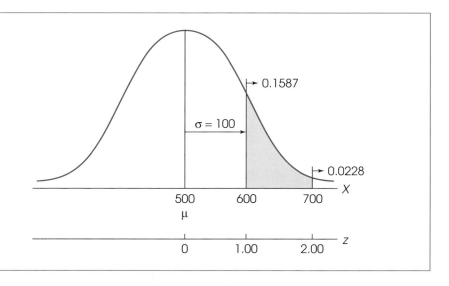

of the distribution located between 600 and 700. The first step is to transform each X value into a z-score:

$$\text{For } X = 600: z = \frac{X - \mu}{\sigma} = \frac{600 - 500}{100} = \frac{100}{100} = 1.00$$

$$\text{For } X = 700: z = \frac{X - \mu}{\sigma} = \frac{700 - 500}{100} = \frac{200}{100} = 2.00$$

The problem now is to find the proportion of the normal distribution that is located between $z = +1.00$ and $z = +2.00$. Several different techniques can be used to find this proportion, and we will examine two possibilities.

First, we consider a method that focuses on the proportions in the tail of the distribution. Using column C of the unit normal table, we find that the proportion in the tail beyond $z = +1.00$ is 0.1587. This includes the shaded portion that we are trying to find but it also includes an extra portion in the tail beyond $z = +2.00$. Using the table again, we find that the extra portion beyond $z = +2.00$ is 0.0228 (see Figure 6.10). To obtain the final answer, we begin with the proportion beyond $z = 1.00$ and subtract the extra portion beyond $z = 2.00$:

$$p(600 < X < 700) = 0.1587 - 0.0228 = 0.1359 \text{ (or 13.59\%)}$$

The second method for finding the proportion involves finding how much of the distribution is located *outside* the section we want to measure. For this example, we do not want the portion in the tail beyond $z = 2.00$ and we do not want the portion in the body to the left of $z = 1.00$ (these areas form the unshaded portions in Figure 6.10). According to the table, the portion in the tail beyond $z = 2.00$ is 0.0228. In addition, the portion in the body to the left of $z = 1.00$ is 0.8413. Thus, the total area that we do not want is

$$0.0228 + 0.8413 = .8641$$

Because the area in the whole distribution is equal to 1.0000, we can simply subtract out the portion we do not want in order to determine the section that we do want. In this example,

$$p(600 < X < 700) = 1.0000 - 0.8641 = 0.1359$$

Note that both methods produce exactly the same answer.

Finding scores corresponding to specific proportions or probabilities   In the previous two examples, the problem was to find the proportion or probability corresponding to specific X values. The two-step process for finding these proportions is shown in Figure 6.11. Thus far, we have only considered examples that move in a clockwise direction around the triangle shown in the figure; that is, we start with an X value that is transformed into a z-score, and then we use the unit normal table to look up the appropriate proportion. You should realize, however, that it is possible to reverse this two-step process so that we move backwards, or counterclockwise, around the triangle. This reverse process will allow us to find the score (X value) corresponding to a specific proportion in the distribution. Following the lines in Figure 6.11, we will begin with a spe-

FIGURE 6.11

Determining probabilities or proportions for a normal distribution is shown as a two-step process with z-scores as an intermediate stop along the way. Note that you cannot move directly along the dashed line between X values and probabilities or proportions. Instead, you must follow the solid lines around the corner.

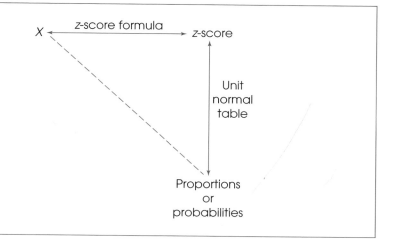

cific proportion, use the unit normal table to look up the corresponding z-score, and then transform the z-score into an X value. The following example demonstrates this process.

E X A M P L E   6 . 7

Scores on the SAT form a normal distribution with $\mu = 500$ and $\sigma = 100$. What is the minimum score necessary to be in the top 15% of the SAT distribution? This problem is shown graphically in Figure 6.12.

In this problem, we begin with a proportion (15% = 0.15), and we are looking for a score. According to the map in Figure 6.11, we can move from p (proportion) to X (score) by going via z-scores. The first step is to use the unit normal table to find the z-score that corresponds to a proportion of 0.15. Because the proportion is located beyond z in the tail of the distribution, we will look in column C for a proportion of 0.1500. Note that you may not find 0.1500 exactly, but locate the closest value

FIGURE 6.12

The distribution of SAT scores. The problem is to locate the score that separates the top 15% from the rest of the distribution. A line is drawn to divide the distribution roughly into 15% and 85% sections.

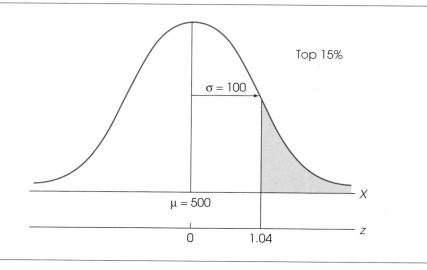

possible. In this case, the closest value in the table is 0.1492, and the z-score that corresponds to this proportion is $z = 1.04$.

The next step is to determine whether the z-score is positive or negative. Remember, the table does not specify the sign of the z-score. Looking at the graph in Figure 6.12, you should realize that the score we want is above the mean, so the z-score is positive, $z = +1.04$.

Now you are ready for the last stage of the solution—that is, changing the z-score into an X value. Using z-score equation 5.2 (p. 109) and the known values of μ, σ, and z, we obtain

$$X = \mu + z\sigma$$

$$= 500 + 1.04(100)$$

$$= 500 + 104$$

$$= 604$$

The conclusion for this example is that you must have an SAT score of at least 604 to be in the top 15% of the distribution.

LEARNING CHECK

1. For a normal distribution with a mean of 80 and a standard deviation of 10, find each probability value requested.
   a. $p(X > 85) = ?$
   b. $p(X < 95) = ?$
   c. $p(X > 70) = ?$
   d. $p(75 < X < 100) = ?$

2. For a normal distribution with a mean of 100 and a standard deviation of 20, find each value requested.
   a. What score separates the top 40% from the bottom 60% of the distribution?
   b. What is the minimum score needed to be in the top 5% of this distribution?
   c. What scores form the boundaries for the middle 60% of this distribution?

3. What is the probability of selecting a score greater than 45 from a positively skewed distribution with $\mu = 40$ and $\sigma = 10$? (Be careful.)

ANSWERS

1. a. $p = 0.3085$ (30.85%)   b. $p = 0.9332$ (93.32%)
   c. $p = 0.8413$ (84.13%)   d. $p = 0.6687$ (66.87%)

2. a. $z = +0.25; X = 105$ b. $z = +1.64; X = 132.8$
   c. $z = \pm0.84$; boundaries are 83.2 and 116.8

3. You cannot obtain the answer. The unit normal table cannot be used to answer this question because the distribution is not normal.

ON THE WEB

REMEMBER THAT a practice quiz for Chapter 6 is available on the Wadsworth Web site at **www.wadsworth.com**. You can use the quiz to test your knowledge on the material in this chapter and determine which parts of the chapter may need more study. In addition, you may want to go back and look once again at the workshop on z-scores. This workshop includes some information about proportions and probabilities that you should recognize now that you are familiar with the unit normal table. For more information about finding the quizzes and workshops, see page 24.

SUMMARY

1. The probability of a particular event A is defined as a fraction or proportion:

$$p(A) = \frac{\text{number of outcomes classified as } A}{\text{total number of possible outcomes}}$$

2. This definition is accurate only for a random sample. There are two requirements that must be satisfied for a random sample:
   a. Every individual in the population has an equal chance of being selected.
   b. When more than one individual is being selected, the probabilities must stay constant. This means there must be sampling with replacement.

3. All probability problems can be restated as proportion problems. The "probability of selecting a king from a deck of cards" is equivalent to the "proportion of the deck that consists of kings." For frequency distributions, probability questions can be answered by determining proportions of area. The "probability of selecting an individual with an IQ greater than 108" is equivalent to the "proportion of the whole population that has IQs above 108."

4. For normal distributions, these probabilities (proportions) can be found in the unit normal table. This table provides a listing of the proportions of a normal distribution that correspond to each z-score value. With this table, it is possible to move between X values and probabilities using a two-step procedure:
   a. The z-score formula (Chapter 5) allows you to transform X to z or to change z back to X.
   b. The unit normal table allows you to look up the probability (proportion) corresponding to each z-score or the z-score corresponding to each probability.

KEY TERMS

probability   simple random sample   sampling with replacement   unit normal table

FOCUS ON PROBLEM SOLVING

1. We have defined probability as being equivalent to a proportion, which means that you can restate every probability problem as a proportion problem. This definition is particularly useful when you are working with frequency distribution graphs where the population is represented by the whole graph and probabilities (proportions) are represented by portions of the graph. When working problems with the normal distribution, you always should start with a sketch of the distribution. You should shade the portion of the graph that reflects the proportion you are looking for.

2. When using the unit normal table, you must remember that the proportions in the table (columns B and C) correspond to specific portions of the distribution. This is important because you will often need to translate the proportions from a problem into specific proportions provided in the table. Also remember that the table allows you to move back and forth between z-scores and proportions. You can look up a given z-score to find a proportion, or you can look up a given proportion to find the corresponding z-score. However, you cannot go directly from an X value to a probability in the unit normal table. You must first compute the z-score for X. Likewise, you cannot go directly from a probability value to a raw score. First, you have to find the z-score associated with the probability (see Figure 6.11).

3. Remember that the unit normal table shows only positive z-scores in column A. However, since the normal distribution is symmetrical, the probability values in columns B and C also apply to the half of the distribution that is below the mean. To be certain that you have the correct sign for z, it helps to sketch the distribution showing μ and X.

4. A common error for students is to use negative values for proportions on the left-hand side of the normal distribution. Proportions (or probabilities) are always positive: 10% is 10% whether it is in the left or the right tail of the distribution.

5. The proportions in the unit normal table are accurate only for normal distributions. If a distribution is not normal, you cannot use the table.

DEMONSTRATION 6.1

FINDING PROBABILITY FROM THE UNIT NORMAL TABLE

A population is normally distributed with a mean of $\mu = 45$ and a standard deviation of $\sigma = 4$. What is the probability of randomly selecting a score that is greater than 43? In other words, what proportion of the distribution consists of scores greater than 43?

STEP 1   Sketch the distribution.

You should always start by sketching the distribution, identifying the mean and the standard deviation ($\mu = 45$ and $\sigma = 4$ in this example). You should also find the approximate location of the specified score and draw a vertical line through the distribution at that score. The score of $X = 43$ is lower than the mean, and, therefore, it should be placed somewhere to the left of the mean. Figure 6.13(a) shows the preliminary sketch.

STEP 2   Shade in the distribution.

Read the problem again to determine whether you want the proportion greater than the score (to the right of your vertical line) or less than the score (to the left of the line). Then shade in the appropriate portion of the distribution. In this demonstration, we are considering scores greater than 43. Thus, we shade in the distribution to the right of this score [Figure 6.13(b)]. Note that if the shaded area covers more than one-half of the distribution, then the probability should be greater than 0.5000.

STEP 3   Transform the X value into a z-score.

Remember, to get a probability from the unit normal table, we must first convert the X value to a z-score.

$$z = \frac{X - \mu}{\sigma} = \frac{43 - 45}{4} = \frac{-2}{4} = -0.5$$

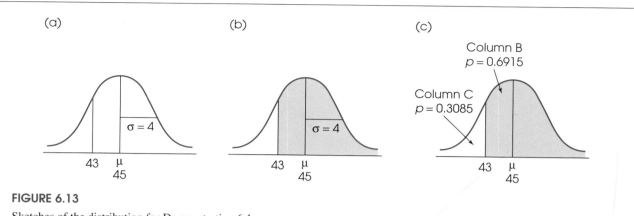

FIGURE 6.13

Sketches of the distribution for Demonstration 6.1.

STEP 4   Consult the unit normal table.

Look up the z-score (ignoring the sign) in the unit normal table. Find the two proportions in the table that are associated with the z-score, and write the two proportions in the appropriate regions on the figure. Remember, column B gives the proportion of area in the body of the distribution (more than 50%), and column C gives the area in the tail beyond z. Figure 6.13(c) shows the proportions for different regions of the normal distribution.

STEP 5   Determine the probability.

If one of the proportions in step 4 corresponds exactly to the entire shaded area, then that proportion is your answer. Otherwise, you will need to do some additional arithmetic. In this example, the proportion in the shaded area is given in column B:

$$p(X > 43) = 0.6915$$

PROBLEMS

1. In a psychology class of 90 students, there are 30 males and 60 females. Of the 30 men, only 5 are freshmen. Of the 60 women, 10 are freshmen. If you randomly sample an individual from this class,
  a. What is the probability of obtaining a female?
  b. What is the probability of obtaining a freshman?
  c. What is the probability of obtaining a male freshman?

2. A jar contains 10 black marbles and 40 white marbles.
  a. If you randomly select a marble from the jar, what is the probability that you will get a white marble?
  b. If you are selecting a random sample of $n = 3$ marbles and the first 2 marbles are both white, what is the probability that the third marble will be black?

3. What requirements must be satisfied to have a *random sample*?

4. What is sampling with replacement, and why is it used?

5. For each of the following z-score values, sketch a normal distribution and draw a vertical line at the location of the z-score. Then, determine whether the tail is to the right or the left of the z-score and find the proportion of the distribution located in the tail.
  a. $z = 1.00$
  b. $z = -2.00$
  c. $z = 1.50$
  d. $z = -0.75$

6. For each of the following z-score values, sketch a normal distribution and draw a vertical line at the location of the z-score. Then, determine whether the body is to the right or the left of the z-score and find the proportion of the distribution located in the body.
   a. $z = 0.25$
   b. $z = -1.50$
   c. $z = 1.75$
   d. $z = -0.40$

7. Find each of the following probabilities for a normal distribution that has been transformed into z-scores.
   a. $p(z > 1.50)$
   b. $p(z > -2.00)$
   c. $p(z < 0.50)$
   d. $p(z < -0.75)$

8. Find each of the following probabilities for a normal distribution.
   a. $p(z > -0.25)$
   b. $p(z > 1.75)$
   c. $p(z < 0.90)$
   d. $p(z < -1.25)$

9. For a normal distribution, identify the z-score location that separates the distribution into the two sections described in each of the following:
   a. What z-score separates the top 10% of the distribution (right side) from the bottom 90% (left side)?
   b. What z-score separates the top 40% from the bottom 60%?
   c. What z-score separates the top 80% from the bottom 20%?

10. For a normal distribution, identify the z-score location that would separate the distribution into sections as described in each of the following:
    a. What z-score would separate the distribution so that there is 20% in the tail on the right-hand side?
    b. What z-score would separate the distribution so that there is 25% in the tail on the right-hand side?
    c. What z-score would separate the distribution so that there is 15% in the tail on the left-hand side?
    d. What z-score would separate the distribution so that there is 30% in the tail on the left-hand side?

11. For each of the following pairs of z-scores, find the proportion of a normal distribution that is located between the two z-score values.
    a. Between $z = 1.50$ and $z = 2.00$
    b. Between $z = -1.00$ and $z = -0.50$
    c. Between $z = 0$ and $z = 2.00$
    d. Between $z = -1.50$ and $z = 0.25$

12. For each of the following pairs of z-scores, find the proportion of a normal distribution that is located between the two z-score values.
    a. Between $z = -0.25$ and $z = 0.25$
    b. Between $z = -0.50$ and $z = 0.50$
    c. Between $z = -1.00$ and $z = 1.00$
    d. Between $z = -1.96$ and $z = 1.96$

13. For a normal distribution, find the z-score values that divide the distribution as described in each of the following.
    a. What z-scores separate the middle 80% from the extreme 20% in the tails?
    b. What z-scores separate the middle 85% from the extreme 15% in the tails?
    c. What z-scores separate the middle 90% from the extreme 10% in the tails?
    d. What z-scores separate the middle 95% from the extreme 5% in the tails?

14. Identify the z-score values that separate each of the following sections from the rest of the scores in a normal distribution.
    a. The middle 30%
    b. The middle 50%
    c. The middle 70%
    d. The middle 95%

15. Answer each of the following for a positively skewed distribution. (*Caution:* This is a trick question.)
    a. Find the proportion of the distribution located in the tail beyond $z = 2.00$.
    b. What z-score value separates the top 40% of the distribution from the rest?

16. A normal distribution has $\mu = 80$ and $\sigma = 20$. For each of the following scores, indicate whether the tail of the distribution is located to the right or the left of the score, and find the proportion of the distribution located in the tail.
    a. $X = 85$
    b. $X = 92$
    c. $X = 70$
    d. $X = 64$

17. A normal distribution has $\mu = 60$ and $\sigma = 12$. For each of the following scores, indicate whether the body of the distribution is located to the right or the left of the score, and find the proportion of the distribution located in the body.
    a. $X = 75$
    b. $X = 69$
    c. $X = 57$
    d. $X = 48$

18. The distribution of IQ scores is normal with $\mu = 100$ and $\sigma = 15$.
    a. What proportion of the population have IQ scores above 130?
    b. What proportion of the population have IQ scores below 90?
    c. What proportion of the population have IQ scores above 110?

19. The distribution of scores on the SAT is approximately normal with $\mu = 500$ and $\sigma = 100$.
    a. What proportion of the population have SAT scores above 650?
    b. What proportion of the population have SAT scores below 540?
    c. What is the minimum SAT score needed to be in the highest 20% of the population?
    d. What SAT score separates the top 60% from the rest of the distribution?

20. The distribution of SAT scores is normal with $\mu = 500$ and $\sigma = 100$.
    a. What SAT score, X value, separates the top 10% from the rest of the distribution?
    b. What SAT score, X value, separates the top 30% from the rest of the distribution?
    c. What SAT score, X value, separates the top 40% from the rest of the distribution?

21. A population forms a normal distribution with $\mu = 68$ and $\sigma = 6$. Find the following probabilities:
    a. The probability of selecting a score with a value less than 60
    b. The probability of selecting a score with a value greater than 58
    c. The probability of selecting a score with a value greater than 74

22. For a normal distribution with $\mu = 100$ and $\sigma = 16$,
    a. What is the probability of randomly selecting a score greater than 104?
    b. What is the probability of randomly selecting a score greater than 96?
    c. What is the probability of randomly selecting a score less than 108?
    d. What is the probability of randomly selecting a score less than 92?

23. A normal distribution has $\mu = 225$ with $\sigma = 15$. Find the following probabilities:
    a. $p(X > 227)$
    b. $p(X > 212)$
    c. $p(X < 230)$
    d. $p(X < 220)$

24. A normal distribution has a mean of 80 and a standard deviation of 10. For this distribution, find each of the following probability values:
    a. $p(X > 75) = ?$
    b. $p(X < 65) = ?$
    c. $p(X < 100) = ?$
    d. $p(65 < X < 95) = ?$
    e. $p(84 < X < 90) = ?$

25. A normal distribution has $\mu = 75$ with $\sigma = 9$. Find the following probabilities:
    a. $p(X < 86) = ?$
    b. $p(X > 60) = ?$
    c. $p(X > 80) = ?$
    d. $p(X > 94) = ?$
    e. $p(63 < X < 88) = ?$
    f. The probability of randomly selecting a score within 3 points of the mean.

26. The distribution of SAT scores is normal with $\mu = 500$ and $\sigma = 100$.
    a. What SAT scores, X values, separate the middle 60% from the rest of the distribution?
    b. What SAT scores, X values, separate the middle 80% from the rest of the distribution?
    c. What SAT scores, X values, separate the middle 95% from the rest of the distribution?

CHAPTER 7

PROBABILITY AND SAMPLES: THE DISTRIBUTION OF SAMPLE MEANS

TOOLS YOU WILL NEED

The following items are considered essential background material for this chapter. If you doubt your knowledge of any of these items, you should review the appropriate chapter and section before proceeding.

- Random sampling (Chapter 6)
- Probability and the normal distribution (Chapter 6)
- z-Scores (Chapter 5)

CONTENTS

7.1   SAMPLES AND SAMPLING ERROR

The preceding two chapters presented the topics of z-scores and probability. Whenever a score is selected from a population, you should be able to compute a z-score that describes exactly where the score is located in the distribution. Also, if the population is normal, you should be able to determine the probability value for each score. In a normal distribution, for example, a z-score of $+2.00$ corresponds to an extreme score out in the tail of the distribution, and a score this large has a probability of only $p = .0228$.

However, the z-scores and probabilities that we have considered so far are limited to situations where the sample consists of a single score. Most research studies use much larger samples, such as $n = 25$ preschool children or $n = 100$ laboratory rats. In this chapter, we will extend the concepts of z-scores and probability to cover situations with larger samples. Thus, a researcher will be able to compute a z-score that describes an entire sample. A z value near zero indicates a central, representative sample; a z value beyond $+2.00$ or -2.00 indicates an extreme sample. Also, it will be possible to determine exact probabilities for samples, no matter how many scores the sample contains.

In general, the difficulty of working with samples is that a sample provides an incomplete picture of the population. Suppose, for example, a researcher selects a sample of $n = 25$ students from the State College. Although the sample should be representative of the entire student population, there will almost certainly be some segments of the population that are not included in the sample. In addition, any statistics that are computed for the sample will not be identical to the corresponding parameters for the entire population. For example, the average IQ for the sample of 25 students will not be the same as the overall mean IQ for the entire population. This difference, or *error* between sample statistics and the corresponding population parameters, is called *sampling error.*

DEFINITION   *Sampling error* is the discrepancy, or amount of error, between a sample statistic and its corresponding population parameter.

Furthermore, samples are variable; they are not all the same. If you take two separate samples from the same population, the samples will be different. They will contain different individuals, they will have different scores, and they will have different sample means. How can you tell which sample is giving the best description of the population? Can you even predict how well a sample will describe its population? What is the probability of selecting a sample that has a certain sample mean? These questions can be answered once we establish the set of rules that relate samples to populations.

7.2   THE DISTRIBUTION OF SAMPLE MEANS

As noted, two separate samples probably will be different even though they are taken from the same population. The samples will have different individuals, different scores, different means, and the like. In most cases, it is possible to obtain thousands of different samples from one population. With all these different samples coming from the same population, it may seem hopeless to try to establish some simple rules for the relationships between samples and populations. Fortunately, the huge set of possible samples forms a relatively simple, orderly, and predictable pattern that makes it possible to predict the characteristics of a sample with some accuracy. The ability to predict sample characteristics is based on the *distribution of sample means.*

DEFINITION

The *distribution of sample means* is the collection of sample means for all the possible random samples of a particular size (*n*) that can be obtained from a population.

You should notice that the distribution of sample means contains *all the possible samples.* It is necessary to have all the possible values in order to compute probabilities. For example, if the entire set contains exactly 100 samples, then the probability of obtaining any specific sample is 1 out of 100; $p = 1/100$.

Also, you should notice that the distribution of sample means is different from distributions we have considered before. Until now we always have discussed distributions of scores; now the values in the distribution are not scores, but statistics (sample means). Because statistics are obtained from samples, a distribution of statistics is referred to as a sampling distribution.

DEFINITION

A *sampling distribution* is a distribution of statistics obtained by selecting all the possible samples of a specific size from a population.

Thus, the distribution of sample means is an example of a sampling distribution. In fact, it often is called the sampling distribution of $\overline{X}$.

If you actually wanted to construct the distribution of sample means, you would first select a random sample of a specific size (*n*) from a population, calculate the sample mean, and write it down on a piece of paper. Then select another random sample of *n* scores from the population. Again, you calculate the sample mean and write it down. You continue selecting samples and calculating means, over and over. Eventually, you will have the complete set of all the possible random samples, and the means that you have written on your paper will form the distribution of sample means. Although we demonstrate this process in Example 7.1, we will soon describe a much easier way to construct the distribution of sample means.

EXAMPLE 7.1   Consider a population that consists of only four scores: 2, 4, 6, 8. This population is pictured in the frequency distribution histogram in Figure 7.1.

FIGURE 7.1

Frequency distribution histogram for a population of four scores: 2, 4, 6, 8.

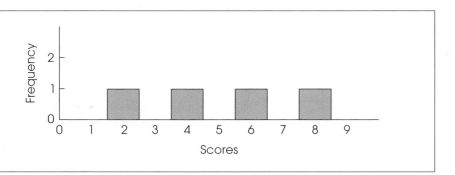

TABLE 7.1

All the possible samples of $n = 2$ scores that can be obtained from the population presented in Figure 7.1.

Notice that the table lists *random samples*. This requires sampling with replacement so it is possible to select the same score twice. Also note that samples are listed systematically. The first four samples are all the possible samples that have $X = 2$ as the first score, the next four samples all have $X = 4$ as the first score, and so on. This way we are sure to have all the possible samples listed, although the samples probably would not be selected in this order.

Sample	First score	Second score	Sample mean $(\overline{X})$
1	2	2	2
2	2	4	3
3	2	6	4
4	2	8	5
5	4	2	3
6	4	4	4
7	4	6	5
8	4	8	6
9	6	2	4
10	6	4	5
11	6	6	6
12	6	8	7
13	8	2	5
14	8	4	6
15	8	6	7
16	8	8	8

We are going to use this population as the basis for constructing the distribution of sample means for $n = 2$. Remember, this distribution is the collection of sample means from all the possible random samples of $n = 2$ from this population. We begin by looking at all the possible samples. Each of the 16 different samples is listed in Table 7.1.

Next, we compute the mean, $\overline{X}$, for each of the 16 samples (see the last column of Table 7.1). The 16 sample means form the distribution of sample means. These 16 values are organized in a frequency distribution histogram in Figure 7.2.

Remember, random sampling requires sampling with replacement.

FIGURE 7.2

The distribution of sample means for $n = 2$. This distribution shows the 16 sample means from Table 7.1.

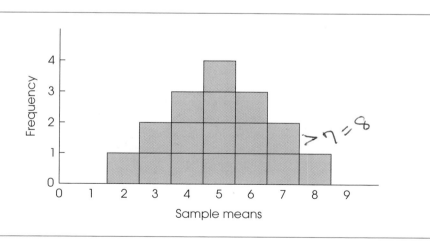

Note that the distribution of sample means has some predictable and some very useful characteristics:

1. The sample means tend to pile up around the population mean. For this example, the population mean is $\mu = 5$, and the sample means are clustered

around a value of 5. It should not surprise you that the sample means tend to approximate the population mean. After all, samples are supposed to be representative of the population.

2. The distribution of sample means is approximately normal in shape. This characteristic will be discussed in detail later and will be extremely useful because you already know a great deal about probabilities and the normal distribution (Chapter 6).

Remember, our goal in this chapter is to answer probability questions about samples with $n > 1$.

3. Finally, note that we can use the distribution of sample means to answer probability questions about sample means. For example, if you take a sample of $n = 2$ scores from the original population, what is the probability of obtaining a sample mean greater than 7? In symbols, $p(\overline{X} > 7) = ?$.

Because probability is equivalent to proportion, the probability question can be restated as follows: Of all the possible sample means, what proportion has values greater than 7? In this form, the question is easily answered by looking at the distribution of sample means. All the possible sample means are pictured (Figure 7.2), and only 1 out of the 16 means has a value greater than 7. The answer therefore is 1 out of 16, or $p = \frac{1}{16}$.

THE CENTRAL LIMIT THEOREM

Example 7.1 demonstrates the construction of the distribution of sample means for a relatively simple, specific situation. In most cases, however, it will not be possible to list all the samples and compute all the possible sample means. As the size (n) of the samples increases, the number of possible samples increases rapidly. Therefore, it is necessary to develop the general characteristics of the distribution of sample means that can be applied in any situation. Fortunately, these characteristics are specified in a mathematical proposition known as the *central limit theorem*. This important and useful theorem serves as a cornerstone for much of inferential statistics. Following is the essence of the theorem.

DEFINITION

Central limit theorem: For any population with mean μ and standard deviation σ, the distribution of sample means for sample size n will have a mean of μ and a standard deviation of $\sigma/\sqrt{n}$ and will approach a normal distribution as n approaches infinity.

The value of this theorem comes from two simple facts. First, it describes the distribution of sample means for *any population,* no matter what shape, mean, or standard deviation. Second, the distribution of sample means "approaches" a normal distribution very rapidly. By the time the sample size reaches $n = 30$, the distribution is almost perfectly normal.

Note that the central limit theorem describes the distribution of sample means by identifying the three basic characteristics that describe any distribution: shape, central tendency, and variability. We will examine each of these.

THE SHAPE OF THE DISTRIBUTION OF SAMPLE MEANS

It has been observed that the distribution of sample means tends to be a normal distribution. In fact, this distribution will be almost perfectly normal if either one of the following two conditions is satisfied.

1. The population from which the samples are selected is a normal distribution.

2. The number of scores (n) in each sample is relatively large, around 30 or more.

(As *n* gets larger, the distribution of sample means will closely approximate a normal distribution. In most situations when $n > 30$, the distribution is almost perfectly normal regardless of the shape of the original population.)

The fact that the distribution of sample means tends to be normal should not be surprising. Whenever you take a sample from a population, you expect the sample mean to be near the population mean. When you take lots of different samples, you expect the sample means to "pile up" around μ, resulting in a normal-shaped distribution.

THE MEAN OF THE DISTRIBUTION OF SAMPLE MEANS: THE EXPECTED VALUE OF $\overline{X}$

You probably noticed in Example 7.1 that the distribution of sample means is centered around the mean of the population from which the samples were obtained. In fact, the average value of all the sample means is exactly equal to the value of the population mean. This fact should be intuitively reasonable; the sample means are expected to be close to the population mean, and they do tend to pile up around μ. The formal statement of this phenomenon is that the mean of the distribution of sample means always will be identical to the population mean. This mean value is called the *expected value of $\overline{X}$*.

DEFINITION

The mean of the distribution of sample means is equal to μ (the population mean) and is called the *expected value of $\overline{X}$*.

The expected value of $\overline{X}$ is often identified by the symbol $\mu_{\overline{X}}$, signifying the "mean of the sample means." However, $\mu_{\overline{X}}$ is always equal to μ, so we will continue to use the symbol μ to refer to the mean for the population of scores and the mean for the distribution of sample means.

In commonsense terms, a sample mean is "expected" to be near its population mean. When all of the possible sample means are obtained, the average value will be identical to μ.

The fact that the average value of $\overline{X}$ is equal to μ was first introduced in Chapter 4 (page 93) in the context of *biased* versus *unbiased* statistics. The sample mean is an example of an unbiased statistic, which means that on average the sample statistic produces a value that is exactly equal to the corresponding population parameter. In this case, the average value of all the sample means is exactly equal to μ.

THE STANDARD ERROR OF $\overline{X}$

So far we have considered the shape and the central tendency of the distribution of sample means. To completely describe this distribution, we need one more characteristic, variability. The measure we will be working with is the standard deviation for the distribution of sample means, and it is called the *standard error of $\overline{X}$*. Like any measure of standard deviation, the standard error defines the standard, or typical, distance from the mean. In this case, we are measuring the standard distance between a single sample mean, $\overline{X}$, and the population mean, μ. Remember, a sample is not expected to provide a perfectly accurate reflection of its population. Although a sample mean should be representative of the population mean, there typically will be some error between the sample and the population. The standard error measures exactly how much difference should be expected, on average, between $\overline{X}$ and μ.

DEFINITION

The standard deviation of the distribution of sample means is called the *standard error of $\overline{X}$*. The standard error measures the standard amount of difference one should expect between $\overline{X}$ and μ simply due to chance.

$$\text{Standard error} = \sigma_{\overline{X}} = \text{standard distance between } \overline{X} \text{ and } \mu$$

The notation that is used to identify the standard error is $\sigma_{\overline{X}}$. The σ indicates that we are measuring a standard deviation or a standard distance from the mean. The subscript

7.1 THE ERROR BETWEEN $\overline{X}$ AND μ

CONSIDER A population consisting of $N = 3$ scores: 1, 8, 9. The mean for this population is $\mu = 6$. Using this population, try to find a random sample of $n = 2$ scores with a sample mean ($\overline{X}$) exactly equal to the population mean. (Try selecting a few samples; record the scores and the sample mean for each of your samples.)

You may have guessed that we constructed this problem so that it is impossible to obtain a sample mean that is identical to μ. The point of the exercise is to emphasize the notion of sampling error. Samples are not identical to their populations, and a sample mean generally will not provide a perfect estimate of the population mean. The purpose of standard error is to provide a quantitative measure of the difference (or error) between sample means and the population mean. Standard error is the standard distance between $\overline{X}$ and μ.

$\overline{X}$ indicates that we are measuring the standard deviation for a distribution of sample means. The standard error is an extremely valuable measure because it specifies precisely how well a sample mean estimates its population mean—that is, how much error you should expect, on the average, between $\overline{X}$ and μ. Remember, one basic reason for taking samples is to use the sample data to answer questions about the population. Specifically, we can use the sample mean as an estimate of the population mean. Although we do not expect a sample mean to be exactly the same as the population mean, it should provide a good estimate. The standard error tells how good the estimate will be (see Box 7.1).

The magnitude of the standard error is determined by two factors: (1) the size of the sample and (2) the standard deviation of the population from which the sample is selected. We will examine each of these factors.

The sample size It should be intuitively reasonable that the size of a sample should influence how accurately the sample represents its population. Specifically, a large sample should be more accurate than a small sample. In general, as the sample size increases, the error between the sample mean and the population mean should decrease. This rule is also known as the *law of large numbers*.

DEFINITION   The *law of large numbers* states that the larger the sample size (n), the more probable it is that the sample mean will be close to the population mean.

The population standard deviation As we noted earlier, when the sample size decreases, the standard error increases. At the extreme, the smallest possible sample and the largest possible error occur when the sample consists of $n = 1$ score. At this extreme, the sample is a single score, X, and the sample mean also equals X. In this case, the standard error measures the standard distance between the score, X, and the population mean, μ. However, we already know that the standard distance between X and μ is the standard deviation. By definition, σ is the standard distance between X and μ. Thus, when $n = 1$, the standard error and the standard deviation are identical.

When $n = 1$,

$$\text{standard error} = \sigma_{\overline{X}} = \sigma = \text{standard deviation}$$

You can think of the standard deviation as the "starting point" for standard error. When $n = 1$, σ and $\sigma_{\overline{X}}$ are the same. As the sample size increases, the standard error decreases in relation to n.

The formula for standard error incorporates both the standard deviation and the sample size:

$$\text{standard error} = \sigma_{\overline{X}} = \frac{\sigma}{\sqrt{n}} \tag{7.1}$$

Note that the formula satisfies all the requirements for the concept of standard error. Specifically, as the sample size increases, the error decreases. As n decreases, the error increases. At the extreme, when $n = 1$, the standard error is equal to the standard deviation. In mathematical terms, the standard error is *directly* related to the population standard deviation and it is *inversely* related to the sample size. That is, when the standard deviation increases, the standard error also increases, but when the sample size increases, the standard error decreases.

In Equation 7.1 and in most of the preceding discussion, we have defined standard error in terms of the population standard deviation. However, the population standard deviation (σ) and the population variance (σ^2) are directly related, and it is easy to substitute variance into the equation for standard error. Using the simple equality $\sigma = \sqrt{\sigma^2}$, the equation for standard error can be rewritten as follows:

$$\text{standard error} = \sigma_{\overline{X}} = \frac{\sigma}{\sqrt{n}} = \frac{\sqrt{\sigma^2}}{\sqrt{n}} = \sqrt{\frac{\sigma^2}{n}} \tag{7.2}$$

Throughout the rest of this chapter (and in Chapter 8), we will continue to define standard error in terms of the standard deviation (Equation 7.1). However, in later chapters (starting in Chapter 9), the formula based on variance (Equation 7.2) will become more useful.

LEARNING CHECK

1. A population of scores is normal with $\mu = 80$ and $\sigma = 20$.

   a. Describe the distribution of sample means for samples of size $n = 16$ selected from this population. (Describe shape, central tendency, and variability for the distribution.)

   b. How would the distribution of sample means be changed if the sample size were $n = 100$ instead of $n = 16$?

2. As sample size increases, the value of the standard error also increases. (True or false?)

3. Under what circumstances will the distribution of sample means be a normal-shaped distribution?

ANSWERS

1. a. The distribution of sample means would be normal with a mean (expected value) of $\mu = 80$ and a standard error of $\sigma_{\overline{X}} = 20/\sqrt{16} = 5$.

   b. The distribution would still be normal with a mean of 80 but the standard error would be reduced to $\sigma_{\overline{X}} = 20/\sqrt{100} = 2$.

2. False. Standard error decreases as n increases.

3. The distribution of sample means will be normal if the sample size is relatively large (around $n = 30$ or more) or if the population of scores is normal. ◆

7.3 PROBABILITY AND THE DISTRIBUTION OF SAMPLE MEANS

The primary use of the distribution of sample means is to find the probability associated with any specific sample. Recall that probability is equivalent to proportion. Because the distribution of sample means presents the entire set of all possible $\overline{X}$'s, we can use proportions of this distribution to determine probabilities. The following example demonstrates this process.

EXAMPLE 7.2   The population of scores on the SAT forms a normal distribution with $\mu = 500$ and $\sigma = 100$. If you take a random sample of $n = 25$ students, what is the probability that the sample mean would be greater than $\overline{X} = 540$?

First, you can restate this probability question as a proportion question: Out of all the possible sample means, what proportion has values greater than 540? You know about "all the possible sample means"; this is simply the distribution of sample means. The problem is to find a specific portion of this distribution. The parameters of this distribution are the following:

Caution: Whenever you have a probability question about a sample mean, you must use the distribution of sample means.

   a. The distribution is normal because the population of SAT scores is normal.

   b. The distribution has a mean of 500 because the population mean is $\mu = 500$.

   c. The distribution has a standard error of $\sigma_{\overline{X}} = 20$:

$$\sigma_{\overline{X}} = \frac{\sigma}{\sqrt{n}} = \frac{100}{\sqrt{25}} = \frac{100}{5} = 20$$

This distribution of sample means is shown in Figure 7.3.

We are interested in sample means greater than 540 (the shaded area in Figure 7.3), so the next step is to find the z-score value that defines the exact location of $\overline{X} = 540$ in the distribution. The value 540 is located above the mean by 40 points, which is exactly 2 standard deviations (in this case, exactly 2 standard errors). Thus, the z-score for $\overline{X} = 540$ is $z = +2.00$.

FIGURE 7.3

The distribution of sample means for $n = 25$. Samples were selected from a normal population with $\mu = 500$ and $\sigma = 100$.

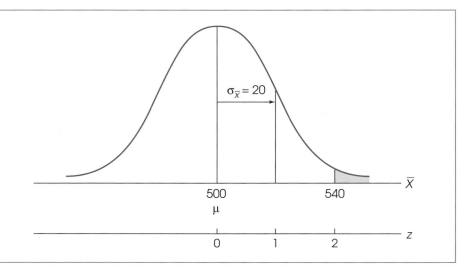

Because this distribution of sample means is normal, you can use the unit normal table to find the probability associated with $z = +2.00$. The table indicates that 0.0228 of the distribution is located in the tail of the distribution beyond $z = +2.00$. Our conclusion is that it is very unlikely, $p = 0.0228$ (2.28%), to obtain a random sample of $n = 25$ students with an average SAT score greater than 540.

looking at for tail greater than 540

A Z-SCORE FOR SAMPLE MEANS

As demonstrated in Example 7.2, it is possible to use a z-score to describe the position of any specific sample within the distribution of sample means. The z-score tells exactly where a specific sample is located in relation to all the other possible samples that could have been obtained. A z-score of $z = +2.00$, for example, indicates that the sample mean is much larger than usually would be expected: It is greater than the expected value of $\overline{X}$ by twice the standard distance. The z-score for each sample mean can be computed by using the standard z-score formula with a few minor changes. First, the value we are locating is a sample mean, rather than a score so the formula uses $\overline{X}$ in place of X. Second, the standard deviation for this distribution is measured by the standard error, so the formula uses $\sigma_{\overline{X}}$ in place of σ. The resulting formula, giving the z-score value corresponding to any sample mean, is

Caution: When computing z for a single score, use the standard deviation, σ. When computing z for a sample mean, you must use the standard error, $\sigma_{\overline{X}}$.

$$z = \frac{\overline{X} - \mu}{\sigma_{\overline{X}}}$$

(7.3)

Every sample mean has a z-score that describes its position in the distribution of sample means. Using z-scores and the unit normal table, it is possible to find the probability associated with any specific sample mean (as in Example 7.2). The following example demonstrates that it also is possible to make quantitative predictions about the kinds of samples that should be obtained from any population.

EXAMPLE 7.3

Once again, the population of SAT scores forms a normal distribution with $\mu = 500$ and $\sigma = 100$. What kind of sample mean is likely to be obtained as the average SAT score for a random sample of $n = 25$ students? Specifically, what range of values would be expected for the sample mean 80% of the time? We begin by looking at the distribution of sample means. Remember that this distribution is the collection of all the possible sample means, and it will show which samples are likely to be obtained and which are not.

Remember that when answering probability questions, it always is helpful to sketch a distribution and shade in the portion you are trying to find.

As demonstrated in Example 7.2, the distribution of sample means for $n = 25$ will be normal, will have an expected value of $\mu = 500$, and will have a standard error of $\sigma_{\overline{X}} = 20$. Looking at this distribution, shown again in Figure 7.4, it is clear that the most likely value to expect for a sample mean is around 500. To be more precise, we can identify the range of values that would be expected 80% of the time by locating the middle 80% of the distribution. Because the distribution is normal, we can use the unit normal table. To find the middle 80%, we need to separate the extreme 20% in the tails. This corresponds to 10% (or .1000) in each of the two tails. Looking up a proportion of .1000 in the unit normal table (column C) gives a z-score of 1.28. Thus, the middle 80% is bounded by z-scores of $z = \pm 1.28$. By definition, $z = 1.28$ indicates a location exactly 1.28 standard error units from the mean. This distance is $1.28 \times 20 = 25.6$ points. The mean is 500, so 25.6 points in either direction would give a range from 474.4 to 525.6. This is the middle 80% of all the possible sample

FIGURE 7.4

The middle 80% of the distribution of sample means for n = 25. Samples were selected from a normal population with μ = 500 and σ = 100.

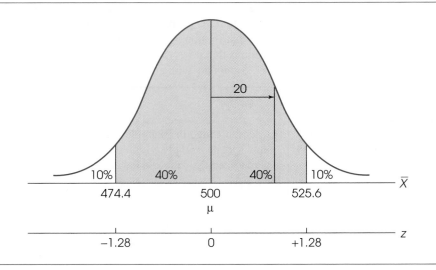

means, so you can expect any particular sample mean to be in this range 80% of the time.

LEARNING CHECK

1. A population has μ = 80 and σ = 12. Find the z-score corresponding to each of the following sample means:
   a. $\overline{X}$ = 84 for a sample of n = 9 scores
   b. $\overline{X}$ = 74 for a sample of n = 16 scores
   c. $\overline{X}$ = 81 for a sample of n = 36 scores

2. A random sample of n = 25 scores is selected from a normal population with μ = 90 and σ = 10.
   a. What is the probability that the sample mean will have a value greater than 94?
   b. What is the probability that the sample mean will have a value less than 91?

3. A positively skewed distribution has μ = 60 and σ = 8.
   a. What is the probability of obtaining a sample mean greater than $\overline{X}$ = 62 for a sample of n = 4 scores? (Be careful. This is a trick question.)
   b. What is the probability of obtaining a sample mean greater than $\overline{X}$ = 62 for a sample of n = 64 scores?

ANSWERS

1. a. The standard error is $12/\sqrt{9}$ = 4. The z-score is z = +1.00.
   b. The standard error is $12/\sqrt{16}$ = 3. The z-score is z = −2.00.
   c. The standard error is $12/\sqrt{36}$ = 2. The z-score is z = +0.50.

2. a. The standard error is $10/\sqrt{25}$ = 2. A mean of $\overline{X}$ = 94 corresponds to z = +2.00, and p = 0.0228.
   b. A mean of $\overline{X}$ = 91 corresponds to z = +0.50, and p = 0.6915.

3. a. The distribution of sample means does not satisfy either of the criteria for being normal. Therefore, you cannot use the unit normal table, and it is impossible to find the probability.

  b. With $n = 64$, the distribution of sample means is normal. The standard error is $8/\sqrt{64} = 1$, the z-score is $+2.00$, and the probability is 0.0228.   ◆

7.4 MORE ABOUT STANDARD ERROR

At the beginning of this chapter, we introduced the idea that it is possible to obtain thousands of different samples from a single population. Each sample will have its own individuals, its own scores, and its own sample mean. The distribution of sample means provides a method for organizing all of the different sample means into a single picture that shows how the sample means are related to each other and how they are related to the overall population mean. Figure 7.5 shows a prototypical distribution of sample means. To emphasize the fact that the distribution contains many different samples, we have constructed this figure so that the distribution is made up of hundreds of small boxes, each box representing a single sample mean. Note that the sample means tend to pile up around the population mean (μ), forming a normal-shaped distribution, as predicted by the central limit theorem.

FIGURE 7.5

An example of a typical distribution of sample means. Each of the small boxes represents the mean obtained for one sample. The normal curve is superimposed on the frequency distribution.

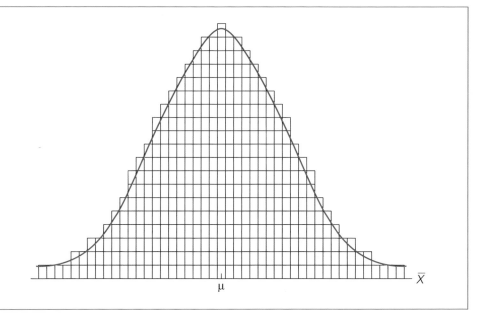

The distribution shown in Figure 7.5 provides a concrete example for reviewing the general concepts of *sampling error* and *standard error*. Although the following points may seem obvious, they are intended to provide you with a better understanding of these two statistical concepts.

1. Sampling Error: The general concept of sampling error is that a sample typically will not provide a perfectly accurate representation of its population. More specifically, there typically will be some discrepancy (or error) between a statistic computed for a sample and the corresponding parameter for the population. As you look at Figure 7.5, note that the individual sample means tend to *underestimate* or *overestimate* the population mean. In fact, 50% of the samples will have means that are smaller than μ (the entire left-hand side of the distribution). Similarly, 50% of the samples will produce means that overestimate the true population mean. In general, there will be some discrepancy, or *sampling error,* between the mean for a sample and the mean for the population from which the sample was obtained.

   2. Standard Error: Again, looking at Figure 7.5, note that most of the sample means are relatively close to the population mean (those in the center of the distribution). These samples provide a fairly accurate representation of the population. On the other hand, some samples will produce means that are out in the tails of the distribution, relatively far away from the population mean. These extreme sample means do not accurately represent the population. For each individual sample, you can measure the error (or distance) between the sample mean and the population mean. For some samples, the error will be relatively small, but for other samples, the error will be relatively large. The *standard error* provides a way to measure the "average" or standard distance between a sample mean and the population mean.

   Thus, the standard error provides a method for defining and measuring sampling error. The advantage of knowing the standard error is that it gives researchers a good indication of how accurately their sample data represent the populations they are studying. In most research situations, for example, the population mean is unknown, and the researcher selects a sample to help obtain information about the unknown population. Specifically, the sample mean provides information about the value of the unknown population mean. The sample mean is not expected to give a perfectly accurate representation of the population mean; there will be some error, and the standard error tells *exactly how much error,* on average, should exist between the sample mean and the unknown population mean.

STANDARD ERROR AND STATISTICAL INFERENCE

Inferential statistics are methods that use sample data as the basis for drawing general conclusions about populations. Most inferential statistics are used in the context of a research study. Typically, the researcher begins with a general question about how a treatment will affect the individuals in a population. This process is demonstrated in the following example.

EXAMPLE 7.4

Suppose that a psychologist is planning a research study to evaluate the effect of a new growth hormone. It is known that regular, adult rats (with no hormone) weigh an average of $\mu = 400$ grams. Of course, not all rats are the same size, and the distribution of their weights is normal with $\sigma = 20$. The psychologist plans to select a sample of $n = 25$ newborn rats, inject them with the hormone, and then measure their weights when they become adults. The structure of this research study is shown in Figure 7.6.

   The psychologist will make a decision about the effect of the hormone by comparing the sample of treated rats with the regular rats in the original population. For example, if the treated rats weigh an average of $\overline{X} = 800$ grams, does it appear that the

FIGURE 7.6

The structure of the research study described in Example 7.4. The purpose of the study is to determine whether or not the treatment (a growth hormone) has an effect on weight for rats.

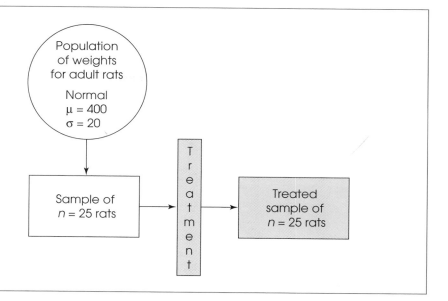

hormone had an effect? The answer should be obviously, yes. In this case, the rats in the treated sample are twice as big as the rats in the original population and the psychologist has a clear indication that the hormone affects weight.

Now suppose that the sample mean is 500 grams. Does it still look like the hormone has an effect? What about a sample mean of 450 grams? How about $\overline{X} = 410$ grams?

The point of this exercise is that the psychologist must decide whether or not the sample provides enough evidence to conclude that the hormone has an effect. That is, the psychologist must determine whether the rats in the treated sample are noticeably different from regular rats. The distribution of sample means and the standard error can help researchers make this kind of comparison. In particular, the distribution of sample means can be used to show exactly what would be expected for a sample of regular rats who do not receive any hormone injections. For this example, the distribution of sample means for $n = 25$ regular, untreated rats will have the following characteristics:

a. It will be a normal distribution, because the population of rat weights is normal.

b. It will have an expected value of 400, because the population mean is $\mu = 400$.

c. It will have a standard error of $\sigma_{\overline{X}} = 20/\sqrt{25} = 20/5 = 4$, because the population standard deviation is $\sigma = 20$ and the sample size is $n = 25$.

The distribution of sample mean is shown in Figure 7.7. Note that nearly all of the sample means for $n = 25$ untreated rats (no hormone) are between 392 grams and 408 grams. Although a few samples do have means outside this range, it is very unlikely to occur. Therefore, if the psychologist obtains a mean of $\overline{X} = 450$ (or even $\overline{X} = 410$) for

FIGURE 7.7

The distribution of sample means for samples of $n = 25$ untreated rats (from Example 7.2). Note that a sample of regular, untreated rats will usually produce a sample mean with a value between 392 grams and 408 grams.

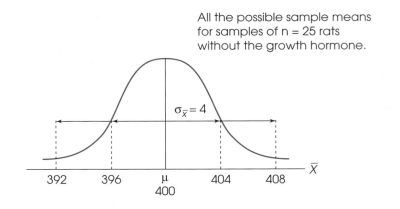

All the possible sample means for samples of n = 25 rats without the growth hormone.

$\sigma_{\bar{X}} = 4$

392   396 μ 404   408 $\bar{X}$
                400

the hormone-injected rats, it is a pretty clear indication that the rats in the treated sample are different from rats in a regular sample.

In Example 7.4 we used the distribution of sample means to provide a description of what is reasonable to expect for a regular sample. Then we evaluated the effect of a treatment by determining whether or not the treated sample was noticeably different from a regular (untreated) sample. This procedure forms the foundation for the inferential technique know as *hypothesis testing* that is introduced in the next chapter.

IN THE LITERATURE:
REPORTING STANDARD ERROR

As we will see later, the standard error plays a very important role in inferential statistics. Because of its crucial role, the standard error for a sample mean, rather than the sample standard deviation, is often reported in scientific papers. Scientific journals vary in how they refer to the standard error, but frequently the symbols *SE* and *SEM* (for standard error of the mean) are used. The standard error is reported in two ways. Much like the standard deviation, it may be reported in a table along with sample means (see Table 7.2). Alternatively, the standard error may be reported in graphs.

TABLE 7.2

The mean self-consciousness scores for subjects who were working in front of a video camera and those who were not (controls)

	n	Mean	*SE*
Control	17	32.23	2.31
Camera	15	45.17	2.78

Figure 7.8 illustrates the use of a bar graph to display information about the sample mean and the standard error. In this experiment, two samples (groups A and B) are given different treatments, and then the subjects' scores on a dependent variable are recorded. The mean for group A is $\overline{X} = 15$, and for group B, it is $\overline{X} = 30$. For both samples, the standard error of $\overline{X}$ is $\sigma_{\overline{X}} = 4$. Note that the mean is represented by the height of the bar and the standard error is depicted on the graph by brackets at the top of each bar. Each bracket extends 1 standard error above and 1 standard error below the sample mean. Thus, the graph illustrates the mean for each group plus or minus 1 standard error ($\overline{X} \pm SE$). When you glance at Figure 7.8, not only do you get a "picture" of the sample means, but also you get an idea of how much error you should expect for those means.

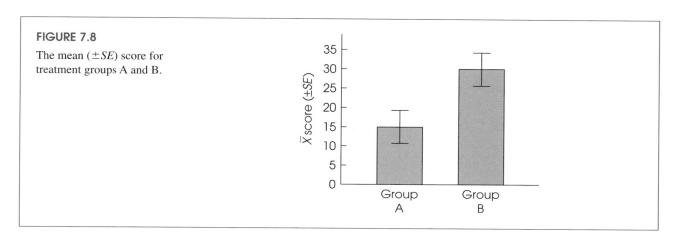

FIGURE 7.8

The mean ($\pm SE$) score for treatment groups A and B.

Figure 7.9 shows how sample means and standard error are displayed on a line graph. In this study, two samples (groups A and B) receive different treatments and then are tested on a task for four trials. The number of mistakes committed on each trial is recorded for all subjects. The graph shows the mean ($\overline{X}$) number of mistakes committed for each group on each trial. The brackets show the size of the standard error for each sample mean. Again, the brackets extend 1 standard error above and below the value of the mean.   ❏

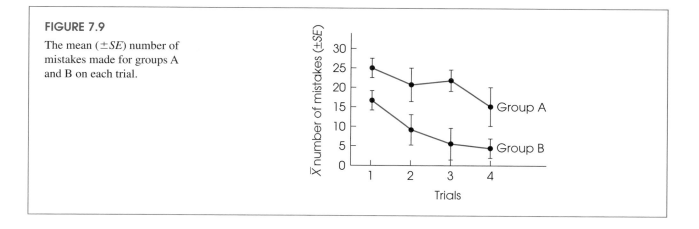

FIGURE 7.9

The mean ($\pm SE$) number of mistakes made for groups A and B on each trial.

LEARNING CHECK

1. A population has a standard deviation of $\sigma = 20$.

   a. If a single score is selected from this population, how close to the population mean, on average, would you expect the score to be?

   b. If a sample of $n = 4$ scores is selected from the population, how close to the population mean, on average, would you expect the sample mean to be?

   c. If a sample of $n = 25$ scores is selected from the population, how close to the population mean, on average, would you expect the sample mean to be?

2. Can the magnitude of the standard error ever be larger than the population standard deviation? Explain your answer.

3. A researcher plans to select a random sample of $n = 36$ individuals from a population with a standard deviation of $\sigma = 18$. On average, how much error should the researcher expect between the sample mean and the population mean?

4. A researcher plans to select a random sample from a population with a standard deviation of $\sigma = 20$.

   a. How large a sample is needed to have a standard error of 10 points or less?

   b. How large a sample is needed if the researcher wants the standard error to be 2 points or less?

A N S W E R S

1. **a.** The standard deviation, $\sigma = 20$, measures the standard distance between a score and the mean.

   b. The standard error is $20/\sqrt{4} = 10$ points.

   c. The standard error is $20/\sqrt{25} = 4$ points.

2. No. The standard error is always less than or equal to the standard deviation. The two values are equal only when $n = 1$.

3. The standard error is $18/\sqrt{36} = 3$ points.

4. **a.** A sample of $n = 4$ or larger.

   b. A sample of $n = 100$ or larger.

ON THE WEB

NOW THAT you have finished Chapter 7, you can test your knowledge with the practice quiz available on the Wadsworth Web site at **www.wadsworth.com**. In addition, there is a workshop on standard error that may give you another perspective on this important statistical concept. For more information about finding the quizzes and workshops, see page 24.

SUMMARY

1. The distribution of sample means is defined as the set of $\overline{X}$'s for all the possible random samples for a specific sample size (n) that can be obtained from a given population. According to the *central limit theorem*, the parameters of the distribution of sample means are as follows:

   a. *Shape.* The distribution of sample means will be normal if either of the following two conditions is satisfied:

   (1) The population from which the samples are selected is normal.

   (2) The size of the samples is relatively large (around $n = 30$ or more).

   b. *Central Tendency.* The mean of the distribution of sample means will be identical to the mean of the population from which the samples are selected. The mean of the distribution of sample means is called the expected value of $\overline{X}$.

   c. *Variability.* The standard deviation of the distribution of sample means is called the standard error of $\overline{X}$ and is defined by the formula

$$\sigma_{\overline{X}} = \frac{\sigma}{\sqrt{n}} \quad \sigma_{\overline{X}} = \sqrt{\frac{\sigma^2}{n}}$$

   Standard error measures the standard distance between a sample mean ($\overline{X}$) and the population mean (μ).

2. One of the most important concepts in this chapter is the standard error. The standard error is the standard deviation of the distribution of sample means. It measures the standard distance between a sample mean ($\overline{X}$) and the population mean (μ). The standard error tells how much error to expect if you are using a sample mean to estimate a population mean.

3. The location of each $\overline{X}$ in the distribution of sample means can be specified by a z-score:

$$z = \frac{\overline{X} - \mu}{\sigma_{\overline{X}}}$$

   Because the distribution of sample means tends to be normal, we can use these z-scores and the unit normal table to find probabilities for specific sample means. In particular, we can identify which sample means are likely and which are very unlikely to be obtained from any given population. This ability to find probabilities for samples is the basis for the inferential statistics in the chapters ahead.

4. In general terms, the standard error measures how much discrepancy you should expect, due to chance, between a sample statistic and a population parameter. Statistical inference involves using sample statistics to make a general conclusion about a population parameter. Thus, standard error plays a crucial role in inferential statistics.

KEY TERMS

sampling error

distribution of sample means

sampling distribution

central limit theorem

expected value of $\overline{X}$

standard error of $\overline{X}$

law of large numbers

FOCUS ON PROBLEM SOLVING

1. Whenever you are working probability questions about sample means, you must use the distribution of sample means. Remember, every probability question can be restated as a proportion question. Probabilities for sample means are equivalent to proportions of the distribution of sample means.

2. When computing probabilities for sample means, the most common error is to use standard deviation (σ) instead of standard error ($\sigma_{\overline{X}}$) in the z-score formula. Standard deviation measures the typical deviation (or "error") for a single score. Standard error measures the typical deviation (or error) for a sample. Remember, the larger the sample is, the more accurately the sample represents the population—that is, the larger the sample, the smaller the error.

$$\text{Standard error} = \sigma_{\overline{X}} = \frac{\sigma}{\sqrt{n}}$$

3. Although the distribution of sample means is often normal, it is not always a normal distribution. Check the criteria to be certain the distribution is normal before you use the unit normal table to find probabilities (see item 1a of the Summary). Remember, all probability problems with the normal distribution are easier if you sketch the distribution and shade in the area of interest.

DEMONSTRATION 7.1

PROBABILITY AND THE DISTRIBUTION OF SAMPLE MEANS

For a normally distributed population with $\mu = 60$ and $\sigma = 12$, what is the probability of selecting a random sample of $n = 36$ scores with a sample mean greater than 64?

In symbols, for $n = 36$, $p(\overline{X} > 64) = ?$

We may rephrase the probability question as a proportion question. Out of all the possible sample means for $n = 36$, what proportion have values greater than 64?

STEP 1   Sketch the distribution.

We are looking for a specific proportion of *all possible sample means*. Therefore, we will have to sketch the distribution of sample means. We should include the expected value, the standard error, and the specified sample mean.

The expected value for this demonstration is $\mu = 60$. The standard error is

$$\sigma_{\overline{X}} = \frac{\sigma}{\sqrt{n}} = \frac{12}{\sqrt{36}} = \frac{12}{6} = 2$$

Remember, we must use the standard error, *not* the standard deviation, because we are dealing with the distribution of sample means.

Find the approximate location of the sample mean, and place a vertical line through the distribution. In this demonstration, the sample mean is 64. It is larger than the expected value of $\mu = 60$ and therefore is placed on the right side of the distribution. Figure 7.10(a) depicts the preliminary sketch.

STEP 2   Shade the appropriate area of the distribution.

Determine whether the problem asks for a proportion greater than ($>$) or less than ($<$) the specified sample mean. Then shade the appropriate area of the distribution. In this

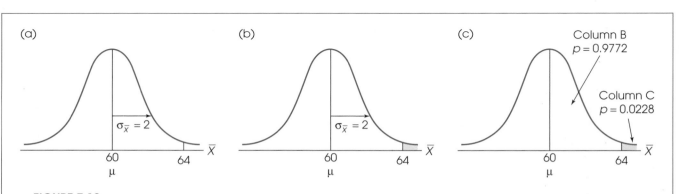

FIGURE 7.10

Sketches of the distribution for Demonstration 7.1.

demonstration, we are looking for the area greater than $\overline{X} = 64$, so we shade the area on the right-hand side of the vertical line [Figure 7.10(b)].

STEP 3   Compute the z-score for the sample mean.

Use the z-score formula for sample means. Remember that it uses standard error in the denominator.

$$z = \frac{\overline{X} - \mu}{\sigma_{\overline{X}}} = \frac{64 - 60}{2} = \frac{4}{2} = 2.00$$

STEP 4   Consult the unit normal table.

Look up the z-score in the unit normal table, and note the two proportions in columns B and C. Jot them down in the appropriate areas of the distribution [Figure 7.10(c)]. For this demonstration, the value in column C (the tail beyond z) corresponds exactly to the proportion we want (shaded area). Thus, for $n = 36$,

$$p(\overline{X} > 64) = p(z > +2.00) = 0.0228$$

PROBLEMS

1. Briefly define each of the following:
   a. Distribution of sample means
   b. Expected value of $\overline{X}$
   c. Standard error of $\overline{X}$

2. For each of the following, assume that the sample was selected from a population with $\mu = 75$ and $\sigma = 20$.
   a. What is the expected value of $\overline{X}$ for a sample of $n = 4$ scores?
   b. What is the standard error of $\overline{X}$ for a sample of $n = 4$ scores?
   c. What is the expected value of $\overline{X}$ for a sample of $n = 25$ scores?
   d. What is the standard error of $\overline{X}$ for a sample of $n = 25$ scores?

3. Describe the distribution of sample means (shape, expected value, and standard error) for samples of size $n = 36$ selected from a population with $\mu = 65$ and $\sigma = 12$.

4. The distribution of SAT scores is normal with $\mu = 500$ and $\sigma = 100$.
   a. If you selected a random sample of $n = 4$ scores from this population, how much error would you expect between the sample mean and the population mean?
   b. If you selected a random sample of $n = 25$ scores, how much error would you expect between the sample mean and the population mean?
   c. How much error would you expect for a sample of $n = 100$ scores?

5. IQ scores form normal distributions with $\sigma = 15$. However, the mean IQ varies from one population to another. For example, the mean IQ for registered voters is different from the mean for nonregistered voters. A researcher would like to use a sample to obtain information about the mean IQ for the population of licensed clinical psychologists in the state of California. Which sample mean should provide a more accurate representation of the population: a sample of $n = 9$ or a sample of $n = 25$? In each case, compute exactly how much error the researcher should expect between the sample mean and the population mean.

6. A distribution of scores has $\sigma = 6$, but the value of the mean is unknown. A researcher plans to select a sample from the population in order to learn more about the unknown mean.
   a. If the sample consists of a single score ($n = 1$), how accurately should the score represent the population mean? That is, how much error, on average, should the researcher expect between the score and the population mean?
   b. If the sample consists of $n = 9$ scores, how accurately should the sample mean represent the population mean?
   c. If the sample consists of $n = 36$ scores, how much error, on average, would be expected between the sample mean and the population mean?

7. A population has $\mu = 60$ and $\sigma = 10$. Find the z-score corresponding to each of the following sample means:
   a. A sample of $n = 4$ with $\overline{X} = 55$
   b. A sample of $n = 25$ with $\overline{X} = 64$
   c. A sample of $n = 100$ with $\overline{X} = 62$

8. The following samples were each selected from a population with $\mu = 35$ and $\sigma = 8$. Calculate the z-score corresponding to each sample mean.
   a. A sample of $n = 4$ scores with $\overline{X} = 37$.
   b. A sample of $n = 16$ scores with $\overline{X} = 37$.
   c. A sample of $n = 64$ scores with $\overline{X} = 37$.

9. For each of the following, assume that the sample was selected from a normal population with $\mu = 65$ and $\sigma = 10$.
   a. For a sample of $n = 4$, would a sample mean of $\overline{X} = 70$ be considered an extreme value compared to other samples of $n = 4$ scores? Explain your answer.
   b. For a sample of $n = 25$, would a sample mean of $\overline{X} = 70$ be considered an extreme value compared to other samples of $n = 25$ scores? Explain your answer.

10. If you are taking a random sample from a normal population with $\mu = 100$ and $\sigma = 16$, which of the following outcomes is more likely? Explain your answer. (*Hint:* Calculate the z-score for each sample mean.)
    a. A sample mean greater than 106 for a sample of $n = 4$
    b. A sample mean greater than 103 for a sample of $n = 36$

11. A normal population has $\mu = 100$ and $\sigma = 20$.
    a. Sketch the distribution of sample means for random samples of $n = 25$.
    b. Using z-scores, find the boundaries that separate the middle 95% of the sample means from the extreme 5% in the tails of the distribution.
    c. A sample mean of $\overline{X} = 106$ is computed for a sample of $n = 25$ scores. Is this sample mean in the extreme 5%?

12. A normal population has $\mu = 80$ and $\sigma = 12$.
    a. Using this population, sketch the distribution of sample means for $n = 4$. Mark the location of the mean (expected value), and show the standard error in your sketch.
    b. Using your sketch from part (a), what proportion of samples of $n = 4$ will have sample means greater than 86? (Locate the position of $\overline{X} = 86$, find the corresponding z-score, and use the unit normal table to determine the proportion.)
    c. Sketch the distribution of sample means based on $n = 16$.
    d. Using your sketch from part (c), what proportion of samples of $n = 16$ will have sample means greater than 86?

13. A normal population has $\mu = 55$ and $\sigma = 8$.
    a. Sketch the distribution of sample means for samples of size $n = 16$ selected from this population.

b. What proportion of samples based on $n = 16$ will have sample means greater than 59?
   c. What proportion of samples with $n = 16$ will have sample means less than 56?
   d. What proportion of samples with $n = 16$ will have sample means between 53 and 57?

14. A normal population has $\mu = 35$ and $\sigma = 8$.
    a. Sketch the distribution of sample means for samples of $n = 4$ selected from this population. Show the expected value of $\overline{X}$ and the standard error in your sketch.
    b. For a sample of $n = 4$, what is the probability of selecting a random sample with a mean greater than $\overline{X} = 32$?
    c. Sketch the distribution of sample means for samples of $n = 16$ selected from this population. Show the expected value of $\overline{X}$ and the standard error in your sketch.
    d. For a sample of $n = 16$, what is the probability of selecting a random sample with a mean greater than $\overline{X} = 32$?

15. A normal population has $\mu = 80$ and $\sigma = 20$.
    a. Sketch the distribution of sample means for samples of $n = 25$ selected from this population. Show the expected value of $\overline{X}$ and the standard error in your sketch.
    b. What is the probability of obtaining a sample mean greater than $\overline{X} = 85$ for a random sample of $n = 25$ scores?
    c. Sketch the distribution of sample means for samples of $n = 100$ selected from this population. Show the expected value of $\overline{X}$ and the standard error in your sketch.
    d. What is the probability of obtaining a sample mean greater than $\overline{X} = 85$ for a random sample of $n = 100$ scores?

16. A normal population has $\mu = 70$ and $\sigma = 12$.
    a. Sketch the population distribution. What proportion of the scores have values greater than $X = 73$?
    b. Sketch the distribution of sample means for samples of size $n = 16$. What proportion of the sample means have values greater than 73?

17. For a normal population with $\mu = 70$ and $\sigma = 20$, what is the probability of obtaining a sample mean greater than 75
    a. For a random sample of $n = 4$ scores?
    b. For a random sample of $n = 16$ scores?
    c. For a random sample of $n = 100$ scores?

18. Standard error measures the standard distance between a sample mean and the population mean. For a population with $\sigma = 30$,
    a. How large a sample would be needed to have a standard error of 10 points or less?
    b. How large a sample would be needed to have a standard error of 5 points or less?
    c. Can the standard error ever be larger than the population standard deviation? Explain your answer.

19. For a population with a standard deviation of $\sigma = 20$:
    a. How large a sample would be needed to have a standard error less than 10 points?
    b. How large a sample would be needed to have a standard error less than 4 points?
    c. How large a sample would be needed to have a standard error less than 2 points?

20. A population has $\mu = 300$ and $\sigma = 80$.
    a. If a random sample of $n = 25$ scores is selected from this population, how much error would be expected between the sample mean and the population mean?
    b. If the sample size were 4 times larger, $n = 100$, how much error would be expected?
    c. If the sample size were increased again by a factor of 4 to $n = 400$, how much error would be expected?
    d. Comparing your answers to parts (a), (b), and (c), what is the relationship between sample size and standard error? (Note that the sample size was increased by a factor of 4 each time.)

21. Scores on a personality test form a normal distribution with $\mu = 80$ and $\sigma = 12$. If a random sample of $n = 16$ people is selected and the mean score is computed for this sample, then
    a. Sketch the distribution of all the possible sample means that could be obtained.
    b. Of all the possible sample means, what proportion will be greater than 85?
    c. What proportion of the sample means will be less than 83?
    d. What proportion of the sample means will be less than 74?
    e. Of all the possible sample means, what proportion will be within 4 points of the population mean? (That is, what proportion will be between 76 and 84?)

22. The average age for registered voters in the county is $\mu = 39.7$ years with $\sigma = 11.8$. The distribution of ages is approximately normal. During a recent jury trial in the county courthouse, a statistician noted that the average age for the 12 jurors was $\overline{X} = 50.4$ years.
    a. How likely is it to obtain a jury this old or older by chance?
    b. Is it reasonable to conclude that this jury is not a random sample of registered voters?

23. Boxes of sugar are filled by machine with considerable accuracy. The distribution of box weights is normal and has a mean of 32 ounces with a standard deviation of only 2 ounces. A quality control inspector takes a sample of $n = 16$ boxes and finds the sample contains, on the average, $\overline{X} = 31$ ounces of sugar. If the machine is working properly, what is the probability of obtaining a sample of 16 boxes that averages 31 ounces or less? Should the inspector suspect that the filling machinery needs repair?

24. A researcher evaluated the effectiveness of relaxation training in reducing anxiety. One sample of anxiety-ridden people received relaxation training, while a second sample did not. Then anxiety scores were measured for all subjects, using a standardized test. Use the information that is summarized in the following table to complete this exercise.

The effect of relaxation training on anxiety scores		
Group	Mean anxiety score	SE
Control group	36	7
Relaxation training	18	5

    a. Construct a bar graph that incorporates all of the information in the table.
    b. Looking at your graph, do you think the relaxation training really worked? Explain your answer.

25. Research examining sleep behavior demonstrates a relationship between age and average amount of sleep. The following data show the mean amount of sleep and the standard error for five samples representing five different ages. Sketch a line graph showing these data including the standard error for each sample mean.
    1 year: $\overline{X} = 13$ hours with SE $= 2$
    5 years: $\overline{X} = 11$ hours with SE $= 1\frac{1}{2}$
    10 years: $\overline{X} = 10$ hours with SE $= 1\frac{1}{2}$
    15 years: $\overline{X} = 8\frac{1}{2}$ hours with SE $= 1$
    20 years: $\overline{X} = 8$ hours with SE $= 1$

CHAPTER 8

INTRODUCTION TO HYPOTHESIS TESTING

TOOLS YOU WILL NEED

The following items are considered essential background material for this chapter. If you doubt your knowledge of any of these items, you should review the appropriate chapter or section before proceeding.

- z-Scores (Chapter 5)
- Distribution of sample means (Chapter 7)
  - Expected value
  - Standard error
  - Probability of sample means

CONTENTS

8.1   THE LOGIC OF HYPOTHESIS TESTING

Usually, it is impossible or impractical for a researcher to observe every individual in a population. Therefore, researchers usually collect data from a sample and then use the sample data to help answer questions about the population. In this chapter, we introduce a statistical procedure that allows researchers to use sample data to draw inferences about the population of interest. As we develop this new statistical procedure, we will use the statistical techniques that were introduced in the preceding three chapters; that is, we will combine the concepts of z-scores, probability, and the distribution of sample means to create a new statistical procedure known as a *hypothesis test.*

DEFINITION

A *hypothesis test* is a statistical method that uses sample data to evaluate a hypothesis about a population parameter.

In very simple terms, the logic underlying the hypothesis-testing procedure is as follows:

1. First, we state a hypothesis about a population. Usually the hypothesis concerns the value of the population mean. For example, we might hypothesize that the mean IQ for registered voters in the United States is $\mu = 110$.

2. Before we actually select a sample, we use the hypothesis to predict the characteristics that the sample should have. For example, if we hypothesize that the population mean IQ is $\mu = 110$, then we would predict that our sample should have a mean *around* 110. Remember, the sample should be similar to the population but you should always expect a certain amount of error.

3. Next, we obtain a random sample from the population. For example, we might select a random sample of $n = 200$ registered voters and compute the mean IQ for the sample.

4. Finally, we compare the obtained sample data with the prediction that was made from the hypothesis. If the sample mean is consistent with the prediction, we will conclude that the hypothesis is reasonable. But if there is a big discrepancy between the data and the prediction, we will decide that the hypothesis is wrong.

A hypothesis test is typically used in the context of a research study. That is, a researcher completes a research study and then uses a hypothesis test to evaluate the results. Depending on the type of research and the type of data, the details of the hypothesis test will change from one research situation to another. In later chapters, we will examine different versions of hypothesis testing that are used for different kinds of research. For now, however, we will focus on the basic elements that are common to all hypothesis tests. To accomplish this general goal, we will examine a hypothesis test as it applies to the simplest possible research study. In particular, we will look at the situation in which a researcher is using one sample to examine one unknown population.

Figure 8.1 shows the general research situation that we will use to introduce the process of hypothesis testing. Note that the researcher begins with a known population. This is the set of individuals as they exist *before treatment.* For this example, we are assuming that the original set of scores forms a normal distribution with $\mu = 26$ and $\sigma = 4$. The purpose of the research is to determine the effect of the treatment on the individuals in the population. That is, the goal is to determine what happens to the population *after the treatment is administered.* Specifically, the purpose is to determine whether or not the treatment has an effect on the population mean.

To simplify the hypothesis-testing situation, one basic assumption is made about the effect of the treatment: If the treatment has any effect, it is simply to add a constant amount to (or subtract a constant amount from) each individual's score. Recall from Chapters 3 and 4 that adding (or subtracting) a constant will change the mean but will not change the shape of the population, nor will it change the standard deviation. Thus, we will assume that the population after treatment has the same shape as the original population and the same standard deviation as the original population. This assumption is incorporated into the situation shown in Figure 8.1.

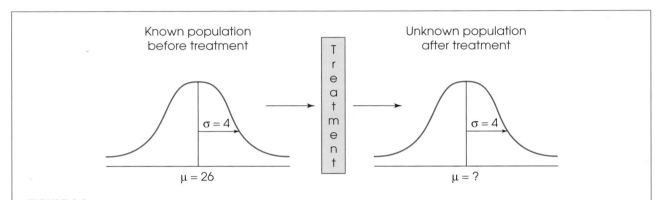

FIGURE 8.1

The basic experimental situation for hypothesis testing. It is assumed that the parameter μ is known for the population before treatment. The purpose of the experiment is to determine whether or not the treatment has an effect on the population mean.

A hypothesis test is a formalized procedure that follows a standard series of operations. In this way, researchers have a standardized method for evaluating the results of their research studies. Other researchers will recognize and understand exactly how the data were evaluated and how conclusions were reached. To emphasize the formal structure of a hypothesis test, we will present hypothesis tests as a four-step process that will be used throughout the rest of the book. The following example will be used to provide a concrete foundation for introducing the hypothesis-testing procedure.

EXAMPLE 8.1   Psychologists have noted that stimulation during infancy can have profound effects on the development of infant rats. It has been demonstrated that stimulation (for example, increased handling) results in eyes opening sooner, more rapid brain maturation, faster growth, and larger body weight (see Levine, 1960). Based on the data, one might theorize that increased stimulation early in life can be beneficial. Suppose a researcher who is interested in this developmental theory would like to determine whether or not stimulation during infancy has an effect on human development.

It is known from national health statistics that the mean weight for 2-year-old children is μ = 26 pounds. The distribution of weights is normal with σ = 4 pounds. The researcher's plan is to obtain a sample of n = 16 newborn infants and give their parents detailed instructions for giving their children increased handling and stimulation. At age 2, each of the 16 infants will be weighed, and the mean weight for the sample will be computed. If the mean weight for the sample is substantially more (or less) than the general population mean, then the researcher can conclude that the increased handling did have an effect on development. On the other hand, if the mean weight for the sample is around 26 pounds (the same as the general population mean), then the researcher must conclude that increased handling does not appear to have any effect.

Figure 8.1 depicts the research situation that was described in the preceding example. Note that the mean weight for the population after treatment is unknown. Specifically, we do not know what will happen to the mean weight for 2-year-old children if the whole population receives special handling. However, we do have a sample of $n = 16$ children who have received special handling, and we can use this sample to draw inferences about the unknown population. The following four steps outline the hypothesis-testing procedure that allows us to use the sample data to answer questions about the unknown population.

STEP 1: STATE THE HYPOTHESES

As the name implies, the process of hypothesis testing begins by stating a hypothesis about the unknown population. Actually, we state two opposing hypotheses. Note that both hypotheses are stated in terms of population parameters.

The first and most important of the two hypotheses is called the *null hypothesis.* The null hypothesis states that the treatment has no effect. In general, the null hypothesis states that there is no change, no effect, no difference—nothing happened, hence the name *null.* The null hypothesis is identified by the symbol H_0. (The H stands for *hypothesis,* and the zero subscript indicates that this is the *zero-effect,* null hypothesis.) For the study in Example 8.1, the null hypothesis states that increased handling during infancy has *no effect* on body weight for the population of infants. In symbols, this hypothesis is

The goal of inferential statistics is to make general statements about the population by using sample data. Therefore, when testing hypotheses, we make our predictions about the population parameters.

$$H_0: \mu_{\text{infants handled}} = 26 \text{ pounds} \qquad \text{(Even with extra handling, the mean weight at 2 years is still 26 pounds.)}$$

DEFINITION

The *null hypothesis* (H_0) states that in the general population there is no change, no difference, or no relationship. In the context of an experiment, H_0 predicts that the independent variable (treatment) will have *no effect* on the dependent variable for the population.

The second hypothesis is simply the opposite of the null hypothesis, and it is called the *scientific* or *alternative hypothesis* (H_1). This hypothesis states that the treatment has an effect on the dependent variable.

DEFINITION

The *alternative hypothesis* (H_1) states that there is a change, a difference, or a relationship for the general population. In the context of an experiment, H_1 predicts that the independent variable (treatment) *will have an effect* on the dependent variable.

The null hypothesis and the alternative hypothesis are mutually exclusive and exhaustive. They cannot both be true. The data will determine which one should be rejected.

For this example, the alternative hypothesis predicts that handling does alter growth for the population. In symbols, H_1 is represented as

$$H_1: \mu_{\text{infants handled}} \neq 26 \qquad \text{(With handling, the mean will be different from 26 pounds.)}$$

Note that the alternative hypothesis simply states that there will be some type of change. It does not specify whether the effect will be increased or decreased growth. In some circumstances, it is appropriate to specify the direction of the effect in H_1. For example, the researcher might hypothesize that increased handling will increase growth ($\mu > 26$ pounds). This type of hypothesis results in a directional hypothesis test, which will be examined in detail later in this chapter. For now we will concentrate on nondirectional tests, where the hypotheses simply state that the treatment has some effect (H_1) or has no effect (H_0). For this example, we are examining whether handling in infancy does alter growth in some way (H_1) or has no effect (H_0). Also note that both hypotheses refer to a population whose mean is unknown—namely, the population of infants who receive extra handling early in life.

STEP 2: SET THE CRITERIA FOR A DECISION

The researcher will eventually use the data from the sample to evaluate the credibility of the null hypothesis. The data will either provide support for the null hypothesis or tend to refute the null hypothesis. In particular, if there is a big discrepancy between the data and the hypothesis, we will conclude that the hypothesis is wrong.

To formalize the decision process, we will use the null hypothesis to predict exactly what kind of samples should be obtained if the treatment has no effect. In particular, we will examine all the possible sample means that could be obtained if the null hypothesis is true. For our example, the null hypothesis states that the mean is still $\mu = 26$ and the researcher is planning to obtain a sample of $n = 16$ children. Therefore, we will examine the distribution of sample means for $n = 16$, centered at a value of $\mu = 26$ pounds. The distribution is then divided into two sections:

1. Sample means that are likely to be obtained if H_0 is true—that is, sample means that are close to the null hypothesis.

2. Sample means that are very unlikely to be obtained if H_0 is true—that is, sample means that are very different from the null hypothesis.

The distribution of sample means divided into these two sections is shown in Figure 8.2. Note that the high-probability samples are located in the center of the distribution and have sample means close to the value specified in the null hypothesis. On the other hand, the low-probability samples are located in the extreme tails of the distribution. After the distribution has been divided in this way, we can compare our sample data with the values in the distribution. Specifically, we can determine whether our sample mean is consistent with the null hypothesis (like the values in the center of the distribution) or whether our sample mean is very different from the null hypothesis (like the values in the extreme tails).

The alpha level   To find the boundaries that separate the high-probability samples from the low-probability samples, we must define exactly what is meant by "low" probability and "high" probability. This is accomplished by selecting a specific probability value, which is known as the *level of significance* or the *alpha level* for the hypothesis test. The alpha (α) value is a small probability that is used to identify the low-probability samples. By convention, commonly used alpha levels are $\alpha = .05$ (5%), $\alpha = .01$ (1%), and $\alpha = .001$ (0.1%). For example, with $\alpha = .05$, we will separate the most unlikely 5% of the sample means (the extreme values) from the most likely 95% of the sample means (the central values).

The extremely unlikely values, as defined by the alpha level, make up what is called the *critical region*. These extreme values in the tails of the distribution define outcomes

FIGURE 8.2

The set of potential samples is divided into those that are likely to be obtained and those that are very unlikely if the null hypothesis is true.

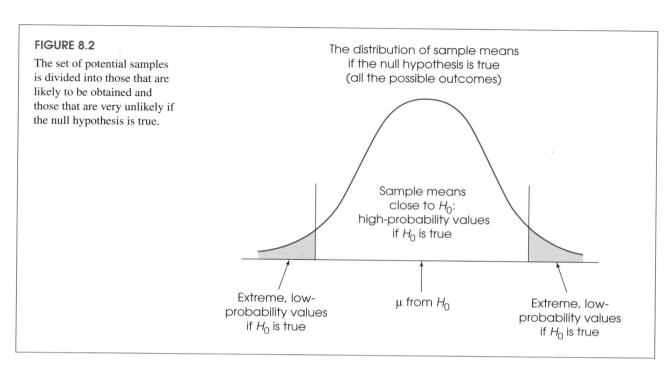

The distribution of sample means if the null hypothesis is true (all the possible outcomes)

Sample means close to H_0: high-probability values if H_0 is true

Extreme, low-probability values if H_0 is true

μ from H_0

Extreme, low-probability values if H_0 is true

that are inconsistent with the null hypothesis; that is, they are very unlikely to occur if the null hypothesis is true. Whenever the data from a research study produce a sample mean that is located in the critical region, we will conclude that the data are inconsistent with the null hypothesis, and we will reject the null hypothesis.

D E F I N I T I O N S

The *alpha level* or the *level of significance* is a probability value that is used to define the very unlikely sample outcomes if the null hypothesis is true.

The *critical region* is composed of extreme sample values that are very unlikely to be obtained if the null hypothesis is true. The boundaries for the critical region are determined by the alpha level. If sample data fall in the critical region, the null hypothesis is rejected.

The boundaries for the critical region   To determine the exact location for the boundaries that define the critical region, we will use the alpha-level probability and the unit normal table. In most cases, the distribution of sample means is normal, and the unit normal table will provide the precise z-score location for the critical region boundaries. With $\alpha = .05$, for example, we must find the boundaries that separate the extreme 5% from the middle 95%. Because the extreme 5% is split between two tails of the distribution, there is exactly 2.5% (or 0.0250) in each tail. In the unit normal table, you can look up a proportion of 0.0250 in column C (the tail) and find that the z-score boundary is $z = 1.96$. Thus, for any normal distribution, the extreme 5% is in the tails of the distribution beyond $z = 1.96$ and $z = -1.96$. These values define the boundaries of the critical region for a hypothesis test using $\alpha = .05$ (see Figure 8.3).

Similarly, an alpha level of $\alpha = .01$ means that 1% or .0100 is split between the two tails. In this case, the proportion in each tail is .0050, and the corresponding z-score

FIGURE 8.3

The critical region (very unlikely outcomes) for α = .05.

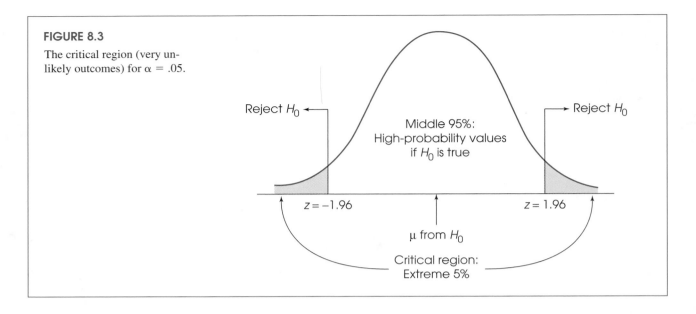

boundaries are $z = \pm 2.58$ (± 2.57 is equally good). For α = .001, the boundaries are
located at $z = \pm 3.30$. You should verify these values in the unit normal table and be sure
that you understand exactly how they are obtained.

**STEP 3: COLLECT DATA
AND COMPUTE
SAMPLE STATISTICS**

The next step in hypothesis testing is to obtain the sample data. At this time, the researcher would select a random sample of infants, and would train their parents to
provide the additional daily handling that constitutes the treatment for this study. Then
the body weight for each infant would be measured at 2 years of age. Note that the data
are collected *after* the researcher has stated the hypotheses and established the criteria
for a decision. This sequence of events helps ensure that a researcher makes an honest,
objective evaluation of the data and does not tamper with the decision criteria after the
experimental outcome is known.

Next, the raw data from the sample are summarized with the appropriate statistics:
For this example, the researcher would compute the sample mean. Now it is possible for
the researcher to compare the sample mean (the data) with the null hypothesis. This is
the heart of the hypothesis test: comparing the data with the hypothesis.

The comparison is accomplished by computing a z-score that describes exactly
where the sample mean is located relative to the hypothesized population mean from
H_0. The z-score formula for a sample mean is

$$z = \frac{\overline{X} - \mu}{\sigma_{\overline{X}}}$$

In the formula, the value of the sample mean ($\overline{X}$) is obtained from the sample data, and
the value of μ is obtained from the null hypothesis. Thus, the z-score formula can be expressed in words as follows:

$$z = \frac{\text{sample mean} - \text{hypothesized population mean}}{\text{standard error between } \overline{X} \text{ and } \mu}$$

Note that the top of the z-score formula measures how much difference there is between the data and the hypothesis. The bottom of the formula measures the standard distance that ought to exist between the sample mean and the population mean.

STEP 4: MAKE A DECISION   In the final step, the researcher uses the z-score value obtained in step 3 to make a decision about the null hypothesis according to the criteria established in step 2. There are two possible decisions, and both are stated in terms of the null hypothesis (see Box 8.1).

One possible decision is to *reject the null hypothesis.* This decision is made whenever the sample data fall in the critical region. By definition, a sample value in the critical region indicates that there is a big discrepancy between the sample and the null hypothesis (the sample is in the extreme tail of the distribution). This kind of outcome is very unlikely to occur if the null hypothesis is true, so our conclusion is to reject H_0. In this case, the data provide convincing evidence that the null hypothesis is wrong, and we conclude that the treatment really did have an effect on the individuals in the sample. For the example we have been considering, suppose the sample of $n = 16$ infants produced a sample mean of $\overline{X} = 30$ pounds at age 2. With $n = 16$ and $\sigma = 4$, the standard error for the sample mean would be

$$\sigma_{\overline{X}} = \frac{\sigma}{\sqrt{n}} = \frac{4}{\sqrt{16}} = \frac{4}{4} = 1$$

The z-score for the sample is

$$z = \frac{\overline{X} - \mu}{\sigma_{\overline{X}}} = \frac{30 - 26}{1} = \frac{4}{1} = 4.00$$

8.1   **REJECTING THE NULL HYPOTHESIS VERSUS PROVING THE ALTERNATIVE HYPOTHESIS**

IT MAY seem awkward to pay so much attention to the null hypothesis. After all, the purpose of most experiments is to show that a treatment does have an effect, and the null hypothesis states that there is no effect. The reason for focusing on the null hypothesis, rather than the alternative hypothesis, comes from the limitations of inferential logic. Remember, we want to use the sample data to draw conclusions, or inferences, about a population. Logically, it is much easier to demonstrate that a universal (population) hypothesis is false than to demonstrate that it is true. This principle is shown more clearly in a simple example. Suppose you make the universal statement "all dogs have four legs" and you intend to test this hypothesis by using a sample of one dog. If the dog in your sample does have four legs, have you

proved the statement? It should be clear that one four-legged dog does not prove the general statement to be true. On the other hand, suppose the dog in your sample has only three legs. In this case, you have proved the statement to be false. Again, it is much easier to show that something is false than to prove that it is true.

Hypothesis testing uses this logical principle to achieve its goals. It would be difficult to state "the treatment has an effect" as the hypothesis and then try to prove that this is true. Therefore, we state the null hypothesis, "the treatment has no effect," and try to show that it is false. The end result still is to demonstrate that the treatment does have an effect. That is, we find support for the alternative hypothesis by disproving (rejecting) the null hypothesis.

With an alpha level of $\alpha = .05$, this z-score is far beyond the boundary of 1.96. Because the sample z-score is in the critical region, we would reject the null hypothesis and conclude that the special handling did have an effect on the infants' weights.

The second possibility occurs when the sample data are not in the critical region. In this case, the data are reasonably close to the null hypothesis (in the center of the distribution). Because the data do not provide strong evidence that the null hypothesis is wrong, our conclusion is to *fail to reject the null hypothesis*. This conclusion means that the treatment does not appear to have an effect. For example, suppose that our sample of $n = 16$ infants produced a sample mean of $\overline{X} = 27$ pounds. As before, the null hypothesis says that the population mean is $\mu = 26$, and the standard error is still $\sigma_{\overline{X}} = 1$. These values produce a z-score of

$$z = \frac{\overline{X} - \mu}{\sigma_{\overline{X}}} = \frac{27 - 26}{1} = \frac{1}{1} = 1.00$$

The z-score of 1.00 is not in the critical region. Therefore, we would fail to reject the null hypothesis and conclude that the special handling does not appear to have an effect on weight.

The two possible decisions may be easier to understand if you think of a research study as an attempt to gather evidence to prove that a treatment works. From this perspective, the research study has two possible outcomes:

1. You gather enough evidence to demonstrate convincingly that the treatment really works. That is, you reject the null hypothesis and conclude that the treatment does have an effect.

2. The evidence you gather from the research study is not convincing. In this case, all you can do is conclude that there is not enough evidence. The research study has failed to demonstrate that the treatment has an effect, and the statistical decision is to fail to reject the null hypothesis.

A CLOSER LOOK AT THE z-SCORE STATISTIC

The z-score statistic that is used in the hypothesis test is the first specific example of what is called a *test statistic*. The term *test statistic* simply indicates that the sample data are converted into a single, specific statistic that is used to test the hypotheses. In the chapters that follow, we will introduce several other test statistics that are used in a variety of different research situations. However, each of the new test statistics will have the same basic structure and will serve the same purpose as the z-score. We have already described the z-score equation as a formal method for comparing the sample data and the population hypothesis. In this section, we will discuss the z-score from two other perspectives that may give you a better understanding of hypothesis testing and the role that z-scores play in this inferential technique. In each case, keep in mind that the z-score will serve as a general model for other test statistics that will come in future chapters.

The z-score formula as a recipe   The z-score formula, like any formula, can be viewed as a recipe. If you follow instructions and use all the right ingredients, the formula will produce a z-score. In the hypothesis-testing situation, however, you do not have all the necessary ingredients. Specifically, you do not know the value for the population mean (μ), which is one component or ingredient in the formula.

This situation is similar to trying to follow a cake recipe in which one of the ingredients is not clearly listed. For example, there may be a grease stain that obscures one part of your recipe. In this situation, what do you do? One possibility is to make a hypothesis about the missing ingredient. You might, for example, hypothesize that the missing ingredient is 2 cups of flour. To test the hypothesis, you simply add the rest of the ingredients along with the hypothesized flour and see what happens. If the cake turns out to be good, then you can be reasonably confident that your hypothesis was correct. But if the cake is terrible, then you conclude that your hypothesis was wrong.

In a hypothesis test with z-scores, you do essentially the same thing. You do not know the value for the population mean, μ. Therefore, you make a hypothesis (the null hypothesis) about the unknown value μ and plug it into the formula along with the rest of the ingredients. To evaluate your hypothesis, you simply look at the result. If the formula produces a z-score near zero (which is where z-scores are supposed to be), then you conclude that your hypothesis was correct. On the other hand, if the formula produces an unlikely result (an extremely large or small value), then you conclude that your hypothesis was wrong.

The z-score formula as a ratio   In the context of a hypothesis test, the z-score formula has the following structure:

$$z = \frac{\overline{X} - \mu}{\sigma_{\overline{X}}} = \frac{\text{sample mean} - \text{hypothesized population mean}}{\text{standard error between } \overline{X} \text{ and } \mu}$$

Note that the numerator of the formula involves a direct comparison between the sample data and the null hypothesis. In particular, the numerator measures the obtained difference between the sample mean and the hypothesized population mean. The standard error in the denominator of the formula measures how much difference ought to exist between the sample mean and the population mean just by chance. Thus, the z-score formula (and most other test statistics) forms a ratio

$$z = \frac{\text{obtained difference}}{\text{difference due to chance}}$$

In general, the purpose of a test statistic is to determine whether the result of the research study (the obtained difference) is more than would be expected by chance alone. Whenever the test statistic has a value greater than 1.00, it means that the obtained result (numerator) is greater than chance (denominator). However, you should realize that most researchers are not satisfied with results that are simply more than chance. Instead, conventional research standards require results that are substantially more than chance. Specifically, most hypothesis tests require that the test statistic ratio have a value of at least 2 or 3; that is, the obtained difference must be 2 or 3 times bigger than chance before the researcher will reject the null hypothesis.

LEARNING CHECK

1. What does the null hypothesis predict about a population or a treatment effect?

2. Define the *critical region* for a hypothesis test.

3. As the alpha level gets smaller, the size of the critical region also gets smaller. (True or false?)

4. A small value (near zero) for the z-score statistic is evidence that the null hypothesis should be rejected. (True or false?)

5. A decision to reject the null hypothesis means that you have demonstrated that the treatment has no effect. (True or false?)

ANSWERS

1. The null hypothesis predicts that the treatment has no effect and the population is unchanged.

2. The critical region consists of sample outcomes that are very unlikely to be obtained if the null hypothesis is true.

3. True. As alpha gets smaller, the critical region is moved farther out into the tails of the distribution.

4. False. A *z*-score near zero indicates that the data support the null hypothesis.

5. False. Rejecting the null hypothesis means that you have concluded that the treatment does have an effect.   ◆

8.2 UNCERTAINTY AND ERRORS IN HYPOTHESIS TESTING

Hypothesis testing is an *inferential process,* which means that it uses limited information as the basis for reaching a general conclusion. Specifically, a sample provides only limited or incomplete information about the whole population, and yet a hypothesis test uses the information from a sample to make a decision about the entire population. In this situation, there is always the possibility that an incorrect conclusion will be made. Although sample data are usually representative of the population, there is always a chance that the sample is misleading and will cause a researcher to make the wrong decision about the research results. In a hypothesis test, there are two different kinds of errors that can be made.

TYPE I ERRORS

It is possible that the data will lead you to reject the null hypothesis when in fact the treatment has no effect. Remember, samples are not expected to be identical to their populations, and some extreme samples can be very different from the populations they are supposed to represent. If a researcher selects one of these extreme samples, just by chance, then the data from the sample may give the appearance of a strong treatment effect, even though there is no real effect. In the previous section, for example, we discussed a research study examining how increased handling during infancy affects body weight. Suppose the researcher selected a sample of $n = 16$ infants who were genetically destined to be bigger than average even without any special treatment. When these infants are measured at 2 years of age, they will look bigger than average even though the special handling (the treatment) may have had no effect. In this case, the researcher is likely to conclude that the treatment has had an effect, when in fact it really did not. This is an example of what is called a *Type I error*.

DEFINITION

A *Type I error* occurs when a researcher rejects a null hypothesis that is actually true. In a typical research situation, a Type I error means that the researcher concludes that a treatment does have an effect when in fact the treatment has no effect.

You should realize that a Type I error is not a stupid mistake in the sense that a researcher is overlooking something that should be perfectly obvious. On the contrary, the researcher is looking at sample data that appear to show a clear treatment effect. The researcher then makes a careful decision based on the available information. The problem is that the information from the sample is misleading. In general, a researcher never knows for certain whether a hypothesis is true or false. Instead, we must rely on the data to tell us whether the hypothesis *appears* to be true or false.

In most research situations, the consequences of a Type I error can be very serious. Because the researcher has rejected the null hypothesis and believes that the treatment has a real effect, it is likely that the researcher will report or even publish the research results. A Type I error, however, means that this is a false report. Thus, Type I errors lead to false reports in the scientific literature. Other researchers may try to build theories or develop other experiments based on the false results. A lot of precious time and resources may be wasted.

Fortunately, the hypothesis test is structured to control and minimize the risk of committing a Type I error. Although extreme and misleading samples are possible, they are relatively unlikely. For an extreme sample to produce a Type I error, the sample mean must be in the critical region. However, the critical region is structured so that it is *very unlikely* to obtain a sample mean in the critical region when H_0 is true. Specifically, the alpha level determines the probability of obtaining a sample mean in the critical region when H_0 is true. Thus, the alpha level defines the probability or risk of a Type I error. This fact leads to an alternative definition of the alpha level.

DEFINITION
The *alpha level* for a hypothesis test is the probability that the test will lead to a Type I error. That is, the alpha level determines the probability of obtaining sample data in the critical region even though the null hypothesis is true.

In summary, whenever the sample data are in the critical region, the appropriate decision for a hypothesis test is to reject the null hypothesis. Normally this is the correct decision because the treatment has caused the sample to be different from the original population; that is, the treatment effect has literally pushed the sample mean into the critical region. In this case, the hypothesis test has correctly identified a real treatment effect. Occasionally, however, sample data will be in the critical region just by chance, without any treatment effect. When this occurs, the researcher will make a Type I error; that is, the researcher will conclude that a treatment effect exists, when in fact it does not. Fortunately, the risk of a Type I error is small and is under the control of the researcher. Specifically, the probability of a Type I error is equal to the alpha level.

TYPE II ERRORS

Whenever a researcher rejects the null hypothesis, there is a risk of a Type I error. Similarly, whenever a researcher fails to reject the null hypothesis, there is a risk of a *Type II error*. By definition, a Type II error is failing to reject a false null hypothesis. In more straightforward English, a Type II error means that a treatment effect really exists, but the hypothesis test fails to detect it.

DEFINITION
A *Type II error* occurs when a researcher fails to reject a null hypothesis that is really false. In a typical research situation, a Type II error means that the hypothesis test has failed to detect a real treatment effect.

A Type II error occurs when the sample mean is not in the critical region even though the treatment has had an effect on the sample. Often this happens when the effect of the treatment is relatively small. In this case, the treatment does influence the sample, but the magnitude of the effect is not big enough to move the sample mean into the critical region. Because the sample is not substantially different from the original population (it is not in the critical region), the statistical decision is to fail to reject the null hypothesis and to conclude that there is not enough evidence to say there is a treatment effect.

The consequences of a Type II error are usually not very serious. A Type II error means that the research data do not show the results that the researcher had hoped to obtain. The researcher can accept this outcome and conclude that the treatment either has no effect or has only a small effect that is not worth pursuing. Or the researcher can repeat the experiment (usually with some improvements) and try to demonstrate that the treatment really does work.

Unlike a Type I error, it is impossible to determine a single, exact probability value for a Type II error. Instead, the probability of a Type II error depends on a variety of factors and therefore is a function, rather than a specific number. Nonetheless, the probability of a Type II error is represented by the symbol β, the Greek letter beta.

In summary, a hypothesis test always leads to one of two decisions:

1. The sample data provide sufficient evidence to reject the null hypothesis and conclude that the treatment has an effect.

2. The sample data do not provide enough evidence to reject the null hypothesis. In this case, you fail to reject H_0 and conclude that the treatment does not appear to have an effect.

In either case, there is a chance that the data are misleading and the decision is wrong. The complete set of decisions and outcomes is shown in Table 8.1.

TABLE 8.1

Possible outcomes of a statistical decision

		Actual situation	
		No effect, H_0 true	Effect exists, H_0 false
Experimenter's decision	Reject H_0	Type I error	Decision correct
	Retain H_0	Decision correct	Type II error

SELECTING AN ALPHA LEVEL

As you have seen, the alpha level for a hypothesis test serves two very important functions. First, alpha helps determine the boundaries for the critical region by defining the concept of "very unlikely" outcomes. More important, alpha determines the probability of a Type I error. When you select a value for alpha at the beginning of a hypothesis, your decision influences both of these functions.

The primary concern when selecting an alpha level is to minimize the risk of a Type I error. Thus, alpha levels tend to be very small probability values. By convention, the largest permissible value is $\alpha = .05$. An alpha level of .05 means that there is a 5% risk, or a 1 in 20 probability, of committing a Type I error. For many research situations, the .05 level of significance is viewed as an unacceptably large risk. Consider, for example, a scientific journal containing 20 research articles, each evaluated with an alpha level of .05. With a 5% risk of a Type I error, 1 out of the 20 articles is probably a false report. For this reason, most scientific publications require a more stringent alpha level, such as .01 or .001. (For more information on the origins of the .05 level of significance, see the excellent short article by Cowles and Davis, 1982.)

At this point, it may appear that the best strategy for selecting an alpha level is to choose the smallest possible value in order to minimize the risk of a Type I error. However, a different kind of risk develops as the alpha level is lowered. Specifically, a lower alpha level means less risk of a Type I error, but it also means that the hypothesis test demands more evidence from the research results.

The trade-off between the risk of a Type I error and the demands of the test is controlled by the boundaries of the critical region. For the hypothesis test to conclude that the treatment does have an effect, the sample data must be in the critical region. If the treatment really has an effect, it should cause the sample to be different from the original population; essentially, the treatment should push the sample into the critical region. However, as the alpha level is lowered, the boundaries for the critical region move farther out and become more difficult to reach. Figure 8.4 shows how the boundaries for the critical region move farther away as the alpha level decreases. Note that lower alpha levels produce more extreme boundaries for the critical region. Thus, an extremely small alpha level would mean almost no risk of a Type I error but would push the critical region so far out that it would become essentially impossible to ever reject the null hypothesis; that is, it would require an enormous treatment effect before the sample data would reach the critical boundaries.

FIGURE 8.4

The locations of the critical region boundaries for three different levels of significance: $\alpha = .05$, $\alpha = .01$, and $\alpha = .001$.

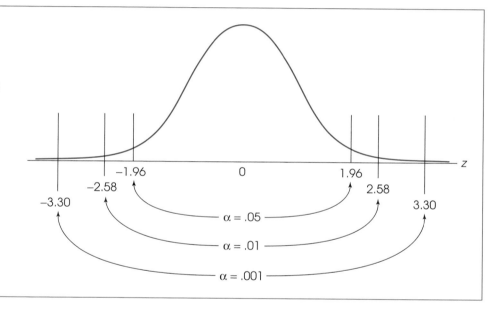

In general, researchers try to maintain a balance between the risk of a Type I error and the demands of the hypothesis test. Alpha levels of .05, .01, and .001 are considered reasonably good values because they provide a relatively low risk of error without placing excessive demands on the research results.

LEARNING CHECK

1. What is a Type I error?

2. Why is the consequence of a Type I error considered serious?

3. If the alpha level is changed from $\alpha = .05$ to $\alpha = .01$, the probability of a Type I error increases. (True or false?)

4. Define a Type II error.

5. What research situation is likely to lead to a Type II error?

ANSWERS   1. A Type I error is rejecting a true null hypothesis—that is, saying that the treatment has an effect when in fact it does not.

2. A Type I error often results in a false report, in which a researcher reports or publishes a treatment effect that does not exist.

3. False. The probability of a Type I error is α.

4. A Type II error is failing to reject a false null hypothesis. In terms of a research study, a Type II error occurs when a study fails to detect a treatment effect that really exists.

5. A Type II error is likely to occur when the treatment effect is very small. In this case, a research study is more likely to overlook or fail to detect the effect.   ◆

8.3   AN EXAMPLE OF A HYPOTHESIS TEST

At this point, we have introduced all the elements of a hypothesis test. In this section, we present a complete example of the hypothesis-testing process and discuss how the results from a hypothesis test are presented in a research report. For purposes of demonstration, the following scenario will be used to provide a concrete background for the hypothesis-testing process.

EXAMPLE 8.2   Alcohol appears to be involved in a variety of birth defects, including low birth weight and retarded growth. A researcher would like to investigate the effect of prenatal alcohol on birth weight. A random sample of $n = 16$ pregnant rats is obtained. The mother rats are given daily doses of alcohol. At birth, one pup is selected from each litter to produce a sample of $n = 16$ newborn rats. The average weight for the sample is $\bar{X} = 15$ grams. The researcher would like to compare the sample with the general population of rats. It is known that regular newborn rats (not exposed to alcohol) have an average weight of $\mu = 18$ grams. The distribution of weights is normal with $\sigma = 4$. Figure 8.5 shows the overall research situation. Note that the researcher's question

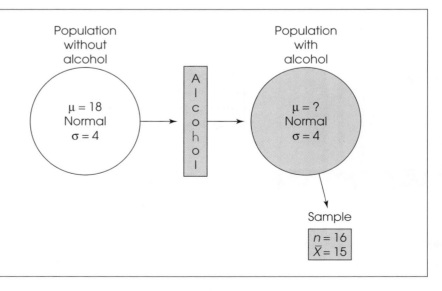

FIGURE 8.5

The structure of a research study to determine whether prenatal alcohol affects birth weight.

concerns the unknown population that is exposed to alcohol and the data consist of a sample from this unknown population. The following steps outline the hypothesis test that evaluates the effect of alcohol exposure on birth weight.

STEP 1   *State the hypotheses, and select the alpha level.* Both hypotheses concern the population that is exposed to alcohol where the population mean is unknown (the population on the right-hand side of Figure 8.5). The null hypothesis states that exposure to alcohol has no effect on birth weight. Thus, the population of rats with alcohol exposure should have the same mean birth weight as the regular, unexposed rats. In symbols,

$$H_0: \mu_{\text{alcohol exposure}} = 18 \qquad \text{(Even with alcohol exposure, the rats still average 18 grams at birth.)}$$

The alternative hypothesis states that alcohol exposure does affect birth weight, so the exposed population should be different from the regular rats. In symbols,

$$H_1: \mu_{\text{alcohol exposure}} \neq 18 \qquad \text{(Alcohol exposure will change birth weight.)}$$

Note that both hypotheses concern the unknown population. For this test, we will use an alpha level of $\alpha = .05$. That is, we are taking a 5% risk of committing a Type I error.

STEP 2   *Set the decision criteria by locating the critical region.* By definition, the critical region consists of outcomes that are very unlikely if the null hypothesis is true. To locate the critical region, we will go through a three-stage process that is portrayed in Figure 8.6. We begin with the population of birth weight scores for rats that have been exposed to alcohol. According to the null hypothesis, the mean for this population is $\mu = 18$ grams. In addition, it is known that the population of birth weight scores is normal with $\sigma = 4$ (see Figure 8.5). Next, we use the hypothesized population to determine the complete set of sample outcomes that could be obtained if the null hypothesis is true. Because the researcher plans to use a sample of $n = 16$ rats, we construct the distribution of sample means for $n = 16$. This distribution of sample means is often called the *null distribution* because it specifies exactly what kinds of research outcomes should be obtained according to the null hypothesis. For this example, the null distribution is centered at $\mu = 18$ (from H_0) and has a standard error of $\sigma_{\overline{X}} = \sigma/\sqrt{n} = 4/\sqrt{16} = 1$. Finally, we use the null distribution to identify the critical region, which consists of those outcomes that are very unlikely if the null hypothesis is true. With $\alpha = .05$, the critical region consists of the extreme 5% of the distribution. As we saw earlier, for any normal distribution, z scores of $z = \pm1.96$ separate the middle 95% from the extreme 5% (a proportion of 0.0250 in each tail). Thus, if the null hypothesis is true, the most unlikely outcomes correspond to z-score values beyond ±1.96. This is the critical region for our test.

STEP 3   *Collect the data, and compute the test statistic.* At this point, we would select our sample of $n = 16$ pups whose mothers had received alcohol during pregnancy. The birth weight would be recorded for each pup and the sample mean computed. As noted, we obtained a sample mean of $\overline{X} = 15$ grams. The sample mean is then converted to a z-score, which is our test statistic.

$$z = \frac{\overline{X} - \mu}{\sigma_{\overline{X}}} = \frac{15 - 18}{1} = \frac{-3}{1} = -3.00$$

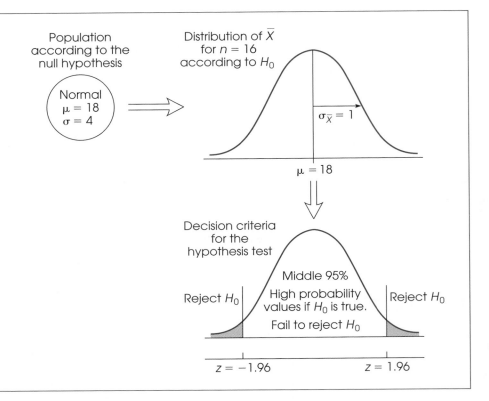

FIGURE 8.6

Locating the critical region as a three-step process. You begin with the population of scores that is predicted by the null hypothesis. Then you construct the distribution of sample means for the sample size that is being used. The distribution of sample means corresponds to all the possible outcomes that could be obtained if H_0 is true. Finally, you use z-scores to separate the extreme outcomes (as defined by the alpha level) from the high-probability outcomes. The extreme values determine the critical region.

STEP 4   *Make a decision.* The z-score computed in step 3 has a value of -3.00, which is beyond the boundary of -1.96. Therefore, the sample mean is located in the critical region. This is a very unlikely outcome if the null hypothesis is true, so our decision is to reject the null hypothesis. In addition to this statistical decision concerning the null hypothesis, it is customary to state a conclusion about the results of the research study. For this example, we conclude that prenatal exposure to alcohol does have a significant effect on birth weight.

IN THE LITERATURE:
REPORTING THE RESULTS OF THE STATISTICAL TEST

A special jargon and notational system are used in published reports of hypothesis tests. When you are reading a scientific journal, for example, you typically will not be told explicitly that the researcher evaluated the data using a z-score as a test statistic with an alpha level of .05. Nor will you be told that "the null hypothesis is rejected." Instead, you will see a statement such as

> The treatment with medication had a significant effect on people's depression scores, $z = 3.85$, $p < .05$.

Let us examine this statement piece by piece. First, what does the term *significant* mean? In statistical tests, this word indicates that the result is different from what would be expected due to chance. A *significant* result means that the null hypothesis has been rejected, which means that the obtained result is very unlikely to have occurred merely by chance. That is, the data are significant because the sample mean falls in the critical region and is not what we would have expected to obtain if H_0 were true.

DEFINITION

Findings are said to be *statistically significant* when the null hypothesis has been rejected. Thus, if results achieve statistical significance, the researcher concludes that a treatment effect occurred.

Next, what is the meaning of $z = 3.85$? The z indicates that a z-score was used as the test statistic to evaluate the sample data and that its value is 3.85. Finally, what does $p < .05$ mean? This part of the statement is a conventional way of specifying the alpha level that was used for the hypothesis test. More specifically, we are being told that the result of the experiment would occur by chance with a probability (p) that is less than .05 (alpha). That is, the probability of a Type I error is less than .05.

The APA style does not use a leading zero in a probability value that refers to a level of significance.

In circumstances where the statistical decision is to *fail to reject H_0*, the report might state that

There was no evidence that the medication had an effect on depression scores, $z = 1.30$, $p > .05$.

In this case, we are saying that the obtained result, $z = 1.30$, is not unusual (not in the critical region) and is relatively likely to occur by chance (the probability is greater than .05). Thus, H_0 was not rejected.

Sometimes students become confused trying to differentiate between $p < .05$ and $p > .05$. Remember that you reject the null hypothesis with extreme, low-probability values, located in the critical region in the tails of the distribution. Thus, a significant result that rejects the null hypothesis corresponds to $p < .05$. See Figure 8.7.

FIGURE 8.7

Sample means that fall in the critical region (shaded areas) have a probability *less than* alpha ($p < \alpha$). H_0 should be rejected. Sample means that do not fall in the critical region have a probability *greater than* alpha ($p > \alpha$).

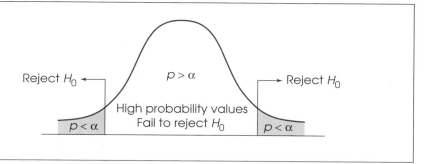

Finally, you should note that in scientific reports, the researcher does not actually state that "the null hypothesis was rejected." Instead, the researcher reports that the effect of the treatment was statistically significant. Likewise, when H_0 is not rejected, one simply states that the treatment effect was not statistically significant or that there was no evidence for a treatment effect. In fact, when you read scientific reports, you will note that the terms *null hypothesis* and *alternative hypothesis* are rarely mentioned. Nevertheless, H_0 and H_1 are part of the logic of hypothesis testing even if they are not formally stated in a scientific report. Because of their central role in the process of hypothesis testing, you should be able to identify and state these hypotheses.   ❏

ASSUMPTIONS FOR HYPOTHESIS TESTS WITH z-SCORES

Typically, the mathematics that are used for a hypothesis test are based on a set of assumptions. When these assumptions are satisfied, you can be confident that the test produces a justified conclusion. However, if the assumptions are not satisfied, the hypothesis test may be compromised. In practice, researchers are not overly concerned about the assumptions underlying a hypothesis test because the tests usually work well even when the assumptions are violated. However, you should be aware of the fundamental conditions that are associated with each type of statistical test to ensure that the test is being used appropriately. The assumptions for hypothesis tests with z-scores are summarized below.

Random sampling   It is assumed that the subjects used to obtain the sample data were selected randomly. Remember, we wish to generalize our findings from the sample to the population. We accomplish this task when we use sample data to test a hypothesis about the population. Therefore, the sample must be representative of the population from which it has been drawn. Random sampling helps to ensure that it is representative.

Independent observations   The values in the sample must consist of *independent* observations. In everyday terms, two observations are independent if there is no consistent,

---

8.2   INDEPENDENT OBSERVATIONS

INDEPENDENT OBSERVATIONS are a basic requirement for nearly all hypothesis tests. The critical concern is that each observation or measurement is not influenced by any other observation or measurement. An example of independent observations is the set of outcomes obtained in a series of coin tosses. Assuming that the coin is balanced, each toss has a 50–50 chance of coming up either heads or tails. More important, each toss is *independent* of the tosses that came before. On the fifth toss, for example, there is a 50% chance of heads no matter what happened on the previous four tosses; the coin does not remember what happened earlier and is not influenced by the past. (*Note:* Many people fail to believe in the independence of events. For example, after a series of four tails in a row, it is tempting to think that the probability of heads must increase because the coin is overdue to come up heads. This is a mistake, called the "gambler's fallacy." Remember, the coin does not know what happened on the preceding tosses and cannot be influenced by previous outcomes.)

In most research situations, the requirement for independent observations is typically satisfied by using a random sample of separate, unrelated individuals. Thus, the measurement obtained for each individual is not influenced by other subjects in the sample. The following two situations demonstrate circumstances where the observations are *not* independent.

1. A researcher is interested in examining television preferences for children. To obtain a sample of $n = 20$ children, the researcher selects 4 children from family A, 3 children from family B, 5 children from family C, 2 children from family D, and 6 children from family E.

   It should be obvious that the researcher does *not* have 20 independent observations. Within each family, the children probably share television preference (at least they watch the same shows). Thus, the response for each child is likely to be related to the responses of his or her siblings.

2. A researcher is interested in people's ability to judge distances. A sample of 20 people is obtained. All 20 subjects are gathered together in the same room. The researcher asks the first subject to estimate the distance between New York and Miami. The second subject is asked the same question, then the third subject, the fourth subject, and so on.

   Again, the observations that the researcher obtains are not independent: The response of each subject is probably influenced by the responses of the previous subjects. For example, consistently low estimates by the first few subjects could create pressure to conform and thereby increase the probability that the following subjects would also produce low estimates.

predictable relationship between the first observation and the second. More precisely, two events (or observations) are independent if the occurrence of the first event has no effect on the probability of the second event. Specific examples of independence and nonindependence are examined in Box 8.2. Usually, this assumption is satisfied by using a *random* sample, which also helps ensure that the sample is representative of the population and that the results can be generalized to the population.

The value of σ is unchanged by the treatment   A critical part of the z-score formula in a hypothesis is the standard error, $\sigma_{\overline{X}}$. To compute the value for the standard error, we must know the sample size (n) and the population standard deviation (σ). In a hypothesis test, however, the sample comes from an *unknown* population (see Figures 8.1 and 8.5). If the population is really unknown, it would suggest that we do not know the standard deviation and, therefore, we cannot calculate the standard error. To solve this dilemma, we must make an assumption. Specifically, we assume that the standard deviation for the unknown population (after treatment) is the same as it was for the population before treatment.

Actually, this assumption is the consequence of a more general assumption that is part of many statistical procedures. This general assumption states that the effect of the treatment is to add a constant amount to (or subtract a constant amount from) every score in the population. You should recall that adding (or subtracting) a constant will change the mean but will have no effect on the standard deviation. You also should note that this assumption is a theoretical ideal. In actual experiments, a treatment generally will not show a perfect and consistent additive effect.

Normal sampling distribution   To evaluate hypotheses with z-scores, we have used the unit normal table to identify the critical region. This table can be used only if the distribution of sample means is normal.

LEARNING CHECK

1. A researcher would like to know whether room temperature will affect eating behavior. The lab temperature is usually kept at 72°, and under these conditions, the rats eat an average of $\mu = 10$ grams of food each day. The amount of food varies from one rat to another, forming a normal distribution with $\sigma = 2$. The researcher selects a sample of $n = 4$ rats and places them in a room where the temperature is kept at 65°. The daily food consumption for these rats averaged $\overline{X} = 13$ grams. Do these data indicate that temperature has a significant effect on eating? Test at the .05 level of significance.

2. In a research report, the term *significant effect* is used when the null hypothesis is rejected. (True or false?)

3. In a research report, the results of a hypothesis test include the phrase "$p < .01$." This means that the test failed to reject the null hypothesis. (True or false?)

ANSWERS

1. The null hypothesis states that temperature has no effect, or $\mu = 10$ grams even at the lower temperature. With $\alpha = .05$, the critical region consists of z-scores beyond $z = \pm 1.96$. The sample data produce $z = 3.00$. The decision is to reject H_0 and conclude that temperature has a significant effect on eating behavior.

2. True

3. False. The probability is *less than* .01, which means it is very unlikely that the result occurred by chance. In this case, the data are in the critical region, and H_0 is rejected.   ◆

8.4   DIRECTIONAL (ONE-TAILED) HYPOTHESIS TESTS

The hypothesis-testing procedure presented in Section 8.2 was the standard, or *two-tailed,* test format. The *two-tailed* comes from the fact that the critical region is located in both tails of the distribution. This format is by far the most widely accepted procedure for hypothesis testing. Nonetheless, there is an alternative that will be discussed in this section.

Usually a researcher begins an experiment with a specific prediction about the direction of the treatment effect. For example, a special training program is expected to *increase* student performance, or alcohol consumption is expected to *slow* reaction times. In these situations, it is possible to state the statistical hypotheses in a manner that incorporates the directional prediction into the statement of H_0 and H_1. The result is a directional test, or what commonly is called a *one-tailed test.*

DEFINITION

In a *directional hypothesis test,* or a *one-tailed test,* the statistical hypotheses (H_0 and H_1) specify either an increase or a decrease in the population mean score. That is, they make a statement about the direction of the effect.

Suppose, for example, a researcher is using a sample of $n = 16$ laboratory rats to examine the effect of a new diet drug. It is known that under regular circumstances these rats eat an average of 10 grams of food each day. The distribution of food consumption is normal with $\sigma = 4$. The expected effect of the drug is to reduce food consumption. The purpose of the experiment is to determine whether or not the drug really works.

THE HYPOTHESES FOR A DIRECTIONAL TEST

Because a specific direction is expected for the treatment effect, it is possible for the researcher to perform a directional test. The first (and most critical) step is to state the statistical hypotheses. Remember that the null hypothesis states that there is no treatment effect and that the alternative hypothesis says that there is an effect. For this example, the predicted effect is that the drug will reduce food consumption. Thus, the two hypotheses would state:

H_0: Food consumption is not reduced

H_1: Food consumption is reduced

To express these directional hypotheses in symbols, it usually is easier to begin with the alternative hypothesis. Again, we know that regular rats eat an average of $\mu = 10$ grams of food, and H_1 says that food consumption will be reduced by the diet drug. Therefore, expressed in symbols, H_1 states

H_1: $\mu < 10$ (With the drug, food consumption is less than 10 grams per day.)

The null hypothesis states that the drug does not reduce food consumption:

H_0: $\mu \geq 10$ (With the drug, food consumption is at least 10 grams per day.)

THE CRITICAL REGION FOR DIRECTIONAL TESTS

The critical region is determined by sample values that are very unlikely if the null hypothesis is true. In other words, the critical region is defined by sample values that refute the null hypothesis because they provide evidence that the treatment really does work. In this example, the treatment is intended to reduce food consumption. Therefore, only sample values substantially less than $\mu = 10$ would indicate that the treatment worked and thereby lead to rejecting H_0. Thus, the critical region is located entirely in one tail of the distribution (see Figure 8.8), which is why the directional test commonly is called *one-tailed*.

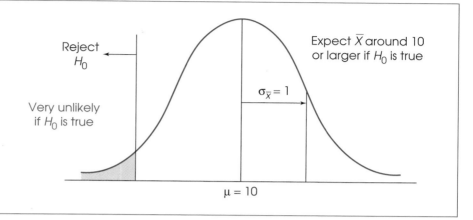

FIGURE 8.8

The distribution of sample means for $n = 16$ if H_0 is true. The null hypothesis states that the diet pill has no effect, so the population mean will be 10 or larger.

Reject H_0

Very unlikely if H_0 is true

Expect $\overline{X}$ around 10 or larger if H_0 is true

$\sigma_{\overline{X}} = 1$

$\mu = 10$

Note that a directional (one-tailed) test requires two changes in the step-by-step hypothesis-testing procedure.

1. In the first step of the hypothesis test, the directional prediction is incorporated into the statement of the hypotheses.

2. In the second step of the process, the critical region is located entirely in one tail of the distribution.

After these two changes, the remainder of a one-tailed test proceeds exactly the same as a regular two-tailed test. Specifically, you calculate the z-score statistic and then make a decision about H_0 depending on whether or not the z-score is in the critical region.

Next we present a complete example of a one-tailed test. Once again, we will use the experiment examining the effect of extra handling on the physical growth of infants to demonstrate the hypothesis-testing procedure.

EXAMPLE 8.3   It is known that under regular circumstances the population of 2-year-old children has an average weight of $\mu = 26$ pounds. The distribution of weights is normal with $\sigma = 4$. The researcher selects a random sample of $n = 4$ newborn infants and instructs the parents to provide each child with extra handling. The researcher predicts that the extra handling will stimulate the infants' growth and produce an *increase* in their weight at age 2. The researcher records the weight of each child at age 2 and obtains a sample mean of $\overline{X} = 29.5$ pounds.

STEP 1   *State the hypotheses.* Because the researcher is predicting that extra handling will produce an increase in weight, it is possible to do a directional test. The null hypothesis states that the treatment does not have the predicted effect. In symbols,

$$H_0: \mu \leq 26 \qquad \text{(There is no increase in weight.)}$$

The alternative hypothesis states that extra handling will increase physical growth. In symbols,

$$H_1: \mu > 26 \qquad \text{(There is an increase in weight.)}$$

STEP 2   *Locate the critical region.* To find the critical region, we look at all the possible sample means for $n = 4$ that could be obtained if H_0 were true. This is the distribution of sample means. It will be normal (because the population is normal), it will have a standard error of $\sigma_{\overline{X}} = 4/\sqrt{4} = 2$, and it will have a mean of $\mu = 26$ if the null hypothesis is true. The distribution is shown in Figure 8.9.

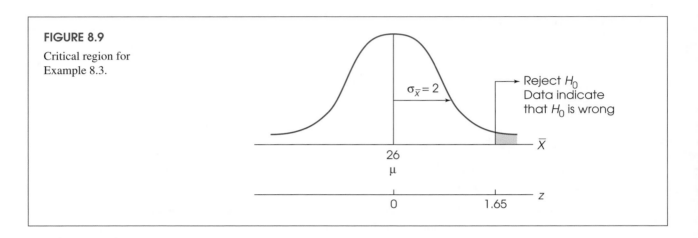

FIGURE 8.9

Critical region for Example 8.3.

If the extra handling does increase growth, as predicted, then the sample should have an average weight substantially greater than 26 pounds. That is, a large value for the sample mean would indicate that H_0 is wrong and should be rejected. There-fore, the critical region is determined by large values in the extreme right-hand tail of the distribution. To find the boundary for the critical region, we must determine the z-score value that separates the extreme .05 (5%) in the tail from the rest of the distribution. Checking the unit normal table, you should find that a proportion of .05 in the tail corresponds to a z-score of $z = 1.65$. (*Note:* A z-score of 1.64 is equally good, but we will use the more extreme value, $z = 1.65$). The critical region and the z-score boundary are shown in Figure 8.9.

> The entire 5% (.05) is in one tail. It is not divided between two tails.

STEP 3   *Obtain the sample data.* The mean for the sample is $\overline{X} = 29.5$. This value corresponds to a z-score of

$$z = \frac{\overline{X} - \mu}{\sigma_{\overline{X}}} = \frac{29.5 - 26}{2} = \frac{3.5}{2} = 1.75$$

STEP 4   *Make a statistical decision.* A z-score of $z = +1.75$ indicates that our sample mean is in the critical region. This is a very unlikely outcome if H_0 is true, so the statisti-cal decision is to reject H_0. The conclusion is that extra handling does result in in-creased growth for infants.

COMPARISON OF ONE-TAILED VERSUS TWO-TAILED TESTS

The general goal of hypothesis testing is to determine whether or not a particular treatment has any effect on a population. The test is performed by selecting a sample, administering the treatment to the sample, and then comparing the result with the original population. If the treated sample is noticeably different from the original population, then we conclude that the treatment has an effect, and we reject H_0. On the other hand, if the treated sample is still similar to the original population, then we conclude that there is no evidence for a treatment effect, and we fail to reject H_0. The critical factor in this decision is the *size of the difference* between the treated sample and the original population. A large difference is evidence that the treatment worked; a small difference is not sufficient to say that the treatment has any effect.

The major distinction between one-tailed and two-tailed tests is in the criteria they use for rejecting H_0. A one-tailed test allows you to reject the null hypothesis when the difference between the sample and the population is relatively small, provided the difference is in the specified direction. A two-tailed test, on the other hand, requires a relatively large difference independent of direction. This point is illustrated in the following example.

EXAMPLE 8.4

Consider again the experiment examining extra handling and infant growth (see Example 8.3). If we had used a standard two-tailed test, then the hypotheses would have been

H_0: $\mu = 26$ pounds   (There is no treatment effect.)

H_1: $\mu \neq 26$ pounds   (Handling does affect growth.)

With $\alpha = .05$, the critical region would consist of any z-score beyond the $z = \pm 1.96$ boundaries.

If we obtained the sample data, $\overline{X} = 29.5$ pounds, which corresponds to a z-score of $z = 1.75$, our statistical decision would be "fail to reject H_0."

Note that with the two-tailed test (Example 8.4), the difference between the data ($\overline{X} = 29.5$) and the hypothesis ($\mu = 26$) is not big enough to conclude that the hypothesis is wrong. In this case, we are saying that the data do not provide sufficient evidence to justify rejecting H_0. However, with the one-tailed test (Example 8.3), the same data led us to reject H_0.

All researchers agree that one-tailed tests are different from two-tailed tests. However, there are several ways to interpret the difference. One group of researchers contends that a two-tailed test is more rigorous and, therefore, more convincing than a one-tailed test. Remember that the two-tailed test demands more evidence to reject H_0 and thus provides a stronger demonstration that a treatment effect has occurred.

Other researchers feel that one-tailed tests are preferred because they are more sensitive. That is, a relatively small treatment effect may be significant with a one-tailed test but fail to reach significance with a two-tailed test. Also, there is the argument that one-tailed tests are more precise because they test hypotheses about a specific directional effect instead of an indefinite hypothesis about a general effect.

In general, two-tailed tests should used in research situations where there is no strong directional expectation or where there are two competing predictions. For example, a two-tailed test would be appropriate for a study in which one theory predicts an increase in scores but another theory predicts a decrease. On the other hand, one-tailed tests should be used only in situations where the directional prediction is made before the research is conducted and there is a strong justification for making the directional prediction. In particular, you should never use a one-tailed test as a second attempt to salvage a significant result from a research study where the first analysis with a two-tailed test failed to reach significance.

LEARNING CHECK ◆

1. A researcher predicts that a treatment will lower scores. If this researcher uses a one-tailed test, will the critical region be in the right- or left-hand tail of the distribution?

2. A psychologist is examining the effects of early sensory deprivation on the development of perceptual discrimination. A sample of $n = 9$ newborn kittens is obtained. These kittens are raised in a completely dark environment for 4 weeks, after which they receive normal visual stimulation. At age 6 months, the kittens are tested on a visual discrimination task. The average score for this sample is $\overline{X} = 32$. It is known that under normal circumstances cats score an average of $\mu = 40$ on this task. The distribution of scores is normal with $\sigma = 12$. The researcher is predicting that the early sensory deprivation will reduce the kittens' performance on the discrimination task. Use a one-tailed test with $\alpha = .01$ to test this hypothesis.

ANSWERS

1. The left-hand tail

2. The hypotheses are H_0: $\mu \geq 40$ and H_1: $\mu < 40$. The critical region is determined by z-scores less than -2.33. The z-score for these sample data is $z = -2.00$. Fail to reject H_0.

8.5 THE GENERAL ELEMENTS OF HYPOTHESIS TESTING: A REVIEW

The z-score hypothesis test presented in this chapter is one specific example of the general process of hypothesis testing. In later chapters, we will examine many other hypothesis tests. Although the details of the hypothesis test will vary from one situation to another, all of the different tests use the same basic logic and consist of the same elements. In this section, we will present a generic hypothesis test that outlines the basic elements and logic common to all tests. The better you understand the general process of a hypothesis test, the better you will understand inferential statistics.

Hypothesis tests consist of five basic elements organized in a logical pattern. The elements and their relationships to each other are as follows:

1. Hypothesized Population Parameter. The first step in a hypothesis test is to state a null hypothesis. Note that the null hypothesis typically provides a specific value for an unknown population parameter. The specific value predicted by the null hypothesis is the first element of hypothesis testing.

2. Sample Statistic. The sample data are used to calculate a sample statistic that corresponds to the hypothesized population parameter. Thus far we have considered only situations in which the null hypothesis specifies a value for the population mean, and the appropriate sample statistic is the sample mean. Similarly, if the hypothesis specified a value for the population variance, then the appropriate statistic would be the sample variance.

3. Estimate of Error. To evaluate our findings, we must know what types of sample data are likely to occur simply due to chance. Typically, a measure of standard error is used to provide this information. The general purpose of standard error is to provide a measure of how much difference is expected between a sample statistic and the corresponding population parameter. Remember that samples (statistics) are not expected to provide a perfectly accurate picture of populations (parameters). There always will be some error or discrepancy between a statistic and a parameter; this is the concept of sampling error. The standard error tells how much error is expected simply by chance.

In Chapter 7, we introduced the standard error of $\overline{X}$. This is the first specific example of the general concept of standard error, and it provides a measure of how much error is expected between a sample mean (statistic) and the corresponding population mean (parameter). In later chapters, you will encounter other examples of standard error, each of which measures the standard distance (expected by chance) between a specific statistic and its corresponding parameter. Although the exact formula for standard error will change from one situation to another, you should recall that standard error is basically determined by two factors:

a. The variability of the scores. Standard error is directly related to the variability of the scores: The larger the variability, the larger the standard error.

b. The size of the sample. Standard error is inversely related to sample size: The larger the sample, the smaller the standard error.

4. The Test Statistic. In this chapter, the test statistic is a z-score:

$$z = \frac{\overline{X} - \mu}{\sigma_{\overline{X}}}$$

This z-score statistic provides a model for other test statistics that will follow. In particular, a test statistic typically forms a ratio. The numerator of the ratio is simply the obtained difference between the sample statistic and the hypothesized parameter. The denominator of the ratio is the standard error measuring how much difference is expected by chance. Thus, the generic form of a test statistic is

$$\text{test statistic} = \frac{\text{obtained difference}}{\text{difference expected by chance}}$$

In general, the purpose of a test statistic is to determine whether or not the result of an experiment (the obtained difference) is more than expected by chance alone. Thus, a test statistic that has a value greater than 1.00 indicates that the obtained result (numerator) is greater than chance (denominator). In addition, the test statistic provides a measure of *how much* greater than chance. A value of 3.00, for example, indicates that the obtained difference is three times greater than would be expected by chance.

5. The Alpha Level. The final element in a hypothesis test is the alpha level, or level of significance. The alpha level provides a criterion for interpreting the test statistic. As we noted, a test statistic greater than 1.00 indicates that the obtained result is greater than expected by chance. However, researchers demand that the likelihood of a result be not simply "more than chance," but *significantly more than chance*. The alpha level provides a criterion for "significance."

Earlier in this chapter (page 182), we noted that when a significant result is reported in the literature, it always is accompanied by a *p* value; for example, $p < .05$ means that there is less than a 5% probability that the result occurred by chance. In general, a *significant* result means that the researcher is very confident that the result is not simply due to chance. A result that is significant at the .05 (5%) level, for example, means that the researcher is 95% confident that the obtained difference is greater than what one would expect by chance alone. Similarly, the .01 (1%) level indicates 99% confidence, and the .001 (.1%) level indicates 99.9% confidence.

To gain more confidence (rejecting H_0 with a smaller alpha), the results must demonstrate a larger difference (treatment effect). As you know, the alpha level is used to obtain a critical value for the test statistic. With the *z*-score test, for example, $\alpha = .05$ produces a critical value of ±1.96. In general, the alpha level determines how big the test statistic ratio must be before you can claim a *significant* result. The following values are *not* intended to be precise; rather, they should provide you with a *rough idea* of how the alpha level is related to the test statistic:

a. For $\alpha = .05$, the criterion for significance is a test statistic ratio of at least 2.00. That is, the obtained difference (numerator) must be at least *twice as big* as chance (denominator). *Note:* The exact value for the *z*-score test is 1.96.

b. For $\alpha = .01$, the criterion for significance is a test statistic ratio of at least 2.50. That is, the obtained difference must be at least *two and one-half times bigger* than chance. *Note:* The exact value for the *z*-score test is 2.58.

c. For $\alpha = .001$, the criterion for significance is a test statistic ratio of at least 3.00. That is, the obtained difference must be at least *three times bigger* than chance. *Note:* The exact value for the *z*-score test is 3.30.

Again, these values are *approximate* and provide a rough "rule of thumb." You always will need to consult a statistical table (for example, the unit normal table) to determine the exact critical values for your hypothesis test. Finally, we remind you to watch for the five basic elements described in this section as you encounter different examples of hypothesis testing throughout the rest of the book.

ON THE WEB

REMEMBER THAT a practice quiz for Chapter 8 is available on the Wadsworth Web site at **www.wadsworth.com**. You can use the quiz to test your knowledge on hypothesis testing and determine which parts of the chapter may need more study. In addition, there is a workshop on hypothesis tests that may give you a better understanding of this important statistical technique. For more information about the quizzes and workshops, see page 24.

SUMMARY

1. Hypothesis testing is an inferential procedure that uses the data from a sample to draw a general conclusion about a population. The procedure begins with a hypothesis about an unknown population. Then a sample is selected, and the sample data provide evidence that either supports or refutes the hypothesis.

2. In this chapter, we introduced hypothesis testing using the simple situation in which a sample mean is used to test a hypothesis about an unknown population mean. We begin with an unknown population, generally a population that has received a treatment. The question is to determine whether or not the treatment has had an effect on the population mean (see Figure 8.1).

3. Hypothesis testing is structured as a four-step process that will be used throughout the remainder of the book.
    a. State the null hypothesis (H_0), and select an alpha level. The null hypothesis states that there is no effect or no change. In this case, H_0 states that the mean for the treated population is the same as the mean before treatment. The alpha level, usually $\alpha = .05$ or $\alpha = .01$, provides a definition of the term *very unlikely* and determines the risk of a Type I error. An alternative hypothesis (H_1), which is the exact opposite of the null hypothesis, is also stated.
    b. Locate the critical region. The critical region is defined as sample outcomes that would be very unlikely to occur if the null hypothesis is true. The alpha level defines "very unlikely." For example, with $\alpha = .05$, the critical region is defined as sample means in the extreme 5% of the distribution of sample means. When the distribution is normal, the extreme 5% corresponds to z-scores beyond $z = \pm 1.96$.
    c. Collect the data, and compute the test statistic. The sample mean is transformed into a z-score by the formula

$$z = \frac{\overline{X} - \mu}{\sigma_{\overline{X}}}$$

The value of μ is obtained from the null hypothesis. The z-score test statistic identifies the location of the sample mean in the distribution of sample means. Expressed in words, the z-score formula is

$$z = \frac{\text{sample mean} - \text{hypothesized population mean}}{\text{standard error}}$$

d. Make a decision. If the obtained z-score is in the critical region, we reject H_0 because it is very unlikely that these data would be obtained if H_0 were true. In this case, we conclude that the treatment has changed the population mean. If the z-score is not in the critical region, we fail to reject H_0 because the data are not significantly different from the null hypothesis. In this case, the data do not provide sufficient evidence to indicate that the treatment has had an effect.

4. Whatever decision is reached in a hypothesis test, there is always a risk of making the incorrect decision. There are two types of errors that can be committed.
   A Type I error is defined as rejecting a true H_0. This is a serious error because it results in falsely reporting a treatment effect. The risk of a Type I error is determined by the alpha level and therefore is under the experimenter's control.
   A Type II error is defined as failing to reject a false H_0. In this case, the experiment fails to report an effect that actually occurred. The probability of a Type II error cannot be specified as a single value and depends in part on the size of the treatment effect. It is identified by the symbol β (beta).

5. When a researcher expects that a treatment will change scores in a particular direction (increase or decrease), it is possible to do a directional or one-tailed test. The first step in this procedure is to incorporate the directional prediction into the hypotheses. For example, if the prediction is that a treatment will increase scores, the null hypothesis says that there is no increase and the alternative hypothesis states that there is an increase. To locate the critical region, you must determine what kind of data would refute the null hypothesis by demonstrating that the treatment worked as predicted. These outcomes will be located entirely in one tail of the distribution, so the entire critical region (5% or 1% depending on α) will be in one tail.

6. A one-tailed test is used when there is prior justification for making a directional prediction. These a priori reasons may be previous reports and findings or theoretical considerations. In the absence of the a priori basis, a two-tailed test is appropriate. In this situation, one might be unclear regarding what to expect in the study, or one might be testing competing theories.

KEY TERMS

hypothesis testing   alpha level   Type I error   statistically significant

null hypothesis   critical region   Type II error   directional test

alternative hypothesis   test statistic   beta   one-tailed test

level of significance

FOCUS ON PROBLEM SOLVING

1. Hypothesis testing involves a set of logical procedures and rules that enable us to make general statements about a population when all we have are sample data. This logic is reflected in the four steps that have been used throughout this chapter. Hypothesis-testing problems will become easier to tackle when you learn to follow the steps.

STEP 1   State the hypotheses, and set the alpha level.

STEP 2   Locate the critical region.

STEP 3   Compute the z-score for the sample data.

STEP 4   Make a decision about H_0 based on the result of step 3.

A nice benefit of mastering these steps is that all hypothesis tests that will follow use the same basic logic outlined in this chapter.

2. Students often ask, "What alpha level should I use?" Or a student may ask, "Why is an alpha of .05 used rather than something else?" There is no single correct answer to either of these questions. Keep in mind the idea of setting an alpha level in the first place: *to reduce the risk of committing a Type I error*. Therefore, you would not want to set alpha to something like .20. In that case, you would be taking a 20% risk of committing a Type I error—reporting an effect when one actually does not exist. Most researchers would find this level of risk unacceptable. Instead, researchers generally agree to the convention that $\alpha = .05$ is the greatest risk one should take of making a Type I error. Thus, the .05 level of significance is frequently used and has become the "standard" alpha level. However, some researchers prefer to take even less risk and use alpha levels of .01 and smaller.

3. Take time to consider the implications of your decision about the null hypothesis. The null hypothesis states that there is no effect. Therefore, if your decision is to reject H_0, you should conclude that the sample data provide evidence for a treatment effect. However, it is an entirely different matter if your decision is to fail to reject H_0. Remember that when you fail to reject the null hypothesis, the results are inconclusive. It is impossible to *prove* that H_0 is correct; therefore, you cannot state with certainty that "there is no effect" when H_0 is not rejected. At best, all you can state is that "there is insufficient evidence for an effect" (see Box 8.1).

4. It is very important that you understand the structure of the z-score formula (page 174). It will help you understand many of the other hypothesis tests that will be covered later.

5. When you are doing a directional hypothesis test, read the problem carefully and watch for key words (such as increase or decrease, raise or lower, and more or less) that tell you which direction the researcher is predicting. The predicted direction will determine the alternative hypothesis (H_1) and the critical region. For example, if a treatment is expected to

increase scores, H_1 would contain a *greater than* symbol, and the critical region would be in the tail associated with high scores.

DEMONSTRATION 8.1

HYPOTHESIS TEST WITH z

A researcher begins with a known population—in this case, scores on a standardized test that are normally distributed with $\mu = 65$ and $\sigma = 15$. The researcher suspects that special training in reading skills will produce a change in the scores for the individuals in the population. Because it is not feasible to administer the treatment (the special training) to everyone in the population, a sample of $n = 25$ individuals is selected, and the treatment is given to this sample. Following treatment, the average score for this sample is $\overline{X} = 70$. Is there evidence that the training has an effect on test scores?

STEP 1   State the hypothesis, and select an alpha level.

Remember that the goal of hypothesis testing is to use sample data to make general conclusions about a population. The hypothesis always concerns an unknown population. For this demonstration, the researcher does not know what would happen if the entire population were given the treatment. Nevertheless, it is possible to make hypotheses about the treated population.

Specifically, the null hypothesis says that the treatment has no effect. According to H_0, the unknown population (after treatment) is identical to the original population (before treatment). In symbols,

$$H_0: \mu = 65 \qquad \text{(After special training, the mean is still 65.)}$$

The alternative hypothesis states that the treatment does have an effect that causes a change in the population mean. In symbols,

$$H_1: \mu \neq 65 \qquad \text{(After special training, the mean is different from 65.)}$$

At this time, you also select the alpha level. Traditionally, alpha is set at .05 or .01. If there is particular concern about a Type I error or if a researcher desires to present overwhelming evidence for a treatment effect, a smaller alpha level can be used (such as $\alpha = .001$). For this demonstration, we will set alpha to .05. Thus, we are taking a 5% risk of committing a Type I error.

STEP 2   Locate the critical region.

Recall that the critical region is defined as the set of outcomes that is very unlikely to be obtained if the null hypothesis is true. Therefore, obtaining sample data from this region would lead us to reject the null hypothesis and conclude that there is an effect. Remember, the critical region is a region of rejection.

We begin by looking at all possible outcomes that could be obtained and then use the alpha level to determine the outcomes that are unlikely. For this demonstration, we look at the distribution of sample means for samples of $n = 25$—that is, all possible sample means that could be obtained if H_0 were true. The distribution of sample means will be normal because the original population is normal. It will have an expected value of $\mu = 65$ and a standard error of

$$\sigma_{\overline{X}} = \frac{\sigma}{\sqrt{n}} = \frac{15}{\sqrt{25}} = \frac{15}{5} = 3$$

With $\alpha = .05$, we want to identify the most unlikely 5% of this distribution. The most unlikely part of a normal distribution is in the tails. Therefore, we divide our alpha level evenly between the two tails, 2.5% or $p = .0250$ per tail. In column C of the unit normal table, find $p = .0250$. Then find its corresponding z-score in column A. The entry is $z = 1.96$. The boundaries for the critical region are -1.96 (on the left side) and $+1.96$ (on the right side). The distribution with its critical region is shown in Figure 8.10.

FIGURE 8.10 .

The critical region for Demonstration 8.1 consists of the extreme tails with boundaries of $z = -1.96$ and $z = +1.96$.

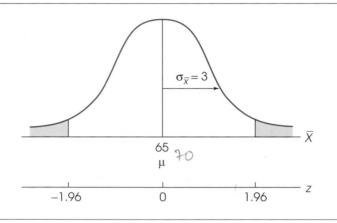

STEP 3   Obtain the sample data, and compute the test statistic.
For this demonstration, the researcher obtained a sample mean of $\overline{X} = 70$. This sample mean corresponds to a z-score of

$$z = \frac{\overline{X} - \mu}{\sigma_{\overline{X}}} = \frac{70 - 65}{3} = \frac{5}{3} = +1.67$$

STEP 4   Make a decision about H_0, and state the conclusion.
The z-score we obtained is not in the critical region. This indicates that our sample mean of $\overline{X} = 70$ is not an extreme or unusual value to be obtained from a population with $\mu = 65$. Therefore, our statistical decision is to *fail to reject* H_0. Our conclusion for the study is that the data do not provide sufficient evidence that the special training changes test scores.

PROBLEMS

1. In the z-score formula as it is used in a hypothesis test,
   a. Explain what is measured by $\overline{X} - \mu$ in the numerator.
   b. Explain what is measured by the standard error in the denominator.

2. The value that is obtained for the z-score in a hypothesis test is determined by several factors. For each of the following, indicate whether the effect would be to produce a larger z-score value (farther from zero) or a smaller z-score value (closer to zero). In each case, assume that all the other components of the z-score remain constant.
   a. Increase the sample size.
   b. Increase the population standard deviation.
   c. Increase the difference between the sample mean and the value of μ specified in the null hypothesis.

3. What happens to the boundaries for the critical region when the alpha level is lowered, for example, from .05 to .01? Also, what happens to the probability of a Type I error when the alpha level is lowered?

$z = \dfrac{\overline{X} - \mu}{\sigma_{\overline{x}}} = \dfrac{76 - 70}{4} = 4 = 1.5$

4. Briefly explain the advantage of using an alpha level of .01 versus a level of .05. In general, what is the disadvantage of using a smaller alpha level?

5. Discuss the errors that can be made in hypothesis testing.
   a. What is a Type I error? Why might it occur?
   b. What is a Type II error? How does it happen?

6. The term *error* is used two different ways in the context of a hypothesis test. First, there is the concept of standard error, and, second, there is the concept of a Type I error.
   a. What factor can a researcher control that will reduce the risk of a Type I error?
   b. What factor can a researcher control that will reduce the standard error?

7. A researcher did a one-tailed hypothesis test using an alpha level of .01. For this test, H_0 was rejected. A colleague analyzed the same data but used a two-tailed test with $\alpha = .05$. In this test, H_0 was *not* rejected. Can both analyses be correct? Explain your answer.

8. A researcher would like to test the effectiveness of a newly developed growth hormone. The researcher knows that under normal circumstances laboratory rats reach an average weight of $\mu = 950$ grams at 10 weeks of age. The distribution of weights is normal with $\sigma = 30$. A random sample of $n = 25$ newborn rats is obtained, and the hormone is given to each rat. When the rats in the sample reached 10 weeks old, each rat was weighed. The mean weight for this sample was $\overline{X} = 974$.
   a. Identify the independent and the dependent variables for this study.
   b. State the null hypothesis in a sentence that includes the independent variable and the dependent variable.
   c. Using symbols, state the hypotheses (H_0 and H_1) that the researcher is testing.
   d. Sketch the appropriate distribution, and locate the critical region for $\alpha = .05$.
   e. Calculate the test statistic (z-score) for the sample.
   f. What decision should be made about the null hypothesis, and what decision should be made about the effect of the hormone?

9. A researcher is evaluating the effectiveness of a new physical education program for elementary school children. The program is designed to reduce competition and increase individual self-esteem. A sample of $n = 16$ children is selected and the children are placed in the new program. After 3 months, each child is given a standardized self-esteem test. For the general population of elementary school children, the scores on the self-esteem test form a normal distribution with $\mu = 40$ and $\sigma = 8$.
   a. If the researcher obtained a sample mean of $\overline{X} = 42$, would this be enough evidence to conclude that the

program has a significant effect? Assume a two-tailed test with $\alpha = .05$.
   b. If the sample mean was $\overline{X} = 44$, would this be enough to demonstrate a significant effect? Again, assume a two-tailed test with $\alpha = .05$.
   c. Briefly explain why you reach different conclusions for part (a) and part (b).

10. The State College is evaluating a new English composition course for freshmen. A random sample of $n = 25$ freshmen is obtained and the students are placed in the course during their first semester. One year later, a writing sample is obtained for each student and the writing samples are graded using a standardized evaluation technique. The average score for the sample is $\overline{X} = 76$. For the general population of college students, writing scores form a normal distribution with a mean of $\mu = 70.$ $= \mu$ σ $\alpha = 0.05$
   a. If the writing scores for the population have a standard deviation of $\sigma = 20$, does the sample provide enough evidence to conclude that the new composition course has a significant effect? Assume a two-tailed test with $\alpha = .05$. 0.025 $? = 1.96$
   b. If the population standard deviation is $\sigma = 10$, is the sample sufficient to demonstrate a significant effect? Again, assume a two-tailed test with $\alpha = .05$. $\sigma_{\overline{x}} = \dfrac{\sigma}{\sqrt{n}} = \dfrac{20}{\sqrt{25}} = \dfrac{20}{5} = 4$
   c. Briefly explain why you reach different conclusions for part (a) and part (b).

11. Suppose that scores on the Scholastic Achievement Test (SAT) form a normal distribution with $\mu = 500$ and $\sigma = 100$. A high school counselor has developed a special course designed to boost SAT scores. A random sample of $n = 16$ students is selected to take the course and then the SAT. The sample had an average score of $\overline{X} = 554$. Does the course have an effect on SAT scores?
   a. What are the dependent and independent variables for this experiment?
   b. Perform the hypothesis test using the four steps outlined in the chapter. Use $\alpha = .05$.
   c. If $\alpha = .01$ were used instead, what z-score values would be associated with the critical region?
   d. For part (c), what decision should be made regarding H_0? Compare to part (b), and explain the difference.

12. A mood questionnaire has been standardized so that the scores form a normal distribution with $\mu = 50$ and $\sigma = 15$. A psychologist would like to use this test to examine how the environment affects mood. A sample of $n = 25$ individuals is obtained, and the individuals are given the mood test in a darkly painted, dimly lit room with plain metal desks and no windows. The average score for the sample is $\overline{X} = 43$.
   a. Do the sample data provide sufficient evidence to conclude that the environment has a significant effect on mood? Test at the .05 level of significance.

b. Repeat the hypothesis test using the .01 level of significance.

c. Compare the results from part (a) and part (b). How does the level of significance influence the outcome of a hypothesis test?

13. A normal population has a mean of $\mu = 100$. A sample of $n = 36$ is selected from the population, and a treatment is administered to the sample. After treatment, the sample mean is computed to be $\overline{X} = 106$.

a. Assuming that the population standard deviation is $\sigma = 12$, use the data to test whether or not the treatment has a significant effect. Test with $\alpha = .05$.

b. Repeat the hypothesis test, but this time assume that the population standard deviation is $\sigma = 30$.

c. Compare the results from part (a) and part (b). How does the population standard deviation influence the outcome of a hypothesis test?

14. A sample of $n = 4$ individuals is selected from a normal population with $\mu = 70$ and $\sigma = 10$. A treatment is administered to the individuals in the sample, and after the treatment, the sample mean is found to be $\overline{X} = 75$.

a. On the basis of the sample data, can you conclude that the treatment has a significant effect? Use a two-tailed test with $\alpha = .05$.

b. Suppose that the sample consisted of $n = 25$ individuals and produced a mean of $\overline{X} = 75$. Repeat the hypothesis test at the .05 level of significance.

c. Compare the results from part (a) and part (b). How does the sample size influence the outcome of a hypothesis test?

15. A pegboard task requires that subjects place small metal pegs into a board with holes arranged in rows. Normative data show that when people work as fast as possible, the scores are normally distributed, and the mean time to complete the task is $\mu = 185$ seconds with $\sigma = 16$. Because this task measures eye–hand coordination, the researcher tests a sample of $n = 18$ subjects that have recently been diagnosed with multiple sclerosis (MS). For the sample of subjects with MS, the mean completion time is $\overline{X} = 212$ seconds. Is eye–hand coordination significantly different for those newly diagnosed with MS? Test with $\alpha = .01$ for two tails.

16. On a perceptual task, subjects must sort cards with shapes (star, cross, triangle, or square) into separate piles. Normative data reveal a normal distribution with an average completion time of $\mu = 92$ seconds and $\sigma = 11$. A sample of $n = 5$ subjects with frontal lobe damage is tested on the task. For these subjects, the average time to complete the task is $\overline{X} = 115$ seconds. Do these people differ significantly from the norm? Use the .01 level of significance for two tails.

17. A psychologist has developed a standardized test for measuring the vocabulary skills of 4-year-old children. The scores on the test form a normal distribution with $\mu = 60$ and $\sigma = 10$. A researcher would like to use this test to investigate the hypothesis that children who grow up as single children develop vocabulary skills at a different rate than children in large families. A sample of $n = 25$ single children is obtained, and the mean test score for this sample is $\overline{X} = 63$.

a. On the basis of this sample, can the researcher conclude that vocabulary skills for single children are significantly different from those of the general population? Test at the .05 level of significance.

b. Perform the same test assuming that the researcher had used a sample of $n = 100$ single children and obtained the same sample mean, $\overline{X} = 63$.

c. You should find that the larger sample (part b) produces a different conclusion than the smaller sample (part a). Explain how the sample size influences the outcome of the hypothesis test.

18. In 1975, a nationwide survey revealed that U.S. grade-school children spent an average of $\mu = 8.4$ hours per week doing homework. The distribution of homework times was normal with $\sigma = 3.2$. Last year, a sample of $n = 100$ grade-school students was given the same survey. For this sample, the mean number of homework hours was $\overline{X} = 7.1$. Has there been a significant change in the homework habits of grade-school children? Test with $\alpha = .05$.

19. A psychologist examined the effect of chronic alcohol abuse on memory. In this experiment, a standardized memory test was used. Scores on this test for the general population form a normal distribution with $\mu = 50$ and $\sigma = 6$. A sample of $n = 22$ alcohol abusers has a mean score of $\overline{X} = 47$. Is there evidence for memory impairment among alcoholics? Use $\alpha = .01$ for a one-tailed test.

20. A psychologist would like to determine whether there is any relationship between people's personality traits and the colors they choose when buying a new car. Based on records from the Department of Motor Vehicles, the psychologist obtains a sample of $n = 25$ people who recently purchased a new red car. These people were all given a brief questionnaire measuring introversion/extroversion. The average score for this sample was $\overline{X} = 54.5$. The personality questionnaire is standardized so that the population forms a normal distribution with a mean of $\mu = 50$ and $\sigma = 10$ (higher scores indicate more extroversion).

a. Using a two-tailed test with $\alpha = .05$, does the sample provide sufficient evidence to conclude that people who select red cars have personality traits that are significantly different from the general population?

b. What conclusion is obtained for a two-tailed test with $\alpha = .01$?

c. If the researcher used a one-tailed test, predicting that people with red cars are more extroverted, are the results significant at the .01 level?

21. A researcher would like to determine whether there is any relationship between students' grades and where they choose to sit in the classroom. Specifically, the researcher suspects that the better students choose to sit in the front of the room. To test this hypothesis, the researcher asks her colleagues to help identify a sample of $n = 100$ students who all sit in the front row in at least one class. At the end of the semester, the grades are obtained for these students and the average grade point average is $\overline{X} = 3.25$. For the same semester, the average grade point average for the entire college is $\mu = 2.95$ with $\sigma = 1.10$.

a. Use a two-tailed test with $\alpha = .01$ to determine whether students who sit in the front of the classroom have significantly different grade point averages than other students.

b. Use a one-tailed test with $\alpha = .01$ to determine whether students who sit in the front of the classroom have significantly higher grade point averages than other students.

22. A sample of $n = 9$ scores is obtained from a normal population with $\sigma = 12$. The sample mean is $\overline{X} = 60$.

a. Use the sample data to test the hypothesis that the population mean is $\mu = 65$. Test at the .05 level of significance.

b. Use the sample data to test the hypothesis that the population mean is $\mu = 55$. Test at the .05 level of significance.

c. In parts (a) and (b) of this problem, you should find that $\mu = 65$ and $\mu = 55$ are both acceptable hypotheses. Explain how two different values can both be acceptable.

23. A developmental psychologist has prepared a training program that, according to a psychological theory, should improve problem-solving ability. For the population of six-year-olds, the average score on a standardized problem-solving test is known to be $\mu = 80$ with $\sigma = 10$. To test the effectiveness of the training program, a random sample of $n = 18$ six-year-old children is selected. After training, the average score for this sample is $\overline{X} = 84.44$. Can the experimenter conclude that the program has an effect? Test with alpha set at .05.

a. Perform the hypothesis test showing all four steps. When you state the hypotheses, explain what they

predict in terms of the independent and dependent variables used in this experiment.

b. Would the same decision have been made about H_0 if a one-tailed had been used with $\alpha = .05$? How about $\alpha = .025$?

24. On a standardized anagram task (anagrams are sets of scrambled letters that must be arranged to form words), people successfully complete an average of $\mu = 26$ anagrams with $\sigma = 4$. This distribution is normal. A researcher would like to demonstrate that the arousal from anxiety is distracting and will decrease task performance. A sample of $n = 14$ anxiety-ridden subjects is tested on the task. The average number of anagrams solved is $\overline{X} = 23.36$.

a. Do the anxiety-ridden subjects show a decrease in task performance? Test with alpha set at .01 for one tail.

b. If a two-tailed test with $\alpha = .01$ is used, what conclusion should be drawn?

25. Researchers have often noted increases in violent crimes when it is very hot. In fact, Reifman, Larrick, and Fein (1991) noted that this relationship even extends to baseball. That is, there is a much greater chance of a batter being hit by a pitch when the temperature increases. Consider the following hypothetical data. Suppose over the past 30 years, during any given week of the major league season, an average of $\mu = 12$ players are hit by wild pitches. Assume the distribution is nearly normal with $\sigma = 3$. For a sample of $n = 4$ weeks in which the daily temperature was extremely hot, the weekly average of hit-by-pitch players was $\overline{X} = 15.5$. Are players more likely to get hit by pitches during hot weeks? Set alpha to .05 for a one-tailed test.

26. A psychologist develops a new inventory to measure depression. Using a very large standardization group of "normal" individuals, the mean score on this test is $\mu = 55$ with $\sigma = 12$, and the scores are normally distributed. To determine whether the test is sensitive in detecting those individuals that are severely depressed, a random sample of patients who are described as depressed by a therapist is selected and given the test. Presumably, the higher the score on the inventory, the more depressed the patient is. The data are as follows: 59, 60, 60, 67, 65, 90, 89, 73, 74, 81, 71, 71, 83, 83, 88, 83, 84, 86, 85, 78, 79. Do patients score significantly differently on the test? Test with the .01 level of significance for two tails.

CHAPTER 9

INTRODUCTION TO THE *t* STATISTIC

TOOLS YOU WILL NEED

The following items are considered essential background material for this chapter. If you doubt your knowledge of any of these items, you should review the appropriate chapter or section before proceeding.

- Sample standard deviation (Chapter 4)

- Degrees of freedom (Chapter 4)

- Hypothesis testing (Chapter 8)

CONTENTS

9.1   OVERVIEW

In the previous chapter, we presented the statistical procedures that permit researchers to use a sample mean to test hypotheses about a population mean. These statistical procedures were based on a few basic notions, which we summarize as follows:

Remember, the expected value of the distribution of sample means is μ, the population mean.

1. A sample mean $(\overline{X})$ is expected to approximate its population mean (μ). This permits us to use the sample mean to test a hypothesis about the population mean.

2. The standard error provides a measure of how well a sample mean approximates the population mean. Specifically, the standard error determines how much difference between $\overline{X}$ and μ is reasonable to expect just by chance.

$$\text{Standard error} = \sigma_{\overline{X}} = \frac{\sigma}{\sqrt{n}} \quad \text{or} \quad \sigma_{\overline{X}} = \sqrt{\frac{\sigma^2}{n}}$$

3. To quantify our inferences about the population, we compare the obtained sample mean $(\overline{X})$ with the hypothesized population mean (μ) by computing a z-score test statistic:

$$z = \frac{\overline{X} - \mu}{\sigma_{\overline{X}}} = \frac{\text{obtained difference between data and hypothesis}}{\text{standard distance expected by chance}}$$

The goal of the hypothesis test is to determine whether or not the obtained difference is significantly greater than would be expected by chance. When the z-scores form a normal distribution, we are able to use the unit normal table (Appendix B) to find the critical region for the hypothesis test.

The shortcoming of using the z-score as an inferential statistic is that the z-score formula requires more information than is usually available. Specifically, z-scores require that we know the value of the population standard deviation, (or variance), which is needed to compute the standard error. Most often the standard deviation of the population is not known, and the standard error of sample means cannot be computed. Without the standard error, we have no way of quantifying the expected amount of distance (or error) between $\overline{X}$ and μ. We have no way of making precise, quantitative inferences about the population based on z-scores. For situations in which the population standard deviation is not known, we use the t statistic rather than a z-score.

THE t STATISTIC—A SUBSTITUTE FOR z

As previously noted, the limitation of z-scores in hypothesis testing is that the population standard deviation (or variance) must be known. More often than not, however, the variability of the scores in the population is not known. In fact, the whole reason for conducting a hypothesis test is to gain knowledge about an *unknown* population. This situation appears to create a paradox: You want to use a z-score to find out about an unknown population, but you must know about the population before you can compute a z-score. Fortunately, there is a relatively simple solution to this problem. When the variability for the population is not known, we use the sample variability in its place.

In Chapter 4, the sample variance was developed specifically to provide an unbiased estimate of the corresponding population variance. You should recall the formulas for sample variance and sample standard deviation as follows:

The concept of degrees of freedom, $df = n - 1$, was introduced in Chapter 4 (p. 91) and is discussed later in this chapter (p. 204).

$$\text{sample variance} = s^2 = \frac{SS}{n - 1} = \frac{SS}{df}$$

$$\text{sample standard deviation} = s = \sqrt{\frac{SS}{n - 1}} = \sqrt{\frac{SS}{df}}$$

Using the sample values, we can now *estimate* the standard error. You should recall from Chapter 7 (p. 151) that the value of the standard error can be computed using either standard deviation or variance:

$$\text{standard error} = \sigma_{\bar{X}} = \frac{\sigma}{\sqrt{n}} = \sqrt{\frac{\sigma^2}{n}}$$

Now, we will estimate the standard error by simply substituting the sample variance or standard deviation in place of the unknown population value:

$$\text{estimated standard error} = s_{\bar{X}} = \frac{s}{\sqrt{n}} = \sqrt{\frac{s^2}{n}} \qquad (9.1)$$

Note that the symbol for the estimated standard error is $s_{\bar{X}}$ instead of $\sigma_{\bar{X}}$, indicating that the estimated value is computed from sample data rather than the actual population parameter.

DEFINITION

The *estimated standard error* $(s_{\bar{X}})$ is used as an estimate of the real standard error $\sigma_{\bar{X}}$ when the value of σ is unknown. It is computed from the sample variance or sample standard deviation and provides an estimate of the standard distance between a sample mean $\bar{X}$ and the population mean μ.

Finally, you should recognize that we have shown formulas for standard error (actual or estimated) using both the standard deviation and the variance. In the past (Chapters 7 and 8), we concentrated on the formula using the standard deviation. At this point, however, we will shift our focus to the formula based on variance. Thus, throughout the remainder of this chapter and in following chapters, the *estimated standard error of* $\bar{X}$ typically will be presented and computed using

Additional information about the estimated standard error is presented in Box 9.1.

$$s_{\bar{X}} = \sqrt{\frac{s^2}{n}}$$

There are two reasons for making this shift from standard deviation to variance:

1. From this point on, we will emphasize a distinction between the sample standard deviation as a *descriptive statistic* and the sample variance as an *inferential statistic*. On one hand, when we are describing or summarizing the scores in a sample, we will use the sample mean and the sample standard deviation. On the other hand, when we want to use the sample to draw inferences about the population, we will use variance and standard error.

<table>
<tr><td>

9.1

</td><td>

ANOTHER LOOK AT STANDARD DEVIATION, STANDARD ERROR, AND VARIANCE

</td></tr>
</table>

MANY STUDENTS find the sample standard deviation (s) and the estimated standard error ($s_{\overline{X}}$) to be very confusing concepts. Therefore, we will present a brief summary of these two statistical measures including some discussion of their similarities and their differences.

The standard deviation is primarily a *descriptive statistic*. Specifically, the sample standard deviation is used along with the sample mean to provide a summary description for a set of scores. The sample mean identifies the center of the set of scores and the sample standard deviation describes how the scores are scattered around the mean. A small value for the standard deviation indicates that the scores are clustered close to the mean, and a large value indicates that the scores are widely scattered.

The estimated standard error is primarily an *inferential statistic*. Standard error measures the standard distance between a sample mean ($\overline{X}$) and the population mean (μ). That is, the standard error measures how accurately the sample represents the population.

Finally, we would like to point out two important similarities between the standard deviation and the standard error.

1. Both values are used to measure *standard distance*. The sample standard deviation measures the standard distance between a score and the mean. The estimated standard error measures the standard distance between a sample and a population.

2. Both of these standard distances are found by taking the square root of the sample variance, s^2.

$$\begin{array}{ll} \text{sample} \\ \text{standard} = s = \sqrt{s^2} \\ \text{deviation} \end{array} \qquad \begin{array}{ll} \text{estimated} \\ \text{standard} = s_{\overline{X}} = \sqrt{s^2/n} \\ \text{error} \end{array}$$

To compute the sample standard deviation, you simply take the square root of the variance. To compute the estimated standard error, however, you must also consider the sample size. Because a larger sample means a smaller error, you must include the sample size (n) in the calculation.

The term *unbiased* means that on average the sample statistic provides an accurate representation of the corresponding population parameter.

2. Recall from Chapter 4 (page 92) that the sample variance is an *unbiased statistic* whereas the sample standard deviation is not. In the formula for estimated standard error, we are using a sample value to substitute for an unknown population value. In this situation, it seems much more appropriate to use the unbiased sample variance instead of the biased sample standard deviation.

Now we can substitute the estimated standard error in the denominator of the z-score formula. This result is a new test statistic called a *t statistic*:

$$t = \frac{\overline{X} - \mu}{s_{\overline{X}}} \tag{9.2}$$

DEFINITION

The *t statistic* is used to test hypotheses about an unknown population mean μ when the value of σ is unknown. The formula for the *t* statistic has the same structure as the z-score formula, except that the *t* statistic uses the estimated standard error in the denominator.

The only difference between the *t* formula and the z-score formula is that the z-score uses the actual population variance, σ^2 (or the standard deviation), and the *t* formula uses the corresponding sample variance (or standard deviation) when the population value is not known.

when σ is known: when σ is not known:

$$z = \frac{\overline{X} - \mu}{\sigma_{\overline{X}}} = \frac{\overline{X} - \mu}{\sqrt{\sigma^2/n}} \qquad t = \frac{\overline{X} - \mu}{s_{\overline{X}}} = \frac{\overline{X} - \mu}{\sqrt{s^2/n}}$$

DEGREES OF FREEDOM AND THE *t* STATISTIC

In this chapter, we have introduced the *t* statistic as a substitute for a *z*-score. The basic difference between these two is that the *t* statistic uses sample variance (s^2) and the *z*-score uses the population variance (σ^2). To determine how well a *t* statistic approximates a *z*-score, we must determine how well the sample variance approximates the population variance.

In Chapter 4, we introduced the concept of degrees of freedom (p. 91). Reviewing briefly, you must know the sample mean before you can compute sample variance. This places a restriction on sample variability such that only $n - 1$ scores in a sample are free to vary. The value $n - 1$ is called the *degrees of freedom* (or *df*) for the sample variance:

$$\text{degrees of freedom} = df = n - 1 \tag{9.3}$$

DEFINITION

Degrees of freedom describe the number of scores in a sample that are free to vary. Because the sample mean places a restriction on the value of one score in the sample, there are $n - 1$ degrees of freedom for the sample (see Chapter 4).

The greater the value of *df* is for a sample, the better s^2 represents σ^2, and the better the *t* statistic approximates the *z*-score. This should make sense because the larger the sample (*n*) is, the better the sample represents its population. Thus, the degrees of freedom associated with s^2 also describe how well *t* represents *z*.

THE *t* DISTRIBUTIONS

Every sample from a population can be used to compute a *z*-score or a *t* statistic. If you select all the possible samples of a particular size (*n*), then the entire set of resulting *z*-scores will form a *z*-score distribution. In the same way, the set of all possible *t* statistics will form a *t* *distribution*. As we saw in Chapter 7, the distribution of *z*-scores computed from sample means tends to be a normal distribution. For this reason, we consulted the unit normal table to find the critical region when using *z*-scores to test hypotheses about a population. The *t* distribution will approximate a normal distribution in the same way that a *t* statistic approximates a *z*-score. How well a *t* distribution approximates a normal distribution is determined by degrees of freedom. In general, the greater the sample size (*n*) is, the larger the degrees of freedom ($n - 1$) are, and the better the *t* distribution approximates the normal distribution (see Figure 9.1).

THE SHAPE OF THE *t* DISTRIBUTION

The exact shape of a *t* distribution changes with degrees of freedom. In fact, statisticians speak of a "family" of *t* distributions. That is, there is a different sampling distribution of *t* (a distribution of all possible sample *t* values) for each possible number of degrees of freedom. As *df* gets very large, the *t* distribution gets closer in shape to a normal *z*-score distribution. A quick glance at Figure 9.1 reveals that distributions of *t* are bell-shaped and symmetrical and have a mean of zero. However, the *t* distribution has more

FIGURE 9.1

Distributions of the *t* statistic for different values of degrees of freedom are compared to a normal *z*-score distribution. Like the normal distribution, *t* distributions are bell-shaped and symmetrical and have a mean of zero. However, *t* distributions have more variability, indicated by the flatter and more spread-out shape. The larger the value of *df* is, the more closely the *t* distribution approximates a normal distribution.

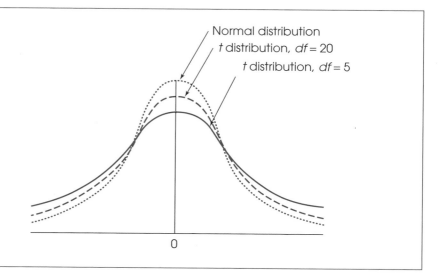

variability than a normal *z* distribution, especially when *df* values are small (Figure 9.1). The *t* distribution tends to be flatter and more spread out, whereas the normal *z* distribution has more of a central peak.

Why is the *t* distribution flatter and more variable than a normal *z* distribution? For a particular population, the top of the *z*-score formula, $\overline{X} - \mu$, can take on different values because $\overline{X}$ will vary from one sample to another. However, the value of the bottom of the *z*-score formula, $\sigma_{\overline{X}}$, is constant. The standard error will not vary from sample to sample because it is derived from the population variance. The implication is that samples that have the same value for $\overline{X}$ should also have the same *z*-score.

On the other hand, the standard error in the *t* formula is not a constant because it is estimated. That is, $s_{\overline{X}}$ is based on the sample variance, which will vary in value from sample to sample. The result is that samples can have the same value for $\overline{X}$, yet different values of *t* because the estimated error will vary from one sample to another. Therefore, a *t* distribution will have more variability than the normal *z* distribution. It will look flatter and more spread out. When the value of *df* increases, the variability in the *t* distribution decreases, and it more closely resembles the normal distribution because with greater *df*, $s_{\overline{X}}$ will more closely estimate $\sigma_{\overline{X}}$, and when *df* is very large, they are nearly the same.

DETERMINING PROPORTIONS AND PROBABILITIES FOR *t* DISTRIBUTIONS

Just as we used the unit normal table to locate proportions associated with *z*-scores, we will use a *t*-distribution table to find proportions for *t* statistics. The complete *t*-distribution table is presented in Appendix B, Table B.2, and a portion of this table is reproduced in Table 9.1. The two rows at the top of the table show proportions of the *t* distribution contained in either one or two tails, depending on which row is used. The first column of the table lists degrees of freedom for the *t* statistic. Finally, the numbers in the body of the table are the *t* values that mark the boundary between the tails and the rest of the *t* distribution.

For example, with *df* = 3, exactly 5% of the *t* distribution is located in the tail beyond *t* = 2.353 (see Figure 9.2). To find this value, locate *df* = 3 in the first column and locate 0.05 (5%) in the one-tail proportion row. When you line up these two values in the table,

TABLE 9.1

A portion of the *t*-distribution table. The numbers in the table are the values of *t* that separate the tail from the main body of the distribution. Proportions for one or two tails are listed at the top of the table, and *df* values for *t* are listed in the first column.

		Proportion in one tail				
	0.25	0.10	0.05	0.025	0.01	0.005
		Proportion in two tails combined				
df	0.50	0.20	0.10	0.05	0.02	0.01
1	1.000	3.078	6.314	12.706	31.821	63.657
2	0.816	1.886	2.920	4.303	6.965	9.925
3	0.765	1.638	2.353	3.182	4.541	5.841
4	0.741	1.533	2.132	2.776	3.747	4.604
5	0.727	1.476	2.015	2.571	3.365	4.032
6	0.718	1.440	1.943	2.447	3.143	3.707

you should find $t = 2.353$. Similarly, 5% of the *t* distribution is located in the tail beyond $t = -2.353$ (see Figure 9.2). Finally, you should notice that a total of 10% is contained in the two tails beyond $t = \pm2.353$ (check the proportion value in the "two-tails" row at the top of the table).

FIGURE 9.2

The *t* distribution with $df = 3$. Note that 5% of the distribution is located in the tail beyond $t = 2.353$. Also, 5% is in the tail beyond $t = -2.353$. Thus, a total proportion of 10% (0.10) is in the two tails beyond $t = \pm2.353$.

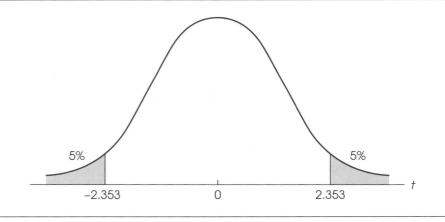

A close inspection of the *t*-distribution table in Appendix B will demonstrate a point we made earlier: As the value for *df* increases, the *t* distribution becomes more and more similar to a normal distribution. For example, examine the column containing *t* values for a 0.05 proportion in two tails. You will find that when $df = 1$, the *t* values that separate the extreme 5% (0.05) from the rest of the distribution are $t = \pm12.706$. As you read down the column, however, you should find that the critical *t* values become smaller and smaller, ultimately reaching ±1.96. You should recognize ±1.96 as the *z*-score values that separate the extreme 5% in a normal distribution. Thus, as *df* increases, the proportions in a *t* distribution become more like the proportions in a normal distribution. When the sample size (and degrees of freedom) is sufficiently large, the difference between a *t* distribution and the normal distribution becomes negligible.

Caution: The *t*-distribution table printed in this book has been abridged and does not include entries for every possible *df* value. For example, the table lists *t* values for $df = 40$ and for $df = 60$, but does not list any entries for *df* values between 40 and 60. Occasionally, you will encounter a situation in which your *t* statistic has a *df* value that is not listed in the table. In these situations, you should look up the critical *t* for both of the surrounding *df* values listed and then use the *larger* value for *t*. If, for example, you have *df* = 53 (not listed), you should look up the critical *t* value for *both df* = 40 and *df* = 60 and *then use the larger t value.* If your sample *t* statistic is greater than the larger value listed, you can be certain that the data are in the critical region, and you can confidently reject the null hypothesis.

LEARNING CHECK ◆

1. Under what circumstances is a *t* statistic used instead of a *z*-score for a hypothesis test?

2. To conduct a hypothesis test with a *z*-score statistic, you must know the variance or the standard deviation for the population of scores. (True or false?)

3. In general, a distribution of *t* statistics is flatter and more spread out than the standard normal distribution. (True or false?)

4. A sample of *n* = 15 scores would produce a *t* statistic with *df* = 16. (True or false?)

5. For *df* = 15, find the value(s) of *t* associated with each of the following:
   a. The top 5% of the distribution
   b. The middle 95% versus the extreme 5% of the distribution
   c. The middle 99% versus the extreme 1% of the distribution

ANSWERS

1. A *t* statistic is used instead of a *z*-score when the population standard deviation or variance is not known.

2. True

3. True

4. False. With *n* = 15, the *df* value would be 14.

5. a. *t* = +1.753
   b. *t* = ±2.131
   c. *t* = ±2.947   ◆

9.2 HYPOTHESIS TESTS WITH THE *t* STATISTIC

We use the *t*-statistic formula in exactly the same way that we use the *z*-score formula to test a hypothesis about a population mean. Once again, the *t* formula and its structure are

$$t = \frac{\overline{X} - \mu}{s_{\overline{X}}} = \frac{\text{sample mean} - \text{population mean}}{\text{estimated standard error}}$$

In the hypothesis-testing situation, we begin with a population with an unknown mean and an unknown variance, often a population that has received some treatment (Figure 9.3). The goal is to use a sample from the treated population (a treated sample) as the basis for determining whether or not the treatment has any effect. As always, the null hypothesis states that the treatment has no effect; specifically, H_0 states that the popula-

FIGURE 9.3

The basic experimental situation for using the *t* statistic or the *z*-score. It is assumed that the parameter μ is known for the population before treatment. The purpose of the experiment is to determine whether or not the treatment has an effect. We ask, Is the population mean after treatment the same as or different from the mean before treatment? A sample is selected from the treated population to help answer this question.

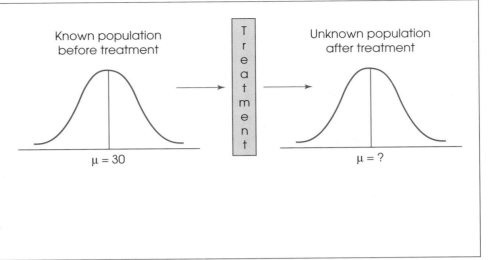

Known population before treatment

Treatment

Unknown population after treatment

$\mu = 30$

$\mu = ?$

tion mean is unchanged. Thus, the null hypothesis provides a specific value for the unknown population mean. The sample data provide a value for the sample mean. Finally, the variance and the estimated standard error are computed from the sample data. When these values are used in the *t* formula, the result becomes

$$t = \frac{\begin{array}{c}\text{sample mean} \\ \text{(from the data)}\end{array} - \begin{array}{c}\text{population mean} \\ \text{(hypothesized from } H_0)\end{array}}{\text{estimated standard error}}$$

As with the *z*-score formula, the *t* statistic forms a ratio. The numerator measures the actual difference between the data and the hypothesis. The denominator measures how much difference is expected just by chance (error). When the obtained difference between the data and the hypothesis (numerator) is much greater than chance (denominator), we will obtain a large value for *t* (either large positive or large negative). In this case, we conclude that the data are not consistent with the hypothesis, and our decision is to "reject H_0." On the other hand, when the difference between the data and the hypothesis is small relative to the standard error, we will obtain a *t* statistic near zero, and our decision will be "fail to reject H_0."

We will now review the basic steps of the hypothesis-testing procedure.

STEPS AND PROCEDURES   For hypothesis tests with a *t* statistic, we use the same steps that we used with *z*-scores (Chapter 8). The major difference is that we are now required to estimate the standard error because σ is unknown. Consequently, we compute a *t* statistic rather than a *z*-score, and consult the *t*-distribution table rather than the unit normal table, to find the critical region.

STEP 1   The hypotheses are stated, and the alpha level is set. The experimenter states the null hypothesis—that is, what should happen if no treatment effect exists. On the other hand, the alternative hypothesis predicts the outcome if an effect does occur. These hypotheses are always stated in terms of the population parameter, μ.

STEP 2   Locate the critical region. The exact shape of the *t* distribution and therefore the critical *t* values vary with degrees of freedom. Thus, to find a critical region in a *t* distribution, it is necessary to determine the value for *df*. Then the critical region can be located by consulting the *t*-distribution table (Appendix B).

STEP 3   The sample data are collected, and the test statistic is computed. When σ is unknown, the test statistic is a *t* statistic (Formula 9.2).

STEP 4   The null hypothesis is evaluated. If the *t* statistic we obtained in step 3 falls in the critical region (exceeds the value of a critical *t*), then H_0 is rejected. We can conclude that a treatment effect exists. However, if the obtained *t* value does not lie in the critical region, then we fail to reject H_0, and we conclude that we failed to observe evidence for an effect in our study.

HYPOTHESIS-TESTING EXAMPLE

The following research situation will be used to demonstrate the procedures of hypothesis testing with the *t* statistic.

EXAMPLE 9.1   Many studies have shown that direct eye contact and even patterns that look like eyes are avoided by many animals. Some insects, such as moths, have even evolved large eye-spot patterns on their wings to help ward off predators. This research example, modeled after Scaife's (1976) study, examines how eye-spot patterns affect the behavior of moth-eating birds.

A sample of $n = 16$ insectivorous birds is selected. The animals are tested in a box that has two separate chambers (see Figure 9.4). The birds are free to roam from one chamber to another through a doorway in a partition. On the wall of one chamber, two large eye-spot patterns have been painted. The other chamber has plain walls. The birds are tested one at a time by placing them in the doorway in the center of the apparatus. Each animal is left in the box for 60 minutes, and the amount of time spent in the plain chamber is recorded. Suppose that the sample of $n = 16$ birds spent an average of $\overline{X} = 35$ minutes in the plain side with $SS = 1215$. Can we conclude that eye-spot patterns have an effect on behavior? Note that while it is possible to predict a value for μ, we have no information about the population standard deviation.

FIGURE 9.4

Apparatus used in Example 9.1.

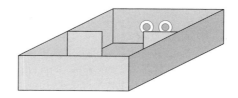

STEP 1   State the hypotheses, and select an alpha level. The null hypothesis states that the eye-spot patterns have no effect on behavior. In this case, the animals should show no preference for either side of the box. That is, they should spend half of the 60-minute test period in the plain chamber. In symbols, the null hypothesis would state that

$$H_0: \mu_{\text{plain side}} = 30 \text{ minutes}$$

Directional hypotheses could be used and would specify whether the average time on the plain side is more or less than 30 minutes.

The alternative hypothesis would state that the eye patterns have an effect on behavior. There are two possibilities: (1) The animals may avoid staying in the chamber with the eye spots as we suspect, or (2) for some reason, the animals may show a preference for the patterns painted on the wall. A nondirectional hypothesis (for a two-tailed test) would be represented in symbols as follows:

$$H_1: \mu_{\text{plain side}} \neq 30 \text{ minutes}$$

We will set the level of significance at $\alpha = .05$ for two tails.

STEP 2   Locate the critical region. The test statistic is a *t* statistic because the population standard deviation is not known. The exact shape of the *t* distribution and therefore the proportions under the *t* distribution depend on the number of degrees of freedom associated with the sample. To find the critical region, *df* must be computed:

$$df = n - 1 = 16 - 1 = 15$$

For a two-tailed test at the .05 level of significance and with 15 degrees of freedom, the critical region consists of *t* values greater than $+2.131$ or less than -2.131. Figure 9.5 depicts the critical region in this *t* distribution.

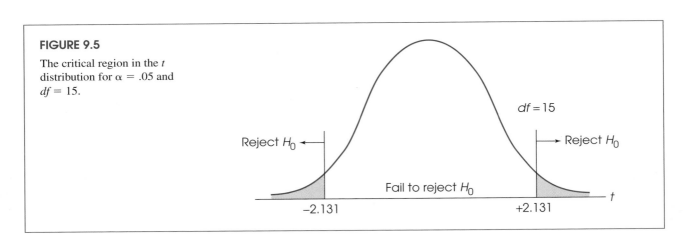

FIGURE 9.5

The critical region in the *t* distribution for $\alpha = .05$ and $df = 15$.

STEP 3   Calculate the test statistic. The *t* statistic typically requires much more computation than is necessary for a *z*-score. Therefore, we recommend that you divide the calculations into a three-stage process as follows.

a. First, calculate the sample variance. Remember, the population variance is unknown, and you must use the sample value in its place. (This is why we are using a *t* statistic instead of a *z*-score.)

$$s^2 = \frac{SS}{n - 1} = \frac{SS}{df}$$

$$= \frac{1215}{15}$$

$$= 81$$

b. Next, use the sample variance (s^2) to compute the estimated standard error. This value will be the denominator of the *t* statistic and measures how much error is expected by chance between a sample mean and the corresponding population mean.

$$s_{\bar{X}} = \sqrt{\frac{s^2}{n}}$$

$$= \sqrt{\frac{81}{16}}$$

$$= 2.25$$

c. Finally, compute the *t* statistic for the sample data.

$$t = \frac{\bar{X} - \mu}{s_{\bar{X}}}$$

$$= \frac{35 - 30}{2.25}$$

$$= \frac{5}{2.25}$$

$$= 2.22$$

STEP 4 Make a decision regarding H_0. The obtained *t* statistic of 2.22 falls into the critical region on the right-hand side of the *t* distribution (Figure 9.5). Our statistical decision is to reject H_0 and conclude that the presence of eye-spot patterns does influence behavior. As can be seen from the sample mean, there is a tendency for animals to avoid the eyes and spend more time on the plain side of the box. The data indicate that the birds spent *significantly* more time on the plain side than would be expected merely by chance (see Box 9.2).

IN THE LITERATURE:
REPORTING THE RESULTS OF A *t* TEST

In Chapter 8, we noted the conventional style for reporting the results of a hypothesis test, according to APA format. First, recall that a scientific report typically uses the term *significant* to indicate that the null hypothesis has been rejected and the term *not significant* to indicate failure to reject H_0. Additionally, there is a prescribed format for reporting the calculated value of the test statistic, degrees of freedom, and alpha level for a *t* test. This format parallels the style introduced in Chapter 8 (page 182). For Example 9.1, we calculated a *t* statistic of $+2.22$ with $df = 15$ and decided to reject H_0 with alpha set at .05. In a scientific report, this information is conveyed in a concise statement, as follows:

The statement $p < .05$ was explained in Chapter 8, page 183.

The subjects spent more time on the plain side of the apparatus ($M = 35$, $SD = 9$). These data demonstrate that the birds spent significantly more time in the chamber without eye-spot patterns; $t(15) = +2.22$, $p < .05$, two-tailed.

9.2   A FINAL ANALOGY FOR THE ESTIMATED STANDARD ERROR

THE ROLE of standard error in a hypothesis test: You should realize by now that the standard error (or the estimated standard error) is a critical part of a hypothesis test. The role of the standard error is demonstrated in the following analogy. Suppose I claim to have ESP, which allows me to predict the outcome of a coin toss. To demonstrate my powers, I have someone toss a balanced coin 100 times and I try to predict the outcome each time. If I were just guessing, I should get 50 out of 100 predictions correct just by chance. Suppose that I actually get 52 correct. Is this enough evidence to convince you that I have ESP?

I hope you realize that predicting 52 out of 100 coin tosses is not convincing evidence of ESP. Specifically, you would expect to get *around* 50 correct just by chance, and a score of 52 is well within the margin of error. This "margin of error" is exactly what is measured by the standard error. To provide convincing evidence that I have ESP, I would need to predict a number of coin tosses that far exceeds the margin of error.

Now consider a similar situation using a sample mean and a population mean. Suppose that a population is known to have a mean of $\mu = 50$. A sample is selected from this population and a treatment is administered to the sample. After treatment, the sample mean is found to be $\overline{X} = 52$. Does this sample provide convincing evidence that the treatment has an effect?

Again, you should realize that a sample mean of $\overline{X} = 52$ *by itself* is not convincing. Specifically, you would expect the sample to average around 50 just by chance. The obtained value, $\overline{X} = 52$, may be within the margin of error. In this case, you would need to compute the standard error to determine exactly how much difference is reasonable to expect just by chance. To demonstrate that the treatment has a *significant* effect, you need to show that the difference between the sample mean and the population mean far exceeds the standard error.

The magnitude of the standard error: We can also use the coin tossing example to look once more at the two factors that determine the size of the standard error.

1. The first factor is the sample size. Obviously, the bigger the sample, the more accurately the sample represents the population. In terms of standard error, the bigger the sample, the smaller is the error.

2. The second factor is the variability of the scores or the variance. If I am trying to predict a coin toss, there are only two possible outcomes, and I can expect an accuracy rate of around 50%. However, suppose that I am trying to predict the outcome from rolling a die (one half of a pair of dice). Now there are six possible outcomes. Note that we have increased the number of different things that can happen; in statistical terms, we have increased the variance. Also, note that my error rate will go up. With six different outcomes, I no longer expect to predict correctly 50% of the time. In other words, as the variance increases, error also increases.

If you examine the formula for estimated standard error, you will find both of these factors. As the sample size (n) increases, the error decreases. However, as the sample variance (s^2) increases, the error also increases.

In the first statement, the mean ($M = 35$) and the standard deviation ($SD = 9$) are reported as previously noted (Chapter 4, page 97). The next statement provides the results of the statistical analysis. Note that the degrees of freedom are reported in parentheses immediately after the symbol t. The value for the obtained t statistic follows (2.22), and next is the probability of committing a Type I error (less than 5%). Finally, the type of test (one- versus two-tailed) is noted.   ❏

DIRECTIONAL HYPOTHESES AND ONE-TAILED TESTS

As we noted in Chapter 8, the nondirectional (two-tailed) test is commonly used for research that is intended for publication in a scientific journal. On the other hand, a directional (one-tailed) test may be used in some research situations, such as exploratory investigations or pilot studies. The following example demonstrates a directional hypothesis test with a *t* statistic, using the same experimental situation that was presented in Example 9.1.

EXAMPLE 9.2   The research question is whether eye-spot patterns will affect the behavior of birds placed in a special testing box. The researcher is expecting the birds to avoid the eye-spot patterns. Therefore, the researcher predicts that the birds will spend most of the hour on the plain side of the box.

STEP 1   State the hypotheses, and select an alpha level. With most directional tests, it is usually easier to state the hypothesis in words, including the directional prediction, and then convert the words into symbols. For this example, the researcher is predicting that the eye-spot patterns will cause the birds to *increase* the amount of time that they spend on the plain side of the box; that is, more than half of the hour should be spent on the plain side. In general, the null hypothesis states that the predicted effect will not happen. For this study, the null hypothesis states that the birds will *not* spend more than half of the hour on the plain side. In symbols,

$$H_0: \mu_{\text{plain side}} \leq 30 \text{ minutes} \qquad \text{(Not more than half of the hour on the plain side)}$$

Similarly, the alternative states that the treatment will work. In this case, H_1 states that the birds will spend more than half of the hour on the plain side. In symbols,

$$H_1: \mu_{\text{plain side}} > 30 \text{ minutes} \qquad \text{(More than half of the hour on the plain side)}$$

We will set the level of significance at $\alpha = .05$.

STEP 2   Locate the critical region. In this example, the researcher is predicting that the sample mean ($\overline{X}$) will be greater than 30. The null hypothesis states that the population mean is $\mu = 30$ (or less). If you examine the structure of the *t*-statistic formula, it should be clear that a positive *t* statistic would support the researcher's prediction and refute the null hypothesis.

$$t = \frac{\overline{X} - \mu}{s_{\overline{X}}}$$

The problem is to determine how large a positive value is necessary to reject H_0. To find the critical value, you must look in the *t*-distribution table using the one-tail proportions. With a sample of $n = 16$, the *t* statistic will have $df = 15$; using $\alpha = .05$, you should find a critical *t* value of 1.753. Figure 9.6 depicts the critical region in the *t* distribution.

STEP 3   Calculate the test statistic. The computation of the *t* statistic is the same for either a one-tailed or a two-tailed test. Earlier (in Example 9.1), we found that the data for this experiment produce a test statistic of $t = 2.22$.

STEP 4   Make a decision. The test statistic is in the critical region, so we reject H_0. In terms of the experimental variables, we have decided that the birds spent significantly more time on the plain side of the box than on the side with eye-spot patterns.

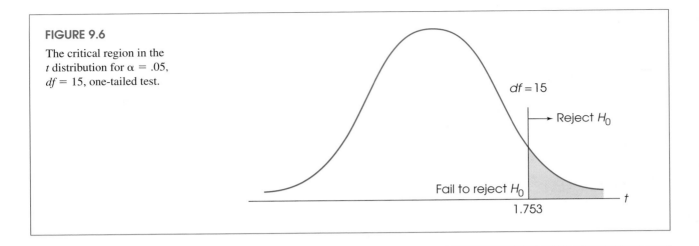

FIGURE 9.6

The critical region in the *t* distribution for α = .05, *df* = 15, one-tailed test.

ASSUMPTIONS OF THE *t* TEST   Two basic assumptions are necessary for hypothesis tests with the *t* statistic.

1. The values in the sample must consist of *independent* observations.

   In everyday terms, two observations are independent if there is no consistent, predictable relationship between the first observation and the second. More precisely, two events (or observations) are independent if the occurrence of the first event has no effect on the probability of the second event. Specific examples of independence and nonindependence were examined in Box 8.2 (page 184).

2. The population sampled must be normal.

   This assumption is a necessary part of the mathematics underlying the development of the *t* statistic and the *t*-distribution table. However, violating this assumption has little practical effect on the results obtained for a *t* statistic, especially when the sample size is relatively large. With very small samples, a normal population is important. With larger samples, this assumption can be violated without affecting the validity of the hypothesis test. If you have reason to suspect that the population is not normal, use a large sample to be safe.

THE VERSATILITY OF THE *t* TEST   The obvious advantage of hypothesis testing with the *t* statistic (as compared to *z*-scores) is that you do not need to know the value of the population standard deviation. This means that we still can do a hypothesis test even though we have little or no information about the population.

Both the *t*-statistic and *z*-score tests were introduced as methods for determining whether or not a treatment has any effect on a dependent variable. For both tests, we assumed that you start with a *known* population mean before treatment, and the research question (hypotheses) concerned the *unknown* population mean after treatment (see Figures 8.1 and 9.3). With the *t* statistic, however, we no longer need a known population before treatment. All we need to compute a *t* statistic is a sample and a sensible null hypothesis. For example, the hypothesis tests evaluating the effects of eye-spot patterns did not involve a population before treatment and a population after treatment. Instead, we simply had one unknown population, one sample, and a logical null hypothesis. Some similar examples follow. Note in each case that the hypothesis is not dependent on knowing the actual population mean before treatment and that the rest of the *t* statistic can be computed entirely from the obtained sample data.

1. A researcher would like to examine the accuracy of people's judgment of time when they are distracted. Individuals are placed in a waiting room where many distracting events occur for a period of 12 minutes. The researcher then asks each person to judge how much time has passed. The goal is to determine whether the distractions cause people to overestimate or underestimate the amount of time. The null hypothesis would state that distraction has no effect and that time judgments are accurate. That is,

$$H_0: \mu = 12 \text{ minutes}$$

2. A researcher has developed a 7-point rating scale to measure people's opinions concerning different issues. The research presents an issue to each subject and asks for an opinion on the scale where a rating of 1 indicates "strongly disapprove" and a rating of 7 indicates "strongly approve." A rating of 4 (the center of the scale) indicates "neutral or no opinion." For any given issue, the null hypothesis would state that there is no consistently positive or consistently negative opinion in the population. Instead, the null hypothesis states that the overall population opinion is neutral,

$$H_0: \mu = 4.00$$

LEARNING CHECK

1. A researcher would like to evaluate the effect of a new cold medication on reaction time. It is known that under regular circumstances the distribution of reaction times is normal with $\mu = 200$. A sample of $n = 4$ subjects is obtained. Each person is given the new cold medication, and 1 hour later reaction time is measured for each individual. The average reaction time for this sample is $\overline{X} = 215$ with $SS = 300$. On the basis of these data, can the researcher conclude that the cold medication has an effect on reaction time? Test at the .05 level of significance.

   a. State the hypotheses.

   b. Locate the critical region.

   c. Compute the *t* statistic.

   d. Make a decision.

2. Suppose the researcher in the previous problem predicted that the medication would increase reaction time and decided to use a one-tailed test to evaluate this prediction.

   a. State the hypotheses for the one-tailed test.

   b. Locate the one-tailed critical region for $\alpha = .05$.

ANSWERS

1. **a.** $H_0: \mu = 200$ (The medication has no effect on reaction time.)
   $H_1: \mu \neq 200$ (Reaction time is changed.)

   b. With $df = 3$ and $\alpha = .05$, the critical region consists of *t* values beyond ± 3.182.

   c. The sample variance is $s^2 = 100$, the standard error is 5, and $t = 3.00$.

   d. The *t* statistic is not in the critical region. Fail to reject the null hypothesis, and conclude that the data do not provide enough evidence to say that the medication affects reaction time.

2. a. H_0: $\mu \leq 200$ (Reaction time is not increased.)
   H_1: $\mu > 200$ (Reaction time is increased.)

b. With $df = 3$ and $\alpha = .05$, the one-tailed critical region consists of values beyond
   $t = +2.353$.

◆

ON THE WEB

NOW THAT you have finished Chapter 9, you can test your knowledge with the practice quiz on the Wadsworth Web site at **www.wadsworth.com.** In addition, there is a workshop on the *t* test for one sample that provides

another look at the material presented in this chapter. For more information about the quizzes and workshops, see page 24.

SUMMARY

1. The *t* statistic is used instead of a *z*-score for hypothesis testing when the population standard deviation (or variance) is unknown.

2. To compute the *t* statistic, you must first calculate the sample variance (or standard deviation) as a substitute for the unknown population value.

$$s^2 = \frac{SS}{df} \qquad s = \sqrt{\frac{SS}{df}}$$

Next, the standard error is *estimated* by substituting s^2 or s in the formula for standard error. The estimated standard error is calculated in the following manner:

$$s_{\overline{X}} = \sqrt{\frac{s^2}{n}} \quad \text{or} \quad s_{\overline{X}} = \frac{s}{\sqrt{n}}$$

Finally, a *t* statistic is computed using the estimated standard error. The *t* statistic is used as a substitute for a *z*-score that cannot be computed when the population variance or standard deviation is unknown.

$$t = \frac{\overline{X} - \mu}{s_{\overline{X}}}$$

3. The structure of the *t* formula is similar to that of the *z*-score in that

$$z \text{ or } t = \frac{\text{sample mean} - \text{population mean}}{\text{(estimated) standard error}}$$

For a hypothesis test, you hypothesize a value for the unknown population mean and plug the hypothesized value into the equation along with the sample mean and the estimated standard error, which are computed from the sample data. If the hypothesized mean produces an extreme value for *t*, you conclude that the hypothesis was wrong.

4. The *t* distribution is an approximation of the normal *z* distribution. To evaluate a *t* statistic that is obtained for a sample mean, the critical region must be located in a *t* distribution. There is a family of *t* distributions, with the exact shape of a particular distribution of *t* values depending on degrees of freedom $(n - 1)$. Therefore, the critical *t* values will depend on the value for *df* associated with the *t* test. As *df* increases, the shape of the *t* distribution approaches a normal distribution.

KEY TERMS

estimated standard error   *t* statistic   degrees of freedom   *t* distribution

FOCUS ON PROBLEM SOLVING

1. The first problem we confront in analyzing data is determining the appropriate statistical test. Remember that you can use a z-score for the test statistic only when the value for σ is known. If the value for σ is not provided, then you must use the t statistic.

2. For a t test, students sometimes use the unit normal table to locate the critical region. This, of course, is a mistake. The critical region for a t test is obtained by consulting the t-distribution table. Note that to use this table you first must compute the value for degrees of freedom (df).

3. For the t test, the sample variance is used to find the value for estimated standard error. Remember, when computing the sample variance, use $n - 1$ in the denominator (see Chapter 4). When computing estimated standard error, use $\sqrt{n}$ in the denominator.

DEMONSTRATION 9.1

A HYPOTHESIS TEST WITH THE t STATISTIC

A psychologist has prepared an "Optimism Test" that is administered yearly to graduating college seniors. The test measures how each graduating class feels about its future—the higher the score, the more optimistic the class. Last year's class had a mean score of $\mu = 15$. A sample of $n = 9$ seniors from this year's class was selected and tested. The scores for these seniors are as follows:

$$7, \quad 12, \quad 11, \quad 15, \quad 7, \quad 8, \quad 15, \quad 9, \quad 6$$

On the basis of this sample, can the psychologist conclude that this year's class has a different level of optimism than last year's class? Note that this hypothesis test will use a t statistic because the population standard deviation (σ) is not known.

STEP 1   State the hypotheses, and select an alpha level.
The statements for the null hypothesis and the alternative hypothesis follow the same form for the t statistic and the z-score test.

$$H_0: \mu = 15 \qquad \text{(There is no change.)}$$

$$H_1: \mu \neq 15 \qquad \text{(This year's mean is different.)}$$

For this demonstration, we will use $\alpha = .05$, two tails.

STEP 2   Locate the critical region.
Remember that for hypothesis tests with the t statistic, we must now consult the t-distribution table to find the critical t values. With a sample of $n = 9$ students, the t statistic will have degrees of freedom equal to

$$df = n - 1 = 9 - 1 = 8$$

For a two-tailed test with $\alpha = .05$ and $df = 8$, the critical t values are $t = \pm 2.306$. These critical t values define the boundaries of the critical region. The obtained t value must be more extreme than either of these critical values to reject H_0.

STEP 3   Obtain the sample data, and compute the test statistic.

For the t formula, we need to determine the values for the following:

1. The sample mean, $\overline{X}$
2. The estimated standard error, $s_{\overline{X}}$

We also have to compute sum of squares (*SS*) and the variance for the sample in order to get the estimated standard error.

The sample mean. For these data, the sum of the scores is

$$\Sigma X = 7 + 12 + 11 + 15 + 7 + 8 + 15 + 9 + 6 = 90$$

Therefore, the sample mean is

$$\overline{X} = \frac{\Sigma X}{n} = \frac{90}{9} = 10$$

Sum of squares. We will use the definitional formula for sum of squares,

$$SS = \Sigma(X - \overline{X})^2$$

The following table summarizes the steps in the computation of *SS*.

X	$X - \overline{X}$	$(X - \overline{X})^2$
7	$7 - 10 = -3$	9
12	$12 - 10 = +2$	4
11	$11 - 10 = +1$	1
15	$15 - 10 = +5$	25
7	$7 - 10 = -3$	9
8	$8 - 10 = -2$	4
15	$15 - 10 = +5$	25
9	$9 - 10 = -1$	1
6	$6 - 10 = -4$	16

For this demonstration problem, the sum of squares value is

$$SS = \Sigma(X - \overline{X})^2 = 9 + 4 + 1 + 25 + 9 + 4 + 25 + 1 + 16$$
$$= 94$$

Sample variance. The variance for the sample is

$$s^2 = \frac{SS}{n - 1} = \frac{94}{8} = 11.75$$

Estimated standard error. The estimated standard error for these data is

$$s_{\overline{X}} = \sqrt{\frac{s^2}{n}} = \sqrt{\frac{11.75}{9}} = 1.14$$

The t statistic. Now that we have the estimated standard error and the sample mean, we can compute the *t* statistic. For this demonstration,

$$t = \frac{\overline{X} - \mu}{s_{\overline{X}}} = \frac{10 - 15}{1.14} = \frac{-5}{1.14} = -4.39$$

STEP 4   Make a decision about H_0 and draw a conclusion.

The *t* statistic we obtained ($t = -4.39$) is in the critical region. Thus, our sample data are unusual enough to reject the null hypothesis at the .05 level of significance. We can conclude that there is a significant difference in level of optimism between this year's and last year's graduating classes, $t(8) = -4.39$, $p < .05$, two-tailed.

PROBLEMS

1. What factor determines whether you should use a *z*-score or a *t* statistic for a hypothesis test?

2. A sample of $n = 25$ scores has a mean of $\overline{X} = 42$ and a sample variance of $s^2 = 100$.
   a. Compute the sample standard deviation (s) and the estimated standard error for the sample mean ($s_{\overline{X}}$).
   b. Briefly describe what is measured by the sample standard deviation and by the estimated standard error.

3. Several different factors influence the value obtained for a *t* statistic. For each of the following, describe how the value of *t* is affected. In each case, assume all other factors are held constant.
   a. What happens to the value of *t* when the variability of the scores in the sample increases?
   b. What happens to the value of *t* when the number of scores in the sample increases?
   c. What happens to the value of *t* when the difference between the sample mean and the hypothesized population mean increases?

4. Why is a *t* distribution generally more variable than a normal distribution?

5. What is the relationship between the value for degrees of freedom and the shape of the *t* distribution? What happens to the critical value of *t* for a particular alpha level when *df* increases in value?

6. A sample has a mean of $\overline{X} = 63$ and a variance of $s^2 = 36$.
   a. If the sample consists of $n = 4$ scores, then compute the sample standard deviation (s) and the estimated standard error for the sample mean ($s_{\overline{X}}$).
   b. If the sample consists of $n = 16$ scores, then compute the sample standard deviation (s) and the estimated standard error for the sample mean ($s_{\overline{X}}$).

7. The following sample was obtained from a population with unknown parameters.

Scores: 8, 0, 8, 8

   a. Compute the sample mean and standard deviation. (Note that these are descriptive values that summarize the sample data.)
   b. Compute the estimated standard error for $\overline{X}$. (Note that this is an inferential value that describes how accurately the sample mean represents the unknown population mean.)

8. The following sample was obtained from a population with unknown parameters.

Scores: 9, 1, 13, 1

   a. Compute the sample mean and standard deviation. (Note that these are descriptive values that summarize the sample data.)
   b. Compute the estimated standard error for $\overline{X}$. (Note that this is an inferential value that describes how accurately the sample mean represents the unknown population mean.)

9. The following sample was obtained from an unknown population. Scores:

3, 11, 3, 3

   a. Compute the sample mean and the sample standard deviation. (Note that these values are descriptive statistics that summarize the sample data.)
   b. How accurately does the sample mean represent the unknown population mean? Compute the estimated standard error for $\overline{X}$. (Note that this value is an inferential statistic that allows you to use the sample data to answer questions about the population.)

10. One characteristic of *t* statistics is that you must first compute the sample variance or sample standard deviation before it is possible to calculate the value for *t*. For each of the following samples:

> Sample 1: 2, 10, 2, 2
>
> Sample 2: 1, 5, 1, 1

   a. Calculate the sample variance and the sample standard deviation. (Note that the standard deviation is a descriptive statistic that describes how the scores are scattered around the mean.)
   b. Calculate the estimated standard error. (Note that the standard error is an inferential statistic that measures how accurately the sample mean represents the population mean.)
   c. Although the two samples are the same size, you should find that one provides a more accurate representation of the population than the other (one has less error). In general, explain how sample variance is related to the magnitude of the estimated standard error.

11. For each of the following samples:

> Sample 1: 7, 1, 1
>
> Sample 2: 8, 6, 3, 5, 5, 13, 7, 6, 10

   a. Calculate the sample variance and the sample standard deviation. (Note that the standard deviation is a descriptive statistic that describes how the scores are scattered around the mean.)
   b. Calculate the estimated standard error. (Note that the standard error is an inferential statistic that measures how accurately the sample mean represents the population mean.)
   c. Although the two samples have exactly the same variance, you should find that one provides a more accurate representation of the population than the other (one has less error). In general, explain how sample size is related to the magnitude of the estimated standard error.

12. A random sample of $n = 9$ individuals is obtained from a population with a mean of $\mu = 80$. A treatment is administered to each individual in the sample and, after treatment, each individual is measured. The average score for the treated sample is $\overline{X} = 86$ with $SS = 288$.
   a. How much difference is there between the mean for the treated sample and the mean for the original population? (*Note:* In a hypothesis test, this value forms the numerator of the *t* statistic.)
   b. How much difference is expected just by chance between the sample mean and its population mean; that is, find the standard error for $\overline{X}$. (*Note:* In a hy-

pothesis test, this value is the denominator of the *t* statistic.)
   c. Based on the sample data, does the treatment have a significant effect? Use a two-tailed test with $\alpha = .05$.

13. A standardized reading achievement test for fifth-grade students has a nationwide mean of $\mu = 70$. A teacher would like to know whether the students in her fifth-grade class are significantly different from the national average. The test is given to the entire class of $n = 25$ students and the average score is $\overline{X} = 75$ with $SS = 2400$.
   a. Using a two-tailed test with $\alpha = .05$, is this class significantly different from the national average?
   b. Using a two-tailed test with $\alpha = .01$, is the class significantly different from the national average?
   c. Explain why you reach a different conclusion when $\alpha = .01$ instead of .05.

14. A newspaper article reported that the typical American family spent an average of $\mu = \$81$ for Halloween candy and costumes last year. A sample of $n = 16$ families this year produced a mean of $\overline{X} = \$85$ with $SS = 6000$. Do these data indicate a significant change in holiday spending? Use a two-tailed test with $\alpha = .05$.

15. A researcher suspects that there is a direct relationship between hand–eye coordination and academic success in mathematics. A sample of $n = 16$ students who have demonstrated above average performance on a second-grade mathematics achievement test is selected. These students are given a standardized hand–eye coordination task where the average score for this age group is $\mu = 55$. The 16 students in the sample produced a mean of $\overline{X} = 61$ with $SS = 540$.
   a. Are the data sufficient to conclude that the high math achievement students have hand–eye coordination scores that are significantly *different from* the general population? Use a two-tailed test with $\alpha = .01$.
   b. Are the data sufficient to conclude that the high math achievement students have hand–eye coordination scores that are significantly *better than* the general population? Use a one-tailed test with $\alpha = .01$.

16. A major corporation in the Northeast noted that last year its employees averaged $\mu = 5.8$ absences during the winter season (December to February). In an attempt to reduce absences, the company offered free flu shots to all employees this year. For a sample of $n = 100$ people who took the shots, the average number of absences this winter was $\overline{X} = 3.6$ with $SS = 396$. Do these data indicate a significant decrease in the number of absences? Use a one-tailed test with $\alpha = .05$.

17. A social psychologist suspects that the increased availability of e-mail may have an effect on the methods that

people use to communicate. The researcher obtained records from 1995 indicating that the average American spent $\mu = 2.1$ hours per month on long distance phone calls. A random sample of $n = 36$ people was obtained and their phone records were monitored for all of last year. The people in the sample averaged $\overline{X} = 1.9$ hours of long distance calls per month with $SS = 12.6$. Do these data indicate a significant change in the use of long distance telephone? Use a two-tailed test with $\alpha = .05$.

18. A random sample has a mean of $\overline{X} = 81$ with $s = 10$. Use this sample to test the null hypothesis that $\mu = 85$ for each of the following situations.
   a. Assume that the sample size is $n = 25$, and use $\alpha = .05$ for the hypothesis test.
   b. Assume that the sample size is $n = 400$, and use $\alpha = .05$ for the hypothesis test.
   c. In general, how does sample size contribute to the outcome of a hypothesis test?

19. A random sample of $n = 16$ scores has a mean of $\overline{X} = 48$. Use this sample to test the null hypothesis that the population mean is $\mu = 45$ for each of the following situations:
   a. Assume that the sample has a variance of $s^2 = 4$ and use a two-tailed test with $\alpha = .05$.
   b. Assume the sample has a variance of $s^2 = 400$ and use a two-tailed test with $\alpha = .05$.
   c. In general, how does the magnitude of the sample variance contribute to the outcome of a hypothesis test?

20. A researcher would like to examine the effects of humidity on eating behavior. It is known that laboratory rats normally eat an average of $\mu = 21$ grams of food each day. The researcher selects a random sample of $n = 100$ rats and places them in a controlled atmosphere room where the relative humidity is maintained at 90%. The daily food consumption for the sample averages $\overline{X} = 18.7$ with $SS = 2475$. On the basis of this sample, can the researcher conclude that humidity affects eating behavior? Use a two-tailed test at the .05 level.

21. A psychologist would like to determine whether there is a relation between depression and aging. It is known that the general population averages $\mu = 40$ on a standardized depression test. The psychologist obtains a sample

of $n = 36$ individuals who are all over the age of 70. The average depression score for this sample is $\overline{X} = 44.5$ with $SS = 5040$. On the basis of this sample, can the psychologist conclude that depression for elderly people is significantly different from depression in the general population? Test at the .05 level of significance.

22. One of the original tests of ESP involves using Zener cards. Each card shows 1 of 5 different symbols (square, circle, star, wavy lines, cross). One person randomly picks a card and concentrates on the symbol it shows. A second person, in a different room, attempts to identify the symbol that was selected. Chance performance on this task (just guessing) should lead to correct identification of 1 out of 5 cards. A psychologist used the Zener cards to evaluate a sample of $n = 9$ subjects who claimed to have ESP. Each subject was tested on a series of 100 cards, and the number correct for each individual is as follows: 18, 23, 24, 22, 19, 28, 15, 26, 25.
   Chance performance on a series of 100 cards would be $\mu = 20$ correct. Did this sample perform significantly better than chance? Use a one-tailed test at the .05 level of significance.

23. Several years ago, a survey in a school district revealed that the average age at which students first tried an alcoholic drink was $\mu = 14$ years. To determine whether anything has changed, a random sample of students was asked questions about alcohol use. The age at which drinking behavior first began was reported by members of the sample as follows:

11, 13, 14, 12, 10

Has there been a change in the mean age at which drinking began? Use $\alpha = .05$ for two tails.

24. On a standardized spatial skills task, normative data reveal that people typically get $\mu = 15$ correct solutions. A psychologist tests $n = 7$ individuals who have brain injuries in the right cerebral hemisphere. For the following data, determine whether or not right-hemisphere damage results in significantly reduced performance on the spatial skills task. Test with alpha set at .05 with one tail. The data are as follows: 12, 16, 9, 8, 10, 17, 10.

CHAPTER 10

THE *t* TEST FOR TWO INDEPENDENT SAMPLES

TOOLS YOU WILL NEED

The following items are considered essential background material for this chapter. If you doubt your knowledge of any of these items, you should review the appropriate chapter or section before proceeding.

- Sample variance (Chapter 4)
- The *t* statistic (Chapter 9)
  - Distribution of *t* values
  - *df* for the *t* statistic
  - Estimated standard error

CONTENTS

10.1 OVERVIEW

Until this point, all the inferential statistics we have considered involve using one sample as the basis for drawing conclusions about one population. Although these *single-sample* techniques are used occasionally in real research, most research studies require the comparison of two (or more) sets of data. For example, a social psychologist may want to compare men and women in terms of their attitudes toward abortion, an educational psychologist may want to compare two methods for teaching mathematics, and a clinical psychologist may want to evaluate a therapy technique by comparing depression scores for patients before therapy with their scores after therapy. In each case, the research question concerns a mean difference between two sets of data.

There are two general research strategies that can be used to obtain the two sets of data to be compared:

1. The two sets of data could come from two completely separate samples. For example, the study could involve a sample of men compared with a sample of women. Or the study could compare one sample of students taught by method A and a second sample taught by method B.

2. The two sets of data could both come from the same sample. For example, the study could obtain one set of scores by measuring depression for a sample of patients before they begin therapy and then obtain a second set of data by measuring the same individuals after 6 weeks of therapy.

The first research strategy, using completely separate samples, is called an *independent-measures* research design or a *between-subjects* design. These terms emphasize the fact that the design involves separate and independent samples and makes a comparison between two groups of individuals. In this chapter, we will examine the statistical techniques used to evaluate the data from an independent-measures design. More precisely, we will introduce the hypothesis test that allows researchers to use the data from two separate samples to evaluate the mean difference between two populations or between two treatment conditions.

The second research strategy, where the two sets of data are obtained from the same sample, is called a *repeated-measures* research design or a *within-subjects* design. The statistical analysis for repeated measures will be introduced in Chapter 11. Also, at the end of Chapter 11, we will discuss some of the advantages and disadvantages of independent-measures versus repeated-measures research designs.

The typical structure of an independent-measures research study is shown in Figure 10.1. Note that the research study is using two separate samples to answer a question about two populations.

DEFINITION

A research design that uses a separate sample for each treatment condition (or for each population) is called an *independent-measures* research design or a *between-subjects* design.

FIGURE 10.1

Do the achievement scores for children taught by method A differ from the scores for children taught by method B? In statistical terms, are the two population means the same or different? Because neither of the two population means is known, it will be necessary to take two samples, one from each population. The first sample will provide information about the mean for the first population, and the second sample will provide information about the second population.

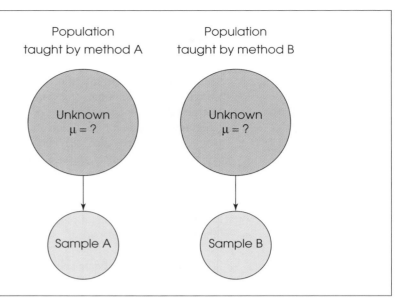

10.2 THE *t* STATISTIC FOR AN INDEPENDENT-MEASURES RESEARCH DESIGN

Because an independent-measures study involves two separate samples, we will need some special notation to help specify which data go with which sample. This notation involves the use of subscripts, which are small numbers written beside a sample statistic. For example, the number of scores in the first sample would be identified by n_1; for the second sample, the number of scores would be n_2. The sample means would be identified by $\overline{X}_1$ and $\overline{X}_2$. The sums of squares would be SS_1 and SS_2.

THE HYPOTHESES FOR AN INDEPENDENT-MEASURES TEST

The goal of an independent-measures research study is to evaluate the mean difference between two populations (or between two treatment conditions). Using subscripts to differentiate the two populations, the mean for the first population is μ_1, and the second population mean is μ_2. The difference between means is simply $\mu_1 - \mu_2$. As always, the null hypothesis states that there is no change, no effect, or, in this case, no difference. Thus, in symbols, the null hypothesis for the independent-measures test is

$$H_0: \mu_1 - \mu_2 = 0 \quad \text{(There is no difference between the population means.)}$$

Note that the null hypothesis could also be stated as $\mu_1 = \mu_2$. However, the first version of H_0 produces a specific numerical value (zero) that will be used in the calculation of the *t* statistic. Therefore, we prefer to phrase the null hypothesis in terms of the difference between the two population means.

The alternative hypothesis states that there is a mean difference between the two populations,

$$H_1: \mu_1 - \mu_2 \neq 0 \quad \text{(There is a mean difference.)}$$

Equivalently, the alternative hypothesis can simply state that the two population means are not equal: $\mu_1 \neq \mu_2$.

THE FORMULAS FOR AN INDEPENDENT-MEASURES HYPOTHESIS TEST

The independent-measures hypothesis test will be based on another *t* statistic. The formula for this new *t* statistic will have the same general structure as the *t* statistic formula introduced in Chapter 9. To help distinguish between the two *t* formulas, we will refer to the original formula (Chapter 9) as the *single-sample t statistic* and we will refer to the new formula as the *independent-measures t statistic*. Because the new independent-measures *t* will include data from two separate samples and hypotheses about two populations, the formulas may appear to be a bit overpowering. However, the new formulas will be easier to understand if you view them in relation to the single-sample *t* formulas from Chapter 9. In particular, there are two points to remember:

1. The basic structure of the *t* statistic is the same for both the independent-measures and the single-sample hypothesis tests. In both cases,

$$t = \frac{\text{sample statistic} - \text{hypothesized population parameter}}{\text{estimated standard error}}$$

2. The independent-measures *t* is basically a *two-sample t that doubles all the elements of the single-sample t formulas.*

To demonstrate the second point, we will examine the two *t* formulas piece by piece.

The overall *t* formula   The single-sample *t* uses one sample mean to test a hypothesis about one population mean. The sample mean and the population mean appear in the numerator of the *t* formula, which measures how much difference there is between the sample data and the population hypothesis.

$$t = \frac{\text{sample mean} - \text{population mean}}{\text{standard error for the sample mean}} = \frac{\overline{X} - \mu}{s_{\overline{X}}}$$

The independent-measures *t* uses two sample means to evaluate a hypothesis about two population means. In the numerator of the *t* formula, the sample statistic is now a sample mean difference and the corresponding population parameter is the population mean difference.

$$t = \frac{\text{sample mean difference} - \text{population mean difference}}{\text{standard error for the sample mean difference}}$$

$$= \frac{(\overline{X}_1 - \overline{X}_2) - (\mu_1 - \mu_2)}{s_{(\overline{X}_1 - \overline{X}_2)}}$$

The standard error   In each of the *t*-score formulas, the standard error in the denominator measures how accurately the sample statistic represents the population parameter. In the single-sample *t* formula, the standard error measures the amount of error expected for a sample mean and is represented by the symbol $s_{\overline{X}}$. For the independent-measures *t* formula, the standard error measures the amount of error that is expected when you use a sample mean difference $(\overline{X}_1 - \overline{X}_2)$ to represent a population mean difference $(\mu_1 - \mu_2)$. The standard error for the sample mean difference is represented by the symbol $s_{(\overline{X}_1 - \overline{X}_2)}$.

Caution: Do not let the notation for standard error confuse you. In general, standard error measures how accurately a statistic represents a parameter. The symbol for standard error takes the form, $s_{\text{statistic}}$. When the statistic is a sample mean, $\overline{X}$, the symbol for standard error is $s_{\overline{X}}$. For the independent-measures test, the statistic is a sample mean difference $(\overline{X}_1 - \overline{X}_2)$, and the symbol for standard error is $s_{(\overline{X}_1 - \overline{X}_2)}$. In each case, the standard error tells how much discrepancy is reasonable to expect just by chance between the statistic and the corresponding population parameter.

To develop the formula for $s_{(\overline{X}_1 - \overline{X}_2)}$ we will consider the following three points:

1. Each of the two sample means represents it own population mean, but in each case there is some error.

    $\overline{X}_1$ approximates μ_1 with some error.

    $\overline{X}_2$ approximates μ_2 with some error.

    Thus, there are two sources of error.

2. The amount of error associated with each sample mean can be measured by computing the standard error of $\overline{X}$. In Chapter 9 (Equation 9.1), we calculated the standard error for a single sample mean as

$$s_{\overline{X}} = \sqrt{\frac{s^2}{n}}$$

3. For the independent-measures t statistic, we want to know the total amount of error involved in using *two* sample means to approximate *two* population means. To do this, we will find the error from each sample separately and then add the two errors together. The resulting formula for standard error is

$$s_{(\overline{X}_1 - \overline{X}_2)} = \sqrt{\frac{s_1^2}{n_1} + \frac{s_2^2}{n_2}} \tag{10.1}$$

Because the independent-measures t statistic uses two sample means, the formula for the estimated standard error simply combines the error for the first sample mean and the error for the second sample mean.

POOLED VARIANCE

Although Equation 10.1 accurately presents the concept of standard error for the independent-measures t statistic, this formula is limited to situations in which the two samples are exactly the same size (that is, $n_1 = n_2$). When the two sample sizes are different, the formula is *biased* and, therefore, inappropriate. The bias comes from the fact that Equation 10.1 treats the two sample variances equally. However, when the sample sizes are different, the two sample variances are not equally good and should not be treated equally. In Chapter 7, we introduced the law of large numbers, which states that statistics obtained from large samples tend to be better (more accurate) estimates of population parameters than statistics obtained from small samples. This same fact holds for sample variances: The variance obtained from a large sample will be a more accurate estimate of σ^2 than the variance obtained from a small sample.

To correct for the bias in the sample variances, the independent-measures t statistic will combine the two sample variances into a single value called the *pooled variance*. The pooled variance is obtained by averaging or "pooling" the two sample variances using a procedure that allows the bigger sample to carry more weight in determining the final value.

Recall that when there is only one sample, the sample variance is computed as

$$s^2 = \frac{SS}{df}$$

For the independent-measures *t* statistic, there are two *SS* values and two *df* values (one from each sample). The values from the two samples are combined to compute what is called the *pooled variance*. The pooled variance is identified by the symbol s_p^2 and is computed as

$$s_p^2 = \frac{SS_1 + SS_2}{df_1 + df_2} \qquad\qquad (10.2)$$

With one sample, variance is computed as *SS* divided by *df*. With two samples, the two *SS*s are divided by the two *df*s to compute pooled variance. The pooled variance is actually an average of the two sample variances, and the value of the pooled variance will always be located between the two sample variances. A more detailed discussion of the pooled variance is presented in Box 10.1.

 10.1   A CLOSER LOOK AT THE POOLED VARIANCE

THE POOLED variance is actually an average of the two sample variances, but the formula is structured so that each sample is weighted by the magnitude of its *df* value. Thus, the larger sample carries more weight in determining the final value. The following examples demonstrate this point.

Equal Sample Size   We begin with two samples that are exactly the same size. The first sample has $n = 6$ scores with $SS = 50$ and the second sample has $n = 6$ scores with $SS = 30$. Individually, the two sample variances are

$$\text{Variance for sample 1:} \quad s^2 = \frac{SS}{df} = \frac{50}{5} = 10$$

$$\text{Variance for sample 2:} \quad s^2 = \frac{SS}{df} = \frac{30}{5} = 6$$

The pooled variance for these two samples is

$$s_p^2 = \frac{SS_1 + SS_2}{df_1 + df_2} = \frac{50 + 30}{5 + 5} = \frac{80}{10} = 8.00$$

Note that the pooled variance is exactly halfway between the two sample variances. Because the two samples are exactly the same size, the pooled variance is simply the average of the two individual sample variances.

Unequal Sample Sizes   Now consider what happens when the samples are not the same size. This time the first sample has $n = 3$ scores with $SS = 20$ and the second sample has $n = 9$ scores with $SS = 48$. Individually, the two sample variances are

$$\text{Variance for sample 1:} \quad s^2 = \frac{SS}{df} = \frac{20}{2} = 10$$

$$\text{Variance for sample 2:} \quad s^2 = \frac{SS}{df} = \frac{48}{8} = 6$$

The pooled variance for these two samples is

$$s_p^2 = \frac{SS_1 + SS_2}{df_1 + df_2} = \frac{20 + 48}{2 + 8} = \frac{68}{10} = 6.80$$

This time the pooled variance is not located halfway between the two sample variances. Instead, the pooled value is closer to the variance for the large sample ($s^2 = 6$) than to the variance for the small sample ($s^2 = 10$). The larger sample carries more weight when the pooled variance is computed.

Using the pooled variance in place of the individual sample variances, we can now obtain an unbiased measure of the standard error for a sample mean difference. The resulting formula for the independent-measures standard error is

$$\text{two-sample standard error} = s_{(\overline{X}_1 - \overline{X}_2)} = \sqrt{\frac{s_p^2}{n_1} + \frac{s_p^2}{n_2}} \qquad (10.3)$$

Conceptually, this standard error measures how accurately the difference between two sample means represents the difference between the two population means. The formula combines the error for the first sample mean with the error for the second sample mean. Note that the pooled variance from the two samples is used to compute the standard error for the two samples.

THE FINAL FORMULA AND DEGREES OF FREEDOM

The complete equation for the independent-measures *t* statistic is as follows:

$$t = \frac{(\overline{X}_1 - \overline{X}_2) - (\mu_1 - \mu_2)}{s_{(\overline{X}_1 - \overline{X}_2)}}$$

$$= \frac{\text{sample mean difference} - \text{population mean difference}}{\text{estimated standard error}} \qquad (10.4)$$

In the formula, the estimated standard error in the denominator is calculated using Formula 10.3, and requires calculation of the pooled variance using Formula 10.2.

The degrees of freedom for the independent-measures *t* statistic are determined by the *df* values for the two separate samples:

$$df \text{ for the } t \text{ statistic} = df \text{ for the first sample} + df \text{ for the second sample}$$

$$= df_1 + df_2$$

$$= (n_1 - 1) + (n_2 - 1) \qquad (10.5)$$

The independent-measures *t* statistic will be used for hypothesis testing. Specifically, we will use the difference between sample means $(\overline{X}_1 - \overline{X}_2)$ as the basis for testing hypotheses about the difference between population means $(\mu_1 - \mu_2)$. In this context, the overall structure of the *t* statistic can be reduced to the following:

$$t = \frac{\text{data} - \text{hypothesis}}{\text{error}}$$

This same structure is used for both the single-sample *t* from Chapter 9 and the new independent-measures *t* that was introduced in the preceding pages. Table 10.1 identifies each component of these two *t* statistics and should help reinforce the point that we made earlier in the chapter; that is, the independent-measures *t* statistic simply doubles each aspect of the single-sample *t* statistic.

LEARNING CHECK

1. Describe the general characteristics of an independent-measures research study.

2. Identify the two sources of error that are reflected in the standard error for the independent-measures *t* statistic.

TABLE 10.1

The basic elements of a *t* statistic for the single-sample *t* and the independent-measures *t*

	Sample data	Hypothesized population parameter	Estimated standard error	Sample variance
Single-sample *t* statistic	$\overline{X}$	μ	$\sqrt{\dfrac{s^2}{n}}$	$s^2 = \dfrac{SS}{df}$
Independent-measures *t* statistic	$(\overline{X}_1 - \overline{X}_2)$	$(\mu_1 - \mu_2)$	$\sqrt{\dfrac{s_p^2}{n_1} + \dfrac{s_p^2}{n_2}}$	$s_p^2 = \dfrac{SS_1 + SS_2}{df_1 + df_2}$

3. An independent-measures *t* statistic is used to evaluate the mean difference between two treatments using a sample of $n = 10$ in one treatment and a separate sample of $n = 15$ in the other treatment. What is the *df* value for the *t* test?

4. The first sample from an independent-measures research study has $n = 5$ scores with $SS = 40$. The second sample has $n = 5$ scores with $SS = 32$.

   a. Compute the variance for each of the two samples.

   b. Compute the pooled variance for the two samples. (Because the two samples are exactly the same size, you should find that the pooled variance is equal to the average of the two sample variances.)

5. The first sample from an independent-measures research study has $n = 5$ scores with $SS = 40$. The second sample has $n = 7$ scores with $SS = 48$.

   a. Compute the variance for each of the two samples.

   b. Compute the pooled variance for the two samples. (Because the two samples are not the same size, you should find that the pooled variance is not halfway between the two sample variances. Because the larger sample carries more weight, the pooled variance is closer to the variance from the larger sample.)

ANSWERS

1. An independent-measures study uses a separate sample to represent each of the treatment conditions or populations being compared.

2. The two sources of error come from the fact that two sample means are being used to represent two population means. Thus, $\overline{X}_1$ represents its population mean with some error and $\overline{X}_2$ represents its population mean with some error. The two errors combine in the standard error for the independent-measures *t* statistic.

3. The *t* statistic has $df = df_1 + df_2 = 9 + 14 = 23$.

4. a. The first sample has a variance of 10 and the second sample has a variance of 8.

   b. The pooled variance is 9 (exactly halfway between 10 and 8).

5. a. The first sample has a variance of 10 and the second sample has a variance of 8.

   b. The pooled variance is 8.8, which is weighted toward the variance for the larger sample. ◆

10.3 HYPOTHESIS TESTS WITH THE INDEPENDENT-MEASURES *t* STATISTIC

The independent-measures *t* statistic uses the data from two separate samples to help decide whether or not there is a significant mean difference between two populations or between two treatment conditions. A complete example of a hypothesis test with two independent samples follows.

EXAMPLE 10.1

In recent years, psychologists have demonstrated repeatedly that using mental images can greatly improve memory. Here we present a hypothetical experiment designed to examine this phenomenon.

The psychologist first prepares a list of 40 pairs of nouns (for example, dog/bicycle, grass/door, lamp/piano). Next, two groups of subjects are obtained (two separate samples). Subjects in one group are given the list for 5 minutes and instructed to memorize the 40 noun pairs. Subjects in another group receive the same list of words, but in addition to the regular instructions, they are told to form a mental image for each pair of nouns (imagine a dog riding a bicycle, for example). Note that the two samples are identical except that one group is using mental images to help learn the list.

Remember that an independent-measures design means there are separate samples for each treatment condition.

Later each group is given a memory test in which they are given the first word from each pair and asked to recall the second word. The psychologist records the number of words correctly recalled for each individual. The data from this experiment are as follows. On the basis of these data, can the psychologist conclude that mental images affected memory?

Data (number of words recalled)

Group 1 (images)		Group 2 (no images)	
18	31	24	13
19	29	23	17
23	26	16	20
29	21	17	15
30	24	19	26
$n = 10$		$n = 10$	
$\overline{X} = 25$		$\overline{X} = 19$	
$SS = 200$		$SS = 160$	

STEP 1   State the hypotheses, and select the alpha level.

Directional hypotheses could be used and would specify whether imagery should increase or decrease recall scores.

$$H_0: \mu_1 - \mu_2 = 0 \quad \text{(No difference; imagery has no effect.)}$$

$$H_1: \mu_1 - \mu_2 \neq 0 \quad \text{(Imagery produces a difference.)}$$

We will set $\alpha = .05$.

STEP 2 This is an independent-measures design. The *t* statistic for these data will have degrees of freedom determined by

$$df = df_1 + df_2$$
$$= (n_1 - 1) + (n_2 - 1)$$
$$= 9 + 9$$
$$= 18$$

The *t* distribution for $df = 18$ is presented in Figure 10.2. For $\alpha = .05$, the critical region consists of the extreme 5% of the distribution and has boundaries of $t = +2.101$ and $t = -2.101$.

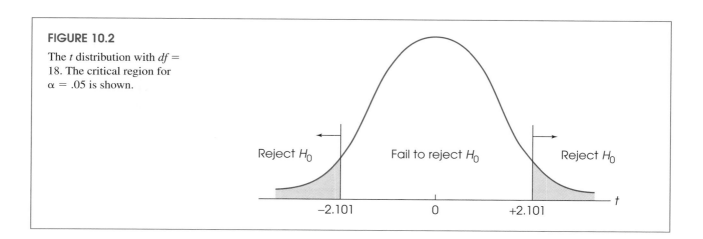

FIGURE 10.2

The *t* distribution with $df = 18$. The critical region for $\alpha = .05$ is shown.

Reject H_0 Fail to reject H_0 Reject H_0

−2.101   0   +2.101   *t*

STEP 3 Obtain the data, and compute the test statistic. The data are as given, so all that remains is to compute the *t* statistic. Because the independent-measures *t* formula is relatively complex, the calculations can be simplified by dividing the process into three parts.
    First, find the pooled variance for the two samples:

Caution: The pooled variance combines the two samples to obtain a single estimate of variance. In the formula, the two samples are combined in a single fraction.

$$s_p^2 = \frac{SS_1 + SS_2}{df_1 + df_2}$$
$$= \frac{200 + 160}{9 + 9}$$
$$= \frac{360}{18}$$
$$= 20$$

Second, use the pooled variance to compute the estimated standard error:

Caution: The standard error adds the errors from two separate samples. In the formula, these two errors are added as two separate fractions. In this case, the two errors are equal because the sample sizes are the same.

$$s_{(\overline{X}_1 - \overline{X}_2)} = \sqrt{\frac{s_p^2}{n_1} + \frac{s_p^2}{n_2}} = \sqrt{\frac{20}{10} + \frac{20}{10}}$$

$$= \sqrt{2 + 2}$$

$$= \sqrt{4}$$

$$= 2$$

Third, compute the *t* statistic:

$$t = \frac{(\overline{X}_1 - \overline{X}_2) - (\mu_1 - \mu_2)}{s_{(\overline{X}_1 - \overline{X}_2)}} = \frac{(25 - 19) - 0}{2}$$

$$= \frac{6}{2}$$

$$= 3.00$$

STEP 4 Make a decision. The obtained value ($t = 3.00$) is in the critical region. In this example, the obtained sample mean difference is three times greater than would be expected by chance (the standard error). This result is very unlikely if H_0 is true. Therefore, we reject H_0 and conclude that using mental images produced a significant difference in memory performance. More specifically, the group using images recalled significantly more words than the group with no images.

ON THE COMPUTER

IN EXAMPLE 10.1 we presented a complete demonstration of a hypothesis test using the independent-measures *t* statistic. You should recognize that the data presented in the example were deliberately constructed so that all the calculations were relatively easy. In a real research situation, the data would probably contain many more scores and would certainly not produce such simple numbers for the sample means and the *SS* values. However, in a real research situation you probably would use a computer to do the arithmetic for you. Although there are many computer programs available for statistical calculations, we will introduce two examples that are commonly used in the behavioral sciences: Minitab and SPSS. We are not going to teach you how to use these programs, but we will present examples of the output that the programs produce. You should be able to read the computer printouts and identify the critical elements of the hypothesis test. To demonstrate the

independent-measures hypothesis test as it is done on a computer, we entered the data from Example 10.1 into Minitab and SPSS. The two computer printouts are shown in Figure 10.3. Various elements of each printout have been highlighted in the figure, and are discussed next. You should be able to relate the items from the computer printouts to the calculations and results from the hypothesis test in Example 10.1.

① Summary statistics are reported for each of the two samples. Both programs report the number of scores, the sample mean, the sample standard deviation, and the estimated standard error for each sample.

② The outcome of the hypothesis test. You should recognize the obtained value of $t = 3.00$ and $df = 18$. Instead of reporting the α level in a traditional format such as $p < .05$ or $p < .01$, the computer

SPSS Printout				
t-tests for Independent Samples of GROUP				

Variable	Number of Cases	Mean	SD	SE of Mean
MEMORY				
① GROUP 1	10	25.0000	4.714	1.491
GROUP 2	10	19.0000	4.216	1.333

Mean Difference = 6.0000

Levene's Test for Equality of Variances: F = .384 P = .543

② t-test for Equality of Means

Variances	t-value	df	2-Tail Sig	SE of Diff	95% CI for Diff
Equal	3.00	18	.008	2.000	(1.798, 10.202)
③ Unequal **④**	3.00	17.78	.008	2.000	(1.794, 10.206)

Minitab Printout				
Two-sample T for Image vs No Image				

	N	Mean	StDev	SE Mean
① Image	10	25.00	4.71	1.5
No Image	10	19.00	4.22	1.3

Difference = mu Image − mu No Image
Estimate for difference: 6.00
④ 95% CI for difference: (1.80, 10.20)
② T-Test of difference = 0 (vs not =): T-Value = 3.00 P-Value = 0.008 DF = 18
③ Both use Pooled StDev = 4.47

FIGURE 10.3

Computer printouts showing the independent-measures *t* hypothesis test as it is performed by the SPSS program (top) and the Minitab program (bottom). Both printouts show the test results for the same data that were analyzed in Example 10.1. The highlighted and numbered sections in each printout are discussed in the text.

calculates the exact probability that the *t* statistic was obtained simply by chance (the probability of a Type I error). For these data, there is a probability of $p = 0.008$ that you would obtain a *t* statistic of $t = 3.00$ (or greater) just by chance. Because this probability value is smaller than $\alpha = .01$, we can conclude that the data show a significant difference with $\alpha = .01$ $(p < .01)$.

③ Both programs have performed the hypothesis test by combining the two sample variances into a single pooled variance. The Minitab printout

(*continues*)

ON THE COMPUTER (*continued*)

shows the pooled standard deviation (square root of the pooled variance). The SPSS printout shows two different versions of the hypothesis test: one with equal variances (pooled together) and one with unequal variances. In this book we only consider the equal-variance (pooled) version.

④ Both programs provide an estimate of how much difference there is between the two treatment conditions. Specifically, the programs have computed a 95% confidence interval (CI) for the mean difference. Estimation and confidence intervals will be discussed in Chapter 12.

IN THE LITERATURE:
REPORTING THE RESULTS OF AN INDEPENDENT-MEASURES *t* TEST

In Chapter 4 (page 97), we demonstrated how the mean and the standard deviation are reported in APA format. In Chapter 9 (page 211), we illustrated the APA style for reporting the results of a *t* test. Now we will use the APA format to report the results of Example 10.1, an independent-measures *t* test. A concise statement might read as follows:

> The group using mental images recalled more words ($M = 25$, $SD = 4.71$) than the group that did not use mental images ($M = 19$, $SD = 4.22$). This difference was significant, $t(18) = 3.00$, $p < .05$, two-tailed.

You should note that standard deviation is not a step in the computations for the independent-measures *t* test, yet it is useful when providing descriptive statistics for each treatment group. It is easily computed when doing the *t* test because you need *SS* and *df* for both groups to determine the pooled variance. Note that the format for reporting *t* is exactly the same as that described in Chapter 9.   ❏

HYPOTHESIS TESTS AND EFFECT SIZE

By now it should be very clear that most researchers conduct a hypothesis test with the hope that the conclusion will be to reject the null hypothesis. Specifically, the goal is to demonstrate that a treatment has a *significant effect* or to show that there is a *significant difference* between two treatment conditions. However, you should be very cautious about how you interpret the concept of statistical significance or the idea of rejecting a null hypothesis. When the conclusion from a hypothesis test is that there is a significant effect (reject H_0), it simply means that the result from the study is bigger than would be expected just by chance.

Looking back at Example 10.1, you will note that the group using mental images had memory scores that averaged 6 points higher than the group that did not use images. This 6-point difference was found to be statistically significant. In other situations, 6 points (or more) may not be sufficient for significance. At the other extreme, when the standard error is very small (which happens with large samples), then the treatment effect can also be very small and still be statistically significant.

The general point of this argument is that statistical significance does not necessarily provide any information about how big the treatment effect actually is. To try to avoid this problem, it is often recommended that when researchers report a statistically significant effect, they also include a report of how big the effect actually is (see the guidelines presented by the APA Task Force on Statistical Inference; Wilkinson, 1999).

Reporting effect size   The simplest and most direct method for reporting the size of a treatment effect is simply to report the actual results of the research study. For example, the results presented in Example 10.1 show a 6-point difference between the imagery group and the no-imagery group. You should realize, however, that in some situations a 6-point difference may be relatively large and in other situations a 6-point difference may be relatively small. For example, two men who differ in weight by 6 pounds would be considered to be essentially the same weight. On the other hand, if two men differ in height by 6 inches, it is considered to be a relatively large difference. Therefore, statisticians have developed several different methods for computing a standardized measure of effect size. We will consider two examples that are representative of the most commonly used methods for computing a measure of effect size.

Cohen's *d*   Cohen (1969) recommended that the magnitude of effect size be standardized by measuring the mean difference between two treatments in terms of the standard deviation. The resulting measure of effect size is defined as *Cohen's d* and is computed as

$$d = \frac{\mu_1 - \mu_2}{\sigma}$$

(10.6)

You should recognize that Cohen's *d* is similar to a *z*-score because it uses the standard deviation to standardize distances. For example, a value of $d = 2.00$ indicates that the mean difference is two times bigger than the standard deviation (see Figure 10.4). On the other hand, a value of $d = 0.5$ indicates that the mean difference is only one-half as large as the standard deviation. Cohen also provided objective criteria for evaluating the size of an effect as follows:

Magnitude of *d*	Evaluation of effect size
$0 < d < 0.2$	Small effect (mean difference less than 0.2 standard deviation)
$0.2 < d < 0.8$	Medium effect (mean difference around 0.5 standard deviation)
$d > 0.8$	Large effect (mean difference more than 0.8 standard deviation)

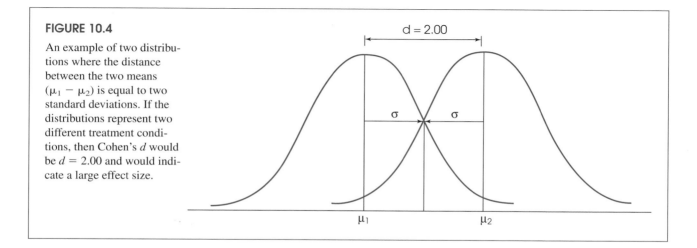

FIGURE 10.4

An example of two distributions where the distance between the two means $(\mu_1 - \mu_2)$ is equal to two standard deviations. If the distributions represent two different treatment conditions, then Cohen's *d* would be $d = 2.00$ and would indicate a large effect size.

Cohen's original formula is stated in terms of population parameters. When this technique is applied to research results, however, the calculations typically use the corresponding sample statistics, resulting in

$$d = \frac{\text{sample mean difference}}{\text{sample standard deviation}}$$

For an independent-measures research design, the formula becomes

$$d = \frac{\overline{X}_1 - \overline{X}_2}{s_p} \tag{10.7}$$

where s_p is the pooled standard deviation (square root of the pooled variance). Using the data from Example 10.1, we obtain the following measure of effect size:

$$d = \frac{\overline{X}_1 - \overline{X}_2}{s_p} = \frac{25 - 19}{\sqrt{20}} = \frac{6}{4.47} = 1.34$$

For this example, the mean difference is larger than one standard deviation. According to Cohen's criteria, using images (as opposed to no images) has a *large effect* on memory.

Percentage of variance accounted for (r^2)   When there is a consistent difference between two treatment conditions, it is possible to predict whether a subject's score will be relatively high or relatively low if you know which treatment the subject is in. For the imagery study in Example 10.1, you know that people who use mental images tend to have higher scores than people who do not use images. The general concept of being able to predict differences forms the basis for another method of calculating effect size. This alternative method for computing effect size measures the degree to which one variable can be predicted from another variable. Typically, the calculation involves measuring the percentage of variance for one variable that can be predicted by knowing a second variable. For example, the subjects in the imagery study all have different memory scores. In statistical terms, their scores are variable. However, some of this variability is predictable by knowing which group the scores come from; subjects in the imagery condition score higher than subjects in the no-imagery condition. By measuring exactly how much of the variability is predictable, we can obtain a measure of how big the effect actually is. One common technique for measuring the percentage of predictable variability is to compute a value for r^2 as follows:

The symbol r is the traditional symbol for a correlation. The concept of r^2 is discussed further in Chapter 15 (page 398).

$$r^2 = \frac{t^2}{t^2 + df} \tag{10.8}$$

For the data in Example 10.1 (the imagery study), we obtained $t = 3.00$ with $df = 18$. These values produce an r^2 of

$$r^2 = \frac{3^2}{3^2 + 18} = \frac{9}{9 + 18} = \frac{9}{27} = 0.333$$

For this example, 0.333 (or 33.3%) of the variance in the memory scores is determined by the imagery versus no-imagery conditions. That is, the memory scores obtained in the research study are partially determined by the two treatment conditions (images

10.2   PERCENTAGE OF VARIANCE ACCOUNTED FOR

ALTHOUGH THE value of r^2 is typically discussed as percentage of *variance,* it actually is measuring the percentage of *SS*. Considering the data in Example 10.1 (the imagery study), if you combine the two groups into a single sample of $n = 20$ scores, you can calculate an overall value of $SS = 540$ for the entire set of $n = 20$ memory scores. (You should check the calculation). This overall *SS* can be partitioned into two components: a predictable component based on the difference between treatments and an unpredictable component that is considered to be error (or chance). The error component has already been calculated and is simply the *SS* values that were used to compute the estimated standard error. These *SS* values are $SS_1 = 200$ and $SS_2 = 160$, and to-

gether they combine for a total error component of $SS = 360$. The predictable component of *SS* can now be found by subtraction: The overall *SS* is 540 and the error component is 360; therefore, the predictable component is $540 - 360 = 180$. Finally, we can compute the percentage that is predictable. For these data, the predictable component is 180 and the overall value is 540, so the proportion is

$$\text{predictable proportion} = \frac{180}{540} = 0.333 = 33.3\%$$

You should recognize that this is exactly the same value we obtained for r^2 using Formula 10.8.

versus no images), and the part that is determined amounts to 33.3% ($\frac{1}{3}$) of the variance in the scores (see Box 10.2).

DIRECTIONAL HYPOTHESES AND ONE-TAILED TESTS

When planning an independent-measures experiment, a researcher usually has some expectation or specific prediction for the outcome. For the memory experiment described in Example 10.1, the psychologist clearly expects the group using images to have higher memory scores than the group without images. This kind of directional prediction can be incorporated into the statement of the hypotheses, resulting in a directional, or one-tailed, test. Recall from Chapter 8 that one-tailed tests can be less conservative than two-tailed tests, and should be used when clearly justified by theory or previous findings. The following example demonstrates the procedure for stating hypotheses and locating the critical region for a one-tailed test using the independent-measures *t* statistic.

EXAMPLE 10.3

We will use the same experimental situation that was described in Example 10.1. The researcher is using an independent-measures design to examine the effect of mental images on memory. The prediction is that the imagery group will have higher memory scores.

STEP 1

State the hypotheses and select the alpha level. As always, the null hypothesis says that there is no effect, and the alternative hypothesis says that there is an effect. For this example, the *predicted* effect is that images will produce higher scores. Thus, the two hypotheses are

H_0: $\mu_{\text{images}} \leq \mu_{\text{no images}}$ (Imagery scores are not higher.)

H_1: $\mu_{\text{images}} > \mu_{\text{no images}}$ (Imagery scores are higher, as predicted.)

Note that it is usually easier to state the hypotheses in words before you try to write them in symbols. Also, it usually is easier to begin with the alternative hypothesis (H_1), which states that the treatment works as predicted. Then the null hypothesis is just the opposite of H_1. Also note that the equal sign goes in the null hypothesis, indicating *no difference* between the two treatment conditions. The idea of zero difference is the essence of the null hypothesis, and the numerical value of zero will be used for $(\mu_1 - \mu_2)$ during the calculation of the *t* statistic.

STEP 2   Locate the critical region. For a directional test, the critical region will be located entirely in one tail of the distribution. Rather than trying to determine which tail, positive or negative, is the correct location, we suggest you identify the criteria for the critical region in a two-step process as follows. First, look at the data and determine whether or not the sample mean difference is in the direction that was predicted. If the answer is no, then the data obviously do not support the predicted treatment effect and you can stop the analysis. On the other hand, if the difference is in the predicted direction, then the second step is to determine whether the difference is large enough to be significant. To test for significance, simply find the one-tailed critical value in the *t* distribution table. If the sample *t* statistic is more extreme (either positive or negative) than the critical value, then the difference is significant.

For this example, the imagery group scored 6 points higher, as predicted. With $df = 18$, the one-tailed critical value for $\alpha = .05$ is $t = 1.734$.

STEP 3   Collect the data and calculate the test statistic. The details of the calculations were shown in Example 10.1. The data produce a *t* statistic of $t = 3.00$.

STEP 4   Make a decision. The *t* statistic of $t = 3.00$ is well beyond the critical boundary of $t = 1.734$. Therefore, we reject the null hypothesis and conclude that scores in the imagery condition are significantly higher than scores in the no-imagery condition, as predicted.

LEARNING CHECK ◆

1. A research report states that there is a significant difference between treatments for an independent-measures design with $t(28) = 2.27$.
   a. How many subjects participated in the research study? (*Hint:* Start with the *df* value.)
   b. Should the report state that $p > .05$ or $p < .05$?

2. A developmental psychologist would like to examine the differences in verbal skills for 6-year-old girls compared with 6-year-old boys. A sample of $n = 5$ girls and $n = 5$ boys is obtained, and each child is given a standardized verbal abilities test. The data are as follows:

Girls	Boys
$\overline{X} = 83$	$\overline{X} = 71$
$SS = 200$	$SS = 120$

   Are these data sufficient to indicate a significant difference in verbal skills for 6-year-old girls and 6-year-old boys? Test at the .05 level of significance.

3. Suppose that the psychologist in the previous question predicted that girls have higher verbal scores at age 5. What value of *t* would be necessary to conclude that girls score significantly higher using a one-tailed test with $\alpha = .01$?

4. Calculate the effect size for the data in Question 2. Compute Cohen's *d* and r^2.

ANSWERS
1. **a.** The $df = 28$, so the total number of subjects is 30.

    b. A significant result is indicated by $p < .05$.

2. Pooled variance $= 40$, the standard error $= 4$, and $t = 3.00$. With $df = 8$, the decision is to reject the null hypothesis.

3. With $df = 8$ and $\alpha = .01$ the critical value is $t = 2.896$.

4. For these data, $d = 1.90$ (a very large effect size) and $r^2 = 0.53$ (or 53%).   ◆

10.4   ASSUMPTIONS UNDERLYING THE INDEPENDENT-MEASURES *t* FORMULA

There are three assumptions that should be satisfied before you use the independent-measures *t* formula for hypothesis testing:

1. The observations within each sample must be independent (see page 184).
2. The two populations from which the samples are selected must be normal.
3. The two populations from which the samples are selected must have equal variances.

The first two assumptions should be familiar from the single-sample *t* hypothesis test presented in Chapter 9. As before, the normality assumption is the less important of the two, especially with large samples. When there is reason to suspect that the populations are far from normal, you should compensate by ensuring that the samples are relatively large.

The third assumption is referred to as *homogeneity of variance* and states that the two populations being compared must have the same variance. You may recall a similar assumption for both the *z*-score and the single-sample *t*. For those tests, we assumed that the effect of the treatment was to add a constant amount to (or subtract a constant amount from) each individual score. As a result, the population standard deviation after treatment was the same as it had been before treatment. We now are making essentially the same assumption but phrasing it in terms of variances.

Remember: Adding a constant to (or subtracting a constant from) each score does not change the standard deviation.

Recall that the pooled variance in the *t*-statistic formula is obtained by averaging together the two sample variances. It makes sense to average these two values only if they both are estimating the same population variance—that is, if the homogeneity of variance assumption is satisfied. If the two sample variances represent different population variances, then the average would be meaningless. (*Note:* There is no meaning to the value obtained by averaging two unrelated numbers. For example, what is the significance of the number obtained by averaging your shoe size and the last two digits of your social security number?)

The importance of the homogeneity assumption increases when there is a large discrepancy between the sample sizes. With equal (or nearly equal) sample sizes, this assumption is less critical but still important.

The homogeneity of variance assumption is quite important because violating this assumption can negate any meaningful interpretation of the data from an independent-measures experiment. Specifically, when you compute the *t* statistic in a hypothesis test, all the numbers in the formula come from the data except for the population mean difference, which you get from H_0. Thus, you are sure of all the numbers in the formula except for one. If you obtain an extreme result for the *t* statistic (a value in the critical region), you conclude that the hypothesized value was wrong. However, consider what happens when you violate the homogeneity of variance assumption. In this case, you have two questionable values in the formula (the hypothesized population value and the meaningless average of the two variances). Now if you obtain an extreme *t* statistic, you do not know which of these two values is responsible. Specifically, you cannot reject the hypothesis because it may have been the pooled variance that produced the extreme *t* statistic. Without satisfying the homogeneity of variance requirement, you cannot accurately interpret a *t* statistic, and the hypothesis test becomes meaningless.

How do you know whether or not the homogeneity of variance assumption is satisfied? One simple test involves just looking at the two sample variances. Logically, if the two population variances are equal, then the two sample variances should be very similar. When the two sample variances are reasonably close, you can be reasonably confident that the homogeneity assumption has been satisfied and proceed with the test. However, if one sample variance is more than three or four times larger than the other, then there is reason for concern. A more objective procedure involves a statistical test to evaluate the homogeneity assumption. Although there are many different statistical methods for determining whether or not the homogeneity of variance assumption has been satisfied, Hartley's *F*-max test is one of the simplest to compute and to understand. An additional advantage is that this test can also be used to check homogeneity of variance with more than two independent samples. Later, in Chapter 13, we will examine statistical methods for comparing several different samples, and Hartley's test will be useful again.

The following example demonstrates the *F*-max test for two independent samples.

EXAMPLE 10.4

The *F*-max test is based on the principle that a sample variance provides an unbiased estimate of the population variance. Therefore, if the population variances are the same, the sample variances should be very similar. The procedure for using the *F*-max test is as follows:

1. Compute the sample variance, $s^2 = SS/df$, for each of the separate samples.

A similar test, Levene's test, was reported in the SPSS printout in Figure 10.3.

2. Select the largest and the smallest of these sample variances and compute

$$F\text{-max} = \frac{s^2(\text{largest})}{s^2(\text{smallest})}$$

A relatively large value for *F*-max indicates a large difference between the sample variances. In this case, the data suggest that the population variances are different and that the homogeneity assumption has been violated. On the other hand, a small value of *F*-max (near 1.00) indicates that the sample variances are similar and that the homogeneity assumption is reasonable.

3. The *F*-max value computed for the sample data is compared with the critical value found in Table B.3 (Appendix B). If the sample value is larger than the table value, then you conclude that the variances are different and that the homogeneity assumption is not valid.

To locate the critical value in the table, you need to know

a. k = number of separate samples. (For the independent-measures *t* test, $k = 2$.)

b. $df = n - 1$ for each sample variance. The Hartley test assumes that all samples are the same size.

c. The alpha level. The table provides critical values for $\alpha = .05$ and $\alpha = .01$. Generally a test for homogeneity would use the larger alpha level.

Example: Two independent samples each have $n = 10$. The sample variances are 12.34 and 9.15. For these data,

$$F\text{-max} = \frac{s^2(\text{largest})}{s^2(\text{smallest})} = \frac{12.34}{9.15} = 1.35$$

With $\alpha = .05$, $k = 2$, and $df = n - 1 = 9$, the critical value from the table is 4.03. Because the obtained F-max is smaller than this critical value, you conclude that the data do not provide evidence that the homogeneity of variance assumption has been violated.

ON THE WEB

NOW THAT you have finished Chapter 10, you can test your knowledge with the practice quiz on the Wadsworth Web site at **www.wadsworth.com**. In addition, you can look at the workshop on the *t* test for between groups and related groups. (The workshop also covers material that will be presented in Chapter 11.) For more information about the quizzes and workshops, see page 24.

SUMMARY

1. The independent-measures *t* statistic uses the data from two separate samples to draw inferences about the mean difference between two populations or between two different treatment conditions.

2. The formula for the independent-measures *t* statistic has the same structure as the original *z*-score or the single-sample *t*:

$$t = \frac{\text{sample statistic} - \text{population parameter}}{\text{estimated standard error}}$$

For the independent-measures *t*, the sample statistic is the sample mean difference $(\overline{X}_1 - \overline{X}_2)$. The population parameter is the population mean difference, $(\mu_1 - \mu_2)$. The estimated standard error for the sample mean difference is computed by combining the errors for the two sample means. The resulting formula is

$$t = \frac{(\overline{X}_1 - \overline{X}_2) - (\mu_1 - \mu_2)}{s_{(\overline{X}_1 - \overline{X}_2)}}$$

where the estimated standard error is

$$s_{(\overline{X}_1 - \overline{X}_2)} = \sqrt{\frac{s_p^2}{n_1} + \frac{s_p^2}{n_2}}$$

The pooled variance in the formula, s_p^2, is the weighted mean of the two sample variances:

$$s_p^2 = \frac{SS_1 + SS_2}{df_1 + df_2}$$

This *t* statistic has degrees of freedom determined by the sum of the *df* values for the two samples:

$$df = df_1 + df_2$$
$$= (n_1 - 1) + (n_2 - 1)$$

3. For hypothesis testing, the null hypothesis normally states that there is no difference between the two population means:

$$H_0: \mu_1 = \mu_2 \quad \text{or} \quad \mu_1 - \mu_2 = 0$$

4. When a hypothesis test with an independent-measures *t* statistic indicates a significant difference, it is recommended that you also compute a measure of the effect size. One measure of effect size is Cohen's *d*, which is a standardized measured of the mean difference. For the independent-measures *t* statistic,

$$d = \frac{\overline{X}_1 - \overline{X}_2}{\sqrt{s_p^2}}$$

A second common measure of effect size is the percentage of variance accounted for by the treatment effect. This measure is identified by r^2 and is computed as

$$r^2 = \frac{t^2}{t^2 + df}$$

5. Appropriate use and interpretation of the *t* statistic require that the data satisfy the homogeneity of variance assumption. This assumption stipulates that the two populations have equal variances. An informal test of this assumption can be made by simply comparing the two sample variances: If the two sample variances are approximately equal, the *t* test is justified. Hartley's *F*-max test provides a statistical technique for determining whether or not the data satisfy the homogeneity assumption.

KEY TERMS

independent-measures research design

between-subjects research design

pooled variance

effect size

Cohen's *d*

percentage of variance accounted for

homogeneity of variance

--- FOCUS ON PROBLEM SOLVING ---

1. As you learn more about different statistical methods, one basic problem will be deciding which method is appropriate for a particular set of data. Fortunately, it is easy to identify situations in which the independent-measures *t* statistic is used. First, the data will always consist of two separate samples (two *n*s, two $\overline{X}$s, two *SS*s, and so on). Second, this *t* statistic is always used to answer questions about a mean difference: On the average, is one group different (better, faster, smarter) than the other group? If you examine the data and identify the type of question that a researcher is asking, you should be able to decide whether or not an independent-measures *t* is appropriate.

2. When computing an independent-measures *t* statistic from sample data, we suggest that you routinely divide the formula into separate stages rather than trying to do all the calculations at once. First, find the pooled variance. Second, compute the standard error. Third, compute the *t* statistic.

3. One of the most common errors for students involves confusing the formulas for pooled variance and standard error. When computing pooled variance, you are "pooling" the two samples together into a single variance. This variance is computed as a *single fraction,* with two *SS* values in the numerator and two *df* values in the denominator. When computing the standard error, you are adding the error from the first sample and the error from the second sample. These two separate errors add as *two separate fractions* under the square root symbol.

--- DEMONSTRATION 10.1 ---

THE INDEPENDENT-MEASURES *t* TEST

In a study of jury behavior, two samples of subjects were provided details about a trial in which the defendant was obviously guilty. Although group 2 received the same details as group 1, the second group was also told that some evidence had been withheld from the jury by the judge. Later the subjects were asked to recommend a jail sentence. The length of term suggested by each subject is presented here. Is there a significant difference between the two groups in their responses?

$$\text{Group 1 scores:} \quad 4 \quad 4 \quad 3 \quad 2 \quad 5 \quad 1 \quad 1 \quad 4$$
$$\text{Group 2 scores:} \quad 3 \quad 7 \quad 8 \quad 5 \quad 4 \quad 7 \quad 6 \quad 8$$

There are two separate samples in this study. Therefore, the analysis will use the independent-measures t test.

STEP 1   State the hypotheses, and select an alpha level.

H_0: $\mu_1 - \mu_2 = 0$ (For the population, knowing evidence has been withheld has no effect on the suggested sentence).

H_1: $\mu_1 - \mu_2 \neq 0$ (For the population, knowledge of withheld evidence has an effect on the jury's response).

We will set the level of significance to $\alpha = .05$, two tails.

STEP 2   Identify the critical region.
For the independent-measures t statistic, degrees of freedom are determined by

$$df = n_1 + n_2 - 2$$
$$= 8 + 8 - 2$$
$$= 14$$

Consult the t-distribution table for a two-tailed test with $\alpha = .05$ and $df = 14$. The critical t values are $+2.145$ and -2.145.

STEP 3   Compute the test statistic.
We are computing an independent-measures t statistic. To do this, we will need the mean and SS for each sample, pooled variance, and estimated standard error.

Sample means and sums of squares   The means $(\overline{X})$ and sums of squares (SS) for the samples are computed as follows:

Sample 1		Sample 2	
X	X^2	X	X^2
4	16	3	9
4	16	7	49
3	9	8	64
2	4	5	25
5	25	4	16
1	1	7	49
1	1	6	36
4	16	8	64
$\Sigma X = 24$	$\Sigma X^2 = 88$	$\Sigma X = 48$	$\Sigma X^2 = 312$

$$n_1 = 8 \qquad\qquad n_2 = 8$$

$$\bar{X}_1 = \frac{\Sigma X}{n} = \frac{24}{8} = 3 \qquad\qquad \bar{X}_2 = \frac{\Sigma X}{n} = \frac{48}{8} = 6$$

$$SS_1 = \Sigma X^2 - \frac{(\Sigma X)^2}{n} \qquad\qquad SS_2 = \Sigma X^2 - \frac{(\Sigma X)^2}{n}$$

$$= 88 - \frac{(24)^2}{8} \qquad\qquad = 312 - \frac{(48)^2}{8}$$

$$= 88 - \frac{576}{8} \qquad\qquad = 312 - \frac{2304}{8}$$

$$= 88 - 72 \qquad\qquad = 312 - 288$$

$$SS_1 = 16 \qquad\qquad SS_2 = 24$$

Pooled variance   For these data, the pooled variance equals

$$s_p^2 = \frac{SS_1 + SS_2}{df_1 + df_2} = \frac{16 + 24}{7 + 7} = \frac{40}{14} = 2.86$$

Estimated standard error   Now we can calculate the estimated standard error for mean differences.

$$s_{(\bar{X}_1 - \bar{X}_2)} = \sqrt{\frac{s_p^2}{n_1} + \frac{s_p^2}{n_2}} = \sqrt{\frac{2.86}{8} + \frac{2.86}{8}} = \sqrt{0.358 + 0.358}$$

$$= \sqrt{0.716} = 0.85$$

The t statistic   Finally, the *t* statistic can be computed.

$$t = \frac{(\bar{X}_1 - \bar{X}_2) - (\mu_1 - \mu_2)}{s_{(\bar{X}_1 - \bar{X}_2)}} = \frac{(3 - 6) - 0}{0.85} = \frac{-3}{0.85}$$

$$= -3.53$$

STEP 4   Make a decision about H_0, and state a conclusion.
      The obtained *t* value of -3.53 falls in the critical region of the left tail (critical $t = \pm2.145$). Therefore, the null hypothesis is rejected. The subjects that were informed about the withheld evidence gave significantly longer sentences, $t(14) = -3.53$, $p < .05$, two tails.

PROBLEMS

1. Describe the general characteristics of a research study for which an independent-measures *t* would be the appropriate test statistic.

2. What is measured by the estimated standard error that is used for the independent-measures *t* statistic?

3. Describe the homogeneity of variance assumption, and explain why it is important for the independent-measures hypothesis test.

4. What happens to the value of the independent-measures *t* statistic as the difference between the two sample means increases? What happens to the *t* value as the variability of the scores in the two samples increases?

5. One sample has $n = 8$ scores with $SS = 56$, and a second sample has $n = 10$ scores with $SS = 108$.
   a. Find the variance for each sample.
   b. Find the pooled variance for the two samples.

6. One sample has $SS = 63$, and a second sample has $SS = 45$.
   a. Assuming that $n = 10$ for both samples, find each of the sample variances, and calculate the pooled variance. You should find that the pooled variance is exactly halfway between the two sample variances.
   b. Now assume that $n = 10$ for the first sample and $n = 16$ for the second. Find each of the sample variances, and calculate the pooled variance. You should find that the pooled variance is closer to the variance for the larger sample ($n = 16$).

7. One sample has $SS = 32$ and a second sample has $SS = 48$.
   a. Calculate the variance for each sample and the pooled variance assuming that $n = 5$ for both samples. You should find that the pooled variance is halfway between the two sample variances.
   b. Now assume that the first sample has $n = 9$ scores and the second has $n = 4$. Calculate the variance for each sample and the pooled variance. This time you should find that the pooled variance is closer to the value for the larger sample.

8. In the independent-measures hypothesis test, the difference between two sample means is used to test a hypothesis about the difference between two population means. The sample mean difference is not expected to be exactly equal to the population mean difference, and the estimated standard error measures how much discrepancy is reasonable to expect on average. For each of the following situations, compute the estimated standard error for the sample mean difference.
   a. First sample has $n = 8$ and $SS = 416$; second sample has $n = 8$ and $SS = 480$.
   b. First sample has $n = 8$ and $SS = 170$; second sample has $n = 4$ and $SS = 70$.

9. One sample has $n = 15$ with $SS = 1660$, and a second sample has $n = 15$ with $SS = 1700$.
   a. Find the pooled variance for the two samples.
   b. Find the standard error for the sample mean difference.
   c. If the sample mean difference is 8 points, is this enough to reject the null hypothesis and conclude that there is a significant difference at the .05 level?
   d. If the sample mean difference is 12 points, is this enough to indicate a significant difference at the .05 level?

10. One sample has $n = 6$ scores with $SS = 500$ and a second sample has $n = 9$ with $SS = 670$.
   a. Calculate the pooled variance for the two samples.
   b. Calculate the estimated standard error for the sample mean difference.

   c. If the sample mean difference is 10 points, is this enough to reject the null hypothesis for an independent-measures hypothesis test using $\alpha = .05$? Assume a two-tailed test.
   d. If the sample mean difference is 15 points, is this enough to reject the null hypothesis for an independent-measures hypothesis test using $\alpha = .05$? Assume a two-tailed test.

11. A researcher is interested in determining whether difficulties experienced during birth have any influence on the eventual development of mother–child relationships. By examining hospital records from 15 years ago, the researcher identifies 12 women who had relatively easy deliveries and another 12 women who had relatively difficult deliveries. All 24 women gave birth to daughters. The researcher then locates the 24 children (now 15 years old) and gives each one a questionnaire measuring the quality of the relationship between mother and daughter. The data for the two samples are as follows:

Easy delivery	Difficult delivery
$\overline{X} = 47$	$\overline{X} = 52$
$SS = 946$	$SS = 1166$

   Do these data provide evidence for a significant connection between mother–daughter relationships and difficulty during childbirth? Use a two-tailed test with a .05 level of significance.

12. A researcher using an independent-measures design to compare two treatments obtained the following data:

Treatment 1	Treatment 2
$n = 4$	$n = 4$
$\overline{X} = 58$	$\overline{X} = 52$
$SS = 84$	$SS = 108$

   a. Calculate the variance for each of the two samples and then compute the pooled variance. (You should find that the pooled variance is exactly halfway between the two sample variances.)
   b. Do these data indicate a significant difference between the two treatments? Use a two-tailed test with $\alpha = .05$.

13. The researcher from the previous problem attempted to repeat the experiment using larger samples. The data for the second attempt are as follows:

Treatment 1	Treatment 2
$n = 16$	$n = 16$
$\overline{X} = 58$	$\overline{X} = 52$
$SS = 420$	$SS = 540$

a. Calculate the variance for each of the two samples and then compute the pooled variance.
b. Do these data indicate a significant difference between the two treatments? Use a two-tailed test with $\alpha = .05$.
c. You should find that these two samples have exactly the same means and variances as the two samples in Problem 12, and the pooled variance is the same for both sets of data. However, in this problem the sample data were sufficient to reject the null hypothesis but in the previous problem the decision was to fail to reject H_0. Explain why the two sets of data lead to different decisions.

14. The data in Problems 12 and 13 produce the same pooled variance (32) and the same sample mean difference (6 points). However, the two problems use different-sized samples and result in different values for t ($t = 1.50$ with $df = 6$ for Problem 12, and $t = 3.00$ with $df = 30$ for Problem 13).
a. With this information, compute the effect size using Cohen's d (standardized mean difference) for both problems.
b. Compute effect size using r^2 (percentage of variance accounted for) for both problems.
c. You should find that one measure of effect size is influenced by sample size and the other is not. Explain how the sample size is included in one formula but not in the other.

15. The animal learning course in the psychology department requires that each student train a rat to perform certain behaviors. The student's grade is partially determined by the rat's performance. The instructor for this course has noticed that some students are very comfortable working with the rats and seem to be very successful training their rats. The instructor suspects that these students may have previous experience with pets that gives them an advantage in the class. To test this hypoth-

esis, the instructor gives the entire class a questionnaire at the beginning of the course. One question determines whether or not each student currently has a pet of any type at home. Based on the responses to this question, the instructor divides the class into two groups and compares the rats' learning scores for the two groups. The data are as follows:

Rats' scores for students with pets	Rats' scores for students without pets
$n = 10$	$n = 15$
$\overline{X} = 78$	$\overline{X} = 66$
$SS = 1420$	$SS = 2030$

a. Are these data sufficient to indicate a significant difference between groups? Use a two-tailed test with $\alpha = .05$.
b. Use Cohen's d to measure the effect size for this study.

16. Friedman and Rosenman (1974) have classified people into two categories: Type A personalities and Type B personalities. Type As are hard-driving, competitive, and ambitious. Type Bs are more relaxed, easy-going people. One factor that differentiates these two groups is the chronically high level of frustration experienced by Type As. To demonstrate this phenomenon, separate samples of Type As and Type Bs are obtained, with $n = 8$ in each sample. The individual subjects are all given a frustration inventory measuring level of frustration. The average score for the Type As is $\overline{X} = 84$ with $SS = 740$, and the Type Bs average $\overline{X} = 71$ with $SS = 660$. Do these data indicate a significant difference between the two groups? Test at the .01 level of significance.

17. In a classic study of problem solving, Duncker (1945) asked subjects to mount a candle on a wall in an upright position so that it would burn normally. One group of subjects was given a candle, a book of matches, and a box of tacks. A second group was given the same items, except the tacks and the box were presented separately as two distinct items. The solution to this problem involves using the tacks to mount the box on the wall, which creates a shelf for the candle. Duncker reasoned that the first group of subjects would have trouble seeing a "new" function for the box (a shelf) because it was already serving a function (holding tacks). For each subject, the amount of time to solve the problem was recorded. Data similar to Duncker's are as follows:

Time to solve problem (in sec.)	
Box of tacks	Tacks and box separate
128	42
160	24
113	68
101	35
94	47

Do these data indicate a significant difference between the two conditions? Test at the .01 level of significance.

18. Siegel (1990) found that elderly people who owned dogs were less likely to pay visits to their doctors after upsetting events than were those who did not own pets. Similarly, consider the following hypothetical data. A sample of elderly dog owners is compared to a similar group (in terms of age and health) who do not own dogs. The researcher records the number of visits to the doctor during the past year for each person. The data are as follows:

Control group	Dog owners
12	8
10	5
6	9
9	4
15	6
12	
14	

a. Is there a significant difference in the number of doctor visits between dog owners and control subjects? Use a two-tailed test with $\alpha = .05$.
b. Calculate the value of r^2 (percentage of variance accounted for) for these data.

19. A researcher reports an independent-measures t statistic of $t = 2.53$ with $df = 24$.
a. How many subjects participated in the researcher's experiment?
b. Can the researcher conclude that there is a significant difference between the two samples with $\alpha = .05$, two tails?
c. Can the researcher conclude that the mean difference is significant at the .01 level, two tails?

20. Consider the following data from an independent measures study:

Treatment 1	Treatment 2
3	12
5	10
7	8
1	14

a. Compute the mean for each sample.
b. Compute SS for each sample, pooled variance, and estimated standard error.
c. Is there evidence for a treatment effect? Test with $\alpha = .05$, two tails.

21. Consider the following data from an independent measures study:

Treatment 1	Treatment 2
0	12
4	10
0	4
12	18

a. Compute the mean for each sample and compare them to the means for treatments 1 and 2 of Problem 20.
b. Compute SS for each sample, pooled variance, and estimated standard error. Compare these results to part (b) of Problem 20.
c. Is there evidence for a treatment effect? Test with $\alpha = .05$, two tails.
d. Compare part (c) of this problem with part (c) of the previous problem. Why is there a different outcome?

22. Consider the following data from an independent measures study:

Treatment 1	Treatment 2
3	7
5	5
7	3
1	9

a. Compute the mean for each sample. Compare these results to those of Problem 20.
b. Compute SS for each sample, pooled variance, and estimated standard error. Compre these results to those of Problem 20.

c. Is there a statistically significant treatment effect? Test with $\alpha = .05$, two tials.

d. Compare the results of part (c) to those of Problem 20. Why do the outcomes of the studies differ?

23. A researcher studies the effect of feedback on estimation of length. Two samples of subjects are given practice estimating the lengths of lines drawn by the researcher on a chalkboard. One group receives no feedback about the accuracy of the estimates. The second group receives feedback ("too long," "too short") for accuracy. Then everyone is tested for accuracy of length estimation. The amount of error, in inches, is measured for all subjects. The following table depicts the data.

No feedback	Feedback
6	3
7	3
4	1
7	5

a. Does feedback have a significant effect on accuracy? Use a two-tailed test with $\alpha = .05$.

b. Calculate Cohen's *d* and r^2 (percentage of variance accounted for) to measure the effect size for this study.

CHAPTER 11

THE *t* TEST FOR TWO RELATED SAMPLES

TOOLS YOU WILL NEED

The following items are considered essential background material for this chapter. If you doubt your knowledge of any of these items, you should review the appropriate chapter or section before proceeding.

- Introduction to the *t* statistic (Chapter 9)
  - Estimated standard error
  - Degrees of freedom
  - *t* distribution
  - Hypothesis tests with the *t* statistic
- Independent-measures design (Chapter 10)

CONTENTS

11.1 OVERVIEW

In the previous chapter, we introduced the independent-measures research design as one strategy for comparing two treatment conditions or two populations. The independent-measures design is characterized by the fact that two separate samples are used to obtain the two sets of data that are to be compared. In this chapter, we will examine an alternative research strategy known as a *repeated-measures* research design. With a repeated-measures design, two sets of data are obtained from the same sample of individuals. For example, a group of patients could be measured before therapy and then measured again after therapy. Or a group of individuals could be tested in a quiet, comfortable environment and then tested again in a noisy, stressful environment to examine the effects of stress on performance. In each case, note that the same variable is being measured twice for the same set of individuals; that is, we are literally repeating measurements on the same sample. Note that a repeated-measures design is often called a *within-subjects* design because it examines treatment differences within a single group of subjects.

DEFINITION

> A *repeated-measures* study is one in which a single sample of individuals is measured more than once on the same dependent variable. The same subjects are used in all of the treatment conditions. A repeated-measures study is often called a *within-subjects* study.

The main advantage of a repeated-measures study is that it uses exactly the same subjects in all treatment conditions. Thus, there is no risk that the subjects in one treatment are substantially different from the subjects in another. With an independent-measures design, on the other hand, there is always a risk that the results are biased because the individuals in one sample are much different (smarter, faster, more extroverted, and so on) than the individuals in the other sample. At the end of this chapter we will present a more detailed comparison of repeated-measures studies and independent-measures studies, considering the advantages and disadvantages of both types of research.

Occasionally, researchers will try to approximate the advantages of a repeated-measures design by using a technique known as *matched subjects*. A matched-subjects design involves two separate samples, but each individual in one sample is matched one-to-one with an individual in the other sample. Typically, the individuals are matched on one or more variables that are considered to be especially important for the study. For example, a researcher studying verbal learning might want to be certain that the two samples are matched in terms of IQ and gender. In this case, a male subject with an IQ of 120 in one sample would be matched with another male with an IQ of 120 in the other sample. Although the subjects in one sample are not *identical* to the subjects in the other sample, the matched-subjects design at least ensures that the two samples are equivalent (or matched) with respect to some specific variables.

DEFINITION

> In a *matched-subjects* study, each individual in one sample is matched with a subject in the other sample. The matching is done so that the two individuals are equivalent (or nearly equivalent) with respect to a specific variable that the researcher would like to control.

In a repeated-measures design, or a matched-subjects design, the data consist of two sets of scores (two samples) with the scores in one sample directly related, one-to-one, with the scores in the second sample. For this reason, the two research designs are statistically equivalent and are grouped together under the common name *related-samples* designs (or correlated-samples designs). In this chapter, we will focus our discussion on repeated-measures designs because they are overwhelmingly the more common example of related-groups designs. However, you should realize that the statistical techniques used for repeated-measures studies can be applied directly to data from a matched-subjects study.

11.2   THE *t* STATISTIC FOR RELATED SAMPLES

The *t* statistic for related samples is structurally similar to the other *t* statistics we have examined. As we shall see, it is essentially the same as the single-sample *t* statistic covered in Chapter 9. One major distinction of the related-samples *t* is that it is based on difference scores rather than raw scores (*X* values). In this section, we examine difference scores and develop the *t* statistic for related samples.

DIFFERENCE SCORES: THE DATA FOR A RELATED-SAMPLES STUDY

Table 11.1 presents hypothetical data from a research study examining how reaction time is affected by a common, over-the-counter cold medication. The first score for each person (X_1) is a measurement of reaction time before the medication was administered. The second score (X_2) is a measure of reaction time one half hour after taking the medication. Because we are interested in how the medication affects reaction time, we have computed the difference between the first score and the second score for each individual. The *difference scores,* or *D* values, are shown in the last column of the table. Typically, the difference scores are obtained by subtracting the first score (before treatment) from the second score (after treatment) for each person:

$$\text{difference score} = D = X_2 - X_1 \tag{11.1}$$

Note that the sign of each *D* score tells you the direction of the change. Person A, for example, shows a decrease in reaction time after taking the medication (a negative change), but person B shows an increase (a positive change).

TABLE 11.1

Reaction time measurements taken before and after taking an over-the-counter cold medication.

Person	Before medication (X_1)	After medication (X_2)	Difference D
A	215	210	−5
B	221	242	21
C	196	219	23
D	202	228	25

$$\Sigma D = 64$$

$$\overline{D} = \frac{\Sigma D}{n} = \frac{64}{4} = 16$$

The sample of difference scores (*D* values) will serve as the sample data for the hypothesis test. To compute the *t* statistic, we will use the number of *D* scores (*n*) as well as the sample mean $(\overline{D})$ and the value of *SS* for the sample of *D* scores.

**THE HYPOTHESES FOR A
RELATED-SAMPLES TEST**

The researcher's goal is to use the sample of difference scores to answer questions about the general population. In particular, the researcher would like to know if there is any difference between the two treatment conditions for the general population. Note that we are interested in a population of *difference scores*. That is, we would like to know what would happen if every individual in the population was measured in two treatment conditions (X_1 and X_2) and a difference score (D) was computed for everyone. Specifically, we are interested in the mean for the population of difference scores. We will identify this population mean difference with the symbol μ_D (using the subscript letter D to indicate that we are dealing with D values rather than X scores).

As always, the null hypothesis states that for the general population there is no effect, no change, or no difference. For a repeated-measures study, the null hypothesis states that the mean difference for the general population is zero. In symbols,

$$H_0: \mu_D = 0$$

Again, this hypothesis refers to the mean for the entire population of difference scores. According to this hypothesis, it is possible that some individuals will show positive difference scores and some will show negative scores, but the differences are random and unsystematic and will balance out to zero.

The alternative hypothesis states that there is a treatment effect that causes the scores in one treatment condition to be systematically higher (or lower) than the scores in the other condition. In symbols,

$$H_1: \mu_D \neq 0$$

According to H_1, the difference scores for the individuals in the population tend to be consistently positive (or negative), indicating a consistent, predictable difference between the two treatments. See Box 11.1 for further discussion of H_0 and H_1.

 **11.1   ANALOGIES FOR H_0 AND H_1 IN
THE REPEATED-MEASURES TEST**

AN ANALOGY *for H_0*: Intelligence is a fairly stable characteristic; that is, you do not get noticeably smarter or dumber from one day to the next. However, if we gave you an IQ test every day for a week, we probably would get seven different numbers. The day-to-day changes in your IQ scores would probably be small and would be random. Some days your IQ score is slightly higher, and some days it is slightly lower. On average, the day-to-day changes in IQ should balance out to zero. This is the situation that is predicted by the null hypothesis for a repeated-measures test. According to H_0, any changes that occur (the D scores) either for an individual or for a sample are just due to chance, and in the long run, they will average out to zero.

An Analogy for H_1: On the other hand, suppose we

elevate the effects of a fitness training program by measuring the strength of the muscles in your right arm. We will measure your grip strength every day over a 4-week period. We probably will find small differences in your scores from one day to the next, just as we did with the IQ scores. However, the day-to-day changes in grip strength will not be random. Although your grip strength may decrease occasionally, there should be a general trend toward increased strength as you go through the training program. Thus, most of the day-to-day changes (the D scores) should show an increase. This is the situation predicted by the alternative hypothesis for the repeated-measures test. According to H_1, the changes that occur are systematic and predictable and will not average out to zero.

THE *t* STATISTIC
FOR RELATED SAMPLES

Figure 11.1 shows the general situation that exists for a repeated-measures hypothesis test. You may recognize that we are facing essentially the same situation that we encountered in Chapter 9. In particular, we have a population for which the mean and the standard deviation are unknown, and we have a sample that will be used to test a hypothesis about the unknown population. In Chapter 9, we introduced a *t* statistic that allowed us to use the sample mean as a basis for testing hypotheses about the population mean. We will use this *t*-statistic formula again here to develop the *repeated-measures t test*. To refresh your memory, the single-sample *t* statistic (Chapter 9) is defined by the formula

$$t = \frac{\overline{X} - \mu}{s_{\overline{X}}}$$

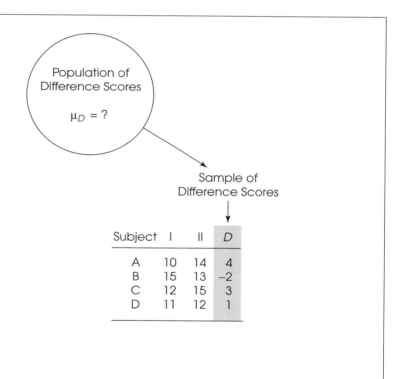

FIGURE 11.1

A sample of $n = 4$ people is selected from the population. Each individual is measured twice, once in treatment I and once in treatment II, and a difference score, D, is computed for each individual. This sample of difference scores is intended to represent the population. Note that we are using a sample of difference scores to represent a population of difference scores. Specifically, we are interested in the mean difference for the general population. The null hypothesis states that for the general population there is no consistent or systematic difference between the two treatments, so the population mean difference is $\mu_D = 0$.

In this formula, the sample mean, $\overline{X}$, is calculated from the data, and the value for the population mean, μ, is obtained from the null hypothesis. The estimated standard error, $s_{\overline{X}}$, is also calculated from the data and provides a measure of how much difference it is reasonable to expect between the sample mean and the population mean.

For the repeated-measures design, the sample data are difference scores and are identified by the letter D rather than X. Therefore, we will substitute Ds in the formula in place of Xs to emphasize that we are dealing with difference scores instead of X values. Also, the population mean that is of interest to us is the population mean difference (the mean amount of change for the entire population), and we identify this parameter with the symbol μ_D. With these simple changes, the *t* formula for the repeated-measures design becomes

$$t = \frac{\overline{D} - \mu_D}{s_{\overline{D}}}$$

(11.2)

In this formula, the *estimated standard error,* $s_{\overline{D}}$ is computed in exactly the same way as $s_{\overline{X}}$ is computed for the single-sample *t* statistic. The change in notation simply indicates that the sample mean is computed for a sample of *D* scores instead of a sample of *X* scores. To calculate the estimated standard error, the first step is to compute the variance (or the standard deviation) for the sample of *D* scores.

$$s^2 = \frac{SS}{n-1} = \frac{SS}{df} \quad \text{or} \quad s = \sqrt{\frac{SS}{df}}$$

The estimated standard error is then computed using the sample variance (or sample standard deviation) and the sample size, *n*.

$$s_{\overline{D}} = \sqrt{\frac{s^2}{n}} \quad \text{or} \quad s_{\overline{D}} = \frac{s}{\sqrt{n}}$$

Note that all of the calculations are done using the difference scores (the *D* scores) and that there is only one *D* score for each subject. With a sample of *n* subjects, the *t* statistic will have $df = n - 1$. Remember that *n* refers to the number of *D* scores, not the number of *X* scores in the original data.

You should also note that the repeated-measures *t* statistic is conceptually similar to the *t* statistics we have previously examined:

$$t = \frac{\text{sample statistic} - \text{population parameter}}{\text{estimated standard error}}$$

In this case, the sample data are represented by the sample mean of the difference scores $(\overline{D})$, the population hypothesis is the value predicted by H_0 for μ_D, and the amount of sampling error is measured by the standard error of sample mean differences $(s_{\overline{D}})$.

LEARNING CHECK

1. What characteristics differentiate a repeated-measures study from an independent-measures research study?

2. How are the difference scores (*D* values) obtained for a repeated-measures hypothesis test?

3. Stated in words and stated in symbols, what is the null hypothesis for a repeated-measures hypothesis test?

ANSWERS

1. A repeated-measures study obtains two sets of data from one sample by measuring each individual twice. An independent-measures study uses two separate samples to obtain two sets of data.

2. The difference score for each subject is obtained by subtracting the subject's first score from the second score. In symbols, $D = X_2 - X_1$.

3. The null hypothesis states that the mean difference for the entire population is zero. That is, if every individual is measured in both treatments and a difference score is computed for each individual, then the average difference score for the entire population will be equal to zero. In symbols, $\mu_D = 0$. ◆

11.3   HYPOTHESIS TESTS FOR THE REPEATED-MEASURES DESIGN

In a repeated-measures study, we are interested in whether or not there is a systematic difference between the scores in the first treatment condition and the scores in the second treatment condition. The hypothesis test will use the difference scores obtained from a sample to evaluate the overall mean difference, μ_D, for the entire population. According to the null hypothesis, there is no consistent or systematic difference between treatments and $\mu_D = 0$. The alternative hypothesis, on the other hand, says that there is a systematic difference and $\mu_D \neq 0$. The purpose of the hypothesis test is to decide between these two options.

The hypothesis test with the repeated-measures t statistic follows the same four-step process that we have used for other tests. The complete hypothesis-testing procedure is demonstrated in Example 11.1.

EXAMPLE 11.1   A researcher in behavioral medicine believes that stress often makes asthma symptoms worse for people who suffer from this respiratory disorder. Because of the suspected role of stress, the investigator decides to examine the effect of relaxation training on the severity of asthma symptoms. A sample of 5 patients is selected for the study. During the week before treatment, the investigator records the severity of their symptoms by measuring how many doses of medication are needed for asthma attacks. Then the patients receive relaxation training. For the week following training, the researcher once again records the number of doses required by each patient. Table 11.2 shows the data and summarizes the findings. Do these data indicate that relaxation training alters the severity of symptoms?

TABLE 11.2

The number of doses of medication needed for asthma attacks before and after relaxation training

Patient	Week before training	Week after training	D	D^2
A	9	4	−5	25
B	4	1	−3	9
C	5	5	0	0
D	4	0	−4	16
E	5	1	−4	16
			$\Sigma D = -16$	$\Sigma D^2 = 66$

Because the data consist of difference scores (D values) instead of X scores, the formulas for the mean and SS also use D in place of X. However, you should recognize the computational formula for SS that was introduced in Chapter 4.

$$\overline{D} = \frac{\Sigma D}{n} = \frac{-16}{5} = -3.2$$

$$SS = \Sigma D^2 - \frac{(\Sigma D)^2}{n} = 66 - \frac{(-16)^2}{5}$$

$$= 66 - 51.2 = 14.8$$

STEP 1   State the hypotheses, and select the alpha level.

$$H_0: \mu_D = 0 \quad \text{(There is no change in symptoms.)}$$

$$H_1: \mu_D \neq 0 \quad \text{(There is a change.)}$$

The level of significance is set at $\alpha = .05$ for a two-tailed test.

STEP 2   Locate the critical region. For this example, $n = 5$, so the t statistic will have $df = n - 1 = 4$. From the t-distribution table, you should find that the critical values are $+2.776$ and -2.776. These values are shown in Figure 11.2.

FIGURE 11.2

The critical regions with $\alpha = .05$ and $df = 4$ begin at $+2.776$ and -2.776 in the t distribution. Obtained values of t that are more extreme than these values will lie in a critical region. In that case, the null hypothesis would be rejected.

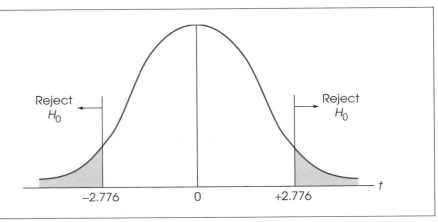

STEP 3   Calculate the t statistic. Table 11.2 shows the sample data and the calculations for $\overline{D} = -3.2$ and $SS = 14.8$. As we have done with the other t statistics, we will present the computation of the t statistic as a three-step process.

First, compute the variance for the sample. Remember that the population variance (σ^2) is unknown, and we must use the sample value in its place.

$$s^2 = \frac{SS}{n - 1} = \frac{14.8}{4} = 3.7$$

Next, use the sample variance to compute the estimated standard error.

$$s_{\overline{D}} = \sqrt{\frac{s^2}{n}} = \sqrt{\frac{3.7}{5}} = \sqrt{0.74} = 0.86$$

Finally, use the sample mean ($\overline{D}$) and the hypothesized population mean (μ_D) along with the estimated standard error to compute the value for the t statistic.

$$t = \frac{\overline{D} - \mu_D}{s_{\overline{D}}} = \frac{-3.2 - 0}{.86} = -3.72$$

STEP 4   Make a decision. The t value we obtained falls in the critical region (see Figure 11.2). The investigator rejects the null hypothesis and concludes that relaxation training does affect the amount of medication needed to control the asthma symptoms.

ON THE COMPUTER

THE DATA from Example 11.1 were entered into the SPSS and Minitab computer programs to demonstrate the repeated-measures t test as it is done on a computer. The two printouts are shown in Figure 11.3. Most elements of the printouts should be easy to understand, especially if you look back to the original calculations and results in the example. Specific items that we have highlighted are as follows.

① Both printouts show the summary statistics for the difference scores (the mean, the standard deviation, and the estimated standard error).

② Both printouts show the results of the t test: $t = -3.72$ with $df = 4$ and $p = 0.020$. As we saw in Chapter 10, the computer programs report an exact value for the alpha level. Instead of reporting $p < .05$, the printouts show $p = 0.020$.

③ The printouts also show a 95% confidence interval (CI) estimating the magnitude of the mean difference. The process of estimation is presented in Chapter 12.

④ Finally, the SPSS printout shows summary statistics for the two sets of scores (before and after).

SPSS Printout						
t-tests for Paired Samples						
Variable	Number of pairs	Corr	2-tail Sig	Mean	SD	SE of Mean
AFTER				2.2000	2.168	.970
	5	.589	.296			
BEFORE				5.4000	2.074	.927

④
②

Paired Differences						
① Mean	SD	SE of Mean		t-value	df	2-tail Sig
−3.2000	1.924	.860		−3.72	4	.020
③ 95% CI (−5.588, −.812)						

Minitab Printout				
Test of mu = 0 vs mu not = 0				
① Variable	N	Mean	StDev	SE Mean
Difference	5	−3.200	1.924	0.860
② Variable	95.0% CI		T	P
Difference	(−5.588, −0.812)		−3.72	0.020
③				

FIGURE 11.3

Computer printouts showing the repeated-measures t using the SPSS computer program (top) and the Minitab program (bottom). The printouts show the test results for the data analyzed in Example 11.1. The highlighted and numbered sections in each printout are discussed in the text.

IN THE LITERATURE:
REPORTING THE RESULTS OF A REPEATED-MEASURES *t* TEST

As we have seen in Chapters 9 and 10, the APA format for reporting the results of *t* tests consists of a concise statement that incorporates the *t* value, degrees of freedom, and alpha level. One typically includes values for means and standard deviations, either in a statement or a table (Chapter 4). For Example 11.1, we observed a mean difference of $\overline{D} = -3.2$ with $s = 1.92$. Also, we obtained a *t* statistic of $t = -3.72$ with $df = 4$, and our decision was to reject the null hypothesis at the .05 level of significance. A published report of this study might summarize the conclusion as follows:

> Relaxation training resulted in a decrease ($M = 3.2$, $SD = 1.92$) in the number of doses of medication needed to control asthma symptoms. This reduction was statistically significant, $t(4) = -3.72$, $p < .05$, two-tailed.

In reporting the mean change, we did not bother to include the negative sign because we explicitly noted that the change was a decrease. ❑

EFFECT SIZE

As we noted in Chapter 10 (page 234), whenever a treatment effect is found to be statistically significant, it is recommended that you also report a measure of the absolute magnitude of the effect. The two commonly used measures of effect size are Cohen's *d* and r^2, the percentage of variance accounted for. Using the data from Example 11.1, we will demonstrate how these two measures are used to calculate effect size.

Cohen's *d* provides a standardized measure of the mean difference between treatments. The standardization process simply divides the actual mean difference by the standard deviation. For the repeated-measures study presented in Example 11.1, the data produce

The negative sign simply indicates that the difference is a decrease in medication.

$$\text{Cohen's } d = \frac{\overline{D}}{s} = \frac{-3.20}{\sqrt{3.7}} = \frac{-3.20}{1.92} = -1.67$$

You should recall that any value greater than 0.80 is considered to be a large effect and these data are clearly in that category.

Percentage of variance is computed using the obtained *t* value and the *df* value from the hypothesis test. For the data in Example 11.1, we obtain

$$r^2 = \frac{t^2}{t^2 + df} = \frac{(-3.72)^2}{(-3.72)^2 + 4} = \frac{13.84}{13.84 + 4} = 0.776$$

For these data, nearly 78% of the variance in the medication scores is accounted for by the difference after training compared with before training.

DIRECTIONAL HYPOTHESES AND ONE-TAILED TESTS

In many repeated-measures and matched-subjects studies, the researcher has a specific prediction concerning the direction of the treatment effect. For example, in the study described in Example 11.1, the researcher expects relaxation training to reduce the severity of asthma symptoms and therefore to reduce the amount of medication needed for asthma attacks. This kind of directional prediction can be incorporated into the statement of hypotheses, resulting in a directional, or one-tailed, hypothesis test. The following example demonstrates how the hypotheses and critical region are determined in a directional test.

EXAMPLE 11.2   We will reexamine the experiment presented in Example 11.1. The researcher is using a repeated-measures design to investigate the effect of relaxation training on the severity of asthma symptoms. The researcher predicts that people will need less medication after training than before, which will produce negative difference scores.

$$D = X_2 - X_1 = \text{after} - \text{before}$$

STEP 1   State the hypotheses, and select the alpha level. As always, the null hypothesis states that there is no effect. For this example, the researcher predicts that relaxation training will reduce the need for medication. The null hypothesis says it will not. In symbols,

$$H_0: \mu_D \geq 0 \quad \text{(Medication is not reduced after training.)}$$

The alternative hypothesis says that the treatment does work. For this example, H_1 states that the training does reduce medication. In symbols,

$$H_1: \mu_D < 0 \quad \text{(Medication is reduced after training.)}$$

It often is easier to start by stating H_1, which says that the treatment works as predicted. Then H_0 is simply the opposite of H_1.

STEP 2   Locate the critical region. The researcher is predicting negative difference scores if the treatment works. Hence, a negative t statistic would tend to support the experimental prediction and refute H_0. With a sample of $n = 5$ subjects, the t statistic will have $df = 4$. Looking in the t-distribution table for $df = 4$ and $\alpha = .05$ for a one-tailed test, we find a critical value of 2.132. Thus, a t statistic that is more extreme than -2.132 will be sufficient to reject H_0. The t distribution with the one-tailed critical region is shown in Figure 11.4.

FIGURE 11.4

The one-tailed critical region for $\alpha = .05$ in the t distribution with $df = 4$.

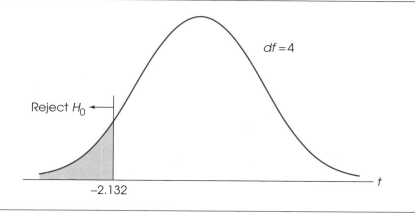

STEP 3   Compute the t statistic. We calculated the t statistic in Example 11.1, where we obtained $t = -3.72$.

STEP 4   Make a decision. The obtained t statistic is well beyond the critical boundary. Therefore, we reject H_0 and conclude that the relaxation training did significantly reduce the amount of medication needed for asthma attacks.

1. A researcher would like to examine the effect of hypnosis on cigarette smoking. The researcher selects a sample of smokers ($n = 4$) for the study, and records the number of cigarettes smoked on the day prior to treatment. The subjects are then hypnotized and given the posthypnotic suggestion that each time they light a cigarette, they will experience a horrible taste and feel nauseous. The data are as follows:

	The number of cigarettes smoked before and after hypnosis	
Subject	Before treatment	After treatment
1	19	12
2	35	36
3	20	13
4	31	24

    a. Find the difference scores (*D* values) for this sample.

    b. The difference scores have $\overline{D} = -5$ and $SS = 48$. Do these data indicate that hypnosis has a significant effect on cigarette smoking? Test with $\alpha = .05$.

    c. Are the data sufficient to conclude that hypnosis significantly *reduces* cigarette smoking? Use a one-tailed test with $\alpha = .05$.

2. Compute the effect size using both Cohen's *d* and r^2 for the hypnosis treatment in Question 1.

3. A computer printout for a repeated-measures *t* test reports a *p* value of $p = .021$.

    a. Can the researcher claim a significant effect with $\alpha = .01$?

    b. Is the effect significant with $\alpha = .05$?

ANSWERS

1. a. The difference scores are $-7, 1, -7, -7$.

    b. For these data, $s^2 = 16$, $s_{\overline{D}} = 2$, and $t = -2.50$. With $\alpha = .05$, we fail to reject H_0; these data do not provide sufficient evidence to conclude that hypnosis has a significant effect on cigarette smoking.

    c. For the directional test, the critical value is $t = -2.353$. The sample data produce a *t* statistic of $t = -2.50$, which is in the critical region. Reject H_0 and conclude that the hypnosis significantly reduced smoking.

2. For these data, $d = -5/4 = -1.25$ and $r^2 = 0.68$.

3. a. The exact *p* value, $p = .021$, is not less than $\alpha = .01$. Therefore, the effect is not significant for $\alpha = .01$ ($p > .01$).

    b. The *p* value is less than .05, so the effect is significant with $\alpha = .05$.

11.4   USES AND ASSUMPTIONS FOR RELATED-SAMPLES *t* TESTS

REPEATED-MEASURES VERSUS INDEPENDENT-MEASURES DESIGNS

In many research situations, it is possible to use either a repeated-measures study or an independent-measures study to compare two treatment conditions. The independent-measures design would use two separate samples (one in each treatment condition) and the repeated-measures design would use only one sample with the same individuals in both treatments. The decision about which design to use is often made by considering the advantages and disadvantages of the two designs. In general, the repeated-measures design has most of the advantages.

Number of subjects   A repeated-measures design typically requires fewer subjects than an independent-measures design. The repeated-measures design uses the subjects more efficiently because each individual is measured in both of the treatment conditions. This can be especially important when there are relatively few subjects available (for example, when you are studying a rare species or individuals in a rare profession).

Study changes over time   The repeated-measures design is especially well suited for studying learning, development, or other changes that take place over time. Remember that this design involves measuring individuals at one time and then returning to measure the same individuals at a later time. In this way, a researcher can observe behaviors that change or develop over time.

Individual differences   The primary advantage of a repeated-measures design is that it reduces or eliminates problems caused by individual differences. *Individual differences* are characteristics such as age, IQ, gender, and personality that vary from one individual to another. These individual differences can influence the scores obtained in a research study and they can affect the outcome of a hypothesis test. Consider the data shown in Table 11.3. The first set of data represents the results from a typical independent-measures study and the second set represents a repeated-measures study. Note that we have identified each subject by name to help demonstrate the effects of individual differences.

For the independent-measures data, note that every score represents a different person. For the repeated-measures study, on the other hand, the same people are measured in both of the treatment conditions. This difference between the two designs has some important consequences.

1. We have constructed the data so that both research studies have exactly the same scores and they both show the same 5-point mean difference between treatments.

TABLE 11.3

Hypothetical data showing the results from an independent-measures study and a repeated-measures study. The two sets of data use exactly the same numerical scores and they both show the same 5-point mean difference between treatments.

Independent-measures study (2 separate samples)		Repeated-measures study (same sample in both treatments)		
Treatment 1	Treatment 2	Treatment 1	Treatment 2	D
(John) $X = 18$	(Sue) $X = 15$	(John) $X = 18$	(John) $X = 15$	-3
(Mary) $X = 27$	(Tom) $X = 20$	(Mary) $X = 27$	(Mary) $X = 20$	-7
(Bill) $X = 33$	(Dave) $X = 28$	(Bill) $X = 33$	(Bill) $X = 28$	-5
$\overline{X} = 26$	$\overline{X} = 21$			$\overline{D} = -5$
$SS = 114$	$SS = 86$			$SS = 8$

In each case, the researcher would like to conclude that the 5-point difference was caused by the treatments. However, with the independent-measures design, there is always the possibility that the subjects in treatment 1 have different characteristics than the subjects in treatment 2. For example, the three subjects in treatment 2 may be more intelligent than the subjects in treatment 1 and their higher intelligence caused them to have higher scores. Note that this problem disappears with the repeated-measures design. Specifically, with repeated measures there is no possibility that the subjects in one treatment are different from the subjects in another treatment because the same subjects are used in all the treatments.

2. Although the two sets of data contain exactly the same scores and have exactly the same 5-point mean difference, you should realize that they are very different in terms of the variance used to compute standard error. For the independent-measures study, you calculate the SS or variance for the scores in each of the two separate samples. Note that in each sample there are big differences between subjects. In treatment 1, for example, Bill has a score of 33 and John's score is only 18. These individual differences produce a relatively large sample variance and a large standard error. For the independent-measures study, the standard error is 5.77, which produces a t statistic of $t = 0.87$. For these data, the hypothesis test concludes that there is no significant difference between treatments.

   In the repeated-measures study, the SS and variance are computed for the difference scores. If you examine the repeated-measures data in Table 11.2, you will see that the big differences between John and Bill that exist in treatment 1 and in treatment 2 are eliminated when you get to the difference scores. Because the individual differences are eliminated, the variance and standard error are dramatically reduced. For the repeated-measures study, the standard error is 1.15 and the t statistic is $t = 4.35$. With the repeated-measures t, the data show a significant difference between treatments. Thus, one big advantage of a repeated-measures study is that it reduces variance by removing individual differences, which increases the chances of finding a significant result.

CARRYOVER EFFECTS AND PROGRESSIVE ERROR

The primary disadvantage of a repeated-measures design is that the structure of the design allows for the possibility that factors other than the treatment effect can cause a subject's score to change from one treatment to the next. For example, a subject may become tired or bored during the first treatment and, therefore, does not perform well in the second treatment. Note that the decline in performance is not caused by the treatment effect; instead, it is caused by fatigue. In this situation, the outcome of the study is contaminated by outside factors that can distort the sample mean difference. Two such factors, specifically associated with repeated-measures designs, are *carryover effects* and *progressive error.*

A carryover effect occurs when a subject's response in the second treatment is altered by lingering aftereffects from the first treatment. Here are some examples of carryover effects:

1. Imagine that a researcher is comparing the effectiveness of two drugs by testing both drugs, one after the other, on the same group of subjects. If the second drug is tested too soon after the first, some of the first drug may still be in the subject's system, and this residual could exaggerate or minimize the effects of the second drug.

2. Imagine a researcher comparing performance on two tasks that vary in difficulty. If subjects are given a very difficult task first, their poor performance may cause them to lose motivation, so that performance suffers when they get to the second task.

In each of these examples, the researcher will observe a difference between the two treatment means. However, the difference in performance is not caused by the treatments; instead, it is caused by carryover effects.

Progressive error occurs when a subject's performance or response changes consistently over time. For example, a subject's performance may decline over time as a result of fatigue, or it may improve over time as a result of practice. In either case, a researcher would observe a mean difference in performance between the first treatment and the second treatment, but the change in performance is not due to the treatments; instead, it is caused by progressive error.

To help distinguish between carryover effects and progressive error, remember that carryover effects are related directly to the first treatment. Progressive error, on the other hand, occurs as a function of time, independent of which treatment condition is presented first or second. Both of these factors, however, can influence the outcome of a repeated-measures study, and they can make it difficult for a researcher to interpret the results: Is the mean difference caused by the treatments, or is it caused by other factors?

One way to deal with carryover effects or progressive error is to *counterbalance* the order of presentation of treatments. That is, the subjects are randomly divided into two groups, with one group receiving treatment 1 followed by treatment 2 and the other group receiving treatment 2 followed by treatment 1. When there is reason to expect strong carryover effects or large progressive error, your best strategy is not to use a repeated-measures design. Instead, use independent measures with a separate sample for each treatment condition, or use a matched-subjects design so that each individual participates in only one treatment condition.

ASSUMPTIONS OF THE RELATED-SAMPLES *t* TEST

The related-samples *t* statistic requires two basic assumptions:

1. The observations within each treatment condition must be independent (see page 184). Note that the assumption of independence refers to the scores *within* each treatment. Inside each treatment, the scores are obtained from different individuals and should be independent of one another.

2. The population distribution of difference scores (*D* values) must be normal.

As before, the normality assumption is not a cause for concern unless the sample size is relatively small. In the case of severe departures from normality, the validity of the *t* test may be compromised with small samples. However, with relatively large samples ($n > 30$), this assumption can be ignored.

LEARNING CHECK

1. What assumptions must be satisfied for repeated-measures *t* tests to be valid?

2. Describe some situations for which a repeated-measures design is well suited.

3. The data from a research study consist of 10 scores in each of two different treatment conditions. How many individual subjects would be needed to produce these data

   a. For an independent-measures design?

   b. For a repeated-measures design?

4. Explain why researchers do not need to worry about carryover effects with an independent-measures research design.

ANSWERS   1. The observations within a treatment are independent. The population distribution of *D* scores is assumed to be normal.

2. The repeated-measures design is suited to situations in which a particular type of subject is not readily available for study. This design is helpful because it uses fewer subjects (only one sample is needed). Certain questions are addressed more adequately by a repeated-measures design—for example, whenever one would like to study changes across time in the same individuals. Also, when individual differences are large, a repeated-measures design is helpful because it reduces the amount of this type of error in the statistical analysis.

3. **a.** The independent-measures design would require 20 subjects (two separate samples with *n* = 10 in each).

   b. The repeated-measures design would require 10 subjects (the same 10 individuals are measured in both treatments).

4. In an independent-measures design, the subjects in the second treatment are completely different from the subjects in the first treatment. Because each subject participates in only one treatment, there is no opportunity for the effects of one treatment to carry over to another.   ◆

ON THE WEB

REMEMBER THAT there is a practice quiz for Chapter 11 on the Wadsworth Web site at **www.wadsworth.com**. In addition, you can review the independent-measures *t* test and the repeated-measures *t* test in the workshop (the *t* test for between groups and related groups). For more information about the quizzes and workshops, see page 24.

SUMMARY

1. In a related-samples research study, the individuals in one treatment condition are directly related, one-to-one, with the individuals in the other treatment condition(s). The most common related-samples study is a repeated-measures design, where the same sample of individuals is tested in all of the treatment conditions. This design literally repeats measurements on the same subjects. An alternative is a matched-subjects design, where the individuals in one sample are matched one-to-one with individuals in another sample. The matching is based on a variable relevant to the study.

2. The repeated-measures *t* test begins by computing a difference between the first and second measurements for each subject (or the difference for each matched pair). The difference scores, or *D* scores, are obtained by

$$D = X_2 - X_1$$

The sample mean, $\overline{D}$, and sample variance, s^2, are used to summarize and describe the set of difference scores.

3. The formula for the repeated-measures *t* statistic is

$$t = \frac{\overline{D} - \mu_D}{s_{\overline{D}}}$$

In the formula, the null hypothesis specifies $\mu_D = 0$, and the estimated standard error is computed by

$$s_{\overline{D}} = \sqrt{\frac{s^2}{n}} \quad \text{or} \quad s_{\overline{D}} = \frac{s}{\sqrt{n}}$$

4. A repeated-measures design may be preferred to an independent-measures study when one wants to observe changes in behavior in the same subjects, as in learning or developmental studies. An important advantage of the repeated-measures design is that it removes or reduces individual differences, which in turn lowers sample variability and tends to increase the chances for obtaining a significant result.

5. For a repeated-measures design, effect size can be measured using either r^2 (the percentage of variance accounted for) or Cohen's d (the standardized mean difference). The value of r^2 is computed the same for both independent- and repeated-measures designs,

$$r^2 = \frac{t^2}{t^2 + df}$$

Cohen's d is defined as the sample mean difference divided by standard deviation for both repeated- and independent-measures designs. For repeated-measures studies,

$$d = \frac{\overline{D}}{s}$$

KEY TERMS

repeated-measures design

within-subjects design

matched-subjects design

difference scores

repeated-measures t statistic

estimated standard error for $\overline{D}$

individual differences

carryover effects

progressive error

FOCUS ON PROBLEM SOLVING

1. Once data have been collected, we must select the appropriate statistical analysis. How can you tell if the data call for a repeated-measures t test? Look at the experiment carefully. Is there only one sample of subjects? Are the same subjects tested a second time? If your answers are yes to both of these questions, then a repeated-measures t test should be done. There is only one situation in which the repeated-measures t test can be used for data from two samples, and that is for *matched-subjects* experiments (page 250).

2. The repeated-measures t test is based on difference scores. In finding difference scores, be consistent with your method. That is, you may use either $X_2 - X_1$ or $X_1 - X_2$ to find D scores, but you must use the same method for all subjects. We suggest that you use $D = X_2 - X_1$ so that the sign of the difference scores ($+$ or $-$) indicates the direction of difference (increase or decrease).

DEMONSTRATION 11.1

A REPEATED-MEASURES *t* TEST

A major oil company would like to improve its tarnished image following a large oil spill. Its marketing department develops a short television commercial and tests it on a sample of

$n = 7$ subjects. People's attitudes about the company are measured with a short question-naire, both before and after viewing the commercial. The data are as follows:

Person	X_1 (Before)	X_2 (After)
A	15	15
B	11	13
C	10	18
D	11	12
E	14	16
F	10	10
G	11	19

Was there a significant change? Note that subjects are being tested twice—once before and once after viewing the commercial. Therefore, we have a repeated-measures design.

STEP 1   State the hypothesis, and select an alpha level.
   The null hypothesis states that the commercial has no effect on people's attitudes, or in symbols,

$$H_0: \mu_D = 0 \quad \text{(The mean difference is zero.)}$$

The alternative hypothesis states that the commercial does alter attitudes about the company, or

$$H_1: \mu_D \neq 0 \quad \text{(There is a mean change in attitudes.)}$$

For this demonstration, we will use an alpha level of .05 for a two-tailed test.

STEP 2   Locate the critical region.
   Degrees of freedom for the repeated-measures *t* test are obtained by the formula

$$df = n - 1$$

For these data, degrees of freedom equal

$$df = 7 - 1 = 6$$

Consult the *t*-distribution table for a two-tailed test with $\alpha = .05$ for $df = 6$. The *t* values for the critical region are $t = \pm 2.447$.

STEP 3   Obtain the sample data, and compute the test statistic.
   To compute the repeated-measures *t* statistic, we will have to determine the values for the difference (*D*) scores, $\overline{D}$, *SS* for the *D* scores, the sample variance for the *D* scores, and the estimated standard error for $\overline{D}$.
   The difference scores. The following table illustrates the computation of the *D* values for our sample data. Remember that $D = X_2 - X_1$.

X_1	X_2	D
15	15	$15 - 15 = 0$
11	13	$13 - 11 = +2$
10	18	$18 - 10 = +8$
11	12	$12 - 11 = +1$
14	16	$16 - 14 = +2$
10	10	$10 - 10 = 0$
11	19	$19 - 11 = +8$

The sample mean of D values. The sample mean for the difference scores is equal to the sum of the D values divided by n. For these data,

$$\Sigma D = 0 + 2 + 8 + 1 + 2 + 0 + 8 = 21$$

$$\overline{D} = \frac{\Sigma D}{n} = \frac{21}{7} = 3$$

Sum of squares for D scores. We will use the computational formula for SS. The following table summarizes the calculations:

D	D^2	
0	0	$\Sigma D = 21$
2	4	$\Sigma D^2 = 0 + 4 + 64 + 1 + 4 + 0 + 64 = 137$
8	64	
1	1	$SS = \Sigma D^2 - \dfrac{(\Sigma D)}{n} = 137 - \dfrac{(21)^2}{7}$
2	4	
0	0	
8	64	$SS = 137 - \dfrac{441}{7} = 137 - 63 = 74$

Variance for the D scores. The variance for the sample of D scores is

$$s^2 = \frac{SS}{df} = \frac{74}{6} = 12.33$$

Estimated standard error for $\overline{D}$. The estimated standard error for the sample mean difference is computed as follows:

$$s_{\overline{D}} = \sqrt{\frac{s^2}{n}} = \sqrt{\frac{12.33}{7}} = \sqrt{1.76} = 1.33$$

The repeated-measures t statistic. We now have the information required to calculate the t statistic.

$$t = \frac{\overline{D} - \mu_D}{s_{\overline{D}}} = \frac{3 - 0}{1.33} = \frac{3}{1.33} = 2.26$$

STEP 4   Make a decision about H_0, and state the conclusion.

The obtained t value is not extreme enough to fall in the critical region. Therefore, we fail to reject the null hypothesis. We conclude that there is no evidence that the commercial will change people's attitudes, $t(6) = 2.26$, $p > .05$, two-tailed. (Note that we state that p is *greater than* .05 because we failed to reject H_0.)

PROBLEMS

1. For the following studies, indicate whether or not a repeated-measures t test is the appropriate analysis. Explain your answers.

   a. A researcher is examining the effectiveness of an SAT training program for high school seniors. One sample of seniors takes the 3-week training program and another sample serves as a control group (no training). Both groups then take the SAT and the researcher compares the mean scores for the two groups.

   b. Another researcher does a similar study. A sample of seniors is obtained and each student takes the SAT. Then the seniors participate in the 3-week training program, after which they take the SAT again. The researcher measures how much the mean changes from the first test to the second.

2. What is the primary advantage of a repeated-measures design over an independent-measures design?

3. Explain the difference between a matched-subjects design and a repeated-measures design.

4. A researcher conducts an experiment comparing two treatment conditions and obtains data with 10 scores for each treatment condition.

   a. If the researcher used an independent-measures design, how many subjects participated in the experiment?

   b. If the researcher used a repeated-measures design, how many subjects participated in the experiment?

   c. If the researcher used a matched-subjects design, how many subjects participated in the experiment?

5. Each of the following describes a sample of difference scores (D scores) from a repeated-measures study:

   Sample 1: $n = 10$, $\overline{D} = +4.00$, $s = 10$

   Sample 2: $n = 10$, $\overline{D} = +12.00$, $s = 10$

   a. For each sample, use the mean and standard deviation to sketch the distribution (or simply describe the distribution). Identify where a value of zero is located relative to the pile of scores.

   b. Which of the two samples would be more likely to reject a null hypothesis stating that the population mean difference is zero($\mu_D = 0$)? Explain your answer.

6. Each of the following describes a sample of difference scores (D scores) from a repeated-measures study:

   Sample 1: $n = 10$, $\overline{D} = +4.00$, $s = 10$

   Sample 2: $n = 10$, $\overline{D} = +4.00$, $s = 2$

   a. For each sample, use the mean and standard deviation to sketch the distribution (or simply describe the distribution). Identify where a value of zero is located relative to the pile of scores.

   b. Which of the two samples would be more likely to reject a null hypothesis stating that the population mean difference is zero ($\mu_D = 0$)? Explain your answer.

7. A sample of $n = 16$ difference scores (D values) from a repeated-measures experiment has $SS = 440$.

   a. Compute the standard error of the mean for this sample.

   b. Would a sample mean difference of $\overline{D} = 3$ be large enough to be significant with $\alpha = .05$? Assume a two-tailed test.

8. A sample of difference scores (D values) from a repeated-measures experiment has a mean of $\overline{D} = 5.00$ with a variance of $s^2 = 16$.

   a. If $n = 4$, is this sample sufficient to reject the null hypothesis using a two-tailed test with $\alpha = .05$?

   b. Would you reject H_0 if $n = 16$? Again, assume a two-tailed test with $\alpha = .05$.

9. A researcher uses a repeated-measures study to evaluate the effectiveness of magnetic therapy for treating chronic pain. A sample of $n = 9$ patients is obtained, each of whom has been treated for severe elbow pain for at least 1 year. Each patient is given a questionnaire to evaluate the current level of pain. The patients are then instructed to wear a magnetic band around their elbows for 2 weeks. After the 2-week period, the patients again complete the questionnaire evaluating pain. For this sample, the reported level of pain decreased by an average of $\overline{D} = 12.5$ points with $SS = 1152$. Do these data indicate a significant change in the level of pain? Use a two-tailed test with $\alpha = .01$.

10. A researcher suspects that increasing the level of lighting during the winter months will have a positive effect on people's moods. To test this hypothesis, the researcher identifies a sample of $n = 36$ college students living on one floor of a dormitory. Each student is given a mood questionnaire at the beginning of February, and then all the lights on the dormitory floor are changed from 75-watt to 100-watt bulbs. After 4 weeks, the researcher again measures each student's mood and records the amount of difference between the two measurements. For this sample, the students' mood scores increased by an average of $\overline{D} = +8.6$ points with $SS = 2835$.
    a. Do these data show a significant change in mood following the increase in lighting? Use a two-tailed test with $\alpha = .05$.
    b. Calculate Cohen's d, the standardized mean difference, to measure effect size for this study.

11. Many over-the-counter cold medications come with a warning that the medicine may cause drowsiness. To evaluate this effect, a researcher measures reaction time for a sample of $n = 36$ subjects. Each subject is then given a dose of a popular cold medicine, and reaction time is measured again. For this sample, reaction time increases after the medication by an average of $\overline{D} = 24$ milliseconds with $s = 8$.
    a. Do these data indicate that the cold medicine has a significant effect on reaction time? Use a two-tailed test with $\alpha = .05$.
    b. Calculate r^2, the percentage of variance in the reaction time scores that is accounted for by the medication.

12. One of the benefits of aerobic exercise is the release of endorphins, which are natural chemicals in the brain that produce a feeling of general well-being. A sample of $n = 16$ subjects is obtained, and each person's tolerance for pain is tested before and after a 50-minute session of aerobic exercise. On average, the pain tolerance for this sample is $\overline{D} = 10.5$ points higher after exercise than it was before. The SS for the sample of difference scores is $SS = 960$.
    a. Do these data indicate that exercise produces a significant increase in pain tolerance? Use a one-tailed test with $\alpha = .01$.
    b. Calculate r^2, the percentage of variance in the pain tolerance scores that is accounted for by the exercise.

13. A psychologist is testing a new drug for its painkilling effects. The pain threshold is measured for a sample of $n = 9$ subjects by determining the intensity of an electric shock that causes discomfort. After the initial baseline is established, each subject receives the drug, and the pain threshold is measured once again. For this sample, the pain threshold has increased by an average of $\overline{D} = 1.6$ milliamperes with $s = 0.4$ after receiving the drug.
    a. Do these data indicate that the drug produces a significant increase in pain tolerance? Use a one-tailed test with $\alpha = .05$.
    b. Calculate r^2, the percentage of variance accounted for by the new drug.

14. The level of lymphocytes (white blood cells) in the blood is associated with susceptibility to disease—lower levels indicate greater susceptibility. In a study of the effects of stress on physical well-being, Schleifer and colleagues (1983) recorded the lymphocyte counts for men who were going through a period of extreme emotional stress (the death of a spouse). For a sample of $n = 20$ men, the lymphocyte counts dropped an average of $\overline{D} = 0.09$ with $s = 0.08$. Do these data indicate a significant change? Test at the .05 level of significance.

15. A researcher studies the effect of cognitive psychotherapy on positive self-regard. The number of positive statements made about oneself is recorded for each subject during the first meeting. After 8 weekly therapy sessions, the measures are repeated for each person. For the following data,
    a. Calculate the difference scores and $\overline{D}$.
    b. Compute SS, sample variance, and estimated standard error.
    c. Is there a significant treatment effect? Use $\alpha = .05$, two tails.

Subject	Before treatment	After treatment
A	3	12
B	5	10
C	7	8
D	1	14

16. Another researcher did the exact same study as described in Problem 15, and the data are presented here.
    a. Calculate the difference scores and D. Compare the results to part (a) of the previous problem.
    b. Compute SS, sample variance, and estimated standard error. Compare these results to those of the previous problem.
    c. Is there a significant treatment effect? Use $\alpha = .05$, two tails.

d. Compare the outcome of part (c) to that of the previous problem. Explain why the outcomes differ.

Subject	Before treatment	After treatment
A	0	12
B	4	10
C	0	4
D	12	18

17. The previous two problems both have a sample mean difference of $\overline{D} = 7$ with $n = 4$ scores. However, for Problem 15 the sample variance is $s^2 = 26.67$, which results in $t = 2.71$ (not significant), and in Problem 16, $s^2 = 12$, which produces $t = 4.05$ (significant).
   a. Compute Cohen's d and r^2 to measure effect size for both sets of data.
   b. Explain how effect size is related to sample variance.

18. The following data are from an experiment comparing two treatments:

Treatment 1	Treatment 2
10	11
2	5
1	2
15	18
7	9
$\overline{X} = 7$	$\overline{X} = 9$
$SS = 134$	$SS = 150$

   a. Assume that the data are from an independent-measures experiment using two separate samples, each with $n = 5$ subjects. Do the data indicate a significant difference between the two treatments? Use a two-tailed test with $\alpha = .05$.
   b. Now assume that the data are from a repeated-measures experiment using the same sample of $n = 5$ subjects in both treatments. Calculate the difference score (D) for each subject and use the sample of difference scores to determine whether there is a significant difference between the two treatments. Again, use a two-tailed test with $\alpha = .05$.
   c. You should find that the repeated-measures test in part (b) reaches a different conclusion than the independent-measures test in part (a). How do you

explain the different outcomes? (*Hint:* Look at the variances or SS values for the two different tests. This is an example of the general fact that repeated-measures designs reduce variance by removing individual differences.)

19. A researcher for a cereal company wanted to demonstrate the health benefits of eating oatmeal. A sample of 9 volunteers was obtained and each subject ate a fixed diet without any oatmeal for 30 days. At the end of the 30-day period, cholesterol was measured for each individual. Then the subjects began a second 30-day period in which they repeated exactly the same diet except for 2 cups of oatmeal each day. After the second 30-day period, cholesterol levels were measured again. The scores for the 9 subjects are as follows:

Subject	A	B	C	D	E	F	G	H	I
1st score	145	187	130	155	152	112	120	208	167
2nd score	145	185	119	140	140	115	111	199	159
Difference	0	−2	−11	−15	−12	+3	−9	−9	−8

Are the data sufficient to demonstrate a significant change in cholesterol level after 30 days with an oatmeal diet? Use a two-tailed test with $\alpha = .05$.

20. A variety of research results suggest that visual images interfere with visual perception. In one study, Segal and Fusella (1970) had subjects watch a screen, looking for brief presentations of a small blue arrow. On some trials, the subjects were also asked to form a mental image (for example, imagine a volcano). The results show that subjects made more errors while forming images than while not forming images. Data similar to the Segal and Fusella results are as follows. Do these data indicate a significant difference between the two conditions? Use a two-tailed test with $\alpha = .05$.

Subject	Errors with image	Errors without image
A	13	4
B	9	2
C	12	10
D	7	8
E	10	6
F	8	6
G	9	4

21. People with agoraphobia are so filled with anxiety about being in public places that they seldom leave their homes. Knowing this is a difficult disorder to treat, a researcher tries a long-term treatment. A sample of individuals report how often they have ventured out of the house in the past month. Then they receive relaxation training and are introduced to trips away from the house at gradually increasing durations. After 2 months of treatment, subjects report the number of trips out of the house they made in the last 30 days. The data are as follows:

Subject	Before treatment	After treatment
A	0	4
B	0	0
C	3	14
D	3	23
E	2	9
F	0	8
G	0	6

Does the treatment have a significant effect on the number of trips a person takes? Test with $\alpha = .05$, two tails.

22. A researcher investigates whether single people who own pets are generally happier than singles without pets. A group of nonpet owners are compared to pet owners using a mood inventory. The pet owners are matched one to one with the nonpet owners for income, number of close friendships, and general health. The data are as follows:

Matched pair	Nonpet owner	Pet owner
A	10	15
B	9	9
C	11	10
D	11	19
E	5	17
F	9	15

Is there a significant difference in the mood scores for nonpet owners versus pet owners? Test with $\alpha = .05$ for two tails.

23. At the Olympic level of competition, even the smallest factors can make the difference between winning and losing. For example, Pelton (1983) has shown that Olympic marksmen shoot much better if they fire between heartbeats, rather than squeezing the trigger during a heartbeat. The small vibration caused by a heartbeat seems to be sufficient to affect the marksman's aim. The following hypothetical data demonstrate this phenomenon. A sample of $n = 6$ Olympic marksmen fires a series of rounds while a researcher records heartbeats. For each marksman, a score is recorded for shots fired during heartbeats and for shots fired between heartbeats. Do these data indicate a significant difference? Test with $\alpha = .05$.

Subject	During heartbeat	Between heartbeats
A	93	98
B	90	94
C	95	96
D	92	91
E	95	97
F	91	97

ESTIMATION

CONTENTS

12.1 AN OVERVIEW OF ESTIMATION

In Chapter 8, we introduced hypothesis testing as a statistical procedure that allows researchers to use sample data to draw inferences about populations. Hypothesis testing is probably the most frequently used inferential technique, but it is not the only one. In this chapter, we will examine the process of estimation, which provides researchers with an additional method for using samples as the basis for drawing general conclusions about populations.

The basic principle underlying all of inferential statistics is that samples are representative of the populations from which they come. The most direct application of this principle is the use of sample values as estimators of the corresponding population values—that is, using statistics to estimate parameters. This process is called *estimation.*

DEFINITION   The inferential process of using sample statistics to estimate population parameters is called *estimation.*

The use of samples to estimate populations is quite common. For example, you often hear news reports such as "Sixty percent of the general public approves of the president's new budget plan." Clearly, the percentage that is reported was obtained from a sample (they don't ask everyone's opinion), and this sample statistic is being used as an estimate of the population parameter.

We already have encountered estimation in earlier sections of this book. For example, the formula for sample variance (Chapter 4) was developed so that the sample value would give an accurate and unbiased estimate of the population variance. Now we will examine the process of using sample means as the basis for estimating population means.

PRECISION AND CONFIDENCE IN ESTIMATION

Before we begin the actual process of estimation, there are a few general points that should be kept in mind. First, a sample will not give a perfect picture of the whole population. A sample is expected to be representative of the population, but there always will be some differences between the sample and the entire population. These differences are referred to as *sampling error.* Second, there are two distinct ways of making estimates. Suppose, for example, you are asked to estimate the age of the authors of this book. If you look in the frontmatter of the book, just before the Contents, you will find pictures of Gravetter and Wallnau. We are roughly the same age, so pick either one of us and estimate how old we are. Note that you could make your estimate using a single value (for example, Gravetter appears to be 52 years old) or you could use a range of values (for example, Wallnau seems to be between 40 and 50 years old). The first estimate, using a single number, is called a *point estimate.*

DEFINITION   For a *point estimate,* you use a single number as your estimate of an unknown quantity.

Point estimates have the advantage of being very precise; they specify a particular value. On the other hand, you generally do not have much confidence that a point estimate is correct. For example, most of you would not be willing to bet that Gravetter is exactly 52 years old.

The second type of estimate, using a range of values, is called an *interval estimate.* Interval estimates do not have the precision of point estimates, but they do give you more confidence. For example, it would be reasonably safe for you to bet that Wallnau is between 35 and 55 years old. At the extreme, you would be very confident betting that Wallnau is between 20 and 70 years old. Note that there is a tradeoff between precision and confidence. As the interval gets wider and wider, your confidence grows. At the same time, however, the precision of the estimate gets worse. We will be using samples to make both point and interval estimates of a population mean. Because the interval estimates are associated with confidence, they usually are called *confidence intervals.*

DEFINITIONS

For an *interval estimate,* you use a range of values as your estimate of an unknown quantity.

When an interval estimate is accompanied by a specific level of confidence (or probability), it is called a *confidence interval.*

Estimation is used in the same general situations in which we have already used hypothesis testing. In fact, there is an estimation procedure that accompanies each of the hypothesis tests we presented in the preceding chapters. Figure 12.1 shows an example of a research situation in which either hypothesis testing or estimation could be used. The figure shows a population with an unknown mean (the population after treatment). A sample is selected from the unknown population. The goal of estimation is to use the sample data to obtain an estimate of the unknown population mean.

FIGURE 12.1

The basic research situation for either hypothesis testing or estimation. The goal is to use the sample data to answer questions about the unknown population mean after treatment.

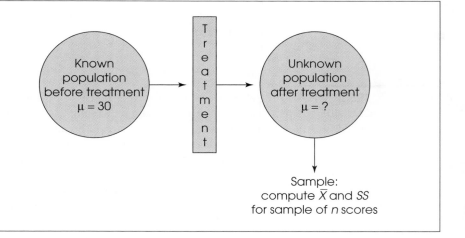

COMPARISON OF HYPOTHESIS TESTS AND ESTIMATION

You should recognize that the situation shown in Figure 12.1 is the same situation in which we have used hypothesis tests in the past. In many ways, hypothesis testing and estimation are similar. They both make use of sample data and either z-scores or t statistics to find out about unknown populations. But these two inferential procedures are designed to answer different questions. Using the situation shown in Figure 12.1 as an example, we could use a hypothesis test to evaluate the effect of the treatment. The test would determine whether or not the treatment has any effect. Note that this is a yes-no question. The null hypothesis says, "No, there is no treatment effect." The alternative hypothesis says, "Yes, there is a treatment effect."

12.1 HYPOTHESIS TESTING VERSUS ESTIMATION: STATISTICAL SIGNIFICANCE VERSUS PRACTICAL SIGNIFICANCE

AS WE already noted, hypothesis tests tend to involve a yes-no decision. Either we decide to reject H_0, or we fail to reject H_0. The language of hypothesis testing reflects this process. The outcome of the hypothesis test is one of two conclusions:

> There is no evidence for a treatment effect (fail to reject H_0)

or

> There is a statistically significant effect (H_0 is rejected).

For example, a researcher studies the effect of a new drug on people with high cholesterol. In hypothesis testing, the question is whether or not the drug has a significant effect on cholesterol levels. Suppose the hypothesis test revealed that the drug did produce a significant decrease in cholesterol. The next question might be, How much of a reduction occurs? This question calls for estimation, in which the size of a treatment effect for the population is estimated.

Estimation can be of great practical importance because the presence of a "statistically significant" effect does not necessarily mean the results are large enough for use in practical applications. Consider the following possibility: Before drug treatment, the sample of patients had a mean cholesterol level of 225. After drug treatment, their cholesterol reading was 210. When analyzed, this 15-point change reached statistical significance (H_0 was rejected). Although the hypothesis test revealed that the drug produced a *statistically significant* change, it may not be *clinically significant*. That is, a cholesterol level of 210 is still quite high. In estimation, we would estimate the population mean cholesterol level for patients who are treated with the drug. This estimated value may reveal that even though the drug does in fact reduce cholesterol levels, it does not produce a large enough change (note that we are looking at a "how much" question) to make it of any practical value. Thus, the hypothesis test might reveal that an effect occurred, but estimation indicates it is small and of little *practical significance* in real-world applications.

The goal of estimation, on the other hand, is to determine the value of the population mean after treatment. Essentially, estimation will determine *how much* effect the treatment has (see Box 12.1). If, for example, we obtained an estimate of $\mu = 38$ for the population after treatment, we could conclude that the effect of the treatment is to increase scores by an average of 8 points (from the original mean of $\mu = 30$ to the post-treatment mean of $\mu = 38$).

WHEN TO USE ESTIMATION   There are three situations in which estimation commonly is used:

1. Estimation is used after a hypothesis test where H_0 is rejected. Remember that when H_0 is rejected, the conclusion is that the treatment does have an effect. The next logical question would be, How much effect? This is exactly the question that estimation is designed to answer.

2. Estimation is used when you already know that there is an effect and simply want to find out how much. For example, the city school board probably knows that a special reading program will help students. However, they want to be sure that the effect is big enough to justify the cost. Estimation is used to determine the size of the treatment effect.

3. Estimation is used when you simply want some basic information about an unknown population. Suppose, for example, you want to know about the political attitudes of students at your college. You could use a sample of students as the basis for estimating the population mean.

THE LOGIC OF ESTIMATION   As we have noted, estimation and hypothesis testing are both *inferential* statistical techniques that involve using sample data as the basis for drawing conclusions about an unknown population. More specifically, a researcher begins with a question about an unknown population parameter. To answer the question, a sample is obtained, and a sample statistic is computed. In general, *statistical inference* involves using sample statistics to help answer questions about population parameters. The general logic underlying the processes of estimation and hypothesis testing is based on the fact that each population parameter has a corresponding sample statistic. In addition, you usually can compute a standard error that measures how much discrepancy is expected, on average, between the statistic and the parameter. For example, a sample mean, $\bar{X}$, corresponds to the population mean, μ, with a standard error measured by $s_{\bar{X}}$.

In the preceding four chapters we presented four different situations for hypothesis testing: the z-score test, the single-sample t, the independent-measures t, and the repeated-measures t. Although it is possible to do estimation in each of these four situations, we will only consider estimation for the three t statistics. Recall that the general structure of a t statistic is as follows:

$$t = \frac{\substack{\text{sample mean} \\ \text{(or mean difference)}} - \substack{\text{population mean} \\ \text{(or mean difference)}}}{\text{estimated standard error}}$$

This general formula is used both for hypothesis testing and for estimation. In each case, the population mean (or mean difference) is unknown. The purpose for a hypothesis test is to evaluate a hypothesis about the unknown population parameter. The purpose for estimation is to determine the value for the unknown population parameter. Because hypothesis testing and estimation have different goals, they will follow different logical paths. These different paths are outlined as follows:

Hypothesis test	Estimation
Goal: To test a hypothesis about a population parameter—usually the null hypothesis, which states that the treatment has no effect.	*Goal:* To estimate the value of an unknown population parameter—usually the value for an unknown population mean.
A. For a hypothesis test, you begin by hypothesizing a value for the unknown population parameter. This value is specified in the null hypothesis.	A. For estimation, you do not attempt to calculate t. Instead, you begin by estimating what the t value ought to be. The strategy for making this estimate is to select a "reasonable" value for t. (*Note:* You are not just picking a value for t; rather, you are estimating
B. The hypothesized value is substituted into the formula, and *the value for t is computed.*	

(*continues*)

(*continued*)

Hypothesis test	Estimation
C. If the hypothesized value produces a "reasonable" value for *t*, we conclude that the hypothesis was "reasonable," and we fail to reject H_0. If the result is an extreme value for *t*, H_0 is rejected. D. A "reasonable" value for *t* is defined by its location in a distribution. In general, "reasonable" values are high-probability outcomes in the center of the distribution. Extreme values with low probability are considered "unreasonable" (see Figure 12.2).	where the sample is located in the distribution.) B. As with hypothesis testing, a "reasonable" value for *t* is defined as a high-probability outcome located near the center of the distribution (see Figure 12.2). C. The "reasonable" value for *t* is substituted into the formula, and *the value for the unknown population parameter is computed.* D. Because you used a "reasonable" value for *t* in the formula, it is assumed that the computation will produce a "reasonable" estimate of the population parameter.

FIGURE 12.2

For estimation or hypothesis testing, the distribution of *t* statistics is divided into two sections: the middle of the distribution, consisting of high-probability outcomes that are considered "reasonable," and the extreme tails of the distribution, consisting of low-probability, "unreasonable" outcomes.

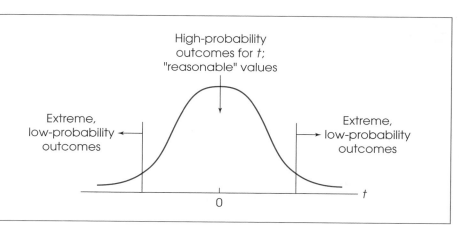

Because the goal of the estimation process is to compute a value for the unknown population mean or mean difference, it usually is easier to regroup the terms in the *t* formula so that the population value is isolated on one side of the equation. In algebraic terms, we are solving the equation for the unknown population parameter. The result takes the following form:

$$\text{population mean \atop (or mean difference)} = \text{sample mean \atop (or mean difference)} \pm t(\text{estimated standard error}) \quad \textbf{(12.1)}$$

This is the general equation that we will use for estimation. Consider the following two points about Equation 12.1:

1. On the right-hand side of the equation, the values for the sample mean and the estimated standard error can be computed directly from the sample data. Thus, only the value of *t* is unknown. If we can determine this missing value, then we can use the equation to calculate the unknown population mean.

2. Although the specific value for the t statistic cannot be determined, we do know what the entire distribution of t statistics looks like. We can use the distribution to *estimate* what the t statistic ought to be.

   a. For a point estimate, the best bet is to use $t = 0$, the exact center of the distribution. There is no reason to suspect that the sample data are biased (either above average or below average), so $t = 0$ is a sensible value. Also, $t = 0$ is the most likely value, with probabilities decreasing steadily as you move away from zero toward the tails of the distribution.

   b. For an interval estimate, we will use a range of t value around zero. For example, to be 90% confident that our estimation is correct, we will simply use the range of t values that forms the middle 90% of the distribution. Note that we are estimating that the sample data correspond to a t statistic somewhere in the middle 90% of the t distribution.

Once we have estimated a value for t, then we have all the numbers on the right-hand side of the equation and we can calculate a value for the unknown population mean. Because one of the numbers on the right-hand side is an estimated value, the population mean that we calculate is also an estimated value.

LEARNING CHECK

1. Estimation procedures basically address a "yes-no" question: whether or not a treatment effect exists. (True or false?)

2. Estimation is primarily used to estimate the value of sample statistics. (True or false?)

3. In general, as precision of an interval estimate increases, confidence decreases. (True or false?)

4. Describe three common applications of estimation.

ANSWERS

1. False. Estimation asks *how much* difference exists.

2. False. Estimation procedures are used to estimate the value for unknown population parameters.

3. True. There is a trade-off between precision and confidence.

4. a. After a hypothesis test results in rejecting H_0, a researcher may want to determine the size of the treatment effect.

   b. If it is already known that a treatment effect exists, estimation can be used to determine how much of an effect is present.

   c. Estimation can be used anytime you want to get information about unknown population parameters.

12.2 ESTIMATION WITH THE t STATISTIC

In the preceding three chapters, we introduced three different versions of the t statistic: the single-sample t in Chapter 9, the independent-measures t in Chapter 10, and the repeated-measures t in Chapter 11. Although the three t statistics were introduced in the context of hypothesis testing, they all can be adapted for use in estimation. As we saw in the previous section, the general form of the *t* equation for estimation is as follows:

$$\begin{matrix} \text{population mean} \\ \text{(or mean difference)} \end{matrix} = \begin{matrix} \text{sample mean} \\ \text{(or mean difference)} \end{matrix} \pm t(\text{estimated standard error})$$

With the single-sample *t*, we will estimate an unknown population mean, μ, using a sample mean, $\overline{X}$. The estimation formula for the single-sample *t* is

$$\mu = \overline{X} \pm t s_{\overline{X}} \tag{12.2}$$

With the independent-measures *t*, we will estimate the size of the difference between two population means, $\mu_1 - \mu_2$, using the difference between two sample means, $\overline{X}_1 - \overline{X}_2$. The estimation formula for the independent-measures *t* is

$$\mu_1 - \mu_2 = \overline{X}_1 - \overline{X}_2 \pm t s_{(\overline{X}_1 - \overline{X}_2)} \tag{12.3}$$

Finally, the repeated-measures *t* statistic will be used to estimate the mean difference for the general population, μ_D, using the mean difference for a sample, $\overline{D}$. The estimation formula for the repeated-measures *t* is

$$\mu_D = \overline{D} \pm t s_{\overline{D}} \tag{12.4}$$

To use the *t* statistic formulas for estimation, we must determine all of the values on the right-hand side of the equation (including an estimated value for *t*) and then use these numbers to compute an estimated value for the population mean or mean difference. Specifically, you first compute the sample mean (or mean difference) and the estimated standard error from the sample data. Next, you estimate a value, or a range of values, for *t*. More precisely, you are estimating where the sample data are located in the *t* distribution. These values complete the right-hand side of the equation and allow us to compute an estimated value for the mean (or the mean difference). The following examples demonstrate the estimation procedure with each of the three *t* statistics.

ESTIMATION OF μ FOR SINGLE-SAMPLE STUDIES

In Chapter 9, we introduced single-sample studies and hypothesis testing with the *t* statistic. Now we will use a single-sample study to estimate the value for μ, using point and interval estimates.

EXAMPLE 12.1

A researcher is evaluating the effectiveness of a special summer reading program for grade-school children. Over the past several years, the researcher has determined that students entering the second grade in the city school district have an average reading achievement score of $\mu = 81$. Although it is reasonable to assume that the special summer reading program will improve reading scores, the question is, How much? To answer this question, a sample of $n = 25$ students is obtained. The students are admitted to the special reading program during the summer after they finish the first grade, and they all take the reading achievement test when they enter the second grade. The average score for the sample is $\overline{X} = 88$ with $SS = 2400$. The researcher would like to use the data to estimate how much effect the special program has on reading achievement scores. Specifically, the researcher would like a point estimate and an 80% confidence interval estimate of the population mean score for students who take the special program. The overall structure for this research study is shown in Figure 12.3.

FIGURE 12.3

The structure of the research study described in Example 12.1. The goal is to use the sample as the basis for estimating the population mean for reading scores after students have attended the special summer program.

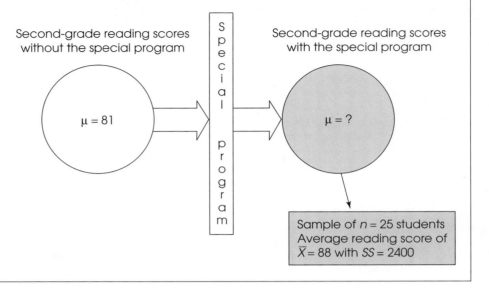

In this example, we are using a single sample to estimate the mean for a single population. In this case, the estimation formula for the single-sample t is

$$\mu = \overline{X} \pm ts_{\overline{X}}$$

To use the equation, we must first compute the estimated standard error and then determine the estimated value(s) to be used for the t statistic.

Compute s^2 and $s_{\overline{X}}$ To compute the estimated standard error, it is first necessary to calculate the sample variance. Using the information provided, we obtain

$$s^2 = \frac{SS}{n-1} = \frac{2400}{24} = 100$$

The estimated standard error is

$$s_{\overline{X}} = \sqrt{\frac{s^2}{n}} = \sqrt{\frac{100}{25}} = 2$$

The point estimate   As noted earlier, a point estimate involves selecting a single value for t. Because the t distribution is always symmetrically distributed with a mean of zero, we will always use $t = 0$ as the best choice for a point estimate. Using the sample data and the estimate of $t = 0$, we obtain

$$\mu = \overline{X} \pm ts_{\overline{X}}$$
$$= 88 \pm 0(2)$$
$$= 88$$

This is our point estimate of the population mean. Note that we simply have used the sample mean, $\overline{X}$, to estimate the population mean, μ. The sample is the only information that we have about the population, and it provides an unbiased estimate of the population mean (Chapter 7, p. 149). That is, on average, the sample mean provides an accurate representation of the population mean. Based on this point estimate, our conclusion is that the special summer reading program will increase reading scores from an average of $\mu = 81$ to an average of $\mu = 88$. We are estimating that the program will have a 7-point effect on reading scores for the general population.

To have 80% in the middle there must be 20% (or .20) in the tails. To find the *t* values, look under two tails, .20 in the *t* table.

The interval estimate   For an interval estimate, select a range of *t* values that is determined by the level of confidence. In this example, we want 80% confidence in our estimate of μ. Therefore, we will estimate that the *t* statistic is located somewhere in the middle 80% of the *t* distribution. With $df = n - 1 = 24$, the middle 80% of the distribution is bounded by *t* values of $+1.318$ and -1.318 (see Figure 12.4). Using the sample data and this estimated range of *t* values, we obtain

$$\mu = \overline{X} \pm ts_{\overline{X}} = 88 \pm 1.318(2) = 88 \pm 2.636$$

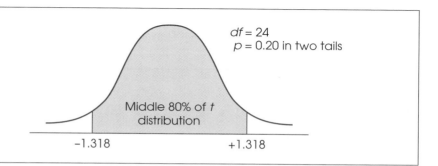

FIGURE 12.4

The 80% confidence interval with $df = 24$ is constructed using *t* values of $t = -1.318$ and $t = +1.318$. The *t* values are obtained from the table using 20% (0.20) as the proportion remaining in the two tails of the distribution.

df = 24
p = 0.20 in two tails

Middle 80% of *t* distribution

−1.318   +1.318

At one end of the interval we obtain 90.636 (88 + 2.636), and at the other end of the interval we obtain 85.364 (88 − 2.636). Thus, we obtain an interval estimate for μ that ranges from 85.364 to 90.636. Our conclusion is that after the special summer program, the population will have a mean reading score between 85.364 and 90.636. In addition, we are 80% confident that the population mean will be within this interval. The confidence comes from the fact that the calculation was based on only one assumption. Specifically, we assumed that the *t* statistic was located between $+1.318$ and -1.318, and we are 80% confident that this assumption is correct because 80% of all the possible *t* values are located in this interval.

Figure 12.5 provides a pictorial presentation of the results from Example 12.1. The original population mean is shown along with the two estimates (point and interval) for the new mean after the special reading program is administered. The estimates clearly indicate that the program should increase scores, and they provide a clear indication of how large the increase should be.

Interpretation of the confidence interval   In the preceding example, we computed an 80% confidence interval to estimate an unknown population mean. We obtained an interval ranging from 85.364 to 90.636, and we are 80% confident that the unknown population mean is located somewhere within this interval. Note that the 80% confidence applies to the specific interval. If we repeated this process over and over, we could eventually obtain hundreds of different samples and calculate hundreds of different confidence inter-

FIGURE 12.5

A representation of the estimates made in Example 12.1. Before a special summer reading program, the population mean reading score was $\mu = 81$. Based on a sample, the special program is estimated to increase the mean to $\mu = 88$ (point estimate), or somewhere between 85.364 and 90.636 (interval estimate).

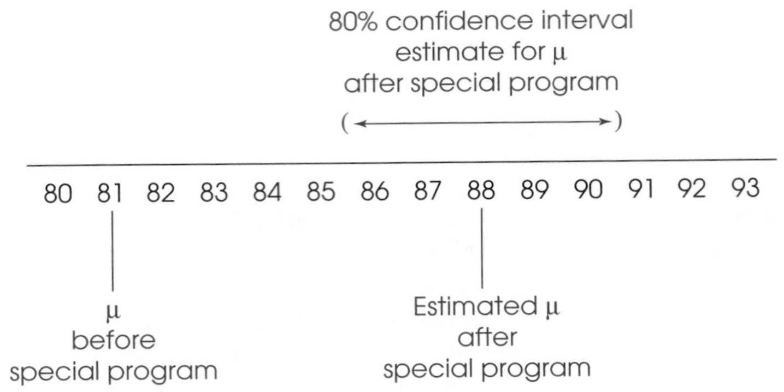

80% confidence interval estimate for μ after special program

$($ ⟵——————⟶ $)$

80 81 82 83 84 85 86 87 88 89 90 91 92 93

μ
before
special program

Estimated μ
after
special program

vals. However, each interval is computed in the same way and each interval is based on the same probabilities. Specifically, there is an 80% probability that the population mean actually is in the interval, and there is a 20% probability that the population mean is not in the interval. Thus, out of all the different confidence intervals that we could calculate, 80% would actually contain the population mean and 20% would not contain the mean.

ESTIMATION OF $\mu_1 - \mu_2$ FOR INDEPENDENT-MEASURES STUDIES

The independent-measures t statistic uses the data from two separate samples to evaluate the mean difference between two populations. In Chapter 10, we used this statistic to answer a yes-no question: Is there any difference between the two population means? With estimation, we ask, *How much* difference? In this case, the independent-measures t statistic is used to estimate the value of $\mu_1 - \mu_2$. The following example demonstrates the process of estimation with the independent-measures t statistic.

E X A M P L E   1 2 . 2

Recent studies have allowed psychologists to establish definite links between specific foods and specific brain functions. For example, lecithin (found in soybeans, eggs, and liver) has been shown to increase the concentration of certain brain chemicals that help regulate memory and motor coordination. This experiment is designed to demonstrate the importance of this particular food substance.

The experiment involves two separate samples of newborn rats (an independent-measures experiment). The 10 rats in the first sample are given a normal diet containing standard amounts of lecithin. The 5 rats in the other sample are fed a special diet, which contains almost no lecithin. After 6 months, each of the rats is tested on a specially designed learning problem that requires both memory and motor coordination. The purpose of the experiment is to demonstrate the deficit in performance that results from lecithin deprivation. The score for each animal is the number of errors it makes before it solves the learning problem. The data from this experiment are as follows:

Regular diet	No-lecithin diet
$n = 10$	$n = 5$
$\overline{X} = 25$	$\overline{X} = 33$
$SS = 250$	$SS = 140$

Because we fully expect that there will be a significant difference between these two treatments, we will not do the hypothesis test (although you should be able to do it). We want to use these data to obtain an estimate of the size of the difference between the two population means; that is, how much does lecithin affect learning perform-ance? We will use a point estimate and a 95% confidence interval.

The basic equation for estimation with an independent-measures experiment is

$$\mu_1 - \mu_2 = (\overline{X}_1 - \overline{X}_2) \pm t s_{(\overline{X}_1 - \overline{X}_2)}$$

The first step is to obtain the known values from the sample data. The sample mean difference is easy; one group averaged $\overline{X} = 25$, and the other averaged $\overline{X} = 33$, so there is an 8-point difference. Note that it is not important whether we call this a +8 or a −8 difference. In either case, the size of the difference is 8 points, and the regular diet group scored lower. Because it is easier to do arithmetic with positive numbers, we will use

$$\overline{X}_1 - \overline{X}_2 = 8$$

Compute the standard error   To find the standard error, we first must pool the two variances:

$$s_p^2 = \frac{SS_1 + SS_2}{df_1 + df_2} = \frac{250 + 140}{9 + 4} = \frac{390}{13} = 30$$

Next, the pooled variance is used to compute the standard error:

$$s_{(\overline{X}_1 - \overline{X}_2)} = \sqrt{\frac{s_p^2}{n_1} + \frac{s_p^2}{n_2}} = \sqrt{\frac{30}{10} + \frac{30}{5}} = \sqrt{3 + 6} = \sqrt{9} = 3$$

Recall that this standard error combines the error from the first sample and the error from the second sample. Because the first sample is much larger, $n = 10$, it should have less error. This difference shows up in the formula. The larger sample contributes an error of 3 points, and the smaller sample contributes 6 points, which combine for a total error of 9 points under the square root.

Sample 1 has $df = 9$, and sample 2 has $df = 4$. The *t* statistic has $df = 9 + 4 = 13$.

Estimate the value(s) for *t*   The final value needed on the right-hand side of the equation is *t*. The data from this experiment would produce a *t* statistic with $df = 13$. With 13 degrees of freedom, we can sketch the distribution of all the possible *t* values. This distribution is shown in Figure 12.6. The *t* statistic for our data is somewhere in

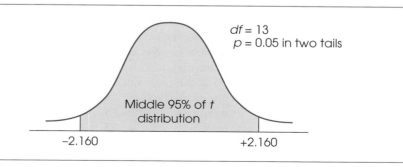

FIGURE 12.6

The distribution of *t* values with $df = 13$. Note that *t* values pile up around zero and that 95% of the values are located between −2.160 and +2.160.

this distribution. The problem is to estimate where. For a point estimate, the best bet is to use $t = 0$. This is the most likely value, located exactly in the middle of the distribution. To gain more confidence in the estimate, you can select a range of t values. For 95% confidence, for example, you would estimate that the t statistic is somewhere in the middle 95% of the distribution. Checking the table, you find that the middle 95% is bounded by values of $t = +2.160$ and $t = -2.160$.

Using these t values and the sample values computed earlier, we now can estimate the magnitude of the performance deficit caused by lecithin deprivation.

Compute the point estimate   For a point estimate, use the single-value (point) estimate of $t = 0$:

$$\mu_1 - \mu_2 = (\overline{X}_1 - \overline{X}_2) \pm ts_{(\overline{X}_1 - \overline{X}_2)}$$
$$= 8 \pm 0(3)$$
$$= 8$$

Note that the result simply uses the sample mean difference to estimate the population mean difference. The conclusion is that lecithin deprivation produces an average of 8 more errors on the learning task. (Based on the fact that the normal animals averaged around 25 errors, an 8-point increase would mean a performance deficit of approximately 30%.)

Construct the interval estimate   For an interval estimate, or confidence interval, use the range of t values. With 95% confidence, at one extreme,

$$\mu_1 - \mu_2 = (\overline{X}_1 - \overline{X}_2) + ts_{(\overline{X}_1 - \overline{X}_2)}$$
$$= 8 + 2.160(3)$$
$$= 8 + 6.48$$
$$= 14.48$$

and at the other extreme,

$$\mu_1 - \mu_2 = (\overline{X}_1 - \overline{X}_2) - ts_{(\overline{X}_1 - \overline{X}_2)}$$
$$= 8 - 2.160(3)$$
$$= 8 - 6.48$$
$$= 1.52$$

This time we conclude that the effect of lecithin deprivation is to increase errors, with an average increase somewhere between 1.52 and 14.48 errors. We are 95% confident of this estimate because our only estimation was the location of the t statistic, and we used the middle 95% of all the possible t values.

Note that the result of the point estimate is to say that lecithin deprivation will increase errors by *exactly* 8 points. To gain confidence, you must lose precision and say that errors will increase by *around* 8 points (for 95% confidence, we say that the average increase will be 8 ± 6.48).

ESTIMATION OF μ_D FOR REPEATED-MEASURES STUDIES

Finally, we turn our attention to the repeated-measures study. Remember that this type of study has a single sample of subjects, which is measured in two different treatment conditions. By finding the difference between the score for treatment 1 and the score for treatment 2, we can determine a difference score for each subject.

$$D = X_2 - X_1$$

The mean for the sample of D scores, $\overline{D}$, is used to estimate the population mean μ_D, which is the mean for the entire population of difference scores.

E X A M P L E   1 2 . 3

A pharmaceutical company has developed a new medication to lower cholesterol and would like to determine how much effect the new drug has. A random sample of $n = 16$ patients who have been diagnosed with high cholesterol is obtained. Cholesterol levels are recorded for all 16 individuals, who then are given the drug for a 6-week period. After taking the new medication for 6 weeks, each individual's cholesterol is measured again and the difference between the first score and the second score is recorded. For this sample, cholesterol levels declined by an average of $\overline{D} = 21$ points with $SS = 1215$. The company would like to use these data to estimate the drug's effect for the general population, using a point estimate and a 90% confidence interval estimate for μ_D.

You should recognize that this study requires a repeated-measures t statistic. For estimation, the repeated-measures t equation is as follows:

$$\mu_D = \overline{D} \pm t s_{\overline{D}}$$

The sample mean is $\overline{D} = 21$, so all that remains is to compute the estimated standard error and estimate the appropriate value(s) for t.

Compute the standard error To find the standard error, we first must compute the sample variance:

$$s^2 = \frac{SS}{n-1} = \frac{1215}{15} = 81$$

Now the estimated standard error is

$$s_{\overline{D}} = \sqrt{\frac{s^2}{n}} = \sqrt{\frac{81}{16}} = \frac{9}{4} = 2.25$$

To complete the estimate of μ_D, we must identify the value of t. We will consider the point estimate and the interval estimate separately.

Compute the point estimate To obtain a point estimate, a single value of t is selected to approximate the location of $\overline{D}$. Remember that the t distribution is symmetrical and bell-shaped with a mean of zero (see Figure 12.7). Because $t = 0$ is the most frequently occurring value in the distribution, this is the t value used for the point estimate. Using this value in the estimation formula gives

$$\mu_D = \overline{D} \pm t s_{\overline{D}} = 21 \pm 0(2.25) = 21$$

For this example, our best estimate is that the new medication will lower cholesterol levels in the general population by an average of $\mu_D = 21$ points. As noted several times before, the sample mean, $\overline{D} = 21$, provides the best point estimate of μ_D.

Construct the interval estimate   The psychologist also wanted to make an interval estimate in order to be 90% confident that the interval contains the value of μ_D. To get the interval, it is necessary to determine what t values form the boundaries of the middle 90% of the t distribution. To use the t distribution table, we first must determine the proportion associated with the tails of this distribution. With 90% in the middle, the remaining area in both tails must be 10%, or $p = .10$. Also note that our sample has $n = 16$ scores, so the t statistic will have $df = n - 1 = 15$. Using $df = 15$ and $p = 0.10$ for two tails, you should find the values $+1.753$ and -1.753 in the t table. These values form the boundaries for the middle 90% of the t distribution. (See Figure 12.7.) We are confident that the t value for our sample is in this range because 90% of all the possible t values are there. Using these values in the estimation formula, we obtain the following: On one end of the interval,

$$\mu_D = \overline{D} - ts_{\overline{D}}$$
$$= 21 - 1.753(2.25)$$
$$= 21 - 3.94$$
$$= 17.06$$

FIGURE 12.7

The t values for the 90% confidence interval are obtained by consulting the t tables for $df = 15$, $p = 0.10$ for two tails.

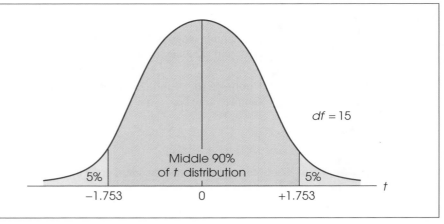

Therefore, the company can conclude that the new medication will reduce cholesterol levels in the general population by an average of around 21 points. The company can be 90% confident that the average reduction will be between 17.06 and 24.94 points.

and on the other end of the interval,

$$\mu_D = 21 + 1.753(2.25)$$
$$= 21 + 3.94$$
$$= 24.94$$

Therefore, the company can conclude that the new medication will reduce cholesterol levels in the general population by an average of around 21 points. The company can be 90% confident that the average reduction will be between 17.06 and 24.94 points.

LEARNING CHECK

1. A professor notices that students who get an A in physics have high grade point averages (GPAs) in their engineering courses. The professor selects a sample of $n = 16$ engineering majors who have earned As in physics. The mean GPA in engineering courses for this sample is $\overline{X} = 3.30$ with $SS = 10$. Use this sample to find the 99% confidence interval for the population mean.

2. A psychologist studies the change in mood from the follicular phase (prior to ovulation) to the luteal phase (after ovulation) during the menstrual cycle. In a repeated-measures study, a sample of $n = 9$ women take a mood questionnaire during each phase. On average, the participants show an increase in dysphoria (negative moods) of $\overline{D} = 18$ points with $SS = 152$. Determine the 95% confidence interval for population mean change in mood.

3. In families with several children, the first-born tend to be more reserved and serious, whereas the last-born tend to be more outgoing and happy-go-lucky. A psychologist is using a standardized personality inventory to measure the magnitude of this difference. Two samples are used: 8 first-born children and 8 last-born children. Each child is given the personality test. The results are as follows:

First-born	Last-born
$\overline{X} = 11.4$	$\overline{X} = 13.9$
$SS = 26$	$SS = 30$

   a. Use these sample statistics to make a point estimate of the population mean difference in personality for first-born versus last-born children.

   b. Make an interval estimate of the population mean difference so that you are 80% confident that the true mean difference is in your interval.

ANSWERS

1. $s^2 = 0.667$, $s_{\overline{X}} = .20$, $df = 15$, $t = \pm 2.947$; estimate that μ is between 2.71 and 3.89.

2. $s^2 = 19$, $s_{\overline{D}} = 1.45$, $df = 8$, $t = \pm 2.306$; estimate that μ_D is between 14.66 and 21.34.

3. a. For a point estimate, use the sample mean difference: $\overline{X}_1 - \overline{X}_2 = 2.5$ points.

   b. Pooled variance $= 4$, estimated standard error $= 1$, $df = 14$, $t = \pm 1.345$. The 80% confidence interval is 1.16 to 3.85.

12.3 A FINAL LOOK AT ESTIMATION

FACTORS AFFECTING THE WIDTH OF A CONFIDENCE INTERVAL

Two characteristics of the confidence interval should be noted. First, notice what happens to the width of the interval when you change the level of confidence (the percent confidence). To gain more confidence in your estimate, you must increase the width of the interval. Conversely, to have a smaller interval, you must give up confidence. This is the basic trade-off between precision and confidence that was discussed earlier. In the estimation formula, the percentage of confidence influences the width of the interval by way of the t value. The larger the level of confidence (the percentage), the larger the t value and the larger the interval. This relationship can be seen in Figure

12.7. In the figure, we have identified the middle 90% of the *t* distribution in order to find a 90% confidence interval. It should be obvious that if we were to increase the confidence level to 95%, it would be necessary to increase the range of *t* values and thereby increase the width of the interval.

Second, note what would happen to the interval width if you had a different sample size. This time the basic rule is as follows: The bigger the sample (*n*), the smaller the interval. This relationship is straightforward if you consider the sample size as a measure of the amount of information. A bigger sample gives you more information about the population and allows you to make a more precise estimate (a narrower interval). The sample size controls the magnitude of the standard error in the estimation formula. As the sample size increases, the standard error decreases, and the interval gets smaller.

With *t* statistics, the sample size has an additional effect on the width of a confidence interval. Remember that the exact shape of the *t* distribution depends on degrees of freedom. As the sample size gets larger, *df* also get larger, and the *t* values associated with any specific percentage of confidence get smaller. This fact simply enhances the general relationship that the larger a sample, the smaller a confidence interval.

ESTIMATION, EFFECT SIZE, AND HYPOTHESIS TESTS

The process of estimation, especially the estimation of mean differences, provides a relatively simple and direct method for evaluating effect size. For example, the outcome of the study in Example 12.3 indicates that the new medication will reduce cholesterol levels by an estimated 21 points. In this case, the estimation process produces a very clear and understandable indication of how large the treatment effect actually is.

In addition to describing the size of a treatment effect, estimation can be used to get an indication of the "significance" of the effect. Example 12.2 presented an independent-measures research study examining the effect of lecithin on problem-solving performance for rats. Based on the results of this study, it was estimated that the mean difference in performance produced by lecithin was $\mu_1 - \mu_2 = 8$ points. The 95% confidence interval estimated the mean difference to be between 1.52 points and 14.48 points. The confidence interval estimate is shown in Figure 12.8. In addition to the confidence interval for $\mu_1 - \mu_2$, we have marked the spot where the mean difference is equal to zero. You should recognize that a mean difference of zero is exactly what would be predicted by the null hypothesis if we were doing a hypothesis test. You also should realize that a zero difference ($\mu_1 - \mu_2 = 0$) is *outside* the 95% confidence interval. In other words, $\mu_1 - \mu_2 = 0$ is not an acceptable value if we want 95% confidence in our estimate. This conclusion is equivalent to rejecting H_0 with $\alpha = .05$. On the other

FIGURE 12.8

The 95% confidence interval for the population mean difference ($\mu_1 - \mu_2$) from Example 12.2. Note that $\mu_1 - \mu_2 = 0$ is excluded from the confidence interval, indicating that a zero difference is not an acceptable value (H_0 would be rejected in a hypothesis test).

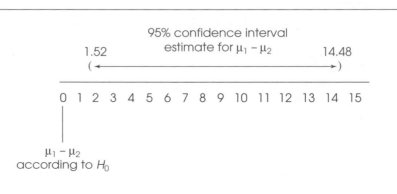

hand, if a mean difference of zero was included within the confidence interval, then we would have to accept $\mu_1 - \mu_2 = 0$ as a reasonable conclusion, which is the same as failing to reject H_0.

ON THE WEB

REMEMBER THAT a practice quiz for Chapter 12 is available on the Wadsworth Web site at **www. wadsworth.com.** You can use the quiz to test your knowledge on the material in this chapter and determine where you may need more study. For more information about finding the quizzes and workshops, see page 24.

SUMMARY

1. Estimation is a procedure that uses sample data to obtain an estimate of a population mean or mean difference. The estimate can be either a point estimate (single value) or an interval estimate (range of values). Point estimates have the advantage of precision, but they do not give much confidence. Interval estimates provide confidence, but you lose precision as the interval grows wider.

2. Estimation and hypothesis testing are similar processes: Both use sample data to answer questions about populations. However, these two procedures are designed to answer different questions. Hypothesis testing will tell you whether or not a treatment effect exists (yes or no). Estimation will tell you how much treatment effect there is.

3. The estimation process begins by solving the t-statistic equation for the unknown population mean (or mean difference).

$$\begin{array}{c} \text{population mean} \\ \text{(or mean difference)} \end{array} = \begin{array}{c} \text{sample mean} \\ \text{(or mean difference)} \end{array}$$
$$\pm\ t(\text{estimated standard error})$$

Except for the value of t, the numbers on the right-hand side of the equation are all obtained from the sample data. By using an estimated value for t, you can then compute an estimated value for the population mean (or mean difference). For a point estimate, use $t = 0$. For an interval estimate, first select a level of confidence and then look up the corresponding range of t values from the t-distribution table. For example, for 90% confidence, use the range of t values that determine the middle 90% of the distribution.

4. For a single-sample study, the mean from one sample is used to estimate the mean for the corresponding population.

$$\mu = \overline{X} \pm ts_{\overline{X}}$$

For an independent-measures study, the means from two separate samples are used to estimate the mean difference between two populations.

$$(\mu_1 - \mu_2) = (\overline{X}_1 - \overline{X}_2) \pm ts_{(\overline{X}_1 - \overline{X}_2)}$$

For a repeated-measures study, the mean from a sample of difference scores (D values) is used to estimate the mean difference for the general population.

$$\mu_D = \overline{D} \pm ts_{\overline{D}}$$

5. The width of a confidence interval is an indication of its precision: A narrow interval is more precise than a wide interval. The interval width is influenced by the sample size and the level of confidence.
   a. As sample size (n) gets larger, the interval width gets smaller (greater precision).
   b. As the percentage of confidence increases, the interval width gets larger (less precision).

KEY TERMS

estimation   point estimate   interval estimate   confidence interval

—— **FOCUS ON PROBLEM SOLVING** ————————————————————————

1. Although hypothesis tests and estimation are similar in some respects, remember that they are separate statistical techniques. A hypothesis test is used to determine whether or not there is evidence for a treatment effect. Estimation is used to determine how much effect a treatment has.

2. When students perform a hypothesis test and estimation with the same set of data, a common error is to take the t statistic from the hypothesis test and use it in the estimation formula. For estimation, the t value is determined by the level of confidence and must be looked up in the appropriate table.

3. Now that you are familiar with several different formulas for hypothesis tests and estimation, one problem will be determining which formula is appropriate for each set of data. When the data consist of a single sample selected from a single population, the appropriate statistic is the single-sample t. For an independent-measures design, you will always have two separate samples. In a repeated-measures design, there is only one sample, but each individual is measured twice so that difference scores can be computed.

—— **DEMONSTRATION 12.1** ————————————————————————

ESTIMATION WITH A SINGLE-SAMPLE *t* STATISTIC

A sample of $n = 16$ is randomly selected from a population with unknown parameters. For the following sample data, estimate the value of μ using a point estimate and a 90% confidence interval:

$$\text{Sample data:}\quad 13,\ \ 10,\ \ 8,\ \ 13,\ \ 9,\ \ 14,\ \ 12,\ \ 10,$$
$$11,\ \ 10,\ \ 15,\ \ 13,\ \ 7,\ \ 6,\ \ 15,\ \ 10$$

Note that we have a single sample and we do not know the value for σ. Thus, the single-sample t statistic should be used for these data. The formula for estimation is

$$\mu = \overline{X} \pm ts_{\overline{X}}$$

STEP 1   Compute the sample mean.
The sample mean is the basis for our estimate of μ. For these data,

$$\Sigma X = 13 + 10 + 8 + 13 + 9 + 14 + 12 + 10 +$$
$$11 + 10 + 15 + 13 + 7 + 6 + 15 + 10$$
$$= 176$$

$$\overline{X} = \frac{\Sigma X}{n} = \frac{176}{16} = 11$$

STEP 2   Compute the estimated standard error, $s_{\overline{X}}$.
To compute the estimated standard error, we must first find the value for SS and the sample variance.
Sum of squares. We will use the definitional formula for SS. The following table demonstrates the computations:

X	$X - \bar{X}$	$(X - \bar{X})^2$
13	$13 - 11 = +2$	4
10	$10 - 11 = -1$	1
8	$8 - 11 = -3$	9
13	$13 - 11 = +2$	4
9	$9 - 11 = -2$	4
14	$14 - 11 = +3$	9
12	$12 - 11 = +1$	1
10	$10 - 11 = -1$	1
11	$11 - 11 = 0$	0
10	$10 - 11 = -1$	1
15	$15 - 11 = +4$	16
13	$13 - 11 = +2$	4
7	$7 - 11 = -4$	16
6	$6 - 11 = -5$	25
15	$15 - 11 = +4$	16
10	$10 - 11 = -1$	1

To obtain SS, we sum the squared deviation scores in the last column.

$$SS = \Sigma(X - \bar{X})^2 = 112$$

Variance. The sample variance is computed for these data.

$$s^2 = \frac{SS}{n-1} = \frac{112}{16-1} = \frac{112}{15} = 7.47$$

Estimated standard error. We can now determine the estimated standard error.

$$s_{\bar{X}} = \sqrt{\frac{s^2}{n}} = \sqrt{\frac{7.47}{16}} = \sqrt{0.467} = 0.68$$

STEP 3   Compute the point estimate for μ.

For a point estimate, we use $t = 0$. Using the estimation formula, we obtain

$$\mu = \bar{X} \pm ts_{\bar{X}}$$
$$= 11 \pm 0(0.68)$$
$$= 11 \pm 0 = 11$$

The point estimate for the population mean is $\mu = 11$.

STEP 4   Determine the confidence interval for μ.

For these data, we want the 90% confidence interval. Therefore, we will use a range of t values that form the middle 90% of the distribution. For this demonstration, degrees of freedom are

$$df = n - 1 = 16 - 1 = 15$$

If we are looking for the middle 90% of the distribution, then 10% ($p = 0.10$) would lie in both tails outside of the interval. To find the t values, we look up $p = 0.10$, two tails, for

$df = 15$ in the t-distribution table. The t values for the 90% confidence interval are $t = \pm 1.753$.

Using the estimation formula, one end of the confidence interval is

$$\mu = \overline{X} - ts_{\overline{X}}$$
$$= 11 - 1.753(0.68)$$
$$= 11 - 1.19 = 9.81$$

For the other end of the confidence interval, we obtain

$$\mu = \overline{X} + ts_{\overline{X}}$$
$$= 11 + 1.753(0.68)$$
$$= 11 + 1.19 = 12.19$$

Thus, the 90% confidence interval for μ is from 9.81 to 12.19.

─────── **DEMONSTRATION 12.2** ───────────────────────────

ESTIMATION WITH THE INDEPENDENT-MEASURES t STATISTIC

Samples are taken from two school districts, and knowledge of American history is tested with a short questionnaire. For the following sample data, estimate the amount of mean difference between the students of these two districts. Specifically, provide a point estimate and a 95% confidence interval for $\mu_1 - \mu_2$.

District A scores: 18,   15,   24,   15

District B scores: 9,   12,   13,   6

STEP 1   Compute the sample means.
The estimate of population mean difference $(\mu_1 - \mu_2)$ is based on the sample mean difference $(\overline{X}_1 - \overline{X}_2)$.
For district A,

$$\Sigma X = 18 + 15 + 24 + 15 = 72$$

$$\overline{X}_1 = \frac{\Sigma X}{n} = \frac{72}{4} = 18$$

For district B,

$$\Sigma X = 9 + 12 + 13 + 6 = 40$$

$$\overline{X}_2 = \frac{\Sigma X}{n} = \frac{40}{4} = 10$$

STEP 2   Calculate the estimated standard error for mean difference, $s_{(\overline{X}_1 - \overline{X}_2)}$.
To compute the estimated standard error, we first need to determine the values of SS for both samples and pooled variance.
Sum of squares. The computations for sum of squares, using the definitional formula, are shown for both samples in the following tables:

District A		
X	$X - \overline{X}$	$(X - \overline{X})^2$
18	$18 - 18 = 0$	0
15	$15 - 18 = -3$	9
24	$24 - 18 = +6$	36
15	$15 - 18 = -3$	9

District B		
X	$X - \overline{X}$	$(X - \overline{X})^2$
9	$9 - 10 = -1$	1
12	$12 - 10 = +2$	4
13	$13 - 10 = +3$	9
6	$6 - 10 = -4$	16

For district A,

$$SS_1 = \Sigma(X - \overline{X})^2 = 0 + 9 + 36 + 9 = 54$$

For district B,

$$SS_2 = \Sigma(X - \overline{X})^2 = 1 + 4 + 9 + 16 = 30$$

Pooled variance. For pooled variance, we use the *SS* and *df* values from both samples. For district A, $df_1 = n_1 - 1 = 3$. For district B, $df_2 = n_2 - 1 = 3$. Pooled variance is

$$s_p^2 = \frac{SS_1 + SS_2}{df_1 + df_2} = \frac{54 + 30}{3 + 3} = \frac{84}{6} = 14$$

Estimated standard error. The estimated standard error for mean difference can now be calculated.

$$s_{(\overline{X}_1 - \overline{X}_2)} = \sqrt{\frac{s_p^2}{n_1} + \frac{s_p^2}{n_2}} = \sqrt{\frac{14}{4} + \frac{14}{4}} = \sqrt{3.5 + 3.5}$$

$$= \sqrt{7} = 2.65$$

STEP 3   Compute the point estimate for $\mu_1 - \mu_2$.

For the point estimate, we use a *t* value of zero. Using the sample means and estimated standard error from previous steps, we obtain

$$\mu_1 - \mu_2 = (\overline{X}_1 - \overline{X}_2) \pm ts_{(\overline{X}_1 - \overline{X}_2)}$$

$$= (18 - 10) \pm 0(2.65)$$

$$= 8 \pm 0 = 8$$

STEP 4   Determine the confidence interval for $\mu_1 - \mu_2$.

For the independent-measures *t* statistic, degrees of freedom are determined by

$$df = n_1 + n_2 - 2$$

For these data, *df* is

$$df = 4 + 4 - 2 = 6$$

With a 95% level of confidence, 5% of the distribution falls in the tails outside the interval. Therefore, we consult the *t*-distribution table for $p = 0.05$, two tails, with $df = 6$. The *t* values from the table are $t = \pm 2.447$. On one end of the confidence interval, the population mean difference is

$$\mu_1 - \mu_2 = (\overline{X}_1 - \overline{X}_2) - ts_{(\overline{X}_1 - \overline{X}_2)}$$

$$= (18 - 10) - 2.447(2.65)$$

$$= 8 - 6.48$$

$$= 1.52$$

On the other end of the confidence interval, the population mean difference is

$$\mu_1 - \mu_2 = (\overline{X}_1 - \overline{X}_2) + ts_{(\overline{X}_1 - \overline{X}_2)}$$

$$= (18 - 10) + 2.447(2.65)$$

$$= 8 + 6.48$$

$$= 14.48$$

Thus, the 95% confidence interval for population mean difference is from 1.52 to 14.48.

PROBLEMS

1. Explain how the purpose of estimation differs from the purpose of a hypothesis test.

2. Explain why it would *not* be reasonable to use estimation after a hypothesis test where the decision was "fail to reject H_0."

3. Explain how each of the following factors affects the width of a confidence interval:
   a. Increasing the sample size
   b. Increasing the sample variability
   c. Increasing the level of confidence (the percentage of confidence)

4. For the following studies, state whether estimation or hypothesis testing is required. Also, is an independent- or a repeated-measures *t* statistic appropriate?
   a. An educator wants to determine how much mean difference can be expected for the population in SAT scores following an intensive review course. Two samples are selected. The first group takes the review course, and the second receives no treatment. SAT scores are subsequently measured for both groups.
   b. A psychiatrist would like to determine whether a new medication has any effect on psychotic symptoms. A sample of patients is assessed and then placed on the

drug therapy for 2 weeks. The severity of their symptoms is assessed again at the end of the treatment.
   c. A researcher would like to determine how much people's moods are affected by seasonal changes. A sample of 100 adults is obtained and each individual is given a mood-analysis questionnaire in the summer and again in the winter.
   d. A researcher would like to determine whether participation in sports has an effect on self-esteem for high school students. The researcher obtains a sample of 50 students who are active in varsity sports and a comparison sample of 50 students who do not participate in any high school sports. Each student is given a self-esteem questionnaire.

5. A college administrator would like to determine how much time students spend on homework assignments during a typical week. A questionnaire is sent to a sample of $n = 25$ students and their responses indicate a mean of $\overline{X} = 7.4$ hours per week with $SS = 216$.
   a. Use the data to make a point estimate of the mean amount of homework for the entire student population.
   b. Make an interval estimate of the population mean so that you are 90% confident the real mean is in your interval.

6. A sample of $n = 16$ scores is obtained from an unknown population. The sample has a mean of $\overline{X} = 46$ with $SS = 6000$.
   a. Use the sample data to make an 80% confidence interval estimate of the unknown population mean.
   b. Make a 90% confidence interval estimate of μ.
   c. Make a 95% confidence interval estimate of μ.
   d. In general, how is the width of a confidence interval related to the percentage of confidence?

7. A sample is obtained from an unknown population. The sample mean is $\overline{X} = 34$ with a sample variance of $s^2 = 36$.
   a. Assuming $n = 4$, use the data to make a 90% confidence interval estimate of the unknown population mean.
   b. Assuming $n = 16$, use the data to make a 90% confidence interval estimate of μ.
   c. Assuming $n = 36$, use the data to make a 90% confidence interval estimate of μ.
   d. In general, how is the width of a confidence interval related to the size of the sample?

8. A researcher has constructed a 90% confidence interval of 87 ± 10, based on a sample of $n = 25$ scores. Note that this interval is 20 points wide (from 77 to 97). How large a sample would be needed to produce a 90% interval that is only 10 points wide? Assume that all other factors are held constant.

9. The manufacturers of a popular medicinal herb claim that their product increases the speed and accuracy of mental processing. To test this claim, a researcher obtains a random sample of $n = 20$ adults. Half of the subjects are given the herb for 30 days and the other half take a placebo. Then, all the subjects are given a decision-making test and their response times are recorded. The subjects taking the herb had an average time of $\overline{X} = 24.5$ seconds with $SS = 43$, and the subjects with the placebo had an average time of $\overline{X} = 28.1$ seconds with $SS = 47$. Use these data to
   a. Make a point estimate of population mean difference in response time.
   b. Make an interval estimate of the mean difference so you are 80% confident that the real mean difference is in your interval.

10. To determine how well people are complying with posted speed limits, the State Highway Patrol measured automobile speeds on a section of highway where the posted limit is 55 mph. For a sample of $n = 100$ cars during daylight hours and good weather conditions, they obtained an average speed of $\overline{X} = 62$ miles per hour with $SS = 2475$. Using these data,
    a. Make a point estimate of the average speed for the general population for this section of highway.

    b. Make an interval estimate of the population mean speed so you are 90% confident that the real mean is in your interval.

11. In an extension of the highway speed study in Problem 10, the researchers also wanted to determine how much people adjust speed in response to weather conditions. In addition to the sample of speeds obtained in Problem 10, they also recorded speeds for $n = 100$ cars during daylight hours when there was moderate rain. For this second sample, they obtained a mean of $\overline{X} = 58.5$ mph with $SS = 2970$. Use the two samples to estimate how much difference there is in highway speeds between dry conditions and rainy conditions.
    a. Make a point estimate of the population mean difference.
    b. Make an interval estimate of the mean difference so you are 95% confident that the true mean difference is in your interval.

12. It is well known that the ability to maintain focused attention declines over time. For this reason, people who must maintain a high level of attention (such as air traffic controllers) require frequent rest breaks. To determine how much decline occurs during the first 30 minutes of focused attention, a researcher tests a sample of $n = 25$ subjects on a visual detection task. The subjects are required to watch a blank TV screen and respond each time a small dot of light appears. The researcher recorded the number of errors during the first 15 minutes and during the second 15 minutes, and recorded a difference score for each subject. On average, this sample made $\overline{D} = 5.7$ more errors during the second 15 minute period than during the first, with $SS = 864$. Using these data,
    a. Make a point estimate of the mean decline in performance for the general population.
    b. Make an interval estimate of the mean difference so you are 95% confident that the true mean is in your interval.
    c. Based on the interval estimate from part (b), do these data indicate a *significant* change in performance (assume a two-tailed test with $\alpha = .05$)?

13. A developmental psychologist would like to determine how much fine motor skill improves for children from age 3 to age 4. A random sample of $n = 15$ three-year-old children and a second sample of $n = 15$ four-year-olds are obtained. Each child is given a manual dexterity test that measures fine motor skills. The average score for the older children was $\overline{X} = 40.6$ with $SS = 430$ and the average for the younger children was $\overline{X} = 35.4$ with $SS = 410$. Using these data,
    a. Make a point estimate of the population mean difference in fine motor skill.

b. Make an interval estimate so you are 95% confident that the real mean difference is in your interval.

c. Make an interval estimate so you are 99% confident that the real mean difference is in your interval.

d. Based on your answers from (b) and (c), do these data indicate a significant change using a two-tailed test with $\alpha = .05$? Is the difference significant with $\alpha = .01$?

14. An educational psychologist has observed that children seem to lose interest and enthusiasm for school as they progress through the elementary grades. To measure the extent of this phenomenon, the psychologist selects a sample of $n = 15$ second-grade children and a sample of $n = 15$ fifth-graders. Each child is given a questionnaire measuring his or her attitude toward school. Higher scores indicate a more positive attitude. The second-grade children average $\overline{X} = 85$ with $SS = 1620$, and the fifth-graders average $\overline{X} = 71$ with $SS = 1740$. Use these data to estimate how much the enthusiasm for school declines from second to fifth grade. Make a point estimate and a 90% confidence interval estimate of the mean difference.

15. The counseling center at the college offers a short course in study skills for students who are having academic difficulty. To evaluate the effectiveness of this course, a sample of $n = 25$ students is selected, and each student's grade point average is recorded for the semester before the course and for the semester immediately following the course. On average, these students show an increase of $\overline{D} = 0.72$ with $SS = 24$. Use these data to estimate how much effect the course has on grade point average. Make a point estimate and a 95% confidence interval estimate of the mean difference.

16. A psychologist has developed a new personality questionnaire for measuring self-esteem and would like to estimate the population parameters for the test scores. The questionnaire is administered to a sample of $n = 25$ subjects. This sample has an average score of $\overline{X} = 43$ with $SS = 2400$.

a. Provide an estimate for the population variance.

b. Make a point estimate for the population mean.

c. Make an interval estimate of μ so you are 90% confident that the value for μ is in your interval.

17. A common test of short-term memory requires subjects to repeat a random string of digits that was presented a few seconds earlier. The number of digits is increased on each trial until the subject begins to make mistakes. The longest string that can be reported accurately determines the subject's score. The following data were obtained from a sample of $n = 11$ subjects. The scores are 7, 9, 8, 10, 8, 6, 7, 8, 7, 6, 5.

a. Compute the mean and variance for the sample.

b. Use the data to make a point estimate of the population mean.

c. Make an 80% confidence interval estimate of μ.

18. Most adolescents experience a growth spurt when they are between 12 and 15 years old. This period of dramatic growth generally occurs around age 12 for girls and around age 14 for boys. A researcher studying physical development selected a random sample of $n = 9$ girls and a second sample of $n = 16$ boys and recorded the gain in height (in millimeters) between the 14th birthday and 15th birthday for each subject. The girls showed an average gain of $\overline{X} = 40$ millimeters with $SS = 1152$, and the boys gained an average of $\overline{X} = 95$ millimeters with $SS = 2160$.

a. Estimate the population mean growth in 1 year for 14-year-old boys. Make a point estimate and an 80% confidence interval estimate.

b. Estimate the population mean growth in 1 year for 14-year-old girls. Make a point estimate and an 80% confidence interval estimate.

c. Estimate the mean difference in growth for boys versus girls during this 1-year period. Again, make a point estimate and an 80% confidence interval estimate.

19. A therapist has demonstrated that five sessions of relaxation training significantly reduced anxiety levels for a sample of $n = 16$ clients. However, the therapist is concerned about the long-term effects of the training. Six months after therapy is completed, the patients are recalled, and their anxiety levels are measured again. On average, the anxiety scores for these patients are $\overline{D} = 5.5$ points higher after six months than they had been at the end of therapy. The difference scores had $SS = 960$. Use these data to estimate the mean amount of relapse that occurs after therapy ends. Make a point estimate and an 80% confidence interval estimate of the population mean difference.

20. In a classic study of problem solving, Katona (1940) demonstrated that people who are required to figure out a problem on their own will learn more than people who are given the solution. One group of subjects is presented with a series of problems that they must figure out. A second group sees the same problems but gets an explanation of the solutions. Later, both groups are given a new set of similar problems and their problem-solving scores are as follows:

On their own	Given solutions
$n = 10$	$n = 15$
$\overline{X} = 78$	$\overline{X} = 66$
$SS = 1420$	$SS = 2030$

a. Make a point estimate of the mean difference between the two training methods.

b. Make a 95% confidence interval estimate of the mean difference.

21. A researcher would like to estimate how much reaction time is affected by a common over-the-counter cold medication. The researcher measures reaction time for a sample of $n = 36$ subjects. Each subject is then given a dose of the cold medication and reaction time is measured again. For this sample, reaction time increased after the medication by an average of $\overline{D} = 24$ milliseconds with $s = 8$.

a. Make a point estimate of the mean difference in reaction time caused by the medicine.

b. Make a 95% confidence interval estimate of the population mean difference.

22. Problem 18 in Chapter 10 presented hypothetical data showing that elderly people who own dogs are significantly less likely to pay visits to their doctors than those who do not own pets. The data are presented again here.

Doctor visits during past year	
Control group	Dog owners
12	8
10	5
6	9
9	4
15	6
12	
14	

Use these data to estimate how much difference there is in the number of doctor visits for people with dogs compared to those without.

a. Make a point estimate of the population mean difference.

b. Make a 90% confidence interval estimate of the mean difference.

23. Problem 23 in Chapter 11 presented data showing that Olympic marksmen score significantly higher for shots fired between heartbeats than they do for shots fired during heartbeats. The scores for the two conditions are as follows:

Subject	During heartbeats	Between heartbeats
A	93	98
B	90	94
C	95	96
D	92	91
E	95	97
F	91	97

Use these data to estimate how much a marksman's score changes for shots fired during heartbeats compared with shots fired between heartbeats.

a. Make a point estimate of the population mean difference.

b. Make a 95% confidence interval estimate of the mean difference.

CHAPTER 13

INTRODUCTION TO ANALYSIS OF VARIANCE

TOOLS YOU WILL NEED

The following items are considered essential background material for this chapter. If you doubt your knowledge of any of these items, you should review the appropriate chapter or section before proceeding.

- Variability (Chapter 4)
  - Sum of squares
  - Sample of variance
  - Degrees of freedom
- Introduction to hypothesis testing (Chapter 8)
  - The logic of hypothesis testing
- Independent-measures t statistic (Chapter 10)

CONTENTS

13.1 INTRODUCTION

Analysis of variance (ANOVA) is a hypothesis-testing procedure that is used to evaluate mean differences between two or more treatments (or populations). As with all inferential procedures, ANOVA uses sample data as the basis for drawing general conclusions about populations. It may appear that analysis of variance and *t* tests are simply two different ways of doing exactly the same job: testing for mean differences. In some respects, this is true—both tests use sample data to test hypotheses about population means. However, ANOVA has a tremendous advantage over *t* tests. Specifically, *t* tests are limited to situations in which there are only two treatments to compare. The major advantage of ANOVA is that it can be used to compare *two or more treatments.* Thus, ANOVA provides researchers with much greater flexibility in designing experiments and interpreting results.

Figure 13.1 shows a typical research situation for which analysis of variance would be used. Note that the study involves three samples representing three populations. The goal of the analysis is to determine whether the mean differences observed among the samples provide enough evidence to conclude that there are mean differences among the three populations. Specifically, we must decide between two interpretations:

1. There really are no differences between the populations (or treatments). The observed differences between samples are simply due to chance (sampling error).

2. The populations (or treatments) really do have different means, and these population mean differences are part of the reason that the samples have different means.

You should recognize that these two interpretations correspond to the two hypotheses (null and alternative) that are part of the general hypothesis-testing procedure.

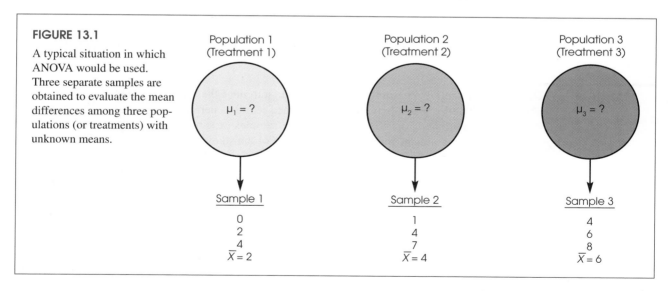

FIGURE 13.1

A typical situation in which ANOVA would be used. Three separate samples are obtained to evaluate the mean differences among three populations (or treatments) with unknown means.

Population 1 (Treatment 1)

$\mu_1 = ?$

Population 2 (Treatment 2)

$\mu_2 = ?$

Population 3 (Treatment 3)

$\mu_3 = ?$

Sample 1

0
2
4
$\overline{X} = 2$

Sample 2

1
4
7
$\overline{X} = 4$

Sample 3

4
6
8
$\overline{X} = 6$

Before we continue, it is necessary to introduce some terminology that is used to describe the research situation shown in Figure 13.1. Recall (from Chapter 1) that when a researcher manipulates a variable to create treatment conditions, the variable is called an *independent variable.* For example, Figure 13.1 could represent a study examining behavior in three different temperature conditions that have been created by the researcher. On the other hand, when a researcher uses a nonmanipulated variable to designate groups, the variable is called a *quasi-independent variable.* For example, the three groups in Figure 13.1 could represent 6-year-old, 8-year-old, and 10-year-old children. In the context of analysis of variance, an independent variable or a quasi-independent variable is called a *factor.* Thus, Figure 13.1 could represent a study where temperature is the factor being evaluated or it could represent a study where age is the factor that is being examined.

DEFINITION   In analysis of variance, the variable (independent or quasi-independent) that designates the groups being compared is called a *factor.*

In addition, the individual groups or treatment conditions that are used to make up a factor are called the *levels* of the factor. For example, a study that examined performance under three different temperature conditions would have three levels of temperature.

DEFINITION   The individual conditions or values that make up a factor are called the *levels* of the factor.

Although analysis of variance can be used in a wide variety of research situations, we will introduce analysis of variance in its simplest form. Specifically, we will only consider research designs that involve one factor—that is, designs with only one independent variable (or only one quasi-independent variable). Also, we will only consider research design that use a separate sample for each of the treatment conditions or groups being compared. Recall that studies using a separate sample for each treatment condition are called independent-measures or between-subject designs (page 223). Thus, in this chapter we will limit our discussion to *single-factor, independent-measures* research studies. In Chapter 14, we will consider ANOVA in more complex situations including research designs with two factors as well as research using repeated-measures designs.

STATISTICAL HYPOTHESES FOR ANOVA

The following example will be used to introduce the statistical hypotheses for ANOVA. Suppose that a psychologist examined learning performance under three temperature conditions: 50°, 70°, and 90°. Three samples of subjects are selected, one sample for each treatment condition. The purpose of the study is to determine whether room temperature affects learning performance. In statistical terms, we want to decide between two hypotheses: the null hypothesis (H_0), which says that temperature has no effect, and the alternative hypothesis (H_1), which states that temperature does affect learning. In symbols, the null hypothesis states

$$H_0: \mu_1 = \mu_2 = \mu_3$$

In words, the null hypothesis states that temperature has no effect on performance. That is, the population means for the three temperature conditions are all the same. In general, H_0 states that there is no treatment effect. Once again, note that the hypotheses are always stated in terms of population parameters, even though we use sample data to test them.

For the alternative hypothesis, we may state that

H_1: At least one population mean is different from the others.

In general, H_1 states that the treatment conditions are not all the same; that is, there is a real treatment effect.

Note that we have not given any specific alternative hypothesis. This is because many different alternatives are possible, and it would be tedious to list them all. One alternative, for example, would be that the first two populations are identical, but that the third is different. Another alternative states that the last two means are the same, but that the first is different. Other alternatives might be

H_1: $\mu_1 \neq \mu_2 \neq \mu_3$ (All three means are different.)

H_1: $\mu_1 = \mu_3$, but μ_2 is different.

We should point out that a researcher typically entertains only one (or at most a few) of these alternative hypotheses. Usually a theory or the outcomes of previous studies will dictate a specific prediction concerning the treatment effect. For the sake of simplicity, we will state a general alternative hypothesis rather than trying to list all the possible specific alternatives.

THE TEST STATISTIC FOR ANOVA

The test statistic for ANOVA is very similar to the t statistics used in earlier chapters. For the t statistic, we computed a ratio with the following structure:

$$t = \frac{\text{obtained difference between sample means}}{\text{difference expected by chance (error)}}$$

For analysis of variance, the test statistic is called an F-ratio and has the following structure:

$$F = \frac{\text{variance (differences) between sample means}}{\text{variance (differences) expected by chance (error)}}$$

Note that the F-ratio is based on *variance* instead of sample mean *difference*. The reason for this change is that ANOVA is used when there are more than two sample means and it is impossible to compute a sample mean difference. For example, if there are only two samples and they have means of $\overline{X} = 20$ and $\overline{X} = 30$, then it is easy to show that there is a 10-point difference between the sample means. However, if we add a third sample with a mean of $\overline{X} = 35$, the concept of a sample mean difference becomes difficult to define and impossible to calculate. The solution to this problem is to use variance to define and measure the size of the differences among the sample means. Consider the following two sets of sample means:

Set 1	Set 2
$\overline{X}_1 = 20$	$\overline{X}_1 = 28$
$\overline{X}_2 = 30$	$\overline{X}_2 = 30$
$\overline{X}_3 = 35$	$\overline{X}_3 = 31$

13.1   TYPE I ERRORS AND MULTIPLE-HYPOTHESIS TESTS

IF WE already have *t* tests for comparing mean differences, you might wonder why analysis of variance is necessary. Why create a whole new hypothesis-testing procedure that simply duplicates what the *t* tests can already do? The answer to this question is based in a concern about Type I errors.

Remember that each time you do a hypothesis test, you select an alpha level that determines the risk of a Type I error. With $\alpha = .05$, for example, there is a 5%, or a 1-in-20, risk of a Type I error. Thus, for every 20 hypothesis tests, you expect to make one Type I error. The more tests you do, the more risk there is of a Type I error. For this reason, researchers often make a distinction between the *testwise* alpha level and the *experimentwise* alpha level. The testwise alpha level is simply the alpha level you select for each individual hypothesis test. The experimentwise alpha level is the total probability of a Type I error accumulated from all of the separate tests in the experiment. As the number of separate tests increases, so does the experimentwise alpha level.

For an experiment involving three treatments, you would need three separate *t* tests to compare all of the mean differences:

Test 1 compares treatment 1 versus treatment 2.
Test 2 compares treatment 1 versus treatment 3.
Test 3 compares treatment 2 versus treatment 3.

The three separate tests accumulate to produce a relatively large experimentwise alpha level. The advantage of analysis of variance is that it performs all three comparisons simultaneously in the same hypothesis test. Thus, no matter how many different means are being compared, ANOVA uses one test with one alpha level to evaluate the mean differences and thereby avoids the problem of an inflated experimentwise alpha level. We discuss this topic in more detail in Section 13.6.

If you compute the variance for the three numbers in each set, then the variance you obtain for set 1 is $s^2 = 58.33$ and the variance for set 2 is $s^2 = 2.33$. Note that the two variances provide an accurate representation of the size of the differences. In set 1 there are relatively large differences between sample means and the variance is relatively large. In set 2 the mean differences are small and the variance is small. Thus, the variance in the numerator of the *F*-ratio provides a single number that describes the differences between all the sample means.

In much the same way, the variance in the denominator of the *F*-ratio and the standard error in the denominator of the *t* statistic both measure the differences that would be expected by chance. In the *t* statistic, the standard error measures standard distance or standard deviation. In the *F*-ratio, this standard deviation (*s*) is simply converted to a variance (s^2).

Finally, you should realize that the *t* statistic and the *F*-ratio provide the same basic information. In each case, the numerator of the ratio measures the actual difference obtained from the sample data, and the denominator measures the difference that would be expected by chance. With either the *F*-ratio or the *t* statistic, a large value provides evidence that the sample mean difference is more than chance (see Box 13.1).

13.2   THE LOGIC OF ANALYSIS OF VARIANCE

The formulas and calculations required in ANOVA are somewhat complicated, but the logic that underlies the whole procedure is fairly straightforward. Therefore, this

TABLE 13.1

Hypothetical data from an experiment examining learning performance under three temperature conditions*

Treatment 1 50° (sample 1)	Treatment 2 70° (sample 2)	Treatment 3 90° (sample 3)
0	4	1
1	3	2
3	6	2
1	3	0
0	4	0
$\overline{X} = 1$	$\overline{X} = 4$	$\overline{X} = 1$

*Note that there are three separate samples, with n = 5 in each sample. The dependent variable is the number of problems solved correctly.

section will give a general picture of analysis of variance before we start looking at the details. We will introduce the logic of ANOVA with the help of the hypothetical data in Table 13.1. These data represent the results of an independent-measures experiment comparing learning performance under three temperature conditions.

One obvious characteristic of the data in Table 13.1 is that the scores are not all the same. In everyday language, the scores are different; in statistical terms, the scores are variable. Our goal is to measure the amount of variability (the size of the differences) and to explain where it comes from.

The first step is to determine the total variability for the entire set of data. To compute the total variability, we will combine all the scores from all the separate samples into one group and then obtain one general measure of variability for the complete experiment. Once we have measured the total variability, we can begin to break it apart into separate components. The word *analysis* means dividing into smaller parts. Because we are going to analyze variability, the process is called *analysis of variance.* This analysis process divides the total variability into two basic components:

1. **Between-Treatments Variance.** Looking at the data in Table 13.1, we clearly see that much of the variability in the scores is due to general differences between treatment conditions. For example, the scores in the 70° condition tend to be much higher ($\overline{X} = 4$) than the scores in the 50° condition ($\overline{X} = 1$). We will calculate the variance between treatments to provide a measure of the overall differences between treatment conditions. Note that the variance between treatments is really measuring the differences between sample means.

2. **Within-Treatments Variance.** In addition to the general differences between treatment conditions, there is variability within each sample. Looking again at Table 13.1, the scores in the 70° condition are not all the same; they are variable. The within-treatments variance will provide a measure of the variability inside each treatment condition.

Partitioning the total variability into these two components is the heart of analysis of variance. We will now examine each of the components in more detail.

BETWEEN-TREATMENTS VARIANCE

Remember that calculating variance is simply a method for measuring how big the differences are for a set of numbers. When you see the term *variance,* you can automatically translate it into the term *differences.* Thus, the between-treatments variance is simply measuring how much difference exists between the treatment conditions.

In addition to measuring the differences between treatments, the overall goal of ANOVA is to evaluate the differences between treatments. Specifically, the purpose for the analysis is to distinguish between two alternative explanations:

1. The differences between treatments have been caused by treatment effects.

2. The differences between treatments are simply due to chance.

Thus, there are always two possible explanations for the difference (or variance) that exists between treatments:

1. **Treatment Effect.** The differences are *caused by the treatments.* For the data in Table 13.1, the scores in sample 1 were obtained in a 50° room and the scores in sample 2 were obtained in a 70° room. It is possible that the difference between samples is caused by the different temperatures.

2. **Chance.** The differences are *simply due to chance.* If there is no treatment effect at all, you would still expect some differences between samples. The samples consist of different individuals with different scores, and it should not be surprising that differences exist between samples just by chance. In general, "chance differences" can be defined as unplanned and unpredictable differences that are not caused or explained by any action on the part of the researcher. Researchers commonly identify two primary sources for chance differences.

   a. *Individual differences:* Individual subjects enter a research study with different characteristics. Although it is reasonable to expect that different subjects will produce different scores, it is impossible to predict exactly what the differences will be.

   b. *Experimental error:* Whenever you make a measurement, there is potential for some degree of error. Thus, if you measure the same individual under the same conditions, it is possible that you will obtain two different measurements. Because these differences are unexplained and unpredictable, they are considered to be chance.

Thus, when we compute the between-treatments variance, we are measuring differences that could be caused by a treatment effect or could simply be due to chance. To demonstrate that there really is a treatment effect, we must establish that the differences between treatments are bigger than would be expected by chance alone. To accomplish this goal, we will determine how big the differences are when there is no treatment effect involved; that is, we will measure how much difference (or variance) occurs by chance alone. To measure chance differences, we compute the variance within treatments.

WITHIN-TREATMENTS VARIANCE

Inside each treatment condition, we have a set of individuals who are treated exactly the same; that is, the researcher does not do anything that would cause these individuals to have different scores. In Table 13.1, for example, the data show that five individuals were tested in a 70° room (treatment 2). Although these five individuals were all treated exactly the same, their scores are different. Why are the scores different? The answer is that the differences within a treatment are simply due to chance.

Thus, the within-treatments variance provides a measure of how much difference is reasonable to expect just by chance. In particular, the within-treatments variance measures the differences that exist when there is no treatment that could cause differences.

Figure 13.2 shows the overall analysis of variance and identifies the sources of variability that are measured by each of the two basic components.

FIGURE 13.2

The independent-measures analysis of variance partitions, or analyzes, the total variability into two components: variance between treatments and variance within treatments.

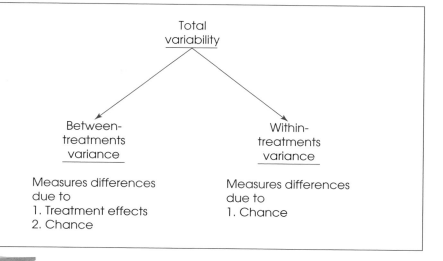

The value obtained for the F-ratio will help determine whether or not any treatment effects exist. Consider the following two possibilities:

THE F-RATIO: THE TEST STATISTIC FOR ANOVA

Once we have analyzed the total variability into two basic components (between treatments and within treatments), we simply compare them. The comparison is made by computing a statistic called an *F-ratio*. For the independent-measures ANOVA, the F-ratio has the following structure:

$$F = \frac{\text{variance between treatments}}{\text{variance within treatments}} \tag{13.1}$$

When we express each component of variability in terms of its sources (see Figure 13.2), the structure of the F-ratio is

$$F = \frac{\text{treatment effect } + \text{ differences due to chance}}{\text{differences due to chance}} \tag{13.2}$$

The value obtained for the F-ratio will help determine whether or not any treatment effects exist. Consider the following two possibilities:

1. When the treatment has no effect, then the differences between treatments (numerator) are entirely due to chance. In this case, the numerator and the denominator of the F-ratio are both measuring chance differences and should be roughly the same size. With the numerator and denominator roughly equal, the F-ratio should have a value around 1.00. In terms of the formula, when the treatment effect is zero, we obtain

$$F = \frac{0 + \text{ differences due to chance}}{\text{differences due to chance}}$$

   Thus, an F-ratio near 1.00 indicates that the differences between treatments (numerator) are about the same as the differences that are expected by chance (the denominator). With an F-ratio near 1.00, we will conclude that there is no evidence to suggest that the treatment has any effect.

2. When the treatment does have an effect, causing differences between samples, then the between-treatment differences (numerator) should be larger than chance

(denominator). In this case, the numerator of the *F*-ratio should be noticeably larger than the denominator, and we should obtain an *F*-ratio noticeably larger than 1.00. Thus, a large *F*-ratio indicates that the differences between treatments are greater than chance; that is, the treatment does have a significant effect.

In more general terms, the denominator of the *F*-ratio measures only uncontrolled and unexplained (often called *unsystematic*) variability. For this reason, the denominator of the *F*-ratio is called the *error term*. The numerator of the *F*-ratio always includes the same unsystematic variability as in the error term, but it also includes any systematic differences caused by the treatment effect. The goal of ANOVA is to find out whether or not a treatment effect exists.

DEFINITION   For ANOVA, the denominator of the *F*-ratio is called the *error term*. The error term provides a measure of the variance due to chance. When the treatment effect is zero (H_0 is true), the error term measures the same sources of variance as the numerator of the *F*-ratio, so the value of the *F*-ratio is expected to be nearly equal to 1.00.

LEARNING CHECK ◆

1. ANOVA is a statistical procedure that compares two or more treatment conditions for differences in variance. (True or false?)

2. In ANOVA, what value is expected, on the average, for the *F*-ratio when the null hypothesis is true?

3. What happens to the value of the *F*-ratio if differences between treatments are increased? What happens to the *F*-ratio if variability inside the treatments is increased?

4. In ANOVA, the total variability is partitioned into two parts. What are these two variability components called, and how are they used in the *F*-ratio?

ANSWERS

1. False. Although ANOVA uses variability in the computations, the purpose of the test is to evaluate differences in *means* between treatments.

2. When H_0 is true, the expected value for the *F*-ratio is 1.00 because the top and bottom of the ratio are both measuring the same variance.

3. As differences between treatments increase, the *F*-ratio will increase. As variability within treatments increases, the *F*-ratio will decrease.

4. The two components are between-treatments variability and within-treatments variability. Between-treatments variance is the numerator of the *F*-ratio, and within-treatments variance is the denominator.   ◆

13.3 ANOVA NOTATION AND FORMULAS

Because ANOVA is most often used to examine data from more than two treatment conditions (and more than two samples), we will need a notational system to help keep track of all the individual scores and totals. To help introduce this notational system, we

TABLE 13.2

Hypothetical data from an experiment examining learning performance under three temperature conditions*

Temperature conditions			
1 50°	2 70°	3 90°	
0	4	1	$\Sigma X^2 = 106$
1	3	2	$G = 30$
3	6	2	$N = 15$
1	3	0	$k = 3$
0	4	0	
$T_1 = 5$	$T_2 = 20$	$T_3 = 5$	
$SS_1 = 6$	$SS_2 = 6$	$SS_3 = 4$	
$n_1 = 5$	$n_2 = 5$	$n_3 = 5$	
$\overline{X}_1 = 1$	$\overline{X}_2 = 4$	$\overline{X}_3 = 1$	

*Summary values and notation for an analysis of variance are also presented.

will use the hypothetical data from Table 13.1 again. The data are reproduced in Table 13.2 along with some of the notation and statistics that will be described.

1. The letter k is used to identify the number of treatment conditions—that is, the number of levels of the factor. For an independent-measures study, k also specifies the number of separate samples. For the data in Table 13.2, there are three treatments, so $k = 3$.

2. The number of scores in each treatment is identified by a lowercase letter n. For the example in Table 13.2, $n = 5$ for all the treatments. If the samples are of different sizes, you can identify a specific sample by using a subscript. For example, n_2 is the number of scores in treatment 2.

3. The total number of scores in the entire study is specified by a capital letter N. When all the samples are the same size (n is constant), $N = kn$. For the data in Table 13.2, there are $n = 5$ scores in each of the $k = 3$ treatments, so $N = 3(5) = 15$.

4. The total (ΣX) for each treatment condition is identified by the capital letter T. The total for a specific treatment can be identified by adding a numerical subscript to the T. For example, the total for the second treatment in Table 13.2 is $T_2 = 20$.

Because ANOVA formulas require ΣX for each treatment and ΣX for the entire set of scores, we have introduced new notation (T and G) to help identify which ΣX is being used. Remember that T stands for *treatment total,* and G stands for *grand total.*

5. The sum of all the scores in the research study (the grand total) is identified by G. You can compute G by adding up all N scores or by adding up the treatment totals: $G = \Sigma T$.

6. Although there is no new notation involved, we also have computed SS and $\overline{X}$ for each sample, and we have calculated ΣX^2 for the entire set of $N = 15$ scores in the study. These values are given in Table 13.2 and will be important in the formulas and calculations for ANOVA.

ANOVA FORMULAS   Because analysis of variance requires extensive calculations and many formulas, one common problem for students is simply keeping track of the different formulas and numbers. Therefore, we will examine the general structure of the procedure and look at the organization of the calculations before we introduce the individual formulas.

1. The final calculation for ANOVA is the F-ratio, which is composed of two variances:

$$F = \frac{\text{variance between treatments}}{\text{variance within treatments}}$$

2. Recall that variance for sample data has been defined as

$$\text{sample variance} = s^2 = \frac{SS}{df}$$

Therefore, we will need to compute an SS and a df for the variance between treatments (numerator of F), and we will need another SS and df for the variance within treatments (denominator of F). To obtain these SS and df values, we must go through two separate analyses: First, compute SS for the total study, and analyze it into two components (between and within). Then compute df for the total study, and analyze it into two components (between and within).

Thus, the entire process of analysis of variance will require nine calculations: three values for SS, three values for df, two variances (between and within), and a final F-ratio. However, these nine calculations are all logically related and are all directed toward finding the final F-ratio. Figure 13.3 shows the logical structure of ANOVA calculations.

FIGURE 13.3

The structure and sequence of calculations for the analysis of variance.

The final goal for the analysis of variance is an F-ratio	$F = \dfrac{\text{Variance between treatments}}{\text{Variance within treatments}}$
Each variance in the F-ratio is computed as SS/df	$\begin{array}{l}\text{Variance} \\ \text{between} = \dfrac{SS\text{ between}}{df\text{ between}} \\ \text{treatments}\end{array}$ $\begin{array}{l}\text{Variance} \\ \text{within} = \dfrac{SS\text{ within}}{df\text{ within}} \\ \text{treatments}\end{array}$
To obtain each of the SS and df values, the total variability is analyzed into the two components	SS total $\diagup\diagdown$ SS between SS within df total $\diagup\diagdown$ df between df within

ANALYSIS OF SUM OF SQUARES (SS)

The ANOVA requires that we first compute a total sum of squares and then partition this value into two components: between treatments and within treatments. This analysis is outlined in Figure 13.4. We will examine each of the three components separately.

FIGURE 13.4

Partitioning the sum of squares (SS) for the independent-measures analysis of variance.

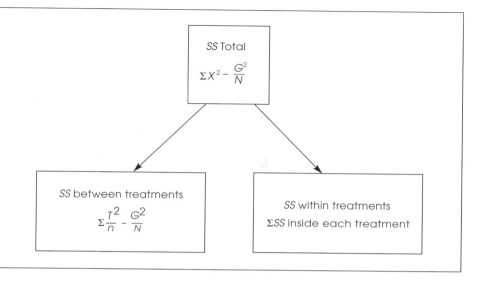

1. **Total Sum of Squares, SS_{total}.** As the name implies, SS_{total} is the sum of squares for the entire set of N scores. We calculate this value by using the computational formula for SS:

$$SS = \Sigma X^2 - \frac{(\Sigma X)^2}{N}$$

To make this formula consistent with the ANOVA notation, we substitute the letter G in place of ΣX and obtain

$$SS_{\text{total}} = \Sigma X^2 - \frac{G^2}{N} \tag{13.3}$$

Applying this formula to the set of data in Table 13.2, we obtain

$$SS_{\text{total}} = 106 - \frac{30^2}{15}$$

$$= 106 - 60$$

$$= 46$$

2. **Within-Treatments Sum of Squares, SS_{within}.** Now we are looking at the variability inside each of the treatment conditions. We have already computed the SS within each of the three treatment conditions (Table 13.2): $SS_1 = 6$, $SS_2 = 6$, and $SS_3 = 4$. To find the overall within-treatment sum of squares, we simply add these values together:

$$SS_{\text{within}} = \Sigma SS_{\text{inside each treatment}} \tag{13.4}$$

For the data in Table 13.2, this formula gives

$$SS_{\text{within}} = 6 + 6 + 4$$

$$= 16$$

3. Between-Treatments Sum of Squares, $SS_{between}$. Before we introduce the equation for $SS_{between}$, consider what we have found so far. The total variability for the data in Table 13.2 is $SS_{total} = 46$. We intend to partition this total into two parts (see Figure 13.4). One part, SS_{within}, has been found to be equal to 16. This means that $SS_{between}$ must be equal to 30 in order for the two parts (16 and 30) to add up to the total (46). The equation for the between-treatments sum of squares should produce a value of $SS_{between} = 30$.

Recall that the variability between treatments measures the differences between treatment means. Conceptually, the most direct way of measuring the amount of variability among the treatment means is to compute the sum of squares for the set of means, but this method is usually awkward, especially when treatment means are not whole numbers. Therefore, we will use a computational formula for $SS_{between}$ that uses the treatment totals (T) instead of the treatment means.

$$SS_{between} = \Sigma \frac{T^2}{n} - \frac{G^2}{N} \tag{13.5}$$

Note the similarity between this formula and the one for SS_{total} (Equation 13.3). When computing SS_{total} we are measuring the variability (differences) for a set of scores or X values, and the formula begins by squaring each of the X values. Now, we are measuring the variability (differences) for a set of treatment totals or T values, and the formula begins by squaring each of the T values. Also, note that $SS_{between}$ is intended to measure the differences between treatments, and the treatment totals (the T values) provide an accurate method to measure and describe differences between treatments.

Using this new formula with the data in Table 13.2, we obtain

$$SS_{between} = \frac{5^2}{5} + \frac{20^2}{5} + \frac{5^2}{5} - \frac{30^2}{15}$$
$$= 5 + 80 + 5 - 60$$
$$= 90 - 60$$
$$= 30$$

At this point in the analysis, we have computed all three of the SS values and it is appropriate to verify our calculations by checking to see that the two components add up to the total. Using the data from Table 13.2,

$$SS_{total} = SS_{between} + SS_{within}$$
$$46 = 30 + 16$$

The formula for each SS and the relationships among these three values are shown in Figure 13.4.

THE ANALYSIS OF DEGREES OF FREEDOM (df)

The analysis of degrees of freedom (df) follows the same pattern as the analysis of SS. First, we will find df for the total set of N scores, and then we will partition this value into two components: degrees of freedom between treatments and degrees of freedom

within treatments. In computing degrees of freedom, there are two important considerations to keep in mind:

1. Each df value is associated with a specific SS value.

2. Normally, the value of df is obtained by counting the number of items that were
used to calculate SS and then subtracting 1. For example, if you compute SS for a
set of n scores, then $df = n - 1$.

With this in mind, we will examine the degrees of freedom for each part of the
analysis:

1. Total Degrees of Freedom, df_{total}. To find the df associated with SS_{total}, you
must first recall that this SS value measures variability for the entire set of N scores.
Therefore, the df value is

$$df_{total} = N - 1 \tag{13.6}$$

For the data in Table 13.2, the total number of scores is $N = 15$, so the total degrees
of freedom are

$$df_{total} = 15 - 1$$
$$= 14$$

2. Within-Treatments Degrees of Freedom, df_{within}. To find the df associated
with SS_{within}, we must look at how this SS value is computed. Remember, we first find
SS inside each of the treatments and then add these values together. Each of the treatment SS values measures variability for the n scores in the treatment, so each SS will
have $df = n - 1$. When all these individual treatment values are added together, we
obtain

$$df_{within} = \Sigma(n - 1) = \Sigma df_{in\ each\ treatment} \tag{13.7}$$

For the experiment we have been considering, each treatment has $n = 5$ scores.
This means there are $n - 1 = 4$ degrees of freedom inside each treatment. Because
there are three different treatment conditions, this gives a total of 12 for the within-
treatments degrees of freedom. Note that this formula for df simply adds up the
number of scores in each treatment (the n values) and subtracts 1 for each treatment. If
these two stages are done separately, you obtain

$$df_{within} = N - k \tag{13.8}$$

(Adding up all the n values gives N. If you subtract 1 for each treatment, then alto-
gether you have subtracted k because there are k treatments.) For the data in Table
13.2, $N = 15$ and $k = 3$, so

$$df_{within} = 15 - 3$$
$$= 12$$

3. Between-Treatments Degrees of Freedom, $df_{between}$. The df associated with
$SS_{between}$ can be found by considering the SS formula. This SS formula measures the
variability for the set of treatment totals. To find $df_{between}$, simply count the number of

T values and subtract 1. Because the number of treatments is specified by the letter k, the formula for df is

$$df_{\text{between}} = k - 1 \qquad\qquad (13.9)$$

For the data in Table 13.2, there are three different treatment conditions (three T values), so the between-treatments degrees of freedom are computed as follows:

$$df_{\text{between}} = 3 - 1$$
$$= 2$$

Note that the two parts we obtained from this analysis of degrees of freedom add up to equal the total degrees of freedom:

$$df_{\text{total}} = df_{\text{within}} + df_{\text{between}}$$
$$14 = 12 + 2$$

The complete analysis of degrees of freedom is shown in Figure 13.5.

FIGURE 13.5

Partitioning degrees of freedom (df) for the independent-measures analysis of variance.

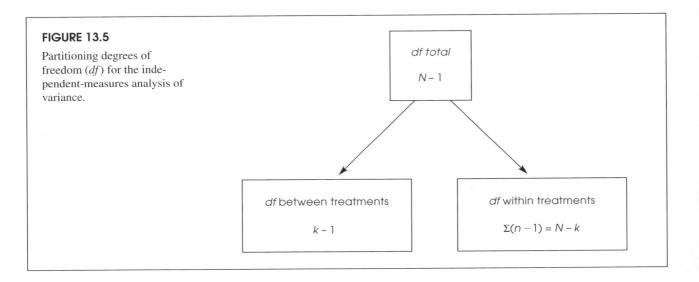

CALCULATION OF
VARIANCES (*MS*)
AND THE *F*-RATIO

The next step in the analysis of variance procedure is to compute the variance between treatments and the variance within treatments in order to calculate the F-ratio (see Figure 13.3).

In ANOVA, it is customary to use the term *mean square,* or simply *MS*, in place of the term *variance*. Recall (from Chapter 4) that variance is defined as the mean of the squared deviations. In the same way that we use *SS* to stand for the sum of the squared deviations, we now will use *MS* to stand for the mean of the squared deviations. For the final F-ratio we will need an *MS* (variance) between treatments for the numerator and an *MS* (variance) within treatments for the denominator. In each case,

$$MS \text{ (variance)} = s^2 = \frac{SS}{df} \qquad\qquad (13.10)$$

For the data we have been considering,

$$MS_{between} = s^2_{between} = \frac{SS_{between}}{df_{between}} = \frac{30}{2} = 15$$

and

$$MS_{within} = s^2_{within} = \frac{SS_{within}}{df_{within}} = \frac{16}{12} = 1.33$$

We now have a measure of the variance (or differences) between the treatments and a measure of the variance within the treatments. The F-ratio simply compares these two variances:

$$F = \frac{MS_{between}}{MS_{within}} \qquad\qquad (13.11)$$

For the experiment we have been examining, the data give an F-ratio of

$$F = \frac{15}{1.33} = 11.28$$

It is useful to organize the results of the analysis in one table called an *ANOVA summary table*. The table shows the source of variability (between treatments, within treatments, and total variability), SS, df, MS, and F. For the previous computations, the ANOVA summary table is constructed as follows:

Source	SS	df	MS	
Between treatments	30	2	15	$F = 11.28$
Within treatments	16	12	1.33	
Total	46	14		

Although these tables are no longer commonly used in published reports, they do provide a concise method for presenting the results of an analysis. (Note that you can conveniently check your work: Adding the first two entries in the SS column $(30 + 16)$ yields the total SS. The same applies to the df column.) When using analysis of variance, you might start with a blank ANOVA summary table and then fill in the values as they are calculated. With this method, you will be less likely to "get lost" in the analysis, wondering what to do next.

For this example, the obtained value of $F = 11.28$ indicates that the numerator of the F-ratio is substantially bigger than the denominator. If you recall the conceptual structure of the F-ratio as presented in Equations 13.1 and 13.2, the F value we obtained indicates that the differences between treatments are more than 11 times bigger than what would be expected by chance. Stated in terms of the experimental variables, it appears that temperature does have an effect on learning performance. However, to properly evaluate the F-ratio, we must examine the F distribution.

13.4   THE DISTRIBUTION OF *F*-RATIOS

In analysis of variance, the *F*-ratio is constructed so that the numerator and the denominator of the ratio are measuring exactly the same variance when the null hypothesis is true (see Equation 13.2). In this situation, we expect the value of *F* to be around 1.00. The problem now is to define precisely what we mean by "around 1.00." What values are considered to be close to 1.00, and what values are far away? To answer this question, we need to look at all the possible *F* values—that is, the *distribution of F-ratios*.

Before we examine this distribution in detail, you should note two obvious characteristics:

1. Because *F*-ratios are computed from two variances (the numerator and the denominator of the ratio), *F* values will always be positive numbers. Remember that variance is always positive.

2. When H_0 is true, the numerator and denominator of the *F*-ratio are measuring the same variance. In this case, the two sample variances should be about the same size, so the ratio should be near 1. In other words, the distribution of *F*-ratios should pile up around 1.00.

With these two factors in mind, we can sketch the distribution of *F*-ratios. The distribution is cut off at zero (all positive values), piles up around 1.00, and then tapers off to the right (see Figure 13.6). The exact shape of the *F* distribution depends on the degrees of freedom for the two variances in the *F*-ratio. You should recall that the precision of a sample variance depends on the number of scores or the degrees of freedom. In general, the variance for a large sample (large *df*) provides a more accurate estimate of the population variance. Because the precision of the *MS* values depends on *df*, the shape of the *F* distribution also will depend on the *df* values for the numerator and denominator of the *F*-ratio. With very large *df* values, nearly all the *F*-ratios will be clustered very near to 1.00. With smaller *df* values, the *F* distribution is more spread out.

FIGURE 13.6

The distribution of *F*-ratios with $df = 2, 12$. Of all the values in the distribution, only 5% are larger than $F = 3.88$, and only 1% are larger than $F = 6.93$.

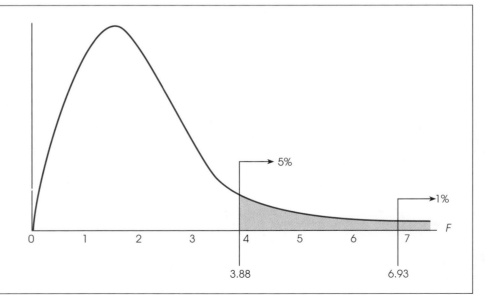

THE F DISTRIBUTION TABLE

For analysis of variance, we expect F near 1.00 if H_0 is true, and we expect a large value for F if H_0 is not true. In the F distribution, we need to separate those values that are reasonably near 1.00 from the values that are significantly greater than 1.00. These critical values are presented in an F distribution table in Appendix B, pages A-29–A-31. A portion of the F distribution table is shown in Table 13.3. To use the table, you must know the df values for the F-ratio (numerator and denominator), and you must know the alpha level for the hypothesis test. It is customary for an F table to have the df values for the numerator of the F-ratio printed across the top of the table. The df values for the denominator of F are printed in a column on the left-hand side. For the temperature experiment we have been considering, the numerator of the F-ratio (between treatments) has $df = 2$, and the denominator of the F-ratio (within treatments) has $df = 12$. This F-ratio is said to have "degrees of freedom equal to 2 and 12." The degrees of freedom would be written as $df = 2, 12$. To use the table, you would first find $df = 2$ across the top of the table and $df = 12$ in the first column. When you line up these two values they point to a pair of numbers in the middle of the table. These numbers give the critical cutoffs for $\alpha = .05$ and $\alpha = .01$. With $df = 2, 12$, for example, the numbers in the table are 3.88 and 6.93. These values indicate that the most unlikely 5% of the distribution ($\alpha = .05$) begins at a value of 3.88. The most extreme 1% of the distribution begins at a value of 6.93 (see Figure 13.6).

TABLE 13.3

A portion of the F distribution table. Entries in roman type are critical values for the .05 level of significance, and bold type values are for the .01 level of significance. The critical values for $df = 2, 12$ have been highlighted (see text).

Degrees of freedom: denominator	Degrees of freedom: numerator					
	1	2	3	4	5	6
10	4.96	4.10	3.71	3.48	3.33	3.22
	10.04	**7.56**	**6.55**	**5.99**	**5.64**	**5.39**
11	4.84	3.98	3.59	3.36	3.20	3.09
	9.65	**7.20**	**6.22**	**5.67**	**5.32**	**5.07**
12	4.75	3.88	3.49	3.26	3.11	3.00
	9.33	**6.93**	**5.95**	**5.41**	**5.06**	**4.82**
13	4.67	3.80	3.41	3.18	3.02	2.92
	9.07	**6.70**	**5.74**	**5.20**	**4.86**	**4.62**
14	4.60	3.74	3.34	3.11	2.96	2.85
	8.86	**6.51**	**5.56**	**5.03**	**4.69**	**4.46**

In the temperature experiment, we obtained an F-ratio of 11.28. According to the critical cutoffs in Figure 13.6, this value is extremely unlikely (it is in the most extreme 1%). Therefore, we would reject H_0 with α set at either .05 or .01 and conclude that temperature does have a significant effect on learning performance.

LEARNING CHECK

1. Calculate SS_{total}, $SS_{between}$, and SS_{within} for the following set of data:

Treatment 1	Treatment 2	Treatment 3	
$n = 10$	$n = 10$	$n = 10$	$N = 30$
$T = 10$	$T = 20$	$T = 30$	$G = 60$
$SS = 27$	$SS = 16$	$SS = 23$	$\Sigma X^2 = 206$

2. A researcher uses an ANOVA to compare three treatment conditions with a sample of $n = 8$ in each treatment. For this analysis, find df_{total}, $df_{between}$, and df_{within}.

3. With $\alpha = .05$, what value forms the boundary for the critical region in the distribution of F-ratios with $df = 2, 24$?

ANSWERS   1. $SS_{total} = 86$; $SS_{between} = 20$; $SS_{within} = 66$

2. $df_{total} = 23$; $df_{between} = 2$; $df_{within} = 21$

3. The critical value is 3.40.   ◆

13.5   EXAMPLES OF HYPOTHESIS TESTING WITH ANOVA

Although we have now seen all the individual components of ANOVA, the following example demonstrates the complete ANOVA process using the standard four-step procedure for hypothesis testing.

EXAMPLE 13.1   The data depicted in Table 13.4 were obtained from an independent-measures experiment designed to measure the effectiveness of three pain relievers (A, B, and C). A fourth group that received a placebo (sugar pill) also was tested.

TABLE 13.4

The effect of drug treatment on the amount of time (in seconds) a stimulus is endured

Placebo	Drug A	Drug B	Drug C	
0	1	3	7	$N = 20$
2	4	6	3	$G = 60$
0	1	4	5	$\Sigma X^2 = 262$
0	1	3	6	
3	3	4	4	
$T = 5$	$T = 10$	$T = 20$	$T = 25$	
$SS = 8$	$SS = 8$	$SS = 6$	$SS = 10$	

The purpose of the analysis is to determine whether these sample data provide evidence of any significant differences among the four drugs. The dependent variable is the amount of time (in seconds) that subjects can withstand a painfully hot stimulus.

Before we begin the hypothesis test, note that we have already computed several summary statistics for the data in Table 13.4. Specifically, the treatment totals (T) and SS values are shown for each sample, and the grand total (G) as well as N and ΣX^2 are shown for the entire set of data. Having these summary values will simplify the computations in the hypothesis test, and we suggest that you always compute these summary statistics before you begin an analysis of variance.

STEP 1   The first step is to state the hypotheses and select an alpha level:

$$H_0: \mu_1 = \mu_2 = \mu_3 = \mu_4 \quad \text{(There is no treatment effect.)}$$

H_1: At least one of the treatment means is different.

We will use $\alpha = .05$.

STEP 2   To locate the critical region for the F-ratio, we first must determine degrees of freedom for $MS_{between}$ and MS_{within} (the numerator and denominator of F). For these data, the total degrees of freedom are

Often it is easier to postpone finding the critical region until after step 3, where you compute the df values as part of the calculations for the F-ratio.

$$df_{total} = N - 1$$
$$= 20 - 1$$
$$= 19$$

Analyzing this total into two components, we obtain

$$df_{between} = k - 1$$
$$= 4 - 1$$
$$= 3$$

$$df_{within} = \Sigma df_{inside\ each\ treatment} = 4 + 4 + 4 + 4 = 16$$

The F-ratio for these data have $df = 3, 16$. The distribution of all the possible F-ratios with $df = 3, 16$ is presented in Figure 13.7. Note that an F-ratio larger than 3.24 is extremely rare ($p < .05$) if H_0 is true.

FIGURE 13.7

The distribution of F-ratios with $df = 3, 16$. The critical value for $\alpha = .05$ is $F = 3.24$.

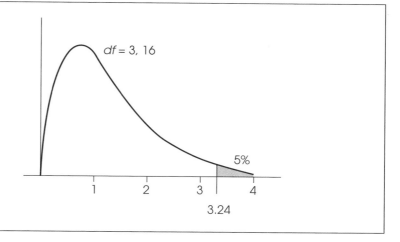

STEP 3   To compute the F-ratio for these data, you must go through the series of calculations outlined in Figure 13.3. The calculations can be summarized as follows:

a. Analyze the SS to obtain $SS_{between}$ and SS_{within}.

b. Use the SS values and the df values (from step 2) to calculate the two variances, $MS_{between}$ and MS_{within}.

c. Finally, use the two MS values (variances) to compute the F-ratio.

Analysis of SS. First, we will compute the total *SS* and then the two components, as indicated in Figure 13.4.

$$SS_{total} = \Sigma X^2 - \frac{G^2}{N}$$

$$= 262 - \frac{60^2}{20}$$

$$= 262 - 180$$

$$= 82$$

$$SS_{within} = \Sigma SS_{inside\ each\ treatment} = 8 + 8 + 6 + 10 = 32$$

$$SS_{between} = \Sigma\frac{T^2}{n} - \frac{G^2}{N}$$

$$= \frac{5^2}{5} + \frac{10^2}{5} + \frac{20^2}{5} + \frac{25^2}{5} - \frac{60^2}{20}$$

$$= 5 + 20 + 80 + 125 - 180$$

$$= 50$$

Calculation of mean squares. Now we must compute the variance or *MS* for each of the two components:

The *df* values ($df_{between} = 3$ and $df_{within} = 16$) were computed in step 2 when we located the critical region.

$$MS_{between} = \frac{SS_{between}}{df_{between}} = \frac{50}{3} = 16.67$$

$$MS_{within} = \frac{SS_{within}}{df_{within}} = \frac{32}{16} = 2.00$$

Calculation of F. Finally, we compute the *F*-ratio:

$$F = \frac{MS_{between}}{MS_{within}} = \frac{16.67}{2.00} = 8.33$$

STEP 4   Finally, we make the statistical decision. The *F* value we obtained, $F = 8.33$, is in the critical region (see Figure 13.7). It is very unlikely ($p < .05$) that we will obtain a value this large if H_0 is true. Therefore, we reject H_0 and conclude that there is a significant treatment effect.

Example 13.1 demonstrated the complete, step-by-step application of the ANOVA procedure. There are two additional points that can be made using this example.

First, you should look carefully at the statistical decision. We have rejected H_0 and concluded that not all the treatments are the same. But we have not determined which ones are different. Is drug A different from the placebo? Is drug A different from drug B? Unfortunately, these questions remain unanswered. We do know that at least one difference exists (we rejected H_0), but additional analysis is necessary to find out exactly where this difference is. We address this problem in Section 13.6.

Second, as noted earlier, all of the components of the analysis (the *SS, df, MS,* and *F*) can be presented together in one summary table. The summary table for the analysis in Example 13.1 is as follows:

Source	SS	df	MS	
Between treatments	50	3	16.67	F = 8.33
Within treatments	32	16	2.00	
Total	82	19		

Although these tables are very useful for organizing the components of an analysis of variance, they are not commonly used in published reports. In the following section, we present the current method for reporting the results from an ANOVA.

IN THE LITERATURE:
REPORTING THE RESULTS OF ANALYSIS OF VARIANCE

The APA format for reporting the results of ANOVA begins with a presentation of the treatment means and standard deviations in the narrative of the article, a table, or a graph. These descriptive statistics are not needed in the calculations of the actual analysis of variance, but you can easily determine the treatment means from n and T ($\overline{X} = T/n$) and the standard deviations from the SS of each treatment [$s = \sqrt{SS/(n-1)}$]. Next, report the results of the ANOVA. For the study described in Example 13.1, the report might state

The means and standard deviations are shown in Table 1. The analysis of variance revealed a significant difference, $F(3, 16) = 8.33, p < .05$.

TABLE 1

Amount of time (seconds) the stimulus was endured

	Placebo	Drug A	Drug B	Drug C
M	1.00	2.00	4.00	5.00
SD	1.41	1.41	1.22	1.58

Note how the *F*-ratio is reported. In this example, degrees of freedom for between and within treatments are $df = 3, 16$, respectively. These values are placed in parentheses immediately following the symbol *F*. Next, the calculated value for *F* is reported, followed by the probability of committing a Type I error. Because H_0 has been rejected and alpha was set at .05, *p* is *less than* .05. ❑

ON THE COMPUTER

BECAUSE IT requires extensive calculations, it is common for an analysis of variance to be performed on a computer. Figure 13.8 shows the printouts from computer analysis of the data from Example 13.1 using the SPSS and the Minitab versions of ANOVA. You should be able to identify and understand most of the elements in each printout, especially if you refer to the calculations we performed in Example 13.1. A few specific elements have been highlighted and numbered and are discussed in the following list.

① Both printouts include an ANOVA summary table showing the *SS*, *df*, and *MS* values as well as the *F*-ratio and an exact probability, *p*. As noted in previous computer versions of a hypothesis test, the computer calculates the exact probability of a Type I error instead of using an α level. In this case, $p = .001$ (or $p = .0015$).

② Both printouts provide summary statistics (including the mean and standard deviation) for all four samples. The summaries also present 95% confidence interval estimates for the four treatment means. SPSS lists an upper and lower limit for each confidence interval and Minitab provides a graphic display of the confidence intervals.

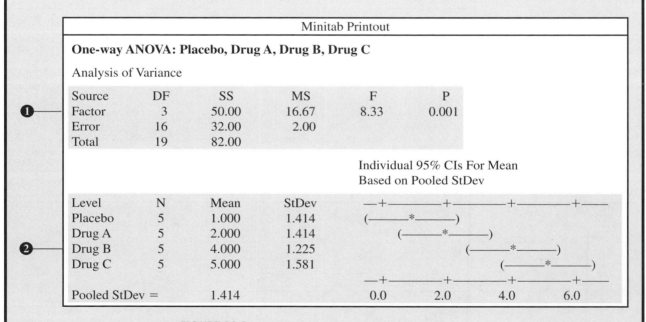

FIGURE 13.8

Computer printouts showing the analysis of variance output from the Minitab program (above) and the SPSS program (opposite). Both printouts show the results for the data that were analyzed in Example 13.1. The highlighted and numbered sections in each printout are discussed in the text.

EFFECT SIZE   As we have noted previously, a *significant* mean difference simply indicates that the difference observed in the sample data is very unlikely to have occurred just by chance. Thus, the term significant does not necessarily mean *large,* it simply means larger than chance. To provide an indication of how large the effect actually is, it is rec-

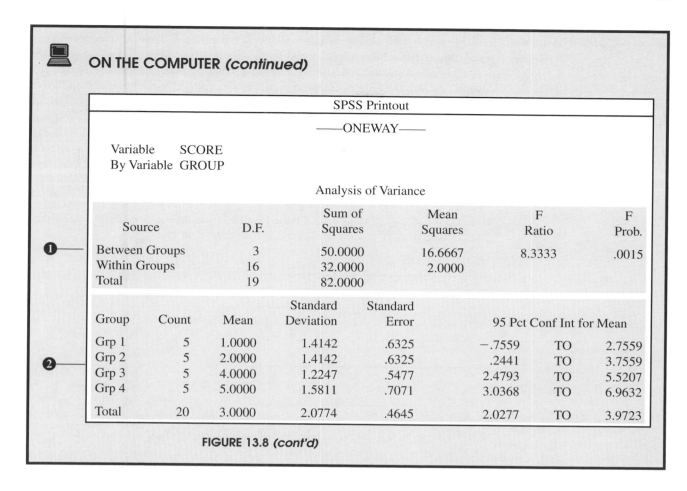

ON THE COMPUTER *(continued)*

SPSS Printout

——ONEWAY——

Variable   SCORE
By Variable GROUP

Analysis of Variance

Source	D.F.	Sum of Squares	Mean Squares	F Ratio	F Prob.
Between Groups	3	50.0000	16.6667	8.3333	.0015
Within Groups	16	32.0000	2.0000		
Total	19	82.0000			

Group	Count	Mean	Standard Deviation	Standard Error	95 Pct Conf Int for Mean		
Grp 1	5	1.0000	1.4142	.6325	−.7559	TO	2.7559
Grp 2	5	2.0000	1.4142	.6325	.2441	TO	3.7559
Grp 3	5	4.0000	1.2247	.5477	2.4793	TO	5.5207
Grp 4	5	5.0000	1.5811	.7071	3.0368	TO	6.9632
Total	20	3.0000	2.0774	.4645	2.0277	TO	3.9723

FIGURE 13.8 *(cont'd)*

ommended that researchers report a measure of effect size in addition to the measure of significance.

For analysis of variance, the simplest and most direct way to measure effect size is to compute r^2, the percentage of variance accounted for. In simpler terms, r^2 measures how much of the differences between scores is accounted for by the differences between treatments. For analysis of variance, the calculation and the concept of r^2 is extremely straightforward.

This version of r^2 is often called η^2 (the Greek letter eta *squared).*

$$r^2 = \frac{SS_{\text{between}}}{SS_{\text{total}}}$$

(13.12)

Remember that SS_{total} is composed of two parts: SS_{between}, which measures the differences between treatments, and SS_{within}, which measures the difference inside the treatments. With this in mind, it should be clear that r^2 simply measures the proportion of the total variability that is accounted for by differences between treatments. For the data from Example 13.1, we obtain

$$r^2 = \frac{50}{82} = 0.61 \text{ or } 61\%$$

**A CONCEPTUAL VIEW
OF ANOVA**

Because analysis of variance requires relatively complex calculations, students encoun-tering this statistical technique for the first time often tend to be overwhelmed by the formulas and arithmetic and lose sight of the general purpose of the analysis. The fol-lowing two examples are intended to minimize the role of the formulas and shift your attention back to the conceptual goal of the ANOVA process.

E X A M P L E   1 3 . 2

The following data represent the outcome of an experiment using two separate samples to evaluate the mean difference between two treatment conditions. Take a minute to look at the data, and without doing any calculations, try to predict the outcome of an ANOVA for these values. Specifically, predict what values should be obtained for $SS_{between}$, $MS_{between}$, and the F-ratio. If you do not "see" the answer after 20 or 30 seconds, try reading the hints that follow the data.

Treatment I	Treatment II	
4	2	$N = 8$
0	1	$G = 16$
1	0	$\Sigma X^2 = 56$
3	5	
$T = 8$	$T = 8$	
$SS = 10$	$SS = 14$	

If you are having trouble predicting the outcome of the ANOVA, read the following hints, and then go back and look at the data.

Hint 1:   Remember that $SS_{between}$ and $MS_{between}$ provide a measure of how much difference there is *between* treatment conditions.

Hint 2:   Find the mean or total (T) for each treatment, and determine how much difference there is *between* the two treatments.

You should realize by now that the data have been constructed so that there is zero dif-ference between treatments. The two sample means (and totals) are identical, so $SS_{between} = 0$, $MS_{between} = 0$, and the F-ratio is zero.

Conceptually, the numerator of the F-ratio always measures how much difference exists between treatments. In Example 13.2, we constructed an extreme set of scores with zero difference. However, you should be able to look at any set of data and quickly compare the means (or totals) to determine whether there are big differences between treatments or small differences between treatments.

Being able to estimate the magnitude of between-treatment differences is a good first step in understanding ANOVA and should help you to predict the outcome of an analy-sis of variance. However, the *between-treatment* differences are only one part of the analysis. You must also understand the *within-treatment* differences that form the denominator of the F-ratio. The following example is intended to demonstrate the concepts underlying SS_{within} and MS_{within}. In addition, the example should give you a better understanding of how the between-treatment differences and the within-treatment differences act together within the ANOVA.

EXAMPLE 13.3   The purpose of this example is to present a visual image for the concepts of between-treatments variability and within-treatments variability. In the example, we will compare two hypothetical outcomes for the same experiment. In each case, the experiment uses two separate samples to evaluate the mean difference between two treatments. The following data represent the two outcomes, which we will call experiment A and experiment B.

Experiment A		Experiment B	
Treatment		Treatment	
I	II	I	II
8	12	4	12
8	13	11	9
7	12	2	20
9	11	17	6
8	13	0	16
9	12	8	18
7	11	14	3
$\overline{X} = 8$	$\overline{X} = 12$	$\overline{X} = 8$	$\overline{X} = 12$
$s = 0.82$	$s = 0.82$	$s = 6.35$	$s = 6.35$

The data from experiment A are displayed in a frequency distribution graph in Figure 13.9(a). In the figure, we have indicated the *between-treatments* difference by showing the distance between the two means. We also have represented the *within-treatment* differences by using the range of scores for each separate sample. Clearly, the between-treatments value is substantially greater than the within-treatments value. This observation is confirmed by computing the F-ratio for experiment A. (You may check the calculations by performing the ANOVA yourself.)

$$F = \frac{\text{between-treatments difference}}{\text{within-treatments differences}} = \frac{MS_{between}}{MS_{within}} = \frac{56}{0.667} = 83.96$$

An F-ratio of $F = 83.96$ is sufficient to reject the null hypothesis with $\alpha = .05$, so we conclude that there is a significant difference between the two treatments. Note that the statistical conclusion agrees with the simple observation that the data [Figure 13.9(a)] show two distinct sets of scores, and it is easy to see that there is a clear difference between the two treatment conditions.

The data from Experiment B present a very different picture. These data are shown in Figure 13.9(b). Again, the *between-treatments* difference is represented by the distance between the treatment means, and the *within-treatments* differences are indicated by the range of scores within each treatment condition. Now, the between-treatments

FIGURE 13.9

A visual representation of the between-treatments variability and the within-treatments variability that form the numerator and denominator, respectively, of the F-ratio. In (a), the difference between treatments is relatively large and easy to see. In (b), the same 4-point difference between treatments is relatively small and is overwhelmed by the within-treatments variability.

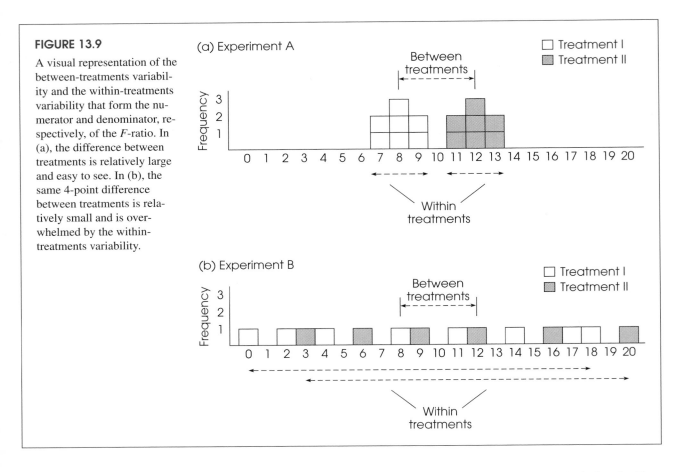

value is small in comparison to the within-treatments differences. Calculating the F-ratio confirms this observation.

$$F = \frac{\text{between-treatments difference}}{\text{within-treatments differences}} = \frac{MS_{\text{between}}}{MS_{\text{within}}} = \frac{56}{40.33} = 1.39$$

For experiment B, the F-ratio is not large enough to reject the null hypothesis, so we conclude that there is no significant difference between the two treatments. Once again, the statistical conclusion is consistent with the appearance of the data in Figure 13.9(b). Looking at the figure, the scores from the two samples appear to be intermixed randomly with no clear distinction between treatments.

AN EXAMPLE WITH UNEQUAL SAMPLE SIZES

In the previous example, all the samples were exactly the same size (equal n's). However, the formulas for ANOVA can be used when the sample size varies within an experiment. With unequal sample sizes, you must take care to be sure that each value of n is matched with the proper T value in the equations. You also should note that the general ANOVA procedure is most accurate when used to examine experimental data with equal sample sizes. Therefore, researchers generally try to plan experiments with equal n's. However, there are circumstances for which it is impossible or impractical to have an equal number of subjects in every treatment condition. In these situations, ANOVA still provides a valid test, especially when the samples are relatively large and when the discrepancy between sample sizes is not extreme.

The following example demonstrates an ANOVA with samples of different sizes.

EXAMPLE 13.4   A psychologist conducts a research study to compare learning performance for three species of monkeys. The animals are tested individually on a delayed-response task. A raisin is hidden in one of three containers while the animal is viewing from its cage window. A shade is then pulled over the window for 1 minute to block the view. After this delay period, the monkey is allowed to respond by tipping over one container. If its response is correct, the monkey is rewarded with the raisin. The number of trials it takes before the animal makes five consecutive correct responses is recorded. The researcher used all of the available animals from each species, which resulted in unequal sample sizes (n). The data are summarized in Table 13.5.

STEP 1   State the hypotheses, and select the alpha level.

$$H_0: \mu_1 = \mu_2 = \mu_3$$

H_1: At least one population is different from the others.

$$\alpha = .05$$

STEP 2   Locate the critical region. To find the critical region, we first must determine the df values for the F-ratio:

$$df_{total} = N - 1 = 20 - 1 = 19$$

$$df_{between} = k - 1 = 3 - 1 = 2$$

$$df_{within} = N - k = 20 - 3 = 17$$

The F-ratio for these data will have $df = 2, 17$. With $\alpha = .05$, the critical value for the F-ratio is 3.59.

STEP 3   Compute the F-ratio. First, compute SS for all three parts of the analysis:

$$SS_{total} = \Sigma X^2 - \frac{G^2}{N}$$

$$= 3400 - \frac{200^2}{20}$$

$$= 3400 - 2000$$

$$= 1400$$

TABLE 13.5

The performance of different species of monkeys on a delayed-response task

Vervet	Rhesus	Baboon	
$n = 4$	$n = 10$	$n = 6$	$N = 20$
$\overline{X} = 9$	$\overline{X} = 14$	$\overline{X} = 4$	$G = 200$
$T = 36$	$T = 140$	$T = 24$	$\Sigma X^2 = 3400$
$SS = 200$	$SS = 500$	$SS = 320$	

$$SS_{\text{between}} = \Sigma \frac{T^2}{n} - \frac{G^2}{N} = \frac{T_1^2}{n_1} + \frac{T_2^2}{n_2} + \frac{T_3^2}{n_3} - \frac{G^2}{N}$$

$$= \frac{36^2}{4} + \frac{140^2}{10} + \frac{24^2}{6} - \frac{200^2}{20}$$

$$= 324 + 1960 + 96 - 2000$$

$$= 380$$

$$SS_{\text{within}} = \Sigma SS_{\text{inside each treatment}}$$

$$= 200 + 500 + 320$$

$$= 1020$$

Finally, compute the *MS* values and the *F*-ratio:

$$MS_{\text{between}} = \frac{SS}{df} = \frac{380}{2} = 190$$

$$MS_{\text{within}} = \frac{SS}{df} = \frac{1020}{17} = 60$$

$$F = \frac{MS_{\text{between}}}{MS_{\text{within}}} = \frac{190}{60} = 3.17$$

STEP 4   Make a decision. Because the obtained *F*-ratio is not in the critical region, we fail to reject H_0 and conclude that these data do not provide evidence of significant differences among the three populations of monkeys in terms of average learning performance.

ASSUMPTIONS FOR THE INDEPENDENT-MEASURES ANOVA

The independent-measures ANOVA requires the same three assumptions that were necessary for the independent-measures *t* hypothesis test:

1. The observations within each sample must be independent (see page 184).
2. The populations from which the samples are selected must be normal.
3. The populations from which the samples are selected must have equal variances (homogeneity of variance).

Ordinarily, researchers are not overly concerned with the assumption of normality, especially when large samples are used, unless there are strong reasons to suspect that the assumption has not been satisfied. The assumption of homogeneity of variance is an important one. If a researcher suspects that it has been violated, it can be tested by Hartley's *F*-max test for homogeneity of variance (Chapter 10, page 240).

LEARNING CHECK   1. The following data summarize the results of an experiment using three separate samples to compare three treatment conditions:

Treatment 1	Treatment 2	Treatment 3	
$n = 5$	$n = 5$	$n = 5$	$\Sigma X^2 = 325$
$T = 5$	$T = 10$	$T = 30$	
$SS = 45$	$SS = 25$	$SS = 50$	

Do these data provide evidence of any significant mean differences among the treatments? Test with $\alpha = .05$.

2. A researcher reports an F-ratio with $df = 2, 30$ for an independent-measures analysis of variance. How many treatment conditions were compared in the experiment? How many subjects participated in the experiment?

ANSWERS   1. The following summary table presents the results of the analysis:

Source	SS	df	MS	
Between	70	2	35	$F = 3.5$
Within	120	12	10	
Total	190	14		

The critical value for F is 3.88. The obtained value for F is not in the critical region, and we fail to reject H_0.

3. There were 3 treatment conditions ($df_{between} = k - 1 = 2$). A total of $N = 33$ individuals participated ($df_{within} = 30 = N - k$). ◆

13.6 POST HOC TESTS

As noted earlier, the primary advantage of ANOVA (compared to t tests) is it allows researchers to test for significant mean differences when there are *more than two* treatment conditions. Analysis of variance accomplishes this feat by comparing all the individual mean differences simultaneously within a single test. Unfortunately, the process of combining several mean differences into a single test statistic creates some difficulty when it is time to interpret the outcome of the test. Specifically, when you obtain a significant F-ratio (reject H_0), it simply indicates that somewhere among the entire set of mean differences there is at least one that is greater than would be expected by chance. In other words, the overall F-ratio only tells you that a significant difference exists; it does not tell exactly which means are significantly different and which are not.

Consider, for example, a research study that uses three samples to compare three treatment conditions. Suppose that the three sample means are $\overline{X}_1 = 3$, $\overline{X}_2 = 5$, and $\overline{X}_3 = 10$. In this hypothetical study there are three mean differences:

1. There is a 2-point difference between $\overline{X}_1$ and $\overline{X}_2$.
2. There is a 5-point difference between $\overline{X}_2$ and $\overline{X}_3$.
3. There is a 7-point difference between $\overline{X}_1$ and $\overline{X}_3$.

If an analysis of variance was used to evaluate these data, a significant F-ratio would indicate that at least one of the sample mean differences is too large to be reasonably explained just by chance and therefore indicates a significant difference between treatments. In this example, the 7-point difference is the biggest of the three and, therefore, it must indicate a significant difference between the first treatment and the third treatment ($\mu_1 \neq \mu_3$). But what about the 5-point difference? Is it also large enough to be significant? And what about the 2-point difference between $\overline{X}_1$ and $\overline{X}_2$? Is it also significant? The purpose of *post hoc tests* is to answer these questions.

DEFINITION   *Post hoc tests* (or *posttests*) are additional hypothesis tests that are done after an analysis of variance to determine exactly which mean differences are significant and which are not.

As the name implies, post hoc tests are done after an analysis of variance. More specifically, these tests are done after ANOVA when

1. You reject H_0 and
2. There are three or more treatments ($k \geq 3$).

Rejecting H_0 indicates that at least one difference exists among the treatments. With $k = 3$ or more, the problem is to find where the differences are. Note that when you have two treatments, rejecting H_0 indicates that the two means are not equal ($\mu_1 \neq \mu_2$). In this case there is no question about *which* means are different and there is no need to do posttests.

POSTTESTS AND TYPE I ERRORS

In general, a post hoc test enables you to go back through the data and compare the individual treatments two at a time. In statistical terms, this is called making *pairwise comparisons*. For example, with $k = 3$, we would compare μ_1 versus μ_2, then μ_2 versus μ_3, and then μ_1 versus μ_3. In each case, we are looking for a significant mean difference. The process of conducting pairwise comparisons involves performing a series of separate hypothesis tests, and each of these tests includes the risk of a Type I error. As you do more and more separate tests, the risk of a Type I error accumulates and is called the *experimentwise alpha level* (see Box 13.1).

DEFINITION   The *experimentwise alpha level* is the overall probability of a Type I error that accumulates over a series of separate hypothesis tests. Typically, the experimentwise alpha level is substantially greater than the value of alpha used for any one of the individual tests.

We have seen, for example, that a research study with three treatment conditions produces three separate mean differences, each of which could be evaluated using a post hoc test. If each test uses $\alpha = .05$, then there is a 5% risk of a Type I error for the first posttest, another 5% risk for the second test, and one more 5% risk for the third test. Although the probability of error does not simply sum across the three tests, it should be clear that increasing the number of separate tests will definitely increase the total, experimentwise probability of a Type I error.

Whenever you are conducting posttests, you must be concerned about the experimentwise alpha level. Statisticians have worked with this problem and have developed several methods for trying to control Type I errors in the context of post hoc tests.

PLANNED VERSUS UNPLANNED COMPARISONS

Statisticians often distinguish between what are called *planned* and *unplanned* comparisons. As the name implies, *planned comparisons* refer to specific mean differences that are relevant to specific hypotheses that the researcher had in mind before the study was conducted. For example, suppose a researcher suspects that a 70° room is the best environment for human problem solving. Any warmer or colder temperature will interfere with performance. The researcher conducts a study comparing three different temperature conditions: 60°, 70°, and 80°. The researcher is predicting that performance in the 70° condition will be significantly better than in the 60° condition (comparison 1) and that 70° will be significantly better than 80° (comparison 2). Because these specific comparisons were planned before the data were collected, many statisticians would argue that the two specific posttests could be conducted without concern about inflating the risk of a Type I error. When the primary interest is in a few specific comparisons, the overall *F*-ratio for all the groups may be viewed as relatively unimportant and the overall ANOVA may not even be conducted. Instead, individual tests (*t* tests or two-group ANOVAs) could be done to evaluate the specific, planned comparisons. Although the planned comparisons could all be done with a standard alpha level, it is often recommended that researchers protect against an inflated experimentwise alpha level by dividing α equally among the planned comparisons. For example, with two comparisons, an alpha level of .05 would be divided equally so that α = .025 is used for each comparison and the overall risk of a Type I error is limited to .05 (.025 for the first test and .025 for the second). This technique for controlling the experimentwise alpha level is referred to as the Dunn test.

Unplanned comparisons, on the other hand, typically involve sifting through the data (a "fishing expedition") by conducting a large number of comparisons in the hope that a significant difference will turn up. In this situation it is necessary that a researcher take deliberate steps to limit the risk of a Type I error. Fortunately, many different procedures for conducting post hoc tests have been developed, each using its own technique to control the experimentwise alpha level. We will examine two commonly used procedures: Tukey's HSD test and the Scheffé test. Incidentally, the safest plan (and the author's recommendation) for posttests is to use one of the special procedures (such as Tukey or Scheffé) for *all* posttests whether they are planned or unplanned.

TUKEY'S HONESTLY SIGNIFICANT DIFFERENCE (HSD) TEST

The first post hoc test we will consider is Tukey's HSD test. We have selected Tukey's HSD test because it is a commonly used test in psychological research. Tukey's test allows you to compute a single value that determines the minimum difference between treatment means that is necessary for significance. This value, called the *honestly significant difference,* or HSD, is then used to compare any two treatment conditions. If the mean difference exceeds Tukey's HSD, you conclude that there is a significant difference between the treatments. Otherwise, you cannot conclude that the treatments are significantly different. The formula for Tukey's HSD is

$$HSD = q\sqrt{\frac{MS_{\text{within}}}{n}}$$

(13.13)

The *q* value used in Tukey's HSD test is called a Studentized range statistic.

where the value of *q* is found in Table B.5 (Appendix B, p. A-32), MS_{within} is the within-treatments variance from the ANOVA, and *n* is the number of scores in each treatment. Tukey's test requires that the sample size, *n*, be the same for all treatments. To locate the appropriate value of *q*, you must know the number of treatments in the overall experiment (k) and the degrees of freedom for MS_{within} (the error term in the F-ratio) and select an alpha level (generally the same α used for the ANOVA).

EXAMPLE 13.5

To demonstrate the procedure for conducting post hoc tests with Tukey's HSD, we will use the hypothetical data shown in Table 13.6. The data represent the results of a study comparing scores in three different treatment conditions. Note that the table displays summary statistics for each sample and the results from the overall ANOVA.

TABLE 13.6

Hypothetical results from a research study comparing three treatment conditions. Summary statistics are presented for each treatment along with the outcome from the analysis of variance.

Treatment A	Treatment B	Treatment C	Source	SS	df	MS
			Between	73.19	2	36.60
$n = 9$	$n = 9$	$n = 9$	Within	96.00	24	4.00
$T = 27$	$T = 49$	$T = 63$	Total	169.19	26	
$\overline{X} = 3.00$	$\overline{X} = 5.44$	$\overline{X} = 7.00$	Overall $F(2, 24) = 9.14$			

With $\alpha = .05$ and $k = 3$ treatments, the value of q for the test is $q = 3.53$ (check the table). Therefore, Tukey's HSD is

$$HSD = q\sqrt{\frac{MS_{within}}{n}} = 3.53\sqrt{\frac{4.00}{9}} = 2.36$$

Thus, the mean difference between any two samples must be at least 2.36 to be significant. Using this value, we can make the following conclusions:

1. Treatment A is significantly different from Treatment B ($\overline{X}_A - \overline{X}_B = 2.44$).
2. Treatment A is also significantly different from Treatment C ($\overline{X}_A - \overline{X}_C = 4.00$).
3. Treatment B is not significantly different from Treatment C ($\overline{X}_B - \overline{X}_C = 1.56$).

THE SCHEFFÉ TEST

Because it uses an extremely cautious method for reducing the risk of a Type I error, the *Scheffé test* has the distinction of being one of the safest of all possible post hoc tests. The Scheffé test uses an F-ratio to test for a significant difference between any two treatment conditions. The numerator of the F-ratio is an MS between treatments that is calculated using *only the two treatments you want to compare*. The denominator is the same MS within treatments that was used for the overall ANOVA. The "safety factor" for the Scheffé test comes from the following two considerations:

1. Although you are comparing only two treatments, the Scheffé test uses the value of k from the original experiment to compute df between treatments. Thus, df for the numerator of the F-ratio is $k - 1$.
2. The critical value for the Scheffé F-ratio is the same as was used to evaluate the F-ratio from the overall ANOVA. Thus, Scheffé requires that every posttest satisfy the same criterion that was used for the complete analysis of variance. The following example uses the data from Table 13.6 to demonstrate the Scheffé posttest procedure.

EXAMPLE 13.6

Remember that the Scheffé procedure requires a separate $SS_{between}$, $MS_{between}$, and F-ratio for each comparison being made. We begin with a comparison of treatment A ($T = 27$) versus treatment B ($T = 49$). The first step is to compute $SS_{between}$ for these two groups.

The value of G is obtained by adding the two treatment totals being compared. In this case, $G = 27 + 49 = 76$.

$$SS_{between} = \Sigma \frac{T^2}{n} - \frac{G^2}{N}$$

$$= \frac{27^2}{9} + \frac{49^2}{9} - \frac{76^2}{18}$$

$$= 81 + 266.78 - 320.89$$

$$= 26.89$$

Although we are comparing only two groups, these two were selected from a study consisting of $k = 3$ samples. The Scheffé test uses the overall study to determine the degrees of freedom between treatments. Therefore, $df_{between} = 3 - 1 = 2$, and the MS between treatments is

$$MS_{between} = \frac{SS_{between}}{df_{between}} = \frac{26.89}{2} = 13.45$$

Finally, the Scheffé procedure uses the error term from the overall ANOVA to compute the F-ratio. In this case, $MS_{within} = 4.00$ with $df_{within} = 24$. Thus, the Scheffé test produces an F-ratio of

$$F_{A \text{ versus } B} = \frac{MS_{between}}{MS_{within}} = \frac{13.45}{4.00} = 3.36$$

With $df = 2, 24$ and $\alpha = .05$, the critical value for F is 3.40 (see Table B.4). Therefore, our obtained F-ratio is not in the critical region and we must conclude that these data show no significant difference between treatment A and treatment B.

The second comparison involves treatment B ($T = 49$) versus treatment C ($T = 63$). This time the data produce $SS_{between} = 10.89$, $MS_{between} = 5.45$, and $F(2, 24) = 1.36$ (check the calculations for yourself). Once again the critical value for F is 3.40, so we must conclude that the data show no significant difference between treatment B and treatment C.

The final comparison is treatment A ($T = 27$) versus treatment C ($T = 63$). This time the data produce $SS_{between} = 72$, $MS_{between} = 36$, and $F(2, 24) = 9.00$ (check the calculations for yourself). Once again the critical value for F is 3.40, and this time we conclude that the data show a significant difference.

Thus, the Scheffé posttest indicates that the only significant difference is between treatment A and treatment C.

There are two interesting points to be made from the posttest outcomes presented in the preceding two examples. First, the Scheffé test was introduced as being one of the safest of the posttest techniques because it provides the greatest protection from Type I errors. To provide this protection, Scheffé simply requires a larger sample mean difference before it is willing to conclude that the difference is significant. In Example 13.5 we found that the difference between treatment A and treatment B was large enough to be significant according to Tukey's test, but this same difference failed to reach significance according to Scheffé (Example 13.6). The discrepancy between the results is an example of Scheffé's extra demands: The Scheffé test simply requires more evidence and, therefore, is less likely to make a Type I error.

The second point concerns the pattern of results from the three Scheffé tests in Example 13.6. You may have noticed that the posttests produce what are apparently contradictory results. Specifically, the tests show no significant difference between A and B and they show no significant difference between B and C. This combination of outcomes might lead you to suspect that there is no significant difference between A and C. However, the test did show a significant difference. The answer to this apparent contradiction lies in the criterion of statistical significance. The differences between A and B and between B and C are too small to satisfy the criterion of significance. However, when these differences are combined, the total difference between A and C is large enough to meet the criterion for significance.

LEARNING CHECK ◆

1. With $k = 2$ treatments, are post hoc tests necessary when the null hypothesis is rejected? Explain why or why not.

2. An analysis of variance comparing three treatments produces an overall F-ratio with $df = 2, 27$. If the Scheffé test was used to compare two of the three treatments, then the Scheffé F-ratio would also have $df = 2, 27$. (True or false?)

3. Using the data and the results from Example 13.1,
   a. Use Tukey's HSD test to determine if there is a significant mean difference between drug B and the placebo. Use $\alpha = .05$.
   b. Use the Scheffé test to determine if there is a significant mean difference between drug B and the placebo. Use $\alpha = .05$.

ANSWERS

1. No. Post hoc tests are used to determine which treatments are different. With only two treatment conditions, there is no uncertainty as to which two treatments are different.

2. True

3. a. For this test, $q = 4.05$ and HSD = 2.55. There is a 3-point mean difference between drug B and the placebo, which is large enough to be significant.
   b. The Scheffé $F = 3.75$, which is greater than the critical value of 3.24. Conclude that the mean difference between drug B and the placebo is significant. ◆

ON THE WEB

AFTER COMPLETING Chapter 13, you can test your knowledge with the practice quiz on the Wadsworth Web site at **www.wadsworth.com**. Also, the Web site contains a workshop called *One Way Anova* that reviews the basic concepts and analysis presented in this chapter. For more information about the quizzes and workshops, see p. 24.

SUMMARY

1. Analysis of variance (ANOVA) is a statistical technique that is used to test for mean differences among two or more treatment conditions. The null hypothesis for this test states that in the general population there are no mean differences among the treatments. The alternative states that at least one mean is different from the others.

2. The test statistic for analysis of variance is a ratio of two variances called an F-ratio. The variances in the F-ratio are called mean squares, or MS values. Each MS is computed by

$$MS = \frac{SS}{df}$$

3. For the independent-measures analysis of variance, the F-ratio is

$$F = \frac{MS_{between}}{MS_{within}}$$

The $MS_{between}$ measures differences between the treatments by computing the variability of the treatment means or totals. These differences are assumed to be produced by
   a. Treatment effects (if they exist)
   b. Differences due to chance

The MS_{within} measures variability inside each of the treatment conditions. Because individuals inside a treatment condition are all treated exactly the same, any differences within treatments cannot be caused by treatment effects. Thus, the within-treatments MS is produced only by differences due to chance. With these factors in mind, the F-ratio has the following structure:

$$F = \frac{\text{treatment effect} + \text{differences due to chance}}{\text{differences due to chance}}$$

When there is no treatment effect (H_0 is true), the numerator and the denominator of the F-ratio are measuring the same variance, and the obtained ratio should be near 1.00. If there is a significant treatment effect, the numerator of the ratio should be larger than the denominator, and the obtained F value should be much greater than 1.00.

4. The F-ratio has two values for degrees of freedom, one associated with the MS in the numerator and one associated with the MS in the denominator. These df values are used to find the critical value for the F-ratio in the F-distribution table.

5. When the decision from an analysis of variance is to reject the null hypothesis and when the experiment contained more than two treatment conditions, it is necessary to continue the analysis with a post hoc test, such as Tukey's HSD test or the Scheffé test. The purpose of these tests is to determine exactly which treatments are significantly different and which are not.

KEY TERMS

analysis of variance (ANOVA)	individual differences	between-treatments variance	post hoc tests
factor	experimental error	within-treatments variance	experimentwise alpha level
levels	F-ratio	mean square (MS)	Tukey's HSD test
treatment effect	error term	ANOVA summary table	Scheffé test

——— FOCUS ON PROBLEM SOLVING ———

1. The words and labels used to describe the different components of variance can help you remember the ANOVA formulas. For example, *total* refers to the total experiment. Therefore, the SS_{total} and df_{total} values are based on the whole set of N scores. The word *within* refers to the variability inside (within) the treatment groups. Thus, the value for SS_{within} is based on an SS value from each group, computed from the scores *within* each group. Finally, *between* refers to the variability (or differences) between treatments. The $SS_{between}$

component measures the differences between treatments (T_1 versus T_2, and so on), and $df_{between}$ is simply the number of T values (k) minus 1.

2. When you are computing SS and df values, always calculate all three components (total, between, and within) separately; then check your work by making sure that the *between-treatments* and *within-treatments* components add up to the *total*.

3. Remember that an F-ratio has two separate values for df: a value for the numerator and one for the denominator. Properly reported, the $df_{between}$ value is stated first. You will need both df values when consulting the F distribution table for the critical F value. You should recognize immediately that an error has been made if you see an F-ratio reported with a single value for df.

4. When you encounter an F-ratio and its df values reported in the literature, you should be able to reconstruct much of the original experiment. For example, if you see "$F(2, 36) = 4.80$," you should realize that the experiment compared $k = 3$ treatment groups (because $df_{between} = k - 1 = 2$), with a total of $N = 39$ subjects participating in the experiment (because $df_{within} = N - k = 36$).

—————— DEMONSTRATION 13.1 ——————————————————————

ANALYSIS OF VARIANCE

A human factors psychologist studied three computer keyboard designs. Three samples of individuals were given material to type on a particular keyboard, and the number of errors committed by each subject was recorded. The data are as follows:

Keyboard A	Keyboard B	Keyboard C	
0	6	6	$N = 15$
4	8	5	$G = 60$
0	5	9	$\Sigma X^2 = 356$
1	4	4	
0	2	6	
$T = 5$	$T = 25$	$T = 30$	
$SS = 12$	$SS = 20$	$SS = 14$	

Are these data sufficient to conclude that there are significant differences in typing performance among the three keyboard designs?

STEP 1   State the hypotheses, and specify the alpha level.
    The null hypothesis states that there is no difference among the keyboards in terms of number of errors committed. In symbols, we would state

$$H_0: \mu_1 = \mu_2 = \mu_3 \quad \text{(Type of keyboard used has no effect.)}$$

As noted previously in this chapter, there are a number of possible statements for the alternative hypothesis. Here we state the general alternative hypothesis:

$$H_1: \text{At least one of the treatment means is different.}$$

That is, the type of keyboard has an effect on typing performance. We will set alpha at $\alpha = .05$.

STEP 2   Locate the critical region.

To locate the critical region, we must obtain the values for $df_{between}$ and df_{within}.

$$df_{between} = k - 1 = 3 - 1 = 2$$

$$df_{within} = N - k = 15 - 3 = 12$$

The F-ratio for this problem will have $df = 2, 12$. Consult the F-distribution table for $df = 2$ in the numerator and $df = 12$ in the denominator. The critical F value for $\alpha = .05$ is $F = 3.88$. The obtained F ratio must exceed this value to reject H_0.

STEP 3   Perform the analysis.

The analysis involves the following steps:

1. Perform the analysis of SS.
2. Perform the analysis of df.
3. Calculate mean squares.
4. Calculate the F-ratio.

Perform the analysis of SS. We will compute SS_{total} followed by its two components.

$$SS_{total} = \Sigma X^2 - \frac{G^2}{N} = 356 - \frac{60^2}{15} = 356 - \frac{3600}{15}$$

$$= 356 - 240 = 116$$

$$SS_{within} = \Sigma SS_{inside\ each\ treatment}$$

$$= 12 + 20 + 14$$

$$= 46$$

$$SS_{between} = \Sigma \frac{T^2}{n} - \frac{G^2}{N}$$

$$= \frac{5^2}{5} + \frac{25^2}{5} + \frac{30^2}{5} - \frac{60^2}{15}$$

$$= \frac{25}{5} + \frac{625}{5} + \frac{900}{5} - \frac{3600}{15}$$

$$= 5 + 125 + 180 - 240$$

$$= 70$$

Analyze degrees of freedom. We will compute df_{total}. Its components, $df_{between}$ and df_{within}, were previously calculated (step 2).

$$df_{total} = N - 1 = 15 - 1 = 14$$

$$df_{between} = 2$$

$$df_{within} = 12$$

Calculate the MS values. The values for $MS_{between}$ and MS_{within} are determined.

$$MS_{between} = \frac{SS_{between}}{df_{between}} = \frac{70}{2} = 35$$

$$MS_{within} = \frac{SS_{within}}{df_{within}} = \frac{46}{12} = 3.83$$

Compute the F-ratio. Finally, we can compute F.

$$F = \frac{MS_{between}}{MS_{within}} = \frac{35}{3.83} = 9.14$$

STEP 4   Make a decision about H_0, and state a conclusion.
   The obtained F of 9.14 exceeds the critical value of 3.88. Therefore, we can reject the null hypothesis. The type of keyboard used has a significant effect on the number of errors committed, $F(2, 12) = 9.14, p < .05$. The following table summarizes the results of the analysis:

Source	SS	df	MS	
Between treatments	70	2	35	$F = 9.14$
Within treatments	46	12	3.83	
Total	116	14		

PROBLEMS

1. Explain why the expected value for an F-ratio is equal to 1.00 when there is no treatment effect.

2. Describe the similarities between an F-ratio and a t statistic.

3. Explain how each of the following would influence the magnitude of the F-ratio obtained from an analysis of variance:
a. Increasing the differences between sample means
b. Increasing the variance for each sample

4. Explain why you should use ANOVA instead of several t tests to evaluate mean differences when an experiment consists of three or more treatment conditions.

5. Describe *when* and *why* post hoc tests are used. Explain why you would not need to do post hoc tests for an experiment with only $k = 2$ treatment conditions.

6. For the following set of data, what value should be obtained for the variance within treatments ($MS_{within} = ?$). Explain your answer. *Note:* You should be able to answer without doing any serious calculations.

Treatments	
1	2
1	3
1	3
1	3
1	3
$T = 4$	$T = 12$
$SS = 0$	$SS = 0$

$G = 16$
$\Sigma X^2 = 40$

7. For the following set of data, what value should be obtained for the variance between treatments ($MS_{between}$ = ?). Explain your answer. *Note:* You should be able to answer without doing any serious calculations.

Treatments		
1	2	
4	2	$G = 18$
0	6	$\Sigma X^2 = 82$
5	1	
$T = 9$	$T = 9$	
$SS = 14$	$SS = 14$	

8. The following data represent the results from an independent-measures experiment comparing three treatment conditions. Use an analysis of variance with $\alpha = .05$ to determine whether these data are sufficient to conclude that there are significant differences between the treatments.

Treatments			
1	2	3	
2	6	6	$N = 12$
4	6	10	$G = 60$
2	2	10	$\Sigma X^2 = 408$
0	6	6	
$T = 8$	$T = 20$	$T = 32$	
$SS = 8$	$SS = 12$	$SS = 16$	

9. In the previous problem, the differences between treatments were significantly greater than would be expected by chance and the statistical decision was to reject the null hypothesis. For the following data, we have taken the original scores from Problem 8 and *reduced the differences between treatments*. Specifically, we increased the scores in treatment 1 by adding 1 point to each individual and we decreased the scores in treatment 3 by subtracting 1 point from each individual.
 a. Before you begin any calculations, predict how the changes in the data should influence the outcome of the analysis. That is, how will the F-ratio for these data compare with the F-ratio obtained in Problem 8?
 b. Use an analysis of variance with $\alpha = .05$ to determine whether there are any significant differences among the three treatments.

Treatments			
1	2	3	
3	6	5	$N = 12$
5	6	9	$G = 60$
3	2	9	$\Sigma X^2 = 368$
1	6	5	
$T = 12$	$T = 20$	$T = 28$	
$SS = 8$	$SS = 12$	$SS = 16$	

10. In Problem 8 the differences between treatments were significantly greater than would be expected by chance and the statistical decision was to reject the null hypothesis. For the following data, we have taken the original scores from Problem 8 and *increased the variance within treatments*. Specifically, we doubled the SS inside each of the three treatment conditions.
 a. Before you begin any calculations, predict how the changes in the data should influence the outcome of the analysis. That is, how will the F-ratio for these data compare with the F-ratio obtained in Problem 8?
 b. Use an analysis of variance with $\alpha = .05$ to determine whether there are any significant differences among the three treatments.

Treatments			
1	2	3	
0	7	4	$N = 12$
4	7	8	$G = 60$
4	1	8	$\Sigma X^2 = 444$
0	5	12	
$T = 8$	$T = 20$	$T = 32$	
$SS = 16$	$SS = 24$	$SS = 32$	

11. A researcher reports an F-ratio with $df = 3, 24$ for an independent-measures research study.
 a. How many treatment conditions were compared in the study?
 b. How many subjects participated in the entire study?

12. The following summary table presents the results of an ANOVA from an experiment comparing four treatment conditions with a sample of $n = 10$ in each treatment. Complete all missing values in the table. (*Hint:* Start with the *df* column.)

Source	SS	df	MS	
Between treatments	—	—	22	$F =$ —
Within treatments	—	—	—	
Total	138	—		

13. A pharmaceutical company has developed a drug that is expected to reduce hunger. To test the drug, three samples of rats are selected with $n = 12$ in each sample. The first sample receives the drug every day. The second sample is given the drug once a week, and the third sample receives no drug at all. The dependent variable is the amount of food eaten by each rat over a 1-month period. The data are analyzed by an analysis of variance, and the results are reported in the following summary table. Fill in all missing values in the table. (*Hint:* Start with the *df* column.)

Source	SS	df	MS	
Between treatments	—	—	—	$F = 6$
Within treatments	99	—	—	
Total	—	—		

14. A common science-fair project involves testing the effects of music on the growth of plants. For one of these projects, a sample of 24 newly sprouted bean plants is obtained. These plants are randomly assigned to four treatments, with $n = 6$ in each group. The four conditions are rock, heavy metal, country, and classical music. The dependent variable is the height of each plant after 2 weeks. The data from this experiment were examined using an ANOVA, and the results are summarized in the following table. Fill in all missing values.

Source	SS	df	MS	
Between treatments	90	—	—	$F =$ —
Within treatments	—	—	5	
Total	—	—		

15. A researcher compares emotionality in different breeds of 4-week-old dogs. Each pup is handled for 25 seconds and the duration of time spent struggling while being handled is measured for each pup. The data are as follows:

German shepherd	Cocker spaniel	American pit bull
4	2	8
3	0	4
5	2	6
4	0	6

a. Compute the means and standard deviations for each group.
b. Do differences in emotionality exist among the dog breeds? Use the .01 level of significance.
c. Compute the value of r^2 (the percentage of variance accounted for) for the data.

16. Suppose the same study described in Problem 15 was done, but the following results were obtained.

German shepherd	Cocker spaniel	American pit bull
6	0	10
1	4	2
7	0	5
2	0	7

a. Compute the means and standard deviations for each group. Compare these results with those of part (a) in Problem 15.
b. Do differences in emotionality exist among the dog breeds? Use the .01 level of significance.
c. Compare the outcome of part (b) of this problem to part (b) of Problem 15. Explain why there is a different outcome.
d. Compute the value of r^2 (the percentage of variance accounted for) for the data and compare your answer with the result from Problem 15.

17. Consider the study described in Problem 15, with the following results:

German shepherd	Cocker spaniel	American pit bull
2	2	5
1	0	1
3	2	3
2	0	3

   a. Compute the means and standard deviations for the three groups. Compare these results to those of part (a) in Problem 15.

   b. Do differences in emotionality exist among the dog breeds? Use the .01 level of significance.

   c. Compare part (b) of this problem with part (b) of Problem 15. Explain why the outcomes are different.

   d. Compute the value of r^2 (the percentage of variance accounted for) for the data and compare your answer with the result from Problem 15.

18. A clinical psychologist has noted that autistic children seem to respond to treatment better if they are in a familiar environment. To evaluate the influence of environment, the psychologist selects a group of 15 autistic children who are currently in treatment and randomly divides them into three groups. One group continues to receive treatment in the clinic as usual. For the second group, treatment sessions are conducted entirely in the child's home. The third group gets half of the treatment in the clinic and half at home. After 6 weeks, the psychologist evaluates the progress for each child. The data are as follows:

Clinic	Home	Both	
1	2	4	$N = 15$
1	7	1	$G = 45$
5	2	2	$\Sigma X^2 = 191$
2	4	2	
1	5	6	
$T = 10$	$T = 20$	$T = 15$	
$SS = 12$	$SS = 18$	$SS = 16$	

Do the data indicate any significant differences between the three settings? Test at the .05 level of significance.

19. A psychologist would like to examine the relative effectiveness of three therapy techniques for treating mild phobias. A sample of $N = 15$ individuals who display a moderate fear of spiders is obtained. These individuals are randomly assigned (with $n = 5$) to each of the three therapies. The dependent variable is a measure of reported fear of spiders after therapy. The data are as follows:

Therapy A	Therapy B	Therapy C	
8	3	1	$G = 45$
5	3	0	$\Sigma X^2 = 221$
5	0	1	
7	2	2	
5	2	1	
$T = 30$	$T = 10$	$T = 5$	
$SS = 8$	$SS = 6$	$SS = 2$	

   a. Do the data indicate that there are any significant differences among the three therapies? Test at the .05 level of significance.

   b. Use Tukey's HSD posttest to determine exactly which treatments are different. Test at the .05 level of significance.

20. A developmental psychologist is examining problem-solving ability for grade-school children. Random samples of 5-year-old, 6-year-old, and 7-year-old children are obtained, with $n = 3$ in each sample. Each child is given a standardized problem-solving task, and the psychologist records the number of errors. The data are as follows:

5-year-olds	6-year-olds	7-year-olds	
5	6	0	$G = 30$
4	4	1	$\Sigma X^2 = 138$
6	2	2	
$T = 15$	$T = 12$	$T = 3$	
$SS = 2$	$SS = 8$	$SS = 2$	

   a. Use the data to test whether there are any significant differences among the three age groups. Use $\alpha = .05$.

   b. Use the Scheffé test to determine which groups are different.

21. The following data represent three separate samples tested in three different treatment conditions.

   a. Using only the first two samples (treatments 1 and 2), use an ANOVA with $\alpha = .05$ to test for a mean difference between the two treatments.

   b. Now use all three samples to test for mean differences among the three treatment conditions, again using $\alpha = .05$.

   c. You should find that the first two treatments are significantly different (part a), but that there are no significant differences when the third treatment is included in the analysis (part b). How can you explain this outcome? (*Hint:* Compute the three sample means. How large is the mean difference when you are comparing only treatment 1 versus treatment 2? How large are the mean differences, on average, when you are comparing all three treatments?)

Treatments		
1	2	3
0	6	4
4	6	0
0	2	4
0	6	4
$T = 4$	$T = 20$	$T = 12$
$SS = 12$	$SS = 12$	$SS = 12$

22. Use an analysis of variance with $\alpha = .05$ to determine whether the following data provide evidence of any significant differences among the three treatments:

Treatment 1	Treatment 2	Treatment 3	
$n = 4$	$n = 5$	$n = 6$	$N = 15$
$T = 2$	$T = 10$	$T = 18$	$G = 30$
$SS = 13$	$SS = 21$	$SS = 26$	$\Sigma X^2 = 135$

23. First-born children tend to develop language skills faster than their younger siblings. One possible explanation for this phenomenon is that first-borns have undivided attention from their parents. If this explanation is correct, then it is also reasonable that twins should show slower language development than single children and that triplets should be even slower. Davis (1937) found exactly this result. The following hypothetical data demonstrate the relationship. The dependent variable is a measure of language skill at age three for each child. Do the data indicate any significant differences? Test with $\alpha = .05$.

Single child	Twin	Triplet
8	4	4
7	6	4
10	7	7
6	4	2
9	9	3

MORE ADVANCED ANALYSIS OF VARIANCE: REPEATED-MEASURES AND TWO-FACTOR DESIGNS

TOOLS YOU WILL NEED

The following items are considered essential background material for this chapter. If you doubt your knowledge of any of these items, you should review the appropriate chapter or section before proceeding.

- Independent-Measures Analysis of Variance (Chapter 13)

- Repeated-Measures Designs (Chapter 11)
  - Individual differences

CONTENTS

14.1   OVERVIEW

In the preceding chapter we introduced analysis of variance (ANOVA) as a hypothesis-testing procedure for evaluating mean differences. The specific advantage of ANOVA, especially in contrast to t tests, is that ANOVA can be used to evaluate the significance of mean differences in situations where there are more than two sample means being compared. However, the presentation of analysis of variance in Chapter 13 was limited to one specific type of research design. In particular, we discussed ANOVA only in relation to single-factor, independent-measures research designs. Recall that *single factor* indicates that the research study involves only one independent variable (or only one quasi-independent variable), and the term *independent-measures* indicates that the study uses a separate sample for each of the different treatment conditions being compared. In fact, ANOVA is an extremely flexible technique, with applications far beyond this single research design. In this chapter, we will begin to explore some more sophisticated research situations in which ANOVA is used. Specifically, we will introduce the following ANOVA topics:

1. **Repeated-Measures ANOVA**   It is possible to compare several different treatment conditions using a repeated-measures research design where the same set of subjects participates in every treatment. We will demonstrate how the analysis of variance procedure can be adapted to test for mean differences from a repeated-measures study.

2. **Two-Factor ANOVA**   Often, research questions are concerned with how behavior is influence by several different variables acting simultaneously. For example, a doctor may want to examine how measurements of cholesterol respond to different levels of diet and medication. In this situation, two variables are manipulated (diet and medication) while a third variable is observed. In statistical terminology, the research study has two independent variables or two factors. In the final section of this chapter, we will show how the general ANOVA procedure from Chapter 13 can be used to test for mean differences in a two-factor research study.

14.2   REPEATED-MEASURES ANALYSIS OF VARIANCE (ANOVA)

Chapter 13 introduced the general logic underlying ANOVA and presented the equations used for analyzing data from a single-factor, independent-measures research study. The term *independent-measures* indicates that the study uses a separate sample for each treatment condition being compared. In this section we will extend the analysis of variance procedure to research situations using *repeated-measures* designs. You should recall that a repeated-measures design uses a single sample, with the same set of individuals participating in all of the different treatment conditions. Table 14.1 shows two sets of data representing typical examples of single-factor, repeated-measures designs. Table 14.1(a) shows results from a study examining the effectiveness of a clinical therapy for treating depression. In this example, measurements of depression were obtained for a single sample of patients when they first entered therapy, when therapy is completed, and again 6 months later to evaluate the long-term effectiveness of the

TABLE 14.1

Two sets of data representing typical examples of single-factor, repeated-measures research designs

(a) Data from a quasi-experimental design evaluating the effectiveness of a clinical therapy for treating depression.

	Depression scores		
Subject	Before therapy	After therapy	6-month follow up
A	71	53	55
B	62	45	44
C	82	56	61
D	77	50	46
E	81	54	55

(b) Data from an experimental study evaluating the effects of different types of distraction on the performance of a visual detection task.

	Visual detection scores		
Subject	No distraction	Visual distraction	Auditory distraction
A	47	22	41
B	57	31	52
C	38	18	40
D	45	32	43

therapy. The goal of the study is to evaluate mean differences in the level of depression as a function of the therapy. Note that the three sets of data are all obtained from the same sample of subjects; this is the essence of a repeated-measures design.

You should recognize the data in Table 14.1(a) as an example of a quasi-experimental research design. In this case, a nonmanipulated variable (time) is the single factor in the study, and the three measurement times define the three levels of the factor. Another common example of this type of design is found in developmental phychology where subject age is the quasi-experimental variable. For example, a psychologist could examine the development of vocabulary skill by measuring vocabulary for a sample of 3-year-old children, then measuring the same children again at age 4 and at age 5. Again, this is a quasi-experimental study (age is not manipulated), with each subject measured three different times.

The single-factor, repeated-measures design can also be used with experimental research where the different treatment conditions are determined by manipulation of an independent variable. Table 14.1(b), for example, shows data from a research study examining visual perception. The subjects' task is to detect a very faint visual stimulus under three different conditions: (1) when there is no distraction, (2) when there is visual distraction from flashing lights, and (3) when there is auditory distraction from banging noises. Note that this study is an experiment because the researcher is manipulating an independent variable (the type of distraction). You should also realize that this is a repeated-measures study because the same sample is being measured in all three treatment conditions.

HYPOTHESES FOR THE REPEATED-MEASURES ANOVA

The hypotheses for the repeated-measures ANOVA are exactly the same as those for the independent-measures ANOVA presented in Chapter 13. Specifically, the null hypothesis states that for the general population there are no mean differences among the treatment conditions being compared. In symbols,

$$H_0: \mu_1 = \mu_2 = \mu_3 = \cdots$$

According to the null hypothesis, on average, all of the treatments have exactly the same effect. As a consequence of H_0, any differences that may exist among the sample means are not caused by the treatments but rather are simply due to chance.

The alternative hypothesis states that there are mean differences among the treatment conditions. Rather than specifying exactly which treatments are different, we will use a generic version of H_1, which simply states that differences exist:

$$H_1: \text{At least one treatment mean } (\mu) \text{ is different from the others.}$$

Note that the alternative says that, on average, the treatments do have different effects. Thus, the treatment conditions may be responsible for causing mean differences among the samples. As always, the goal of the analysis of variance is to use the sample data to determine which of the two hypotheses is more likely to be correct.

THE *F*-RATIO FOR THE REPEATED-MEASURES ANOVA

The test statistic for the repeated-measures analysis of variance has the same structure that was used for the independent-measures ANOVA in Chapter 13. In each case, the F-ratio compares the actual mean differences between treatments (numerator) with the amount of difference that would be expected just by chance (denominator). As always, the F-ratio uses variance to measure the size of the differences. Thus, the F-ratio for the repeated-measures ANOVA has the general structure

$$F = \frac{\text{variance (differences) between treatments}}{\text{variance (differences) expected by chance/error}}$$

A large value for the F-ratio indicates that the differences between treatments are greater than would be expected by chance or error alone. If the F-ratio is larger than the critical value in the F distribution table, we can conclude that the differences between treatments are *significantly* larger than chance.

Although the structure of the F-ratio is the same for independent-measures and repeated-measures designs, there is a fundamental difference between the two designs that produces a corresponding difference in the two F-ratios. Specifically, one of the characteristics of a repeated-measures design is that it eliminates or removes the variance caused by individual differences. This point was first made when we introduced the repeated-measures design in Chapter 11 (page 262), but we will repeat it briefly now.

First, recall that the term *individual differences* refers to subject characteristics such as age, personality, and gender that vary from one person to another and may influence the measurements that you obtain for each person. In some research designs it is possible that the subjects assigned to one treatment will have higher scores simply because they have different characteristics than the subjects assigned to another treatment. For example, the subjects in one treatment may be smarter or older or taller than those in another treatment. In this case, the mean difference between treatments is not necessarily caused by the treatments; instead, it may be caused by individual differences. With a repeated-measures design, however, you never need to worry about this problem. In a repeated-measures study, the subjects in one treatment are exactly the same as the subjects in every other treatment. In terms of the F-ratio for a repeated-measures design, the variance between treatments (the numerator) does not contain any individual differences.

A repeated-measures design also allows you to remove individual differences from the variance in the denominator of the F-ratio. Because the same individuals are measured in every treatment condition, it is possible to measure the size of the individual differences. In Table 14.1(a), for example, subject A has scores that average 10 points higher than subject B. Because there is a consistent difference between subjects across all the treatment conditions, we can be reasonably confident that the 10-point difference is not simply chance or random error, but rather is a systematic and predictable measure of the individual differences between these two subjects. Thus, in a repeated-measures research study, individual differences are not random and unpredictable, but instead they can be measured and separated from other sources of error.

Because individual differences can be eliminated or removed from a repeated-measures study, the structure of the final F-ratio can be modified as follows:

$$F = \frac{\text{variance/differences between treatments (without individual differences)}}{\text{variance/differences expected by chance (with individual differences removed)}}$$

The process of removing individual differences will be an important part of the procedure for a repeated-measures analysis of variance.

THE LOGIC OF THE REPEATED-MEASURES ANOVA

The general purpose of a repeated-measures analysis of variance is to determine whether the differences that are found between treatment conditions are significantly greater than would be expected by chance. In the numerator of the F-ratio, the between-treatments variance measures the size of the actual mean differences between the treatment conditions in a research study. The variance in the denominator of the F-ratio is intended to measure how much difference is reasonable to expect just by chance. In this section we will examine the elements that make up each of these two variances.

Variance between treatments: The numerator of the F-ratio   Logically, any differences that are found between treatment conditions can be explained by only two factors:

1. Treatment Effect. It is possible that the different treatment conditions really do have different effects and, therefore, cause the individuals' scores in one condition to be higher (or lower) than in another. Remember that the purpose for the research study is to determine whether or not a treatment effect exists.

2. Error or Chance. Even if there is no treatment effect, it is still possible for the scores in one treatment condition to be different from the scores in another. For example, suppose that I measure your IQ score on a Monday morning. A week later I come back and measure your IQ again under exactly the same conditions. Will you get exactly the same IQ score both times? In fact, minor differences between the two measurement situations will probably cause you to end up with two different scores. For example, for one of the IQ tests you might be more tired, or hungry, or worried, or distracted than you were on the other test. These differences can cause your scores to vary. The same thing can happen in a repeated-measures research study. The same individuals are being measured two different times and, even though there may be no difference between the two treatment conditions, you can still end up with different scores. Because these differences are unsystematic and unpredictable, they are classified as chance or experimental error.

Thus, it is possible that any differences (or variance) found between treatments could be caused by treatment effects, and it is possible that the differences could simply be due to chance. On the other hand, it is *impossible* that the differences between treatments are caused by individual differences. Because the same individuals are used in every treatment, the individual differences are *automatically eliminated* from the variance between treatments in the numerator of the *F*-ratio.

Variance due to chance/error: The denominator of the *F*-ratio   The denominator of the *F*-ratio is intended to measure the magnitude of the differences (or variance) that would be expected by chance alone. For a repeated-measures analysis of variance, this means that we must measure the variance due to random sources of error without including any individual differences. Remember: Individual differences are eliminated from the numerator of the *F*-ratio and now we must remove them from the denominator to keep the *F*-ratio balanced.

For the independent-measures ANOVA in Chapter 13, we used the variance within treatments for the denominator of the *F*-ratio. Briefly, the logic for using variance within treatments is as follows:

All the individuals within a treatment condition are treated exactly the same.

Therefore, nothing is being done to *cause* their scores to be different.

Therefore, any differences that exist within treatments must be just chance.

Unfortunately this logic does not work for a repeated-measures study. The problem is that the scores within each treatment come from different subjects who have different characteristics like age, IQ, and gender. Therefore, the variance within treatments includes individual differences that are not supposed to be included in the repeated-measures *F*-ratio. The solution to this problem is to measure the variance within treatments, just as we did in Chapter 13, but then *subtract out the individual differences*. The result is a measure of unsystematic error variance that does not include any individual differences. This is exactly what we want for the denominator of the repeated-measures *F*-ratio.

In summary, the *F*-ratio for a repeated-measures ANOVA has the same basic structure as the *F*-ratio for independent measures (Chapter 13) except that it includes no variability due to individual differences. The individual differences are automatically eliminated from the variance between treatments (numerator) because the repeated-measures design uses the same subjects in all treatments. In the denominator, the individual differences are subtracted out during the analysis. As a result, the repeated-measures *F*-ratio has the following structure:

$$F = \frac{\text{variance between treatments}}{\text{variation due to chance/error}}$$

$$= \frac{\text{treatment effect} + \text{chance/error (excluding individual diff's.)}}{\text{chance/error (excluding individual diff's.)}} \tag{14.1}$$

Where there is no treatment effect, the *F*-ratio is balanced because the numerator and denominator are both measuring exactly the same variance. In this case, the *F*-ratio should have a value near 1.00. When research results produce an *F*-ratio near 1.00, we conclude that there is no treatment effect and we fail to reject the null hypothesis. On the other hand, when a treatment effect does exist, it will contribute only to the numerator and should produce a large value for the F-ratio. Thus, a large value for F indicates that there is a real treatment effect and means that we should reject the null hypothesis.

LEARNING CHECK

1. What sources contribute to between-treatments variability for the repeated-measures design?

2. What sources of variability contribute to within-treatments variability?

3. **a.** Describe the structure of the F-ratio for a repeated-measures ANOVA.

   b. Compare it to the F-ratio structure for the independent-measures ANOVA (Chapter 13). How do they differ?

ANSWERS

1. Treatment effect, error/chance

2. Individual differences, error/chance

3. **a.** $F = \dfrac{\text{treatment effect } + \text{ error/chance}}{\text{error/chance}}$

   b. For the independent-measures ANOVA, individual differences contribute variability to both between-treatments variability and the error term of the F-ratio.

THE STRUCTURE OF THE REPEATED-MEASURES ANOVA

The overall structure of the repeated-measures analysis of variance is shown in Figure 14.1. Note that the ANOVA can be viewed as a two-stage process. In the first stage, the total variability is partitioned into two components: variance between treatments and variance within treatments. This stage is identical to the analysis that we conducted for an independent-measures design in Chapter 13.

The second stage of the analysis is intended to remove the individual differences from the denominator of the F-ratio. In the second stage, we begin with the variance within treatments and then measure and subtract out the individual differences. The remaining variance, often called the *residual variance* or *error variance,* provides a measure of how much variance is reasonable to expect by chance after the individual differences have been removed. The second stage of the analysis is what differentiates the repeated-measures ANOVA from the independent-measures ANOVA. Specifically, the repeated-measures design requires that the individual differences be removed.

DEFINITION

In a repeated-measures analysis of variance, the denominator of the F-ratio is called the *residual variance* or the *error variance* and measures how much variance is to be expected just by chance after the individual differences have been removed.

NOTATION AND FORMULAS FOR THE REPEATED-MEASURES ANOVA

We will use the data in Table 14.2 to introduce the notation for the repeated-measures ANOVA. The data represent the results of a study examining the effects of fatigue. A sample of $n = 5$ subjects is obtained, and each subject is given a reading comprehension test in the morning after a good night's sleep. The same subjects are tested again after they have been awake for 24 hours, and tested once more after 48 hours with no sleep. You should recognize that most of the notation in Table 14.2 is identical to the notation used in an independent-measures analysis (Chapter 13). For example, there are $n = 5$

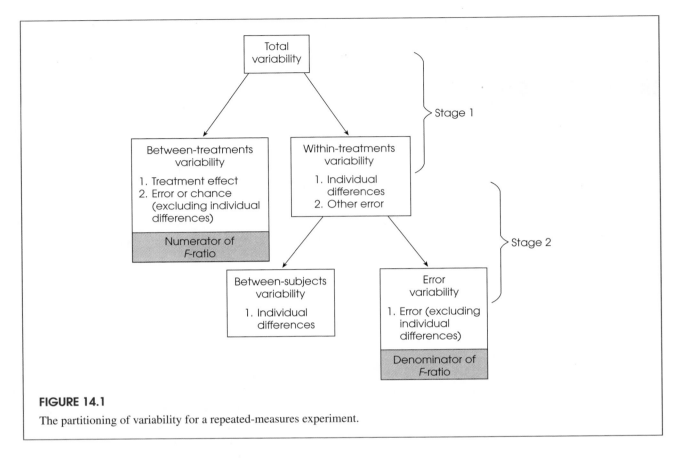

FIGURE 14.1

The partitioning of variability for a repeated-measures experiment.

subjects who are tested in $k = 3$ treatment conditions, producing a total of $N = 15$ scores that sum to a grand total of $G = 60$.

The repeated-measures ANOVA introduces only one new notational symbol. The letter P will be used to represent the total of all the scores for each individual in the study. You can think of the P values as "Person totals" or "Participants totals." In Table 14.2, for example, subject A had scores of 6, 4, and 2 for a total of $P = 12$. The P values will be used to define and measure the magnitude of the individual differences in the second stage of the analysis.

TABLE 14.2

Hypothetical data from a repeated-measures study examining the effects of fatigue on reading comprehension. Reading comprehension scores are obtained for each of five subjects under three different levels of fatigue.

	Reading comprehension scores				
Subject	Well rested	Awake 24 hours	Awake 48 hours	Person totals P	
A	6	4	2	12	$n = 5$
B	4	2	0	6	$k = 3$
C	5	3	1	9	$N = 15$
D	6	6	3	15	$G = 60$
E	9	5	4	18	$\Sigma X^2 = 314$
	$T_1 = 30$	$T_2 = 20$	$T_3 = 10$		
	$SS_1 = 14$	$SS_2 = 10$	$SS_3 = 10$		

EXAMPLE 14.1   The complete analysis of *SS* and degrees of freedom for the data in Table 14.2 is shown in Figure 14.2. The first stage of the analysis is identical to the independent-measures ANOVA presented in Chapter 13. (You should be able to perform all the calculations in the first stage and verify the numbers in Figure 14.2. See Figures 13.4 and 13.5 for reference.) The second stage of the analysis involves measuring the individual differences by computing a between-subjects *SS* and a between-subjects *df*, and then subtracting these values from the corresponding within-treatments values. This second stage is what differentiates the independent-measures ANOVA from the repeated-measures ANOVA.

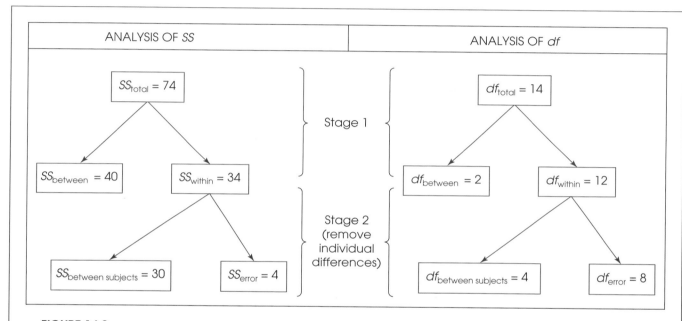

FIGURE 14.2

Results of the repeated-measures analysis for the data in Example 14.1. Stage 1 of the analysis is identical to an independent-measures ANOVA. In the second stage of the analysis, the individual differences are removed by computing a between-subjects *SS* and *df*, and subtracting these values from the corresponding within-treatment values. The calculations for stage 2 are discussed in the text.

STAGE 2 OF THE REPEATED-MEASURES ANALYSIS   The second stage of the analysis involves removing the individual differences from the denominator of the *F*-ratio. Because the same individuals are used in every treatment, it is possible to measure the size of the individual differences. For the data in Table 14.2, for example, subject B tends to have the lowest scores and subject E tends to have the highest scores. These individual differences are reflected in the *P* values, or person totals in the right-hand column. We will use these *P* values to calculate an *SS* between subjects in much the same way that we used the treatment totals, the *T* values, to compute the *SS* between treatments. Specifically, the formula for *SS* between subjects is

$$SS_{\text{between subjects}} = \Sigma \frac{P^2}{k} - \frac{G^2}{N}$$

(14.2)

14.1   THE RELATIONSHIP BETWEEN $SS_{\text{BETWEEN SUBJECTS}}$ AND $SS_{\text{BETWEEN TREATMENTS}}$

THE DATA for a repeated-measures study are normally presented in a matrix, with the treatment conditions determining the columns and the subjects defining the rows. The data in Table 14.2 provide an example of this normal presentation. The calculation of $SS_{\text{between treatments}}$ is intended to provide a measure of the differences between treatment conditions; that is, a measure of the mean differences between *columns* in the data matrix. For the data in Table 14.2, the column totals are 30, 20, and 10. These values are variable and $SS_{\text{between treatments}}$ measures the amount of variability.

The following table reproduces the data from Table 14.2, but now we have turned the data matrix sideways so that the subjects define the columns and the treatment conditions define the rows.

In this new format, the differences between the columns represent the between-subjects variability. The column totals are now P values (instead of T values) and the number of scores in each column is now identified by k (instead of n). With these changes in notation, the formula for $SS_{\text{between treatments}}$ is exactly the same as the formula for $SS_{\text{between subjects}}$.

	Subjects					
	A	B	C	D	E	
Well rested	6	4	5	6	9	$T = 30$
Awake 24 hours	4	2	3	6	5	$T = 20$
Awake 48 hours	2	0	1	3	4	$T = 10$
	$P = 12$	$P = 6$	$P = 9$	$P = 15$	$P = 18$	

Note that the formula for the between-subjects SS has exactly the same structure as the formula for the between-treatments SS. In this case, we use the person totals (P values) instead of the treatment totals (T values). Each P value is squared and divided by the number of scores that were added to obtain the total. In this case, each person has k scores, one for each treatment. Box 14.1 presents another demonstration of the similarity of the formulas for SS between subjects and SS between treatments. For the data in Table 14.2,

$$SS_{\text{between subjects}} = \Sigma \frac{P^2}{k} - \frac{G^2}{N}$$

$$= \frac{12^2}{3} + \frac{6^2}{3} + \frac{9^2}{3} + \frac{15^2}{3} + \frac{18^2}{3} - \frac{60^2}{15}$$

$$= 48 + 12 + 27 + 75 + 108 - 240$$

$$= 270 - 240$$

$$= 30$$

The value of $SS_{\text{between subjects}}$ provides a measure of the size of the individual differences—that is, the differences between subjects. In the second stage of the analysis, we simply subtract out the individual differences to obtain the measure of error that will form the denominator of the F-ratio. Thus, the final step in the analysis of SS is

$$SS_{\text{error}} = SS_{\text{within treatments}} - SS_{\text{between subjects}} \qquad \text{(14.3)}$$

For the data in Table 14.2,

$$SS_{error} = 34 - 30 = 4$$

The analysis of degrees of freedom follows exactly the same pattern that was used to analyze SS. Remember that we are using the P values to measure the magnitude of the individual differences. The number of P values corresponds to the number of subjects, n, so the corresponding df is

$$df_{between\ subjects} = n - 1 \qquad\qquad (14.4)$$

For the data in Table 14.2, there are $n = 5$ subjects and

$$df_{between\ subjects} = 5 - 1 = 4$$

Next, we subtract the individual differences from the within-subjects component to obtain a measure of error. In terms of degrees of freedom,

$$df_{error} = df_{within\ treatments} - df_{between\ subjects} \qquad\qquad (14.5)$$

For the data in Table 14.2,

$$df_{error} = 12 - 4 = 8$$

Remember: The purpose for the second stage of the analysis is to measure the individual differences and then remove the individual differences from the denominator of the F-ratio. This goal is accomplished by computing SS and df between subjects (the individual differences) and then subtracting these values from the within-treatments values. The result is a measure of variability due to error with the individual differences removed. This error variance (SS and df) will be used in the denominator of the F-ratio.

CALCULATION OF THE VARIANCES (MS VALUES) AND THE F-RATIO

The final calculation in the analysis is the F-ratio, which is a ratio of two variances. Each variance is called a mean square or MS and is obtained by dividing the appropriate SS by its corresponding df value. The MS in the numerator of the F-ratio measures the size of the differences between treatments and is calculated as

$$MS_{between\ treatments} = \frac{SS_{between\ treatments}}{df_{between\ treatments}} \qquad\qquad (14.6)$$

For the data in Table 14.2,

$$MS_{between\ treatments} = \frac{40}{2} = 20$$

The denominator of the F-ratio measures how much difference is reasonable to expect just by chance, after the individual differences have been removed. This is the error variance or the residual obtained in stage 2 of the analysis.

$$MS_{error} = \frac{SS_{error}}{df_{error}} \qquad\qquad (14.7)$$

For the data in Table 14.2,

$$MS_{error} = \frac{4}{8} = 0.50$$

Finally, the F-ratio is computed as

$$F = \frac{MS_{between\ treatments}}{MS_{error}} \qquad\qquad (14.8)$$

For the data in Table 14.2,

$$F = \frac{20}{0.50} = 40.00$$

Once again you should note that the repeated-measures ANOVA uses MS_{error} in the denominator of the F-ratio. This MS value is obtained in the second stage of the analysis, after the individual differences have been removed. As a result, individual differences are completely eliminated from the repeated-measures F-ratio so that the general structure is

$$F = \frac{treatment\ effect\ +\ chance/error\ (without\ individual\ differences)}{chance/error\ (without\ individual\ differences)}$$

For the data we have been examining, the F ratio is $F = 40.00$, indicating that the differences between treatments (numerator) are 40 times bigger than you would expect just by chance (denominator). A ratio this large would seem to provide clear evidence that there is a real treatment effect. To verify this conclusion, you must consult the F-distribution table to determine the appropriate critical value for the test. The degrees of freedom for the F-ratio are determined by the two variances that form the numerator and the denominator. For a repeated-measures ANOVA, the df values for the F-ratio are reported as

$$df = df_{between\ treatments},\ df_{error}$$

For the example we have been considering, the F-ratio has $df = 2, 8$ ("degrees of freedom equals two and eight"). Using the F-distribution table (pages A-29–A-31) with $\alpha = .05$, the critical value is $F = 4.46$ and with $\alpha = .01$ the critical value is $F = 8.65$. Our obtained F-ratio, $F = 40.00$, is well beyond either of the critical values, so we can conclude that the differences between treatments are *significantly* greater than chance using either $\alpha = .05$ or $\alpha = .01$.

The summary table for the repeated-measures ANOVA from Example 14.1 is presented in Table 14.3. Although these tables are no longer commonly used in research reports, they provide a concise format for displaying all of the elements of the analysis.

TABLE 14.3

A summary table for the repeated-measures ANOVA for the data from Example 14.1.

Source	SS	df	MS	F
Between treatments	40	2	20.00	$F(2, 8) = 40.00$
Within treatments	34	12		
Between subjects	30	4		
Error	4	8	0.50	
Total	74	14		

IN THE LITERATURE
REPORTING THE RESULTS OF A REPEATED-MEASURES ANOVA

As described in Chapter 13 (page 319), the format for reporting ANOVA results in journal articles consists of

1. A summary of descriptive statistics (at least treatment means and standard deviations, and tables or graphs as needed)
2. A concise statement of the outcome of the analysis of variance

For the study in Example 14.1, the report could state:

> The means and standard deviations for the three fatigue conditions are shown in Table 1. A repeated-measures analysis of variance revealed a significant decrease in reading comprehension as sleep deprivation increased, $F(2, 8) = 40.00$, $p < .01$.
>
> **TABLE 1**
>
> Reading comprehension at different levels of sleep deprivation.
>
> | | Well rested | Awake 24 hours | Awake 48 hours |
> |-----|-------------|----------------|----------------|
> | M | 6.00 | 4.00 | 2.00 |
> | SD | 1.87 | 1.58 | 1.58 |

For the descriptive statistics, the APA format uses M, rather than $\overline{X}$, for the sample mean. Likewise, SD is used in place of s for the sample standard deviation. The report of the ANOVA results indicates a *significant* change. That is, the null hypothesis was rejected. Finally, the F-ratio specifies the degrees of freedom values (between-treatments $df = 2$, error $df = 8$), as well as the probability of committing a Type I error ($p < \alpha$ or $p < .01$). ❑

POST HOC TESTS WITH REPEATED MEASURES

Recall that ANOVA provides an overall test of significance for the treatment. When the null hypothesis is rejected, it indicates only that there is a difference between at least two of the treatment means. If $k = 2$, it is obvious where the difference lies in the experiment. However, when k is greater than 2, the situation becomes more complex. To determine exactly where significant differences exist, the researcher must follow the ANOVA with post hoc tests. In Chapter 13, we used Tukey's HSD and the Scheffé test to make these multiple comparisons among treatment means. These two procedures attempt to control the overall alpha level by making adjustments for the number of potential comparisons.

For a repeated-measures ANOVA, Tukey's HSD and the Scheffé test can be used in the exact same manner as was done for the independent-measures ANOVA, *provided* that you substitute MS_{error} in place of MS_{within} in the formulas and use df_{error} in place of df_{within} when locating the critical value in a statistical table. It should be noted that statisticians are not in complete agreement about the appropriate error term in post hoc tests for repeated-measures designs (for a discussion, see Keppel, 1973, or Keppel and Zedeck, 1989).

ON THE COMPUTER

FIGURE 14.3 shows two computer printouts for the repeated-measures analysis of variance for the data from Example 14.1. You should be able to relate most of the elements in each printout to the corresponding calculations and results in the example. A few specific elements are as follows:

1. You should recognize that the Minitab printout displays a summary table almost identical to Table 14.3 in the text. The printout, however, includes an *F* value and a *P* value for "subjects" that are not part of the normal analysis. Also note that the "treatment" *P*

value of 0.000 has been rounded off and would normally be reported as $p < .001$.

2. We have omitted most of the SPSS printout because it reports statistical results that are well beyond the scope of this text. Instead, we have focused on the portion of the printout that includes the test of significance. Specifically, the line beginning with FATIGUE reports the *SS*, *df*, *MS*, *F*-ratio, and *P* value for the fatigue factor. Again, note that a *P* value of .000 has been rounded off and normally would be reported as $p < .001$.

Minitab Printout

Two-way ANOVA: score versus treatment, subject

Analysis of Variance for score

Source	DF	SS	MS	F	P
treatment	2	40.000	20.000	40.00	0.000
subject	4	30.000	7.500	15.00	0.001
Error	8	4.000	0.500		
Total	14	74.000			

SPSS Printout (abridged)

EFFECT .. FATIGUE
Tests involving 'FATIGUE' Within-Subject Effect.

AVERAGED Tests of Significance for MEAS.1 using UNIQUE sums of squares

Source of Variation	SS	DF	MS	F	Sig of F
WITHIN+RESIDUAL	4.00	8	.50		
FATIGUE	40.00	2	20.00	40.00	.000

FIGURE 14.3

Computer printouts showing the repeated-measures ANOVA output from Minitab (top) and SPSS (bottom). Both printouts show the results for the data from Example 14.1. The printouts are discussed in the text.

LEARNING CHECK

1. $SS_{\text{within treatments}} - SS_{\text{between subjects}} =$ _____

2. What two *df* components are associated with the repeated-measures *F*-ratio? How are they computed?

3. For the following set of data, compute all of the SS components for a repeated-measures ANOVA:

Subject	Treatment 1	2	3	4	
A	2	2	2	2	$G = 32$
B	4	0	0	4	$\Sigma X^2 = 96$
C	2	0	2	0	
D	4	2	2	4	

4. Which two MS components are used to form the F-ratio of the repeated-measures ANOVA? How are they computed?

ANSWERS

1. SS_{error}

2. Between-treatments df and error df; $df_{\text{between treatments}} = k - 1$; $df_{\text{error}} = (N - k) - (n - 1)$

3. $SS_{\text{total}} = 32$, $SS_{\text{between treatments}} = 10$, $SS_{\text{within treatments}} = 22$, $SS_{\text{between subjects}} = 8$, $SS_{\text{error}} = 14$

4. Between-treatments MS and error MS;

$$MS_{\text{between treatments}} = \frac{SS_{\text{between treatments}}}{df_{\text{between treatments}}}$$

$$MS_{\text{error}} = \frac{SS_{\text{error}}}{df_{\text{error}}}$$

◆

14.3 TWO-FACTOR ANALYSIS OF VARIANCE (INDEPENDENT MEASURES)

In most research situations, the goal is to examine the relationship between two variables. Typically, the research study will attempt to isolate the two variables in order to eliminate or reduce the influence of any outside variables that may distort the relationship being studied. A typical experiment, for example, will focus on one independent variable (which is expected to influence behavior) and one dependent variable (which is a measure of the behavior). In real life, however, variables rarely exist in isolation. That is, behavior usually is influenced by a variety of different variables acting and interacting simultaneously. To examine these more complex, real-life situations, researchers often design research studies that include more than one independent variable. Thus, researchers will systematically change two (or more) variables and then observe how the changes influence another (dependent) variable.

In the preceding chapter, we examined analysis of variance for *single-factor* research designs—that is, designs that included only one independent variable or only one quasi-independent variable. When a research study involves more than one factor, it is called a *factorial design*. In this chapter, we consider the simplest version of a factorial design. Specifically, we will examine analysis of variance as it applies to research studies with exactly two factors. In addition, we will limit our discussion to studies that use a separate sample for each treatment condition—that is, independent-measures designs. Finally, we will consider research designs only where the sample size (n) is the same for all treatment conditions. In the terminology of ANOVA, this chapter will examine *two-factor, independent-measures, equal n designs.* The following example demonstrates the general structure of this kind of research study.

EXAMPLE 14.2   Most of us find it difficult to think clearly or to work efficiently on hot summer days. If you listen to people discussing this problem, you will occasionally hear comments like "It's not the heat; it's the humidity." To evaluate this claim scientifically, you would need to design a study in which both heat and humidity are manipulated within the same experiment and then observe behavior under a variety of different heat and humidity combinations. Table 14.4 shows the structure of a hypothetical study intended to examine the heat-versus-humidity question. Note that the study involves two independent variables: The temperature (heat) is varied from 70° to 80° to 90°, and the humidity is varied from low to high. The two independent variables are used to create a *matrix* with the different values of temperature defining the columns and the different levels of humidity defining the rows. The resulting two-by-three matrix shows six different combinations of the variables, producing six treatment conditions. Thus, the research study would require six separate samples, one for each of the *cells* or boxes in the matrix. The dependent variable for our study would be a measure of thinking/working proficiency (such as performance on a problem-solving task) for people observed in each of the six conditions.

TABLE 14.4

The structure of a two-factor experiment presented as a matrix. The factors are humidity and temperature. There are two levels for the humidity factor (low and high), and there are three levels for the temperature factor (70°, 80°, and 90°).

		Factor *B*: Temperature		
		70° room	80° room	90° room
Factor *A*: humidity	Low humidity	Scores for $n = 15$ subjects tested in a 70° room with low humidity	Scores for $n = 15$ subjects tested in an 80° room with low humidity	Scores for $n = 15$ subjects tested in a 90° room with low humidity
	High humidity	Scores for $n = 15$ subjects tested in a 70° room with high humidity	Scores for $n = 15$ subjects tested in an 80° room with high humidity	Scores for $n = 15$ subjects tested in a 90° room with high humidity

The two-factor analysis of variance will test for mean differences in research studies that are structured like the heat-and-humidity example in Table 14.4. For this example, the two-factor ANOVA tests for

1. Mean difference between the two humidity levels.

2. Mean differences between the three temperature levels.

3. Any other mean differences that may result from unique combinations of a specific temperature and a specific humidity level. (For example, high humidity may be especially disruptive when the temperature is also high.)

Thus, the two-factor ANOVA combines three separate hypothesis tests in one analysis. Each of these three tests will be based on its own F-ratio computed from the data. The three F-ratios will all have the same basic structure:

$$F = \frac{\text{variance (differences) between sample means}}{\text{variance (differences) expected by chance}}$$

As always in ANOVA, a large value for the F-ratio indicates that the sample mean differences are greater than chance. To determine whether the obtained F-ratios are *significantly* greater than chance, we will need to compare each F-ratio with the critical values found in the F-distribution table in Appendix B.

MAIN EFFECTS AND INTERACTIONS

As noted in the previous section, a two factor ANOVA actually involves three distinct hypothesis tests. In this section, we will examine these three tests in more detail.

Traditionally, the two independent variables in a two-factor experiment are identified as factor A and factor B. For the experiment presented in Table 14.4, humidity would be factor A, and temperature would be factor B. The goal of the experiment is to evaluate the mean differences that may be produced by either of these factors independently or by the two factors acting together.

MAIN EFFECTS

One purpose of the experiment is to determine whether differences in humidity (factor A) result in differences in performance. To answer this question, we will compare the mean score for all subjects tested with low humidity versus the mean score for all subjects tested with high humidity. Note that this process evaluates mean differences between the rows in Table 14.4.

To make this process more concrete, we have presented a set of hypothetical data in Table 14.5. This table shows the mean score for each of the treatment conditions (cells) as well as the mean for each column (each temperature) and for each row (humidity level). These data indicate that subjects in the low-humidity condition (the top row) obtained an average score of $\overline{X} = 80$. This overall mean was obtained by computing the average of the three means in the top row. In contrast, high humidity resulted in a mean score of $\overline{X} = 70$ (the overall mean for the bottom row). The difference between these means constitutes what is called the *main effect* for humidity, or the *main effect for factor A*.

Similarly, the main effect for factor B (temperature) is defined by the mean differences among columns of the matrix. For the data in Table 14.5, the two groups of subjects tested with a temperature of 70° obtained an overall mean score of $\overline{X} = 80$. Subjects tested with the temperature at 80° averaged only $\overline{X} = 75$, and subjects tested at 90° acheived a mean score of $\overline{X} = 70$. The differences among these means constitute the *main effect* for temperature, or the *main effect for factor B*.

TABLE 14.5

Hypothetical data from an experiment examining two different levels of humidity (factor A) and three different levels of temperature (factor B)

	70°	80°	90°	
Low humidity	$\overline{X} = 85$	$\overline{X} = 80$	$\overline{X} = 75$	$\overline{X} = 80$
High humidity	$\overline{X} = 75$	$\overline{X} = 70$	$\overline{X} = 65$	$\overline{X} = 70$
	$\overline{X} = 80$	$\overline{X} = 75$	$\overline{X} = 70$	

DEFINITION   The mean differences among the levels of one factor are referred to as the *main effect* of that factor. When the design of the research study is represented as a matrix with one factor determining the rows and the second factor determining the columns, then the mean differences among the rows describe the main effect of one factor, and the mean differences among the columns describe the main effect for the second factor.

You should realize that the mean differences among columns or rows simply *describe* the main effects for a two-factor study. As we have observed in earlier chapters, the existence of sample mean differences does not necessarily imply that the differences are *statistically significant*. In the case of a two-factor study, any main effects that are observed in the data must be evaluated with a hypothesis test to determine whether or not they are statistically significant effects. Unless the hypothesis test demonstrates that the main effects are significant, you must conclude that the observed mean differences are simply the result of sampling error.

The evaluation of main effects will make up two of the three hypothesis tests contained in a two-factor ANOVA. We will state hypotheses concerning the main effect of factor A and the main effect of factor B and then calculate two separate F-ratios to evaluate the hypotheses.

For the example we are considering, factor A involves the comparison of two different levels of humidity. The null hypothesis would state that there is no difference between the two levels; that is, humidity has no effect on performance. In symbols,

$$H_0: \mu_{A_1} = \mu_{A_2}$$

The alternative hypothesis is that the two different levels of humidity do produce different scores:

$$H_1: \mu_{A_1} \neq \mu_{A_2}$$

To evaluate these hypotheses, we will compute an F-ratio that compares the actual mean differences between the two humidity levels versus the amount of difference that would be expected by chance or sampling error.

$$F = \frac{\text{variance(differences) between the means for factor } A}{\text{variance (differences) expected by chance/error}}$$

$$F = \frac{\text{variance (differences) between row means}}{\text{variance (differences) expected by chance/error}}$$

Similarly, factor B involves the comparison of the three different temperature conditions. The null hypothesis states that overall there are no differences in mean performance among the three temperatures. In symbols,

$$H_0: \mu_{B_1} = \mu_{B_2} = \mu_{B_3}$$

As always, the alternative hypothesis states that there are differences:

$$H_1: \text{At least one mean is different from the others.}$$

Again, the F-ratio will compare the obtained mean differences among the three temperature conditions versus the amount of difference that would be expected by chance.

$$F = \frac{\text{variance(differences) between the means for factor } B}{\text{variance (differences) expected by chance/error}}$$

$$F = \frac{\text{variance (differences) between column means}}{\text{variance (differences) expected by chance/error}}$$

INTERACTIONS

In addition to evaluating the main effect of each factor individually, the two-factor ANOVA allows you to evaluate other mean differences that may result from unique combinations of the two factors. For example, specific combinations of heat and humidity may have effects that are different from the overall effects of heat or humidity acting alone. Any "extra" mean differences that are not explained by the main effects are called an *interaction between factors*. The real advantage of combining two factors within the same study is the ability to examine the unique effects caused by an interaction.

DEFINITION

An *interaction between two factors* occurs whenever the mean differences between individual treatment conditions, or cells, are different from what would be predicted from the overall main effects of the factors.

To make the concept of an interaction more concrete, we will reexamine the data shown in Table 14.5. For these data, there is no interaction; that is, there are no extra mean differences that are not explained by the main effects. For example, within each temperature condition (each column of the matrix) the subjects scored 10 points higher in the low humidity condition than in the high humidity condition. This 10-point mean difference is exactly what is predicted by the overall main effect for humidity.

Now consider the data shown in Table 14.6. These new data show exactly the same main effects that existed in Table 14.5 (the column means and the row means have not been changed). But now there is an interaction between the two factors. For example, when the temperature is 90° (third column), there is a 20-point difference between the low humidity and the high humidity conditions. This 20-point difference cannot be explained by the 10-point main effect for humidity. Also, when the temperature is 70° (first column), the data show no difference between the two humidity conditions. Again, this zero difference is not what would be expected based on the 10-point main effect for humidity. The extra, unexplained mean differences are an indication that there is an interaction between the two factors.

TABLE 14.6

Hypothetical data from an experiment examining two different levels of humidity (factor A) and three different temperature conditions (factor B). (These data show the same main effects as the data in Table 14.5, but the individual treatment means have been modified to produce an interaction.)

	70°	80°	90°	
Low humidity	$\overline{X} = 80$	$\overline{X} = 80$	$\overline{X} = 80$	$\overline{X} = 80$
High humidity	$\overline{X} = 80$	$\overline{X} = 70$	$\overline{X} = 65$	$\overline{X} = 70$
	$\overline{X} = 80$	$\overline{X} = 75$	$\overline{X} = 70$	

To evaluate the interaction, the two-factor ANOVA first identifies mean differences that cannot be explained by the main effects. After the extra mean differences are identified, they are evaluated by an F-ratio with the following structure:

$$F = \frac{\text{variance (mean differences) not explained by main efffects}}{\text{variance (differences) expected by chance/error}}$$

The null hypothesis for this F-ratio simply states that there is no interaction:

H_0: There is no interaction between factors A and B. All the mean differences between treatment conditions are explained by the main effects of the two factors.

The alternative hypothesis is that there is an interaction between the two factors:

H_1: There is an interaction between factors. The mean differences between treatment conditions are not what would be predicted from the overall main effects of the two factors.

MORE ABOUT INTERACTIONS

In the previous section, we introduced the concept of an interaction as the unique effect produced by two factors working together. This section will present two alternative definitions of an interaction. These alternatives are intended to help you understand the concept of an interaction and to help you identify an interaction when you encounter one in a set of data. You should realize that the new definitions are equivalent to the original and simply present slightly different perspectives on the same concept.

The first new perspective on the concept of an interaction focuses on the notion of independence for the two factors. More specifically, if the two factors are independent, so that one factor does not influence the effect of the other, then there will be no interaction. On the other hand, when the two factors are not independent, so that the effect of one factor is influenced by the other, then there is an interaction. You should realize that the notion of independence is consistent with our earlier discussion of interactions. If one factor influences the effect of the other, then unique combinations of the factors will produce unique effects.

DEFINITION   When the effect of one factor depends on the different levels of a second factor, then there is an *interaction between the factors.*

Returning to the data in Table 14.5, you will notice that the size of the humidity effect (top row versus bottom row) *does not depend on* the temperature. For these data, the change in humidity shows the same 10-point effect for all three levels of temperature. Thus, the humidity effect does not depend on temperature, and there is no interaction. Now consider the data in Table 14.6. This time, the effect of changing humidity *depends on* the temperature, and there is an interaction. At 70°, for example, there is no difference between the high and low humidity conditions. However, there is a 10-point difference between high and low humidity when the temperature is 80°, and there is a 20-point effect at 90°. Thus, the effect of humidity depends on the temperature, which means that there is an interaction between the two factors.

The second alternative definition of an interaction is obtained when the results of a two-factor study are presented in a graph. In this case, the concept of an interaction can

FIGURE 14.4

(a) Graph showing the data from Table 14.5, where there is no interaction. (b) Graph showing the data from Table 14.6, where there is an interaction.

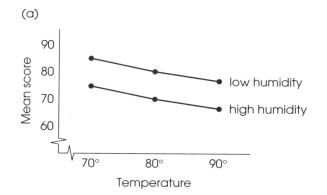

(a)

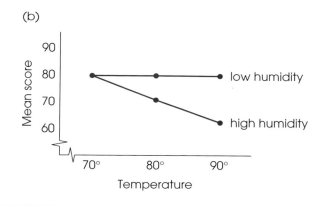

(b)

be defined in terms of the pattern displayed in the graph. Figure 14.4 shows the two sets of data we have been considering. The original data from Table 14.5, where there is no interaction, are presented in Figure 14.4(a). To construct this figure, we selected one of the factors to be displayed on the horizontal axis; in this case, the different levels of temperature are displayed. The dependent variable, mean level of performance, is shown on the vertical axis. Note that the figure actually contains two separate graphs: The top line shows the relationship between temperature and mean performance when the humidity is low, and the bottom line shows the relationship when the humidity is high. In general, the picture in the graph matches the structure of the data matrix; the columns of the matrix appear as values along the X-axis, and the rows of the matrix appear as separate lines in the graph.

For this particular set of data, Figure 14.4(a), note that the two lines are parallel; that is, the distance between lines is constant. In this case, the distance between lines reflects the 10-point difference in mean performance between high and low humidity, and this 10-point difference is the same for all three temperature conditions.

Now look at a graph that is obtained when there is an interaction in the data. Figure 14.4(b) shows the data from Table 14.6. This time, note that the lines in the graph are not parallel. The distance between the lines changes as you scan from left to right. For these data, the distance between the lines corresponds to the humidity effect—that is, the mean difference in performance for low humidity versus high humidity. The fact that this difference depends on temperature indicates an interaction between factors.

DEFINITION   When the results of a two-factor study are presented in a graph, the existence of nonparallel lines (lines that cross or converge) indicates an *interaction between the two factors.*

The $A \times B$ interaction typically is called "*A* by *B*" interaction. If there is an interaction of temperature and humidity, it may be called the "temperature by humidity" interaction.

For many students, the concept of an interaction is easiest to understand using the perspective of interdependency; that is, an interaction exists when the effects of one variable *depend* on another factor. However, the easiest way to identify an interaction within a set of data is to draw a graph showing the treatment means. The presence of nonparallel lines is an easy way to spot an interaction.

LEARNING CHECK ◆ 1. Each of the following matrices represents a possible outcome of a two-factor experiment. For each experiment:

    a. Describe the main effect for factor *A*.

    b. Describe the main effect for factor *B*.

    c. Does there appear to be an interaction between the two factors?

Experiment I

	B_1	B_2
A_1	$\overline{X} = 10$	$\overline{X} = 20$
A_2	$\overline{X} = 30$	$\overline{X} = 40$

Experiment II

	B_1	B_2
A_1	$\overline{X} = 10$	$\overline{X} = 30$
A_2	$\overline{X} = 20$	$\overline{X} = 20$

2. In a graph showing the means from a two-factor experiment, parallel lines indicate that there is no interaction. (True or false?)

3. A two-factor ANOVA consists of three hypothesis tests. What are they?

4. It is impossible to have an interaction unless you also have main effects for at least one of the two factors. (True or false?)

ANSWERS 1. For Experiment I:

    a. There is a main effect for factor *A*; the scores in A_2 average 20 points higher than in A_1.

    b. There is a main effect for factor *B*; the scores in B_2 average 10 points higher than in B_1.

    c. There is no interaction; there is a constant 20-point difference between A_1 and A_2 that does not depend on the levels of factor *B*.

For Experiment II:

    a. There is no main effect for factor *A*; overall, the scores in A_1 and in A_2 both average 20.

    b. There is a main effect for factor *B*; overall, the scores in B_2 average 10 points higher than in B_1.

    c. There is an interaction. The difference between A_1 and A_2 depends on the level of factor *B*. (There is a $+10$ difference in B_1 and a -10 difference in B_2.)

2. True

3. The two-factor ANOVA evaluates the main effects for factor *A*, the main effects for factor *B*, and the interaction between the two factors.

4. False. The existence of main effects and interactions is completely independent. ◆

STRUCTURE OF THE TWO-FACTOR ANALYSIS

The two-factor ANOVA is composed of three distinct hypothesis tests:

1. The main effect of factor A (often called the A-effect). Assuming that factor A is used to define the rows of the matrix, the main effect of factor A evaluates the mean differences between rows.

2. The main effect of factor B (called the B-effect). Assuming that factor B is used to define the columns of the matrix, the main effect of factor B evaluates the mean differences between columns.

3. The interaction (called the $A \times B$ interaction). The interaction evaluates mean differences between treatment conditions that are not predicted from the overall main effects from factor A or factor B.

For each of these three tests, we are looking for mean differences between treatments that are larger than would be expected by chance. In each case, the magnitude of the treatment effect will be evaluated by an F-ratio. All three F-ratios have the same basic structure:

$$F = \frac{\text{variance (mean differences) between treatments}}{\text{variance (differences) expected by chance/error}}$$

The general structure of the two-factor ANOVA is shown in Figure 14.5. Note that the overall analysis is divided into two stages. In the first stage, the total variability is separated into two components: between-treatments variability and within-treatments variability. This first stage is identical to the single-factor analysis of variance introduced in Chapter 13 with each cell in the two-factor data matrix viewed as a separate treatment condition. The second stage of the analysis partitions the between-treatments variability into three components: differences attributed to factor A, differences attributed to factor B, and any remaining mean differences that define the interaction. These three components will form the basis for the three F-ratios in the analysis.

FIGURE 14.5

Structure of the analysis for a two-factor analysis of variance.

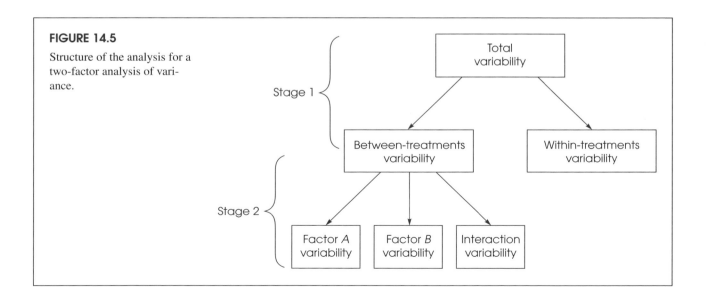

NOTATION AND FORMULAS FOR THE TWO-FACTOR ANOVA

EXAMPLE 14.3   The hypothetical data shown in Table 14.7 will be used to demonstrate the two-factor ANOVA. The data are representative of many studies examining the relationship between arousal and performance. The general result of these studies is that increasing the level of arousal (or motivation) tends to improve the level of performance. For very difficult tasks, however, increasing arousal beyond a certain point tends to lower the level of performance. (This relationship is generally known as the Yerkes–Dodson law). The data are displayed in a matrix where the levels of task difficulty make up the rows and the levels of arousal make up the columns. There are two levels of task difficulty (easy and difficult), which we have designated factor A, and three levels of arousal (low, medium, high), which we have designated as factor B. For the easy task, note that performance scores increase consistently as arousal increases. For the difficult task, on the other hand, performance peaks at a medium level of arousal and drops when arousal is increased to a high level. Note that the data matrix has a total of six *cells* or treatment conditions with a separate sample of $n = 5$ subjects in each condition. Most of the notation should be familiar from the single-factor ANOVA presented in Chapter 13. Specifically, the treatment totals are identified by T values, the total number of scores in the entire study is $N = 30$, and the grand total (sum) of all 30 scores is $G = 120$. In addition to these familiar values, we have included the totals for each row and for each column in the matrix. The goal of the ANOVA is to determine whether the mean differences observed in the data are significantly greater than would be expected just by chance.

The complete, two-factor analyses of SS and df for the data in Table 14.7 are shown in Figure 14.6. The first stage of the analysis is identical to the single-factor ANOVA presented in Chapter 13. (You should be able to perform these calculations and verify

TABLE 14.7

Hypothetical data for a two-factor research study comparing two levels of task difficulty (easy and hard) and three levels of arousal (low, medium, and high). The study involves a total of six different treatment conditions with $n = 5$ subjects in each condition.

		Factor B: Arousal level			
		Low	Medium	High	
	Easy	3	2	9	$T_{ROW1} = 90$
		1	5	9	
		1	9	13	
		6	7	6	
		4	7	8	
		$T = 15$	$T = 30$	$T = 45$	$N = 30$
		$SS = 18$	$SS = 28$	$SS = 26$	$G = 120$
Factor A: Task difficulty					$\Sigma X^2 = 840$
	Difficult	0	3	0	
		2	8	0	
		0	3	0	$T_{ROW2} = 30$
		0	3	5	
		3	3	0	
		$T = 5$	$T = 20$	$T = 5$	
		$SS = 8$	$SS = 20$	$SS = 20$	
		$T_{COL1} = 20$	$T_{COL2} = 50$	$T_{COL3} = 50$	

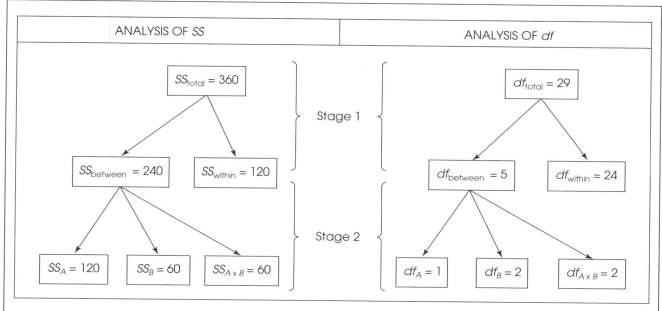

FIGURE 14.6

Results of the two-factor analysis of *SS* and *df* for the data in Example 14.3. The first stage of the analysis is identical to the single-factor analysis presented in Chapter 13. The second stage separates the difference between treatments into three separate components (factor *A*, factor *B*, and the interaction) that will generate the three *F*-ratios in the two-factor ANOVA.

the results shown in the figure. Remember that each of the six cells in the data matrix is treated as a separate treatment condition. See Figures 13.4 and 13.5 for reference.)

STAGE 2 OF THE TWO-FACTOR ANALYSIS

The second stage of the analysis is what differentiates the two-factor ANOVA from the single-factor ANOVA. Therefore, we will present a detailed demonstration of the calculations involved in stage 2.

In the second stage of the analysis we calculate a *SS* and a *df* for each of the two factors and for the interaction. For our hypothetical data, factor *A* defines the rows of the data matrix and factor *B* determines the columns. To compute the *SS* for factor *A*, we will calculate a between-treatment *SS* using the row totals exactly the same as we computed $SS_{\text{between treatments}}$ using the treatment totals (*T* values) earlier. For factor *A*, the row totals are 90 and 30, and each total was obtained by adding up 15 scores. Therefore,

$$SS_{\text{factor } A} = \Sigma \frac{T_{\text{ROW}}^2}{n_{\text{ROW}}} - \frac{G^2}{N} \tag{14.9}$$

For our data,

$$SS_{\text{factor } A} = \frac{90^2}{15} + \frac{30^2}{15} - \frac{120^2}{30}$$

$$= 540 + 60 - 480$$

$$= 120$$

Factor A involves two treatments (or two rows), easy and difficult, so the df value is

$$df_{\text{factor }A} = \text{number of rows} - 1 \tag{14.10}$$
$$= 2 - 1$$
$$= 1$$

Similarly, SS and df for factor B are computed using the column totals.

$$SS_{\text{factor }B} = \Sigma \frac{T^2_{\text{COL}}}{n_{\text{COL}}} - \frac{G^2}{N} \tag{14.11}$$

For our data, the column totals are 20, 50, and 50, and each total was obtained by summing 10 scores. Thus,

$$SS_{\text{factor }B} = \frac{20^2}{10} + \frac{50^2}{10} + \frac{50^2}{10} - \frac{120^2}{30}$$
$$= 40 + 250 + 250 - 480$$
$$= 60$$

$$df_{\text{factor }B} = \text{number of columns} - 1 \tag{14.12}$$
$$= 3 - 1$$
$$= 2$$

The $A \times B$ interaction is defined as the "extra" mean differences not accounted for by the main effects of the two factors. We will use this definition to find the SS and df values for the interaction by simple subtraction. Specifically, the between-treatments variability is partitioned into three parts: the A effect, the B effect, and the interaction (see Figure 14.5). We have already computed the SS and df values for A and B, so we can find the interaction values by subtracting to find out how much is left. Thus,

$$SS_{A \times B} = SS_{\text{between treatments}} - SS_{\text{factor }A} - SS_{\text{factor }B} \tag{14.13}$$

For our hypothetical data,

$$SS_{A \times B} = 240 - 120 - 60$$
$$= 60$$

Similarly,

$$df_{A \times B} = df_{\text{between treatments}} = df_{\text{factor }A} - df_{\text{factor }B} \tag{14.14}$$
$$= 5 - 1 - 2$$
$$= 2$$

MEAN SQUARES AND F-RATIOS FOR THE TWO-FACTOR ANALYSIS

The two-factor ANOVA consists of three separate hypothesis tests with three separate F-ratios. The denominator for each F-ratio is intended to measure the variance (differences) that would be expected just by chance. As we saw in Chapter 13, the within-treatments variance forms the denominator for an independent-measures design. Remember that inside each treatment all the individuals are treated exactly the same, which means any differences that occur are simply due to chance (see Chapter 13, page 304). The within-treatments variance is called a *mean square,* or *MS*, and is computed as follows:

$$MS_{\text{within treatments}} = \frac{SS_{\text{within treatments}}}{df_{\text{within treatments}}}$$

For the data in Table 14.7,

$$MS_{\text{within treatments}} = \frac{120}{24} = 5.00$$

This value will form the denominator for all three *F*-ratios.

The numerators of the three *F*-ratios all measured variance or differences between treatments: differences between levels of factor *A*, or differences between levels of factor *B*, or extra differences that are attributed to the $A \times B$ interaction. These three variances are computed as follows:

$$MS_A = \frac{SS_A}{df_A} \qquad MS_B = \frac{SS_B}{df_B} \qquad MS_{A \times B} = \frac{SS_{A \times B}}{df_{A \times B}}$$

For the data in Table 14.7, the three *MS* values are

$$MS_A = \frac{SS_A}{df_A} = \frac{120}{1} = 120 \qquad MS_B = \frac{SS_B}{df_B} = \frac{60}{2} = 30$$

$$MS_{A \times B} = \frac{SS_{A \times B}}{df_{A \times B}} = \frac{60}{2} = 30$$

Finally, the three *F*-ratios are

$$F_A = \frac{MS_A}{MS_{\text{within}}} = \frac{120}{5} = 24.00 \qquad F_B = \frac{MS_B}{MS_{\text{within}}} = \frac{30}{5} = 6.00$$

$$F_{A \times B} = \frac{MS_{A \times B}}{MS_{\text{within}}} = \frac{30}{5} = 6.00$$

To determine the significance of each *F*-ratio, we must consult the *F*-distribution table using the *df* values for each of the individual *F*-ratios. For this example, the *F*-ratio for factor *A* has $df = 1$ for the numerator and $df = 24$ for the denominator. Checking the table with $df = 1, 24$, we find a critical value of 4.26 for $\alpha = .05$ and a critical value of 7.82 for $\alpha = .01$. Our obtained *F*-ratio, $F = 24.00$ exceeds both of these values, so we conclude that there is a significant difference between the levels of factor *A*. That is, performance on the easy task (top row) is significantly different from performance on the difficult task (bottom row).

Similarly, the *F*-ratio for factor *B* has $df = 2, 24$. The critical values obtained from the table are 3.40 for $\alpha = .05$ and 5.61 for $\alpha = .01$. Again, our obtained *F*-ratio, $F = 6.00$, exceeds both values, so we can conclude that there are significant differences among the levels of factor *B*. For this study, the three levels of arousal result in significantly different levels of performance.

Finally, the F-ratio for the $A \times B$ interaction has $df = 2, 24$ (the same as factor B). With critical values of 3.40 for $\alpha = .05$ and 5.61 for $\alpha = .01$, our obtained F-ratio of $F = 6.00$ is sufficient to conclude that there is a significant interaction between task difficulty and level of arousal.

Table 14.8 is a summary table for the complete two-factor analysis of variance from Example 14.3. Although these tables are no longer commonly used in research reports, they provide a concise format for displaying all of the elements of the analysis.

TABLE 14.8

A summary table for the repeated-measures ANOVA for the data from Example 14.3

Source	SS	df	MS	F
Between treatments	240	5		
Factor A (difficulty)	120	1	120.0	$F(1, 24) = 24.00$
Factor B (arousal)	60	2	30.0	$F(2, 24) = 6.00$
$A \times B$ interaction	60	2	30.0	$F(2, 24) = 6.00$
Within treatments	120	24	5.0	
Total	360	29		

INTERPRETATION OF RESULTS FROM A TWO-FACTOR ANOVA

Because the two-factor analysis of variance involves three separate tests, you must consider the overall pattern of results rather than focusing on the individual main effects or the interaction. In particular, whenever there is a significant interaction, you should be cautious about accepting the main effects at face value (whether they are significant or not). A significant interaction can distort, conceal, or exaggerate the main effects.

Figure 14.7 shows the sample means obtained from the task difficulty and arousal study. Recall that the analysis showed that both main effects and the interaction were all significant. The main effect for factor A (task difficulty) can be seen by the fact that the scores on the easy task are generally higher than scores on the difficult task.

FIGURE 14.7

Sample means for the data in Example 14.3. The data are hypothetical results for a two-factor study examining how performance is related to task difficulty and level of arousal.

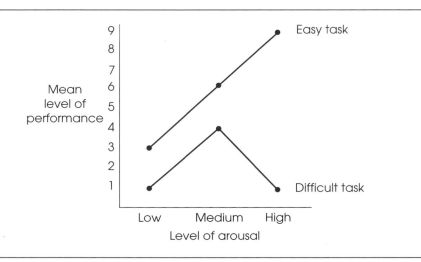

On the other hand, the main effect for factor *B* (arousal) is not that easy to see. Although there is a tendency for scores to increase as the level of arousal increases, this is not a completely consistent trend. In fact, the scores on the difficult task show a sharp *decrease* when arousal is increased from moderate to high. This is an example of the complications that can occur when you have a significant interaction. Remember that an interaction means that a factor does not have a uniformly consistent effect. Instead, the effect of one factor *depends on* the other factor. For the data in Figure 14.7, the effect of increasing arousal depends on the task difficulty. For the easy task, increasing arousal produces increased performance. For the difficult task, however, increasing arousal beyond a moderate level produces decreased performance. This interdependence between factors is the source of the significant interaction.

IN THE LITERATURE
REPORTING THE RESULTS OF A TWO-FACTOR ANOVA

The APA format for reporting the results of a two-factor analysis of variance follows the same basic guidelines as the single-factor report. First, the means and standard deviations are reported. Because a two-factor design typically involves several treatment conditions, these descriptive statistics usually are presented in a table or a graph. Next, the results of all three hypothesis tests (*F*-ratios) are reported. For the research study in Example 14.3, the report would have the following form:

> The means and standard deviations for all treatment conditions are shown in Table 1. The two-factor analysis of variance showed a significant main effect for task difficulty, $F(1, 24) = 24.00$, $p < .01$; a significant main effect for level of arousal, $F(2, 24) = 6.00$, $p < .01$; and a significant interaction between difficulty and arousal, $F(2, 24) = 6.00$, $p < .01$.
>
> **TABLE 1**
> Mean performance score for each treatment condition
>
> | | | Level of arousal | | |
> | --- | --- | --- | --- | --- |
> | | | Low | Medium | High |
> | Difficulty | Easy | $M = 3.00$ $SD = 2.12$ | $M = 6.00$ $SD = 2.65$ | $M = 9.00$ $SD = 2.55$ |
> | | Hard | $M = 1.00$ $SD = 1.41$ | $M = 4.00$ $SD = 2.24$ | $M = 1.00$ $SD = 2.24$ |

You should recognize the elements of this report as being identical to other examples reporting the results from an analysis of variance. Each of the obtained *F*-ratios is reported with its *df* values in parentheses. The term *significant* is used to indicate that the null hypothesis was rejected (the mean differences are greater than what would be expected by chance). Finally, the *p* value reported with each *F*-ratio reflects the alpha level used for the test. For example, $p < .01$ indicates that the probability is less than .01 that the obtained mean difference is simply due to chance or sampling error.

ON THE COMPUTER

FIGURE 14.8 shows two computer printouts of the two-factor analysis of variance for the data in Example 14.3. You should recognize that both the SPSS and the Minitab printouts have the same basic structure as the summary table presented in Table 14.8 in the text. A few specific elements are discussed as follows:

1. The SPSS printout separates the main effects and the interactions (there is only one interaction although it is listed twice). In addition to reporting each main effect (factor A, Difficulty and factor B, Arousal) the

printout includes a combined "Main Effects" factor that is not normally part of the analysis. Also, the overall variability between treatments is listed as "explained" variability, and the printout includes a *MS* value and an *F*-ratio for this source although these values are not normally computed.

2. The Minitab printout is very similar to Table 14.8 in the text except that the printout does not include an overall "between treatments" source, and it lists the within-treatments variability as "error."

SPSS Printout					

ANALYSIS OF VARIANCE

       SCORE
by   DIFFICUL
       AROUSAL

       Unique sums of squares
       All effects entered simultaneously

Source of Variable	Sum of Squares	DF	Mean Square	F	Sig of F
Main Effects	180.000	3	60.000	12.000	.000
DIFFICUL	120.000	1	120.000	24.000	.000
AROUSAL	60.000	2	30.000	6.000	.008
2-Way Interactions	60.000	2	30.000	6.000	.008
DIFFICUL AROUSAL	60.000	2	30.000	6.000	.008
Explained	240.000	5	48.000	9.600	.000
Residual	120.000	24	5.000		
Total	360.000	29	12.414		

30 cases were processed.
0 cases (.0 pct) were missing.

FIGURE 14.8

Computer printouts showing the two-factor ANOVA output from SPSS (above) and Minitab (opposite). Both printouts show the results for the data from Example 14.3. The printouts are discussed in the text.

ON THE COMPUTER *(continued)*

Minitab Printout

Two-sample ANOVA: scores versus row, column

Analysis of Variance for scores

Source	DF	SS	MS	F	P
row	1	120.00	120.00	24.00	0.000
column	2	60.00	30.00	6.00	0.008
Interaction	2	60.00	30.00	6.00	0.008
Error	24	120.00	5.00		
Total	29	360.00			

ASSUMPTIONS FOR THE TWO-FACTOR ANOVA

The validity of the analysis of variance presented in this chapter depends on the same three assumptions we have encountered with other hypothesis tests for independent-measures designs (the t test in Chapter 10 and the single-factor ANOVA in Chapter 13):

1. The observations within each sample must be independent (see p. 184).
2. The populations from which the samples are selected must be normal.
3. The populations from which the samples are selected must have equal variances (homogeneity of variance).

As before, the assumption of normality generally is not a cause for concern, especially when the sample size is relatively large. The homogeneity of variance assumption is more important, and if it appears that your data fail to satisfy this requirement, you should conduct a test for homogeneity before you attempt the ANOVA. Hartley's F-max test (see p. 240) allows you to use the sample variances from your data to determine whether there is evidence for any differences among the population variances.

LEARNING CHECK

1. The following data summarize the results from a two-factor independent-measures experiment:

		Factor B		
		B_1	B_2	B_3
Factor A	A_1	$n = 10$ $T = 0$ $SS = 30$	$n = 10$ $T = 10$ $SS = 40$	$n = 10$ $T = 20$ $SS = 50$
	A_2	$n = 10$ $T = 40$ $SS = 60$	$n = 10$ $T = 30$ $SS = 50$	$n = 10$ $T = 20$ $SS = 40$

a. Calculate the total for each level of factor A (the row totals), and compute SS for factor A.

b. Calculate the total for each level of factor B (the column totals), and compute SS for factor B. (*Note:* You should find that the totals for B are all the same, so there is no variability for this factor.)

c. For these data, $SS_{\text{between treatments}}$ is equal to 100. Given this information, what is the SS for the interaction?

d. Calculate the within-treatments SS, df, and MS for these data. (*Note:* MS_{within} is the denominator for each of the three F-ratios.)

A N S W E R S   **1. a.** The totals for factor A are 30 and 90, and each total is obtained by summing 30 scores. $SS_A = 60$.

b. All three totals for factor B are equal to 40. Because they are all the same, there is no variability, and $SS_B = 0$.

c. The interaction is determined by differences that remain after the main effects have been accounted for. For these data,

$$SS_{A \times B} = SS_{\text{between treatments}} - SS_A - SS_B$$

$$= 100 - 60 - 0$$

$$= 40$$

d. $SS_{\text{within}} = \Sigma SS_{\text{each cell}} = 30 + 40 + 50 + 60 + 50 + 40$

$$= 270$$

$$df_{\text{within}} = \Sigma df_{\text{each cell}} = 9 + 9 + 9 + 9 + 9 + 9$$

$$= 54$$

$$MS_{\text{within}} = \frac{SS_{\text{within}}}{df_{\text{within}}} = \frac{270}{54} = 5.00 \qquad \blacklozenge$$

ON THE WEB

AFTER COMPLETING Chapter 14, you can test your knowledge with the practice quiz on the Wadsworth Web site at **www.wadsworth.com**. Also, there are two workshops that are related to this material. The *One Way Anova* workshop provides a review of the basic analysis, which is identical to the first stage of the repeated-measures ANOVA and the two-factor ANOVA. In addition, there is a *Two Way Anova* workshop, which is directly related to Section 14.3 in this chapter. See p. 24 for more information about quizzes and workshops.

SUMMARY

1. The repeated-measures ANOVA is used to evaluate the mean differences obtained in a research study comparing two or more treatment conditions using the same sample of individuals in each condition. The test statistic is an F-ratio, where the numerator measures the variance (differences) between treatments and the denominator measures the variance (differences) due to chance or error.

$$F = \frac{MS_{\text{between treatments}}}{MS_{\text{error}}}$$

2. The first stage of the repeated-measures ANOVA is identical to the independent-measures analysis and separates the total variability into two components: between-treatments and within-treatments. Because a repeated measures design uses the same subjects in every treatment condition, the differences between treatments cannot be caused by individual differences. Thus, individual differences are automatically eliminated from the between-treatments variance in the numerator of the F-ratio.

3. In the second stage of the repeated-measures analysis, individual differences are computed and removed from the denominator of the F-ratio. To remove the individual differences, you first compute the variability between subjects (SS and df) and then subtract these values from the corresponding within-treatments values. The residual provides a measure of error excluding individual differences, which is the appropriate denominator for the repeated-measures F-ratio.

4. A research study with two independent variables is called a two-factor design. Such a design can be diagrammed as a matrix by listing the levels of one factor across the top and the levels of the other factor down the side. Each *cell* in the matrix corresponds to a specific combination of the two factors.

5. Traditionally, the two factors are identified as factor A and factor B. The purpose of the analysis of variance is to determine whether there are any significant mean differences among the treatment conditions or cells in the experimental matrix. These treatment effects are classified as follows:
   a. The A effect: Differential effects produced by the different levels of factor A.
   b. The B effect: Differential effects produced by the different levels of factor B.
   c. The $A \times B$ interaction: Differences that are produced by unique combinations of A and B. An interaction exists when the effect of one factor depends on the levels of the other factor.

6. The two-factor analysis of variance produces three F-ratios: one for factor A, one for factor B, and one for the $A \times B$ interaction. Each F-ratio has the same basic structure:

$$F = \frac{MS_{\text{treatment effect}}(\text{either } A \text{ or } B \text{ or } A \times B)}{MS_{\text{within}}}$$

KEY TERMS

individual differences	error variability	matrix	main effect
between-subjects variability	two-factor design	cells	interaction

FOCUS ON PROBLEM SOLVING

1. Before you begin a repeated-measures ANOVA, complete all the preliminary calculations needed for the ANOVA formulas. This requires that you find the total for each treatment (Ts), the total for each person (Ps), the grand total (G), the SS for each treatment condition, and ΣX^2 for the entire set of N scores. As a partial check on these calculations, be sure that the T values add up to G and that the P values have a sum of G.

2. To help remember the structure of repeated-measures ANOVA, keep in mind that a repeated-measures experiment eliminates the contribution of individual differences. There are no individual differences contributing to the numerator of the F-ratio ($MS_{\text{between treatments}}$) because the same individuals are used for all treatments. Therefore,

you must also eliminate individual differences in the denominator. This is accomplished by partitioning within-treatments variability into two components: between-subjects variability and error variability. It is the MS value for error variability that is used in the denominator of the F-ratio.

3. Before you begin a two-factor ANOVA, take time to organize and summarize the data. It is best if you summarize the data in a matrix with rows corresponding to the levels of one factor and columns corresponding to the levels of the other factor. In each cell of the matrix, show the number of scores (n), the total and mean for the cell, and the SS within the cell. Also compute the row totals and column totals that will be needed to calculate main effects.

4. For a two-factor ANOVA, there are three separate F-ratios. These three F-ratios use the same error term in the denominator (MS_{within}). On the other hand, these F-ratios will have different numerators and may have different df values associated with each of these numerators. Therefore, you must be careful when you look up the critical F values in the table. The two factors and the interaction may have different critical F values.

———— DEMONSTRATION 14.1 ————

REPEATED-MEASURES ANOVA

The following data were obtained from a research study examining the effect of sleep deprivation on motor skills performance. A sample of five subjects was tested on a motor skills task after 24 hours of sleep deprivation, tested again after 36 hours, and tested once more after 48 hours. The dependent variable is the number of errors made on the motor skills task. Do these data indicate that the number of hours of sleep deprivation has a significant effect on motor skills performance?

Subject	24 hours	36 hours	48 hours	P totals	
A	0	0	6	6	$N = 15$
B	1	3	5	9	$G = 45$
C	0	1	5	6	$\Sigma X^2 = 245$
D	4	5	9	18	
E	0	1	5	6	

	$T = 5$	$T = 10$	$T = 30$		
	$SS = 12$	$SS = 16$	$SS = 12$		

STEP 1   State the hypotheses and specify alpha.
The null hypothesis states that for the general population there are no differences among the three deprivation conditions. Any differences that exist among the samples are simply due to chance or error. In symbols,

$$H_0 = \mu_1 = \mu_2 = \mu_3$$

The alternative hypothesis states that there are differences among the conditions.

$$H_0: \text{At least one of the treatment means is different.}$$

We will use $\alpha = .05$.

STEP 2   The repeated-measures analysis.

Rather than compute the df values and look for a critical value for F at this time, we will proceed directly to the ANOVA.

STAGE 1   The first stage of the analysis is identical to the independent-measures ANOVA presented in Chapter 13.

$$SS_{total} = \Sigma X^2 - \frac{G^2}{N}$$

$$= 245 - \frac{45^2}{15} = 110$$

$$SS_{within} = \Sigma SS_{inside\ each\ treatment} = 12 + 16 + 12 = 40$$

$$SS_{between} = \Sigma \frac{T^2}{n} - \frac{G^2}{N}$$

$$= \frac{5^2}{5} + \frac{10^2}{5} + \frac{30^2}{5} - \frac{45^2}{15}$$

$$= 70$$

and the corresponding degrees of freedom are

$$df_{total} = N - 1 = 14$$

$$df_{within} = \Sigma df = 4 + 4 + 4 = 12$$

$$df_{between} = k - 1 = 2$$

STAGE 2   The second stage of the repeated-measures analysis measures and removes the individual differences from the denominator of the F-ratio.

$$SS_{between\ subjects} = \Sigma \frac{P^2}{k} - \frac{G^2}{N}$$

$$= \frac{6^2}{3} + \frac{9^2}{3} + \frac{6^2}{3} + \frac{18^2}{3} + \frac{6^2}{3} - \frac{45^2}{15}$$

$$= 36$$

$$SS_{error} = SS_{within} - SS_{between\ subjects}$$

$$= 40 - 36$$

$$= 4$$

and the corresponding df values are

$$df_{between\ subject} = n - 1 = 4$$

$$df_{error} = df_{within} - df_{between\ subjects}$$

$$= 12 - 4$$

$$= 8$$

The mean square values that will form the F-ratio are as follows:

$$MS_{between} = \frac{SS_{between}}{df_{between}} = \frac{70}{2} = 35$$

$$MS_{error} = \frac{SS_{error}}{df_{error}} = \frac{4}{8} = 0.50$$

Finally, the F-ratio is

$$F = \frac{MS_{between}}{MS_{error}} = \frac{35}{0.50} = 70.00$$

STEP 3   Make a decision and state a conclusion.   With $df = 2, 8$ and $\alpha = .05$, the critical value is $F = 4.46$. Our obtained F-ratio ($F = 70.00$) is well into the critical region, so our decision is to reject the null hypothesis and conclude that there are significant differences among the three levels of sleep deprivation.

——— **DEMONSTRATION 14.2** ———

TWO-FACTOR ANOVA

The following data are representative of the results obtained in a research study examining the relationship between eating behavior and body weight (Schachter, 1968). The two factors in this study were:

1. The subject's weight (normal or obese)
2. The subject's state of hunger (full stomach or empty stomach)

All subjects were led to believe that they were taking part in a taste test for several types of crackers, and they were allowed to eat as many crackers as they wanted. The dependent variable was the number of crackers eaten by each subject. There were two specific predictions for this study. First, it was predicted that normal subjects' eating behavior would be determined by their state of hunger. That is, people with empty stomachs would eat more and people with full stomachs would eat less. Second, it was predicted that eating behavior for obese subjects would not be related to their state of hunger. Specifically, it was predicted that obese subjects would eat the same amount whether their stomachs were full or empty. Note that the researchers are predicting an interaction: The effect of hunger will be different for the normal subjects and the obese subjects. The data are as follows:

		Factor B: Hunger		
		Empty stomach	Full stomach	
Factor A: **Weight**	Normal	$n = 20$ $\overline{X} = 22$ $T = 440$ $SS = 1540$	$n = 20$ $\overline{X} = 15$ $T = 300$ $SS = 1270$	$T_{normal} = 740$
	Obese	$n = 20$ $\overline{X} = 17$ $T = 340$ $SS = 1320$	$n = 20$ $\overline{X} = 18$ $T = 360$ $SS = 1266$	$T_{obese} = 700$
		$T_{empty} = 780$	$T_{full} = 660$	

$G = 1440$
$N = 80$
$\Sigma X^2 = 31,836$

STEP 1   State the hypotheses and select alpha.   For a two-factor study, there are three separate hypotheses, the two main effects and the interaction.

For factor A, the null hypothesis states that there is no difference in the amount eaten for normal subjects versus obese subjects. In symbols,

$$H_0: \mu_{normal} = \mu_{obese}$$

For factor B, the null hypothesis states that there is no difference in the amount eaten for full-stomach versus empty-stomach conditions. In symbols,

$$H_0: \mu_{full} = \mu_{empty}$$

For the $A \times B$ interaction, the null hypothesis can be stated two different ways. First, the difference in eating between the full-stomach and empty-stomach conditions will be the same for normal and obese subjects. Second, the difference in eating between the normal and obese subjects will be the same for the full-stomach and empty-stomach conditions. In more general terms,

$$H_0: \text{The effect of factor } A \text{ does not depend on the levels of factor } B \text{ (and } B$$
$$\text{does not depend on } A).$$

We will use $\alpha = .05$ for all tests.

STEP 2   The two-factor analysis.

Rather than compute the df values and look up critical values for F at this time, we will proceed directly to the ANOVA.

STAGE 1   The first stage of the analysis is identical to the independent-measures ANOVA presented in Chapter 13, where each cell in the data matrix is considered a separate treatment condition.

$$SS_{total} = \Sigma X^2 - \frac{G^2}{N}$$

$$= 31,836 - \frac{1440^2}{80} = 5916$$

$$SS_{within} = \Sigma SS_{inside\ each\ treatment} = 1540 + 1270 + 1320 + 1266 = 5396$$

$$SS_{between} = \Sigma \frac{T^2}{n} - \frac{G^2}{N}$$

$$= \frac{440^2}{20} + \frac{300^2}{20} + \frac{340^2}{20} + \frac{360^2}{20} - \frac{1440^2}{80}$$

$$= 520$$

The corresponding degrees of freedom are

$$df_{total} = N - 1 = 79$$

$$df_{within} = \Sigma df = 19 + 19 + 19 + 19 = 76$$

$$df_{between} = \text{number of treatments} - 1 = 3$$

STAGE 2   The second stage of the analysis partitions the between-treatments variability into three components: the main effect for factor A, the main effect for factor B, and the $A \times B$ interaction.

For factor A (normal/obese),

$$SS_A = \Sigma \frac{T^2_{\text{ROWS}}}{n_{\text{ROWS}}} - \frac{G^2}{N}$$

$$= \frac{740^2}{40} + \frac{700^2}{40}^2 - \frac{1440^2}{80}$$

$$= 20$$

For factor B (full/empty),

$$SS_B = \Sigma \frac{T^2_{\text{COLS}}}{n_{\text{COLS}}} - \frac{G^2}{N}$$

$$= \frac{780^2}{40} + \frac{660^2}{40} - \frac{1440^2}{80}$$

$$= 180$$

For the $A \times B$ interaction,

$$SS_{A \times B} = SS_{\text{between}} - SS_A - SS_B$$

$$= 520 - 20 - 180$$

$$= 320$$

The corresponding degrees of freedom are

$$df_A = \text{number of rows} - 1 = 1$$
$$df_B = \text{number of columns} - 1 = 1$$
$$df_{A \times B} = df_{\text{between}} - df_A - df_B$$

$$= 3 - 1 - 1$$
$$= 1$$

The MS values needed for the F-ratios are

$$MS_A = \frac{SS_A}{df_A} = \frac{20}{1} = 20$$

$$MS_B = \frac{SS_B}{df_B} = \frac{180}{1} = 180$$

$$MS_{A \times B} = \frac{SS_{A \times B}}{df_{A \times B}} = \frac{320}{1} = 320$$

$$MS_{\text{within}} = \frac{SS_{\text{within}}}{df_{\text{within}}} = \frac{5396}{76} = 71$$

Finally, the F-ratios are

$$F_A = \frac{MS_A}{MS_{\text{within}}} = \frac{20}{71} = 0.28$$

$$F_B = \frac{MS_B}{MS_{\text{within}}} = \frac{180}{71} = 2.54$$

$$F_{A \times B} = \frac{MS_{A \times B}}{MS_{\text{within}}} = \frac{320}{71} = 4.51$$

STEP 3 Make a decision and state a conclusion.   All three F-ratios have $df = 1, 76$. With $\alpha = .05$, the critical F value is 3.98 for all three tests.

For these data, factor A (weight) has no significant effect; $F(1, 76) = 0.28$. Statistically, there is no difference in the number of crackers eaten by normal versus obese subjects.

Similarly, factor B (fullness) has no significant effect; $F(1, 76) = 2.54$. Statistically, the number of crackers eaten by full subjects is no different from the number eaten by hungry subjects. (*Note:* This conclusion concerns the combined group of normal and obese subjects. The interaction concerns these two groups separately.)

These data produce a significant interaction; $F(1, 76) = 4.51, p < .05$. This means that the effect of fullness does depend on weight. A closer look at the original data shows that the degree of fullness did affect the normal subjects, but it had no effect on the obese subjects.

PROBLEMS

1. How does the denominator of the F-ratio (the error term) differ for a repeated-measures analysis of variance compared to an independent-measures ANOVA?

2. A researcher conducts a repeated-measures experiment using a sample of $n = 12$ subjects to evaluate the differences among three treatment conditions. If the results are examined with an ANOVA, what are the df values for the F-ratio?

3. A researcher conducts a repeated-measures ANOVA for a study comparing four treatment conditions using a sample of $n = 10$ subjects. What are the df values for the F-ratio?

4. A researcher reports an F-ratio with $df = 3, 36$ for a repeated-measures ANOVA.
  a. How many treatment conditions were evaluated in this experiment?
  b. How many subjects participated in this experiment?

5. A researcher reports an F-ratio with $df = 2, 40$ from a repeated-measures experiment.
  a. How many treatment conditions were compared in this experiment?
  b. How many subjects participated in the experiment?

6. The following data were obtained from a repeated-measures study comparing three treatment conditions.

| | | Treatments | | |
Subject	I	II	III	P
A	6	8	10	24	$G = 48$
B	5	5	5	15	$\Sigma X^2 = 294$
C	1	2	3	6	
D	0	1	2	3	

$$T = 12 \quad T = 16 \quad T = 20$$
$$SS = 26 \quad SS = 30 \quad SS = 38$$

Use a repeated-measures analysis of variance with $\alpha = .05$ to determine whether these data are sufficient to demonstrate significant differences between the treatments.

7. In the previous problem, the data show large and consistent differences between subjects. For example, subject A has the largest score in every treatment and subject D always has the smallest score. In the second stage of the ANOVA, the large individual differences get subtracted out of the denominator of the F-ratio, which results in a larger value for F.

The following data were created by using the same numbers that appeared in Problem 6. However, we have now eliminated the consistent individual differences by scrambling the scores within each treatment.

Subject	Treatments			P
	I	II	III	
A	6	2	3	11
B	5	1	5	11
C	1	5	10	15
D	0	8	2	11

$G = 48$
$\Sigma X^2 = 294$

$T = 12$ $T = 16$ $T = 20$
$SS = 26$ $SS = 30$ $SS = 38$

a. Use a repeated-measures analysis of variance with $\alpha = .05$ to determine whether these data are sufficient to demonstrate significant differences between the treatments.

b. Explain how the results of this analysis compare with the results from Problem 6.

8. It has been demonstrated that when subjects must memorize a list of words serially (in the order of presentation), words at the beginning and end of the list are remembered better than words in the middle. This observation has been called the *serial-position effect*. The following data represent the number of errors made in recall of the first eight, second eight, and last eight words in the list:

Person	Serial position			P
	First	Middle	Last	
A	1	5	0	6
B	3	7	2	12
C	5	6	1	12
D	3	2	1	6

$\Sigma X^2 = 164$

$T = 12$ $T = 20$ $T = 4$
$SS = 8$ $SS = 14$ $SS = 2$

a. Compute the mean number of errors for each position, and draw a graph of the data.

b. Is there evidence for a significant effect of serial position? Test at the .05 level of significance. Based on the ANOVA, explain the results of the study.

9. The following data are from an experiment comparing three different treatment conditions:

A	B	C	
0	1	2	$N = 15$
2	5	5	$\Sigma X^2 = 354$
1	2	6	
5	4	9	
2	8	8	

$T = 10$ $T = 20$ $T = 30$
$SS = 14$ $SS = 30$ $SS = 30$

a. If the experiment uses an *independent-measures design,* can the researcher conclude that the treatments are significantly different? Test at the .05 level of significance.

b. If the experiment were done with a *repeated-measures design,* should the researcher conclude that the treatments are significantly different? Set alpha at .05 again.

c. Explain why the results are different in the analyses of parts (a) and (b).

10. A psychologist studies the effect of practice on maze learning for rats. Rats are tested in the maze in one daily session for 4 days. The psychologist records the number of errors made in each daily session. The data are as follows:

Rat	Session				P
	1	2	3	4	
1	3	1	0	0	4
2	3	2	2	1	8
3	6	3	1	2	12

$\Sigma X^2 = 78$

$T = 12$ $T = 6$ $T = 3$ $T = 3$
$SS = 6$ $SS = 2$ $SS = 2$ $SS = 2$

Is there evidence for a practice effect? Use the .05 level of significance to test for mean differences between sessions.

11. One of the main advantages of a repeated-measures design is that the variability caused by individual differences is removed before the test statistic is computed. To demonstrate this fact, we have taken the data from Problem 10 and exaggerated the individual differences by adding 6 points to each of the scores for rat 3. As the following data show, this rat now has scores substantially different from those of the other two rats.

a. How will increasing the individual differences affect the between-treatments variance? Compare the mean differences for these data versus the data in Problem 10. Compare the $MS_{between}$ for these data with the corresponding value from Problem 10.

b. How will the increased individual differences affect the error term for the F-ratio? Calculate MS_{error} for these data, and compare the result with MS_{error} from Problem 10.

c. Compare the F-ratio for the following data, and compare the result with the F-ratio from Problem 10. What happened to the individual differences that were added to the data?

| | | Session | | | | |
Rat	1	2	3	4	P	
1	3	1	0	0	4	$\Sigma X^2 = 366$
2	3	2	2	1	8	
3	12	9	7	8	36	

$$T = 18 \quad T = 12 \quad T = 9 \quad T = 9$$
$$SS = 54 \quad SS = 38 \quad SS = 26 \quad SS = 38$$

12. A psychologist is asked by a dog food manufacturer to determine whether animals will show a preference among three new food mixes recently developed. The psychologist takes a sample of $n = 6$ dogs. They are deprived of food overnight and presented simultaneously with three bowls of the mixes on the next morning. After 10 minutes, the bowls are removed, and the amount of food (in ounces) consumed is determined for each type of mix. The data are as follows:

| | | Mix | | | |
Subject	I	II	III	P	
A	3	2	1	6	$G = 48$
B	0	5	1	6	$\Sigma X^2 = 196$
C	2	4	3	9	
D	0	7	5	12	
F	0	3	3	6	
G	1	3	5	9	

$$T = 6 \quad T = 24 \quad T = 18$$
$$SS = 8 \quad SS = 16 \quad SS = 16$$

Is there evidence for a significant preference? Test at the .05 level of significance.

13. To determine the long-term effectiveness of relaxation training on anxiety, a researcher uses a repeated-measures study. A random sample of $n = 10$ subjects is first tested for the severity of anxiety with a standardized test. In addition to this pretest, subjects are tested again 1 week, 1 month, 6 months, and 1 year after treatment. The investigator used ANOVA to evaluate these data, and portions of the results are presented in the following summary table. Fill in the missing values. (*Hint:* Start with the df values.)

Source	SS	df	MS	
Between treatments	____	____	____	$F = 5$
Within treatments	500	____		
Between subjects	____	____		
Error	____	____	10	
Total	____	____		

14. A teacher studies the effectiveness of a reading skills course on comprehension. A sample of $n = 15$ students is studied. The instructor assesses their comprehension with a standardized reading test. The test is administered at the beginning of the course, at midterm, and at the end of the course. The instructor uses analysis of variance to determine whether or not a significant change has occurred in the students' reading performance. The following summary table presents a portion of the ANOVA results. Provide the missing values in the table. (Start with the df values.)

Source	SS	df	MS	
Between treatments	____	____	24	$F = 8$
Within treatments	120	____		
Between subjects	____	____		
Error	____	____	____	
Total	____	____		

15. The structure of a two-factor study can be presented as a matrix with one factor determining the rows and the second factor determining the columns. With this structure in mind, identify the three separate hypothesis tests that make up a two-factor ANOVA, and explain the purpose of each test.

For each of the following sets of data, determine whether or not the data indicate the presence of a main effect for factor A, a main effect for factor B, and/or an $A \times B$ interaction. *Note:* It may help to sketch a graph showing the sample means.

a.

		Factor B	
		B_1	B_2
Factor A	A_1	$\overline{X} = 10$	$\overline{X} = 50$
	A_2	$\overline{X} = 30$	$\overline{X} = 70$

b.

		Factor B	
		B_1	B_2
Factor A	A_1	$\overline{X} = 20$	$\overline{X} = 20$
	A_2	$\overline{X} = 10$	$\overline{X} = 50$

c.

		Factor B	
		B_1	B_2
Factor A	A_1	$\overline{X} = 40$	$\overline{X} = 40$
	A_2	$\overline{X} = 10$	$\overline{X} = 10$

17. The results of a two-factor experiment are examined using an ANOVA, and the researcher reports an F-ratio for factor A with $df = 1, 54$ and an F-ratio for factor B with $df = 2, 108$. Explain why this report cannot be correct.

18. A psychologist conducts a two-factor study comparing the effectiveness of two different therapy techniques (factor A) for treating mild and severe phobias (factor B). The dependent variable is a measure of fear for each subject. If the study uses $n = 10$ subjects in each of the four conditions, then identify the df values for each of the three F-ratios.
a. What are the df values for the F-ratio for factor A?
b. What are the df values for the F-ratio for factor B?
c. What are the df values for the F-ratio for the $A \times B$ interaction?

19. The following matrix presents the results of a two-factor experiment with two levels of factor A, two levels of factor B, and $n = 10$ subjects in each treatment condition. Each value in the matrix is the mean score for the subjects in that treatment condition. Note that one of the mean values is missing.

		Factor B	
		B_1	B_2
Factor A	A_1	10	40
	A_2	30	?

a. What value should be assigned to the missing mean so that the resulting data would show no main effect for factor A?
b. What value should be assigned to the missing mean so that the data would show no main effect for factor B?
c. What value should be assigned to the missing mean so that the data would show no interaction?

20. The following data were obtained from an independent-measures experiment using $n = 5$ subjects in each treatment condition:

		Factor B	
		B_1	B_2
Factor A	A_1	$T = 15$ $SS = 80$	$T = 25$ $SS = 90$
	A_2	$T = 5$ $SS = 70$	$T = 55$ $SS = 80$

$$\Sigma X^2 = 1100$$

a. Compute the means for each cell, and draw a graph showing the results of this experiment. Your graph should be similar to those shown in Figure 14.4.
b. Just from looking at your graph, does there appear to be a main effect for factor A? What about factor B? Does there appear to be an interaction?
c. Use an analysis of variance with $\alpha = .05$ to evaluate these data.

21. The following data are from a study examining the extent to which different personality types are affected by distraction. Individuals were selected to represent two different personality types: introverts and extroverts. Half the individuals in each group were tested on a monotonous task in a relatively quiet, calm room. The individuals in the other half of each group were tested in a noisy room filled with distractions. The dependent variable was the number of errors committed by each individual. The results of this study are as follows:

	Factor B (personality)	
	Introvert	Extrovert
Quiet	$n = 5$ $T = 10$ $SS = 15$	$n = 5$ $T = 10$ $SS = 25$
Noisy	$n = 5$ $T = 20$ $SS = 10$	$n = 5$ $T = 40$ $SS = 30$

Factor A (distraction) — Quiet / Noisy

$$\Sigma X^2 = 520$$

Use a two-factor ANOVA with $\alpha = .05$ to evaluate these results.

22. Shrauger (1972) conducted an experiment that examined the effect of an audience on the performance of two different personality types. Hypothetical data from this experiment are as follows. The dependent variable is the number of errors made by each subject.

		Alone	Audience
Self-esteem	High	3 6 2 2 4 7	9 4 5 8 4 6
	Low	7 7 2 6 8 6	10 14 11 15 11 11

Use an ANOVA with $\alpha = .05$ to evaluate these data. Describe the effect of the audience and the effect of personality on performance.

23. A researcher conducted a two-factor research study using two levels of factor A and four levels of factor B with a separate sample of $n = 6$ subjects in each of the eight treatment conditions (cells). The following table summarizes the results of the analysis, but it is not complete. Fill in the missing values. (*Hint:* Start with the *df* values.)

Source	SS	df	MS	
Between treatments	280	_____		
Main effect for A	_____	_____	_____	$F =$ _____
Main effect for B	_____	_____	48	$F =$ _____
$A \times B$ interaction	120	_____	_____	$F =$ _____
Within treatments	_____	_____	_____	
Total	600	_____		

24. A researcher conducted a two-factor research study using two levels of factor A and three levels of factor B with a separate sample of $n = 10$ subjects in each of the six treatment conditions (cells). The following table summarizes the results of the analysis, but it is not complete. Fill in the missing values. (*Hint:* Start with the *df* values.)

Source	SS	df	MS	
Between treatments	60	_____		
Main effect for A	_____	_____	0	$F =$ _____
Main effect for B	_____	_____	_____	$F =$ _____
$A \times B$ interaction	40	_____	_____	$F =$ _____
Within treatments	_____	_____	2	
Total	_____	_____		

CHAPTER 15

CORRELATION AND REGRESSION

CONTENTS

15.1   INTRODUCTION

Correlation is a statistical technique that is used to measure and describe a relationship between two variables. Usually the two variables are simply observed as they exist naturally in the environment—there is no attempt to control or manipulate the variables. For example, a researcher interested in the relationship between nutrition and IQ could observe (and record) the dietary patterns for a group of preschool children and then measure IQ scores for the same group. Note that the researcher is not trying to manipulate the children's diet or IQ but is simply observing what occurs naturally. You also should note that a correlation requires two separate scores for each individual (one score from each of the two variables). These scores normally are identified as X and Y. The pairs of scores can be listed in a table, or they can be presented in a graph called a scatterplot (see Figure 15.1). In the scatterplot, the X values are placed on the horizontal axis of a graph, and the Y values are placed on the vertical axis. Each individual is then identified by a single point on the graph so that the coordinates of the point (the X and Y values) match the individual's X score and Y score. The value of the scatterplot is that it allows you to see any patterns or trends that exist in the data (see Figure 15.1).

FIGURE 15.1

The same set of $n = 6$ pairs of scores (X and Y values) is shown in a table and in a scatterplot. Note that the scatterplot allows you to see the relationship between X and Y.

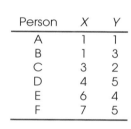

Person	X	Y
A	1	1
B	1	3
C	3	2
D	4	5
E	6	4
F	7	5

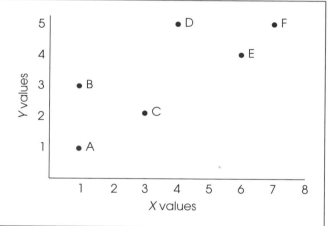

THE CHARACTERISTICS OF A RELATIONSHIP

A correlation measures three characteristics of the relationship between X and Y. These three characteristics are as follows.

1. The Direction of the Relationship. Correlations can be classified into two basic categories: positive and negative.

DEFINITIONS

In a *positive correlation,* the two variables tend to change in the same direction: When the X variable increases, the Y variable also increases; if the X variable decreases, the Y variable also decreases.

In a *negative correlation,* the two variables tend to go in opposite directions. As the X variable increases, the Y variable decreases. That is, it is an inverse relationship.

The direction of a relationship is identified by the sign of the correlation. A positive value (+) indicates a positive relationship; a negative value (−) indicates a negative relationship. The following example provides a description of positive and negative relationships.

E X A M P L E   1 5 . 1   Suppose you run the drink concession at the football stadium. After several seasons, you begin to notice a relationship between the temperature at game time and the beverages you sell. Specifically, you have noted that when the temperature is low, you sell relatively little beer. However, as the temperature goes up, beer sales also go up (see Figure 15.2). This is an example of a positive correlation. At the same time, you have noted a relationship between temperature and coffee sales: On cold days you sell a lot of coffee, but coffee sales go down as the temperature goes up. This is an example of a negative relationship.

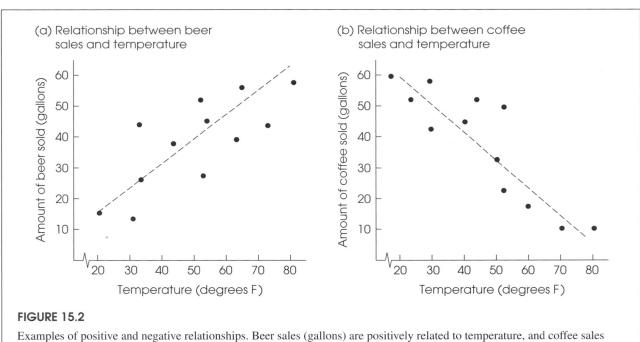

FIGURE 15.2

Examples of positive and negative relationships. Beer sales (gallons) are positively related to temperature, and coffee sales (gallons) are negatively related to temperature.

2. The Form of the Relationship. In the preceding coffee and beer examples, the relationships tend to have a linear form; that is, the points in the scatterplot tend to form a straight line. Note that we have drawn a line through the middle of the data points in each figure to help show the relationship. The most common use of correlation is to measure straight-line relationships. However, you should note that other forms of relationships do exist and that there are special correlations used to measure them. (We will examine an alternative in Section 15.5.)

3. The Degree of the Relationship. Finally, a correlation measures how well the data fit the specific form being considered. For example, a linear correlation measures how well the data points fit on a straight line. The degree of relationship is measured by the numerical value of the correlation. A *perfect correlation* always is identified by a correlation of 1.00 and indicates a perfect fit. At the other extreme, a correlation of 0 indicates no fit at all. Intermediate values represent the degree to which the data points approximate the perfect fit. The numerical value of the correlation also reflects the degree to which there is a consistent, predictable relationship between the two variables. Again, a correlation of 1.00 (or −1.00) indicates a perfectly consistent relationship.

Examples of different values for linear correlations are shown in Figure 15.3. In each example we have sketched a line around the data points. This line, called an *envelope* because it encloses the data, often helps you to see the overall trend in the data.

> A correlation of −1.00 also indicates a perfect fit. The direction of the relationship (positive or negative) should be considered separately from the degree of the relationship.

FIGURE 15.3

Examples of different values for linear correlations: (a) a strong positive relationship, approximately +0.90; (b) a relatively weak negative correlation, approximately −0.40; (c) a perfect negative correlation, −1.00; (d) no linear trend, 0.00.

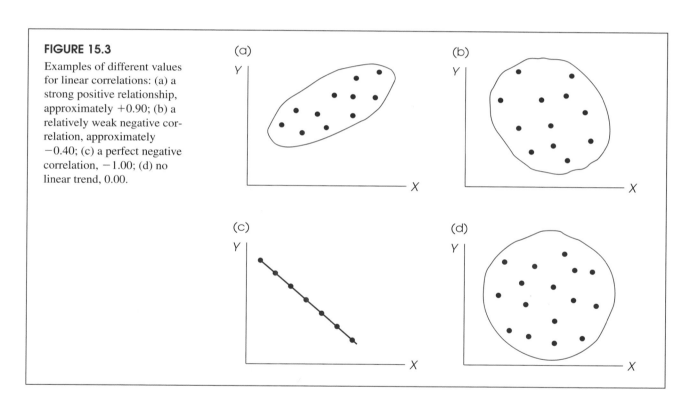

LEARNING CHECK

1. If the world were fair, would you expect a positive or negative relationship between grade point average (X) and weekly studying hours (Y) for college students?

2. Data suggest that, on average, children from large families have lower IQs than children from small families. Do these data indicate a positive or a negative relationship between family size and average IQ?

3. If you are measuring linear relationships, correlations of $+0.50$ and -0.50 are equally good in terms of how well the data fit on a straight line. (True or false?)

4. It is impossible to have a correlation greater than $+1.00$ or less than -1.00. (True or false?)

ANSWERS   **1.** Positive. More hours studying should be associated with higher grade point averages.

2. Negative.

3. True. The degree of fit is measured by the magnitude of the correlation independent of sign.

4. True. Correlations are always from $+1.00$ to -1.00.   ◆

15.2   THE PEARSON CORRELATION

By far the most common correlation is the Pearson correlation (or the Pearson product–moment correlation).

DEFINITION   The *Pearson correlation* measures the degree and the direction of the linear relationship between two variables.

The Pearson correlation is identified by the letter r. Conceptually, this correlation is computed by

$$r = \frac{\text{degree to which } X \text{ and } Y \text{ vary together}}{\text{degree to which } X \text{ and } Y \text{ vary separately}}$$

$$= \frac{\text{covariability of } X \text{ and } Y}{\text{variability of } X \text{ and } Y \text{ separately}}$$

When there is a perfect linear relationship, every change in the X variable is accompanied by a corresponding change in the Y variable. In Figure 15.3(c), for example, every time the value of X increases, there is a perfectly predictable decrease in the value of Y. The result is a perfect linear relationship, with X and Y always varying together. In this case, the covariability (X and Y together) is identical to the variability of X and Y separately, and the formula produces a correlation with a magnitude of 1.00 or -1.00. At the other extreme, when there is no linear relationship, a change in the X variable does not correspond to any predictable change in the Y variable. In this case, there is no covariability, and the resulting correlation is zero.

THE SUM OF PRODUCTS OF DEVIATIONS   To calculate the Pearson correlation, it is necessary to introduce one new concept: the *sum of products of deviations*. In the past, we have used a similar concept, SS (the sum of squared deviations), to measure the amount of variability for a single variable. The sum of products, or SP, provides a parallel procedure for measuring the amount of covariability between two variables. The value for SP can be calculated with either a definitional formula or a computational formula.

The *definitional formula* for the sum of products of deviations is

$$SP = \Sigma(X - \overline{X})(Y - \overline{Y}) \tag{15.1}$$

The definitional formula instructs you to perform the following sequence of operations:

1. Find the X deviation and the Y deviation for each individual.
2. Find the product of the deviations for each individual.
3. Sum the products.

Notice that this process "defines" the value being calculated: the sum of the products of the deviations.

The *computational formula* for the sum of products of deviations is

Caution: The n in this formula refers to the number of pairs of scores.

$$SP = \Sigma XY - \frac{\Sigma X \Sigma Y}{n} \tag{15.2}$$

Because the computational formula uses the original scores (X and Y values), it usually results in easier calculations than those required with the definitional formula. However, both formulas will always produce the same value for SP.

You may have noted that the formulas for SP are similar to the formulas you have learned for SS (sum of squares). The relationship between the two sets of formulas is described in Box 15.1. The following example demonstrates the calculation of SP with both formulas.

15.1 COMPARING THE *SP* AND *SS* FORMULAS

IT WILL help you to learn the formulas for SP if you note the similarity between the two SP formulas and the corresponding formulas for SS that were presented in Chapter 4. The definitional formula for SS is

$$SS = \Sigma(X - \overline{X})^2$$

In this formula, you must square each deviation, which is equivalent to multiplying it by itself. With this in mind, the formula can be rewritten as

$$SS = \Sigma(X - \overline{X})(X - \overline{X})$$

The similarity between the SS formula and the SP formula should be obvious—the SS formula uses squares and the SP formula uses products. This same relationship exists for the computational formulas. For SS, the computational formula is

$$SS = \Sigma X^2 - \frac{(\Sigma X)^2}{n}$$

As before, each squared value can be rewritten so that the formula becomes

$$SS = \Sigma XX - \frac{\Sigma X \, \Sigma X}{n}$$

Again, note the similarity in structure between the SS formula and the SP formula. If you remember that SS uses squares and SP uses products, the two new formulas for the sum of products should be easy to learn.

EXAMPLE 15.2   The set of $n = 4$ pairs of scores shown in the following table will be used to calculate SP, using first the definitional formula and then the computational formula.

For the definitional formula, you need deviation scores for each of the X values and each of the Y values. Note that the mean for the Xs is $\overline{X} = 3$ and the mean for the Ys is $\overline{Y} = 5$. The deviations and the products of deviations also are shown in the following table:

Caution: The signs ($+$ and $-$) are critical in determining the sum of products, SP.

Scores		Deviations		Products
X	Y	$X - \overline{X}$	$Y - \overline{Y}$	$(X - \overline{X})(Y - \overline{Y})$
1	3	-2	-2	$+4$
2	6	-1	$+1$	-1
4	4	$+1$	-1	-1
5	7	$+2$	$+2$	$+4$
				$+6 = SP$

For these scores, the sum of the products of the deviations is $SP = +6$.

For the computational formula, you need the sum of the X values, the sum of the Y values, and the sum of the XY products for each pair. These values are as follows:

	X	Y	XY
	1	3	3
	2	6	12
	4	4	16
	5	7	35
Totals	12	20	66

Substituting the sums in the formula gives

$$SP = \Sigma XY - \frac{\Sigma X \, \Sigma Y}{n}$$

$$= 66 - \frac{12(20)}{4}$$

$$= 66 - 60$$

$$= 6$$

Note that both formulas produce the same result, $SP = 6$.

CALCULATION OF THE PEARSON CORRELATION   As noted earlier, the Pearson correlation consists of a ratio comparing the covariability of X and Y (the numerator) with the variability of X and Y separately (the denominator). In the formula for the Pearson r, we will use SP to measure the covariability of X and Y.

The variability of X and Y will be measured by computing SS for the X scores and SS for the Y scores separately. With these definitions, the formula for the Pearson correlation becomes

Note that you *multiply SS for X* and *SS for Y* in the denominator of the Pearson formula.

$$r = \frac{SP}{\sqrt{SS_X SS_Y}}$$ (15.3)

The following example demonstrates the use of this formula with a simple set of scores.

EXAMPLE 15.3

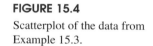

X	Y
0	1
10	3
4	1
8	2
8	3

The Pearson correlation is computed for the set of $n = 5$ pairs of scores shown in the margin.

Before starting any calculations, it is useful to put the data in a scatterplot and make a preliminary estimate of the correlation. These data have been graphed in Figure 15.4. Looking at the scatterplot, it appears that there is a very good (but not perfect) positive correlation. You should expect an approximate value of $r = +.8$ or $+.9$. To find the Pearson correlation, we will need SP, SS for X, and SS for Y. The following table presents the calculations for each of these values using the definitional formulas. (Note that the mean for the X values is $\overline{X} = 6$ and the mean for the Y scores is $\overline{Y} = 2$.)

FIGURE 15.4

Scatterplot of the data from Example 15.3.

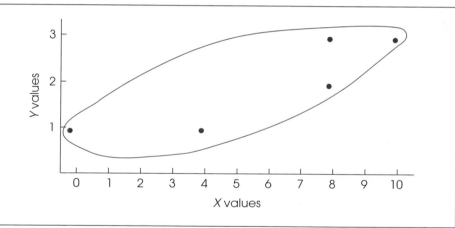

Scores		Deviations		Squared deviations		Products
X	Y	$X - \overline{X}$	$Y - \overline{Y}$	$(X - \overline{X})^2$	$(Y - \overline{Y})^2$	$(X - \overline{X})(Y - \overline{Y})$
0	1	−6	−1	36	1	+6
10	3	+4	+1	16	1	+4
4	1	−2	−1	4	1	+2
8	2	+2	0	4	0	0
8	3	+2	+1	4	1	+2
				64 = SS for X	4 = SS for Y	+14 = SP

By using these values, the Pearson correlation is

$$r = \frac{SP}{\sqrt{SS_X SS_Y}} = \frac{14}{\sqrt{64(4)}} = \frac{14}{16} = +0.875$$

Note that the value we obtained is in agreement with the prediction based on the scatterplot.

THE PEARSON CORRELATION AND z-SCORES

The Pearson correlation measures the relationship between an individual's location in the X distribution and his or her location in the Y distribution. For example, a positive correlation means that individuals who score high on X also tend to score high on Y. Similarly, a negative correlation indicates that individuals with high X scores tend to have low Y scores.

You should recall from Chapter 5 that z-scores provide a precise way to identify the location of an individual score within a distribution. Because the Pearson correlation measures the relationship between locations and because z-scores are used to specify locations, the formula for the Pearson correlation can be expressed entirely in terms of z-scores:

$$r = \frac{\Sigma \, z_X z_Y}{n} \tag{15.4}$$

In this formula, z_X identifies each individual's z-score position within the X distribution, and z_Y identifies his or her position within the Y distribution. The product of the z-scores (like the product of the deviation scores) determines the strength and direction of the correlation.

Because z-scores are considered to be the best way to describe a location within a distribution, Formula 15.4 often is considered to be the best way to define the Pearson correlation. However, realize that this formula requires a lot of tedious calculations (changing each score to a z-score), so it rarely is used to calculate a correlation.

LEARNING CHECK ◆

1. Describe what is measured by a Pearson correlation.

2. Can SP ever have a value less than zero?

3. Calculate the sum of products of deviations (SP) for the following set of scores. Use the definitional formula and then the computational formula. Verify that you get the same answer with both formulas.

X	Y
1	0
3	1
7	6
5	2
4	1

Remember: It is useful to sketch a scatterplot and make an estimate of the correlation before you begin calculations.

4. Compute the Pearson correlation for the following data:

X	Y
2	9
1	10
3	6
0	8
4	2

ANSWERS

1. The Pearson correlation measures the degree and the direction of linear relationship between two variables.

2. Yes. SP can be positive, negative, or zero depending on the relationship between X and Y.

3. $SP = 19$

4. $r = -\dfrac{16}{20} = -.80$ ◆

15.3 USING AND INTERPRETING THE PEARSON CORRELATION

WHERE AND WHY CORRELATIONS ARE USED

Although correlations have a number of different applications, a few specific examples are presented next to give an indication of the value of this statistical measure.

1. Prediction. If two variables are known to be related in some systematic way, it is possible to use one of the variables to make accurate predictions about the other. For example, when you applied for admission to college, you were required to submit a great deal of personal information, including your scores on the Scholastic Achievement Test (SAT). College officials want this information so they can predict your chances of success in college. It has been demonstrated over several years that SAT scores and college grade point averages are correlated. Students who do well on the SAT tend to do well in college; students who have difficulty with the SAT tend to have difficulty in college. Based on this relationship, college admissions officers can make a prediction about the potential success of each applicant. You should note that this prediction is not perfectly accurate. Not everyone who does poorly on the SAT will have trouble in college. Thus, you also submit letters of recommendation, high school grades, and other information with your application.

2. Validity. Suppose a psychologist develops a new test for measuring intelligence. How could you show that this test truly measures what it claims; that is, how could you demonstrate the validity of the test? One common technique for demonstrating validity is to use a correlation. If the test actually measures intelligence, then the scores on the test should be related to other measures of intelligence—for example, standardized IQ tests, performance on learning tasks, problem-solving ability, and so on. The psychologist could measure the correlation between the new test and each of these other measures of intelligence to demonstrate that the new test is valid.

15.2   RELIABILITY AND ERROR IN MEASUREMENT

THE IDEA of reliability of measurement is tied directly to the notion that each individual measurement includes an element of error. Expressed as an equation,

$$\text{measured score} = \text{true score} + \text{error}$$

For example, if I try to measure your intelligence with an IQ test, the score that I get is determined partially by your actual level of intelligence (your true score) but it also is influenced by a variety of other factors such as your current mood, your level of fatigue, your general health, and so on. These other factors are lumped together as *error*, and are typically a part of any measurement.

It is generally assumed that the error component changes randomly from one measurement to the next and this causes your score to change. For example, your IQ score is likely to be higher when you are well rested and feeling good compared to a measurement that is taken when you are tired and depressed. Although your actual intelligence hasn't changed, the error component causes your score to change from one measurement to another.

As long as the error component is relatively small, then your scores will be relatively consistent from one measurement to the next, and the measurements are said to be reliable. If you are feeling especially happy and well rested, it may affect your IQ score by a few points, but it is not going to boost your IQ from 110 to 170.

On the other hand, if the error component is relatively large, then you will find huge differences from one measurement to the next and the measurements are not reliable. Suppose, for example, that I am trying to measure the strength of your leg by determining how far you can kick a football. Your first kick goes off the side of your foot then hits the ground at a bad angle and bounces backwards. The next time you hit the ball squarely and get a good roll. In this situation, it is likely that I will find enormous differences between measurements: one kick can easily be two or three times longer than another. When measurements are unreliable you cannot trust any single measurement to provide an accurate indication of the individual's true score.

Correlations can be used to help researchers measure and describe reliability. By taking two measurements for each individual, it is possible to compute the correlation between the first score and the second score. A strong, positive correlation indicates a good level of reliability: people who scored high on the first measurement also scored high on the second. A weak correlation indicates that there is not a consistent relationship between the first score and the second score; that is, a weak correlation indicates poor reliability.

3. Reliability. In addition to evaluating the validity of a measurement procedure, correlations are used to determine reliability. A measurement procedure is considered reliable to the extent that it produces stable, consistent measurements. That is, a reliable measurement procedure will produce the same (or nearly the same) scores when the same individuals are measured under the same conditions. For example, if your IQ were measured as 113 last week, you would expect to obtain nearly the same score if your IQ were measured again this week. One way to evaluate reliability is to use correlations to determine the relationship between two sets of measurements. When reliability is high, the correlation between two measurements should be strong and positive. Further discussion of the concept of reliability is presented in Box 15.2.

4. Theory Verification. Many psychological theories make specific predictions about the relationship between two variables. For example, a theory may predict a relationship between brain size and learning ability; a developmental theory may predict a relationship between the parents' IQs and the child's IQ; a social psychologist may have a theory predicting a relationship between personality type and behavior in a social situation. In each case, the prediction of the theory could be tested by determining the correlation between the two variables.

INTERPRETING CORRELATIONS

When you encounter correlations, there are four additional considerations that you should bear in mind:

1. Correlation simply describes a relationship between two variables. It does not explain why the two variables are related. Specifically, a correlation should not and cannot be interpreted as proof of a cause-and-effect relationship between the two variables.

2. The value of a correlation can be affected greatly by the range of scores represented in the data.

3. One or two extreme data points, often called *outliers,* can have a dramatic effect on the value of a correlation.

4. When judging how "good" a relationship is, it is tempting to focus on the numerical value of the correlation. For example, a correlation of +.5 is halfway between 0 and 1.00 and therefore appears to represent a moderate degree of relationship. However, a correlation should not be interpreted as a proportion. Although a correlation of 1.00 does mean that there is a 100% perfectly predictable relationship between X and Y, a correlation of .5 does not mean that you can make predictions with 50% accuracy. To describe how accurately one variable predicts the other, you must square the correlation. Thus, a correlation of $r = .5$ provides only $r^2 = .5^2 = 0.25$, or 25% accuracy.

We will now discuss each of these four points in detail.

CORRELATION AND CAUSATION

One of the most common errors in interpreting correlations is to assume that a correlation necessarily implies a cause-and-effect relationship between the two variables. We constantly are bombarded with reports of relationships: Cigarette smoking is related to heart disease; alcohol consumption is related to birth defects; carrot consumption is related to good eyesight. Do these relationships mean that cigarettes cause heart disease or carrots cause good eyesight? The answer is *no.* Although there may be a causal relationship, the simple existence of a correlation does not prove it. This point should become clear in the following hypothetical example.

EXAMPLE 15.4

Suppose we select a variety of different cities and towns throughout the United States and measure the number of churches (X variable) and the number of serious crimes (Y variable) for each. A scatterplot showing hypothetical data for this study is presented in Figure 15.5. Note that this scatterplot shows a strong, positive correlation between churches and crime. You also should note that these are realistic data. It is reasonable that the small towns would have less crime and fewer churches and that the large cities would have large values for both variables. Does this relationship mean that churches cause crime? Does it mean that crime causes churches? It should be clear that both answers are no. Although a strong correlation exists between churches and crime, the real cause of the relationship is the size of the population.

FIGURE 15.5

Hypothetical data showing the logical relationship between the number of churches and the number of serious crimes for a sample of U.S. cities.

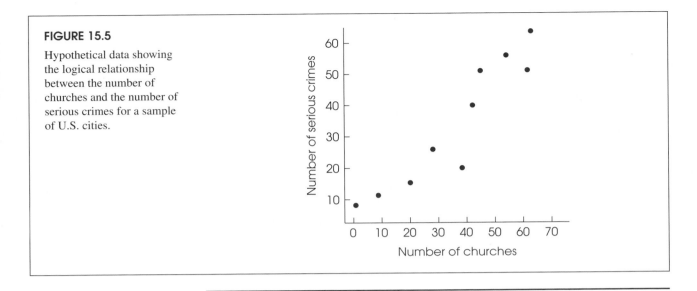

CORRELATION AND RESTRICTED RANGE

Whenever a correlation is computed from scores that do not represent the full range of possible values, you should be cautious in interpreting the correlation. Suppose, for example, you are interested in the relationship between IQ and creativity. If you select a sample of your fellow college students, your data probably would represent only a limited range of IQ scores (most likely from 110 to 130). The correlation within this restricted range could be completely different from the correlation that would be obtained from a full range of IQ scores. Two extreme examples are shown in Figure 15.6.

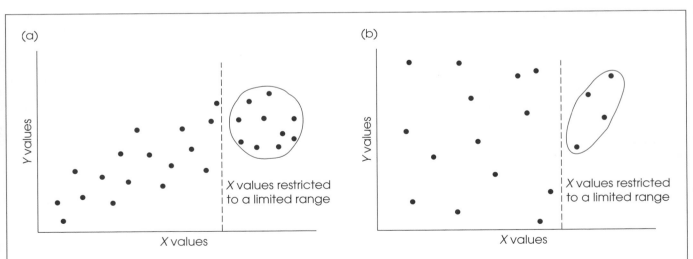

FIGURE 15.6

(a) In this example the full range of X and Y values shows a strong, positive correlation but the restricted range of scores produces a correlation near zero. (b) Here the full range of X and Y values shows a correlation near zero but the scores in the restricted range produce a strong, positive correlation.

Figure 15.6(a) shows an example where there is a strong, positive relationship between X and Y when the entire range of scores is considered. However, this relationship is obscured when the data are limited to a *restricted range*. In Figure 15.6(b), there is no consistent relationship between X and Y for the full range of scores. However, when the range of X values is restricted, the data show a strong, positive relationship.

To be safe, you should not generalize any correlation beyond the range of data represented in the sample. For a correlation to provide an accurate description for the general population, there should be a wide range of X and Y values in the data.

OUTLIERS   An outlier is an individual with X and/or Y values that are substantially different (larger or smaller) from the values obtained for the other individuals in the data set. The data point of a single outlier can have a dramatic influence on the value obtained for the correlation. This effect is illustrated in Figure 15.7. Figure 15.7(a) shows a set of $n = 5$ data points where the correlation between the X and Y variables is nearly zero (actually $r = -0.08$). In Figure 15.7(b), one extreme data point (14, 12) has been added to the original data set. When this outlier is included in the analysis, a strong, positive correlation emerges (now $r = +0.85$). Note that the single outlier drastically alters the value for the correlation and thereby can affect one's interpretation of the relationship between variables X and Y. Without the outlier, one would conclude there is no relationship between the two

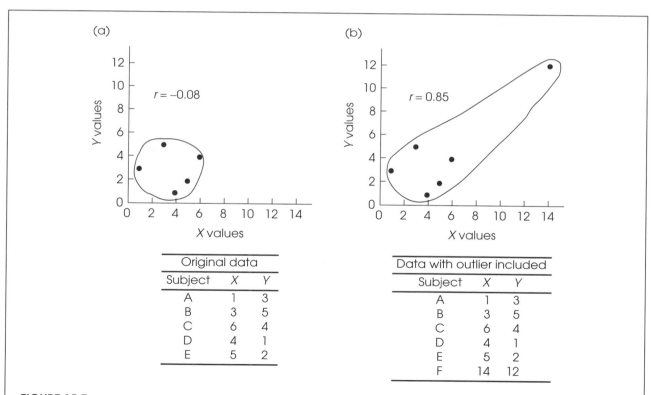

FIGURE 15.7

A demonstration of how one extreme data point (an outlier) can influence the value of a correlation.

variables. With the extreme data point, $r = +0.85$ implies that as X increases, Y will increase—and do so consistently. The problem of outliers is a good reason why you should always look at a scatterplot, instead of simply basing your interpretation on the numerical value of the correlation. If you only "go by the numbers," you might overlook the fact that one extreme data point inflated the size of the correlation.

CORRELATION AND THE STRENGTH OF THE RELATIONSHIP

A correlation measures the degree of relationship between two variables on a scale from 0 to 1.00. Although this number provides a measure of the degree of relationship, many researchers prefer to square the correlation and use the resulting value to measure the strength of the relationship.

One of the common uses of correlation is for prediction. If two variables are correlated, you can use the value of one variable to predict the other. For example, college admissions officers do not guess which applicants are likely to do well; they use other variables (SAT scores, high school grades, etc.) to predict which students are most likely to be successful. These predictions are based on correlations. By using correlations, the admissions officers expect to make more accurate predictions than would be obtained by guessing. In general, the squared correlation (r^2) measures the gain in accuracy that is obtained from using the correlation for prediction rather than guessing.

DEFINITION

The value r^2 is called the *coefficient of determination* because it measures the proportion of variability in one variable that can be determined from the relationship with the other variable. A correlation of $r = .80$ (or $-.80$), for example, means that $r^2 = 0.64$ (or 64%) of the variability in the Y scores can be predicted from the relationship with X.

In earlier chapters (see pages 236, 258, and 321) we introduced r^2 as a method for measuring effect size for research studies where mean differences were used to compare treatments. Specifically, we measured how much of the variance in the scores was accounted for by the differences between treatments. In experimental terminology, r^2 measures how much of the variance in the dependent variable is accounted for by the independent variable. Now we are doing the same thing, except that there is no independent or dependent variable. Instead, we simply have two variables, X and Y, and we use r^2 to measure how much of the variance in one variable can be determined from its relationship with the other variable. The following example demonstrates this concept.

EXAMPLE 15.5

Figure 15.8 shows three sets of data representing different degrees of linear relationship. The first set of data [Figure 15.8(a)] shows the relationship between IQ and shoe size. In this case, the correlation is $r = 0$ (and $r^2 = 0$), and you have no ability to predict a person's IQ based on his or her shoe size. Knowing a person's shoe size provides no information (0%) about the person's IQ. In this case, the two measurements are completely independent and there is no overlap between the information they provide.

Now consider the data in Figure 15.8(b). These data show a reasonably good, positive correlation, $r = +0.80$, between SAT scores and college grade point averages (GPA). Students who score high on the SAT tend to have higher grades than students with low SAT scores. From this relationship, it is possible to predict a student's GPA

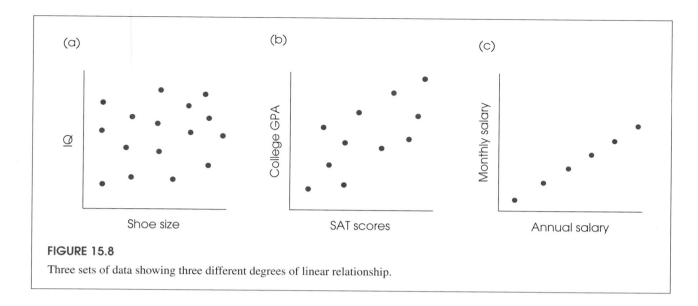

FIGURE 15.8

Three sets of data showing three different degrees of linear relationship.

based on his or her SAT score. However, you should realize that the prediction is not perfect. Although students with high SAT scores *tend* to have high GPAs, this is not always true. Thus, knowing a student's SAT score provides some information about the student's grades, or knowing a student's grades provides some information about the student's SAT score. Although we are measuring two separate variables (SAT and GPA), the two scores for each student actually provide much the same information. In other words, there is some overlap or redundancy between the two measures. With a correlation of $r = +0.80$, we obtain $r^2 = 0.64$, which means that there is a 64% overlap between the two measures.

Finally, consider the data in Figure 5.8(c). This time we show a perfect linear relationship ($r = +1.00$) between monthly salary and yearly salary for a group of college employees. With $r = 1.00$ and $r^2 = 1.00$, there is 100% predictability. If you know a person's monthly salary, you can predict perfectly the person's annual salary. In this case, there is complete overlap between the two measures because a person's monthly salary provides exactly the same information as the person's annual salary.

15.4 HYPOTHESIS TESTS WITH THE PEARSON CORRELATION

The Pearson correlation is generally computed for sample data. As with most sample statistics, however, a sample correlation is often used to answer questions about the general population. That is, the sample correlation is used as the basis for drawing inferences about the corresponding population correlation. For example, a psychologist would like to know whether there is a relationship between IQ and creativity. This is a general question concerning a population. To answer the question, a sample would be selected, and the sample data would be used to compute the correlation value. You should recognize this process as an example of inferential statistics: using samples to draw inferences about populations. In the past, we have been concerned primarily with using sample means as the basis for answering questions about population means. In this section, we will examine the procedures for using a sample correlation as the basis for testing hypotheses about the corresponding population correlation.

The basic question for this hypothesis test is whether or not a correlation exists in the population. The null hypothesis is "No, there is no correlation in the population" or "The population correlation is zero." The alternative hypothesis is "Yes, there is a real, nonzero correlation in the population." Because the population correlation is traditionally represented by ρ (the Greek letter rho), these hypotheses would be stated in symbols as

H_0: ρ = 0   (There is no population correlation.)

H_1: ρ ≠ 0   (There is a real correlation.)

Directional hypotheses for a one-tailed test would specify either a positive correlation (ρ > 0) or a negative correlation (ρ < 0).

The correlation from the sample data (*r*) will be used to evaluate these hypotheses. As always, samples are not expected to be identical to the populations from which they come; there will be some discrepancy (sampling error) between a sample statistic and the corresponding population parameter. Specifically, you should always expect some error between a sample correlation (*r*) and the population correlation (ρ) it represents. One implication of this fact is that even when there is no correlation in the population (ρ = 0), you are still likely to obtain a nonzero value for the sample correlation. This is particularly true for small samples. Figure 15.9 illustrates how a small sample from a population with a near-zero correlation could result in a correlation that deviates from zero. The colored dots in the figure represent the entire population and the three circled dots represent a random sample. Note that the three sample points show a relatively good, positive correlation even though there is no linear trend (ρ = 0) for the

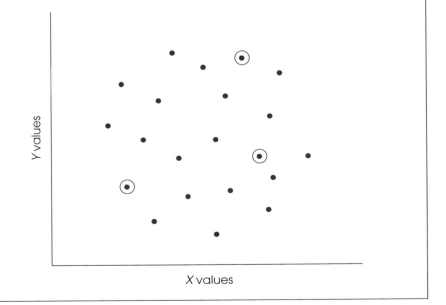

FIGURE 15.9

Scatterplot of a population of *X* and *Y* values with a near-zero correlation. However, a small sample of *n* = 3 data points from this population shows a relatively strong, positive correlation. These data points in the sample are circled.

population. The goal of the hypothesis test is to decide between the following two alternatives:

1. The nonzero sample correlation is simply due to chance. That is, there is no correlation in the population, and the sample value is simply the result of sampling error. This is the situation shown in Figure 15.9 and it is the alternative specified by H_0.

2. The nonzero sample correlation accurately represents a real, nonzero correlation in the population. This is the alternative stated in H_1.

The table lists critical values in terms of degrees of freedom: $df = n - 2$. Remember to subtract 2 when using this table.

Although it is possible to conduct the hypothesis test by computing either a t statistic or an F-ratio, the computations have been completed and are summarized in Table B.6 in Appendix B. To use this table, you must know the sample size (n), the magnitude of the sample correlation (independent of sign), and the alpha level. The values given in the table indicate how large a sample correlation must be before it is *significantly* greater than chance (significantly more than sampling error). That is, in order to reject H_0, the magnitude of the sample correlation must *equal or exceed* the value given in the table. The following examples demonstrate the use of the table.

EXAMPLE 15.6   A researcher is using a regular, two-tailed test with $\alpha = .05$ to determine whether or not a nonzero correlation exists in the population. A sample of $n = 30$ individuals is obtained. With $\alpha = .05$ and $n = 30$, the table lists a value of 0.361. Thus, the sample correlation (independent of sign) must have a value greater than or equal to 0.361 to reject H_0 and conclude that there is a significant correlation in the population. Any sample correlation between 0.361 and -0.361 is considered within the realm of sampling error and therefore not significant.

EXAMPLE 15.7   This time the researcher is using a directional, one-tailed test to determine whether or not there is a positive correlation in the population.

H_0: $\rho \leq 0$ (There is not a positive correlation)

H_1: $\rho > 0$ (There is a positive correlation.)

With $\alpha = .05$ and a sample of $n = 30$, the table lists a value of 0.306 for a one-tailed test. Thus, the researcher must obtain a sample correlation that is positive (as predicted) and has a value greater than or equal to 0.306 to reject H_0 and conclude that there is a significant positive correlation in the population.

IN THE LITERATURE:
REPORTING CORRELATIONS

When correlations are computed, the results are reported using APA format. The statement should include the sample size, the calculated value for the correlation, whether or not it is a statistically significant relationship, the probability level, and the type of test used (one- or two-tailed). For example, a correlation might be reported as follows:

A correlation for the data revealed that amount of education and annual income were significantly related, $r = +.65$, $n = 30$, $p < .01$, two tails.

Sometimes a study might look at several variables, and correlations between all possible variable pairings are computed. Suppose, for example, a study measured people's annual income, amount of education, age, and intelligence. With four variables, there are six possible pairings. Correlations were computed for every pair of variables. These results are most easily reported in a table called a *correlation matrix,* using footnotes to indicate which correlations are significant. For example, the report might state:

The analysis examined the relationships among income, amount of education, age, and intelligence for $n = 30$ subjects. The correlations between pairs of variables are reported in Table 1. Significant correlations are noted in the table.

TABLE 1

Correlation matrix for income, amount of education, age, and intelligence

	Education	Age	IQ
Income	+.65*	+.41**	+.27
Education		+.11	+.38**
Age			−.02

$n = 30$
*$p < .01$, two tails
**$p < .05$, two tails

1. A researcher obtains a correlation of $r = -.41$ for a sample of $n = 25$ individuals. Does this sample provide sufficient evidence to conclude that there is a significant, nonzero correlation in the population? Assume a nondirectional test with $\alpha = .05$.

2. For a sample of $n = 20$, how large a correlation is needed to conclude at the .05 level that there is a nonzero correlation in the population? Assume a nondirectional test.

3. As sample size gets smaller, what happens to the magnitude of the correlation necessary for significance? Explain why this occurs.

ANSWERS 1. Yes. For $n = 25$, the critical value is $r = .396$. The sample value is in the critical region.

2. For $n = 20$, the critical value is $r = .444$.

3. As the sample size gets smaller, the magnitude of the correlation needed for significance gets larger. With a small sample, it is easy to get a relatively good correlation just by chance (see Figure 15.9). Therefore, a small sample requires a very large correlation before you can be confident there is a real (nonzero) relationship in the population. ◆

ON THE COMPUTER

FIGURE 15.10 shows the computer printouts from correlations computed by the Minitab program and the SPSS program. In each case, the correlation is for the same data that were used in Example 15.3 (page 391). The two printouts demonstrate examples of the two common formats that are used to report correlations in the literature. The Minitab printout reports the correlation and the *p* value (probability of chance) in a simple text format. The SPSS printout, on the other hand, uses a correlation matrix. With more than two variables, a correlation matrix can be a convenient format for presenting lots of information. In this example, however, the correlation involves only two variables, *X* and *Y*, and the matrix is largely obvious and redundant. For example, the correlation between *X* and *X* (upper left) and the correlation between *Y* and *Y* (lower right) are obviously both equal to 1.00. Also, the correlation between *X* and *Y* is exactly the same as the correlation between *Y* and *X*, both equal to 0.8750.

Minitab Printout
Correlations: X, Y
Pearson correlation of X and Y = 0.875 P-Value = 0.052

SPSS Printout		
	—Correlation Coefficients—	
	XSCORE	YSCORE
XSCORE	1.0000 (5) P=.	.8750 (5) P= .052
YSCORE	.8750 (5) P= .052	1.0000 (5) P= .
(Coefficient / (Cases) / 2-tailed Significance)		
" . " is printed if a coefficient cannot be computed		

FIGURE 15.10

Computer printouts showing correlations obtained from Minitab (top) and SPSS (bottom). Both printouts show the correlations obtained for the data used in Example 15.3.

15.5   THE SPEARMAN CORRELATION

The Pearson correlation specifically measures the degree of linear relationship between two variables. It is the most commonly used measure of relationship and is used with data from an interval or a ratio scale of measurement. However, other correlation measures have been developed for nonlinear relationships and for other types of data (scales of measurement). One of these useful measures is called the *Spearman correlation.* The Spearman correlation is used in two situations.

First, the Spearman correlation is designed to measure the relationship between variables measured on an ordinal scale of measurement. Recall that in Chapter 1 we noted that an ordinal scale of measurement involves placing observations into rank order. Rank-order data are fairly common because they are often easier to obtain than interval or ratio scale data. For example, a teacher may feel confident about rank-ordering students' leadership abilities but would find it difficult to measure leadership on some other scale.

In addition to measuring relationships for ordinal data, the Spearman correlation can be used as a valuable alternative to the Pearson correlation, even when the original raw scores are on an interval or a ratio scale. As we have noted, the Pearson correlation measures the degree of *linear relationship* between two variables—that is, how well the data points fit on a straight line. However, a researcher often expects the data to show a consistent relationship but not necessarily a linear relationship. Consider the situation in which a researcher is investigating the relationship between amount of practice (*X*) and level of performance (*Y*). For these data, the researcher expects a strong, positive relationship: More practice leads to better performance. However, the expected relationship probably does not fit a linear form, so a Pearson correlation would not be appropriate (see Figure 15.11). In this situation, the Spearman correlation can be used to obtain a measure of the consistency of the relationship, independent of its specific form.

The reason that the Spearman correlation measures consistency, rather than form, comes from a simple observation: When two variables are consistently related, their ranks will be linearly related. For example, a perfectly consistent positive relationship means that every time the *X* variable increases, the *Y* variable also increases. Thus, the smallest value of *X* is paired with the smallest value of *Y*, the second-smallest value of

FIGURE 15.11

Hypothetical data showing the relationship between practice and performance. Although this relationship is not linear, there is a consistent positive relationship. An increase in performance tends to accompany an increase in practice.

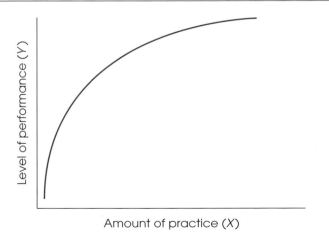

X is paired with the second-smallest value of *Y*, and so on. This phenomenon is demonstrated in the following example.

EXAMPLE 15.8

TABLE 15.1

Scores for Example 15.8

Person	X	Y
A	4	9
B	2	2
C	10	10
D	3	8

The data in Table 15.1 represent *X* and *Y* scores for a sample of $n = 4$ people. Note that person B has the lowest *X* score and the lowest *Y* score. Similarly, person D has the second-lowest score for both *X* and *Y*, person A has the third-lowest scores, and person C has the highest scores. These data show a perfectly consistent relationship: Each increase in *X* is accompanied by an increase in *Y*. However, the relationship is not linear, as we can see in the graph of the data in Figure 15.12(a).

Now we convert the raw scores to ranks: The lowest *X* is assigned a rank of 1, the next lowest *X* a rank of 2, and so on. This procedure is repeated for the *Y* scores. What happens when the *X* and *Y* scores are converted to ranks? Again, person B has the lowest *X* and *Y* scores, so this individual is ranked first on both variables. Similarly, person D is ranked second on both variables, person A is ranked third, and person C is ranked fourth (Table 15.2). When the ranks are plotted on a graph [see Figure 15.12(b)], the result is a perfect linear relationship.

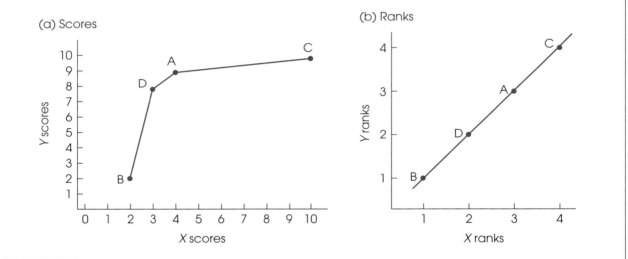

FIGURE 15.12

Scatterplots showing (a) the scores and (b) the ranks for the data in Example 15.8. Note that there is a consistent, positive relationship between the *X* and *Y* scores, although it is not a linear relationship. Also note that the scatterplot of the ranks shows a perfect linear relationship.

TABLE 15.2

Ranks for Example 15.8

Person	X Rank	Y Rank
A	3	3
B	1	1
C	4	4
D	2	2

The preceding example has demonstrated that a consistent relationship among scores produces a linear relationship when the scores are converted to ranks. Thus, if you want to measure the consistency of a relationship for a set of scores, you can simply convert the scores to ranks and then use the Spearman correlation to measure the correlation for the ranked data. The degree of relationship for the ranks (the Spearman correlation) provides a measure of the degree of consistency for the original scores.

To summarize, the Spearman correlation measures the relationship between two variables when both are measured on ordinal scales (ranks). There are two general situations in which the Spearman correlation is used:

1. Spearman is used when the original data are ordinal; that is, when the X and Y values are ranks.

2. Spearman is used when a researcher wants to measure the consistency of a relationship between X and Y, independent of the specific form of the relationship. In this case, the original scores are first converted to ranks; then the Spearman correlation is used to measure the relationship for the ranks. Incidentally, when there is a consistently one-directional relationship between two variables, the relationship is said to be *monotonic*. Thus, the Spearman correlation can be used to measure the degree of monotonic relationship between two variables.

The word *monotonic* describes a sequence that is consistently increasing (or decreasing). Like the word *monotonous,* it means constant and unchanging.

CALCULATION OF THE SPEARMAN CORRELATION

The calculation of the Spearman correlation is remarkably simple, provided you know how to compute a Pearson correlation. First, be sure that you have ordinal data (ranks) for the X and the Y scores. If necessary, you may have to place X scores and/or Y scores in rank order if they are not already. Ranking is accomplished as follows: The smallest X is assigned a rank of 1, the next smallest a rank of 2, and so on. Then the same is done for the Y scores. (Note that the X and Y scores are ranked separately.) Finally, the Spearman correlation is computed by simply using the Pearson correlation formula *for the ranks* of X and Y.

That's all there is to it. When you use the Pearson correlation formula for ordinal data, the result is called a Spearman correlation. The Spearman correlation is identified by the symbol r_S to differentiate it from the Pearson correlation. The complete process of computing the Spearman correlation, including ranking scores, is demonstrated in Example 15.9.

EXAMPLE 15.9

The following data show a nearly perfect monotonic relationship between X and Y. When X increases, Y tends to decrease, and there is only one reversal in this general trend. To compute the Spearman correlation, we first rank the X and Y values, and we then compute the Pearson correlation for the ranks.

We have listed the X values in order so that the trend is easier to recognize.

Original data			Ranks		
X	Y		X	Y	XY
3	12		1	5	5
4	5		2	3	6
5	6		3	4	12
10	4		4	2	8
13	3		5	1	5
					$36 = \Sigma XY$

The scatterplots for the original data and the ranks are shown in Figure 15.13. To compute the correlation, we will need SS for X, SS for Y, and SP. Remember that all these values are computed with the ranks, not the original scores.

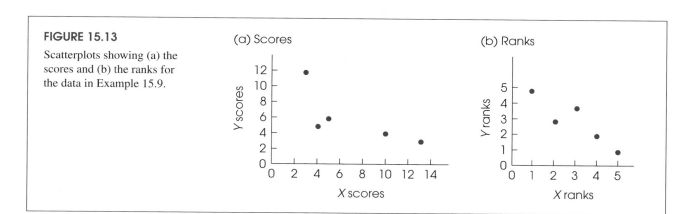

FIGURE 15.13

Scatterplots showing (a) the scores and (b) the ranks for the data in Example 15.9.

The X ranks are simply the integers 1, 2, 3, 4, and 5. These values have $\Sigma X = 15$ and $\Sigma X^2 = 55$. The SS for the X ranks is

$$SS_X = \Sigma X^2 - \frac{(\Sigma X)^2}{n}$$

$$= 55 - \frac{(15)^2}{5}$$

$$= 55 - 45$$

$$= 10$$

Note that the ranks for Y are identical to the ranks for X; that is, they are the integers 1, 2, 3, 4, and 5. Therefore, the SS for Y will be identical to the SS for X:

$$SS_Y = 10$$

To compute the SP value, we need ΣX, ΣY, and ΣXY for the ranks. The XY values are listed in the table with the ranks, and we already have found that both the Xs and the Ys have a sum of 15. Using these values, we obtain

$$SP = \Sigma XY - \frac{(\Sigma X)(\Sigma Y)}{n}$$

$$= 36 - \frac{(15)(15)}{5}$$

$$= 36 - 45$$

$$= -9$$

The final Spearman correlation is

$$r_S = \frac{SP}{\sqrt{(SS_X)(SS_Y)}}$$

$$= \frac{-9}{\sqrt{10(10)}}$$

$$= -0.9$$

The Spearman correlation indicates that the data show a strong (nearly perfect) negative trend.

RANKING TIED SCORES

When you are converting scores into ranks for the Spearman correlation, you may encounter two (or more) identical scores. Whenever two scores have exactly the same value, their ranks should also be the same. This is accomplished by the following procedure:

1. List the scores in order from smallest to largest. Include tied values in this list.
2. Assign a rank (first, second, etc.) to each position in the ordered list.
3. When two (or more) scores are tied, compute the mean of their ranked positions, and assign this mean value as the final rank for each score.

The process of finding ranks for tied scores is demonstrated here. The scores are listed in order from smallest to largest.

Scores	Rank position	Final rank	
3	1	1.5	⎫ Mean of 1 and 2
3	2	1.5	⎭
5	3	3	
6	4	5	⎫
6	5	5	⎬ Mean of 4, 5, and 6
6	6	5	⎭
12	7	7	

Note that this example has seven scores and uses all seven ranks. For $X = 12$, the largest score, the appropriate rank is 7. It cannot be given a rank of 6 because that rank has been used for the tied scores.

SPECIAL FORMULA FOR THE SPEARMAN CORRELATION

After the original X values and Y values have been ranked, the calculations necessary for SS and SP can be greatly simplified. First, note that the X ranks and the Y ranks are really just a set of integers: 1, 2, 3, 4, . . . , n. To compute the mean for these integers, you can locate the midpoint of the series by $\overline{X} = (n + 1)/2$. Similarly, the SS for this series of integers can be computed by

$$SS = \frac{n(n^2 - 1)}{12} \quad \text{(Try it out.)}$$

Also, because the X ranks and the Y ranks are the same values, the SS for X will be identical to the SS for Y.

Because calculations with ranks can be simplified and because the Spearman correlation uses ranked data, these simplifications can be incorporated into the final calculations for the Spearman correlation. Instead of using the Pearson formula after ranking the data, you can put the ranks directly into a simplified formula:

Caution: In this formula, you compute the value of the fraction and then subtract from 1. The 1 is not part of the fraction.

$$r_S = 1 - \frac{6\Sigma D^2}{n(n^2 - 1)} \qquad (15.5)$$

where D is the difference between the X rank and the Y rank for each individual. This special formula will produce the same result that would be obtained from the Pearson formula. However, you should note that this special formula can be used only after the scores have been converted to ranks and only when there are no ties among the ranks. If there are relatively few tied ranks, the formula still may be used, but it loses accuracy as the number of ties increases. The application of this formula is demonstrated in the following example.

EXAMPLE 15.10

To demonstrate the special formula for the Spearman correlation, we will use the same data that were presented in Example 15.9. The ranks for these data are shown again here:

Ranks		Difference	
X	Y	D	D^2
1	5	4	16
2	3	1	1
3	4	1	1
4	2	−2	4
5	1	−4	16
			$38 = \Sigma D^2$

Using the special formula for the Spearman correlation, we obtain

$$r_S = 1 - \frac{6\Sigma D^2}{n(n^2 - 1)}$$

$$= 1 - \frac{6(38)}{5(25 - 1)}$$

$$= 1 - \frac{228}{120}$$

$$= 1 - 1.90$$

$$= -0.90$$

Note that this is exactly the same answer that we obtained in Example 15.9, using the Pearson formula on the ranks.

LEARNING CHECK ◆ 1. Describe what is measured by a Spearman correlation, and explain how this correlation is different from the Pearson correlation.

2. Identify the two procedures that can be used to compute the Spearman correlation.

3. Compute the Spearman correlation for the following set of scores:

X	Y
2	7
12	38
9	6
10	19

ANSWERS 1. The Spearman correlation measures the consistency of the direction of the relationship between two variables. The Spearman correlation does not depend on the form of the relationship, whereas the Pearson correlation measures how well the data fit a linear form.

2. After the X and Y values have been ranked, you can compute the Spearman correlation by using either the special formula or the Pearson formula.

3. $r_S = 0.80$ ◆

15.6   INTRODUCTION TO REGRESSION

Earlier in this chapter, we introduced the Pearson correlation as a technique for describing and measuring the linear relationship between two variables. Figure 15.14 presents hypothetical data showing the relationship between SAT scores and college grade point average (GPA). Note that the figure shows a good, but not perfect, positive relationship. Also note that we have drawn a line through the middle of the data points. This line serves several purposes:

FIGURE 15.14

Hypothetical data showing the relationship between SAT scores and GPA with a regression line drawn through the data points. The regression line defines a precise, one-to-one relationship between each X value (SAT score) and its corresponding Y value (GPA).

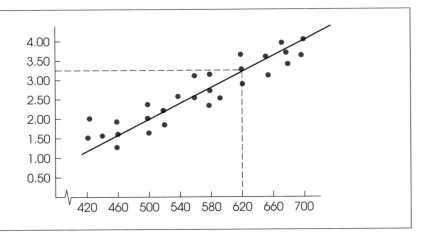

1. The line makes the relationship between SAT and GPA easier to see.

2. The line identifies the center, or *central tendency,* of the relationship, just as the mean describes central tendency for a set of scores. Thus, the line provides a simplified description of the relationship. For example, if the data points were removed, the straight line would still give a general picture of the relationship between SAT and GPA.

3. Finally, the line can be used for prediction. The line establishes a precise, one-to-one relationship between each X value (SAT score) and a corresponding Y value (GPA). For example, an SAT score of 620 corresponds to a GPA of 3.25 (see Figure 15.14). Thus, the college admissions officers could use the straight-line relationship to predict that a student entering college with an SAT score of 620 should achieve a college GPA of approximately 3.25.

Our goal in this section is to develop a procedure that identifies and defines the straight line that provides the best fit for any specific set of data. You should realize that this straight line does not have to be drawn on a graph; it can be presented in a simple equation. Thus, our goal is to find the equation for the line that best describes the relationship for a set of X and Y data.

LINEAR EQUATIONS

In general, a *linear relationship* between variables X and Y can be expressed by the equation $Y = bX + a$, where b and a are fixed constants.

For example, a local tennis club charges a fee of $5 per hour plus an annual membership fee of $25. With this information, the total cost of playing tennis can be computed using a *linear equation* that describes the relationship between the total cost (Y) and the number of hours (X):

$$Y = 5X + 25$$

Note that a positive slope means that Y increases when X increases, and a negative slope indicates that Y decreases when X increases.

In the general linear equation, the value of b is called the *slope.* The slope determines how much the Y variable will change when X is increased by one point. For the tennis club example, the slope is $b = \$5$ and indicates that your total cost will increase by $5 for each hour you play. The value of a in the general equation is called the *Y-intercept* because it determines the value of Y when $X = 0$. (On a graph, the a value identifies the point where the line intercepts the Y-axis.) For the tennis club example, $a = \$25$; there is a $25 charge even if you never play tennis.

Figure 15.15 shows the general relationship between cost and number of hours for the tennis club example. Note that the relationship results in a straight line. To obtain this graph, we picked any two values of X and then used the equation to compute the corresponding values for Y. For example,

when $X = 10$:	when $X = 30$:
$Y = bX + a$	$Y = bX + a$
$= \$5(10) + \$25$	$= \$5(30) + \$25$
$= \$50 + \$25$	$= \$150 + \$25$
$= \$75$	$= \$175$

FIGURE 15.15

Relationship between total cost and number of hours playing tennis. The tennis club charges a $25 membership fee plus $5 per hour. The relationship is described by a linear equation:

total cost = $5(number of hours) + $25

$$Y = bX + a$$

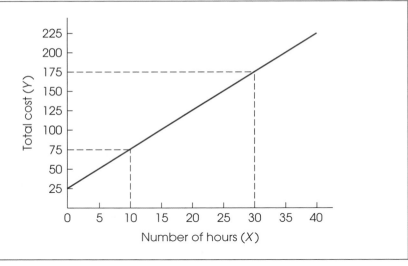

When drawing a graph of a linear equation, it is wise to compute and plot at least three points to be certain you have not made a mistake.

Next, these two points are plotted on the graph: one point at $X = 10$ and $Y = 75$, the other point at $X = 30$ and $Y = 175$. Because two points completely determine a straight line, we simply drew the line so that it passed through these two points.

Because a straight line can be extremely useful for describing a relationship between two variables, a statistical technique has been developed that provides a standardized method for determining the best-fitting straight line for any set of data. The statistical procedure is regression, and the resulting straight line is called the regression line.

DEFINITION

The statistical technique for finding the best-fitting straight line for a set of data is called *regression,* and the resulting straight line is called the *regression line.*

The goal for regression is to find the best-fitting straight line for a set of data. To accomplish this goal, however, it is first necessary to define precisely what is meant by "best fit." For any particular set of data, it is possible to draw lots of different straight lines that all appear to pass through the center of the data points. Each of these lines can be defined by a linear equation of the form

$$Y = bX + a$$

where b and a are constants that determine the slope and Y-intercept of the line, respectively. Each individual line has its own unique values for b and a. The problem is to find the specific line that provides the best fit to the actual data points.

LEARNING CHECK

1. Identify the slope and Y-intercept for the following linear equation:

$$Y = -3X + 7$$

2. Use the linear equation $Y = 2X - 7$ to determine the value of Y for each of the following values of X: 1, 3, 5, 10.

3. If the slope constant (b) in a linear equation is positive, then a graph of the equation will be a line tilted from lower left to upper right. (True or false?)

ANSWERS   **1.** Slope $= -3$ and Y-intercept $= +7$.

2.

X	Y
1	−5
3	−1
5	3
10	13

3. True. A positive slope indicates that Y increases (goes up in the graph) when X increases (goes to the right in the graph).   ◆

THE LEAST-SQUARES SOLUTION

To determine how well a line fits the data points, the first step is to define mathematically the distance between the line and each data point. For every X value in the data, the linear equation will determine a Y value on the line. This value is the predicted Y and is called $\hat{Y}$ ("Y hat"). The distance between this predicted value and the actual Y value in the data is determined by

$$\text{distance} = Y - \hat{Y}$$

Note that we simply are measuring the vertical distance between the actual data point (Y) and the predicted point on the line. This distance measures the error between the line and the actual data (see Figure 15.16).

FIGURE 15.16

The distance between the actual data point (Y) and the predicted point on the line ($\hat{Y}$) is defined as $Y - \hat{Y}$. The goal of regression is to find the equation for the line that minimizes these distances.

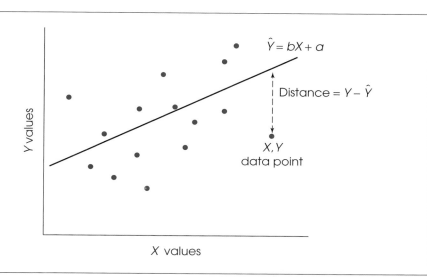

Because some of these distances will be positive and some will be negative, the next step is to square each distance to obtain a uniformly positive measure of error. Finally, to determine the total error between the line and the data, we sum the squared errors for all of the data points. The result is a measure of overall squared error between the line and the data:

$$\text{total squared error} = \Sigma(Y - \hat{Y})^2$$

Now we can define the *best-fitting* line as the one that has the smallest total squared error. For obvious reasons, the resulting line is commonly called the *least-squared-error* solution.

In symbols, we are looking for a linear equation of the form

$$\hat{Y} = bX + a$$

For each value of X in the data, this equation will determine the point on the line $(\hat{Y})$ *that gives the best prediction of Y*. The problem is to find the specific values for a and b that will make this the best-fitting line.

The calculations that are needed to find this equation require calculus and some sophisticated algebra, so we will not present the details of the solution. The results, however, are relatively straightforward, and the solutions for b and a are as follows:

A commonly used alternative formula for the slope is

$$b = r\frac{s_Y}{s_X}$$

where s_X and s_Y are the standard deviations for X and Y, respectively.

$$b = \frac{SP}{SS_X} \tag{15.6}$$

where SP is the sum of products and SS_X is the sum of squares for the X scores.

$$a = \overline{Y} - b\overline{X} \tag{15.7}$$

Note that these two formulas determine the linear equation that provides the best prediction of Y values. This equation is called the regression equation for Y.

DEFINITION

The *regression equation for Y* is the linear equation

$$\hat{Y} = bX + a$$

where the constants b and a are determined by Equations 15.6 and 15.7, respectively. This equation results in the least squared error between the data points and the line.

You should notice that the values of SS and SP are needed in the formulas for b and a, just as they are needed to compute the Pearson correlation. Now we present an example demonstrating the calculation and use of this best-fitting line.

EXAMPLE 15.11

The following table shows X and Y scores for a sample of $n = 5$ individuals. These data will be used to demonstrate the procedure for determining the linear regression equation for predicting Y values.

X	Y	$X - \overline{X}$	$Y - \overline{Y}$	$(X - \overline{X})(Y - \overline{Y})$	$(X - \overline{X})^2$
7	11	2	5	10	4
4	3	−1	−3	3	1
6	5	1	−1	−1	1
3	4	−2	−2	4	4
5	7	0	1	0	0
				$16 = SP$	$10 = SS_X$

For these data, $\Sigma X = 25$, so $\overline{X} = 5$. Also, $\Sigma Y = 30$, so $\overline{Y} = 6$. These means have been used to compute the deviation scores for each X and Y value. The final two columns show the products of the deviation scores and the squared deviations for X. Based on these values,

$$SP = \Sigma(X - \overline{X})(Y - \overline{Y}) = 16$$
$$SS_X = \Sigma(X - \overline{X})^2 = 10$$

Our goal is to find the values for b and a in the linear equation so that we obtain the best-fitting straight line for these data.

By using Formulas 15.6 and 15.7, the solutions for b and a are

$$b = \frac{SP}{SS_X} = \frac{16}{10} = 1.6$$

$$\begin{aligned} a &= \overline{Y} - b\overline{X} \\ &= 6 - 1.6(5) \\ &= 6 - 8 \\ &= -2 \end{aligned}$$

The resulting regression equation is

$$\hat{Y} = 1.6X - 2$$

The original data and the regression line are shown in Figure 15.17.

FIGURE 15.17

The scatterplot for the data in Example 15.11 is shown with the best-fitting straight line. The predicted Y values ($\hat{Y}$) are on the regression line. Unless the correlation is perfect ($+1.00$ or -1.00), there will be some error between the actual Y values and the predicted Y values. The larger the correlation is, the smaller the error will be.

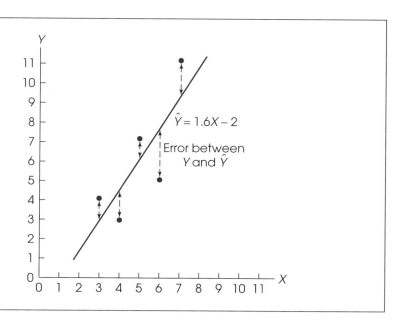

As we noted at the beginning of this section, one common use of regression equations is for prediction. For any given value of X, we can use the equation to compute a predicted value for Y. For the equation from Example 15.11, an individual with an X score of $X = 5$ would be predicted to have a Y score of

$$\hat{Y} = 1.6X - 2$$
$$= 1.6(5) - 2$$
$$= 8 - 2$$
$$= 6$$

Although regression equations can be used for prediction, a few cautions should be considered whenever you are interpreting the predicted values:

1. The predicted value is not perfect (unless $r = +1.00$ or -1.00). If you examine Figure 15.17, it should be clear that the data points do not fit perfectly on the line. In general, there will be some error between the predicted Y values (on the line) and the actual data. Although the amount of error will vary from point to point, on average the errors will be directly related to the magnitude of the correlation. With a correlation near 1.00 (or -1.00), the data points will generally be close to the line (small error), but as the correlation gets nearer to zero, the magnitude of the error will increase.

2. The regression equation should not be used to make predictions for X values that fall outside the range of values covered by the original data. For Example 15.11, the X values ranged from $X = 3$ to $X = 7$, and the regression equation was calculated as the best-fitting line within this range. Because you have no information about the X-Y relationship outside this range, the equation should not be used to predict Y for any X value lower than 3 or greater than 7.

LEARNING CHECK ◆

1. Sketch a scatterplot for the following data—that is, a graph showing the X, Y data points:

X	Y
1	4
3	9
5	8

a. Find the regression equation for predicting Y and X. Draw this line on your graph. Does it look like the best-fitting line?

b. Use the regression equation to find the predicted Y value corresponding to each X in the data.

ANSWERS

1. a. $SS_X = 8$, $SP = 8$, $b = 1$, $a = 4$. The equation is

$$\hat{Y} = X + 4$$

b. The predicted Y values are 5, 7, and 9.   ◆

ON THE WEB

REMEMBER THAT a practice quiz for Chapter 15 is available on the Wadsworth Web site at **www.wadsworth.com**. You can use the quiz to test your knowledge on correlation and regression and determine where you may need more study. In addition, you can visit the workshop on correlation at the same Web site. For more information about finding the quizzes and workshops, see page 24.

SUMMARY

1. A correlation measures the relationship between two variables, X and Y. The relationship is described by three characteristics:

    a. *Direction.* A relationship can be either positive or negative. A positive relationship means that X and Y vary in the same direction. A negative relationship means that X and Y vary in opposite directions. The sign of the correlation ($+$ or $-$) specifies the direction.

    b. *Form.* The most common form for a relationship is a straight line. However, special correlations exist for measuring other forms. The form is specified by the type of correlation used. For example, the Pearson correlation measures linear form.

    c. *Degree.* The magnitude of the correlation measures the degree to which the data points fit the specified form. A correlation of 1.00 indicates a perfect fit, and a correlation of 0 indicates no degree of fit.

2. The most commonly used correlation is the Pearson correlation, which measures the degree of linear relationship. The Pearson correlation is identified by the letter r and is computed by

$$r = \frac{SP}{\sqrt{SS_X SS_Y}}$$

In this formula, SP is the sum of products of deviations and can be calculated with either a definitional formula or a computational formula:

definitional formula: $SP = \Sigma(X - \overline{X})(Y - \overline{Y})$

computational formula: $SP = \Sigma XY - \dfrac{\Sigma X \Sigma Y}{n}$

3. A correlation between two variables should not be interpreted as implying a causal relationship. Simply because X and Y are related does not mean that X causes Y or that Y causes X.

4. To evaluate the strength of a relationship, you should square the value of the correlation. The resulting value, r^2, is called the *coefficient of determination* because it measures the portion of the variability in one variable that can be predicted using the relationship with the second variable.

5. The Spearman correlation (r_S) measures the consistency of direction in the relationship between X and Y—that is, the degree to which the relationship is one-directional, or monotonic. The Spearman correlation is computed by a two-stage process:

    a. Rank the X scores and the Y scores.

    b. Compute the Pearson correlation using the ranks.

    Note: After the X and Y values are ranked, you may use a special formula to determine the Spearman correlation:

$$r_S = 1 - \frac{6\Sigma D^2}{n(n^2 - 1)}$$

where D is the difference between the X rank and the Y rank for each individual. The formula is accurate only when there are no tied scores in the data.

6. When there is a general linear relationship between two variables, X and Y, it is possible to construct a linear equation that allows you to predict the Y value corresponding to any known value of X:

$$\text{predicted } Y \text{ value} = \hat{Y} = bX + a$$

The technique for determining this equation is called regression. By using a *least-squares* method to minimize the error between the predicted Y values and the actual Y values, the best-fitting line is achieved when the linear equation has

$$b = \frac{SP}{SS_X} \quad \text{and} \quad a = \overline{Y} - b\overline{X}$$

KEY TERMS

correlation	sum of products of	ranks	regression
positive correlation	deviations	monotonic relationship	regression line
negative correlation	restricted range	linear equation	predicted Y
perfect correlation	coefficient of determination	slope	least-squared error
Pearson correlation	Spearman correlation	Y-intercept	regression equation for Y
	linear relationship		

FOCUS ON PROBLEM SOLVING

1. A correlation always has a value from $+1.00$ to -1.00. If you obtain a correlation outside this range, then you have made a computational error.

2. When interpreting a correlation, do not confuse the sign ($+$ or $-$) with its numerical value. The sign and the numerical value must be considered separately. Remember that the sign indicates the direction of the relationship between X and Y. On the other hand, the numerical value reflects the strength of the relationship or how well the points approximate a linear (straight-line) relationship. Therefore, a correlation of -0.90 is as strong as a correlation of $+.90$. The signs tell us that the first correlation is an inverse relationship.

3. Before you begin to calculate a correlation, you should sketch a scatterplot of the data and make an estimate of the correlation. (Is it positive or negative? Is it near 1 or near 0?) After computing the correlation, compare your final answer with your original estimate.

4. The definitional formula for the sum of products (SP) should be used only when you have a small set (n) of scores and the means for X and Y are both whole numbers. Otherwise, the computational formula will produce quicker, easier, and more accurate results.

5. For computing a correlation, n is the number of individuals (and therefore the number of *pairs* of X and Y values).

6. When using the special formula for the Spearman correlation, remember that the fraction is computed separately and then subtracted from 1. Students often include the 1 as a part of the numerator, or they get so absorbed in computing the fractional part of the equation that they forget to subtract it from 1. Be careful using this formula.

7. When computing a Spearman correlation, be sure that both X and Y values have been ranked. Sometimes the data will consist of one variable already ranked with the other variable on an interval or a ratio scale. If one variable is ranked, do not forget to rank the other. When interpreting a Spearman correlation, remember that it measures how monotonic (consistent) the relationship is between X and Y.

8. To draw a graph from a linear equation, choose any three values for X, put each value in the equation, and calculate the corresponding values for Y. Then plot the three X, Y points on the graph. It is a good idea to use $X = 0$ for one of the three values because this will give you the Y-intercept. You can get a quick idea of what the graph should look like if you know the Y-intercept and the slope. Remember that the Y-intercept is the point where the line crosses the Y-axis, and the slope identifies the tilt of the line. For example, suppose the Y-intercept is 5 and the slope is -3. The line passes through the point $(0, 5)$, and its slope indicates that the Y value goes down 3 points each time X increases by 1.

9. Rather than memorizing the formula for the Y-intercept in the regression equation, simply remember that the graphed line of the regression equation always goes through the point $\overline{X}$, $\overline{Y}$. Therefore, if you plug the mean value for X ($\overline{X}$) into the regression equation, the result equals the mean value for Y ($\overline{Y}$).

$$\overline{Y} = b\overline{X} + a$$

If you simply solve this equation for a, you get the formula for the Y-intercept.

$$a = \overline{Y} - b\overline{X}$$

DEMONSTRATION 15.1

CORRELATION AND REGRESSION

For the following data, calculate the Pearson correlation and find the regression equation:

Person	X	Y
A	0	4
B	2	1
C	8	10
D	6	9
E	4	6

STEP 1   Sketch a scatterplot.

We have constructed a scatterplot for the data (Figure 15.18) and placed an envelope around the data points to make a preliminary estimate of the correlation. Note that the envelope is narrow and elongated. This indicates that the correlation is large—perhaps 0.80 to

FIGURE 15.18

The scatterplot for the data of Demonstration 15.1. An envelope is drawn around the points to estimate the magnitude of the correlation. A line is drawn through the middle of the envelope to roughly estimate the Y-intercept for the regression equation.

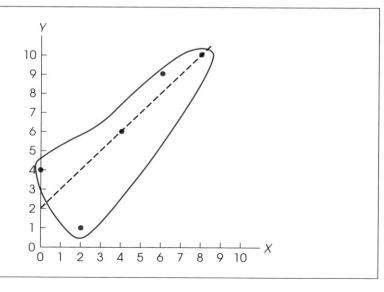

0.90. Also, the correlation is positive because increases in X are generally accompanied by increases in Y.

We can sketch a straight line through the middle of the envelope and data points. Now we can roughly approximate the slope and Y-intercept of the best-fit line. This is only an educated guess, but it will tell us what values are reasonable when we actually compute the regression line. The line has a positive slope (as X increases, Y increases), and it intersects the Y-axis in the vicinity of $+2$.

STEP 2   Obtain the values for SS and SP.

To compute the Pearson correlation, we must find the values for SS_X, SS_Y, and SP. These values are needed for the regression equation as well. The following table illustrates these calculations with the computational formulas for SS and SP:

X	Y	X^2	Y^2	XY
0	4	0	16	0
2	1	4	1	2
8	10	64	100	80
6	9	36	81	54
4	6	16	36	24
$\Sigma X = 20$	$\Sigma Y = 30$	$\Sigma X^2 = 120$	$\Sigma Y^2 = 234$	$\Sigma XY = 160$

For SS_X, we obtain

$$SS_X = \Sigma X^2 - \frac{(\Sigma X)^2}{n} = 120 - \frac{20^2}{5} = 120 - \frac{400}{5} = 120 - 80$$
$$= 40$$

For Y, the sum of squares is

$$SS_Y = \Sigma Y^2 - \frac{(\Sigma Y)^2}{n} = 234 - \frac{30^2}{5} = 234 - \frac{900}{5} = 234 - 180$$
$$= 54$$

The sum of products equals

$$SP = \Sigma XY - \frac{\Sigma X \Sigma Y}{n} = 160 - \frac{20(30)}{5} = 160 - \frac{600}{5} = 160 - 120$$
$$= 40$$

STEP 3   Compute the Pearson correlation.

For these data, the Pearson correlation is

$$r = \frac{SP}{\sqrt{SS_X SS_Y}} = \frac{40}{\sqrt{40(54)}} = \frac{40}{\sqrt{2160}} = \frac{40}{46.48}$$
$$= 0.861$$

In step 1, our preliminary estimate for the correlation was between $+0.80$ and $+0.90$. The calculated correlation is consistent with this estimate.

STEP 4 Compute the values for the regression equation.
The general form of the regression equation is

$$\hat{Y} = bX + a$$

We will need to compute the values for the slope (b) of the line and the Y-intercept (a). For slope, we obtain

$$b = \frac{SP}{SS_X} = \frac{40}{40} = +1$$

The formula for the Y-intercept is

$$a = \overline{Y} - b\overline{X}$$

Thus, we will need the values for the sample means. For these data, the sample means are

$$\overline{X} = \frac{\Sigma X}{n} = \frac{20}{5} = 4 \qquad \overline{Y} = \frac{\Sigma Y}{n} = \frac{30}{5} = 6$$

Now we can compute the Y-intercept.

$$a = 6 - 1(4) = 6 - 4 = 2$$

Finally, the regression equation is

$$\hat{Y} = bX + a = 1X + 2$$

or

$$\hat{Y} = X + 2$$

PROBLEMS

1. What information is provided by the sign ($+$ or $-$) of the Pearson correlation?

2. What information is provided by the numerical value of the Pearson correlation?

3. What is the major distinction between the Pearson and Spearman correlations?

4. For each of the following sets of scores, calculate SP using the definitional formula and then using the computational formula:

Set 1	
X	Y
1	2
3	2
5	3
7	5

Set 2	
X	Y
3	5
6	1
4	2
7	0

5. For the following set of data,

X	Y
1	0
2	2
4	6
5	8
3	4

a. Sketch a graph showing the location of the five X, Y points.
b. Just looking at your graph, estimate the value of the Pearson correlation.
c. Compute the Pearson correlation.

6. For this problem, we have used the same X and Y values that appeared in Problem 5, but we have changed the X, Y pairings:

X	Y
1	6
2	8
4	2
5	0
3	4

a. Sketch a graph showing these reorganized data.
b. Estimate the Pearson correlation just by looking at your graph.
c. Compute the Pearson correlation. (*Note:* Much of the calculation for this problem was done already in Problem 5.)

If you compare the results of Problem 5 and Problem 6, you will see that the correlation measures the relationship between X and Y. These two problems use the same X and Y values, but they differ in the way X and Y are related.

7. With a very small sample, a single point can have a large influence on the magnitude of a correlation. For the following data set,

X	Y
0	1
10	3
4	1
8	2
8	3

a. Sketch a graph showing the X, Y points.
b. Estimate the value of the Pearson correlation.
c. Compute the Pearson correlation.
d. Now we will change the value of one of the points. For the first individual in the sample ($X = 0$ and $Y = 1$), change the Y value to $Y = 6$. What happens to the graph of the X, Y points? What happens to the Pearson correlation? Compute the new correlation.

8. In the following data, there are three scores (X, Y, and Z) for each of the $n = 5$ individuals:

X	Y	Z
3	5	5
4	3	2
2	4	6
1	1	3
0	2	4

a. Sketch a graph showing the relationship between X and Y. Compute the Pearson correlation between X and Y.
b. Sketch a graph showing the relationship between Y and Z. Compute the Pearson correlation between Y and Z.
c. Given the results of parts (a) and (b), what would you predict for the correlation between X and Z?
d. Sketch a graph showing the relationship between X and Z. Compute the Pearson correlation for these data.
e. What general conclusion can you make concerning relationships among correlations? If X is related to Y and Y is related to Z, does this necessarily mean that X is related to Z?

9. a. Compute the Pearson correlation for the following set of data:

X	Y
4	8
3	10
3	7
5	6
6	8
8	4
9	2
10	3

b. Add 5 points to each X value, and compute the Pearson correlation again.
c. When you add a constant to each score, what happens to SS for X and Y? What happens to SP? What happens to the correlation between X and Y?
d. Now multiply each X in the original data by 3, and calculate the Pearson correlation once again.
e. When you multiply by a constant, what happens to SS for X and Y? What happens to SP? What happens to the correlation between X and Y?

10. It is well known that similarity in attitudes, beliefs, and interests plays an important role in interpersonal attraction (see Byrne, 1971, for example). Thus, correlations for attitudes between married couples should be strong. Suppose a researcher developed a questionnaire that measures how liberal or conservative one's attitudes are. Low scores indicate that the person has liberal attitudes, while high scores indicate conservatism. The following hypothetical data are scores for married couples.

Couple	Wife	Husband
A	11	14
B	6	7
C	18	15
D	4	7
E	1	3
F	10	9
G	5	9
H	3	3

a. Compute the Pearson correlation for these data.
b. Do the data indicate a significant correlation between attitudes for husbands and wives? Use a two-tailed test with $\alpha = .05$.

11. A researcher has developed a new test of self-esteem. To evaluate the reliability of the test, the researcher obtains a sample of $n = 8$ subjects. Each individual takes the test on a Monday morning, then returns 2 weeks later to take the test again. The two scores for each individual are reported in the following table. Use a Pearson correlation to measure the degree of consistency between the first and second measure for this sample.

First test	Second test
13	15
5	4
12	13
11	11
9	10
14	13
8	8
8	6

12. A high school counselor would like to know whether there is a relationship between mathematical skill and verbal skill. After selecting a sample of $n = 25$ students, the counselor records achievement test scores in mathematics and English for each student. The Pearson correlation for this sample is $r = +0.50$. Do these data provide sufficient evidence for a real relationship in the population? Test at the .05 level, two tails.

13. A psychologist would like to determine whether there is any consistent relationship between intelligence and creativity. The psychologist obtains a random sample of $n = 18$ people, and administers a standardized IQ test and a creativity test to each individual. Using these data, the psychologist obtains a Pearson correlation of $r = +0.20$ between IQ and creativity.
a. Do the sample data provide sufficient evidence to conclude that a real (nonzero) correlation exists in the population? Test at the .05 level of significance.
b. If the same correlation, $r = 0.20$, was obtained for a sample of $n = 102$ people, what decision would you make about the population correlation?

14. While grading essay exams, a professor noticed huge differences in the writing skills of the students. To investigate a possible cause for the differences, the professor asked the students how many English courses they had completed. The number of courses completed and the professor's ranking of the essay are reported for each student in the following table.

Quality of essay (professor's ranking)	Number of English courses
1 (best)	7
2	4
3	1
4	3
5	1
6	1
7	0
8	2

Compute the Spearman correlation between writing ability and English background. (*Note:* You must convert the data before computing the correlation.)

15. A common concern for students (and teachers) is the assignment of grades for essays or term papers. Because there are no absolute right or wrong answers, these grades must be based on a judgment of quality. To demonstrate that these judgments actually are valid, an English instructor asked a colleague to rank-order a set

of term papers. The ranks and the instructor's grades for these papers are as follows:

Rank	Grade
1	A
2	B
3	A
4	B
5	B
6	C
7	D
8	C
9	C
10	D
11	E

  a. Calculate the Spearman correlation for these data. (*Note:* You must convert the letter grades to ranks.)

  b. Based on this correlation, does it appear that there is reasonable agreement between these two instructors in their judgment of the papers?

16. In the following data, X and Y are related by the equation $Y = X^2$:

X	Y
0	0
1	1
2	4
3	9
4	16
5	25

  a. Sketch a graph showing the relationship between X and Y. Describe the relationship shown in your graph.

  b. Compute the Spearman correlation for these data.

17. A psychology instructor asked each student to report the number of hours he or she spent preparing for an exam. In addition, the instructor recorded the number of errors made on each student's exam. The data are as follows.

Hours	Errors
0	19
1	6
2	2
4	1
4	4
5	0
3	3
5	5

  a. Calculate the Pearson correlation for the data.

  b. Convert the hours and errors to ranks and compute the Spearman correlation.

  c. Explain the difference between the values obtained for the two correlations. *Hint:* Sketch a scatterplot for the original data and for the ranks.

18. Researchers who measure reaction time for human subjects often observe a relationship between the reaction time scores and the number of errors that the subjects commit. This relationship is known as the *speed–accuracy trade-off*. The following data are from a reaction time study where the researcher recorded the average reaction time (milliseconds) and the total number of errors for each individual in a sample of $n = 8$ subjects.

Subject	Reaction time	Errors
A	184	10
B	213	6
C	234	2
D	197	7
E	189	13
F	221	10
G	237	4
H	192	9

  a. Compute the Pearson correlation for the data.

  b. In words, describe the speed–accuracy trade-off.

19. Sketch a graph of the equation $Y = 2X + 4$.

20. For the following set of data, find the linear regression equation for predicting Y from X:

X	Y
0	9
2	9
4	7
6	3

21. a. Find the regression equation for the following data:

X	Y
1	2
4	7
3	5
2	1
5	14
3	7

b. Compute the predicted Y value for each X in the data.

22. Find the regression equation for the following data:

X	Y
3	12
0	8
4	18
2	12
1	8

23. Many researchers have found a negative relationship between children's IQs and the size of the family in which the children live. The following hypothetical data represent eight families.
   a. Compute the Pearson correlation between family size and average IQ.
   b. Find the regression equation for using the number of children to predict the average IQ.

Number of children (X)	Children's average IQ (Y)
4	104
2	111
2	101
1	131
3	103
5	96
1	123
2	115

24. A college professor claims that the scores on the first exam provide an excellent indication of how students will perform throughout the term. To test this claim, first-exam scores and final grades were recorded for a sample of $n = 12$ students in an introductory psychology class. The data are as follows:

First exam	Final grade
62	74
73	93
88	68
82	79
85	91
77	72
94	96
65	61
91	92
74	82
85	93
98	95

Is the professor right? Is there a significant correlation between scores on the first exam and final grades? Test with $\alpha = .01$.

CHAPTER 16

THE CHI-SQUARE STATISTIC: TESTS FOR GOODNESS OF FIT AND INDEPENDENCE

TOOLS YOU WILL NEED

The following items are considered essential background material for this chapter. If you doubt your knowledge of any of these items, you should review the appropriate chapter or section before proceeding.

- Proportions (math review, Appendix A)
- Frequency distributions (Chapter 2)

CONTENTS

16.1 PARAMETRIC AND NONPARAMETRIC STATISTICAL TESTS

All the statistical tests we have examined thus far are designed to test hypotheses about specific population parameters. For example, we used t tests to assess hypotheses about μ and later about $\mu_1 - \mu_2$. In addition, these tests typically make assumptions about the shape of the population distribution and about other population parameters. Recall that, for analysis of variance, the population distributions are assumed to be normal and homogeneity of variance is required. Because these tests all concern parameters and require assumptions about parameters, they are called *parametric tests*.

Another general characteristic of parametric tests is that they require a numerical score for each individual in the sample. The scores then are added, squared, averaged, and otherwise manipulated using basic arithmetic. In terms of measurement scales, parametric tests require data from an interval or a ratio scale (see Chapter 1).

Often, researchers are confronted with experimental situations that do not conform to the requirements of parametric tests. In these situations, it may not be appropriate to use a parametric test. Remember that when the assumptions of a test are violated, the test may lead to an erroneous interpretation of the data. Fortunately, there are several hypothesis-testing techniques that provide alternatives to parametric tests. These alternatives are called *nonparametric tests*.

In this chapter, we will introduce two commonly used examples of nonparametric tests. Both tests are based on a statistic known as chi-square and both tests use sample data to evaluate hypotheses about the proportions or relationships that exist within populations. You should note that the two chi-square tests, like most nonparametric tests, do not state hypotheses in terms of a specific parameter and that they make few (if any) assumptions about the population distribution. For the latter reason, nonparametric tests sometimes are called *distribution-free tests*.

One of the most obvious differences between parametric and nonparametric tests is the type of data that they use. All of the parametric tests that we have examined so far require numerical scores. For nonparametric tests, on the other hand, the subjects are usually just classified into categories such as Democrat and Republican, or High, Medium, and Low IQ. Note that these classifications involve measurement on nominal or ordinal scales, and they do not produce numerical values that can be used to calculate means and variances. Instead, the data for many nonparametric tests are simply frequencies—for example, the number of Democrats and the number of Republicans in a sample of $n = 100$ registered voters.

Finally, you should be warned that nonparametric tests generally are not as sensitive as parametric tests; nonparametric tests are more likely to fail in detecting a real difference between two treatments. Therefore, whenever the experimental data give you a choice between a parametric and a nonparametric test, you should always choose the parametric alternative.

16.2   THE CHI-SQUARE TEST FOR GOODNESS OF FIT

Parameters such as the mean and the standard deviation are the most common way to describe a population, but there are situations in which a researcher has questions about the proportions or relative frequencies for a distribution. For example,

The name of the test comes from the Greek letter χ (chi, pronounced "kye"), which is used to identify the test statistic.

How does the number of women lawyers compare with the number of men in the profession?

Of the three leading brands of soft drinks, which is preferred by most Americans? Which brands are second and third, and how big are the differences in popularity among the three?

To what extent are different ethnic groups represented in the population of your college or university?

Note that each of the preceding examples asks a question about proportions in the population. The *chi-square test for goodness of fit* is specifically designed to answer this type of question. In general terms, this chi-square test is a hypothesis-testing procedure that uses the proportions obtained for a sample distribution to test hypotheses about the corresponding proportions in the population distribution.

DEFINITION

The *chi-square test for goodness of fit* uses sample data to test hypotheses about the shape or proportions of a population distribution. The test determines how well the obtained sample proportions fit the population proportions specified by the null hypothesis.

Recall from Chapter 2 that a frequency distribution is defined as a tabulation of the number of individuals located in each category of the scale of measurement. In a frequency distribution graph, the categories that make up the scale of measurement are listed on the X-axis. In a frequency distribution table, the categories are listed in the first column. With chi-square tests, however, it is customary to present the scale of measurement as a series of boxes, with each box corresponding to a separate category on the scale. The frequency corresponding to each category is simply presented as a number written inside the box. Figure 16.1 shows how a distribution of eye colors for a set of $n = 40$ students can be presented as a graph, a table, or a series of boxes. The scale of measurement for this example consists of four categories of eye color (blue, brown, green, other).

THE NULL HYPOTHESIS FOR THE GOODNESS-OF-FIT TEST

For the chi-square test of goodness of fit, the null hypothesis specifies the proportion (or percentage) of the population in each category. For example, a hypothesis might state that 90% of all lawyers are men and only 10% are women. The simplest way of presenting this hypothesis is to put the hypothesized proportions in the series of boxes representing the scale of measurement:

	Men	Women
H_0:	90%	10%

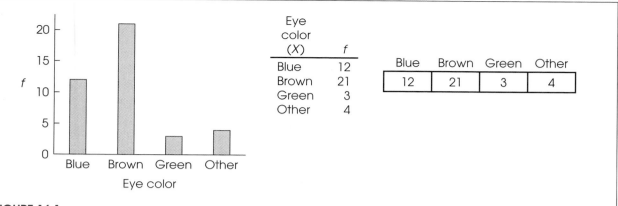

FIGURE 16.1

Distribution of eye colors for a sample of $n = 40$ individuals. The same frequency distribution is shown as a bar graph, as a table, and with the frequencies written in a series of boxes.

Although it is conceivable that a researcher could choose any proportions for the null hypothesis, there usually is some well-defined rationale for stating a null hypothesis. Generally H_0 will fall into one of the following categories:

1. No Preference. The null hypothesis often states that there is no preference among the different categories. In this case, H_0 states that the population is divided equally among the categories. For example, a hypothesis stating that there is no preference among the three leading brands of soft drinks would specify a population distribution as follows:

	Brand X	Brand Y	Brand Z
H_0:	$\frac{1}{3}$	$\frac{1}{3}$	$\frac{1}{3}$

(Preferences in the population are equally divided among the three soft drinks.)

The no-preference hypothesis is used in situations where a researcher wants to determine whether there are any preferences among categories or any variations from one category to another.

2. No Difference from a Comparison Population. The null hypothesis can state that the frequency distribution for one population is not different from the distribution that is known to exist for another population. For example, suppose it is known that 60% of Americans favor the president's foreign policy and 40% are in opposition. A researcher might wonder whether this same pattern of attitudes exists among Europeans. The null hypothesis would state that there is no difference between the two populations and would specify that the Europeans are distributed as follows:

	Favor	Oppose
H_0:	60%	40%

(Proportions for the European population are not different from the American proportions.)

The no-difference hypothesis is used when a specific population distribution is already known. You may have a known distribution from an earlier time, and the question is whether there has been any change in the distribution. Or you may have a known distribution for one population, and the question is whether a second population has the same distribution.

Because the null hypothesis for the goodness-of-fit test specifies an exact distribution for the population, the alternative hypothesis (H_1) simply states that the population distribution has a different shape from that specified in H_0. If the null hypothesis states that the population is equally divided among three categories, the alternative hypothesis will say that the population is not divided equally.

THE DATA FOR THE GOODNESS-OF-FIT TEST

The data for a chi-square test are remarkably simple. There is no need to calculate a sample mean or SS; you just select a sample of n individuals and count how many are in each category. The resulting values are called *observed frequencies*. The symbol for observed frequency is f_o. For example, the following data represent observed frequencies for a sample of $n = 40$ subjects. Each person was given a personality questionnaire and classified into one of three personality categories: A, B, or C.

Category A	Category B	Category C	
15	19	6	$n = 40$

Note that each individual in the sample is classified into one and only one of the categories. Thus, the frequencies in this example represent three completely separate groups of individuals: 15 who were classified as category A, 19 classified as B, and 6 classified as C. Also note that the observed frequencies add up to the total sample size: $\Sigma f_o = n$.

DEFINITION

The *observed frequency* is the number of individuals from the sample who are classified in a particular category. Each individual is counted in one and only one category.

EXPECTED FREQUENCIES

The general goal of the chi-square test for goodness of fit is to compare the data (the observed frequencies) with the null hypothesis. The problem is to determine how well the data fit the distribution specified in H_0—hence the name *goodness of fit*.

The first step in the chi-square test is to construct a hypothetical sample that represents how the sample distribution would look if it was in perfect agreement with the proportions stated in the null hypothesis. Suppose, for example, the null hypothesis states that the population is distributed in three categories with the following proportions:

	Category A	Category B	Category C
H_0:	25%	50%	25%

If this hypothesis is correct, how would you expect a random sample of $n = 40$ individuals to be distributed among the three categories? It should be clear that your best strategy is to predict that 25% of the sample would be in category A, 50% would be in category B, and 25% would be in category C. To find the exact frequency expected for each category, multiply the sample size (n) by the proportion (or percentage) from the null hypothesis. For this example, you would expect

$$25\% \text{ of } 40 = 0.25(40) = 10 \text{ individuals in category A}$$

$$50\% \text{ of } 40 = 0.50(40) = 20 \text{ individuals in category B}$$

$$25\% \text{ of } 40 = 0.25(40) = 10 \text{ individuals in category C}$$

The frequency values predicted from the null hypothesis are called *expected frequencies*. The symbol for expected frequency is f_e, and the expected frequency for each category is computed by

$$\text{expected frequency} = f_e = pn \qquad (16.1)$$

where p is the proportion stated in the null hypothesis and n is the sample size.

DEFINITION

The *expected frequency* for each category is the frequency value that is predicted from the null hypothesis and the sample size (n). The expected frequencies define an ideal, *hypothetical* sample distribution that would be obtained if the sample proportions were in perfect agreement with the proportions specified in the null hypothesis.

Note that the no-preference null hypothesis will always produce equal f_e values for all categories because the proportions (p) are the same for all categories. On the other hand, the no-difference null hypothesis typically will not produce equal values for the expected frequencies because the hypothesized proportions typically vary from one category to another. You also should note that the expected frequencies are calculated, hypothetical values and the numbers that you obtain may be decimals or fractions. The observed frequencies, on the other hand, always represent real individuals and always will be whole numbers.

THE CHI-SQUARE STATISTIC

The general purpose of any hypothesis test is to determine whether the sample data support or refute a hypothesis about the population. In the chi-square test for goodness of fit, the sample is expressed as a set of observed frequencies (f_o values), and the null hypothesis is used to generate a set of expected frequencies (f_e values). The *chi-square statistic* simply measures how well the data (f_o) fit the hypothesis (f_e). The symbol for the chi-square statistic is χ^2. The formula for the chi-square statistic is

$$\text{chi-square} = \chi^2 = \Sigma \frac{(f_o - f_e)^2}{f_e} \qquad (16.2)$$

As the formula indicates, the value of chi-square is computed by the following steps:

1. Find the difference between f_o (the data) and f_e (the hypothesis) for each category.
2. Square the difference. This ensures that all values are positive.
3. Next, divide the squared difference by f_e. A justification for this step is given in Box 16.1.
4. Finally, sum the values from all the categories.

16.1   THE CHI-SQUARE FORMULA

THE NUMERATOR of the chi-square formula is fairly easy to understand. Specifically, the numerator simply measures how much difference there is between the data (the f_o values) and the hypothesis (represented by the f_e values). A large value indicates that the data do not fit the hypothesis, and will lead us to reject the hypothesis.

The denominator of the formula, on the other hand, is not so easy to understand. Why must we divide by f_e before we sum the category values? The answer to this question is that the obtained discrepancy between f_o and f_e is viewed as *relatively* large or *relatively* small depending on the size of the expected frequency. This point is demonstrated in the following analogy.

Suppose you were going to throw a party and you *expected* 1000 people to show up. However, at the party you counted the number of guests and *observed* that 1040 actually showed up. Forty more guests than expected are no major problem when all along you were planning for 1000. There will still probably be enough beer and potato chips for everyone. On the other hand, suppose you had a party and you expected 10 people to attend but instead 50 actually showed up. Forty more guests in this case spell big trouble. How "significant" the discrepancy is depends in part on what you were originally expecting. With very large expected frequencies, allowances are made for more error between f_o and f_e. This is accomplished in the chi-square formula by dividing the squared discrepancy for each category, $(f_o - f_e)^2$, by its expected frequency.

THE CHI-SQUARE DISTRIBUTION AND DEGREES OF FREEDOM

It should be clear from the chi-square formula that the value of chi-square measures the discrepancy between the observed frequencies (data) and the expected frequencies (H_0). When there are large differences between f_o and f_e, the value of chi-square will be large, and we will conclude that the data do not fit the hypothesis. Thus, a large value for chi-square will lead us to reject H_0. On the other hand, when the observed frequencies are very close to the expected frequencies, chi-square will be small, and we will conclude that there is a very good fit between the data and the hypothesis. Thus, a small chi-square value indicates that we should fail to reject H_0. To decide whether a particular chi-square value is "large" or "small," we must refer to a *chi-square distribution*. This distribution is the set of chi-square values for all the possible random samples when H_0 is true. Much like other distributions we have examined (*t* distribution, *F* distribution), the chi-square distribution is a theoretical distribution with well-defined characteristics. Some of these characteristics are easy to infer from the chi-square formula.

1. The formula for chi-square involves adding squared values, so you can never obtain a negative value. Thus, all chi-square values are zero or larger.

2. When H_0 is true, you expect the data (f_o values) to be close to the hypothesis (f_e values). Thus, we expect chi-square values to be small when H_0 is true.

These two factors suggest that the typical chi-square distribution will be positively skewed (see Figure 16.2). Note that small values, near zero, are expected when H_0 is true and large values (in the right-hand tail) are very unlikely. Thus, unusually large values of chi-square will form the critical region for the hypothesis test.

Although the typical chi-square distribution is positively skewed, there is one other factor that plays a role in the exact shape of the chi-square distribution—the number of categories. You should recall that the chi-square formula requires that you sum values from every category. The more categories you have, the more likely it is that you will obtain a large sum for the chi-square value. On average, chi-square will be larger when

FIGURE 16.2

Chi-square distributions are positively skewed. The critical region is placed in the extreme tail, which reflects large chi-square values.

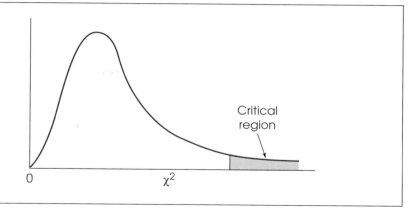

you are summing over 10 categories than when you are summing over only 3 categories. As a result, there is a whole family of chi-square distributions, with the exact shape of each distribution determined by the number of categories used in the study. Technically, each specific chi-square distribution is identified by degrees of freedom (*df*) rather than the number of categories. For the goodness-of-fit test, the degrees of freedom are determined by

$$df = C - 1 \tag{16.3}$$

Caution: The *df* for a chi-square test is *not* related to sample size (*n*), as it is in most other tests.

where *C* is the number of categories. A brief discussion of this *df* formula is presented in Box 16.2. Figure 16.3 shows the general relationship between *df* and the shape of the chi-square distribution. Note that the peak in the chi-square distribution (the mode) gets larger and larger as the value for *df* increases.

FIGURE 16.3

The shape of the chi-square distribution for different values of *df*. As the number of categories increases, the peak (mode) of the distribution has a larger chi-square value.

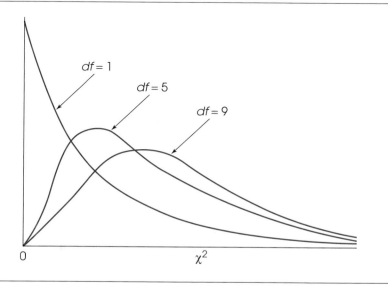

16.2   A CLOSER LOOK AT DEGREES OF FREEDOM

DEGREES OF freedom for the chi-square test literally measure the number of free choices that exist when you are determining the null hypothesis or the expected frequencies. For example, when you are classifying individuals into three categories, you have exactly two free choices in stating the null hypothesis. You may select any two proportions for the first two categories, but then the third proportion is determined. If you hypothesize 25% in the first category and 50% in the second category, then the third category must be 25% to account for 100% of the population.

Category A	Category B	Category C
25%	50%	?

In general, you are free to select proportions for all but one of the categories, but then the final proportion is determined by the fact that the entire set must total 100%. Thus, you have $C - 1$ free choices, where C is the number of categories: Degrees of freedom, df, equal $C - 1$.

LOCATING THE CRITICAL REGION FOR A CHI-SQUARE TEST

Recall that a large value for the chi-square statistic indicates a big discrepancy between the data and the hypothesis, and suggests that we reject H_0. To determine whether a particular chi-square value is significantly large, you must consult the table entitled The Chi-Square Distribution (Appendix B). A portion of the chi-square table is shown in Table 16.1. The first column lists df values for the chi-square test, and the top row of the table lists proportions (alpha levels) in the extreme right-hand tail of the distribution. The numbers in the body of the table are the critical values of chi-square. The table shows, for example, that in a chi-square distribution with $df = 3$, only 5% (.05) of the values are larger than 7.81, and only 1% (.01) are larger than 11.34.

TABLE 16.1

A portion of the table of critical values for the chi-square distribution

	Proportion in critical region				
df	0.10	0.05	0.025	0.01	0.005
1	2.71	3.84	5.02	6.63	7.88
2	4.61	5.99	7.38	9.21	10.60
3	6.25	7.81	9.35	11.34	12.84
4	7.78	9.49	11.14	13.28	14.86
5	9.24	11.07	12.83	15.09	16.75
6	10.64	12.59	14.45	16.81	18.55
7	12.02	14.07	16.01	18.48	20.28
8	13.36	15.51	17.53	20.09	21.96
9	14.68	16.92	19.02	21.67	23.59

EXAMPLE OF THE CHI-SQUARE TEST FOR GOODNESS OF FIT

We will use the same step-by-step process for testing hypotheses with chi-square as we used for other hypothesis tests. In general, the steps consist of stating the hypotheses, locating the critical region, computing the test statistic, and making a decision about H_0. The following example demonstrates the complete process of hypothesis testing with the goodness-of-fit test.

EXAMPLE 16.1   A psychologist examining art appreciation selected an abstract painting that had no obvious top or bottom. Hangers were placed on the painting so that it could be hung with any one of the four sides at the top. The painting was shown to a sample of $n = 50$ subjects, and each was asked to hang the painting in whatever orientation looked best. The following data indicate how many times each of the four sides was placed at the top:

Top up (correct)	Bottom up	Left side up	Right side up
18	17	7	8

The question for the hypothesis test is whether there are any preferences among the four possible orientations. Are any of the orientations selected more (or less) often than would be expected simply by chance?

STEP 1   State the hypotheses and select an alpha level. The hypotheses can be stated as follows:

H_0:   In the general population, there is no preference for any specific orientation. Thus, the four possible orientations are selected equally often, and the population distribution has the following proportions:

Top up (correct)	Bottom up	Left side up	Right side up
25%	25%	25%	25%

H_1:   In the general population, one or more of the orientations is preferred over the others.

We will use $\alpha = .05$.

STEP 2   Locate the critical region. For this example, the value for degrees of freedom is

$$df = C - 1 = 4 - 1 = 3$$

For $df = 3$ and $\alpha = .05$, the table of critical values for chi-square indicates that the critical χ^2 has a value of 7.81. The critical region is sketched in Figure 16.4.

FIGURE 16.4

For Example 16.1, the critical region begins at a chi-square value of 7.81.

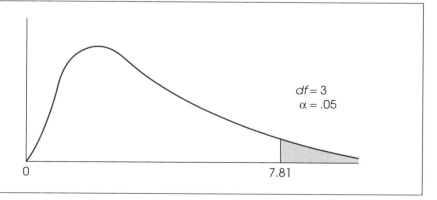

$df = 3$
$\alpha = .05$

0   7.81

STEP 3   Calculate the chi-square statistic. The calculation of chi-square is actually a two-stage process. First, you must compute the expected frequencies from H_0 and then calculate the value of the chi-square statistic. For this example, the null hypothesis specifies a proportion of $p = 25\%$ (or $p = \frac{1}{4}$) for each of the four categories and the sample size is $n = 50$. Thus, the expected frequency for each category is

Expected frequencies are computed and may be decimal values. Observed frequencies are always whole numbers.

$$f_e = pn = \tfrac{1}{4}(50) = 12.5$$

The observed frequencies and the expected frequencies are presented in Table 16.2.

TABLE 16.2

The observed frequencies and the expected frequencies for the chi-square test in Example 16.1.

Observed frequencies	Top up (correct)	Bottom up	Left side up	Right side up
	18	17	7	8

Expected frequencies	Top up (correct)	Bottom up	Left side up	Right side up
	12.5	12.5	12.5	12.5

Using these values, the chi-square statistic may now be calculated.

$$\chi^2 = \Sigma \frac{(f_o - f_e)^2}{f_e}$$

$$= \frac{(18 - 12.5)^2}{12.5} + \frac{(17 - 12.5)^2}{12.5} + \frac{(7 - 12.5)^2}{12.5} + \frac{(8 - 12.5)^2}{12.5}$$

$$= \frac{30.25}{12.5} + \frac{20.25}{12.5} + \frac{30.25}{12.5} + \frac{20.25}{12.5}$$

$$= 2.42 + 1.62 + 2.42 + 1.62$$

$$= 8.08$$

STEP 4   State a decision and a conclusion. The obtained chi-square value is in the critical region. Therefore, H_0 is rejected and the researcher may conclude that the four orientations are not equally likely to be preferred. Instead, there are significant differences among the four orientations, with some selected more often and others less often than would be expected by chance.

IN THE LITERATURE:
REPORTING THE RESULTS FOR CHI-SQUARE

APA style specifies the format for reporting the chi-square statistic in scientific journals. For the results of Example 16.1, the report might state:

The participants showed significant preferences among the four orientations for hanging the painting, $\chi^2 (3, n = 50) = 8.08, p < .05$.

Note that the form of the report is similar to that of other statistical tests we have examined. Degrees of freedom are indicated in parentheses following the chi-square symbol. Also contained in the parentheses is the sample size (n). This additional information is important because the degrees of freedom value is based on the number of categories (C), not sample size. Next, the calculated value of chi-square is presented, followed by the probability that a Type I error has been committed. Because the null hypothesis was rejected, the probability is *less than* the alpha level.

Additionally, the report should provide the observed frequencies (f_o) for each category. This information may be presented in a simple sentence or in a table.   ❏

GOODNESS OF FIT AND THE SINGLE-SAMPLE *t* TEST

We begin this chapter with a general discussion of the difference between parametric tests and nonparametric tests. In this context, the chi-square test for goodness of fit is an example of a nonparametric test; that is, it makes no assumptions about the parameters of the population distribution, and it does not require data from an interval or ratio scale. In contrast, the single-sample *t* test introduced in Chapter 9 is an example of a parametric test: It assumes a normal population, it tests hypotheses about the population mean (a parameter), and it requires numerical scores that can be summed, squared, divided, and so on.

Although the chi-square test and the single-sample *t* are clearly distinct, they are also very similar. In particular, both tests are intended to use the data from a single sample to test hypotheses about a single population.

When the sample data consist of numerical scores, it is usually most appropriate to compute the sample mean and then use a *t* test to evaluate a hypothesis about the population mean. For example, a researcher could measure IQ scores for a sample of registered voters and then use a *t* test to test a hypothesis about the mean IQ for the general population of voters. On the other hand, when the individuals in the sample are simply classified into nonnumerical categories, you probably would use a chi-square test to evaluate a hypothesis about the population proportions. For example, a researcher could measure gender for a sample of registered voters, recording the proportion of males and females in the sample. A chi-square test would then be the appropriate method for using the sample proportions to evaluate a hypothesis about the corresponding population proportions.

LEARNING CHECK

1. A researcher for an insurance company would like to know whether high-performance, overpowered automobiles are more likely to be involved in accidents than other types of cars. For a sample of 50 insurance claims, the investigator classifies the automobiles as high-performance, subcompact, midsize, or full-size. The observed frequencies are as follows:

Observed frequencies of insurance claims

High-performance	Subcompact	Midsize	Full-size	Total
20	14	7	9	50

In determining the f_e values, assume that only 10% of the cars in the population are the high-performance variety. However, subcompacts, midsize cars, and full-size cars make up 40%, 30%, and 20%, respectively. Can the researcher conclude that the observed pattern of accidents does not fit the predicted (f_e) values? Test with $\alpha = .05$.

a. In a few sentences, state the hypotheses.

b. Determine the value for *df*, and locate the critical region.

c. Determine the f_e values, and compute chi-square.

d. Make a decision regarding H_0.

ANSWERS   **1. a.** H_0: In the population, no particular type of car shows a disproportionate number of accidents. H_1: In the population, a disproportionate number of accidents occur with certain types of cars.

b. $df = 3$; the critical χ^2 value is 7.81.

c. The f_e values for high-performance, subcompact, midsize, and full-size cars are 5, 20, 15, and 10, respectively. The obtained chi-square is 51.17.

d. Reject H_0.   ◆

16.3   THE CHI-SQUARE TEST FOR INDEPENDENCE

The chi-square statistic may also be used to test whether or not there is a relationship between two variables. In this situation, each individual in the sample is measured or classified on two separate variables. For example, a group of students could be classified in terms of personality (introvert, extrovert) and in terms of color preference (red, yellow, green, or blue). Usually the data from this classification are presented in the form of a matrix, where the rows correspond to the categories of one variable and the columns correspond to the categories of the second variable. Table 16.3 presents some hypothetical data for a sample of $n = 400$ students who have been classified by personality and color preference. The number in each box, or cell, of the matrix depicts the frequency of that particular group. In Table 16.3, for example, there are 10 students who were classified as introverted and who selected red as their preferred color. To obtain these data, the researcher first selects a random sample of $n = 200$ students. Each student is then given a personality test and is asked to select a preferred color from among the four choices. Note that the classification is based on the measurements for each student; the researcher does not assign students to categories. Also, note that the data consist of frequencies, not scores, from a sample. These sample data will be used to test a hypothesis about the corresponding population frequency distribution. Once again, we will be using the chi-square statistic for the test, but in this case, the test is called the chi-square *test for independence*.

TABLE 16.3

Color preferences according to personality types

	Red	Yellow	Green	Blue	
Introvert	10	3	15	22	50
Extrovert	90	17	25	18	150
	100	20	40	40	$n = 200$

THE NULL HYPOTHESIS FOR THE TEST FOR INDEPENDENCE

The null hypothesis for the chi-square test for independence states that the two variables being measured are independent; that is, for each individual, the value obtained for one variable is not related to (or influenced by) the value for the second variable. This general hypothesis can be expressed in two different conceptual forms, each viewing the data and the test from slightly different perspectives. The data in Table 16.3 describing color preference and personality will be used to present both versions of the null hypothesis.

H_0 version 1   For this version of H_0, the data are viewed as a single sample with each individual measured on two variables. The goal of the chi-square test is to evaluate the relationship between the two variables. For the example we are considering, the goal is to determine whether or not there is a consistent, predictable relationship between personality and color preference. That is, if I know your personality, will it help me to predict your color preference? The null hypothesis states that there is no relationship. The alternative hypothesis, H_1, states that there is a relationship between the two variables.

> H_0: For the general population of students, there is no relationship between color preference and personality.

This version of H_0 demonstrates the similarity between the chi-square test for independence and a correlation. In each case, the data consist of two measurements (X and Y) for each individual, and the goal is to evaluate the relationship between the two variables. The correlation, however, requires numerical scores for X and Y. The chi-square test, on the other hand, simply uses frequencies for individuals classified into categories.

H_0 version 2   For this version of H_0, the data are viewed as two (or more) separate samples representing two (or more) separate populations. The goal of the chi-square test is to determine whether or not there are significant differences between the populations. For the example we are considering, the data in Table 16.3 would be viewed as a sample of $n = 50$ introverts (top row) and a separate sample of $n = 150$ extroverts (bottom row). The chi-square test will determine whether the distribution of color preferences for introverts is significantly different from the distribution of color preferences for extroverts. From this perspective, the null hypothesis is stated as follows:

> H_0: In the general population of students, the distribution of color preferences has the same shape (same proportions) for both categories of personality.

This version of H_0 demonstrates the similarity between the chi-square test and an independent-measures t test (or ANOVA). In each case, the data consist of two (or more) separate samples that are being used to test for differences between two (or more) populations. With the t statistic (or ANOVA) we used sample means to test for differences between population means. The chi-square test, on the other hand, uses sample proportions to test for differences between population proportions. The null hypothesis states that there are no differences between population proportions. The alternative hypothesis, H_1, states that the populations do not have the same shape (same proportions). For the example we are considering, H_1 states that the distribution of color preferences for introverts is different from the distribution of color preferences for extroverts.

Equivalence of H_0 version 1 and H_0 version 2   Although we have presented two different statements of the null hypothesis, you should realize that these two versions are equivalent. The first version of H_0 states that color preference is not related to personality. If this hypothesis is correct, then the distribution of color preferences should not depend on personality. In other words, the distribution of color preferences should be the same for introverts and extroverts, which is the second version of H_0.

For example, if we found that 60% of the introverts preferred red, then H_0 would predict that we also should find that 60% of the extroverts prefer red. In this case, knowing that an individual prefers red does not help you predict his or her personality. Note that finding the *same proportions* indicates *no relationship*.

On the other hand, if the proportions were different, it would suggest that there is a relationship. For example, if red were preferred by 60% of the extroverts but only 10% of the introverts, then there is a clear, predictable relationship between personality and color preference. (If I know your personality, I can predict your color preference.) Thus, finding *different proportions* means that there is *a relationship* between the two variables.

DEFINITION

Two variables are *independent* when there is no consistent, predictable relationship between them. In this case, the frequency distribution for one variable is not related to (or dependent on) the categories of the second variable. As a result, when two variables are independent, the frequency distribution for one variable will have the same shape (same proportions) for all categories of the second variable.

Thus, stating that there is no relationship between two variables (version 1 of H_0) is equivalent to stating that the distributions have equal proportions (version 2 of H_0).

OBSERVED AND EXPECTED FREQUENCIES

The chi-square test for independence uses the same basic logic that was used for the goodness-of-fit test. First, a sample is selected, and each individual is classified or categorized. Because the test for independence considers two variables, every individual is classified on both variables, and the resulting frequency distribution is presented as a two-dimensional matrix (see Table 16.3). As before, the frequencies in the sample distribution are called *observed frequencies* and are identified by the symbol f_o.

The next step is to find the expected frequencies, or f_e values, for this chi-square test. As before, the *expected frequencies* define an ideal hypothetical distribution that is in perfect agreement with the null hypothesis. Once the expected frequencies are obtained, we will compute a chi-square statistic to determine how well the data (observed frequencies) fit the null hypothesis (expected frequencies).

Although you can use either version of the null hypothesis to find the expected frequencies, the logic of the process is much easier when you use H_0 stated in terms of equal proportions. For the example we are considering, the null hypothesis states

H_0: The frequency distribution of color preference has the same shape (same proportions) for both categories of personality.

To find the expected frequencies, we first determine the overall distribution of color preferences and then apply this distribution to both categories of personality. Table 16.4 shows an empty matrix corresponding to the data from Table 16.3. Note that the empty matrix includes all of the row totals and the column totals from the original sample data.

TABLE 16.4

An empty matrix corresponding to the data in Table 16.3.

An empty frequency distribution matrix showing only the row totals and column totals. (These numbers describe the basic characteristics of the sample from Table 16.3.)

	Red	Yellow	Green	Blue	
Introvert					50
Extrovert					150
	100	20	40	40	

The row totals and the column totals are essential for computing the expected frequencies.

The column totals for the matrix describe the overall distribution of color preferences. For these data, 100 people selected red as their preferred color. Because the total sample consists of 200 people, it is easy to determine that the proportion selecting red is 100 out of 200 or 50%. The complete set of color preference proportions is as follows:

100 out of 200 = 50% prefer red

20 out of 200 = 10% prefer yellow

40 out of 200 = 20% prefer green

40 out of 200 = 20% prefer blue

The row totals in the matrix define the two samples of personality types. For example, the matrix in Table 16.4 shows a total of 50 introverts (the top row) and a sample of 150 extroverts (the bottom row). According to the null hypothesis, both personality groups should have the same proportions for color preferences. To find the expected frequencies, we simply apply the overall distribution of color preferences to each sample. Beginning with the sample of 50 introverts in the top row, we obtain expected frequencies of

50% = 0.50 choose red: $f_e = 0.50(50) = 25$

10% = 0.10 choose yellow: $f_e = 0.10(50) = 5$

20% = 0.20 choose green: $f_e = 0.20(50) = 10$

20% = 0.20 choose blue: $f_e = 0.20(50) = 10$

Using exactly the same proportions for the sample of 150 extroverts in the bottom row, we obtain expected frequencies of

50% = 0.50 choose red: $f_e = 0.50(150) = 75$

10% = 0.10 choose yellow: $f_e = 0.10(150) = 15$

20% = 0.20 choose green: $f_e = 0.20(150) = 30$

20% = 0.20 choose blue: $f_e = 0.20(150) = 30$

The complete set of expected frequencies is shown in Table 16.5. Note that the row totals and the column totals for the expected frequencies are the same as those for the original data (the observed frequencies) in Table 16.3.

TABLE 16.5

Expected frequencies corresponding to the data in Table 16.3

Expected frequencies. (This is the distribution predicted by the null hypothesis.)

	Red	Yellow	Green	Blue	
Introvert	25	5	10	10	50
Extrovert	75	15	30	30	150
	100	20	40	40	

A SIMPLE FORMULA FOR DETERMINING EXPECTED FREQUENCIES

Although you should understand that expected frequencies are derived directly from the null hypothesis and the sample characteristics, it is not necessary to go through extensive calculations in order to find f_e values. In fact, there is a simple formula that determines f_e for any cell in the frequency distribution table:

$$f_e = \frac{f_c f_r}{n} \qquad (16.4)$$

where f_c is the frequency total for the column (column total), f_r is the frequency total for the row (row total), and n is the number of individuals in the entire sample. To demonstrate this formula, we will compute the expected frequency for introverts selecting yellow in Table 16.5. First, note that this cell is located in the top row and second column in the table. The column total is $f_c = 20$, the row total is $f_r = 50$, and the sample size is $n = 200$. Using these values in Formula 16.4, we obtain

$$f_e = \frac{f_c f_r}{n} = \frac{20(50)}{200} = 5$$

This is identical to the expected frequency we obtained using percentages from the overall distribution.

THE CHI-SQUARE STATISTIC AND DEGREES OF FREEDOM

The chi-square test of independence uses exactly the same chi-square formula as the test for goodness of fit:

$$\chi^2 = \Sigma \frac{(f_o - f_e)^2}{f_e}$$

As before, the formula measures the discrepancy between the data (f_o values) and the hypothesis (f_e values). A large discrepancy will produce a large value for chi-square and will indicate that H_0 should be rejected. To determine whether a particular chi-square statistic is significantly large, you must first determine degrees of freedom (df) for the statistic and then consult the chi-square distribution in the appendix. For the chi-square test of independence, degrees of freedom are based on the number of cells for which you can freely choose expected frequencies. Recall that the f_e values are partially determined by the sample size (n) and by the row totals and column totals from the original data. These various totals restrict your freedom in selecting expected frequencies. This point is illustrated in Table 16.6. Once three of the f_e values have been selected, all the other f_e values in the table are also determined. In general, the row totals and the column totals restrict the final choices in each row and column. Thus, we may freely choose all but one f_e in each row and all but one f_e in each column. The total number of f_e values that you can freely choose is $(R - 1)(C - 1)$, where R is the number of rows

TABLE 16.6

Degrees of freedom and expected frequencies. (Once three values have been selected, all the remaining expected frequencies are determined by the row totals and the column totals. This example has only three free choices, so $df = 3$.)

Red	Yellow	Green	Blue	
25	5	10	?	50
?	?	?	?	150
100	20	40	40	

and C is the number of columns. The degrees of freedom for the chi-square test of independence are given by the formula

$$df = (R - 1)(C - 1) \tag{16.5}$$

AN EXAMPLE OF THE CHI-SQUARE TEST FOR INDEPENDENCE

The steps for the chi-square test of independence should be familiar by now. First, the hypotheses are stated, and an alpha level is selected. Second, the value for degrees of freedom is computed, and the critical region is located. Third, expected frequencies are determined, and the chi-square statistic is computed. Finally, a decision is made regarding the null hypothesis. The following example demonstrates the complete hypothesis-testing procedure.

EXAMPLE 16.2

A researcher is investigating the relationship between academic performance and self-esteem. A sample of $n = 150$ ten-year-old children is obtained, and each child is classified by level of academic performance and level of self-esteem. The frequency distribution for this sample, the set of observed frequencies, is shown in Table 16.7.

STEP 1

State the hypotheses, and select a level of significance. According to the null hypothesis, the two variables are independent. This general hypothesis can be stated in two different ways:

Version 1

H_0: In the general population, there is no relationship between academic performance and self-esteem.

This version of H_0 emphasizes the similarity between the chi-square test and a correlation. The corresponding alternative hypothesis would state

H_1: There is a consistent, predictable relationship between academic performance and self-esteem.

TABLE 16.7

A frequency distribution showing the level of self-esteem according to the level of academic performance for a sample of $n = 150$ ten-year-old children.

		Level of self-esteem			
		High	Medium	Low	
Academic performance	High	17	32	11	60
	Low	13	43	34	90
		30	75	45	$n = 150$

Version 2

H_0: In the general population, the distribution of self-esteem is the same for high and low academic performers.

The corresponding alternative hypothesis would state

H_1: The distribution for self-esteem for high academic performers is different from the distribution for low academic performers.

The second version of H_0 emphasizes the similarity between the chi-square test and the independent-measures t test.

Remember that the two versions for the hypotheses are equivalent. The choice between them is largely determined by how the researcher wants to describe the outcome. For example, a researcher may want to emphasize the *relationship* between variables or may want to emphasis the *difference* between groups.

For this test, we will use $\alpha = .05$.

STEP 2   Determine the degrees of freedom, and locate the critical region. For the chi-square test for independence,

$$df = (R - 1)(C - 1)$$

Therefore, for this study,

$$df = (2 - 1)(3 - 1) = 2$$

With $df = 2$ and $\alpha = .05$, the critical value for chi-square is 5.99 (see Table B.7, p. A-34).

STEP 3   Determine the expected frequencies, and compute the chi-square statistic. The following table shows an empty matrix with the same row totals and column totals as the original data. The calculation of expected frequencies requires that this table be filled in so the resulting values provide an ideal frequency distribution that perfectly represents the null hypothesis.

Level of self-esteem

		High	Medium	Low	
Academic performance	High				60
	Low				90
		30	75	45	$n = 150$

The column totals indicate that 30 out of 150 subjects are classified as high self-esteem. This value represents a proportion of $\frac{30}{150}$ or 20% of the subjects. Similarly, $\frac{75}{150} = 50\%$ are medium self-esteem, and $\frac{45}{150} = 30\%$ are low self-esteem. The null hypothesis (version 2) states that this distribution of self-esteem is the same for high and low performers. Therefore, we simply apply the same proportions to each group to obtain the expected frequencies. For the 60 students classified as high academic performers, it is expected that

20% of 60 = 12 students would have high self-esteem

50% of 60 = 30 students would have medium self-esteem

30% of 60 = 18 students would have low self-esteem

For the 90 students classified as low academic performers, it is expected that

20% of 90 = 18 students would have high self-esteem

50% of 90 = 45 students would have medium self-esteem

30% of 90 = 27 students would have low self-esteem

These expected frequencies are summarized in Table 16.8.

TABLE 16.8

The expected frequencies (f_e values) that would be predicted if academic performance and self-esteem were completely independent.

Level of self-esteem

		High	Medium	Low	
Academic performance	High	12	30	18	60
	Low	18	45	27	90
		30	75	45	$n = 150$

The chi-square statistic is now used to measure the discrepancy between the data (the observed frequencies in Table 16.7) and the null hypothesis that was used to generate the expected frequencies in Table 16.8.

$$\chi^2 = \frac{(17 - 12)^2}{12} + \frac{(32 - 30)^2}{30} + \frac{(11 - 18)^2}{18}$$
$$+ \frac{(13 - 18)^2}{18} + \frac{(43 - 45)^2}{45} + \frac{(34 - 27)^2}{27}$$
$$= 2.08 + 0.13 + 2.72 + 1.39 + 0.09 + 1.82$$
$$= 8.23$$

STEP 4   Make a decision regarding the null hypothesis and the outcome of the study. The obtained chi-square value exceeds the critical value (5.99). Therefore, the decision is to reject the null hypothesis. In the literature, this would be reported as a significant result with $\chi^2(2, n = 150) = 8.23$, $p < .05$. According to version 1 of H_0, this means that we have decided there is a significant relationship between academic performance and self-esteem. Expressed in terms of version 2 of H_0, the data show a significant difference between the distribution of self-esteem for high academic performers versus low academic performers. To describe the details of the significant result, you must compare the original data (Table 16.7) with the expected frequencies from the null hypothesis (Table 16.8). Looking at the two tables, it should be clear that the high performers had higher self-esteem than would be expected if the two variables were independent and the low performers had lower self-esteem than would be expected.

ON THE COMPUTER

THE DATA used in Example 16.2 were also analyzed with the Minitab and SPSS computer programs, and the two printouts are shown in Figure 16.5. Some specific comments concerning each printout are as follows:

1. The SPSS printout (below) shows the matrix of observed frequencies including the row and column totals. The percentage in each row and each column is also reported along with the corresponding total.

The basic chi-square value (Pearson) as well as the *df* value and the *p* value are reported, along with other statistical tests performed on the data.

2. The Minitab printout (opposite) also shows the matrix of observed frequencies and includes the expected frequency that is computed for each cell. This printout shows the chi-square calculation, summed over all six cells, along with the *df* and *p* values.

SPSS Printout				
ACADEMIC by ESTEEM				

	ESTEEM			Page 1 of 1
Count				Row Total
ACADEMIC	1.00	2.00	3.00	
1.00	17	32	11	60 40.0
2.00	13	43	34	90 60.0
Column Total	30 20.0	75 50.0	45 30.0	150 100.0

Chi-Square	Value	DF	Significance
Pearson	8.23148	2	.01631
Likelihood Ratio	8.44327	2	.01467
Mantel-Haenszel test for linear association	8.10884	1	.00440

Minimum Expected Frequency   12.000

FIGURE 16.5

Two computer printouts showing the output from SPSS (above) and Minitab (opposite) for the chi-square test for independence. The printouts show the results for the data from Example 16.2.

ON THE COMPUTER (continued)

> ### Minitab Printout
>
> **Chi-Square Test: C1, C2, C3**
>
> Expected counts are printed below observed counts
>
> | | C1 | C2 | C3 | Total |
> |---|---|---|---|---|
> | 1 | 17 | 32 | 11 | 60 |
> | | 12.00 | 30.00 | 18.00 | |
> | 2 | 13 | 43 | 34 | 90 |
> | | 18.00 | 45.00 | 27.00 | |
> | Total | 30 | 75 | 45 | 150 |
>
> Chi-Sq = 2.083 + 0.133 + 2.722 +
> 1.389 + 0.089 + 1.815 = 8.231
> DF = 2, P-Value = 0.016

LEARNING CHECK

1. A researcher suspects that color blindness is inherited by a sex-linked gene. This possibility is examined by looking for a relationship between gender and color vision. The researcher tests a sample of 1000 people for color blindness, and then classifies them according to their sex and color vision status (normal, red-green blind, other color blindness). Is color blindness related to gender? The data are as follows:

Observed frequencies of color vision status according to sex

	Normal color vision	Red-green color blindness	Other color blindness	Totals
Male	320	70	10	400
Female	580	10	10	600
Totals	900	80	20	

  a. State the hypotheses.

  b. Determine the value for *df*, and locate the critical region.

  c. Compute the f_e values and then chi-square.

  d. Make a decision regarding H_0.

ANSWERS   1. **a.** H_0: In the population, there is no relationship between gender and color vision.
    H_1: In the population, gender and color vision are related.

  b. *df* = 2; critical χ^2 = 5.99 for α = .05.

c. f_e values are as follows:

Expected frequencies

	Normal	Red-green	Other
Male	360	32	8
Female	540	48	12

Obtained $\chi^2 = 83.44$

d. Reject H_0. ∎

16.4   ASSUMPTIONS AND RESTRICTIONS FOR CHI-SQUARE TESTS

To use a chi-square test for goodness of fit or a test of independence, several conditions must be satisfied. For any statistical test, violation of assumptions and restrictions will cast doubt on the results. For example, the probability of committing a Type I error may be distorted when assumptions of statistical tests are not satisfied. Some important assumptions and restrictions for using chi-square tests are the following:

1. Independent Observations. This is *not* to be confused with the concept of independence between *variables,* as seen in the test for independence (Section 16.3). One consequence of independent observations is that each observed frequency is generated by a different subject. A chi-square test would be inappropriate if a person could produce responses that can be classified in more than one category or contribute more than one frequency count to a single category. (See p. 184 for more information on independence.)

2. Size of Expected Frequencies. A chi-square test should not be performed when the expected frequency of any cell is less than 5. The chi-square statistic can be distorted when f_e is very small. Consider the chi-square computations for a single cell. Suppose the cell has values of $f_e = 1$ and $f_o = 5$. The contribution of this cell to the total chi-square value is

$$\text{cell} = \frac{(f_o - f_e)^2}{f_e} = \frac{(5 - 1)^2}{1} = \frac{4^2}{1} = 16$$

Now consider another instance, where $f_e = 10$ and $f_o = 14$. The difference between the observed and the expected frequencies is still 4, but the contribution of this cell to the total chi-square value differs from that of the first case:

$$\text{cell} = \frac{(f_o - f_e)^2}{f_e} = \frac{(14 - 10)^2}{10} = \frac{4^2}{10} = 1.6$$

It should be clear that a small f_e value can have a great influence on the chi-square value. This problem becomes serious when f_e values are less than 5. When f_e is very small, what would otherwise be a minor discrepancy between f_o and f_e will now result in large chi-square values. The test is too sensitive when f_e values are extremely small. One way to avoid small expected frequencies is to use large samples.

ON THE WEB

REMEMBER THAT a practice quiz for Chapter 16 is available on the Wadsworth Web site at **www.wadsworth.com**. You can use the quiz to test your knowledge on the chi-square tests to determine where you may need more study. In addition, you can review the workshop on chi-square at the same Web site. For more information about finding the quizzes and workshops, see page 24.

SUMMARY

1. Chi-square tests are a type of nonparametric technique that tests hypotheses about the form of the entire frequency distribution. Two types of chi-square tests are the test for goodness of fit and the test for independence. The data for these tests consist of the frequencies observed for various categories of a variable.

2. The test for goodness of fit compares the frequency distribution for a sample to the frequency distribution that is predicted by H_0. The test determines how well the observed frequencies (sample data) fit the expected frequencies (predicted by H_0).

3. The expected frequencies for the goodness-of-fit test are determined by

$$\text{expected frequency} = f_e = pn$$

where p is the hypothesized proportion (according to H_0) of observations falling into a category and n is the size of the sample.

4. The chi-square statistic is computed by

$$\text{chi-square} = \chi^2 = \Sigma \frac{(f_o - f_e)^2}{f_e}$$

where f_o is the observed frequency for a particular category and f_e is the expected frequency for that category. Large values for χ^2 indicate that there is a large discrepancy between the observed (f_o) and the expected (f_e) frequencies, which may warrant rejection of the null hypothesis.

5. Degrees of freedom for the test for goodness of fit are

$$df = C - 1$$

where C is the number of categories in the variable.

6. The test for independence is used to assess the relationship between two variables. The null hypothesis states that the two variables in question are independent of each other. That is, the frequency distribution for one variable does not depend on the categories of the second variable. On the other hand, if a relationship does exist, then the form of the distribution for one variable will depend on the categories of the other variable.

7. For the test for independence, the expected frequencies for H_0 can be directly calculated from the marginal frequency totals:

$$f_e = \frac{f_c f_r}{n}$$

where f_c is the total column frequency and f_r is the total row frequency for the cell in question.

8. Degrees of freedom for the test for independence are computed by

$$df = (R - 1)(C - 1)$$

where R is the number of row categories and C is the number of column categories.

9. For the test for independence, a large chi-square value means there is a large discrepancy between the f_o and the f_e values. Rejecting H_0 in this test provides support for a relationship between the two variables.

10. The chi-square statistic is distorted when f_e values are small. Chi-square tests therefore are restricted to situations in which f_e values are 5 or greater. The test should not be performed when the expected frequency of any cell is less than 5.

KEY TERMS

parametric test	goodness-of-fit test	expected frequencies	distribution of chi-square
nonparametric test	observed frequencies	chi-square statistic	test for independence

FOCUS ON PROBLEM SOLVING

1. The expected frequencies that you calculate must satisfy the constraints of the sample. For the goodness-of-fit test, $\Sigma f_e = \Sigma f_o = n$. For the test for independence, the row totals and the column totals for the expected frequencies should be identical to the corresponding totals for the observed frequencies.

2. It is entirely possible to have fractional (decimal) values for expected frequencies. Observed frequencies, however, are always whole numbers.

3. Whenever $df = 1$, the difference between observed and expected frequencies $(f_o - f_e)$ will be identical (the same value) for all cells. This makes the calculation of chi-square easier.

4. Although you are advised to compute expected frequencies for all categories (or cells), you should realize that it is not essential to calculate all f_e values separately. Remember, df for chi-square identifies the number of f_e values that are free to vary. Once you have calculated that number of f_e values, the remaining f_e values are determined. You can get these remaining values by subtracting the calculated f_e values from their corresponding row or column total.

5. Remember that, unlike previous statistical tests, the degrees of freedom (df) for a chi-square test are *not* determined by the sample size (n). Be careful!

DEMONSTRATION 16.1

TEST FOR INDEPENDENCE

A manufacturer of watches would like to examine preferences for digital versus analog watches. A sample of $n = 200$ people is selected, and these individuals are classified by age and preference. The manufacturer would like to know whether there is a relationship between age and watch preference. The observed frequencies (f_o) are as follows:

		Preference		
		Digital	Analog	Undecided
Age	Under 30	90	40	10
	30 or over	10	40	10

STEP 1   State the hypotheses, and select an alpha level.
The null hypothesis states that there is no relationship between the two variables.

H_0: Preference is independent of age. That is, the frequency distribution of preference has the same form for people under 30 as for people 30 or over.

The alternative hypothesis states that there is a relationship between the two variables.

> H_1: Preference is related to age. That is, the type of watch preferred depends on a person's age.

We will set alpha to $\alpha = .05$.

STEP 2   Locate the critical region.

Degrees of freedom for the chi-square test for independence are determined by

$$df = (C - 1)(R - 1)$$

For these data,

$$df = (3 - 1)(2 - 1) = 2(1) = 2$$

For $df = 2$ with $\alpha = .05$, the critical chi-square value is 5.99. Thus, our obtained chi-square must exceed 5.99 to be in the critical region and to reject H_0.

STEP 3   Compute the test statistic.

Computing the chi-square statistic requires the following preliminary calculations:

1. Obtain the row and the column totals.
2. Calculate the expected frequencies.

Row and column totals. We start by determining the row and the column totals from the original observed frequencies, f_o.

	Digital	Analog	Undecided	Row totals
Under 30	90	40	10	140
30 or over	10	40	10	60
Column totals	100	80	20	$n = 200$

Expected frequencies, f_e. For the test for independence, the following formula is used to obtain expected frequencies:

$$f_e = \frac{f_c f_r}{n}$$

For people under 30, we obtain the following expected frequencies:

$$f_e = \frac{100(140)}{200} = \frac{14,000}{200} = 70 \text{ for digital}$$

$$f_e = \frac{80(140)}{200} = \frac{11,200}{200} = 56 \text{ for analog}$$

$$f_e = \frac{20(140)}{200} = \frac{2800}{200} = 14 \text{ for undecided}$$

For individuals 30 or over, the expected frequencies are as follows:

$$f_e = \frac{100(60)}{200} = \frac{6000}{200} = 30 \text{ for digital}$$

$$f_e = \frac{80(60)}{200} = \frac{4800}{200} = 24 \text{ for analog}$$

$$f_e = \frac{20(60)}{200} = \frac{1200}{200} = 6 \text{ for undecided}$$

The following table summarizes the expected frequencies:

	Digital	Analog	Undecided
Under 30	70	56	14
30 or under	30	24	6

The chi-square statistic. The chi-square statistic is computed from the formula

$$\chi^2 = \Sigma \frac{(f_o - f_e)^2}{f_e}$$

That is, we must

1. Find the $f_o - f_e$ difference for each cell.
2. Square these differences.
3. Divide the squared differences by f_e.
4. Sum the results.

The following table summarizes these calculations:

Cell	f_o	f_e	$(f_o - f_e)$	$(f_o - f_e)^2$	$(f_o - f_e)^2/f_e$
Under 30—digital	90	70	20	400	5.71
Under 30—analog	40	56	−16	256	4.57
Under 30—undecided	10	14	−4	16	1.14
30 or over—digital	10	30	−20	400	13.33
30 or over—analog	40	24	16	256	10.67
30 or over—undecided	10	6	4	16	2.67

Finally, we can sum the last column to get the chi-square value.

$$\chi^2 = 5.71 + 4.57 + 1.14 + 13.33 + 10.67 + 2.67$$
$$= 38.09$$

STEP 4 Make a decision about H_0, and state the conclusion.

The chi-square value is in the critical region. Therefore, we can reject the null hypothesis. There is a relationship between watch preference and age, $\chi^2(2, n = 200) = 38.09$, $p < .05$.

PROBLEMS

1. Parametric tests (such as t or ANOVA) differ from non-parametric tests (such as chi-square) primarily in terms of the assumptions they require and the data they use. Explain these differences.

2. A major snack food company has started an advertising campaign claiming that it makes "America's favorite potato chip." To test this claim, a researcher assembles a sample of 90 volunteers and asks each individual to taste the company's chips along with two other brands. Each individual is asked to select a favorite from the three brands. The following data show the number of individuals selecting each brand. Do the data provide significant support for any preferences among the three brands? Test at the .05 level of significance.

Brand A	Brand B	Brand C
38	28	24

3. Automobile insurance is much more expensive for teenage drivers than for older drivers. To justify this cost difference, insurance companies claim that the younger drivers are much more likely to be involved in costly accidents. To test this claim, a researcher obtains information about registered drivers from the department of motor vehicles and selects a sample of $n = 300$ accident reports from the police department. The motor vehicle department reports the percentage of registered drivers in each age category as follows: 16% are under age 20; 28% are 20 to 29 years old, and 56% are age 30 or older. The number of accident reports for each age group is as follows:

Under age 20	Age 20–29	Age 30 or older
68	92	140

Do the data demonstrate a significantly disproportionate number of accidents among the younger drivers? Test with $\alpha = .05$.

4. A social psychologist suspects that people who serve on juries tend to be much older than citizens in the general population. The psychologist obtains voter registration records and finds that 20% of registered voters are between 18 and 29 years old, 45% are between 30 and 49 years old, and 35% are age 50 or older. The psychologist also monitors jury composition over several weeks and observes the following distribution of ages for actual juries:

Age categories for jurors		
18–29	30–49	50 and over
12	36	32

Are these data sufficient to conclude that the age distribution for jurors is significantly different from the distribution for the population of registered voters? Test with $\alpha = .05$. (*Note:* Jurors are selected from the population of registered voters.)

5. A developmental psychologist would like to determine whether infants display any color preferences. A stimulus consisting of four color patches (red, green, blue, and yellow) is projected onto the ceiling above a crib. Infants are placed in the crib, one at a time, and the psychologist records how much time an infant spends looking at each of the four colors. The color that receives the most attention during a 100-second test period is identified as the preferred color for that infant. The preferred colors for a sample of 60 infants are shown in the following table:

Red	Green	Blue	Yellow
21	11	18	10

Do the data indicate any significant preferences among the four colors? Test at the .05 level of significance.

6. A researcher would like to examine the factors that influence a person's decision when buying a new car. The researcher interviews 60 people who are shopping for a new car and asks each person to select the single most important factor that determines which car they will eventually buy. The frequency distribution for the sample is as follows:

Factors influencing decision		
Style	Safety	Reliability
12	16	32

Do the data indicate any significant preferences among the three factors, or are the three factors equally important in the general population? Test at the .05 level of significance.

7. A researcher is investigating the physical characteristics that influence whether or not a person's face is judged as beautiful. The researcher selects a photograph of a woman and then creates two modifications of the photo

by (1) moving the eyes slightly farther apart and (2) moving the eyes slightly closer together. The original photograph and the two modifications are then shown to a sample of $n = 150$ college students, and each student is asked to select the "most beautiful" of the three faces. The distribution of responses was as follows:

Original photo	Eyes moved apart	Eyes moved together
51	72	27

Do the data indicate any significant preferences among the three versions of the photograph? Test at the .05 level of significance.

8. A researcher would like to determine whether any particular age group has a greater risk of influenza-related death. A sample of 50 such cases is categorized according to the victim's age. The observed frequencies are as follows:

Number of flu-related deaths

Under 30	30–60	Over 60
5	5	40

Note that in the city from which the sample was selected, 30% of the population is in the "under 30" bracket, 40% is in "30–60," and 30% is in "over 60." (This information should help in determining f_e values.) Can the investigator conclude that risk differs with age? Test with the .05 level of significance.

9. A professor in the psychology department would like to determine whether there has been a significant change in grading practices over the years. It is known that the overall grade distribution for the department in 1985 had 14% As, 26% Bs, 31% Cs, 19% Ds, and 10% Fs. A sample of $n = 200$ psychology students from last semester produced the following grade distribution.

A	B	C	D	F
32	61	64	31	12

Do the data indicate a significant change in the grade distribution? Test at the .05 level of significance.

10. A researcher obtained a random sample of $n = 60$ students to determine whether there were any significant preferences among three leading brands of colas. Each student tasted all three brands and then selected his or her favorite. The resulting frequency distribution is as follows:

Brand A	Brand B	Brand C
28	14	18

Are the data sufficient to indicate any preferences among the three brands? Test with $\alpha = .05$.

11. Suppose the researcher from the previous problem repeated the cola-preference study using twice as many students and obtaining observed frequencies that exactly doubled the original values. The resulting data are as follows:

Brand A	Brand B	Brand C
56	28	36

a. Use a chi-square test to determine whether the data indicate any significant preferences among the three brands.
b. You should find that the conclusion from the hypothesis test is that there are significant preferences (reject H_0). However, in Problem 10 the decision was to fail to reject H_0. How do you explain the difference between the two tests?

12. A researcher would like to evaluate the relationship between a person's age and his or her preference between two leading brands of cola. In a sample of 30 people, the researcher found that 15 out of 18 people who were over 30 years old preferred brand A and only 3 out of 12 people under 30 preferred brand A. Are the data sufficient to indicate a significant relationship between age and cola preference? Test at the .05 level of significance.

13. A psychology professor is trying to decide which textbook to use for next year's introductory class. To help make the decision, the professor asks the current students to review three texts and identify which one they prefer. The distribution of preferences for the current class is as follows:

Book 1	Book 2	Book 3
52	41	27

Do the data indicate any significant preferences among the three books? Test with $\alpha = .05$.

14. In Problem 13, a professor asked students to rate three textbooks to determine whether there were any prefer-

ences among them. Although the data appear to indicate an overall preference for book 1, the professor would like to know whether this opinion is shared by students with different levels of academic ability. To answer this question, the median grade was used to separate the students into two groups: the upper half and the lower half of the class. The distribution of preferences for these two groups is as follows:

	Book 1	Book 2	Book 3	
Upper half	17	31	12	60
Lower half	35	10	15	60
	52	41	27	

Do the data indicate that the distribution of preferences for students in the upper half of the class is significantly different from the distribution for students in the lower half? Test at the .05 level of significance.

15. Gender differences in dream content are well documented (see Winget & Kramer, 1979). Suppose a researcher studies aggression content in the dreams of men and women. Each subject reports his or her most recent dream. Then each dream is judged by a panel of experts to have low, medium, or high aggression content. The observed frequencies are shown in the following matrix:

		Aggression content		
		Low	Medium	High
Gender	Female	18	4	2
	Male	4	17	15

Is there a relationship between gender and the aggression content of dreams? Test with $\alpha = .01$.

16. Cialdini, Reno, and Kallgren (1990) examined how people conform to norms concerning littering. The researchers wanted to determine whether a person's tendency to litter depended on the amount of litter already in the area. People were handed a handbill as they entered an amusement park. The entrance area had already been prepared with either no litter, a small amount of litter, or a lot of litter lying on the ground. The people were observed to determine whether or not they dropped their handbills. The frequency data are as follows:

	Amount of existing litter		
	None	Small amount	Large amount
Littering	17	28	49
Not littering	102	91	71

Do the data indicate a significant relationship between littering behavior and the norms established by the amount of litter already on the ground? Test at the .05 level of significance.

17. A local county is considering a budget proposal that would allocate extra funding toward the renovation of city parks. A survey is conducted to measure public opinion concerning the proposal. A total of 300 individuals respond to the survey: 100 who live within the city limits and 200 from the surrounding suburbs. The frequency distribution is as follows:

		Opinion about proposal		
		Favor	Oppose	
Residence	City	68	32	100
	Suburb	86	114	200

Is there a significant difference in the distribution of opinions for city residents compared to those in the suburbs? Test at the .05 level of significance.

18. Last fall the college installed a new e-mail system and conducted a series of training sessions to teach students and staff how to use the system. In the spring semester, the college used a survey to determine the level of satisfaction with the new system. In addition to measuring satisfaction, the survey asked whether or not each individual had attended a training session. The results of the survey are as follows:

	Level of satisfaction			
	Very satisfied	Somewhat satisfied	Somewhat dissatisfied	Very dissatisfied
Attended training	15	35	5	5
No training	5	45	35	15

Do the data indicate a significant difference in the distribution of satisfaction for those who attended training compared with those who did not? Test with $\alpha = .05$.

19. Darley and Latané (1968) conducted a study examining the factors that influence whether a subject will try to help a person in need. Each subject was placed in a preexisting group of either 2 people, 3 people, or 6 people. The subjects were led to believe that they were participating in discussion groups. Suddenly, one of the others in the group pretended to suffer a seizure, and the researcher recorded whether or not the subject tried to help. Darley and Latané predicted that the more people available to help, the less an individual subject would feel the responsibility to help. Hypothetical data similar to the study results are as follows:

Number in the group

	2	3	6
Helping	11	16	4
Not helping	2	10	9

Do the data indicate a significant relationship between helping behavior and the number of potential helpers available in the group? Test at the .01 level of significance.

20. Friedman and Rosenman (1974) have suggested that personality type is related to heart disease. Specifically, type A people, who are competitive, driven, pressured, and impatient, are more prone to heart disease. On the other hand, type B individuals, who are less competitive and more relaxed, are less likely to have heart disease. Suppose an investigator would like to examine the relationship between personality type and disease. For a random sample of individuals, personality type is assessed with a standardized test. These individuals are then examined and categorized as to whether they have a heart disorder. The observed frequencies are as follows:

	No heart disease	Heart disease
Type A	60	110
Type B	126	54

Is there a relationship between personality and disorder? Test at the .05 level of significance.

21. A scientist would like to see whether there is a relationship between handedness and eye preference, and selects a random sample of $n = 150$ subjects. For each subject, the researcher determines two things: (1) whether the person is left-handed or right-handed and (2) which eye the person prefers to use when looking through a camera viewfinder. The observed frequencies are as follows:

Hand preference

		Left	Right
Eye preference	Left	20	40
	Right	10	80

Is there a relationship between the two variables? Test at the .01 level of significance.

22. As part of a campaign to demonstrate sex discrimination in salary within the county government, a sample of $n = 200$ employees was selected, and each individual's salary was recorded. The median salary was computed for the sample and then each individual was classified by gender and relationship to the median. The obtained distribution was as follows:

	Female	Male
Above median	28	72
Below median	52	48

Do the data indicate that the salary distribution for females is significantly different from the distribution for males? Test at the .05 level of significance.

APPENDIX A   BASIC MATHEMATICS REVIEW

CONTENTS

PREVIEW

This appendix reviews some of the basic math skills that are necessary for the statistical calculations presented in this book. Many students already will know some or all of this material. Others will need to do extensive work and review. To help you assess your own skills, we include a skills assessment exam here. You should allow approximately 30 minutes to complete the test. When you finish, grade your test using the answer key on page A-22.

Note that the test is divided into five sections. If you miss more than three questions in any section of the test, you probably need help in that area. Turn to the section of this appendix that corresponds to your problem area. In each section, you will find a general review, some examples, and some additional practice problems. After reviewing the appropriate section and doing the practice problems, turn to the end of the appendix. You will find another version of the skills assessment exam. If you still miss more than three questions in any section of the exam, continue studying. Get assistance from an instructor or a tutor if necessary. At the end of this appendix is a list of recommended books for individuals who need a more extensive review than can be provided here. We must stress that mastering this material now will make the rest of the course much easier.

SKILLS ASSESSMENT PREVIEW EXAM

SECTION 1

(corresponding to Section A.1 of this appendix)

1. $3 + 2 \times 7 = ?$
2. $(3 + 2) \times 7 = ?$
3. $3 + 2^2 - 1 = ?$
4. $(3 + 2)^2 - 1 = ?$
5. $12/4 + 2 = ?$
6. $12/(4 + 2) = ?$
7. $12/(4 + 2)^2 = ?$
8. $2 \times (8 - 2^2) = ?$
9. $2 \times (8 - 2)^2 = ?$
10. $3 \times 2 + 8 - 1 \times 6 = ?$
11. $3 \times (2 + 8) - 1 \times 6 = ?$
12. $3 \times 2 + (8 - 1) \times 6 = ?$

SECTION 2

(corresponding to Section A.2 of this appendix)

1. The fraction ¾ corresponds to a percentage of _____ .
2. Express 30% as a fraction.
3. Convert ¹²⁄₄₀ to a decimal.
4. $\frac{2}{13} + \frac{8}{13} = ?$
5. $1.375 + 0.25 = ?$
6. $\frac{2}{5} \times \frac{1}{4} = ?$
7. $\frac{1}{8} + \frac{2}{3} = ?$
8. $3.5 \times 0.4 = ?$
9. $\frac{1}{5} \div \frac{3}{4} = ?$
10. $3.75/0.5 = ?$
11. In a group of 80 students, 20% are psychology majors. How many psychology majors are in this group?
12. A company reports that two-fifths of its employees are women. If there are 90 employees, how many are women?

SECTION 3

(corresponding to Section A.3 of this appendix)

1. $3 + (-2) + (-1) + 4 = ?$
2. $6 - (-2) = ?$
3. $-2 - (-4) = ?$
4. $6 + (-1) - 3 - (-2) - (-5) = ?$
5. $4 \times (-3) = ?$
6. $-2 \times (-6) = ?$
7. $-3 \times 5 = ?$
8. $-2 \times (-4) \times (-3) = ?$
9. $12 \div (-3) = ?$
10. $-18 \div (-6) = ?$
11. $-16 \div 8 = ?$
12. $-100 \div (-4) = ?$

SECTION 4

(corresponding to Section A.4 of this appendix)

For each equation, find the value of X.

1. $X + 6 = 13$
2. $X - 14 = 15$
3. $5 = X - 4$
4. $3X = 12$
5. $72 = 3X$
6. $X/5 = 3$
7. $10 = X/8$
8. $3X + 5 = -4$
9. $24 = 2X + 2$
10. $(X + 3)/2 = 14$
11. $(X - 5)/3 = 2$
12. $17 = 4X - 11$

SECTION 5

(corresponding to Section A.5 of this appendix)

1. $4^3 = ?$
2. $\sqrt{25 - 9} = ?$
3. If $X = 2$ and $Y = 3$, then $XY^3 = ?$
4. If $X = 2$ and $Y = 3$, then $(X + Y)^2 = ?$
5. If $a = 3$ and $b = 2$, then $a^2 + b^2 = ?$
6. $(-3)^3 = ?$
7. $(-4)^4 = ?$
8. $\sqrt{4} \times 4 = ?$
9. $36/\sqrt{9} = ?$
10. $(9 + 2)^2 = ?$
11. $5^2 + 2^3 = ?$
12. If $a = 3$ and $b = -1$, then $a^2 b^3 = ?$

The answers to the skills assessment exam are at the end of Appendix A, on pp. A-22–A-23.

A.1   SYMBOLS AND NOTATION

Table A.1 presents the basic mathematical symbols that you should know, and it provides examples of their use. Statistical symbols and notation will be introduced and explained throughout this book as they are needed. Notation for exponents and square roots is covered separately at the end of this appendix.

TABLE A.1

Symbol	Meaning	Example
+	Addition	$5 + 7 = 12$
−	Subtraction	$8 - 3 = 5$
×, ( )	Multiplication	$3 \times 9 = 27$, $3(9) = 27$
÷, /	Division	$15 \div 3 = 5$, $15/3 = 5$, $\frac{15}{3} = 5$
>	Greater than	$20 > 10$
<	Less than	$7 < 11$
≠	Not equal to	$5 \neq 6$

Parentheses are a useful notation because they specify and control the order of computations. Everything inside the parentheses is calculated first. For example,

$$(5 + 3) \times 2 = 8 \times 2 = 16$$

Changing the placement of the parentheses also changes the order of calculations. For example,

$$5 + (3 \times 2) = 5 + 6 = 11$$

ORDER OF OPERATIONS

Often a formula or a mathematical expression will involve several different arithmetic operations, such as adding, multiplying, squaring, and so on. When you encounter these situations, you must perform the different operations in the correct sequence. Following is a list of mathematical operations, showing the order in which they are to be performed.

1. Any calculation contained within parentheses is done first.
2. Squaring (or raising to other exponents) is done second.
3. Multiplying and/or dividing is done third. A series of multiplication and/or division operations should be done in order from left to right.
4. Adding and/or subtracting is done fourth.

The following examples demonstrate how this sequence of operations is applied in different situations.

To evaluate the expression

$$(3 + 1)^2 - 4 \times 7/2$$

first, perform the calculation within parentheses:

$$(4)^2 - 4 \times 7/2$$

Next, square the value as indicated:

$$16 - 4 \times 7/2$$

Then perform the multiplication and division:

$$16 - 14$$

Finally, do the subtraction:

$$16 - 14 = 2$$

A sequence of operations involving multiplication and division should be performed in order from left to right. For example, to compute $12/2 \times 3$, you divide 12 by 2 and then multiply the result by 3:

$$12/2 \times 3 = 6 \times 3 = 18$$

Note that violating the left-to-right sequence can change the result. For this example, if you multiply before dividing, you will obtain

$$12/2 \times 3 = 12/6 = 2 \quad \text{(This is wrong.)}$$

A sequence of operations involving only addition and subtraction can be performed in any order. For example, to compute $3 + 8 - 5$, you can add 3 and 8 and then subtract 5:

$$(3 + 8) - 5 = 11 - 5 = 6$$

Or you can subtract 5 from 8 and then add the result to 3:

$$3 + (8 - 5) = 3 + 3 = 6$$

A mathematical expression or formula is simply a concise way to write a set of instructions. When you evaluate an expression by performing the calculation, simply follow the instructions. For example, assume you are given the instructions that follow:

1. First, add 3 and 8.
2. Next, square the result.
3. Next, multiply the resulting value by 6.
4. Finally, subtract 50 from the value you have obtained.

You can write these instructions as a mathematical expression.

1. The first step involved addition. Because addition is normally done last, use parentheses to give this operation priority in the sequence of calculations:

$$(3 + 8)$$

2. The instruction to square a value is noted by using the exponent 2 beside the value to be squared:

$$(3 + 8)^2$$

3. Because squaring has priority over multiplication, you can simply introduce the multiplication into the expression:

$$6 \times (3 + 8)^2$$

4. Addition and subtraction are done last, so simply write in the requested subtraction:

$$6 \times (3 + 8)^2 - 50$$

To calculate the value of the expression, work through the sequence of operations in the proper order:

$$6 \times (3 + 8)^2 - 50 = 6 \times (11)^2 - 50$$
$$= 6 \times (121) - 50$$
$$= 726 - 50$$
$$= 676$$

As a final note, you should realize that the operation of squaring (or raising to any exponent) applies only to the value that immediately precedes the exponent. For example,

$$2 \times 3^2 = 2 \times 9 = 18 \quad \text{(Only the 3 is squared.)}$$

If the instructions require multiplying values and then squaring the product, you must use parentheses to give the multiplication priority over squaring. For example, to multiply 2 times 3 and then square the product, write

$$(2 \times 3)^2 = (6)^2 = 36$$

LEARNING CHECK ◆

1. Evaluate each of the following expressions:
   a. $4 \times 8/2^2$
   b. $4 \times (8/2)^2$
   c. $100 - 3 \times 12/(6 - 4)^2$
   d. $(4 + 6) \times (3 - 1)^2$
   e. $(8 - 2)/(8 - 9)^2$
   f. $6 + (4 - 1)^2 - 3 \times 4^2$
   g. $4 \times (8 - 3) + 8 - 3$

ANSWERS   1. a. 8   b. 64   c. 91   d. 40   e. 6   f. -33 g. 25   ◆

A.2 PROPORTIONS: FRACTIONS, DECIMALS, AND PERCENTAGES

A proportion is a part of a whole and can be expressed as a fraction, a decimal, or a percentage. For example, in a class of 40 students, only 3 failed the final exam.

The proportion of the class that failed can be expressed as a fraction

$$\text{fraction} = \tfrac{3}{40}$$

or as a decimal value

$$\text{decimal} = 0.075$$

or as a percentage

$$\text{percentage} = 7.5\%$$

In a fraction, such as ¾, the bottom value (the denominator) indicates the number of equal pieces into which the whole is split. Here the "pie" is split into 4 equal pieces:

If the denominator has a larger value—say, 8—then each piece of the whole pie is smaller:

A larger denominator indicates a smaller fraction of the whole.

The value on top of the fraction (the numerator) indicates how many pieces of the whole are being considered. Thus, the fraction ¾ indicates that the whole is split evenly into 4 pieces and that 3 of them are being used:

A fraction is simply a concise way of stating a proportion: "Three out of four" is equivalent to ¾. To convert the fraction to a decimal, divide the numerator by the denominator:

$$\tfrac{3}{4} = 3 \div 4 = 0.75$$

To convert the decimal to a percentage, simply multiply by 100, and place a percent sign (%) after the answer:

$$0.75 \times 100 = 75\%$$

The U.S. money system is a convenient way of illustrating the relationship between fractions and decimals. "One quarter," for example, is one-fourth (¼) of a dollar, and its decimal equivalent is 0.25. Other familiar equivalencies are as follows:

	Dime	Quarter	50 cents	75 cents
Fraction	$\frac{1}{10}$	$\frac{1}{4}$	$\frac{1}{2}$	$\frac{3}{4}$
Decimal	0.10	0.25	0.50	0.75
Percentage	10%	25%	50%	75%

FRACTIONS

1. Finding Equivalent Fractions. The same proportional value can be expressed by many equivalent fractions. For example,

$$\frac{1}{2} = \frac{2}{4} = \frac{10}{20} = \frac{50}{100}$$

To create equivalent fractions, you can multiply the numerator and denominator by the same value. As long as both the numerator and the denominator of the fraction are multiplied by the same value, the new fraction will be equivalent to the original. For example,

$$\frac{3}{10} = \frac{9}{30}$$

because both the numerator and the denominator of the original fraction have been multiplied by 3. Dividing the numerator and denominator of a fraction by the same value will also result in an equivalent fraction. By using division, you can reduce a fraction to a simpler form. For example,

$$\frac{40}{100} = \frac{2}{5}$$

because both the numerator and the denominator of the original fraction have been divided by 20.

You can use these rules to find specific equivalent fractions. For example, find the fraction that has a denominator of 100 and is equivalent to ¾. That is,

$$\frac{3}{4} = \frac{?}{100}$$

Note that the denominator of the original fraction must be multiplied by 25 to produce the denominator of the desired fraction. For the two fractions to be equal, both the numerator and the denominator must be multiplied by the same number. Therefore, we also multiply the top of the original fraction by 25 and obtain

$$\frac{3 \times 25}{4 \times 25} = \frac{75}{100}$$

2. Multiplying Fractions. To multiply two fractions, first multiply the numerators and then multiply the denominators. For example,

$$\frac{3}{4} \times \frac{5}{7} = \frac{3 \times 5}{4 \times 7} = \frac{15}{28}$$

3. Dividing Fractions. To divide one fraction by another, invert the second fraction and then multiply. For example,

$$\tfrac{1}{2} \div \tfrac{1}{4} = \tfrac{1}{2} \times \tfrac{4}{1} = \tfrac{1 \times 4}{2 \times 1} = \tfrac{4}{2} = \tfrac{2}{1} = 2$$

4. Adding and Subtracting Fractions. Fractions must have the same denominator before you can add or subtract them. If the two fractions already have a common denominator, simply add (or subtract as the case may be) *only* the values in the numerators. For example,

$$\tfrac{2}{5} + \tfrac{1}{5} = \tfrac{3}{5}$$

Suppose you divided a pie into five equal pieces (fifths). If you first ate two-fifths of the pie and then another one-fifth, the total amount eaten would be three-fifths of the pie:

If the two fractions do not have the same denominator, you must first find equivalent fractions with a common denominator before you can add or subtract. The product of the two denominators will always work as a common denominator for equivalent fractions (although it may not be the lowest common denominator). For example,

$$\tfrac{2}{3} + \tfrac{1}{10} = ?$$

Because these two fractions have different denominators, it is necessary to convert each into an equivalent fraction and find a common denominator. We will use $3 \times 10 = 30$ as the common denominator. Thus, the equivalent fraction of each is

$$\tfrac{2}{3} = \tfrac{20}{30} \qquad \text{and} \qquad \tfrac{1}{10} = \tfrac{3}{30}$$

Now the two fractions can be added:

$$\tfrac{20}{30} + \tfrac{3}{30} = \tfrac{23}{30}$$

5. Comparing the Size of Fractions. When comparing the size of two fractions with the same denominator, the larger fraction will have the larger numerator. For example,

$$\tfrac{5}{8} > \tfrac{3}{8}$$

The denominators are the same, so the whole is partitioned into pieces of the same size. Five of these pieces are more than three of them:

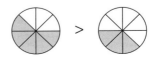

When two fractions have different denominators, you must first convert them to fractions with a common denominator to determine which is larger. Consider the following fractions:

$$\frac{3}{8} \quad \text{and} \quad \frac{7}{16}$$

If the numerator and denominator of $\frac{3}{8}$ are multiplied by 2, the resulting equivalent fraction will have a denominator of 16:

$$\frac{3}{8} = \frac{3 \times 2}{8 \times 2} = \frac{6}{16}$$

Now a comparison can be made between the two fractions:

$$\frac{6}{16} < \frac{7}{16}$$

Therefore,

$$\frac{3}{8} < \frac{7}{16}$$

DECIMALS

1. Converting Decimals to Fractions. Like a fraction, a decimal represents part of the whole. The first decimal place to the right of the decimal point indicates how many tenths are used. For example,

$$0.1 = \frac{1}{10} \qquad 0.7 = \frac{7}{10}$$

The next decimal place represents $\frac{1}{100}$, the next $\frac{1}{1000}$, the next $\frac{1}{10,000}$, and so on. To change a decimal to a fraction, just use the number without the decimal point for the numerator. Use the denominator that the last (on the right) decimal place represents. For example,

$$0.32 = \frac{32}{100} \qquad 0.5333 = \frac{5333}{10,000} \qquad 0.05 = \frac{5}{100} \qquad 0.001 = \frac{1}{1000}$$

2. Adding and Subtracting Decimals. To add and subtract decimals, the only rule is that you must keep the decimal points in a straight vertical line. For example,

$$\begin{array}{r} 0.27 \\ + 1.326 \\ \hline 1.596 \end{array} \qquad \begin{array}{r} 3.595 \\ - 0.67 \\ \hline 2.925 \end{array}$$

3. Multiplying Decimals. To multiply two decimal values, first multiply the two numbers, ignoring the decimal points. Then position the decimal point in the answer so that the number of digits to the right of the decimal point is equal to the total number of decimal places in the two numbers being multiplied. For example,

$$\begin{array}{r} 1.73 \\ \times\ 0.251 \\ \hline 173 \\ 865 \\ 346 \\ \hline 0.43423 \end{array} \begin{array}{l} \text{(two decimal places)} \\ \text{(three decimal places)} \\ \\ \\ \\ \text{(five decimal places)} \end{array} \qquad \begin{array}{r} 0.25 \\ \times\ 0.005 \\ \hline 125 \\ 00 \\ 00 \\ \hline 0.00125 \end{array} \begin{array}{l} \text{(two decimal places)} \\ \text{(three decimal places)} \\ \\ \\ \\ \text{(five decimal places)} \end{array}$$

4. Dividing Decimals. The simplest procedure for dividing decimals is based on the fact that dividing two numbers is identical to expressing them as a fraction:

$$0.25 \div 1.6 \text{ is identical to } \frac{0.25}{1.6}$$

You now can multiply both the numerator and the denominator of the fraction by 10, 100, 1000, or whatever number is necessary to remove the decimal places. Remember that multiplying both the numerator and the denominator of a fraction by the *same* value will create an equivalent fraction. Therefore,

$$\frac{0.25}{1.6} = \frac{0.25 \times 100}{1.6 \times 100} = \frac{25}{160} = \frac{5}{32}$$

The result is a division problem without any decimal places in the two numbers.

PERCENTAGES

1. Converting a Percentage to a Fraction or a Decimal. To convert a percentage to a fraction, remove the percent sign, place the number in the numerator, and use 100 for the denominator. For example,

$$52\% = \frac{52}{100} \qquad 5\% = \frac{5}{100}$$

To convert a percentage to a decimal, remove the percent sign, and divide by 100, or simply move the decimal point two places to the left. For example,

$$83\% = 83. \quad = 0.83$$
$$14.5\% = 14.5 = 0.145$$
$$5\% = 5. \quad = 0.05$$

2. Performing Arithmetic Operations with Percentages. In certain situations, it is best to express percent values as decimals in order to perform certain arithmetic operations. For example, what is 45% of 60? This question may be stated as

$$45\% \times 60 = ?$$

The 45% should be converted to decimal form to find the solution to this question. Therefore,

$$0.45 \times 60 = 27$$

LEARNING CHECK

1. Convert $\frac{3}{25}$ to a decimal.

2. Convert $\frac{3}{8}$ to a percentage.

3. Next to each set of fractions, write "True" if they are equivalent and "False" if they are not:

   a. $\frac{3}{8} = \frac{9}{24}$ _____   **b.** $\frac{7}{9} = \frac{17}{19}$ _____

   c. $\frac{2}{7} = \frac{4}{14}$ _____

4. Compute the following:

   a. $\frac{1}{6} \times \frac{7}{10}$ **b.** $\frac{7}{8} - \frac{1}{2}$ **c.** $\frac{9}{10} \div \frac{2}{3}$ **d.** $\frac{7}{22} + \frac{2}{3}$

5. Identify the larger fraction of each pair:

    a. $\frac{7}{10}, \frac{21}{100}$ **b.** $\frac{3}{4}, \frac{7}{12}$ **c.** $\frac{22}{3}, \frac{19}{3}$

6. Convert the following decimals into fractions:

    a. 0.012   **b.** 0.77   **c.** 0.005

7. $2.59 \times 0.015 = ?$

8. $1.8 \div 0.02 = ?$

9. What is 28% of 45?

ANSWERS   **1.** 0.12   **2.** 37.5%   **3. a.** True   **b.** False   **c.** True

    4. a. $\frac{7}{60}$ **b.** $\frac{3}{8}$ **c.** $\frac{27}{20}$ **d.** $\frac{65}{66}$ **5. a.** $\frac{7}{10}$ **b.** $\frac{3}{4}$ **c.** $\frac{22}{3}$

    6. a. $\frac{12}{1000} = \frac{3}{250}$ **b.** $\frac{77}{100}$ **c.** $\frac{5}{1000} = \frac{1}{200}$ **7.** 0.03885   **8.** 90   **9.** 12.6   ◆

A.3 NEGATIVE NUMBERS

Negative numbers are used to represent values less than zero. Negative numbers may occur when you are measuring the difference between two scores. For example, a researcher may want to evaluate the effectiveness of a propaganda film by measuring people's attitudes with a test both before and after viewing the film:

	Before	After	Amount of change
Person A	23	27	+4
Person B	18	15	−3
Person C	21	16	−5

Note that the negative sign provides information about the direction of the difference: A plus sign indicates an increase in value, and a minus sign indicates a decrease.

    Because negative numbers are frequently encountered, you should be comfortable working with these values. This section reviews basic arithmetic operations using negative numbers. You should also note that any number without a sign (+ or −) is assumed to be positive.

    1. Adding Negative Numbers. When adding numbers that include negative values, simply interpret the negative sign as subtraction. For example,

$$3 + (-2) + 5 = 3 - 2 + 5 = 6$$

When adding a long string of numbers, it often is easier to add all the positive values to obtain the positive sum and then to add all of the negative values to obtain the negative sum. Finally, you subtract the negative sum from the positive sum. For example,

$$-1 + 3 + (-4) + 3 + (-6) + (-2)$$

positive sum $= 6$ negative sum $= 13$

Answer: $6 - 13 = -7$

2. Subtracting Negative Numbers. To subtract a negative number, change it to a positive number, and add. For example,

$$4 - (-3) = 4 + 3 = 7$$

This rule is easier to understand if you think of positive numbers as financial gains and negative numbers as financial losses. In this context, taking away a debt is equivalent to a financial gain. In mathematical terms, taking away a negative number is equivalent to adding a positive number. For example, suppose you are meeting a friend for lunch. You have $7, but you owe your friend $3. Thus, you really have only $4 to spend for lunch. But your friend forgives (takes away) the $3 debt. The result is that you now have $7 to spend. Expressed as an equation,

$$\$4 \text{ minus a } \$3 \text{ debt} = \$7$$
$$4 - (-3) = 4 + 3 = 7$$

3. Multiplying and Dividing Negative Numbers. When the two numbers being multiplied (or divided) have the same sign, the result is a positive number. When the two numbers have different signs, the result is negative. For example,

$$3 \times (-2) = -6$$
$$-4 \times (-2) = +8$$

The first example is easy to explain by thinking of multiplication as repeated addition. In this case,

$$3 \times (-2) = (-2) + (-2) + (-2) = -6$$

You add three negative 2s, which results in a total of negative 6. In the second example, we are multiplying by a negative number. This amounts to repeated subtraction. That is,

$$-4 \times (-2) = -(-2) - (-2) - (-2) - (-2)$$
$$= 2 + 2 + 2 + 2 = 8$$

By using the same rule for both multiplication and division, we ensure that these two operations are compatible. For example,

$$-6 \div 3 = -2$$

which is compatible with

$$3 \times (-2) = -6$$

Also,

$$8 \div (-4) = -2$$

which is compatible with

$$-4 \times (-2) = +8$$

1. Complete the following calculations:

    a. $3 + (-8) + 5 + 7 + (-1) + (-3)$

    b. $5 - (-9) + 2 - (-3) - (-1)$

    c. $3 - 7 - (-21) + (-5) - (-9)$

    d. $4 - (-6) - 3 + 11 - 14$

    e. $9 + 8 - 2 - 1 - (-6)$

    f. $9 \times (-3)$

    g. $-7 \times (-4)$

    h. $-6 \times (-2) \times (-3)$

    i. $-12 \div (-3)$

    j. $18 \div (-6)$

ANSWERS   **1. a.** 3   **b.** 20   **c.** 21   **d.** 4   **e.** 20

          f. -27 **g.** 28   **h.** -36 **i.** 4   **j.** -3

A.4   BASIC ALGEBRA: SOLVING EQUATIONS

An equation is a mathematical statement that indicates two quantities are identical. For example,

$$12 = 8 + 4$$

Often an equation will contain an unknown (or variable) quantity that is identified with a letter or symbol, rather than a number. For example,

$$12 = 8 + X$$

In this event, your task is to find the value of X that makes the equation "true," or balanced. For this example, an X value of 4 will make a true equation. Finding the value of X is usually called *solving the equation.*

    To solve an equation, there are two points to be kept in mind:

1. Your goal is to have the unknown value (X) isolated on one side of the equation. This means that you need to remove all of the other numbers and symbols that appear on the same side of the equation as the X.

2. The equation will remain balanced, provided you treat both sides exactly the same. For example, you could add 10 points to *both* sides, and the solution (the X value) for the equation would be unchanged.

FINDING THE SOLUTION FOR AN EQUATION

We will consider four basic types of equations and the operations needed to solve them.

    1. When X Has a Value Added to It. An example of this type of equation is

$$X + 3 = 7$$

Your goal is to isolate X on one side of the equation. Thus, you must remove the $+3$ on the left-hand side. The solution is obtained by subtracting 3 from *both* sides of the equation:

$$X + 3 - 3 = 7 - 3$$
$$X = 4$$

The solution is $X = 4$. You should always check your solution by returning to the original equation and replacing X with the value you obtained for the solution. For this example,

$$X + 3 = 7$$
$$4 + 3 = 7$$
$$7 = 7$$

2. When X Has a Value Subtracted from It. An example of this type of equation is

$$X - 8 = 12$$

In this example, you must remove the -8 from the left-hand side. Thus, the solution is obtained by adding 8 to *both* sides of the equation:

$$X - 8 + 8 = 12 + 8$$
$$X = 20$$

Check the solution:

$$X - 8 = 12$$
$$20 - 8 = 12$$
$$12 = 12$$

3. When X Is Multiplied by a Value. An example of this type of equation is

$$4X = 24$$

In this instance, it is necessary to remove the 4 that is multiplied by X. This may be accomplished by dividing both sides of the equation by 4:

$$\frac{4X}{4} = \frac{24}{4}$$
$$X = 6$$

Check the solution:

$$4X = 24$$
$$4(6) = 24$$
$$24 = 24$$

4. When X Is Divided by a Value. An example of this type of equation is

$$\frac{X}{3} = 9$$

Now the X is divided by 3, so the solution is obtained by multiplying by 3. Multiplying both sides yields

$$3\left(\frac{X}{3}\right) = 9(3)$$

$$X = 27$$

For the check,

$$\frac{X}{3} = 9$$

$$\frac{27}{3} = 9$$

$$9 = 9$$

SOLUTIONS FOR MORE COMPLEX EQUATIONS

Equations that are more complex can be solved by using a combination of the preceding simple operations. Remember: At each stage you are trying to isolate X on one side of the equation. For example,

$$3X + 7 = 22$$

$$3X + 7 - 7 = 22 - 7 \quad \text{(Remove + 7 by subtracting 7 from both sides.)}$$

$$3X = 15$$

$$\frac{3X}{3} = \frac{15}{3} \quad \text{(Remove 3 by dividing both sides by 3.)}$$

$$X = 5$$

To check this solution, return to the original equation, and substitute 5 in place of X:

$$3X + 7 = 22$$

$$3(5) + 7 = 22$$

$$15 + 7 = 22$$

$$22 = 22$$

Following is another type of complex equation that is frequently encountered in statistics:

$$\frac{X + 3}{4} = 2$$

First, remove the 4 by multiplying both sides by 4:

$$4\left(\frac{X + 3}{4}\right) = 2(4)$$

$$X + 3 = 8$$

Now remove the + 3 by subtracting 3 from both sides:

$$X + 3 - 3 = 8 - 3$$

$$X = 5$$

To check this solution, return to the original equation, and substitute 5 in place of X:

$$\frac{X + 3}{4} = 2$$

$$\frac{5 + 3}{4} = 2$$

$$\frac{8}{4} = 2$$

$$2 = 2$$

LEARNING CHECK

1. Solve for X, and check the solutions:

a. $3X = 18$ **b.** $X + 7 = 9$ **c.** $X - 4 = 18$ **d.** $5X - 8 = 12$

e. $\dfrac{X}{9} = 5$ **f.** $\dfrac{X + 1}{6} = 4$ **g.** $X + 2 = -5$ **h.** $\dfrac{X}{5} = -5$

i. $\dfrac{2X}{3} = 12$ **j.** $\dfrac{X}{3} + 1 = 3$

ANSWERS   **1. a.** $X = 6$ **b.** $X = 2$ **c.** $X = 22$ **d.** $X = 4$ **e.** $X = 45$
f. $X = 23$ **g.** $X = -7$ **h.** $X = -25$ **i.** $X = 18$ **j.** $X = 6$

A.5 EXPONENTS AND SQUARE ROOTS

EXPONENTIAL NOTATION

A simplified notation is used whenever a number is being multiplied by itself. The notation consists of placing a value, called an *exponent,* on the right-hand side of and raised above another number, called a *base.* For example,

$7^3 \leftarrow$ exponent
$\uparrow$
base

The exponent indicates how many times the base is used as a factor in multiplication. Following are some examples:

$$7^3 = 7(7)(7)$$ (Read "7 cubed" *or* "7 raised to the third power.")

$$5^2 = 5(5)$$ (Read "5 squared.")

$$2^5 = 2(2)(2)(2)(2)$$ (Read "2 raised to the fifth power.")

There are a few basic rules about exponents that you will need to know for this course. They are outlined here.

1. Numbers Raised to One or Zero. Any number raised to the first power equals itself. For example,

$$6^1 = 6$$

Any number (except zero) raised to the zero power equals 1. For example,

$$9^0 = 1$$

2. Exponents for Multiple Terms. The exponent applies only to the base that is just in front of it. For example,

$$XY^2 = XYY$$
$$a^2b^3 = aabbb$$

3. Negative Bases Raised to an Exponent. If a negative number is raised to a power, then the result will be positive for exponents that are even and negative for exponents that are odd. For example,

$$(-4)^3 = (-4)(-4)(-4)$$
$$= 16(-4)$$
$$= -64$$

and

$$(-3)^4 = (-3)(-3)(-3)(-3)$$
$$= 9(-3)(-3)$$
$$= 9(9)$$
$$= 81$$

Note: The parentheses are used to ensure that the exponent applies to the entire negative number, including the sign. Without the parentheses there is some ambiguity as to how the exponent should be applied. For example, the expression -3^2 could have two interpretations:

$$-3^2 = (-3)(-3) = 9 \quad \text{or} \quad -3^2 = -(3)(3) = -9$$

4. Exponents and Parentheses. If an exponent is present outside of parentheses, then the computations within the parentheses are done first, and the exponential computation is done last:

$$(3 + 5)^2 = 8^2 = 64$$

Note that the meaning of the expression is changed when each term in the parentheses is raised to the exponent individually:

$$3^2 + 5^2 = 9 + 25 = 34$$

Therefore,

$$X^2 + Y^2 \neq (X + Y)^2$$

5. Fractions Raised to a Power. If the numerator and denominator of a fraction are each raised to the same exponent, then the entire fraction can be raised to that exponent. That is,

$$\frac{a^2}{b^2} = \left(\frac{a}{b}\right)^2$$

For example,

$$\frac{3^2}{4^2} = \left(\frac{3}{4}\right)^2$$

$$\frac{9}{16} = \frac{3}{4}\left(\frac{3}{4}\right)$$

$$\frac{9}{16} = \frac{9}{16}$$

SQUARE ROOTS   The square root of a value equals a number that when multiplied by itself yields the original value. For example, the square root of 16 equals 4 because 4 times 4 equals 16. The symbol for the square root is called a *radical*, $\sqrt{}$. The square root is taken for the number under the radical. For example,

$$\sqrt{16} = 4$$

Finding the square root is the inverse of raising a number to the second power (squaring). Thus,

$$\sqrt{a^2} = a$$

We will typically use positive square roots although you should realize that $\sqrt{9}$ could be either +3 or −3.

For example,

$$\sqrt{3^2} = \sqrt{9} = 3$$

Also,

$$\left(\sqrt{b}\right)^2 = b$$

For example,

$$\left(\sqrt{64}\right)^2 = 8^2 = 64$$

Computations under the same radical are performed *before* the square root is taken. For example,

$$\sqrt{9 + 16} = \sqrt{25} = 5$$

Note that with addition (or subtraction) separate radicals yield a different result:

$$\sqrt{9} + \sqrt{16} = 3 + 4 = 7$$

Therefore,

$$\sqrt{X} + \sqrt{Y} \neq \sqrt{X + Y}$$
$$\sqrt{X} - \sqrt{Y} \neq \sqrt{X - Y}$$

If the numerator and denominator of a fraction each have a radical, then the entire fraction can be placed under a single radical:

$$\frac{\sqrt{16}}{\sqrt{4}} = \sqrt{\frac{16}{4}}$$

$$\frac{4}{2} = \sqrt{4}$$

$$2 = 2$$

Therefore,

$$\frac{\sqrt{X}}{\sqrt{Y}} = \sqrt{\frac{X}{Y}}$$

Also, if the square root of one number is multiplied by the square root of another number, then the same result would be obtained by taking the square root of the product of both numbers. For example,

$$\sqrt{9} \times \sqrt{16} = \sqrt{9 \times 16}$$

$$3 \times 4 = \sqrt{144}$$

$$12 = 12$$

Therefore,

$$\sqrt{a} \times \sqrt{b} = \sqrt{ab}$$

LEARNING CHECK

1. Perform the following computations:
   a. $(-6)^3$
   b. $(3 + 7)^2$
   c. $a^3 b^2$ when $a = 2$ and $b = -5$

    d. a^4b^3 when $a = 2$ and $b = 3$
    e. $(XY)^2$ when $X = 3$ and $Y = 5$
    f. $X^2 + Y^2$ when $X = 3$ and $Y = 5$
    g. $(X + Y)^2$ when $X = 3$ and $Y = 5$
    h. $\sqrt{5} + 4$
    i. $\left(\sqrt{9}\right)^2$
    j. $\dfrac{\sqrt{16}}{\sqrt{4}}$

ANSWERS   **1. a.** -216 **b.** 100   **c.** 200   **d.** 432   **e.** 225
                  f. 34   **g.** 64   **h.** 3   **i.** 9   **j.** 2

PROBLEMS FOR APPENDIX A   Basic Mathematics Review

1. $50/(10 - 8) = ?$

2. $(2 + 3)^2 = ?$

3. $20/10 \times 3 = ?$

4. $12 - 4 \times 2 + 6/3 = ?$

5. $24/(12 - 4) + 2 \times (6 + 3) = ?$

6. Convert $\frac{7}{20}$ to a decimal.

7. Express $\frac{9}{25}$ as a percentage.

8. Convert 0.91 to a fraction.

9. Express 0.0031 as a fraction.

10. Next to each set of fractions, write "True" if they are equivalent and "False" if they are not:

    a. $\dfrac{4}{1000} = \dfrac{2}{100}$ _____

    b. $\dfrac{5}{6} = \dfrac{52}{62}$ _____

    c. $\dfrac{1}{8} = \dfrac{7}{56}$ _____

11. Perform the following calculations:

    a. $\dfrac{4}{5} \times \dfrac{2}{3} = ?$ **b.** $\dfrac{7}{9} \div \dfrac{2}{3} = ?$

    c. $\dfrac{3}{8} + \dfrac{1}{5} = ?$ **d.** $\dfrac{5}{18} - \dfrac{1}{6} = ?$

12. $2.51 \times 0.017 = ?$

13. $3.88 \times 0.0002 = ?$

14. $3.17 + 17.0132 = ?$

15. $5.55 + 10.7 + 0.711 + 3.33 + 0.031 = ?$

16. $2.04 \div 0.2 = ?$

17. $0.36 \div 0.4 = ?$

18. $5 + 3 - 6 - 4 + 3 = ?$

19. $9 - (-1) - 17 + 3 - (-4) + 5 = ?$

20. $5 + 3 - (-8) - (-1) + (-3) - 4 + 10 = ?$

21. $8 \times (-3) = ?$

22. $-22 \div (-2) = ?$

23. $-2(-4) \times (-3) = ?$

24. $84 \div (-4) = ?$

Solve the equations in Problems 25–32 for X.

25. $X - 7 = -2$

26. $9 = X + 3$

27. $\dfrac{X}{4} = 11$

28. $-3 = \dfrac{X}{3}$

29. $\dfrac{X + 3}{5} = 2$

30. $\dfrac{X + 1}{3} = -8$

31. $6X - 1 = 11$

32. $2X + 3 = -11$

33. $(-5)^2 = ?$

34. $(-5)^3 = ?$

35. If $a = 4$ and $b = 3$, then $a^2 + b^4 = ?$

36. If $a = -1$ and $b = 4$, then $(a + b)^2 = ?$

37. If $a = -1$ and $b = 5$, then $ab^2 = ?$

38. $\dfrac{18}{\sqrt{4}} = ?$

39. $\sqrt{\dfrac{20}{5}} = ?$

SKILLS ASSESSMENT FINAL EXAM

SECTION 1

1. $4 + 8/4 = ?$

2. $(4 + 8)/4 = ?$

3. $4 \times 3^2 = ?$

4. $(4 \times 3)^2 = ?$

5. $10/5 \times 2 = ?$

6. $10/(5 \times 2) = ?$

7. $40 - 10 \times 4/2 = ?$

8. $(5 - 1)^2/2 = ?$

9. $3 \times 6 - 3^2 = ?$

10. $2 \times (6 - 3)^2 = ?$

11. $4 \times 3 - 1 + 8 \times 2 = ?$

12. $4 \times (3 - 1 + 8) \times 2 = ?$

SECTION 2

1. Express $^{14}\!/_{80}$ as a decimal.

2. Convert $^9\!/_{25}$ to a percentage.

3. Convert 18% to a fraction.

4. $\frac{3}{5} \times \frac{2}{3} = ?$

5. $\frac{5}{24} + \frac{5}{6} = ?$

6. $\frac{7}{12} \div \frac{5}{6} = ?$

7. $\frac{5}{9} - \frac{1}{3} = ?$

8. $6.11 \times 0.22 = ?$

9. $0.18 \div 0.9 = ?$

10. $8.742 + 0.76 = ?$

11. In a statistics class of 72 students, three-eighths of the students received a *B* on the first test. How many *B*s were earned?

12. What is 15% of 64?

SECTION 3

1. $3 - 1 - 3 + 5 - 2 + 6 = ?$

2. $-8 - (-6) = ?$

3. $2 - (-7) - 3 + (-11) - 20 = ?$

4. $-8 - 3 - (-1) - 2 - 1 = ?$

5. $8(-2) = ?$

6. $-7(-7) = ?$

7. $-3(-2)(-5) = ?$

8. $-3(5)(-3) = ?$

9. $-24 \div (-4) = ?$

10. $36 \div (-6) = ?$

11. $-56/7 = ?$

12. $-7/(-1) = ?$

SECTION 4

Solve for *X*.

1. $X + 5 = 12$

2. $X - 11 = 3$

3. $10 = X + 4$

4. $4X = 20$

5. $\dfrac{X}{2} = 15$

6. $18 = 9X$

7. $\dfrac{X}{5} = 35$

8. $2X + 8 = 4$

9. $\dfrac{X + 1}{3} = 6$

10. $4X + 3 = -13$

11. $\dfrac{X + 3}{3} = -7$

12. $23 = 2X - 5$

SECTION 5

1. $5^3 = ?$

2. $(-4)^3 = ?$

3. $(-2)^5 = ?$

4. $(-2)^6 = ?$

5. If $a = 4$ and $b = 2$, then $ab^2 = ?$

6. If $a = 4$ and $b = 2$, then $(a + b)^3 = ?$

7. If $a = 4$ and $b = 2$, then $a^2 + b^2 = ?$

8. $(11 + 4)^2 = ?$

9. $\sqrt{7^2} = ?$

10. If $a = 36$ and $b = 64$, then $\sqrt{a + b} = ?$

11. $\dfrac{25}{\sqrt{25}} = ?$

12. If $a = -1$ and $b = 2$, then $a^3 b^4 = ?$

ANSWER KEY   Skills Assessment Exams

PREVIEW EXAM

SECTION 1

1. 17

2. 35

3. 6

4. 24

5. 5

6. 2

7. $\dfrac{1}{3}$

8. 8

9. 72

10. 8

11. 24

12. 48

SECTION 2

1. 75%

2. $\dfrac{30}{100}$, or $\dfrac{3}{10}$

3. 0.3

4. $\dfrac{10}{13}$

5. 1.625

6. $\dfrac{2}{20}$, or $\dfrac{1}{10}$

7. $\dfrac{19}{24}$

8. 1.4

9. $\dfrac{4}{15}$

10. 7.5

11. 16

12. 36

SECTION 3

1. 4

2. 8

3. 2

4. 9

5. -12

6. 12

7. -15

8. -24

9. -4

10. 3

11. -2

12. 25

SECTION 4

1. $X = 7$

2. $X = 29$

3. $X = 9$

4. $X = 4$

5. $X = 24$

6. $X = 15$

7. $X = 80$

8. $X = -3$

9. $X = 11$

10. $X = 25$

11. $X = 11$

12. $X = 7$

SECTION 5

1. 64

2. 4

3. 54

4. 25

5. 13

6. -27

7. 256

8. 8

9. 12

10. 121

11. 33

12. -9

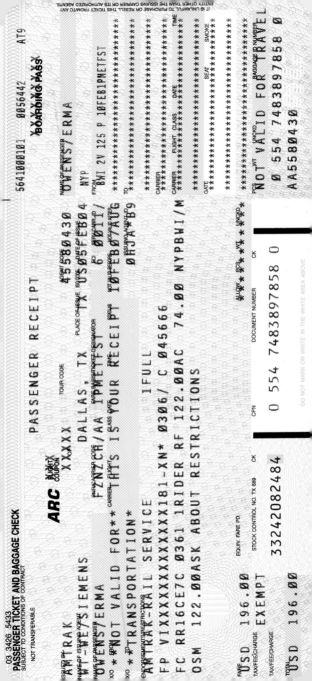

NOT FOR USE IN MAGNETIC STRIPE READERS

PASSENGER TICKET AND BAGGAGE CHECK

PASSENGER COUPON

NOTICE

International (Warsaw Convention) Notice

If the passenger's journey involves an ultimate destination or stop in a country other than the country of departure, the Warsaw Convention may be applicable and the Convention governs and in most cases limits the liability of carriers for death or personal injury and for loss of or damage to baggage. See also the notices entitled "Advice to International Passengers on Limitation of Liability" and "Notice of Baggage Liability Limitations".

Domestic Notice

Air Transportation to be provided between points in the U.S. (including its overseas territories and possessions) is subject to the individual contract terms (including rules, regulations, tariffs and conditions) of the transporting air carriers, which are herein incorporated by reference and made part of the contract of carriage.

Where this coupon is issued for transportation, or services other than air travel, specific terms and conditions may apply. These terms and conditions may be included in the ticket set or may be obtained from this issuing company or agent.

Please make sure you have received the important legal notices entitled "Conditions of Contract", "Notice of Incorporated Terms", "Notice of Baggage Liability Limitations", and "Notice of Overbooking" or the specific terms and conditions relating to non-air transportation or services. If not, contact the nearest office of the company or agent to obtain copies.

FINAL EXAM

SECTION 1

1. 6	**7.** 20
2. 3	**8.** 8
3. 36	**9.** 9
4. 144	**10.** 18
5. 4	**11.** 27
6. 1	**12.** 80

SECTION 2

1. 0.175

2. 24%

3. $\dfrac{18}{100}$, or $\dfrac{9}{50}$

4. $\dfrac{6}{15}$, or $\dfrac{2}{5}$

5. $\dfrac{25}{24}$

6. $\dfrac{42}{60}$, or $\dfrac{7}{10}$

7. $\dfrac{2}{9}$

8. 1.3442

9. 0.2

10. 9.502

11. 27

12. 9.6

SECTION 3

1. 8	**4.** -13
2. -2	**5.** -16
3. -25	**6.** 49

SECTION 3 (continued)

7. -30	**10.** -6
8. 45	**11.** -8
9. 6	**12.** 7

SECTION 4

1. $X = 7$	**7.** $X = 175$
2. $X = 14$	**8.** $X = -2$
3. $X = 6$	**9.** $X = 17$
4. $X = 5$	**10.** $X = -4$
5. $X = 30$	**11.** $X = -24$
6. $X = 2$	**12.** $X = 14$

SECTION 5

1. 125	**7.** 20
2. -64	**8.** 225
3. -32	**9.** 7
4. 64	**10.** 10
5. 16	**11.** 5
6. 216	**12.** -16

SOLUTIONS TO SELECTED PROBLEMS FOR APPENDIX A   Basic Mathematics Review

1. 25

3. 6

5. 21

6. 0.35

7. 36%

9. $\dfrac{31}{10,000}$

10. b. False

11. a. $\dfrac{8}{15}$ **b.** $\dfrac{21}{18}$

  c. $\dfrac{23}{40}$

12. 0.04267

14. 20.1832

17. 0.9

19. 5

21. -24

22. 11

25. $X = 5$

28. $X = -9$

30. $X = -25$

31. $X = 2$

34. -125

36. 9

37. -25

39. 2

SUGGESTED REVIEW BOOKS

There are many basic mathematics review books available if you need a more extensive review than this appendix can provide. The following books are but a few of the many that you may find helpful:

Angel, A. R., & Porter, S. R. (1997). *A survey of mathematics with applications,* 5th ed. Reading, Mass.: Addison-Wesley.

Bloomfield, D. I. (1994). *Introductory algebra.* St. Paul, Minn.: West.

Falstein, L. D. (1986). *Basic mathematics,* 2nd ed. Reading, Mass.: Addison-Wesley.

Goodman, A., & Hirsch, L. (1994). *Understanding elementary algebra.* St. Paul, Minn.: West.

STATISTICAL TABLES

TABLE B.1   THE UNIT NORMAL TABLE*

*Column A lists z-score values. A vertical line drawn through a normal distribution at a
z-score location divides the distribution into two sections.
Column B identifies the proportion in the larger section, called the *body*.
Column C identifies the proportion in the smaller section, called the *tail*.

Note: Because the normal distribution is symmetrical, the proportions for negative z-scores
are the same as those for positive z-scores.

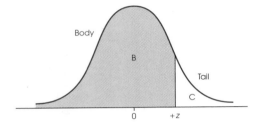
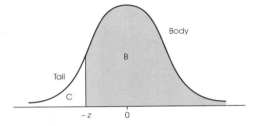

(A)	(B) Proportion in body	(C) Proportion in tail	(A)	(B) Proportion in body	(C) Proportion in tail	(A)	(B) Proportion in body	(C) Proportion in tail
z			z			z		
0.00	.5000	.5000	0.20	.5793	.4207	0.40	.6554	.3446
0.01	.5040	.4960	0.21	.5832	.4168	0.41	.6591	.3409
0.02	.5080	.4920	0.22	.5871	.4129	0.42	.6628	.3372
0.03	.5120	.4880	0.23	.5910	.4090	0.43	.6664	.3336
0.04	.5160	.4840	0.24	.5948	.4052	0.44	.6700	.3300
0.05	.5199	.4801	0.25	.5987	.4013	0.45	.6736	.3264
0.06	.5239	.4761	0.26	.6026	.3974	0.46	.6772	.3228
0.07	.5279	.4721	0.27	.6064	.3936	0.47	.6808	.3192
0.08	.5319	.4681	0.28	.6103	.3897	0.48	.6844	.3156
0.09	.5359	.4641	0.29	.6141	.3859	0.49	.6879	.3121
0.10	.5398	.4602	0.30	.6179	.3821	0.50	.6915	.3085
0.11	.5438	.4562	0.31	.6217	.3783	0.51	.6950	.3050
0.12	.5478	.4522	0.32	.6255	.3745	0.52	.6985	.3015
0.13	.5517	.4483	0.33	.6293	.3707	0.53	.7019	.2981
0.14	.5557	.4443	0.34	.6331	.3669	0.54	.7054	.2946
0.15	.5596	.4404	0.35	.6368	.3632	0.55	.7088	.2912
0.16	.5636	.4364	0.36	.6406	.3594	0.56	.7123	.2877
0.17	.5675	.4325	0.37	.6443	.3557	0.57	.7157	.2843
0.18	.5714	.4286	0.38	.6480	.3520	0.58	.7190	.2810
0.19	.5753	.4247	0.39	.6517	.3483	0.59	.7224	.2776

TABLE B.1 continued

(A) z	(B) Proportion in body	(C) Proportion in tail	(A) z	(B) Proportion in body	(C) Proportion in tail	(A) z	(B) Proportion in body	(C) Proportion in tail
0.60	.7257	.2743	1.05	.8531	.1469	1.50	.9332	.0668
0.61	.7291	.2709	1.06	.8554	.1446	1.51	.9345	.0655
0.62	.7324	.2676	1.07	.8577	.1423	1.52	.9357	.0643
0.63	.7357	.2643	1.08	.8599	.1401	1.53	.9370	.0630
0.64	.7389	.2611	1.09	.8621	.1379	1.54	.9382	.0618
0.65	.7422	.2578	1.10	.8643	.1357	1.55	.9394	.0606
0.66	.7454	.2546	1.11	.8665	.1335	1.56	.9406	.0594
0.67	.7486	.2514	1.12	.8686	.1314	1.57	.9418	.0582
0.68	.7517	.2483	1.13	.8708	.1292	1.58	.9429	.0571
0.69	.7549	.2451	1.14	.8729	.1271	1.59	.9441	.0559
0.70	.7580	.2420	1.15	.8749	.1251	1.60	.9452	.0548
0.71	.7611	.2389	1.16	.8770	.1230	1.61	.9463	.0537
0.72	.7642	.2358	1.17	.8790	.1210	1.62	.9474	.0526
0.73	.7673	.2327	1.18	.8810	.1190	1.63	.9484	.0516
0.74	.7704	.2296	1.19	.8830	.1170	1.64	.9495	.0505
0.75	.7734	.2266	1.20	.8849	.1151	1.65	.9505	.0495
0.76	.7764	.2236	1.21	.8869	.1131	1.66	.9515	.0485
0.77	.7794	.2206	1.22	.8888	.1112	1.67	.9525	.0475
0.78	.7823	.2177	1.23	.8907	.1093	1.68	.9535	.0465
0.79	.7852	.2148	1.24	.8925	.1075	1.69	.9545	.0455
0.80	.7881	.2119	1.25	.8944	.1056	1.70	.9554	.0446
0.81	.7910	.2090	1.26	.8962	.1038	1.71	.9564	.0436
0.82	.7939	.2061	1.27	.8980	.1020	1.72	.9573	.0427
0.83	.7967	.2033	1.28	.8997	.1003	1.73	.9582	.0418
0.84	.7995	.2005	1.29	.9015	.0985	1.74	.9591	.0409
0.85	.8023	.1977	1.30	.9032	.0968	1.75	.9599	.0401
0.86	.8051	.1949	1.31	.9049	.0951	1.76	.9608	.0392
0.87	.8078	.1922	1.32	.9066	.0934	1.77	.9616	.0384
0.88	.8106	.1894	1.33	.9082	.0918	1.78	.9625	.0375
0.89	.8133	.1867	1.34	.9099	.0901	1.79	.9633	.0367
0.90	.8159	.1841	1.35	.9115	.0885	1.80	.9641	.0359
0.91	.8186	.1814	1.36	.9131	.0869	1.81	.9649	.0351
0.92	.8212	.1788	1.37	.9147	.0853	1.82	.9656	.0344
0.93	.8238	.1762	1.38	.9162	.0838	1.83	.9664	.0336
0.94	.8264	.1736	1.39	.9177	.0823	1.84	.9671	.0329
0.95	.8289	.1711	1.40	.9192	.0808	1.85	.9678	.0322
0.96	.8315	.1685	1.41	.9207	.0793	1.86	.9686	.0314
0.97	.8340	.1660	1.42	.9222	.0778	1.87	.9693	.0307
0.98	.8365	.1635	1.43	.9236	.0764	1.88	.9699	.0301
0.99	.8389	.1611	1.44	.9251	.0749	1.89	.9706	.0294
1.00	.8413	.1587	1.45	.9265	.0735	1.90	.9713	.0287
1.01	.8438	.1562	1.46	.9279	.0721	1.91	.9719	.0281
1.02	.8461	.1539	1.47	.9292	.0708	1.92	.9726	.0274
1.03	.8485	.1515	1.48	.9306	.0694	1.93	.9732	.0268
1.04	.8508	.1492	1.49	.9319	.0681	1.94	.9738	.0262

TABLE B.1   continued

(A) z	(B) Proportion in body	(C) Proportion in tail	(A) z	(B) Proportion in body	(C) Proportion in tail	(A) z	(B) Proportion in body	(C) Proportion in tail
1.95	.9744	.0256	2.42	.9922	.0078	2.88	.9980	.0020
1.96	.9750	.0250	2.43	.9925	.0075	2.89	.9981	.0019
1.97	.9756	.0244	2.44	.9927	.0073	2.90	.9981	.0019
1.98	.9761	.0239	2.45	.9929	.0071	2.91	.9982	.0018
1.99	.9767	.0233	2.46	.9931	.0069	2.92	.9982	.0018
2.00	.9772	.0228	2.47	.9932	.0068	2.93	.9983	.0017
2.01	.9778	.0222	2.48	.9934	.0066	2.94	.9984	.0016
2.02	.9783	.0217	2.49	.9936	.0064	2.95	.9984	.0016
2.03	.9788	.0212	2.50	.9938	.0062	2.96	.9985	.0015
2.04	.9793	.0207	2.51	.9940	.0060	2.97	.9985	.0015
2.05	.9798	.0202	2.52	.9941	.0059	2.98	.9986	.0014
2.06	.9803	.0197	2.53	.9943	.0057	2.99	.9986	.0014
2.07	.9808	.0192	2.54	.9945	.0055	3.00	.9987	.0013
2.08	.9812	.0188	2.55	.9946	.0054	3.01	.9987	.0013
2.09	.9817	.0183	2.56	.9948	.0052	3.02	.9987	.0013
2.10	.9821	.0179	2.57	.9949	.0051	3.03	.9988	.0012
2.11	.9826	.0174	2.58	.9951	.0049	3.04	.9988	.0012
2.12	.9830	.0170	2.59	.9952	.0048	3.05	.9989	.0011
2.13	.9834	.0166	2.60	.9953	.0047	3.06	.9989	.0011
2.14	.9838	.0162	2.61	.9955	.0045	3.07	.9989	.0011
2.15	.9842	.0158	2.62	.9956	.0044	3.08	.9990	.0010
2.16	.9846	.0154	2.63	.9957	.0043	3.09	.9990	.0010
2.17	.9850	.0150	2.64	.9959	.0041	3.10	.9990	.0010
2.18	.9854	.0146	2.65	.9960	.0040	3.11	.9991	.0009
2.19	.9857	.0143	2.66	.9961	.0039	3.12	.9991	.0009
2.20	.9861	.0139	2.67	.9962	.0038	3.13	.9991	.0009
2.21	.9864	.0136	2.68	.9963	.0037	3.14	.9992	.0008
2.22	.9868	.0132	2.69	.9964	.0036	3.15	.9992	.0008
2.23	.9871	.0129	2.70	.9965	.0035	3.16	.9992	.0008
2.24	.9875	.0125	2.71	.9966	.0034	3.17	.9992	.0008
2.25	.9878	.0122	2.72	.9967	.0033	3.18	.9993	.0007
2.26	.9881	.0119	2.73	.9968	.0032	3.19	.9993	.0007
2.27	.9884	.0116	2.74	.9969	.0031	3.20	.9993	.0007
2.28	.9887	.0113	2.75	.9970	.0030	3.21	.9993	.0007
2.29	.9890	.0110	2.76	.9971	.0029	3.22	.9994	.0006
2.30	.9893	.0107	2.77	.9972	.0028	3.23	.9994	.0006
2.31	.9896	.0104	2.78	.9973	.0027	3.24	.9994	.0006
2.32	.9898	.0102	2.79	.9974	.0026	3.30	.9995	.0005
2.33	.9901	.0099	2.80	.9974	.0026	3.40	.9997	.0003
2.34	.9904	.0096	2.81	.9975	.0025	3.50	.9998	.0002
2.35	.9906	.0094	2.82	.9976	.0024	3.60	.9998	.0002
2.36	.9909	.0091	2.83	.9977	.0023	3.70	.9999	.0001
2.37	.9911	.0089	2.84	.9977	.0023	3.80	.99993	.00007
2.38	.9913	.0087	2.85	.9978	.0022	3.90	.99995	.00005
2.39	.9916	.0084	2.86	.9979	.0021	4.00	.99997	.00003
2.40	.9918	.0082	2.87	.9979	.0021			
2.41	.9929	.0080						

Generated by the Minitab statistical program using the CDL command.

TABLE B.2   THE *t* DISTRIBUTION

Table entries are values of *t* corresponding to proportions in one tail or in two tails combined.

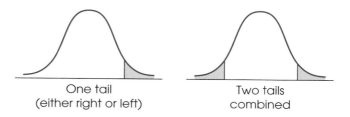

One tail
(either right or left)

Two tails
combined

df	**Proportion in one tail**					
	0.25	0.10	0.05	0.025	0.01	0.005
	Proportion in two tails combined					
	0.50	0.20	0.10	0.05	0.02	0.01
1	1.000	3.078	6.314	12.706	31.821	63.657
2	0.816	1.886	2.920	4.303	6.965	9.925
3	0.765	1.638	2.353	3.182	4.541	5.841
4	0.741	1.533	2.132	2.776	3.747	4.604
5	0.727	1.476	2.015	2.571	3.365	4.032
6	0.718	1.440	1.943	2.447	3.143	3.707
7	0.711	1.415	1.895	2.365	2.998	3.499
8	0.706	1.397	1.860	2.306	2.896	3.355
9	0.703	1.383	1.833	2.262	2.821	3.250
10	0.700	1.372	1.812	2.228	2.764	3.169
11	0.697	1.363	1.796	2.201	2.718	3.106
12	0.695	1.356	1.782	2.179	2.681	3.055
13	0.694	1.350	1.771	2.160	2.650	3.012
14	0.692	1.345	1.761	2.145	2.624	2.977
15	0.691	1.341	1.753	2.131	2.602	2.947
16	0.690	1.337	1.746	2.120	2.583	2.921
17	0.689	1.333	1.740	2.110	2.567	2.898
18	0.688	1.330	1.734	2.101	2.552	2.878
19	0.688	1.328	1.729	2.093	2.539	2.861
20	0.687	1.325	1.725	2.086	2.528	2.845
21	0.686	1.323	1.721	2.080	2.518	2.831
22	0.686	1.321	1.717	2.074	2.508	2.819
23	0.685	1.319	1.714	2.069	2.500	2.807
24	0.685	1.318	1.711	2.064	2.492	2.797
25	0.684	1.316	1.708	2.060	2.485	2.787
26	0.684	1.315	1.706	2.056	2.479	2.779
27	0.684	1.314	1.703	2.052	2.473	2.771
28	0.683	1.313	1.701	2.048	2.467	2.763
29	0.683	1.311	1.699	2.045	2.462	2.756
30	0.683	1.310	1.697	2.042	2.457	2.750
40	0.681	1.303	1.684	2.021	2.423	2.704
60	0.679	1.296	1.671	2.000	2.390	2.660
120	0.677	1.289	1.658	1.980	2.358	2.617
∞	0.674	1.282	1.645	1.960	2.326	2.576

Table III of R. A. Fisher and F. Yates, *Statistical Tables for Biological, Agricultural and Medical Research,* 6th ed. London: Longman Group Ltd., 1974 (previously published by Oliver and Boyd Ltd., Edinburgh). Adapted and reprinted with permission of the Addison Wesley Longman Publishing Co.

STATISTICAL TABLES

TABLE B.3   CRITICAL VALUES FOR THE *F*-MAX STATISTIC*

*The critical values for $\alpha = .05$ are in lightface type, and for $\alpha = .01$, they are in boldface type.

$n - 1$	\multicolumn{11}{c}{k = Number of samples}										
	2	3	4	5	6	7	8	9	10	11	12
4	9.60	15.5	20.6	25.2	29.5	33.6	37.5	41.4	44.6	48.0	51.4
	23.2	**37.**	**49.**	**59.**	**69.**	**79.**	**89.**	**97.**	**106.**	**113.**	**120.**
5	7.15	10.8	13.7	16.3	18.7	20.8	22.9	24.7	26.5	28.2	29.9
	14.9	**22.**	**28.**	**33.**	**38.**	**42.**	**46.**	**50.**	**54.**	**57.**	**60.**
6	5.82	8.38	10.4	12.1	13.7	15.0	16.3	17.5	18.6	19.7	20.7
	11.1	**15.5**	**19.1**	**22.**	**25.**	**27.**	**30.**	**32.**	**34.**	**36.**	**37.**
7	4.99	6.94	8.44	9.70	10.8	11.8	12.7	13.5	14.3	15.1	15.8
	8.89	**12.1**	**14.5**	**16.5**	**18.4**	**20.**	**22.**	**23.**	**24.**	**26.**	**27.**
8	4.43	6.00	7.18	8.12	9.03	9.78	10.5	11.1	11.7	12.2	12.7
	7.50	**9.9**	**11.7**	**13.2**	**14.5**	**15.8**	**16.9**	**17.9**	**18.9**	**19.8**	**21.**
9	4.03	5.34	6.31	7.11	7.80	8.41	8.95	9.45	9.91	10.3	10.7
	6.54	**8.5**	**9.9**	**11.1**	**12.1**	**13.1**	**13.9**	**14.7**	**15.3**	**16.0**	**16.6**
10	3.72	4.85	5.67	6.34	6.92	7.42	7.87	8.28	8.66	9.01	9.34
	5.85	**7.4**	**8.6**	**9.6**	**10.4**	**11.1**	**11.8**	**12.4**	**12.9**	**13.4**	**13.9**
12	3.28	4.16	4.79	5.30	5.72	6.09	6.42	6.72	7.00	7.25	7.48
	4.91	**6.1**	**6.9**	**7.6**	**8.2**	**8.7**	**9.1**	**9.5**	**9.9**	**10.2**	**10.6**
15	2.86	3.54	4.01	4.37	4.68	4.95	5.19	5.40	5.59	5.77	5.93
	4.07	**4.9**	**5.5**	**6.0**	**6.4**	**6.7**	**7.1**	**7.3**	**7.5**	**7.8**	**8.0**
20	2.46	2.95	3.29	3.54	3.76	3.94	4.10	4.24	4.37	4.49	4.59
	3.32	**3.8**	**4.3**	**4.6**	**4.9**	**5.1**	**5.3**	**5.5**	**5.6**	**5.8**	**5.9**
30	2.07	2.40	2.61	2.78	2.91	3.02	3.12	3.21	3.29	3.36	3.39
	2.63	**3.0**	**3.3**	**3.5**	**3.6**	**3.7**	**3.8**	**3.9**	**4.0**	**4.1**	**4.2**
60	1.67	1.85	1.96	2.04	2.11	2.17	2.22	2.26	2.30	2.33	2.36
	1.96	**2.2**	**2.3**	**2.4**	**2.4**	**2.5**	**2.5**	**2.6**	**2.6**	**2.7**	**2.7**

Table 31 of E. Pearson and H. O. Hartley, *Biometrika Tables for Statisticians,* 2nd ed. New York: Cambridge University Press, 1958. Adapted and reprinted with permission of the Biometrika trustees.

TABLE B.4   THE F DISTRIBUTION*

*Table entries in lightface type are critical values for the .05 level of significance. Boldface type values are for the .01 level of significance.

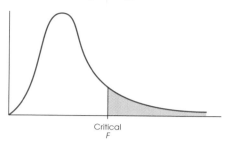

Critical
F

Degrees of Freedom: Denominator	Degrees of freedom: Numerator														
	1	2	3	4	5	6	7	8	9	10	11	12	14	16	20
1	161	200	216	225	230	234	237	239	241	242	243	244	245	246	248
	4052	**4999**	**5403**	**5625**	**5764**	**5859**	**5928**	**5981**	**6022**	**6056**	**6082**	**6106**	**6142**	**6169**	**6208**
2	18.51	19.00	19.16	19.25	19.30	19.33	19.36	19.37	19.38	19.39	19.40	19.41	19.42	19.43	19.44
	98.49	**99.00**	**99.17**	**99.25**	**99.30**	**99.33**	**99.34**	**99.36**	**99.38**	**99.40**	**99.41**	**99.42**	**99.43**	**99.44**	**99.45**
3	10.13	9.55	9.28	9.12	9.01	8.94	8.88	8.84	8.81	8.78	8.76	8.74	8.71	8.69	8.66
	34.12	**30.92**	**29.46**	**28.71**	**28.24**	**27.91**	**27.67**	**27.49**	**27.34**	**27.23**	**27.13**	**27.05**	**26.92**	**26.83**	**26.69**
4	7.71	6.94	6.59	6.39	6.26	6.16	6.09	6.04	6.00	5.96	5.93	5.91	5.87	5.84	5.80
	21.20	**18.00**	**16.69**	**15.98**	**15.52**	**15.21**	**14.98**	**14.80**	**14.66**	**14.54**	**14.45**	**14.37**	**14.24**	**14.15**	**14.02**
5	6.61	5.79	5.41	5.19	5.05	4.95	4.88	4.82	4.78	4.74	4.70	4.68	4.64	4.60	4.56
	16.26	**13.27**	**12.06**	**11.39**	**10.97**	**10.67**	**10.45**	**10.27**	**10.15**	**10.05**	**9.96**	**9.89**	**9.77**	**9.68**	**9.55**
6	5.99	5.14	4.76	4.53	4.39	4.28	4.21	4.15	4.10	4.06	4.03	4.00	3.96	3.92	3.87
	13.74	**10.92**	**9.78**	**9.15**	**8.75**	**8.47**	**8.26**	**8.10**	**7.98**	**7.87**	**7.79**	**7.72**	**7.60**	**7.52**	**7.39**
7	5.59	4.47	4.35	4.12	3.97	3.87	3.79	3.73	3.68	3.63	3.60	3.57	3.52	3.49	3.44
	12.25	**9.55**	**8.45**	**7.85**	**7.46**	**7.19**	**7.00**	**6.84**	**6.71**	**6.62**	**6.54**	**6.47**	**6.35**	**6.27**	**6.15**
8	5.32	4.46	4.07	3.84	3.69	3.58	3.50	3.44	3.39	3.34	3.31	3.28	3.23	3.20	3.15
	11.26	**8.65**	**7.59**	**7.01**	**6.63**	**6.37**	**6.19**	**6.03**	**5.91**	**5.82**	**5.74**	**5.67**	**5.56**	**5.48**	**5.36**
9	5.12	4.26	3.86	3.63	3.48	3.37	3.29	3.23	3.18	3.13	3.10	3.07	3.02	2.98	2.93
	10.56	**8.02**	**6.99**	**6.42**	**6.06**	**5.80**	**5.62**	**5.47**	**5.35**	**5.26**	**5.18**	**5.11**	**5.00**	**4.92**	**4.80**
10	4.96	4.10	3.71	3.48	3.33	3.22	3.14	3.07	3.02	2.97	2.94	2.91	2.86	2.82	2.77
	10.04	**7.56**	**6.55**	**5.99**	**5.64**	**5.39**	**5.21**	**5.06**	**4.95**	**4.85**	**4.78**	**4.71**	**4.60**	**4.52**	**4.41**
11	4.84	3.98	3.59	3.36	3.20	3.09	3.01	2.95	2.90	2.86	2.82	2.79	2.74	2.70	2.65
	9.65	**7.20**	**6.22**	**5.67**	**5.32**	**5.07**	**4.88**	**4.74**	**4.63**	**4.54**	**4.46**	**4.40**	**4.29**	**4.21**	**4.10**
12	4.75	3.88	3.49	3.26	3.11	3.00	2.92	2.85	2.80	2.76	2.72	2.69	2.64	2.60	2.54
	9.33	**6.93**	**5.95**	**5.41**	**5.06**	**4.82**	**4.65**	**4.50**	**4.39**	**4.30**	**4.22**	**4.16**	**4.05**	**3.98**	**3.86**
13	4.67	3.80	3.41	3.18	3.02	2.92	2.84	2.77	2.72	2.67	2.63	2.60	2.55	2.51	2.46
	9.07	**6.70**	**5.74**	**5.20**	**4.86**	**4.62**	**4.44**	**4.30**	**4.19**	**4.10**	**4.02**	**3.96**	**3.85**	**3.78**	**3.67**
14	4.60	3.74	3.34	3.11	2.96	2.85	2.77	2.70	2.65	2.60	2.56	2.53	2.48	2.44	2.39
	8.86	**6.51**	**5.56**	**5.03**	**4.69**	**4.46**	**4.28**	**4.14**	**4.03**	**3.94**	**3.86**	**3.80**	**3.70**	**3.62**	**3.51**
15	4.54	3.68	3.29	3.06	2.90	2.79	2.70	2.64	2.59	2.55	2.51	2.48	2.43	2.39	2.33
	8.68	**6.36**	**5.42**	**4.89**	**4.56**	**4.32**	**4.14**	**4.00**	**3.89**	**3.80**	**3.73**	**3.67**	**3.56**	**3.48**	**3.36**
16	4.49	3.63	3.24	3.01	2.85	2.74	2.66	2.59	2.54	2.49	2.45	2.42	2.37	2.33	2.28
	8.53	**6.23**	**5.29**	**4.77**	**4.44**	**4.20**	**4.03**	**3.89**	**3.78**	**3.69**	**3.61**	**3.55**	**3.45**	**3.37**	**3.25**

TABLE B.4   continued

Degrees of Freedom: Denominator	Degrees of freedom: Numerator														
	1	2	3	4	5	6	7	8	9	10	11	12	14	16	20
17	4.45	3.59	3.20	2.96	2.81	2.70	2.62	2.55	2.50	2.45	2.41	2.38	2.33	2.29	2.23
	8.40	**6.11**	**5.18**	**4.67**	**4.34**	**4.10**	**3.93**	**3.79**	**3.68**	**3.59**	**3.52**	**3.45**	**3.35**	**3.27**	**3.16**
18	4.41	3.55	3.16	2.93	2.77	2.66	2.58	2.51	2.46	2.41	2.37	2.34	2.29	2.25	2.19
	8.28	**6.01**	**5.09**	**4.58**	**4.25**	**4.01**	**3.85**	**3.71**	**3.60**	**3.51**	**3.44**	**3.37**	**3.27**	**3.19**	**3.07**
19	4.38	3.52	3.13	2.90	2.74	2.63	2.55	2.48	2.43	2.38	2.34	2.31	2.26	2.21	2.15
	8.18	**5.93**	**5.01**	**4.50**	**4.17**	**3.94**	**3.77**	**3.63**	**3.52**	**3.43**	**3.36**	**3.30**	**3.19**	**3.12**	**3.00**
20	4.35	3.49	3.10	2.87	2.71	2.60	2.52	2.45	2.40	2.35	2.31	2.28	2.23	2.18	2.12
	8.10	**5.85**	**4.94**	**4.43**	**4.10**	**3.87**	**3.71**	**3.56**	**3.45**	**3.37**	**3.30**	**3.23**	**3.13**	**3.05**	**2.94**
21	4.32	3.47	3.07	2.84	2.68	2.57	2.49	2.42	2.37	2.32	2.28	2.25	2.20	2.15	2.09
	8.02	**5.78**	**4.87**	**4.37**	**4.04**	**3.81**	**3.65**	**3.51**	**3.40**	**3.31**	**3.24**	**3.17**	**3.07**	**2.99**	**2.88**
22	4.30	3.44	3.05	2.82	2.66	2.55	2.47	2.40	2.35	2.30	2.26	2.23	2.18	2.13	2.07
	7.94	**5.72**	**4.82**	**4.31**	**3.99**	**3.76**	**3.59**	**3.45**	**3.35**	**3.26**	**3.18**	**3.12**	**3.02**	**2.94**	**2.83**
23	4.28	3.42	3.03	2.80	2.64	2.53	2.45	2.38	2.32	2.28	2.24	2.20	2.14	2.10	2.04
	7.88	**5.66**	**4.76**	**4.26**	**3.94**	**3.71**	**3.54**	**3.41**	**3.30**	**3.21**	**3.14**	**3.07**	**2.97**	**2.89**	**2.78**
24	4.26	3.40	3.01	2.78	2.62	2.51	2.43	2.36	2.30	2.26	2.22	2.18	2.13	2.09	2.02
	7.82	**5.61**	**4.72**	**4.22**	**3.90**	**3.67**	**3.50**	**3.36**	**3.25**	**3.17**	**3.09**	**3.03**	**2.93**	**2.85**	**2.74**
25	4.24	3.38	2.99	2.76	2.60	2.49	2.41	2.34	2.28	2.24	2.20	2.16	2.11	2.06	2.00
	7.77	**5.57**	**4.68**	**4.18**	**3.86**	**3.63**	**3.46**	**3.32**	**3.21**	**3.13**	**3.05**	**2.99**	**2.89**	**2.81**	**2.70**
26	4.22	3.37	2.98	2.74	2.59	2.47	2.39	2.32	2.27	2.22	2.18	2.15	2.10	2.05	1.99
	7.72	**5.53**	**4.64**	**4.14**	**3.82**	**3.59**	**3.42**	**3.29**	**3.17**	**3.09**	**3.02**	**2.96**	**2.86**	**2.77**	**2.66**
27	4.21	3.35	2.96	2.73	2.57	2.46	2.37	2.30	2.25	2.20	2.16	2.13	2.08	2.03	1.97
	7.68	**5.49**	**4.60**	**4.11**	**3.79**	**3.56**	**3.39**	**3.26**	**3.14**	**3.06**	**2.98**	**2.93**	**2.83**	**2.74**	**2.63**
28	4.20	3.34	2.95	2.71	2.56	2.44	2.36	2.29	2.24	2.19	2.15	2.12	2.06	2.02	1.96
	7.64	**5.45**	**4.57**	**4.07**	**3.76**	**3.53**	**3.36**	**3.23**	**3.11**	**3.03**	**2.95**	**2.90**	**2.80**	**2.71**	**2.60**
29	4.18	3.33	2.93	2.70	2.54	2.43	2.35	2.28	2.22	2.18	2.14	2.10	2.05	2.00	1.94
	7.60	**5.42**	**4.54**	**4.04**	**3.73**	**3.50**	**3.33**	**3.20**	**3.08**	**3.00**	**2.92**	**2.87**	**2.77**	**2.68**	**2.57**
30	4.17	3.32	2.92	2.69	2.53	2.42	2.34	2.27	2.21	2.16	2.12	2.09	2.04	1.99	1.93
	7.56	**5.39**	**4.51**	**4.02**	**3.70**	**3.47**	**3.30**	**3.17**	**3.06**	**2.98**	**2.90**	**2.84**	**2.74**	**2.66**	**2.55**
32	4.15	3.30	2.90	2.67	2.51	2.40	2.32	2.25	2.19	2.14	2.10	2.07	2.02	1.97	1.91
	7.50	**5.34**	**4.46**	**3.97**	**3.66**	**3.42**	**3.25**	**3.12**	**3.01**	**2.94**	**2.86**	**2.80**	**2.70**	**2.62**	**2.51**
34	4.13	3.28	2.88	2.65	2.49	2.38	2.30	2.23	2.17	2.12	2.08	2.05	2.00	1.95	1.89
	7.44	**5.29**	**4.42**	**3.93**	**3.61**	**3.38**	**3.21**	**3.08**	**2.97**	**2.89**	**2.82**	**2.76**	**2.66**	**2.58**	**2.47**
36	4.11	3.26	2.86	2.63	2.48	2.36	2.28	2.21	2.15	2.10	2.06	2.03	1.98	1.93	1.87
	7.39	**5.25**	**4.38**	**3.89**	**3.58**	**3.35**	**3.18**	**3.04**	**2.94**	**2.86**	**2.78**	**2.72**	**2.62**	**2.54**	**2.43**
38	4.10	3.25	2.85	2.62	2.46	2.35	2.26	2.19	2.14	2.09	2.05	2.02	1.96	1.92	1.85
	7.35	**5.21**	**4.34**	**3.86**	**3.54**	**3.32**	**3.15**	**3.02**	**2.91**	**2.82**	**2.75**	**2.69**	**2.59**	**2.51**	**2.40**
40	4.08	3.23	2.84	2.61	2.45	2.34	2.25	2.18	2.12	2.07	2.04	2.00	1.95	1.90	1.84
	7.31	**5.18**	**4.31**	**3.83**	**3.51**	**3.29**	**3.12**	**2.99**	**2.88**	**2.80**	**2.73**	**2.66**	**2.56**	**2.49**	**2.37**
42	4.07	3.22	2.83	2.59	2.44	2.32	2.24	2.17	2.11	2.06	2.02	1.99	1.94	1.89	1.82
	7.27	**5.15**	**4.29**	**3.80**	**3.49**	**3.26**	**3.10**	**2.96**	**2.86**	**2.77**	**2.70**	**2.64**	**2.54**	**2.46**	**2.35**
44	4.06	3.21	2.82	2.58	2.43	2.31	2.23	2.16	2.10	2.05	2.01	1.98	1.92	1.88	1.81
	7.24	**5.12**	**4.26**	**3.78**	**3.46**	**3.24**	**3.07**	**2.94**	**2.84**	**2.75**	**2.68**	**2.62**	**2.52**	**2.44**	**2.32**
46	4.05	3.20	2.81	2.57	2.42	2.30	2.22	2.14	2.09	2.04	2.00	1.97	1.91	1.87	1.80
	7.21	**5.10**	**4.24**	**3.76**	**3.44**	**3.22**	**3.05**	**2.92**	**2.82**	**2.73**	**2.66**	**2.60**	**2.50**	**2.42**	**2.30**
48	4.04	3.19	2.80	2.56	2.41	2.30	2.21	2.14	2.08	2.03	1.99	1.96	1.90	1.86	1.79
	7.19	**5.08**	**4.22**	**3.74**	**3.42**	**3.20**	**3.04**	**2.90**	**2.80**	**2.71**	**2.64**	**2.58**	**2.48**	**2.40**	**2.28**

TABLE B.4   continued

Degrees of Freedom: Denominator	Degrees of freedom: Numerator														
	1	2	3	4	5	6	7	8	9	10	11	12	14	16	20
50	4.03	3.18	2.79	2.56	2.40	2.29	2.20	2.13	2.07	2.02	1.98	1.95	1.90	1.85	1.78
	7.17	**5.06**	**4.20**	**3.72**	**3.41**	**3.18**	**3.02**	**2.88**	**2.78**	**2.70**	**2.62**	**2.56**	**2.46**	**2.39**	**2.26**
55	4.02	3.17	2.78	2.54	2.38	2.27	2.18	2.11	2.05	2.00	1.97	1.93	1.88	1.83	1.76
	7.12	**5.01**	**4.16**	**3.68**	**3.37**	**3.15**	**2.98**	**2.85**	**2.75**	**2.66**	**2.59**	**2.53**	**2.43**	**2.35**	**2.23**
60	4.00	3.15	2.76	2.52	2.37	2.25	2.17	2.10	2.04	1.99	1.95	1.92	1.86	1.81	1.75
	7.08	**4.98**	**4.13**	**3.65**	**3.34**	**3.12**	**2.95**	**2.82**	**2.72**	**2.63**	**2.56**	**2.50**	**2.40**	**2.32**	**2.20**
65	3.99	3.14	2.75	2.51	2.36	2.24	2.15	2.08	2.02	1.98	1.94	1.90	1.85	1.80	1.73
	7.04	**4.95**	**4.10**	**3.62**	**3.31**	**3.09**	**2.93**	**2.79**	**2.70**	**2.61**	**2.54**	**2.47**	**2.37**	**2.30**	**2.18**
70	3.98	3.13	2.74	2.50	2.35	2.23	2.14	2.07	2.01	1.97	1.93	1.89	1.84	1.79	1.72
	7.01	**4.92**	**4.08**	**3.60**	**3.29**	**3.07**	**2.91**	**2.77**	**2.67**	**2.59**	**2.51**	**2.45**	**2.35**	**2.28**	**2.15**
80	3.96	3.11	2.72	2.48	2.33	2.21	2.12	2.05	1.99	1.95	1.91	1.88	1.82	1.77	1.70
	6.96	**4.88**	**4.04**	**3.56**	**3.25**	**3.04**	**2.87**	**2.74**	**2.64**	**2.55**	**2.48**	**2.41**	**2.32**	**2.24**	**2.11**
100	3.94	3.09	2.70	2.46	2.30	2.19	2.10	2.03	1.97	1.92	1.88	1.85	1.79	1.75	1.68
	6.90	**4.82**	**3.98**	**3.51**	**3.20**	**2.99**	**2.82**	**2.69**	**2.59**	**2.51**	**2.43**	**2.36**	**2.26**	**2.19**	**2.06**
125	3.92	3.07	2.68	2.44	2.29	2.17	2.08	2.01	1.95	1.90	1.86	1.83	1.77	1.72	1.65
	6.84	**4.78**	**3.94**	**3.47**	**3.17**	**2.95**	**2.79**	**2.65**	**2.56**	**2.47**	**2.40**	**2.33**	**2.23**	**2.15**	**2.03**
150	3.91	3.06	2.67	2.43	2.27	2.16	2.07	2.00	1.94	1.89	1.85	1.82	1.76	1.71	1.64
	6.81	**4.75**	**3.91**	**3.44**	**3.14**	**2.92**	**2.76**	**2.62**	**2.53**	**2.44**	**2.37**	**2.30**	**2.20**	**2.12**	**2.00**
200	3.89	3.04	2.65	2.41	2.26	2.14	2.05	1.98	1.92	1.87	1.83	1.80	1.74	1.69	1.62
	6.76	**4.71**	**3.88**	**3.41**	**3.11**	**2.90**	**2.73**	**2.60**	**2.50**	**2.41**	**2.34**	**2.28**	**2.17**	**2.09**	**1.97**
400	3.86	3.02	2.62	2.39	2.23	2.12	2.03	1.96	1.90	1.85	1.81	1.78	1.72	1.67	1.60
	6.70	**4.66**	**3.83**	**3.36**	**3.06**	**2.85**	**2.69**	**2.55**	**2.46**	**2.37**	**2.29**	**2.23**	**2.12**	**2.04**	**1.92**
1000	3.85	3.00	2.61	2.38	2.22	2.10	2.02	1.95	1.89	1.84	1.80	1.76	1.70	1.65	1.58
	6.66	**4.62**	**3.80**	**3.34**	**3.04**	**2.82**	**2.66**	**2.53**	**2.43**	**2.34**	**2.26**	**2.20**	**2.09**	**2.01**	**1.89**
∞	3.84	2.99	2.60	2.37	2.21	2.09	2.01	1.94	1.88	1.83	1.79	1.75	1.69	1.64	1.57
	6.64	**4.60**	**3.78**	**3.32**	**3.02**	**2.80**	**2.64**	**2.51**	**2.41**	**2.32**	**2.24**	**2.18**	**2.07**	**1.99**	**1.87**

Table A14 of *Statistical Methods,* 7th ed. by George W. Snedecor and William G. Cochran. Copyright © 1980 by the Iowa State University Press, 2121 South State Avenue, Ames, Iowa 50010. Reprinted with permission of the Iowa State University Press.

STATISTICAL TABLES

TABLE B.5   THE STUDENTIZED RANGE STATISTIC (q)*

*The critical values for q corresponding to $\alpha = .05$ (lightface type) and $\alpha = .01$ (boldface type).

df for error term	k = Number of treatments										
	2	3	4	5	6	7	8	9	10	11	12
5	3.64	4.60	5.22	5.67	6.03	6.33	6.58	6.80	6.99	7.17	7.32
	5.70	**6.98**	**7.80**	**8.42**	**8.91**	**9.32**	**9.67**	**9.97**	**10.24**	**10.48**	**10.70**
6	3.46	4.34	4.90	5.30	5.63	5.90	6.12	6.32	6.49	6.65	6.79
	5.24	**6.33**	**7.03**	**7.56**	**7.97**	**8.32**	**8.61**	**8.87**	**9.10**	**9.30**	**9.48**
7	3.34	4.16	4.68	5.06	5.36	5.61	5.82	6.00	6.16	6.30	6.43
	4.95	**5.92**	**6.54**	**7.01**	**7.37**	**7.68**	**7.94**	**8.17**	**8.37**	**8.55**	**8.71**
8	3.26	4.04	4.53	4.89	5.17	5.40	5.60	5.77	5.92	6.05	6.18
	4.75	**5.64**	**6.20**	**6.62**	**6.96**	**7.24**	**7.47**	**7.68**	**7.86**	**8.03**	**8.18**
9	3.20	3.95	4.41	4.76	5.02	5.24	5.43	5.59	5.74	5.87	5.98
	4.60	**5.43**	**5.96**	**6.35**	**6.66**	**6.91**	**7.13**	**7.33**	**7.49**	**7.65**	**7.78**
10	3.15	3.88	4.33	4.65	4.91	5.12	5.30	5.46	5.60	5.72	5.83
	4.48	**5.27**	**5.77**	**6.14**	**6.43**	**6.67**	**6.87**	**7.05**	**7.21**	**7.36**	**7.49**
11	3.11	3.82	4.26	4.57	4.82	5.03	5.20	5.35	5.49	5.61	5.71
	4.39	**5.15**	**5.62**	**5.97**	**6.25**	**6.48**	**6.67**	**6.84**	**6.99**	**7.13**	**7.25**
12	3.08	3.77	4.20	4.51	4.75	4.95	5.12	5.27	5.39	5.51	5.61
	4.32	**5.05**	**5.50**	**5.84**	**6.10**	**6.32**	**6.51**	**6.67**	**6.81**	**6.94**	**7.06**
13	3.06	3.73	4.15	4.45	4.69	4.88	5.05	5.19	5.32	5.43	5.53
	4.26	**4.96**	**5.40**	**5.73**	**5.98**	**6.19**	**6.37**	**6.53**	**6.67**	**6.79**	**6.90**
14	3.03	3.70	4.11	4.41	4.64	4.83	4.99	5.13	5.25	5.36	5.46
	4.21	**4.89**	**5.32**	**5.63**	**5.88**	**6.08**	**6.26**	**6.41**	**6.54**	**6.66**	**6.77**
15	3.01	3.67	4.08	4.37	4.59	4.78	4.94	5.08	5.20	5.31	5.40
	4.17	**4.84**	**5.25**	**5.56**	**5.80**	**5.99**	**6.16**	**6.31**	**6.44**	**6.55**	**6.66**
16	3.00	3.65	4.05	4.33	4.56	4.74	4.90	5.03	5.15	5.26	5.35
	4.13	**4.79**	**5.19**	**5.49**	**5.72**	**5.92**	**6.08**	**6.22**	**6.35**	**6.46**	**6.56**
17	2.98	3.63	4.02	4.30	4.52	4.70	4.86	4.99	5.11	5.21	5.31
	4.10	**4.74**	**5.14**	**5.43**	**5.66**	**5.85**	**6.01**	**6.15**	**6.27**	**6.38**	**6.48**
18	2.97	3.61	4.00	4.28	4.49	4.67	4.82	4.96	5.07	5.17	5.27
	4.07	**4.70**	**5.09**	**5.38**	**5.60**	**5.79**	**5.94**	**6.08**	**6.20**	**6.31**	**6.41**
19	2.96	3.59	3.98	4.25	4.47	4.65	4.79	4.92	5.04	5.14	5.23
	4.05	**4.67**	**5.05**	**5.33**	**5.55**	**5.73**	**5.89**	**6.02**	**6.14**	**6.25**	**6.34**
20	2.95	3.58	3.96	4.23	4.45	4.62	4.77	4.90	5.01	5.11	5.20
	4.02	**4.64**	**5.02**	**5.29**	**5.51**	**5.69**	**5.84**	**5.97**	**6.09**	**6.19**	**6.28**
24	2.92	3.53	3.90	4.17	4.37	4.54	4.68	4.81	4.92	5.01	5.10
	3.96	**4.55**	**4.91**	**5.17**	**5.37**	**5.54**	**5.69**	**5.81**	**5.92**	**6.02**	**6.11**
30	2.89	3.49	3.85	4.10	4.30	4.46	4.60	4.72	4.82	4.92	5.00
	3.89	**4.45**	**4.80**	**5.05**	**5.24**	**5.40**	**5.54**	**5.65**	**5.76**	**5.85**	**5.93**
40	2.86	3.44	3.79	4.04	4.23	4.39	4.52	4.63	4.73	4.82	4.90
	3.82	**4.37**	**4.70**	**4.93**	**5.11**	**5.26**	**5.39**	**5.50**	**5.60**	**5.69**	**5.76**
60	2.83	3.40	3.74	3.98	4.16	4.31	4.44	4.55	4.65	4.73	4.81
	3.76	**4.28**	**4.59**	**4.82**	**4.99**	**5.13**	**5.25**	**5.36**	**5.45**	**5.53**	**5.60**
120	2.80	3.36	3.68	3.92	4.10	4.24	4.36	4.47	4.56	4.64	4.71
	3.70	**4.20**	**4.50**	**4.71**	**4.87**	**5.01**	**5.12**	**5.21**	**5.30**	**5.37**	**5.44**
∞	2.77	3.31	3.63	3.86	4.03	4.17	4.28	4.39	4.47	4.55	4.62
	3.64	**4.12**	**4.40**	**4.60**	**4.76**	**4.88**	**4.99**	**5.08**	**5.16**	**5.23**	**5.29**

TABLE B.6 CRITICAL VALUES FOR THE PEARSON CORRELATION*

*To be significant, the sample correlation, r, must be greater than or equal to the critical value in the table.

	Level of significance for one-tailed test			
	.05	.025	.01	.005
	Level of significance for two-tailed test			
$df = n - 2$	.10	.05	.02	.01
1	.988	.997	.9995	.9999
2	.900	.950	.980	.990
3	.805	.878	.934	.959
4	.729	.811	.882	.917
5	.669	.754	.833	.874
6	.622	.707	.789	.834
7	.582	.666	.750	.798
8	.549	.632	.716	.765
9	.521	.602	.685	.735
10	.497	.576	.658	.708
11	.476	.553	.634	.684
12	.458	.532	.612	.661
13	.441	.514	.592	.641
14	.426	.497	.574	.623
15	.412	.482	.558	.606
16	.400	.468	.542	.590
17	.389	.456	.528	.575
18	.378	.444	.516	.561
19	.369	.433	.503	.549
20	.360	.423	.492	.537
21	.352	.413	.482	.526
22	.344	.404	.472	.515
23	.337	.396	.462	.505
24	.330	.388	.453	.496
25	.323	.381	.445	.487
26	.317	.374	.437	.479
27	.311	.367	.430	.471
28	.306	.361	.423	.463
29	.301	.355	.416	.456
30	.296	.349	.409	.449
35	.275	.325	.381	.418
40	.257	.304	.358	.393
45	.243	.288	.338	.372
50	.231	.273	.322	.354
60	.211	.250	.295	.325
70	.195	.232	.274	.302
80	.183	.217	.256	.283
90	.173	.205	.242	.267
100	.164	.195	.230	.254

Table VI of R. A. Fisher and F. Yates, *Statistical Tables for Biological, Agricultural and Medical Research,* 6th ed. London: Longman Group Ltd., 1974 (previously published by Oliver and Boyd Ltd., Edinburgh). Adapted and reprinted with permission of Addison Wesley Longman Publishing Co.

STATISTICAL TABLES

TABLE B.7   THE CHI-SQUARE DISTRIBUTION*

*The table entries are critical values of χ^2.

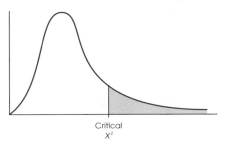

Critical
χ^2

df	Proportion in critical region				
	0.10	0.05	0.025	0.01	0.005
1	2.71	3.84	5.02	6.63	7.88
2	4.61	5.99	7.38	9.21	10.60
3	6.25	7.81	9.35	11.34	12.84
4	7.78	9.49	11.14	13.28	14.86
5	9.24	11.07	12.83	15.09	16.75
6	10.64	12.59	14.45	16.81	18.55
7	12.02	14.07	16.01	18.48	20.28
8	13.36	15.51	17.53	20.09	21.96
9	14.68	16.92	19.02	21.67	23.59
10	15.99	18.31	20.48	23.21	25.19
11	17.28	19.68	21.92	24.72	26.76
12	18.55	21.03	23.34	26.22	28.30
13	19.81	22.36	24.74	27.69	29.82
14	21.06	23.68	26.12	29.14	31.32
15	22.31	25.00	27.49	30.58	32.80
16	23.54	26.30	28.85	32.00	34.27
17	24.77	27.59	30.19	33.41	35.72
18	25.99	28.87	31.53	34.81	37.16
19	27.20	30.14	32.85	36.19	38.58
20	28.41	31.41	34.17	37.57	40.00
21	29.62	32.67	35.48	38.93	41.40
22	30.81	33.92	36.78	40.29	42.80
23	32.01	35.17	38.08	41.64	44.18
24	33.20	36.42	39.36	42.98	45.56
25	34.38	37.65	40.65	44.31	46.93
26	35.56	38.89	41.92	45.64	48.29
27	36.74	40.11	43.19	46.96	49.64
28	37.92	41.34	44.46	48.28	50.99
29	39.09	42.56	45.72	49.59	52.34
30	40.26	43.77	46.98	50.89	53.67
40	51.81	55.76	59.34	63.69	66.77
50	63.17	67.50	71.42	76.15	79.49
60	74.40	79.08	83.30	88.38	91.95
70	85.53	90.53	95.02	100.42	104.22
80	96.58	101.88	106.63	112.33	116.32
90	107.56	113.14	118.14	124.12	128.30
100	118.50	124.34	129.56	135.81	140.17

SOLUTIONS FOR ODD-NUMBERED PROBLEMS IN THE TEXT

Note: Many of the problems in the text require several stages of computation. At each stage, there is an opportunity for rounding answers. Depending on the exact sequence of operations used to solve a problem, different individuals will round their answers at different times and in different ways. As a result, you may obtain answers that are slightly different from those presented here. As long as those differences are small, they probably can be attributed to rounding error and should not be a matter for concern.

CHAPTER 1 INTRODUCTION TO STATISTICS

1. Descriptive statistics are used to simplify and summarize data. Inferential statistics use sample data to make general conclusions about populations.

3. In experimental research the researcher manipulates an independent variable to create the different treatment conditions or groups that will be compared in the study. Then, subjects are randomly assigned to the treatment conditions. In quasi-experimental research, the researcher simply uses a pre-existing (nonmanipulated) variable to define the conditions or groups that will be compared.

5. Because a sample is only a part of the whole population, the characteristics of a sample tend to be different from the characteristics of the population. The discrepancy between a statistic for a sample and the corresponding parameter for the population is called *sampling error*.

7. The independent variable is whether or not the individuals were given aspirin and the dependent variable is whether or not they suffered a second heart attack.

9. The independent variable is the loudness of the buzzer. The dependent variable is reaction time (how quickly subjects respond).

11. **a.** The independent variable is the number of syllables (1, 2, or 3), which is measured on a ratio scale.
    b. The dependent variable is the number of words recalled by each subject, which is also measured on a ratio scale.

13. **a.** The independent variable is the brand of medication, brand X versus brand Y, which is measured on a nominal scale.
    b. The dependent variable is the degree of indigestion, which is measured on an ordinal scale; a series of ordered categories.

15. A discrete variable consists of separate, indivisible categories. A continuous variable is divisible into an infinite number of fractional parts.

17. **a.** nominal scale   **b.** interval scale
    c. ordinal scale   **d.** ratio scale

19. **a.** $\Sigma X = 15$ **b.** $\Sigma Y = 10$ **c.** $\Sigma XY = 40$

21. **a.** Sum the scores, then subtract 4 from the total.
    b. Square each score, then sum the squared values.
    c. Add 4 points to each score, then square the resulting values. Finally, sum the squared values.

23. **a.** $\Sigma X = -3$ **b.** $\Sigma X^2 = 37$ **c.** $\Sigma(X + 3) = 12$

25. **a.** First, subtract 4 points from each score. Second, square each of the resulting values. Third, sum the squared values.
    b. $\Sigma(X - 4)^2 = 34$
    c. $\Sigma(X - 4) = 0$

CHAPTER 2 **FREQUENCY DISTRIBUTIONS**

1.

X	f	p	%
5	3	.15	15%
4	4	.20	20%
3	8	.40	40%
2	3	.15	15%
1	2	.10	10%

3. A bar graph leaves a space between adjacent bars and is used with data from nominal or ordinal scales. In a histogram, adjacent bars touch at the real limits. Histograms are used to display data from interval or ratio scales.

5.

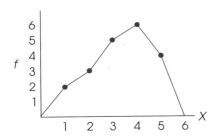

7. a.

X	f
5	10
4	4
3	3
2	1

b.

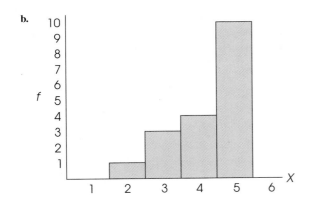

c. (1) The distribution is negatively skewed.
(2) If X = 3 is normal, the majority of the students scored above normal.

9. a. $N = 12$ **b.** $\Sigma X = 43$

11. $N = \Sigma f = 13$, $\Sigma X = 38$, $\Sigma X^2 = 128$

13. a.

X	f
11	1
10	0
9	1
8	0
7	2
6	3
5	3
4	6
3	5
2	4

b.

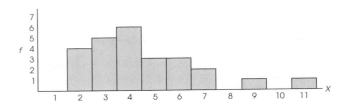

c.

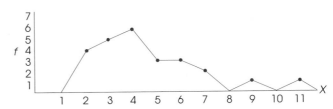

d. Positively skewed.

15. a.

X	f
30–31	1
28–29	0
26–27	2
24–25	1
22–23	4
20–21	5
18–19	2
16–17	3
14–15	1
12–13	1

b.

X	f
30–34	1
25–29	2
20–24	10
15–19	5
10–14	2

17. a.

Set I			Set II	
X	f		X	f
5	1		14–15	1
4	2		12–13	0
3	4		10–11	1
2	2		8–9	2
1	1		6–7	1
			4–5	2
			2–3	1
			0–1	1

b.

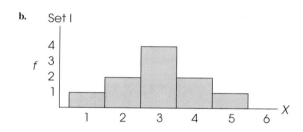

Set I

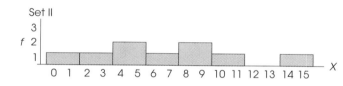

Set II

c. Set I forms a symmetrical distribution, centered at $X = 3$, with most of the scores clustered close to the center. Set II forms a flat distribution with a center near $X = 7$ or $X = 8$, but the scores are spread evenly across the entire scale.

19. a.

X	f
10	1
9	3
8	2
7	1
6	1
5	2
4	3
3	2
2	1

b.

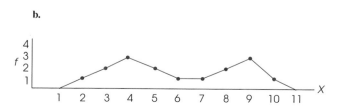

c. (1) The distribution is roughly symmetrical with scores piled up at each end of the scale.
(2) The center is near $X = 6$.
(3) The scores are spread across the entire scale.

21.

X	f
800–899	1
700–799	3
600–699	4
500–599	6
400–499	5
300–399	3
200–299	1
100–199	1

23. a.

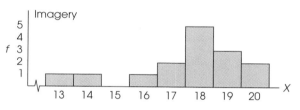

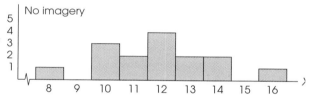

b. For the imagery group, the graph is negatively skewed and is centered about $X = 18$. The graph for the no-imagery group is more symmetrical and is centered around $X = 12$.
c. The imagery instructions seemed to produce higher memory scores.

25. a.

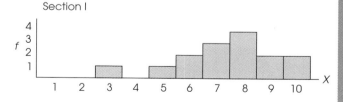

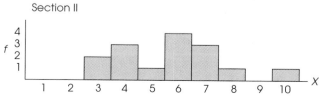

b. The scores in Section I are centered around $X = 8$ and form a negatively skewed distribution. In Section II, the scores are lower (centered around $X = 6$) and the distribution is more symmetrical with some tendency toward a positively skewed distribution.

CHAPTER 3 **CENTRAL TENDENCY**

1. The purpose of central tendency is to identify the center of a distribution, usually by determining a single score that serves as a representative for the entire distribution.

3. a. The mean is the *balance point* of a distribution because the sum of the distances above the mean is exactly equal to the sum of the distances below the mean.

  b. The median is the *midpoint* of a distribution because 50% of the scores are greater than or equal to the median and 50% are less than or equal to the median.

5. The mean, median, and mode are identical for a symmetrical distribution with one mode.

7. With a skewed distribution, the extreme scores in the tail can displace the mean. Specifically, the mean is displaced away from the main pile of scores and moved out toward the tail. The result is that the mean is often not a very representative value.

9. The mean is 50/10 = 5, the median is 5, and the mode is 5.

11. The mean is 116/20 = 5.8, the median is 5.5, and the mode is 5.

13. $\Sigma X = 105$

15. The original $\Sigma X = 160$ and the new $\Sigma X = 120$. The new mean is 120/8 = 15.

17. The original $\Sigma X = 30$ and the new $\Sigma X = 28$. The new mean is 28/4 = 7.

19. The original $\Sigma X = 55$ and the new $\Sigma X = 72$. The score that was added is $X = 17$.

21. For the combined sample $n = 20$ and $\Sigma X = 450 + 120 = 570$. The mean for the combined sample is 570/20 = 28.5.

23. Statement (c) cannot be correct. The mode is the score with the greatest frequency so there must be individuals with scores equal to the mode.

25. a.

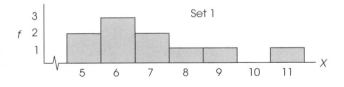

For set 1, the mean is 7, the median is 6.5, and the mode is 6.

  b.

For set 2, the mean is 8.4, the median is 7.5, and the mode is 6.

  c. The greater the amount of skew, the bigger are the differences between the three measures of central tendency.

27. a. Independent variable is the brand of coffee; dependent variable is the flavor rating.

  b. Nominal

  c. Bar graph (coffee brand is a nominal scale)

  d.

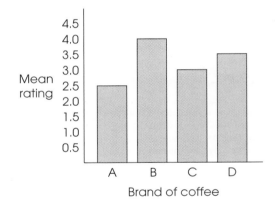

CHAPTER 4 **VARIABILITY**

1. a. *SS* is the sum of squared deviation scores.

  b. Variance is the mean squared deviation.

  c. Standard deviation is the square root of the variance. It provides a measure of the standard distance from the mean.

3. *SS* cannot be less than zero because it is computed by adding squared deviations. Squared deviations are always greater than or equal to zero.

5. An *unbiased* estimate means that on average the sample statistic will provide an accurate representation of the corresponding population parameter. More specifically, if you take all the possible samples and compute the variance for each sample, then the average of all the sample variances will be exactly equal to the population variance.

7. The standard deviation, s, can be found by taking the square root of the variance, s^2. For this example, $s = \sqrt{s^2} = \sqrt{100} = 10$.

9. a. The sample variance is $60/5 = 12$.
  b. The population variance is $60/6 = 10$.

11. a. The definitional formula is easy to use when the mean is a whole number and there are relatively few scores.
  b. The computational formula is preferred when the mean is not a whole number.

13. $SS = 8$, the sample variance is 1, and the standard deviation is 1.

15. $SS = 36$, the population variance is 9, and the standard deviation is 3.

17. a. Your score is 5 points above the mean. If the standard deviation is 2, then your score is an extremely high value (out in the tail of the distribution). However, if the standard deviation is 10, then your score is only slightly above average. Thus, you would prefer $\sigma = 2$.
  b. If you are located 5 points below the mean, then the situation is reversed. A standard deviation of 2 gives you an extremely low score, but with a standard deviation of 10, you are only slightly below average. Here you would prefer $\sigma = 10$.

19. a.

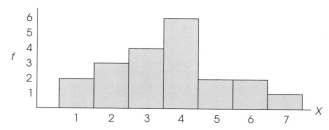

  b. Range = 7
  c. Interquartile range = $(4.5 - 2.5) = 2$ and the semi-interquartile range = 1

21. a. Standard deviation is 10   **b.** $SS = 2400$

23. a. For the original scores, the range is 8, the interquartile range is 4, and the sample standard deviation is 2.45.
  b. After moving the extreme scores closer to the center, the range is reduced to 6 points, the interquartile range stays the same at 4 points, and the standard deviation is reduced to 2.07.
  c. When the central scores are moved to the extremes, the range is still 8, the interquartile range increases to 6, and the standard deviation increases to 3.07.

CHAPTER 5 z-SCORES

1. A z-score describes a precise location within a distribution. The sign of the z-score tells whether the location is above $(+)$ or below $(-)$ the mean, and the magnitude tells the distance from the mean in terms of the number of standard deviations.

3. a. $X = 80$ is in the extreme right-hand tail at $z = 2.00$.
  b. $X = 80$ is slightly above the mean at $z = 0.50$.

5. a.

X	z	X	z	X	z
110	0.50	140	2.00	80	−1.00
60	−2.00	105	0.25	130	1.50

b.

X	z	X	z	X	z
150	2.50	90	−0.50	70	−1.50
105	0.25	80	−1.00	115	0.75

7.

X	z	X	z	X	z
66	0.50	48	−1.00	84	2.00
55	−0.42	70	0.83	75	1.25

9. a.

X	z	X	z	X	z
75	−0.25	90	0.50	110	1.50
95	0.75	60	−1.00	40	−2.00

b.

X	z	X	z	X	z
130	2.50	70	−0.50	50	−1.50
85	0.25	65	−0.75	100	1.00

11. a. $z = 2.00$ **b.** $z = -1.00$ **c.** $z = 1.50$ **d.** $z = -3.00$

13. $\sigma = 6$

15. $\mu = 90$

17. $\mu = 54$ and $\sigma = 8$. The distance between the two scores is 12 points, which is equal to 1.50 standard deviations.

19. a. With $\sigma = 2$, the score $X = 86$ corresponds to $z = 3.00$, which is an extreme value.
  b. With $\sigma = 12$, the score $X = 86$ corresponds to $z = 0.50$, which is a central value.

21. $\sigma = 10$

23. Mary's statistics score corresponds to $z = -0.25$ and her biology score corresponds to $z = -2.00$. She should expect the higher grade in statistics.

25.

Original score	Transformed score
$X = 34$	$X = 80$
$X = 36$	$X = 90$
$X = 37$	$X = 95$
$X = 41$	$X = 115$
$X = 46$	$X = 140$

27. a. $\mu = 3$ and $\sigma = 2$

b. and **c.**

Original X	z-score	Transformed X
0	-1.50	35
4	0.50	55
6	1.50	65
1	-1.00	40
3	0	50
4	0.50	55

CHAPTER 6 **PROBABILITY**

1. a. $p = 60/90 = 0.667$ **b.** $p = 15/90 = 0.167$
   c. $p = 5/90 = 0.056$

3. The two requirements for a random sample are: (1) each individual has an equal chance of being selected, and (2) if more than one individual is selected, the probabilities must stay constant for all sections.

5. a. Tail to the right, $p = 0.1587$
   b. Tail to the left, $p = 0.0228$
   c. Tail to the right, $p = 0.0668$
   d. Tail to the left, $p = .2266$

7. a. $p(z > 1.50) = 0.0668$
   b. $p(z > -2.00) = 0.9772$
   c. $p(z < 0.50) = 0.6915$
   d. $p(z < -0.75) = 0.2266$

9. a. $z = 1.28$ **b.** $z = 0.25$ **c.** $z = -0.84$

11. a. $p = 0.0440$ **b.** $p = 0.1498$ **c.** $p = 0.4772$ **d.** $p = 0.5319$

13. a. $z = \pm 1.28$ **b.** $z = \pm 1.44$
   c. $z = \pm 1.64$ or ± 1.65 **d.** $z = \pm 1.96$

15. a and **b.** You cannot use the unit normal table to find proportions or z-scores because the distribution is not normal.

17. a. Body to the left, $p = 0.8944$
   b. Body to the left, $p = 0.7734$
   c. Body to the right, $p = 0.5987$
   d. Body to the right, $p = 0.8413$

19. a. $z = 1.50, p = 0.0668$ **b.** $z = 0.40, p = 0.6554$
   c. $z = 0.84, X = 584$ **d.** $z = -0.25, X = 475$

21. a. $z = -1.33, p = 0.0918$ **b.** $z = -1.67, p = 0.9525$
   c. $z = 1.00, p = 0.1587$

23. a. $z = 0.13, p = 0.4483$
   b. $z = -0.87, p = 0.8078$
   c. $z = 0.33, p = 0.6293$
   d. $z = -0.33, p = 0.3707$

25. a. $p(z < 1.22) = 0.8888$
   b. $p(z > -1.67) = 0.9525$
   c. $p(z > 0.56) = 0.2877$
   d. $p(z > 2.11) = 0.0174$
   e. $p(-1.33 < z < 1.44) = 0.8333$
   f. $p(-0.33 < z < 0.33) = 0.2586$

CHAPTER 7 **THE DISTRIBUTION OF SAMPLE MEANS**

1. a. The distribution of sample means is the set of sample means for all the possible random samples of a specific size (n) from a specific population.
   b. The expected value of $\overline{X}$ is the mean of the distribution of sample means (μ).
   c. The standard error of $\overline{X}$ is the standard deviation of the distribution of sample means $(\sigma_{\overline{X}} = \sigma/\sqrt{n})$.

3. With $n = 36$, the distribution of sample means will be approximately normal even if the population is not. The expected value is $\mu = 65$ and the standard error is $12/6 = 2$.

5. A sample of $n = 25$ would be more accurate with a standard error of 3 points. A sample of $n = 9$ would have a standard error of 5 points.

7. a. $z = -1.00$ **b.** $z = +2.00$ **c.** $z = +2.00$

9. a. With a standard error of 5, $\overline{X} = 70$ corresponds to $z = 1.00$, which is not extreme.

b. With a standard error of 2, $\overline{X} = 70$ corresponds to $z = 2.50$, which is extreme.

11. a. The distribution is normal with $\mu = 100$ and $\sigma_{\overline{X}} = 4$.
   b. The z-score boundaries are ± 1.96. The $\overline{X}$ boundaries are 92.16 and 107.84.
   c. $\overline{X} = 106$ corresponds to $z = 1.50$. This is not in the extreme 5%.

13. a. The distribution is normal with $\mu = 55$ and $\sigma_{\overline{X}} = 2$.
   b. $z = +2.00, p = 0.0228$ **c.** $z = +0.50, p = 0.6915$
   d. $p(-1.00 < z < +1.00) = 0.6826$

15. a. The distribution is normal with an expected value (mean) of 80 and a standard error of 4.
   b. $\overline{X} = 85$ corresponds to $z = 1.25, p = 0.1056$.
   c. The distribution is normal with an expected value (mean) of 80 and a standard error of 2.
   d. $\overline{X} = 85$ corresponds to $z = 2.50, p = 0.0062$.

17. a. $\sigma_{\bar{X}} = 10$, $z = 0.50$, $p = 0.3085$
  b. $\sigma_{\bar{X}} = 5$, $z = 1.00$, $p = 0.1587$
  c. $\sigma_{\bar{X}} = 2$, $z = 2.50$, $p = 0.0062$

19. a. Larger than $n = 4$ **b.** Larger than $n = 25$
  c. Larger than $n = 100$

21. a. The distribution of sample means is normal with $\mu = 80$ and $\sigma_{\bar{X}} = 3$.
  b. $z = 1.67$, $p = 0.0475$
  c. $z = 1.00$, $p = 0.8413$
  d. $z = -2.00$, $p = 0.0228$
  e. $p(76 < \bar{X} < 84) = p(-1.33 < z < 1.33) = .8164$

23. With $n = 16$, $\sigma_{\bar{X}} = 0.50$, $p(\bar{X} \le 31) = p(z \le -2.00) = .0228$. This is a very unlikely outcome by chance alone. The inspector should suspect some problem with the machinery.

25.

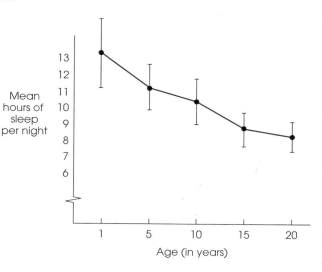

Mean hours of sleep per night vs. Age (in years)

CHAPTER 8 INTRODUCTION TO HYPOTHESIS TESTING

1. a. $\bar{X} - \mu$ measures the difference between the sample data and the hypothesized population mean.
  b. A sample mean is not expected to be identical to the population mean. The standard error indicates how much difference between $\bar{X}$ and μ is expected by chance.

3. Lowering the alpha level causes the boundaries of the critical region to move farther out into the tails of the distribution. Lowering α reduces the probability of a Type I error.

5. a. A Type I error is rejecting a true H_0. This can occur if you obtain a very unusual sample with scores that are much different from the general population.
  b. A Type II error is failing to reject a false H_0. This can happen when the treatment effect is very small. In this case the treated sample is not noticeably different from the original population.

7. The analyses are contradictory. The critical region for the two-tailed tests consists of the extreme 2.5% in each tail of the distribution. The two-tailed conclusion indicates that the data were not in this critical region. However, the one-tailed test indicates that the data were in the extreme 1% of one tail. Data cannot be in the extreme 1% and at the same time fail to be in the extreme 2.5%.

9. a. H_0: $\mu = 40$. The sample mean $\bar{X} = 42$ corresponds to $z = 1.00$. This is not sufficient to reject the null hypothesis. You cannot conclude that the program has a significant effect.
  b. H_0: $\mu = 40$. The sample mean $\bar{X} = 44$ corresponds to $z = 2.00$. This is sufficient to reject the null hypothesis and conclude that the program does have a significant effect.
  c. The 2-point difference between the sample and the hypothesis in part (a) was not sufficient to reject H_0. However, the 4-point difference in part (b) is significantly more than can be accounted for by chance.

11. a. The dependent variable is SAT score and the independent variable is whether they take the special course or not.

b. H_0: $\mu = 500$, $H_1\mu \ne 500$. The critical boundaries are $z = \pm 1.96$. For these data, $z = 2.16$, so our decision is to reject H_0 and conclude that the course did affect SAT scores.
  c. With $\alpha = .01$, the critical region consists of z-score values greater than 2.58 or less than -2.58.
  d. With $\alpha = .01$, the decision is to fail to reject H_0. With $\alpha = .01$, you have less risk of a Type I error. Therefore, the test requires a larger treatment effect in order to reject H_0.

13. a. H_0: $\mu = 100$. The critical boundaries are $z = \pm 1.96$. With $\sigma = 12$, the standard error is $\sigma_{\bar{X}} = 2$ and $z = 3.00$. Reject H_0.
  b. With $\sigma = 30$, $\sigma_{\bar{X}} = 5$ and $z = 1.20$. Fail to reject H_0.
  c. There is a 6-point difference between the sample mean and the hypothesized population value. In part (a), the standard error is 2 points and the 6-point difference is significantly more than is expected by chance. However, in part (b), the standard error is 5 points and the 6-point difference is not sufficient to reject the full hypothesis.

15. The null hypothesis states that the mean completion time for the MS population is not different from the mean time for the regular population; H_0: $\mu = 185$ seconds. With $\alpha = .01$, the critical value is $z = \pm 2.58$. For this sample mean, the standard error is 3.77 and $z = 7.16$. Reject the null hypothesis and conclude that the MS population is significantly different.

17. a. For $n = 25$, $\sigma_{\bar{X}} = 2$ and $z = 1.50$. Fail to reject the null hypothesis. There is no significant difference in vocabulary skills between only children and the general population.
  b. For $n = 100$, $\sigma_{\bar{X}} = 1$ and $z = 3.00$. Reject the null hypothesis, and conclude there is a significant difference in vocabulary skills between only children and the general population.
  c. The larger sample results in a smaller standard error. With $n = 100$, the difference between the data and the null hypothesis is significant.

19. For the one-tailed test, the null hypothesis states that there is no memory impairment, H_0: $\mu \geq 50$. The critical region consists of z-scores less than -2.33. For these data, $\sigma_{\overline{X}} = 1.28$ and $z = -2.34$. Reject H_0, and conclude that the alcoholics have significantly lower memory scores.

21. a. H_0: $\mu = 2.95$; $\sigma_{\overline{X}} = 0.11$ and $z = 2.73$. The calculated z-score is beyond the critical boundary of 2.58, so we reject H_0 and conclude that students who sit in the front have significantly different grade point averages than the general population.

  b. H_0: $\mu \leq 2.95$ (not higher). For the one-tailed test, the critical boundary is 2.33, so we reject H_0 and conclude that students who sit in the front have grade point averages that are significantly higher than the general population.

23. a. The null hypothesis states that the training program has no effect on the problem-solving scores (H_0: $\mu = 80$). The critical region consists of z-score values beyond ± 1.96. For these data, the stan-

dard error is 2.36 and $z = 1.88$. Fail to reject H_0. There is not sufficient evidence to conclude that the training program has any effect.

  b. For a one-tailed test, the null hypothesis would state that training does not improve problem-solving ability; H_0: $\mu \leq 80$. The critical region consists of z-score values greater than $+1.65$. For the one-tailed test, the z-score is in the critical region and the decision is to reject H_0. For $\alpha = .025$, the null hypothesis would not be rejected.

25. H_0: $\mu \leq 12$ (no increase during hot weather). H_1: $\mu > 12$ (there is an increase). The critical region consists of z-score values greater than $+1.65$. For these data, the standard error is 1.50, and $z = 2.33$, which is in the critical region. We reject the null hypothesis and conclude that there is a significant increase in the mean number of hit players during hot weather.

CHAPTER 9 INTRODUCTION TO THE *t* STATISTIC

1. A z-score is used when the population standard deviation (or variance) is known. The t statistic is used when the population variance or standard deviation is unknown. You use the sample data to estimate the variance and the standard error.

3. a. As variability increases, t becomes smaller (closer to zero).

  b. As sample size increases, the standard error decreases, and the t value increases.

  c. The larger the difference between $\overline{X}$ and μ, the larger the t value.

5. As the value of df increases, the t distribution becomes less variable (less spread out) and more like a normal distribution. For $\alpha = .05$, the critical t values move toward ± 1.96 as df increases.

7. a. $\overline{X} = 6$ and $s = 4$ **b.** $s_{\overline{X}} = 2$

9. a. $\overline{X} = 5$ and $s = 4$ **b.** $s_{\overline{X}} = 2$ points

11. a. For sample 1, $s^2 = 9$ and $s = 3$. For sample 2, $s^2 = 9$ and $s = 3$.

  b. For sample 1, and $s_{\overline{X}} = 1.50$. For sample 2, and $s_{\overline{X}} = 1$.

  c. Sample size is one component of the estimated standard error. As sample size increases, the estimated standard error decreases.

13. a. With $\alpha = .05$ and $df = 24$, the critical boundaries are $t = \pm 2.064$. For these data, the estimated standard error is 2 and $t = 2.50$. Reject H_0.

  b. With $\alpha = .01$ and $df = 24$, the critical boundaries are $t = \pm 2.797$. For these data, the estimated standard error is 2 and $t = 2.50$. Fail to reject H_0.

  c. The test with $\alpha = .01$ involves less risk of a Type I error but also requires more evidence from the data. In this problem, the data are sufficient to reject H_0 at the .05 level, but are not sufficient to satisfy the criteria for $\alpha = .01$.

15. a. With $df = 15$, the critical boundaries are ± 2.947. For these data, the sample variance is 36, the estimated standard error is 1.50, and $t = 4.00$. Reject H_0.

  b. For the one-tailed test, the critical boundary is 2.602. For the data, $t = 4$. Reject H_0 and conclude that hand–eye coordination is significantly better for those who are above average in mathematics performance.

17. Because $df = 35$ is not in the table, use $df = 30$ to obtain critical boundaries of ± 2.042. The sample variance is 0.36, the estimated standard error is 0.10, and $t = -2.00$. Fail to reject H_0.

19. a. The critical boundaries are ± 2.131. For these data, the estimated standard error is 0.50 and $t = 6.00$. Reject H_0.

  b. The critical boundaries are ± 2.131. For these data, the estimated standard error is 5.00 and $t = 0.60$. Fail to reject H_0.

  c. The larger variance produces a larger estimated error, which produces a smaller value for t (closer to zero) and reduces the probability of a significant result.

21. H_0: $\mu = 40$. Because $df = 35$ is not in the table, use $df = 30$ to obtain critical values of $t = \pm 2.042$. For these data, $s^2 = 144$, the standard error is 2.00, and $t(35) = 2.25$. Reject H_0 and conclude that depression for the elderly is significantly different from depression for the general population.

23. H_0: $\mu = 14$ (no change). With $df = 4$, the critical boundaries are ± 2.776. For these data, $\overline{X} = 12$, $s^2 = 2.5$, the estimated standard error is 0.71, and $t(4) = -2.82$. Reject H_0 and conclude that there has been a significant change in the mean age at which drinking begins.

CHAPTER 10 THE *t* TEST FOR TWO INDEPENDENT SAMPLES

1. An independent-measures study requires a separate sample for each of the treatments or populations being compared. An independent-measures t statistic is appropriate when a researcher has two

samples and wants to use the sample mean difference to test hypotheses about the population mean difference.

3. The homogeneity of variance assumption specifies that $\sigma_1^2 = \sigma_2^2$ for the two populations from which the samples are obtained. If this assumption is violated, the t statistic can cause misleading conclusions for a hypothesis test.

5. a. The first sample has $s^2 = 8$ and the second has $s^2 = 12$.
  b. The pooled variance is $164/16 = 10.25$.

7. a. The first sample has a variance of 8, the second sample variance is 12, and the pooled variance is 10 (halfway between).
  b. The first sample has a variance of 4, the second sample variance is 16, and the pooled variance is 7.27 (closer to the variance for the larger sample).

9. a. The pooled variance is 120.
  b. The standard error is 4.00.
  c. A mean difference of 8 would produce $t = 8/4 = 2$. With $df = 28$, the critical values are ± 2.048. Fail to reject H_0.
  d. A mean difference of 12 would produce $t = 12/4 = 3$. With $df = 28$, the critical values are ± 2.048. Reject H_0.

11. The null hypothesis states that there is no difference in the mother–child relationship between easy-delivery and difficult-delivery daughters, $H_0: \mu_1 - \mu_2 = 0$. With $df = 22$ and $\alpha = .05$, the critical region consists of t values beyond ± 2.074. For these data, the pooled variance is 96, the estimated standard error is 4, and $t(22) = -1.25$. Fail to reject H_0. The data are not sufficient to indicate a significant difference between the two birth conditions.

13. a. For treatment 1, the variance is $420/15 = 28$ and for treatment 2, the variance is $540/15 = 36$. The pooled variance is $960/30 = 32$.
  b. The null hypothesis states that there is no difference between the two treatments, $H_0: \mu_1 - \mu_2 = 0$. With $df = 30$ and $\alpha = .05$, the critical region consists of t values beyond ± 2.042. For these data, the estimated standard error is 2, and $t(30) = 3.00$. Reject H_0. The data are sufficient to conclude that there is a significant difference between the two treatments.
  c. The samples in this problem are much larger than the samples in Problem 12. The larger samples produce a smaller standard error so that the sample mean difference is now significant.

15. a. The null hypothesis states that there is no difference in the performance scores between the students with pets and those without pets, $H_0: \mu_1 - \mu_2 = 0$. With $df = 23$ and $\alpha = .05$, the critical region consists of t values beyond ± 2.069. For these data, the pooled variance is 150, the estimated standard error is 5, and $t(23) = 2.40$. Reject H_0. The data are sufficient to conclude that there is a significant difference between the two groups.
  b. For these data, $d = 0.98$.

17. The null hypothesis states that there is no difference in difficulty between the two problems, $H_0: \mu_1 - \mu_2 = 0$. With $\alpha = .01$, the critical region consists of t values beyond ± 3.355. With the tacks in the box, $\overline{X} = 119.2$ and $SS = 2746.80$. With the tacks and box separate, $\overline{X} = 43.2$ and $SS = 1066.80$. The pooled variance is 476.7, the standard error is 13.81, and $t(8) = 5.50$. Reject H_0. The data are sufficient to indicate a significant difference between the two conditions.

19. a. There are a total of 26 subjects in the two samples combined.
  b. With $df = 24$ and $\alpha = .05$, the critical region consists of t values beyond ± 2.064. The t statistic is in the critical region. Reject H_0 and conclude that there is a significant difference.
  c. With $df = 24$ and $\alpha = .01$, the critical region consists of t values beyond ± 2.797. The t statistic is not in the critical region. Fail to reject H_0 and conclude that there is no significant difference.

21. a. For treatment 1, the mean is $\overline{X} = 4$ and for treatment 2, the mean is $\overline{X} = 11$. The means are the same as in Problem 20.
  b. For treatment 1, $SS = 96$ and for treatment 2, $SS = 100$. The pooled variance is 32.67 and the estimated standard error is 4.04. The variances and the standard error are much larger than they were in Problem 20.
  c. The null hypothesis states that there is no difference between the two treatments, $H_0: \mu_1 - \mu_2 = 0$. With $df = 6$ and $\alpha = .05$, the critical region consists of t values beyond ± 2.447. For these data, $t(6) = -1.73$. Fail to reject H_0. The data are not sufficient to conclude that there is a significant difference between the two treatments.
  d. The difference between Problem 20 and Problem 21 is the magnitude of the sample variance. In Problem 21, the large variance produces a large standard error with the result that the difference between sample means is not significant.

23. a. The null hypothesis states that feedback will have no effect on estimation of length, $H_0: \mu_1 - \mu_2 = 0$. With $df = 6$ and $\alpha = .05$, the critical region consists of t values beyond ± 2.447. For the no-feedback group, $\overline{X} = 6$ and $SS = 6$. For the feedback group, $\overline{X} = 3$ with $SS = 8$. For these data the pooled variance is 2.33, the estimated standard error is 1.08, and $t(6) = 2.77$. Reject H_0. The data are sufficient to conclude that there is a significant difference between the two feedback conditions.
  b. For these data, Cohen's $d = 1.96$ (a very large effect) and $r^2 = 0.56$ (56%).

SOLUTIONS

CHAPTER 11 **THE t TEST FOR TWO RELATED SAMPLES**

1. a. This is an independent-measures experiment with two separate samples.
  b. This is a repeated-measures design. The same sample is measured twice.

3. For a repeated-measures design, the same subjects are used in both treatment conditions. In a matched-subjects design, two different sets of subjects are used. However, in a matched-subjects design, each subject in one condition is matched with respect to a specific variable with a subject in the second condition so that the two separate samples are equivalent with respect to the matching variable.

5. a. For sample 1, the scores pile up around $\overline{D} = 4$ and the majority of the scores are spread over a range from -6 to 14. A value of zero is located near the center of the distribution. For sample 2, the scores pile up around $\overline{D} = 12$ and the majority of the scores are spread over a range from 2 to 22. A value of zero is an extreme value, not located near the center of the distribution.
  b. Sample 2 is more likely to reject a hypothesis of $\mu_D = 0$. For this sample, there is a clear difference between the center of the sample and the value of zero.

7. a. The estimated standard error is 1.35.
b. $\overline{D} = 3$ produces $t = 2.22$. The obtained t value is beyond the critical boundaries of ± 2.131. Reject H_0.

9. The null hypothesis says that the magnetic therapy has no effect, H_0: $\mu_D = 0$. With $df = 8$ and $\alpha = .01$, the critical values are $t = \pm 3.355$. For these data, the standard error is 4, and $t(8) = 3.13$. Fail to reject H_0 and conclude that the magnetic therapy has no significant effect on chronic pain.

11. a. The null hypothesis says that the medication has no effect, H_0: $\mu_D = 0$. Because $df = 35$ is not in the table, use $df = 30$ to obtain critical values of $t = \pm 2.042$. For these data, the standard error is 1.33, and $t(35) = 18.05$. Reject H_0 and conclude that the medication produces a significant change in reaction time.
b. For these data, $r^2 = 0.90$ (90%).

13. a. The null hypothesis says that the drug does not increase the pain threshold, H_0: $\mu_D \leq 0$. With $\alpha = .05$, the one-tailed critical region consists of t values greater than 1.860. For these data, $s^2 = 0.16$, the standard error is 0.13, and $t(8) = 12.31$. Reject H_0 and conclude that there has been a significant change.
b. For these data, $r^2 = 0.95$ (95%).

15. a. The difference scores are 9, 5, 1, and 13. $\overline{D} = 7$.
b. $SS = 80$, sample variance is 26.67, and the estimated standard error is 2.58.
c. With $df = 3$ and $\alpha = .05$, the critical values are $t = \pm 3.182$. For these data, $t = 2.71$. Fail to reject H_0. There is not a significant treatment effect.

17. a. For Problem 15, Cohen's d is 1.36 and for Problem 16, $d = 2.02$. The percentage of variance accounted for is $r^2 = .71$ for Problem 15 and $r^2 = .85$ for Problem 16.
b. In general, the smaller sample variance (Problem 16) produces the larger effect size.

19. The null hypothesis says that the oatmeal has no effect, H_0: $\mu_D = 0$. With $df = 8$ and $\alpha = .05$, the critical values are $t = \pm 2.306$. For these data, $\overline{D} = -7$, $SS = 288$, the standard error is 2, and $t(8) = -3.50$. Reject H_0 and conclude that the oatmeal has a significant effect on cholesterol.

21. The null hypothesis says that the treatment has no effect on agoraphobia, H_0: $\mu_D = 0$. With $df = 6$ and $\alpha = .05$, the critical values are $t = \pm 2.447$. For these data, $\overline{D} = 8$, $SS = 238$, the estimated standard error is 2.38, and $t(6) = 3.36$. Reject H_0 and conclude that the treatment does have a significant effect on agoraphobia.

23. The null hypothesis says that there is no difference between shots fired during versus between heartbeats, H_0: $\mu_D = 0$. For these data, $\overline{D} = 2.83$, $SS = 34.83$, $s^2 = 6.97$, the standard error is 1.08, and $t(5) = 2.62$. With $\alpha = .05$, the critical region consists of t values beyond ± 2.571. Reject H_0, and conclude that the timing of the shot has a significant effect on the marksmen's scores.

CHAPTER 12 **ESTIMATION**

---

1. The general purpose of a hypothesis test is to determine whether or not a treatment effect exists. A hypothesis test always addresses a "yes-no" question. The purpose of estimation is to determine the size of the effect. Estimation addresses a "how much" question.

3. a. The larger the sample, the narrower the interval.
b. The larger the sample standard deviation (s), the wider the interval.
c. The higher the percentage of confidence, the wider the interval.

5. a. Use the sample mean, $\overline{X} = 7.4$, for the point estimate.
b. Using a single-sample t statistic with $df = 24$, the standard error is 0.60, the t-score boundaries for 90% confidence are ± 1.711, and the interval extends from 6.373 to 8.427.

7. a. Using a single-sample t statistic with $df = 3$, the standard error is 3, the t-score boundaries for 90% confidence are ± 2.353, and the interval extends from 26.941 to 41.059.
b. Using a single-sample t statistic with $df = 15$, the standard error is 1.5, the t-score boundaries for 90% confidence are ± 1.753, and the interval extends from 31.370 to 36.630.
c. Using a single-sample t statistic with $df = 35$, the standard error is 1, the t-score boundaries for 90% confidence are ± 1.697 (using $df = 30$ because 35 is not listed), and the interval extends from 32.303 to 35.697.
d. The larger the sample size, the narrower the confidence interval.

9. a. Use the sample mean difference, 3.6 seconds, for the point estimate.
b. Using an independent-measures t statistic with $df = 18$, the pooled variance is 5, the standard error is 1, the t-score bound-aries for 80% confidence are ± 1.330, and the interval extends from 2.27 to 4.93 seconds.

11. a. Use the sample mean difference, 3.5 miles per hour, for the point estimate.
b. Using an independent-measures t statistic with $df = 198$, the pooled variance is 27.5 and the standard error is 0.74. Using $df = 120$ because 198 is not listed, the t-score boundaries for 95% confidence are ± 1.980, and the interval extends from 2.035 to 4.965 miles per hour.

13. a. Use the sample mean difference, 5.2, for the point estimate.
b. Using an independent-measures t statistic with $df = 28$, the pooled variance is 30, the estimated standard error is 2.00, the t-score boundaries for 95% confidence are ± 2.048, and the interval extends from 1.104 to 9.296.
c. The t score boundaries for 99% confidence are ± 2.763. and the interval extends from -0.326 to 10.726.
d. The change is significant for $\alpha = .05$ because a mean difference of zero is outside the interval and therefore rejected with 95% confidence. However, a mean difference of zero is within the 99% interval and therefore is an acceptable value (fail to reject) with 99% confidence.

15. Use the sample mean difference, 0.72, for the point estimate. Using a repeated-measures t statistic with $df = 24$, the standard error is 0.20, the t-score boundaries for 95% confidence are ± 2.064, and the interval extends from 0.3072 to 1.1328.

17. a. $\overline{X} = 7.36$ and $s^2 = 2.05$

   b. Use $\overline{X} = 7.36$ as the point estimate for μ.

   c. With $df = 10$ and an estimated standard error of 0.43, the t-score boundaries for 80% confidence are $t = \pm 1.372$, and the interval extends from 6.77 and 7.950.

19. Use the sample mean difference, 5.5, for the point estimate. Using a repeated-measures t statistic with $df = 15$, the standard error is 2, the t-score boundaries for 80% confidence are ± 1.341, and the interval extends from 2.818 to 8.182.

21. a. Use the sample mean difference, 24, for the point estimate.

   b. Using a repeated-measures t statistic with $df = 35$, the estimated standard error is 1.33, the t-score boundaries for 95% confidence are ± 2.042, (using $df = 30$ because 35 is not listed), and the interval extends from 21.284 to 26.716.

23. a. Use the sample mean difference, 2.83, for the point estimate.

   b. Using a repeated-measures t statistic with $df = 5$, the estimated standard error is 1.08, the t-score boundaries for 95% confidence are ± 2.571, and the interval extends from 0.053 to 5.607.

CHAPTER 13 ANALYSIS OF VARIANCE

1. When there is no treatment effect, the numerator and the denominator of the F-ratio are both measuring the same source of variability (differences due to chance/error). In this case, the F-ratio is balanced and should have a value near 1.00.

3 a. As the differences between sample means increase, $MS_{between}$ also increases, and the F-ratio increases.

   b. Increases in sample variance cause MS_{within} to increase and, thereby, decrease the F-ratio.

5. Posttests are done after an ANOVA where you reject the null hypothesis with three or more treatments. Posttests determine which treatments are significantly different.

7. There is no difference between treatments. Both treatments have the same total, $T = 9$, and the same mean, $\overline{X} = 3$. With no difference between treatments, $MS_{between} = 0$.

9. a. Reducing the differences between treatments should reduce the value of $MS_{between}$ and should lower the value of the F-ratio.

   b.

Source	SS	df	MS	
Between treatments	32	2	16	$F(2, 9) = 4.00$
Within treatments	36	9	4	
Total	68	11		

With $\alpha = .05$, the critical value is $F = 4.26$. Fail to reject the null hypothesis and conclude that there are no significant differences among the three treatments. Note that the F-ratio is substantially smaller than it was in Problem 6.

11. a. With $df_{between} = 3$, there must be $k = 4$ treatment conditions.

   b. Adding the two df values gives $df_{total} = 27$. Therefore, the total number of subjects must be $N = 28$.

13.

Source	SS	df	MS	
Between treatments	36	2	18	$F(2, 33) = 6.00$
Within treatments	99	33	3	
Total	135	35		

15. a. For the German shepherds, $\overline{X} = 4$ and $s = 0.82$. For the cocker spaniels, $\overline{X} = 1$ and $s = 1.15$. For the pit bulls, $\overline{X} = 6$ and $s = 1.63$.

b.

Source	SS	df	MS	
Between treatments	50.67	2	25.33	$F(2, 9) = 16.24$
Within treatments	14.00	9	1.56	
Total	64.67	11		

With $\alpha = .05$, the critical value is $F = 4.26$. Reject the null hypothesis and conclude that there are significant differences among the three breeds.

   c. For these data, $r^2 = 50.67/64.67 = 0.78$ (78%).

17. a. For the German shepherds, $\overline{X} = 2$ and $s = 0.82$. For the cocker spaniels, $\overline{X} = 1$ and $s = 1.15$. For the pit bulls, $\overline{X} = 3$ and $s = 1.63$. The standard deviations are the same as in Problem 15, but the mean differences are much smaller.

b.

Source	SS	df	MS	
Between treatments	8.00	2	4.00	$F(2, 9) = 2.56$
Within treatments	14.00	9	1.56	
Total	22.00	11		

With $\alpha = .05$, the critical value is $F = 4.26$. Fail to reject the null hypothesis and conclude that there are no significant differences among the three breeds.

   c. The smaller differences between sample means produced a smaller value for $MS_{between}$ and lowered the F-ratio.

   d. For these data, $r^2 = 8/22 = .36$ (36%). Because the mean differences are smaller than in Problem 15, the percentage of variance accounted for is lower.

19. a.

Source	SS	df	MS	
Between treatments	70	2	35.00	$F(2, 12) = 26.32$
Within treatments	16	12	1.33	
Total	86	14		

The critical value is $F = 3.88$. Reject H_0. The data do provide evidence of differences among the three therapies.

   b. For these data, Tukey's HSD is 1.94. According to this criterion, therapy A is significantly different from both B and C, but therapies B and C are not significantly different from each other.

21. a. For treatments 1 and 2 only, the null hypothesis is H_0: $\mu_1 = \mu_2$. The critical value for $\alpha = .05$ is 5.99.

Source	SS	df	MS	
Between treatments	32	1	32	$F(1, 6) = 8.00$
Within treatments	24	6	4	
Total	56	7		

The obtained F-ratio is in the critical region, so we reject H_0 and conclude that there is a significant difference between the two treatments.

b. When the analysis includes all three treatments, the null hypothesis is H_0: $\mu_1 = \mu_2 = \mu_3$. The critical value for $\alpha = .05$ is 4.26.

Source	SS	df	MS	
Between treatments	32	2	16	$F(2, 9) = 4.00$
Within treatments	36	9	4	
Total	68	11		

The obtained F-ratio is not in the critical region, so we fail to reject H_0 and conclude that there are no significant differences among the three treatments.

c. When comparing only treatments 1 and 2, there is a 4-point difference between means, $\overline{X}_1 = 1$ and $\overline{X}_2 = 5$. However, when the third treatment, with $\overline{X}_3 = 3$, is added, the study contains mean differences that are only 2 points (for example $\overline{X}_1$ versus $\overline{X}_3$). Thus, when the third treatment is included, the average difference between means decreases and $MS_{between}$ also decreases. As a result, the mean differences are no longer significant.

23. The means and SS values are:

Single	Twin	Triplet
$\overline{X} = 8$	$\overline{X} = 6$	$\overline{X} = 4$
$SS = 10$	$SS = 18$	$SS = 14$

The null hypothesis states that there are no differences in language development among the three groups, H_0: $\mu_1 = \mu_2 = \mu_3$. The critical value for $\alpha = .05$ is 3.88. The analysis of variance produces

Source	SS	df	MS	
Between treatments	40	2	20	$F(2, 12) = 5.71$
Within treatments	42	12	3.5	
Total	82	14		

Reject H_0, and conclude that there are significant differences in language development among the three groups.

CHAPTER 14 MORE ADVANCED ANALYSIS OF VARIANCE: REPEATED-MEASURES AND TWO-FACTOR DESIGNS

1. For an independent measures design, the variability within treatments is the appropriate error term. For repeated measures, however, you must subtract out variability due to individual differences from the variability within treatments to obtain a measure of error.

3. $df = 3, 27$

5. a. $k = 3$ **b.** $n = 21$

7. a. The null hypothesis states that there are no differences among the three treatments, H_0: $\mu_1 = \mu_2 = \mu_3$. With $df = 2, 6$, the critical value is 5.14.

Source	SS	df	MS	
Between treatments	8	2	4	$F(2, 6) = 0.27$
Within treatments	94	9		
Between subjects	4	3		
Error	90	6	15	
Total	102	11		

Fail to reject H_0. There are no significant differences among the three treatments.

b. In Problem 6, the individual differences were relatively large and consistent. When the individual differences were subtracted out, the error was greatly reduced.

9. a. The null hypothesis states that there are no differences between treatments, H_0: $\mu_1 = \mu_2 = \mu_3$. For an independent-measures design, the critical value is 3.88.

Source	SS	df	MS	
Between treatments	40	2	20.00	$F(2, 12) = 3.24$
Within treatments	74	12	6.17	
Total	114	14		

b. The null hypothesis states that there are no differences between treatments, H_0: $\mu_1 = \mu_2 = \mu_3$. For a repeated-measures design, the critical value is 4.46.

Source	SS	df	MS	
Between treatments	40	2	20.0	$F(2, 8) = 8.00$
Within treatments	74	12		
Between subjects	54	4		
Error	20	8	2.5	
Total	114	14		

c. The independent measures design includes all the individual differences in the error term (MS_{within}). As a result, the F-ratio, $F(2,12) = 3.24$, is not significant. With a repeated-measures design, the individual differences are removed and the result is a significant F-ratio, $F(2,8) = 8.00$, $p < .05$.

11. a. The means have all increased by 2 points compared to the values in Problem 10, but the mean differences have not changed at all. $MS_{between}$ is still equal to 6.00, unchanged.

b. MS_{error} is not changed from the value obtained in Problem 10. The extra variability within treatments is all accounted for as variability between subjects, which is subtracted out before MS_{error} is computed.

c. The null hypothesis states that the mean number of errors does not change across sessions, $H_0: \mu_1 = \mu_2 = \mu_3 = \mu_4$. The critical value is 4.76. The complete analysis for the new data is as follows:

Source	SS	df	MS	
Between treatments	18	3	6.00	$F(3, 6) = 8.96$
Within treatments	156	8		
Between subjects	152	2		
Error	4	6	0.67	
Total	174	11		

Reject H_0 and conclude that there is a significant practice effect.

13.

Source	SS	df	MS	
Between treatments	200	4	50	$F(4, 36) = 5.00$
Within treatments	500	45		
Between subjects	140	9		
Error	360	36	10	
Total	700	49		

15. One hypothesis test evaluates mean differences among the rows, and a second test evaluates mean differences among the columns. The test for an interaction evaluates the significance of any mean differences that are not explained by row and/or column differences.

17. All F-ratios have the same error term, MS_{within}, and, therefore, have the same df value for the denominator.

19. a. 20   **b.** 0   **c.** 60

21. The null hypotheses state that there is no mean difference between levels of factor A ($H_0: \mu_{Quiet} = \mu_{Noisy}$), no difference between levels of factor B ($H_0: \mu_{Introvert} = \mu_{Extrovert}$), and no interaction. All F-ratios have $df = 1$, 16 and the critical value is $F = 4.49$.

Source	SS	df	MS	
Between treatments	120	3		
A (Distraction)	80	1	80	$F(1, 16) = 16$
B (Personality)	20	1	20	$F(1, 16) = 4$
$A \times B$	20	1	20	$F(1, 16) = 4$
Within treatments	80	16	5	
Total	200	19		

Distraction has a significant effect on performance. These results do not provide sufficient evidence to conclude that personality affects performance or that personality interacts with distraction.

23.

Source	SS	df	MS	
Between treatments	280	7		
A	16	1	16	$F(1, 40) = 2.00$
B	144	3	48	$F(3, 40) = 6.00$
$A \times B$	120	3	40	$F(3, 40) = 5.00$
Within treatments	320	40	8	
Total	600	47		

CHAPTER 15 **CORRELATION AND REGRESSION**

1. A positive correlation indicates that X and Y change in the same direction: As X increases, Y also increases. A negative correlation indicates that X and Y tend to change in opposite directions: As X increases, Y decreases.

3. The Pearson correlation measures the degree of linear relationship. The Spearman correlation measures the degree to which the relationship is monotonic or one-directional independent of form.

5. a.

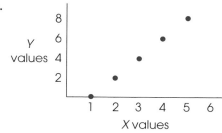

b. It appears to be a perfect positive correlation, $r = 1.00$.
c. $SS_X = 10$, $SS_Y = 40$, $SP = 20$, and $r = 1.00$.

7. a.

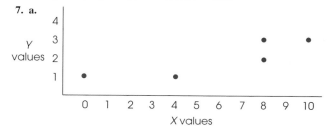

b. It appears to be a strong positive correlation, about $r = +.8$ or $+.9$.
c. $SS_X = 64$, $SS_Y = 4$, $SP = 14$, and $r = +.875$
d. $SS_X = 64$, $SS_Y = 14$, $SP = -16$, and $r = -.535$

9. a. $SS_X = 52$, $SS_Y = 54$, $SP = -47$, and $r = -.887$.
  b. The correlation is still $r = -.887$.
  c. Adding a constant does not change SS or SP or the correlation.
  d. The correlation is still $r = -.887$.
  e. Multiplying each score by 3 will cause all the SS and SP values to be multiplied by 9. However, this multiplication cancels out in the correlation formula, so the correlation is unchanged.

11. For these data, $SS_{1st} = 64$, $SS_{2nd} = 100$, $SP = 76$, and the Pearson correlation is $r = 0.95$.

13. a. The null hypothesis states that there is no correlation in the population. With $n = 18$, the correlation must be greater than 0.468 to be significant at the .05 level. Fail to reject H_0. The data do not provide evidence for a significant correlation.
  b. With $n = 102$, the critical value is 0.195. Reject H_0 and conclude that this sample provides enough evidence to conclude that a significant, nonzero correlation exists in the population.

15. a. $r_s = +0.907$
  b. Yes, there is a strong positive relationship between the grades assigned by the two instructors.

17. a. $SS_X = 24$, $SS_Y = 252$, $SP = -56$, and $r = -.72$.
  b. The ranks are as follows:

Hours	Errors
1	8
2	7
3	3
5.5	2
5.5	5
7.5	1
4	4
7.5	6

The Spearman correlation is $r_s = -.58$ using the Pearson formula on the ranks, or $r_s = -.56$ using the special Spearman formula.
  c. After ranking, the extreme individual (0, 19) is moved back into the rest of the group producing a moderate negative correlation. Ranking the scores reduces the influence of any extreme scores.

19.

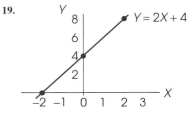

21. a. $\hat{Y} = 3X - 3$
  b. For each X, the predicted Y value would be

X	$\hat{Y}$
1	0
4	9
3	6
2	3
5	12
3	6

23. a. $SS_{number} = 14$, $SS_{IQ} = 996$, $SP = -97$, $r = -0.82$.
  b. The regression equation is: $\hat{Y} = -6.93X + 127.82$.

CHAPTER 16 THE CHI-SQUARE STATISTIC TESTS FOR GOODNESS OF FIT AND INDEPENDENCE

1. Nonparametric tests make few, if any, assumptions about the populations from which the data are obtained. For example, the populations do not need to form normal distributions, nor is it required that different populations in the same study have equal variances (homogeneity of variance assumption). Parametric tests require data measured on an interval or a ratio scale. For nonparametric tests, any scale of measurement is acceptable.

3. H_0 states that the distribution of automobile accidents is the same as the distribution of registered drivers: 16% under age 20, 28% for age 20 to 29, and 56% for age 30 or older. With $df = 2$, the critical value is 5.99. The expected frequencies for these three categories are 48, 84, and 168. Chi-square = 13.76. Reject H_0, and conclude that the distribution of automobile accidents is not identical to the distribution of registered drivers.

5. The null hypothesis states that there are no preferences among the four colors; $p = \frac{1}{4}$ for each color. With $df = 3$, the critical value is 7.81. The expected frequencies are $f_e = 15$ for all categories, and

chi-square = 5.73. Fail to reject H_0, and conclude that there are no significant preferences.

7. The null hypothesis states that there is no preference among the three photographs: $p = \frac{1}{3}$ for all categories. The expected frequencies are $f_e = 50$ for all categories, and chi-square = 20.28. With $df = 2$, the critical value is 5.99. Reject H_0, and conclude that there are significant preferences.

9. The null hypothesis states that the grade distribution for last semester has the same proportions as it did in 1985. For a sample of $n = 200$, the expected frequencies are 28, 52, 62, 38 and 20 for grades of A, B, C, D, and F, respectively. With $df = 4$, the critical value for chi-square is 9.49. For these data, the chi-square statistic is 6.68. Fail to reject H_0 and conclude that there is no evidence that the distribution has changed.

11. a. The null hypothesis states that there is no preference among the three colas; one-third of the population prefers each of the three colas. For a sample of $n = 120$, the expected frequency is 40 for each cola. For $df = 2$ and $\alpha = .05$, the critical value for chi-square is 5.99. For these data, the chi-square statistic is 10.40. Reject H_0 and conclude that there are significant preferences among the colas.

b. A larger sample should be more representative of the population. If the sample continues to be different from the hypothesis as the sample size increases, eventually the difference will be significant.

13. The null hypothesis states that there are no preferences among the three books: $p = \frac{1}{3}$ for all categories. With $df = 2$, the critical value is 5.99. The expected frequencies are $f_e = 40$ for all categories, and chi-square = 7.85. Reject H_0 and conclude that there are significant preferences.

15. The null hypothesis states that there is no relation between dream content and gender; the distribution of aggression content should be the same for males and females. The critical value is 9.21. The expected frequencies are:

	Low	Medium	High
Female	8.8	8.4	6.8
Male	13.2	12.6	10.2

The chi-square statistic is 25.52. Reject H_0 with $\alpha = .01$ and $df = 2$.

17. The null hypothesis states that the distribution of opinions is the same for those who live in the city and those who live in the suburbs. For $df = 1$ and $\alpha = .05$, the critical value for chi-square is 3.84. The expected frequencies are:

	Favor	Oppose
City	51.33	48.67
Suburb	102.67	97.33

For these data, chi-square = 16.68. Reject H_0 and conclude that opinions in the city are different from those in the suburbs.

19. The null hypothesis states that there is no relationship between group size and helping behavior. With $df = 2$, the critical value is 9.21. The expected frequencies are:

	None	Small	Large
Help	7.75	15.50	7.75
Not help	5.25	10.50	5.25

Chi-square = 7.91. Fail to reject H_0 and conclude that there is no relationship between helping and group size.

21. The null hypothesis states that there is no relation between handedness and eye preference. With $df = 1$ and $\alpha = .01$, the critical value is 6.63. The expected frequencies for left-handed subjects are 12 left eye and 18 right eye. For right-handed subjects, the expected frequencies are 48 for left eye and 72 for right eye. Chi-square = 11.11. There is a significant relationship between hand and eye preference.

STATISTICS ORGANIZER

The following pages present an organized summary of the statistical procedures covered in this book. This organizer is divided into four sections, each of which groups together statistical techniques that serve a common purpose. The four groups are

    I. Descriptive Statistics

   II. Parametric Tests for Means and Mean Differences

  III. Nonparametric Chi-square Tests

  IV. Measures of Relationship between Two Variables

Each of the four sections begins with a general overview that discusses the purpose for the statistical techniques that follow and points out some common characteristics of the different techniques. Next, there is a decision map that leads you, step by step, through the task of deciding which statistical technique is appropriate for the data you wish to analyze. Finally, there is a brief description of each technique and the necessary formulas.

I DESCRIPTIVE STATISTICS

The purpose of descriptive statistics is to simplify and organize a set of scores. Scores may be organized in a table or graph, or they may be summarized by computing one or two values that describe the entire set. The most commonly used descriptive techniques are as follows:

A. Frequency Distribution Tables and Graphs

A frequency distribution is an organized tabulation of the number of individuals in each category on the scale of measurement. A frequency distribution can be presented as either a table or a graph. The advantage of a frequency distribution is that it presents the entire set of scores rather than condensing the scores into a single descriptive value. The disadvantage of a frequency distribution is that it can be somewhat complex, especially with large sets of data.

B. Measures of Central Tendency

The purpose of measuring central tendency is to identify a single score that represents an entire data set. The goal is to obtain a single value that is the best example of the average, or most typical, score from the entire set.

Measures of central tendency are used to describe a single data set, and they are the most commonly used measures for comparing two (or more) different sets of data.

C. Measures of Variability

Variability is used to provide a description of how spread out the scores are in a distribution. It also provides a measure of how accurately a single score selected from a distribution represents the entire set.

D. *z*-Scores

Most descriptive statistics are intended to provide a description of an entire set of scores. However, *z*-scores are used to describe individual scores within a distribution. The purpose of a *z*-score is to identify the precise location of an individual within a distribution by using a single number.

CHOOSING DESCRIPTIVE STATISTICS: A DECISION MAP

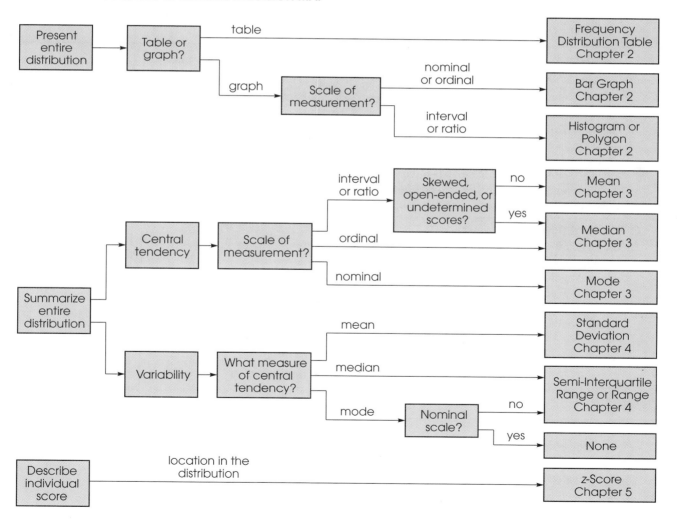

1. The Mean (Chapter 3) The mean is the most commonly used measure of central tendency. It is computed by finding the total (ΣX) for the set of scores and then dividing the total by the number of individuals. Conceptually, the mean is the amount each individual will receive if the total is divided equally.	Population: $\mu = \dfrac{\Sigma X}{N}$ Sample: $\overline{X} = \dfrac{\Sigma X}{n}$
2. The Median (Chapter 3) Exactly 50% of the scores in a data set have values less than or equal to the median. The median is the 50th percentile. The median usually is computed for data sets in situations where the mean cannot be found (undetermined scores, open-ended distribution) or where the mean does not provide a good, representative value (ordinal scale, skewed distribution).	List the scores in order from smallest to largest. a. With an odd number of scores, the median is the middle score. b. With an even number of scores, the median is the average of the middle two scores.
3. The Mode (Chapter 3) The mode is the score with the greatest frequency. The mode is used when the scores consist of measurements on a nominal scale.	No calculation. Simply count the frequency of occurrence for each different score.
4. The Range (Chapter 4) The range is the distance from the lowest to the highest score in a data set. The range is considered to be a relatively crude measure of variability.	Find the upper real limit for the largest score and the lower real limit for the smallest score. The range is the difference between these two real limits.
5. The Semi-Interquartile Range (Chapter 4) The semi-interquartile range is one-half of the range covered by the middle 50% of the distribution. The semi-interquartile range is often used to measure variability in situations where the median is used to report central tendency.	Find the first quartile and the third quartile. The semi-interquartile range is one-half of the distance between the two quartiles.
6. Standard Deviation (Chapter 4) The standard deviation is a measure of the standard distance from the mean. Standard deviation is obtained by first computing SS (the sum of squared deviations) and variance (the mean squared deviation). Standard deviation is the square root of variance.	**Sum of Squares** Definitional: $SS = \Sigma(X - \mu)^2$ Computational: $SS = \Sigma X^2 - \dfrac{(\Sigma X)^2}{N}$ **Variance** Population: $\sigma^2 = \dfrac{SS}{N}$ Sample: $s^2 = \dfrac{SS}{n-1}$ **Standard Deviation** Population: $\sigma = \sqrt{\dfrac{SS}{N}}$ Sample: $s = \sqrt{\dfrac{SS}{n-1}}$
7. z-Scores (Chapter 5) The sign of a z-score indicates whether an individual is above ($+$) or below ($-$) the mean. The numerical value of the z-score indicates how many standard deviations there are between the score and the mean.	$z = \dfrac{X - \mu}{\sigma}$

II PARAMETRIC TESTS: INFERENCES ABOUT POPULATION MEANS OR MEAN DIFFERENCES

All of the hypothesis tests covered in this section use the means obtained from sample data as the basis for testing hypotheses about population means. Although there are a variety of tests used in a variety of research situations, all use the same basic logic, and all of the test statistics have the same basic structure. In each case, the test statistic (z, t, or F) involves computing a ratio with the following structure:

$$\text{test statistic} = \frac{\text{obtained difference between sample means}}{\text{mean difference expected by chance}}$$

The goal of each test is to determine whether the observed sample mean differences are larger than expected by chance. In general terms, a *significant result* means that the results obtained in a research study (sample differences) are more than would be expected by chance. In each case, a large value for the test statistic ratio indicates a significant result; that is, when the actual difference between sample means (numerator) is substantially larger than chance (denominator), you will obtain a large ratio, which indicates that the sample difference is significant.

The actual calculations differ slightly from one test statistic to the next, but all involve the same basic computations.

1. A set of scores (sample) is obtained for each population or each treatment condition.

2. The mean is computed for each set of scores, and some measure of variability (*SS,* standard deviation, or variance) is obtained for each individual set of scores.

3. The differences between the sample means provide a measure of how much difference exists between treatment conditions. Because these mean differences may be caused by the treatment conditions, they are often called *systematic* or *predicted.* These differences are the numerator of the test statistic.

4. The variability within each set of scores provides a measure of unsystematic or unpredicted differences due to chance. Because the individuals within each treatment condition are treated exactly the same, there is nothing that should cause their scores to be different. Thus, any observed differences (variability) within treatments are assumed to be due to error or chance.

With these considerations in mind, each of the test statistic ratios can be described as follows:

$$\text{test statistic} = \frac{\text{differences (variability) between treatments}}{\text{differences (variability) within treatments}}$$

The hypothesis tests reviewed in this section apply to three basic research designs:

1. Single-Sample Designs. Data from a single sample are used to test a hypothesis about a single population.

2. Independent-Measures Designs. A separate sample is obtained to represent each individual population or treatment condition.

3. **Related-Samples Designs.** Related-samples designs include repeated-measures and matched-subjects designs. For a repeated-measures design, there is only one sample, with each individual subject being measured in all of the different treatment conditions. In a matched-subjects design, every individual in one sample is matched with a subject in each of the other samples.

Finally, you should be aware that all parametric tests place stringent restrictions on the sample data and the population distributions being considered. First, these tests all require measurements on an interval or a ratio scale (numerical values that allow you to compute means and differences). Second, each test makes assumptions about population distributions and sampling techniques. Consult the appropriate section of this book to verify that the specific assumptions are satisfied before proceeding with any parametric test.

CHOOSING A PARAMETRIC TEST: A DECISION MAP FOR MAKING INFERENCES ABOUT POPULATION MEANS OR MEAN DIFFERENCES

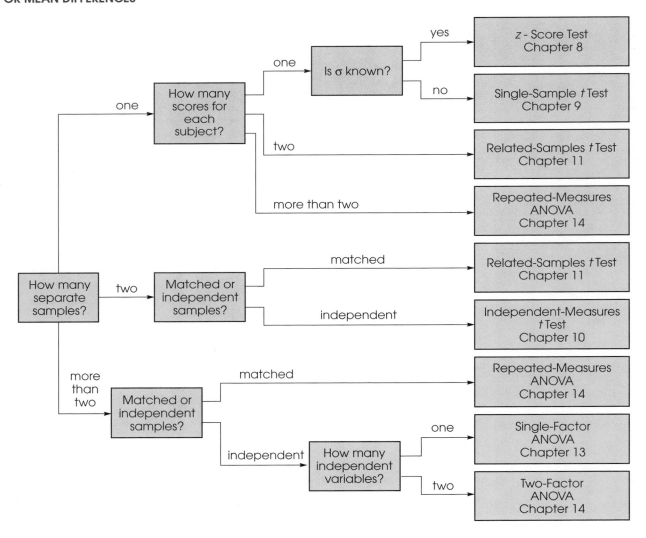

1. **The z-Score Test** (Chapter 8)
   The z-score test uses the data from a single sample to test a hypothesis about the population mean when the population standard deviation (σ) is known. The null hypothesis states a specific value for the unknown population mean.

$$z = \frac{\overline{X} - \mu}{\sigma_{\overline{X}}} \quad \text{where } \sigma_{\overline{X}} = \frac{\sigma}{\sqrt{n}}$$

2. **The Single-Sample *t* Test** (Chapter 9)
   This test uses the data from a single sample to test a hypothesis about a population mean when the population standard deviation is unknown. The sample variance is used to estimate the unknown population variance. The null hypothesis states a specific value for the unknown population mean.

$$t = \frac{\overline{X} - \mu}{s_{\overline{X}}} \quad \text{where } s_{\overline{X}} = \sqrt{\frac{s^2}{n}}$$

$$df = n - 1$$

3. **The Independent-Measures *t* Test**
   (Chapter 10)
   The independent-measures *t* test uses data from two separate samples to test a hypothesis about the difference between two population means. The variability within the two samples is combined to obtain a single (pooled) estimate of population variance. The null hypothesis states that there is no difference between the two population means.

$$t = \frac{(\overline{X}_1 - \overline{X}_2) - (\mu_1 - \mu_2)}{s_{(\overline{X}_1 - \overline{X}_2)}}$$

$$\text{where } s_{(\overline{X}_1 - \overline{X}_2)} = \sqrt{\frac{s_p^2}{n_1} + \frac{s_p^2}{n_2}} \text{ and } s_p^2 = \frac{SS_1 + SS_2}{df_1 + df_2}$$

$$df = df_1 + df_2 = (n_1 - 1) + (n_2 - 1)$$

4. **The Related-Samples *t* Test** (Chapter 11)
   This test evaluates the mean difference between two treatment conditions using the data from a repeated-measures or a matched-subjects experiment. A difference score (D) is obtained for each subject (or each matched pair) by subtracting the score in treatment 1 from the score in treatment 2. The variability of the sample difference scores is used to estimate the population variability. The null hypothesis states that the population mean difference (μ_D) is zero.

$$t = \frac{\overline{D} - \mu_D}{s_{\overline{D}}} \quad \text{where } s_{\overline{D}} = \sqrt{\frac{s^2}{n}}$$

$$df = n - 1$$

5. **Single-Factor, Independent-Measures Analysis of Variance** (Chapter 13) This test uses data from two or more separate samples to test for mean differences among two or more populations. The null hypothesis states that there are no differences among the population means. The test statistic is an F-ratio that uses the variability between treatment conditions (sample mean differences) in the numerator and the variability within treatment conditions (error variability) as the denominator. With only two samples, this test is equivalent to the independent-measures t test.

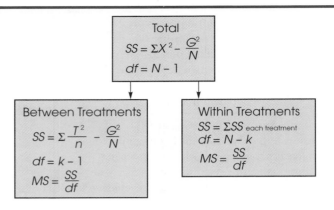

6. **Single-Factor, Repeated-Measures Analysis of Variance** (Chapter 14) This test is used to evaluate mean differences among two or more treatment conditions using sample data from a repeated-measures (or matched-subjects) experiment. The null hypothesis states that there are no differences among the population means. The test statistic is an F-ratio using variability between treatment conditions (mean differences) in the numerator exactly like the independent-measures ANOVA. The denominator of the F-ratio (error term) is obtained by measuring variability within treatments and then subtracting out the variability between subjects. The research design and the test statistic remove variability due to individual differences and thereby provide a more sensitive test for treatment differences than is possible with an independent-measures design.

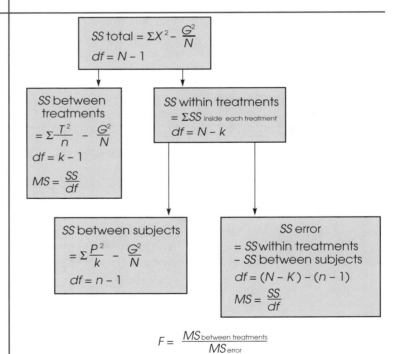

7. **Two-Factor, Independent-Measures Analysis of Variance** (Chapter 15) This test is used to evaluate mean differences among populations or treatment conditions using sample data from research designs with two independent variables (factors). The two-factor ANOVA tests three separate hypotheses: mean differences among the levels of factor A (main effect for factor A), mean differences among the levels of factor B (main effect for factor B), and mean differences resulting from specific combinations of the two factors (interaction). Each of the three separate null hypotheses states that there are no population mean differences. Each of the three tests uses an F-ratio as the test statistic, with the variability between samples (sample mean differences) in the numerator and the variability within samples (error variability) in the denominator.

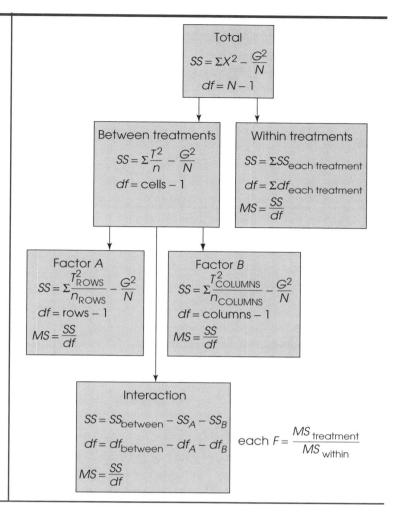

III NONPARAMETRIC CHI-SQUARE TESTS

Chi-square tests consist of techniques used to test hypotheses about the relative frequencies (proportions) one expects to find in a frequency distribution. The sample data for these tests consist of the frequencies of observations that fall into various categories of a variable: for example, the frequency of people preferring soft drink A, the frequency preferring soft drink B, and so on. The hypotheses make statements about what proportion of frequencies you should expect for each category for the population. The chi-square test for goodness of fit tests how well the form (or shape) of a sample frequency distribution matches a hypothesized population distribution. The chi-square test for independence also compares sample frequencies to hypothesized population proportions. However, it determines whether two variables, consisting of two or more categories apiece, are related.

A DECISION MAP FOR CHI-SQUARE TESTS

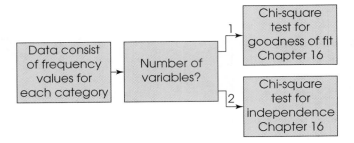

1. **The Chi-Square Test for Goodness of Fit**
   (Chapter 16)
   This chi-square test is used in situations where the measurement procedure results in classifying individuals into distinct categories. The test uses frequency data from a single sample to test a hypothesis about the population distribution. The null hypothesis specifies the proportion or percentage of the population for each category on the scale of measurement.

   $$\chi^2 = \Sigma \frac{(f_o - f_e)^2}{f_e} \quad \text{where } f_e = pn$$

   $$df = C - 1$$

2. **The Chi-Square Test for Independence**
   (Chapter 16)
   This test uses frequency data to determine whether there is a significant relationship between two variables. The null hypothesis states that the two variables are independent. The chi-square test for independence is used when the scale of measurement consists of relatively few categories for both variables and can be used with nominal, ordinal, interval, or ratio scales.

   $$\chi^2 = \Sigma \frac{(f_o - f_e)^2}{f_e} \quad \text{where } f_e = \frac{(\text{row total})(\text{column total})}{n}$$

   $$df = (R - 1)(C - 1)$$

IV   MEASURES OF RELATIONSHIP BETWEEN TWO VARIABLES

As we noted in Chapter 1, a major purpose for scientific research is to investigate and establish orderly relationships between variables. The statistical techniques covered in this section all serve the purpose of measuring and describing relationships. The data for these statistics involve two observations for each individual—one observation for each of the two variables being examined. The goal is to determine whether a consistent, predictable relationship exists and to describe the nature of the relationship.

Each of the different statistical methods described in this section is intended to be used with a specific type of data. To determine which method is appropriate, you must first examine your data and identify what type of variable is involved.

CHOOSING A MEASURE OF RELATIONSHIP BETWEEN TWO VARIABLES: A DECISION MAP

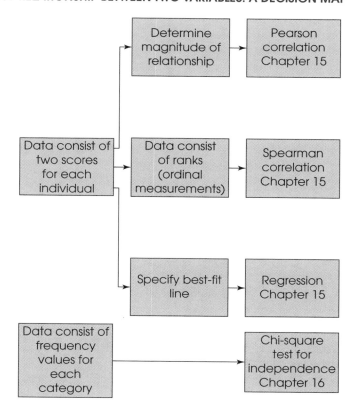

1. **Pearson Correlation** (Chapter 15)	
The Pearson correlation measures the degree of linear relationship between two variables. The sign ($+$ or $-$) of the correlation indicates the direction of the relationship. The magnitude of the correlation (from 0 to 1) indicates the degree to which the data points fit on a straight line.	$$r = \frac{SP}{\sqrt{SS_X SS_Y}}$$ where $SP = \Sigma(X - \bar{X})(Y - \bar{Y}) = \Sigma XY - \frac{(\Sigma X)(\Sigma Y)}{n}$
2. **The Spearman Correlation** (Chapter 15)	
The Spearman correlation measures the degree to which the relationship between two variables is one-directional, or monotonic. The Spearman correlation is used when both variables, X and Y, are ranks (measured on an ordinal scale).	Use the Pearson formula on the ranked data or the special Spearman formula: $$r_S = 1 - \frac{6\Sigma D^2}{n(n^2 - 1)}$$

3. **Linear Regression** (Chapter 15)
   The purpose of linear regression is to find the equation for the best-fitting straight line for predicting Y scores from X scores. The regression process determines the linear equation with the least squared error between the actual Y values and the predicted Y values on the line.

$$\hat{Y} = bX + a \quad \text{where } b = \frac{SP}{SS_X} \quad \text{and} \quad a = \overline{Y} - b\overline{X}$$

4. **The Chi-Square Test for Independence** (Chapter 16)

See Section III, number 2.

REFERENCES

American Psychological Association (APA). (1994). *Publication manual of the American Psychological Association,* 4th ed. Washington, D.C.: Author.

Bransford, J. D., & Johnson, M. K. (1972). Contextual prerequisites for understanding: Some investigations of comprehension and recall. *Journal of Verbal Learning and Verbal Behavior, 11,* 717–726.

Byrne, D. (1971). *The attraction paradigm.* New York: Academic Press.

Cialdini, R. B., Reno, R. R., & Kallgren, C. A. (1990). A focus theory of normative conduct: Recycling the concept of norms to reduce littering in public places. *Journal of Personality and Social Psychology, 58,* 1015–1026.

Cohen, J. (1969). *Statistical power analysis for the behavioral sciences.* New York: Academic Press.

Cowles, M., & Davis, C. (1982). On the origins of the .05 level of statistical significance. *American Psychologist, 37,* 553–558.

Darley, J. M., & Latané, B. (1968). Bystander intervention in emergencies: Diffusion of responsibility. *Journal of Personality and Social Psychology, 8,* 377–383.

Davis, E. A. (1937). *The development of linguistic skills in twins, single twins with siblings, and only children from age 5 to 10 years.* Institute of Child Welfare Series, No. 14. Minneapolis: University of Minnesota Press.

Duncker, K. (1945). On problem-solving. *Psychological Monographs, 58* (No. 270).

Friedman, M., & Rosenman, R. H. (1974). *Type A behavior and your heart.* New York: Knopf.

Hyman, A. (1993, August). *A suggestion for teaching two types of populations and samples.* Poster session presented at the annual meeting of the American Psychological Association. Toronto, Ontario, Canada.

Katona, G. (1940). *Organizing and memorizing.* New York: Columbia University Press.

Keppel, G. (1973). *Design and analysis: A researcher's handbook.* Englewood Cliffs, N.J.: Prentice-Hall.

Keppel, G., and Zedeck, S. (1989). *Data analysis for research designs.* New York: Freeman.

Levine, S. (1960). Stimulation in infancy. *Scientific American, 202,* 80–86.

Pelton, T. (1983). The shootists. *Science83, 4*(4), 84–86.

Reifman, A. S., Larrick, R. P., & Fein, S. (1991). Temper and temperature on the diamond: The heat-aggression relationship in major league baseball. *Personality and Social Psychology Bulletin, 17,* 580–585.

Scaife, M. (1976). The response to eye-like shapes by birds. I. The effect of context: A predator and a strange bird. *Animal Behaviour, 24,* 195–199.

Schachter, S. (1968). Obesity and eating. *Science, 161,* 751–756.

Schleifer, S. J., Keller, S. E., Camerino, M., Thornton, J. C., & Stein, M. (1983). Suppression of lymphocyte stimulation following bereavement. *Journal of the American Medical Association, 250,* 374–377.

Segal, S. J., and Fusella, V. (1970). Influence of imaged pictures and sounds on detection of visual and auditory signals. *Journal of Experimental Psychology, 83,* 458–464.

Shrauger, J. S. (1972). Self-esteem and reactions to being observed by others. *Journal of Personality and Social Psychology, 23,* 192–200.

Siegel, J. M. (1990). Stress life events and use of physician services among the elderly: The moderating role of pet ownership. *Journal of Personality and Social Psychology, 58,* 1081–1086.

Wilkinson, L., and the Task Force on Statistical Inference. (1999). Statistical methods in psychology journals. *American Psychologist, 54,* 594–604.

Winget, C., & Kramer, M. (1979). *Dimensions of dreams.* Gainesville: University Press of Florida.

INDEX

CHOOSING DESCRIPTIVE STATISTICS: A DECISION MAP

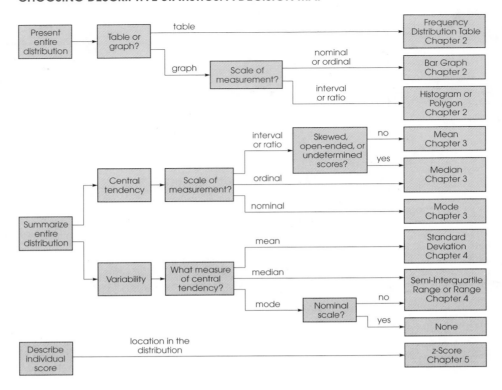

CHOOSING A PARAMETRIC TEST: A DECISION MAP FOR MAKING INFERENCES ABOUT POPULATION MEANS OR MEAN DIFFERENCES

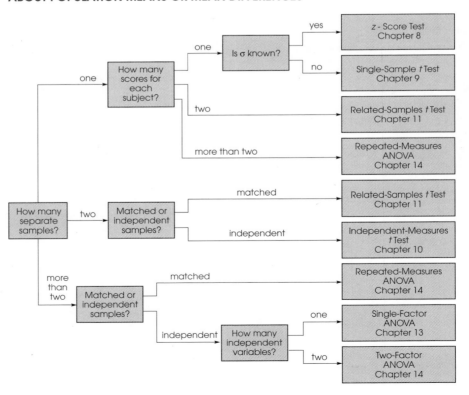